Contents

Davinia West

GNVQ Advanced

Information Technology

Stephen Doyle

Stanley Thornes (Publishers) Ltd.

First published in 1997 by
Stanley Thornes (Publishers) Ltd
Ellenborough House
Wellington Street
CHELTENHAM GL50 1YW

98 99 00 01 / 10 9 8 7 6 5 4 3 2

A catalogue record for this book is available from the British Library

ISBN 07487 2890 2

Typeset by GreenGate Publishing Services, Tonbridge, Kent
Printed and bound in Great Britain by Redwood Books, Trowbridge, Wiltshire

Introduction

What is a GNVQ?

A General National Vocational Qualification (GNVQ) is an alternative qualification to A-levels or GCSEs and can be taken at three levels:

- Foundation GNVQ: equivalent to four GCSEs at grades D–G; these normally take one year of full-time study.
- Intermediate GNVQ: equivalent to four GCSEs at grades A–C; these normally take one year of full-time study.
- Advanced GNVQ: equivalent to two A-levels (Advanced GNVQs are sometimes referred to as 'Vocational A-levels'); these are normally taken over a two-year period of full-time study.

How is a GNVQ assessed?

GNVQ units are assessed both internally by your assessor, who will normally be the person who is teaching the unit, and also externally by someone employed by the awarding body (i.e. City and Guilds, BTEC or RSA).

What happens if you disagree with an assessment?

Each school or college must have an appeals procedure which will deal effectively with any complaints that a student may have. You can appeal on the grounds that an assessment procedure was not properly carried out or that an outcome (pass) was not carried out in a proper manner. You should have been given a copy of the appeals procedure as part of the induction material you were given at the start of the course. If you have not been given this document, then you should ask your tutor for one.

The externally assessed test papers

The external testing is via the end-of-unit tests which consist of a number of objective questions that are answered on a special mark sheet, and your answers to these are sent away for marking. The marking is performed automatically by an optical mark reader.

The purpose of the tests is to assess the knowledge and skills that you have gained during the time you have been studying the unit. Each GNVQ test paper lasts about one hour and the pass mark is 70 per cent.

The external tests take place several times a year, so if you fail or are absent for one of the tests then there will be other times when the test can be retaken. There is no limit to the number of times you can re-sit each test.

There are written tests on seven out of the eight mandatory units. Unit 8 (Information technology projects and teamwork), covered in Chapter 15 of this book, does not have a sample unit test.

The internally assessed work

This work will be set by your tutors and the same people will also be responsible for collecting in and assessing this work. All the work that you do during your GNVQ course will need to be organised into a portfolio of evidence. Because there may be several groups doing the GNVQ Advanced IT course but all with different tutors, the work will need to be verified by a different experienced tutor called a verifier. The main function of the verifier is to make sure that the assessments carried out by each tutor are of a consistent standard.

There is also another checking process which makes use of someone external to the college or school, and their purpose is to make sure that the assessments agree with national standards and do not vary from one college or school to the next. Someone called an external verifier performs this task, and they should visit your school or college at least twice a year to look at students' work.

Assessment at GNVQ level is all about showing the assessor what you have achieved. It is therefore about supplying evidence to prove to the assessor that you have done the necessary work. It is for this reason that you need to collect this evidence and organise it into a portfolio of work.

For the award of an Advanced IT GNVQ you must complete fifteen units:

- Eight compulsory vocational units which are found only in the GNVQ Advanced IT course.
- Three compulsory key skills units (Application of number, Communication and Information technology).
- Four optional units.

This book covers the eight compulsory vocational units, the three key skills units but not the four optional units.

GNVQs are offered by three examination boards: BTEC, RSA and City & Guilds. At the back of each chapter there are a number of objective (multiple choice) questions and some of these are taken from actual RSA question papers. The book is structured so that each unit is covered by more than one chapter, but the objective questions would normally be taken only at the end of a unit.

How is the Advanced GNVQ graded?

When you have completed a unit to the required national standard, you will be given a pass. To pass the whole course you have to pass all the mandatory units.

Each unit on its own is not graded as such, so you can only get a pass mark. To gain a higher grade (a merit or a distinction) you need to show that you have consistently produced high quality work above the standard requirement for a pass. The high quality work must consistently show that you have exhibited skills under the following two headings:

Process
Planning your work, information seeking (how much research you have done, the variety of sources, the level of detail, etc.), information handling (how you have collected, collated and summarised the information obtained from your research) and finally evaluation.

Quality of outcomes
The four individual themes (planning, information seeking, information handling, evaluation and quality of outcomes) determine the eventual grade you will obtain and

will be based on the best third of the evidence you present for each theme. In order to get a merit or a distinction you must achieve a third of the evidence in all four themes.

Key skills

All Advanced GNVQ students have to gain the key skills in Application of number, Communication and Information technology at Level 3. Your course at school or college will try to integrate this work into the subjects you study as far as possible, so you will probably supply the evidence of these skills as part of your other assignments. However, it may be difficult to supply all the evidence needed without doing some separate assignments whose sole purpose is to pick up the key skills.

The portfolio

A portfolio needs to be an organised collection of your work and it should be possible for the assessors to be able to find a particular piece of work quickly. It therefore needs to be kept in sections with dividers between each section, and it should have page numbers with a contents page at the front.

Also included within the portfolio will be the forms which your tutor will fill in when assessing your work. The purpose of these forms is to provide basic information regarding the status of your evidence with respect to each unit.

GNVQ units

What does a unit consist of?

A GNVQ unit consists of the following:

- The name of the unit. For instance, the one shown in Figure 1 is Unit 1: Information technology systems.
- A number of elements, each of which describes briefly what you need to do. Each element has a number of performance criteria (PCs) which you must meet. If you look at Figure 1 you will see that under the performance criteria there are some words or phrases which are emboldened, and each of these words or phrases has a range statement belonging to it which lists what is meant by the statement.

If you look at Element 1.1 (Investigate industrial and commercial information technology systems), performance criteria 1 states that you must describe and give examples of commercial and industrial systems. The range statements then tell us what types of commercial and industrial systems we need to be aware of. The range therefore adds more detail to the performance criteria.

The evidence indicators set out exactly what is required as evidence to fulfil all the performance criteria, and also provide details as to the amount of evidence required.

The amplification section expands on some of the key terms used in the range section and is used primarily to add further detail, define the way certain terms are to be used and provide detail on the depth or scope of the element.

The guidance section is mainly for the benefit of your tutors and gives them further information on how the evidence for the assessment might be produced.

What needs to be covered for the award of the Advanced GNVQ?

For the award of the qualification, it is necessary to study the following mandatory units as well as the units in the key skills. In addition, there are four optional units which are not covered in this book.

Unit 1: Information technology systems (Advanced) **29**

Element 1.1: Investigate industrial and commercial information technology systems

PERFORMANCE CRITERIA
A student must:

1. describe and give examples of **commercial** and **industrial systems**
2. **analyse commercial systems**
3. **evaluate** the selected **commercial systems**
4. **analyse industrial systems**
5. **evaluate** the selected **industrial systems**

RANGE
Commercial systems: booking systems, electronic funds transfer, electronic point of sale systems, stock control, order processing, payroll processing

Industrial systems: design, process control, robotics, environmental control, traffic control

Criteria for analysis: purpose, hardware, software, data, people, processing activities, inputs, outputs, advantages, limitations, impact on environment

Criteria for evaluation: comparison with alternative system, costs, benefits (speed, efficiency, accuracy, quality), identification of potential improvements

EVIDENCE INDICATORS
A report covering all the criteria for analysis and evaluation, relating to:

- two commercial IT systems
- two industrial IT systems.

Notes describing in general terms other types of commercial and industrial systems, with one example of each.

AMPLIFICATION
Information technology systems (element title) the hardware, software, information, staff and accommodation which together enable information technology operations.

Commercial systems (PC1, PC2 and PC3) good examples include airlines, holiday or hotel booking systems, retail stores and mail order companies.

Industrial systems (PC1, PC4 and PC5) for example domestic systems such as washing machines and central heating systems, systems in public areas such as traffic lights, car speeding camera systems and photographic processing facilities, and systems used in the manufacture of electronic circuit boards, bottles, automobiles and plastic pipes.

Impact on environment (PC2 and PC4 range) for example impact on travel, pollution, radiation, better information about environmental conditions.

Selected systems (PC3 and PC5) the systems should be either selected by the teacher/tutor, or by the students and agreed with the teacher/tutor. The systems should be large enough to enable students to consider all the items in the criteria for analysis and evaluation range.

GUIDANCE
Ideally the investigations will be carried out through visits to local commercial and industrial organisations which have extensive computing systems, but they could be completed using case-study material. Any case-study materials should reflect real systems and must adequately cover the range.

Commercial organisations such as supermarkets which use bar codes or magnetic strip systems to determine customer bills and to implement stock control and reordering activities, will provide a good area of study with which students are likely to be familiar.

The use of the Bankers Automated Clearing Services (BACS), enabling payment of wages to be made directly to an employee's bank account, provides another ideal area of study, because it involves electronic funds transfer (EFT) and payroll processing. It is also likely that case-study materials are available for this area of study.

There are a great variety of industrial systems suited to a case study approach, but students may benefit from undertaking an initial study of an area with which they have some experience, such as a domestic heating system. This type of system offers an opportunity to grasp the concepts involved before progressing to more industrially-based systems.

This element builds on the corresponding element at Intermediate level, is closely related to other elements in this unit and has close links with all the elements in Unit 2. There are also close links between the commercial aspects of this element and Units 3 and 7.

Figure 1 Page from the GNVQ syllabus covering Element 1.1: Investigate industrial and commercial information technology systems

Mandatory units

Unit 1: Information technology systems

Element 1.1: Investigate industrial and commercial information technology systems
Element 1.2: Investigate components of an information technology system
Element 1.3: Investigate the operation of a microprocessor system
Element 1.4: Install and configure a stand-alone computer system

Unit 2: Using information technology

Element 2.1: Process commercial documents
Element 2.2: Process presentational and technical graphic designs
Element 2.3: Model data
Element 2.4: Develop a control system

Unit 3: Organisations and information technology
Element 3.1: Investigate the flow of information in organisations
Element 3.2: Investigate data handling systems
Element 3.3: Use information technology for a data handling activity
Element 3.4: Investigate the safety and security requirements for a data handling activity

Unit 4: Communications and networking
Element 4.1: Investigate electronic communications
Element 4.2: Use electronic communications to transfer data
Element 4.3: Investigate computer networks
Element 4.4: Use a computer network

Unit 5: Systems analysis
Element 5.1: Investigate principles of systems analysis and specification
Element 5.2: Undertake systems analysis
Element 5.3: Produce a system specification

Unit 6: Software
Element 6.1: Investigate software
Element 6.2: Examine software production
Element 6.3: Investigate the production of automated procedures

Unit 7: Database development
Element 7.1: Create relational database structures for a given specification
Element 7.2: Create data input forms for a database
Element 7.3: Create database reports

Unit 8: Information technology projects and teamwork
Element 8.1: Explore information technology team projects
Element 8.2: Contribute to an information technology team project
Element 8.3: Evaluate an information technology team project

Key skills units (Level 3)

Application of number
Element 3.1: Collect and record data
Element 3.2: Tackle problems
Element 3.3: Interpret and present data

Communication
Element 3.1: Take part in discussions
Element 3.2: Produce written material
Element 3.3: Use images
Element 3.4: Read and respond to written materials

Information technology
Element 3.1: Prepare information
Element 3.2: Process information
Element 3.3: Present information
Element 3.4: Evaluate the use of information technology

How to use this book

This book covers the material needed for the mandatory units and the key skills and it is organised into chapters which cover one or more elements. Several chapters are grouped together to form one unit.

Included in each chapter is a series of activities which are numbered in the following way: Activity 1.7 means that the activity is in Chapter 1 and that it is the seventh activity in the chapter.

Assignments are also included in each chapter and these take longer to do than the activities. They also cover specific elements. Assignments are coded in the same way as the activities, but with the letter 'A' before the number to show that it is an assignment rather than an activity, so A1.2 means that this is an assignment in Chapter 1 and that it is the second of the assignments in this chapter.

Both the assignments and activities can be placed in your portfolio to supply the evidence for the internal and external assessors.

The grid on page xi shows which activities and assignments cover the various elements, and that on page xii shows how they relate to the key skills.

Important notes

It is important to bear the following in mind:

- A piece of work, be it an assignment or an activity, can provide the evidence for more than one element.
- All your work should be done using a computer wherever possible.
- Your portfolio should be presented in a professional manner. Keep back-up copies of all your work.
- All the evidence that you are providing should be sufficient, authentic (all your own work) and relevant (i.e. tests what the performance criteria require to be tested).
- It may be necessary to include computer disks as part of your portfolio in order to show the assessors how a program or database that you have developed works.
- The assessors and verifiers should find the portfolio easy to read, understand and access. The index should identify what units and elements the evidence refers to.
- You can use screenshots to capture and help explain things which are on the screen that cannot be printed out in the normal way. Ask your tutor to explain how this is done.

Acknowledgements

Thanks to Sarah Wilman and Sandy Marshall of Stanley Thornes for their encouragement and help in producing this book, and also to David Mackin for his help and patience during the editing process.

Thanks are also due to the following for their permission to use copyright material: Dr Martin Wynn of H P Bulmer Ltd; Alan Mather and Paul Winward of Terry & Partners; Peter Buckingham of Britannia Airways Ltd; Peter Jones of Sefton Technical Services; British Aerospace; and Tesco plc.

Thank you also to the Royal Society of Arts for allowing the use of past examination questions.

While every effort has been made to contact the owners of copyright material, this may not have been possible in all cases; any omissions brought to our attention will be remedied in future printings.

GNVQ Advanced Information Technology

How the activities and assignments relate to the mandatory units and elements

The following matrix shows how the activities and assignments relate to the units and elements. By keeping a record of your work, many of these exercises will generate useful evidence for your portfolio.

MANDATORY UNITS	Activities	Assignments
1 Information technology systems		
1.1 Investigate industrial and commercial information technology systems	1.1–1.12	A1.1, A1.2
1.2 Investigate components of an information technology system	2.1–2.4	A2.1
1.3 Investigate the operation of a microprocessor system	2.5	A2.2
1.4 Install and configure a stand-alone computer system	2.6	A2.3
2 Using information technology		
2.1 Process commercial documents	3.1–3.5	A3.1
2.2 Process presentational and technical graphic designs	3.7	A3.2, A3.3
2.3 Model data	4.1–4.15	A4.1
2.4 Develop a control system	4.16–4.20	A4.2, A4.3
3 Organisations and information technology		
3.1 Investigate the flow of information in organisations	5.1–5.7	A5.1
3.2 Investigate data handling systems	6.1	A6.1
3.3 Use information technology for a data handling activity		A14.2
3.4 Investigate the safety and security requirements for a data handling activity	6.2–6.6	A6.2
4 Communications and networking		
4.1 Investigate electronic communications	7.1–7.4	A7.1
4.2 Use electronic communications to transfer data	7.5	A7.2
4.3 Investigate computer networks	8.1–8.4	A8.1
4.4 Use a computer network	8.5	A8.2, A8.3
5 Systems analysis		
5.1 Investigate principles of systems analysis and specification	9.1–9.19, 10.2	A9.1
5.2 Undertake systems analysis	10.2	A10.1
5.3 Produce a system specification	10.1, 10.2	A10.1
6 Software		
6.1 Investigate software	11.1–11.8	A11.1
6.2 Examine software production	12.1, 12.2	A12.1
6.3 Investigate the production of automated procedures	12.3–12.5	A12.2
7 Database development		
7.1 Create relational database structures for a given specification	13.1–13.4	A13.1
7.2 Create data input forms for a database	14.1–14.4	A14.1
7.3 Create database reports	14.5–14.7	A14.2
8 Information technology projects and teamwork		
8.1 Explore information technology team projects	15.1	A15.1
8.2 Contribute to an information technology team project	15.2	A15.2
8.3 Evaluate an information technology team project	15.3	A15.3

How the activities and assignments relate to the key skills

The following matrix shows how the activities and assignments provide opportunities to provide evidence for the key skills. By keeping a record of your work, many of these exercises will generate useful evidence for your portfolio.

Key skills	Activities	Assignments
Application of number		
3.1 Collect and record data	1.12, 4.5, 4.11, 4.12, 4.14, 4.15, 7.3, 8.4	A4.1
3.2 Tackle problems	4.5, 4.6, 4.9, 4.11, 4.12–4.14, 7.3, 8.4	A4.1
3.3 Interpret and present data	1.12, 4.5, 4.7–4.11, 4.12–4.15, 7.3, 8.4	A4.1
Communication		
3.1 Take part in discussions	4.2, 4.17, 4.18, 5.5, 5.6, 7.1, 9.5, 9.6, 9.9, 15.2	A3.3, A7.1, A8.1–A8.3, A9.1, A15.1–A15.3
3.2 Produce written material	1.7, 5.4, 5.7, 6.6, 8.1, 9.4, 10.2, 11.7, 12.1	A1.2, A2.1–A2.3, A3.1–A3.3, A4.1–A4.3, A5.1, A6.1, A6.2, A7.1, A8.1–A8.3, A9.1, A10.1, A11.1, A12.1, A12.2, A13.1, A14.1, A14.2, A15.1–A15.3
3.3 Use images	1.7, 2.2, 2.6, 5.7, 6.6, 9.10, 9.11, 10.2	A1.2, A2.1–A2.3, A3.1–A3.3, A4.1–A4.3, A5.1, A6.1, A6.2, A7.1, A8.1–A8.3, A10.1, A11.1, A12.1, A12.2, A13.1, A14.1, A14.2, A15.1–A15.3
3.4 Read and respond to written materials	1.7, 2.4, 5.7, 8.1, 10.1, 10.2, 12.1	A1.2, A2.2, A2.3, A3.1, A3.2, A4.3, A5.1, A6.1, A6.2, A7.1, A7.2, A8.1–A8.3, A9.1
Information technology		
3.1 Prepare information	3.1–3.4, 3.6, 3.7, 8.3, 9.9, 9.19, 11.1, 11.4, 12.4	A1.2, A2.1–A2.3, A3.1, A3.2, A4.1–A4.3, A5.1, A6.2, A7.1, A8.1–A8.3, A9.1, A10.1, A11.1, A12.1, A12.2, A13.1, A14.1, A14.2, A15.1–A15.3
3.2 Process information	3.1–3.4, 3.7, 3.2, 4.6–4.8, 4.11, 4.15, 5.2, 8.3, 9.1, 9.2, 9.19, 11.1, 14.6	A1.2, A2.1–A2.3, A3.1–A3.3, A4.1–A4.3, A5.1, A6.1, A6.2, A7.1, A8.1–A8.3, A9.1, A10.1, A11.1, A12.1, A12.2, A13.1, A14.1, A14.2, A15.1–A15.3
3.3 Present information	3.1–3.4, 3.7, 4.15, 8.3, 9.8	A1.2, A2.1–A2.3, A3.1–A3.3, A4.1–A4.3 A5.1, A6.1, A6.2, A7.1, A8.1–A8.3, A9.1, A10.1, A11.1, A12.1, A12.2, A13.1, A14.1, A14.2, A15.1–A15.3
3.4 Evaluate the use of information technology	1.7, 1.8, 2.4, 3.2, 7.1, 10.1, 12.4, 15.3	A3.3, A4.1–A4.3, A6.1, A7.1, A7.2, A8.1–A8.3

1 Industrial and commercial information technology systems

What is covered in this chapter

In this chapter we will look at a wide variety of information technology systems in both industry and commerce.

Element 1.1: Investigate industrial and commercial information technology systems

- Commercial systems
- Industrial systems
- Criteria for analysis
- Criteria for evaluation
- Tesco case study
- Britannia Airways case study
- London Transport case study
- H P Bulmer case study
- Sefton traffic control system case study

Resources you will need for your portfolio for Element 1.1
- Your written answers to the activities and assignments in this chapter.

Activity 1.1

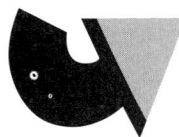

A washing machine can be considered to be an industrial system in spite of most people thinking that it is a relatively simple machine. A look at the steps it automatically performs reveals that its operation is quite complex.

Consider a typical weekly wash. There is a variety of different-coloured clothes to be washed, made of different fabrics with different washing instructions. Imagine you are going to wash the clothes by hand in a sink and then hang them out on the line to dry. Write a list of the steps, in order, that you would take to perform this task.

Commercial systems

Commercial systems are those systems used to help in the administrative activities of a business or organisation. There is a wide range of systems, and many larger organisations will use several of them. You will be expected to know about the following systems in particular:

- booking systems
- electronic funds transfer (EFT)
- electronic point of sale systems (EPOS)
- stock control
- order processing
- payroll processing.

Booking systems

There are many different types of booking systems in use and these include those used in travel agencies for booking holidays and airline, railway and ferry tickets, and those for booking seats at concerts. Such systems need to make sure that double bookings cannot occur and that the correct tickets are printed after payment has been made. Because tickets can be booked at a large number of places it is necessary to use networks in which terminals – usually just a monitor and keyboard – situated anywhere in the country (or even the world) can access a central computer which holds all the booking details.

Electronic funds transfer (EFT)

More and more financial transactions (transactions are pieces of business) are now performed without any paperwork such as cheques. Instead, electronic signals are passed from one computer to another. These may, for example, tell the computer to deduct an amount from one account and then to pass it to another computer where it is added to another account. The main advantage of such a system is that it makes it much quicker and safer to transfer large amounts of money, although the financial institutions do have to make sure that they code the electronic signals so that they cannot be intercepted and altered.

Most large organisations make use of the **BACS (Bankers' Automated Clearing Service)** system to pay their staff, which uses the data from the organisations' payroll programs to transfer money from their bank accounts to the accounts of their employees. Such a system saves time and reduces the number of pieces of paper in circulation.

Activity 1.2

Identify a place where you might go to find out more about how a BACS system works. Wages at your college may be paid in this way.

Electronic point of sale (EPOS) systems

EPOS systems make use of the computerised tills used in shops, garages, etc. As well as providing the customers with itemised bills, they also provide useful management information which may be used for re-ordering stock or for predicting customer trends.

An extension of this system is **EFTPOS**, which stands for electronic fund transfer at point of sale. As well as providing the same services as the standard EPOS system it has the additional facility of electronic funds transfer. Funds can be transferred directly from a person's bank account to a store's account using a card called a debit card. The Switch card is the most popular debit card system in use at present and is accepted at all main retail outlets. It is a much faster method of payment than payment by cheque, and the retailer gets the money much more quickly since it is not necessary to wait several days for the cheque to be cleared.

Stock control

Most organisations require some stock to be kept, even if only supplies of office stationery, and it is important to keep track of the amount of stock so that items are re-ordered when stocks are getting low. Many companies are involved in the manufacture of goods from raw materials or components and the lack of a single item can stop a whole production line and cause a company to lose large amounts of money. Accurate stock-taking must therefore be an integral part of a business. One way to avoid this situation is for a company to buy so much stock that it is unlikely ever to run out. The problem with this approach is that stock costs money, so it means tying money up in stock rather than using it more profitably. Also, the more stock that is held the more difficult it is to find a particular stock item, and the greater the amount of resources needed to deal with it (i.e. storage space and staff).

With a computerised stock control system, a balance is maintained between keeping the amount of stock held at any one time to a minimum while at the same time making sure that the demand for stock can be satisfied. Food retailers such as Tesco have very efficient stock control systems since many of the items they sell have a shelf-life of only a couple of days, so if they buy too much they may have to sell it at a reduced price or even throw it away. There is a case study on Tesco later in this chapter which looks at how it deals with stock control.

Order processing

Any organisation involved in the supply of goods or services has to have an administrative procedure to deal with customers' orders. Order processing systems record the details of each order as it comes in, check to see if the goods are in stock, check to see if the customer owes the organisation any money or if the value of the order will bring the customer's account above their credit limit, and then arrange for the order to be made up and delivered and for the customer to be invoiced for the price of the goods. Order processing is dealt with in more detail in the Tesco and H P Bulmer case studies later in this chapter.

Payroll processing

All employees expect to be paid the correct amount and on time, so payroll processing is crucial to any organisation. Employees can be paid in different ways: for example salaried employees have their annual salary divided by twelve to be paid monthly, whereas other staff have an hourly rate of pay and are paid weekly according to the number of hours they have worked. These hours may be at a basic rate or at an enhanced overtime rate for working weekends, bank holidays, etc. In addition to their basic pay, some employees may receive bonuses, commission and so on.

Not all employees get the same pay, even if they are doing identical jobs. Some may be given more pay because they have worked in the organisation longer. Some people's pay may differ because the amounts deducted vary, for example the amount of tax. This depends on a person's tax code which in turn is determined by an individual's circumstances. Each employee is supplied with a detailed breakdown of the amount they are paid, including deductions, in the form of a payslip.

In addition to the money paid to employees, an organisation has to send money to many other organisations such as the Inland Revenue for income tax and National Insurance contributions, pension agencies for the payment of pension contributions, trade unions for the payment of subscriptions and so on.

Because of the security and cost problems of dealing with the transfer of large amounts of money, many organisations use electronic funds transfer (EFT) using BACS to transfer the money between the organisation's bank account and the employee's account. They can also use the system to make payments to the Inland Revenue of income tax and National Insurance contributions that have been deducted from employees' pay.

Activity 1.3

Investigate the payroll system in an organisation with which you are familiar. You may find that the BACS system is used.

Industrial systems

Industrial systems are systems which use IT for the monitoring of devices and for controlling robots, industrial processes and equipment. In some ways industrial systems are the Cinderellas of the computing world because their use is not as apparent to the general public as the more up-front commercial systems. Industrial systems are very important and without them even the simplest jobs like driving to work or doing the weekly washing can become a much harder task.

Some of the tasks performed by industrial systems include:

- design (buildings, cars, engineering components, structures, chips, etc.);
- process control (washing machines, central heating systems, chemical processes, etc.);
- robotics (paint-spraying, welding, computerised fork-lift trucks, etc.);
- environmental control (flood and tidal warning systems, weather forecasting, pollution monitoring, etc.);
- traffic control.

Design

Because changes in design are so easy to make using a computer, it is hard to find any aspect of designing that is still performed manually. **Computer-aided design (CAD)** packages are used to manipulate the designs of, for example, buildings, cars, engineering components, structures (bridges, tunnels, etc.) and computer chips. Designs can be made up from previously stored shapes and drawings in a fraction of the time it would take to do a manual drawing. In addition, alterations can be made rapidly without the need for redrawing. More information on the use of CAD can be obtained from the case study in Chapter 3 based on a practice of consulting engineers, Terry & Partners.

Process control

Process control seeks to influence how a process advances by the use of data received from sensors. The sensors continually monitor certain quantities and, using a stored program, a microprocessor is able to influence the output in some way. Process control is used in washing machines and central heating systems. In the chemical industry it is used to ensure that chemical reactions produce the most profitable yield of product. Using computers in this way provides more accurate control, and later in this chapter we will look at the way in which process control can be used to perform the sequence of processes needed to wash clothes. Process control in cider-making is studied in the H P Bulmer case study. Chapter 4 examines process control in more depth and includes a case study on how it is used to help fly sophisticated aircraft.

Robotics

Computer-controlled robots are a feature of many assembly lines, particularly in the car industry where they are used to perform a variety of tasks such as assembling, welding, paint-spraying and quality control. Robots have the advantage over manual methods of being able to complete the task to the same high standard, 24 hours per day if necessary, sometimes in conditions that would be dangerous for a human operator.

It is now common to see robots moving materials or stock from one place to another in huge automated warehouses. These robots, which resemble fork-lift trucks, are connected to a central computer which controls them, telling them where to place incoming stock and where to assemble customers' orders. Such a system is looked at in Chapter 4 where there is a case study based on a large stationery wholesaler.

Environmental control

For plants and animals to thrive it is necessary to keep them in the correct environmental conditions. For example, by ensuring that plants receive the correct levels of nutrients, moisture, sunlight and heat, farmers can be certain that they grow at their optimum rate and produce much bigger harvests than if the environmental conditions were left to chance. Computer-controlled sensors pick up data about the environment so that it can be changed if necessary.

Humans also need optimum environmental conditions in order to work efficiently. If an office is too cold or too hot then people will be uncomfortable and unable to concentrate on their work. Air-conditioning systems in offices and cars are computer controlled to provide the optimum working or driving conditions. One of the simplest environment control system is a central heating system which is used to ensure a fairly constant temperature in all the rooms.

Pollution control systems are used by the Environment Agency to ensure the quality of the water in rivers and estuaries. Other types of environmental control systems are those used for monitoring the depths of rivers, and providing a flood warning if the level rises above a certain value and the weather conditions and tides mean that flooding is likely to occur.

Criteria for analysis

Throughout the GNVQ Advanced IT course you will study a wide variety of different systems, some industrial and some commercial. In fact, in many of the case studies in this and later chapters, there are many different systems in use even within the same organisation. You will learn throughout the course to analyse systems either through reading the case studies based on actual companies or organisations, or by researching your own. Either way it is useful to have a checklist outlining some of the things about the system or systems that you need to consider. Such checklists are called the criteria for analysis. It is important to remember that many of the systems you will come across will be very similar, such as payroll or stock-taking, so it is useful to build up a detailed knowledge of such systems. Other systems, such as traffic control systems or systems for controlling pollution, are more specialised and less well known.

It is hard to give a set of criteria for analysis that will be suitable for all the systems you will come across, but the following list should be included when building up your portfolio:

Purpose

All IT systems have been developed for a purpose and this purpose needs to be clearly stated. In this section you need to say specifically what particular system you are looking at. Try to stick with a single system, although many systems overlap with other systems.

Hardware

Since the systems you will be looking at involve IT you need to mention the hardware that is used. **Hardware** is the collective term for the components of the IT system that you can touch, and includes devices such as visual display units, processors, printers, modems, scanners, sensors, motors and robot arms. As well as providing the name of each hardware device, you should also give the specifications of the hardware where possible, such as the amount of **RAM** (**random access memory**), the type of **chip** (**Pentium**, **486**, etc.) and so on.

Software

Software is the name given to the programs that control the hardware. Here you need to look at whether the software used is general purpose software (wordprocessors, databases, spreadsheets, desktop publishing, etc.) or whether it has been written specifically for the application. Many organisations look at the software first and then buy the hardware that it is able to run on.

Data

Data is the name given to the raw facts and figures that are processed by the computer. In many cases the data is input using keyboards but large quantities of data are best input using direct methods such as barcodes or scanning systems. In industrial control systems, the data comes in automatically from sensors which make measurements of certain quantities such as pressure, temperature and light intensity at predetermined intervals. It is important to look at all the methods by which data enters a system.

People

Many information technology systems take over the mundane, repetitive aspects of certain jobs, freeing people to do more interesting and rewarding tasks like dealing with customers. Sometimes an IT system replaces a task that is quite dangerous. Paint-spraying, for example, gives off toxic fumes and is now often performed by robots. In frozen-food warehouses, temperatures are so low that a fork-lift truck driver can spend only an hour or so at a time working in them, but computer-controlled fork-lift trucks are unaffected by low temperatures.

Obviously there are social implications of using an IT system and many companies offset the high initial cost of IT equipment with the savings they make in the number of staff needed to do a job. But you must bear in mind that the use of IT creates a whole range of jobs in its own right: systems analysts, project managers, network managers and programmers are some examples.

Processing activities

A processing activity is something which is done with raw data. In this section you need to include details of the processes that are performed on the data in order to produce the final output.

Inputs

For the processing activities to take place it is necessary to supply an input. The inputs to a system supply the raw data which is then processed in some way to yield the final output.

The inputs to industrial systems usually come via **sensors**, whereas those to commercial systems come via a wide variety of input devices, the commonest of which is the keyboard.

Outputs

For most commercial systems the **outputs** from a system are mainly in the form of paper documents or a screen display. Sometimes the output from one system is a series of electronic signals which may then be used as the input to another system, such as when files are transferred using a network or when **documents** are sent over the Internet using e-mail.

In many industrial systems the outputs may be considered to be the operation of the electric motors, hydraulic pistons, etc. used in a robot arm in a factory.

Advantages

When comparing doing a task using an IT system against performing the same task manually, it is usually fairly easy to see the advantages. For instance, compare using a wordprocessor to produce a letter with using a typewriter that does not have a memory. It is much easier to correct your mistakes using the wordprocessor and this means that the work will be faster. Other advantages include being able to check spelling and grammar quickly, alter the format of the document if necessary and produce as many copies as you like without having to retype it each time.

Many commercial organisations will have been using IT for some time and they will be continually analysing the way they do things to see if improvements could be made by using a different approach or new IT equipment. In situations such as these you will be comparing the new system with the previous one, and discussing the advantages and disadvantages of each.

Limitations

When looking at different systems, you will usually find that they have some limitations. For instance a video library system may record details of members, videos and borrowings perfectly well but be unable to tell you which videos have been taken out the most often over the past year. The video shop manager may well find this information useful if they want to get rid of some of the less popular videos to make more space for new releases. When looking for limitations, it is useful to ask 'is there anything the existing system will not do that you would like it to do?'.

Impact on the environment

Information technology can be used to help improve the environment. Take traffic control systems, for example. These systems make the traffic flow more smoothly so vehicles spend less time in hold-ups, which means that they burn less fuel and produce lower amounts of harmful exhaust gases. Microprocessor-controlled heating systems allow you to control accurately the temperature of each room in a large building and it is easy to turn down the heating of those rooms which are not in use. Such computer-controlled systems therefore save energy and reduce the amount of fuel burnt, which in turn reduces the quantities of carbon dioxide and sulphur dioxide released into the atmosphere.

There are many process control systems used in factories and because these control the processes more accurately there is less waste. In the H P Bulmer case study later in this chapter, you will see that where computers are used to control the fermentation of the crushed apples, there are no longer any ruined batches of cider produced as a result of human error.

Weather forecasting systems use thousands of sensors to monitor the variables which are used to predict the weather. The data from these sensors is processed using some of the most powerful computers in the world to produce a model of the weather and the weather forecast itself. Such systems are able to predict hurricanes, storms and floods, so that precautions, such as moving people away from the area, can be taken.

Commercial IT systems also help improve the environment. With the advent of networking and cheap communications systems, it is now possible for some people to work from home. They therefore no longer have to travel to work, thus reducing fuel consumption and car pollution. In addition, the use of computers in the office means that less paper is used, thus saving trees as well as the energy involved in making the paper.

It has been claimed that by the end of the century computers will account for 10 per cent of the world's power supply. 'Green' computers are now available which have been specially designed with the environment in mind. These computers use less electricity than ordinary computers by 'powering down' the monitor and the disk drives if the computer has been inactive for a certain period of time. Most laser printers, however, are not so environmentally friendly: like photocopiers, they emit the gas ozone which, although useful in the upper regions of the atmosphere, is a poisonous gas when breathed in. Many modern **laser printers**, though, emit little or no ozone. Laser printers do, however, use quite large amounts of power and produce used cartridges which need to be disposed of carefully or preferably recycled.

Activity 1.4

Explain how each of the following systems helps protect the environment:
1 electronic mail systems
2 microprocessor-controlled washing machines.

In Activity 1.1 you identified the steps involved in carrying out a weekly wash by hand. Nowadays most people leave these tasks to automatic washing machines, which are actually industrial IT systems. If we were going to analyse such an industrial system, our criteria for analysis might look something like this:

Criteria for analysis

Purpose: What has the automatic washing machine been designed to do? What tasks does the automatic washing machine perform?

Hardware: What are the main parts of the system? Are there any parts which can also be found in a computer?

Software: Automatic washing machines operate using a series of programs. What media are they stored on? How is a particular program selected? Can a particular instruction within a program be changed easily?

Data: Some data needs to be supplied to the system. What is this data and how is it supplied?

People: Can the system function without humans to operate it? When does the system need a person and what tasks does the person perform? Why is it that the system cannot perform these tasks automatically?

Processing activities: Processing is performed on the input. If you consider the dirty clothes, water (hot and cold), soap powder, power supply and program instructions as the input, what are the processing activities?

Inputs: What inputs need to be given to the system in order to get it to work?

Outputs: What are the results of the processing (i.e. what is the system designed to do)?

Advantages: Compare using an automatic washing machine with doing the washing by hand.

Limitations: Are there any parts of the system that still need to be performed manually? Is the cost of the system a limitation?

Impact on the environment: Are there any energy- or resource-saving features of the system?

Activity 1.5

Try to get access to an automatic washing machine and the instruction manual that goes with it. Under the heading 'Criteria for analysis', produce an outline of the system under each of the subheadings given above, using the information provided to help you.

Criteria for evaluation

We are often required in IT to evaluate an industrial or commercial system. Evaluating means assessing the worth of the system. In other words we are looking at how good it is. There are several criteria we can use when evaluating such systems, including those listed below.

Comparison with alternative systems

One way of assessing the value of a system is to compare it with the way the task was performed before. In some cases this would mean comparing the IT solution with a manual method, but since computer/**microprocessor** systems have been in use for some time you are more likely to be comparing one IT solution with another.

Costs

The cost of any system has to be weighed against its benefits but it is often difficult to work these out in financial terms. For instance, using point-of-sale terminals in super-markets may reduce the amount of time customers spend waiting to pay for their goods, but what is this type of benefit worth financially? Some customers may never shop at the store again if they have to wait too long, while others will be content to wait in the queue.

Sometimes new systems are developed simply to supply the managers of the organisation with more information on which they can base decisions about the way they run the business. More up-to-date management information is clearly a benefit, but it is difficult to quantify it in monetary terms.

In Britain, accountants use something called 'payback' which is the time it takes to recover the cost of a new system from the savings made when it was implemented. In Britain the normal payback period is three years although in many other countries it is longer.

Benefits

The benefits of a new system usually fall into one or more of the following categories:
- speed
- efficiency
- accuracy
- quality.

Identification of potential improvements

Sometimes it is not possible to implement a complete solution to a problem. There may not be enough qualified staff to implement the new system or there may not be enough money in the budget, so often a compromise is reached. It is therefore important to be able to identify any potential improvements to a system. All systems need to be periodically reviewed to make sure that they are still meeting the original objectives, and if they are not either the system needs to be modified or a new system put into place.

If we were to evaluate an automatic washing machine, we might consider the following points:

> ### Criteria for evaluation
> **Comparison with alternative systems**: Make a comparison with doing the washing manually.
> **Costs**: What is the cost of the new system?
> **Benefits**: What are the benefits of using an automatic washing machine? Usually these will be in terms of one or more of the following: speed, efficiency, accuracy or quality. You may be able to think of other benefits that are more applicable to this system.
> **Identification of potential improvements**: Sometimes, when looking for a way of solving a particular problem, the same solution can be applied to other problems that you might not have initially identified. For instance, you might decide that to save energy the washing machine could be used with only half a load. At the same time this would be cheaper because less washing powder would be used, and there would be less waste water.

Activity 1.6

Produce an evaluation of the washing machine you looked at in Activity 1.5 using each of the subheadings above.

In the rest of this chapter we will use case studies to look at the information technology systems used by real companies and organisations. Throughout the book you will come across other case studies and you will also be finding out about some of your own. Building up your knowledge about systems is important: if you get a job in information technology then you could be designing real systems of your own.

Tesco case study

Everyone is familiar with Tesco, one of Britain's top food retailers. Tesco used to have many small, high street shops but now concentrates on developing the huge superstores we see today. Each one stocks over 14 000 food lines and has a sales area of over 2400 square metres.

The laser scanning system (barcode reading system)

Tesco was one of the first high street stores to use a **barcode reader**, which is now called a **laser scanner**. The objectives of the scanning system were to improve the service to customers and to increase company productivity and profits.

The scanning system uses a laser beam to read the **barcode** on the goods. What it is actually doing is reading the numeric code at the bottom of the barcode without needing the number to be typed in. As the barcode is passed across the scanner this number is read, the price and description of the goods are then obtained from the computer, the sale is registered and an itemised receipt is produced.

Benefits of the system to the customers
There are numerous benefits to customers, including the following:
- With the old system, prices were entered into the cash register manually. With the scanning system this is done automatically, which eliminates typing errors.
- The scanning system is reckoned to be 15 per cent more efficient than the manual system, so customers spend less time waiting to be served.
- Produce such as loose tomatoes are weighed at the checkout so the customers no longer have to queue twice – once at the pricing point and again at the checkout.

- Customers can have their cheques and credit card vouchers printed automatically.
- Customers using a debit card such as Switch can withdraw up to £50 in cash from any checkout.
- More promotions can be offered, such as 'buy two and get one free' ('multisaver').
- An itemised receipt is produced like that in Figure 1.1. Notice the detail it contains.

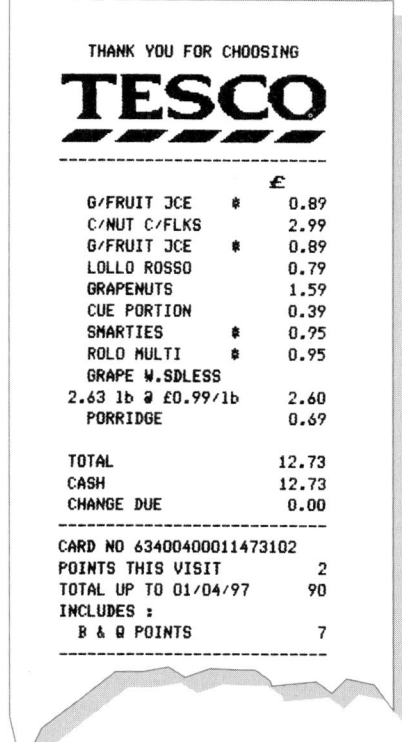

THANK YOU FOR CHOOSING

TESCO

	£
G/FRUIT JCE ⬤	0.89
C/NUT C/FLKS	2.99
G/FRUIT JCE ⬤	0.89
LOLLO ROSSO	0.79
GRAPENUTS	1.59
CUE PORTION	0.39
SMARTIES ⬤	0.?5
ROLO MULTI ⬤	0.95
GRAPE W.SDLESS	
2.63 lb @ £0.99/lb	2.60
PORRIDGE	0.69
TOTAL	12.73
CASH	12.73
CHANGE DUE	0.00

CARD NO 63400400011473102
POINTS THIS VISIT   2
TOTAL UP TO 01/04/97   90
INCLUDES :
   B & Q POINTS   7

Figure 1.1 An itemised receipt

Benefits of the system to the company

- **Improved checkout accuracy**: it is no longer possible for the till operator to key in the wrong price, so there are fewer errors and less fraud.
- **Faster and more efficient throughput**: there is, on average, a 15 per cent saving in time to register the goods in a shopping trolley compared with the manual system.
- **Improved customer service**: new services such as the Clubcard, multisavers, etc. mean that customers enjoy a better service.
- **Improved productivity**: there is no longer a need to price each item individually. Prices are provided on the front of the shelves on which the items are displayed. Weighing and pricing at the checkouts eliminates the need for separate price points.
- **Sales-based ordering**: sales information from the checkout is used to create the orders for stock replacement.
- **Reduced stock levels**: more efficient stock control means lower stock levels are needed, so less money is tied up in stock and there is less likelihood of running out of certain items on the sales floor.
- **Reduced wastage**: perishable goods such as fresh meat and salads can be ordered accurately using the sales information obtained from the checkout.
- **Promotional and sales analysis**: scanned data can be used to assess the effectiveness of special promotions and can provide information about the sales of certain goods.

Disadvantages of the system to the company

- The stores become totally reliant on their computerised systems and the loss of use of a system, even for a short time, can result in chaos.
- Shelf prices need to be checked carefully to ensure that the prices on the shelves match those on the computer.

The barcoding system

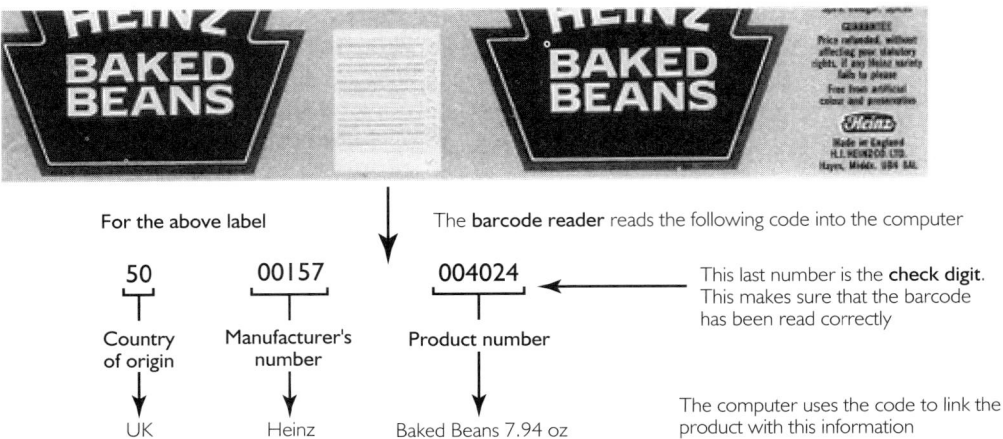

Figure 1.2 A barcode from a tin of Heinz baked beans

Figure 1.2 shows a barcode from a tin of Heinz baked beans. The number at the bottom is called the European Article Number (EAN) and this number is allocated to all product manufacturers by the Article Number Association (ANA).

- The first two digits represent the country where the goods are produced.
- The next five digits identify the suppliers of the goods.
- The following five digits identify the product.
- The final number is a **check digit** and is used to check that the other 12 have been entered correctly.

EFTPOS and the use of debit cards

EFTPOS (electronic funds transfer at point of sale) is the method used by Tesco to transfer money from customers' credit card companies or debit cards directly to the Tesco bank account. A **debit card** is rather like a cheque since the money comes straight out of a person's bank account, except there is no limit to the amount a person can spend using one of these cards – provided that the money is available in the account. With cheques there is a limit, usually £50 or £100, to the amount a customer can write.

Using checkout information for planning bakery production

Sales information from the checkout is used by the in-store bakeries to plan the production for the same day of the following week. This reduces waste and means stores are less likely to run out of bread.

Sales-based ordering

Sales-based ordering is the automatic re-ordering of goods from the warehouse using the sales information from the checkouts. If, for example, 200 tins of baked beans were sold from a certain store in one day, then 200 tins would be automatically re-ordered and delivered to the store the following day from one of the Tesco distribution centres.

Stock control

All ordering is performed by computer and there are fast electronic communication lines between the shops, the distribution centres and head office. There are also direct links to the major suppliers which means that the orders can go straight through to production lines. The advantage with this is that the stock arrives just when it is needed, so it is always fresh. Another advantage of this system is that money does not need to be tied up in stock and may be used for more productive purposes.

Electronic shelf labelling

Tesco is developing a system using liquid-crystal shelf labels containing the price, description and ordering information of goods. The label is operated from a computer using radio signals, which means that if a price is changed on the computer database, the price displayed on the shelf is changed automatically at the same time. This avoids human errors such as a price change on the computer not being transferred to the shelf.

Electronic data interchange (EDI)

Electronic data interchange is a method of speeding up the transfer of orders to suppliers. Using **EDI** eliminates the need for paperwork since the ordering is carried out between the supplier's computer and Tesco's computer. This system is less expensive and quicker than sending the orders by phone, post or fax and cuts out errors such as lost or wrongly printed orders. Tesco can send information to suppliers regarding sales forecasts and information about stock levels so that the suppliers can plan their production appropriately.

Once an electronic order has been placed, the invoice is generated automatically by the supplier's computer. This is sent back and checked by the Tesco computer before payment is made. The H P Bulmer case study later in this chapter looks at EDI in more detail.

The hardware

We have looked at the systems in use by Tesco, and as you can imagine the computers used to run them need to be extremely sophisticated and powerful. The mainframe computers are situated in two computer centres and each one is capable of running all of the company's systems on its own. They can deliver 216 **MIPS** (million instructions per second) and are among the fastest commercial computers in the world.

Since computers are so vital to Tesco's operations, there are back-up procedures in place so that, if one of the computer centres were completely destroyed, the other would be able to re-establish the vital systems within 48 hours. The back-up procedures are tested each year so that staff know exactly what to do if a disaster were to occur.

Designing store layout using CAD

It is no longer necessary to use drawing boards for planning new stores and redesigning existing ones. Instead, computer-aided design (CAD) is used. This has reduced the time taken to plan new stores: a data bank holds designs and plans from existing stores which can be adapted, rather than new ones having to be generated each time. CAD is also able to show three-dimensional views of the stores, and colours, lighting and different finishes on materials can be altered simply by moving the mouse.

When a new store is planned, photographs of the proposed site can be used in conjunction with CAD to see what the area will look like with the Tesco store in place.

CAD is also used to design the warehouse layouts, and the roads and areas surrounding the distribution centres. This is important since the access roads need to be suitable for large articulated vehicles, and there must be ample room around the distribution centres for them to turn round.

Warehouse systems

Computers are used in the warehouse to monitor complex stock control procedures and make the best use of space, time and labour. Like all areas of retailing, better operating methods need to be found to ensure Tesco's continued success. As with all the other systems Tesco has in place, paperwork has been eliminated wherever possible, so the thick binders containing lists of stock items are replaced by computer terminals. These terminals are mounted on fork-lift trucks and give the operators information regarding the movement of the pallets so that stock items can be moved quickly and efficiently. If some stock goes out of the warehouse, for example, then a slot is available for the new stock arriving and notification of this is obtained from the terminal. Efficient use of the available space means the trucks have to travel shorter distances and the whole process is therefore faster. The computer system also monitors where each fork-lift truck is situated in the warehouse so that a particular job can be given to the ones best able to complete it in the least amount of time.

Electronic mail

Tesco, like most other large companies, has realised the benefits of using **electronic mail**. Conventional methods of communication can have a variety of problems such as lost post, unanswered telephones, engaged fax machines, people not at their desks, etc. Electronic mail eliminates many of these problems.

Some of the advantages to Tesco of using electronic mail are as follows:

- Unlike with a telephone call the recipient does not need to be there when the message is sent. People can receive their mail at any terminal connected to the system.
- The sender can be sure that the messages are received.
- It is possible to send mail to a whole department or a group of people without knowing anyone by name.
- The electronic mail system is used as a company information and noticeboard. You can, for example, find out about the latest job vacancies and appointments and look at the latest share price.
- It is possible to send electronic mail to the major suppliers, thus speeding up orders, etc.

Tesco and the Internet

Tesco has now become the first UK supermarket to offer a shopping and delivery service on the **Internet** for all the items it sells. At present, the service is being trialled at one of the larger London stores and customers who have a Tesco loyalty Clubcard are able to browse through and select items from a range of 20 000 product lines. Each customer then selects their method of payment and a suitable time for the goods to be delivered to the person's home. For the delivery, there is a fixed charge of £5 and this is added to the customer's bill. At present the delivery service is available over quite a large area within the vicinity of the store. To pay by credit card, the customer keys in his or her details which are then sent over the Internet. The customer then signs an authorisation slip when the goods are delivered the next day.

The Internet business consultant for Tesco hopes that the Internet shopping service will attract working people who dislike spending the little time they have in the super-market. Customers can also shop 'off-line' using software and a product list available on **CD-ROM**, and send in the order via **CompuServe** or another of the popular Internet service providers. You can take a look at this service yourself at the Internet address http//www.Tesco.co.uk/superstore.

Activities 1.7

Task 1

You are required to do some research into sales-based ordering systems. These systems are used to keep track of the current stock position as the customers buy the goods at the computerised till (point-of-sale terminal). As soon as the number of stock items falls below a certain level (called the re-order level) an order is automatically issued by the computer which is then checked and sent to the supplier.

In particular, you need to investigate the following:
- how the data is captured at the till (in most cases this will be with a barcode reader but there are other methods);
- the advantages to the management of the shop;
- the advantages to the shoppers;
- the advantages to the till operators;
- the disadvantages to the till operators;
- how the point-of-sale system links up with the stock control system.

Use the following sources to get your information:
- local shops;
- textbooks;
- the Internet (most of the large retail chains have a Web site);
- articles in *Computer Weekly*, *Computing* or similar publications (e.g. the *Guardian* computer section).

Produce your findings in the form of a report.

Task 2

Many of the larger retail chains have their own Web sites. As we have seen, Tesco has now extended this so that goods can be ordered over the Internet. Investigate other retailer's sites on the Internet and produce your findings in the form of a brief article to be submitted to a magazine for publication. Ideally your report should provide a comparison between the different sites and facilities offered.

Britannia Airways case study

If you have ever taken a holiday abroad with Thomson Holidays, then you will have probably flown on a plane owned by Britannia Airways. Britannia Airways is a sub-sidiary company owned by Thomson Holidays. It is a charter airline as opposed to a scheduled airline, which means that it books whole aeroplanes full of passengers through a holiday company rather than individual seats on planes.

Since the cost of travelling to and from the destination is only part of the total price of the holiday, costs need to be kept low for the company to be profitable, while still providing a high level of customer service. Information technology is therefore used throughout Britannia to reduce costs, maximise efficiency and customer satisfaction, and increase profits.

Central to Britannia's operations is the planning and managing of the flight programme. This involves the flying staff (pilots and air stewards/stewardesses), the aircraft planning department, engineering, finance and some other areas. Before IT systems were introduced, the only way that information could be passed from one of these areas to another was by paper (memos, letters, etc.). An integrated approach was needed to enable a system in one area to communicate with the systems in other areas.

The first step in trying to develop such a system was to build a business model which charted the main business areas. Britannia's business cycle starts with the production of an outline flying schedule which is then discussed at an annual International Air Transport Association (IATA) conference at which airport take-off and landing slots are agreed. When this is done a revised schedule is produced from which the operations, crew, engineering, procurement (the buying of supplies and services) and finance departments of the business make their plans. The objectives of the new system were to automate all the elements of this process.

Britannia conducted a worldwide search for a software package around which it could base the core system. The integrated flight plan software was chosen out of a possible 45, and was then used as the basis for choosing the hardware. The advantage of the software chosen was that it was based on open systems so it was not necessary to purchase hardware from a particular company. Britannia's computer hardware and software carried a price tag of around £6.5 million, but the system soon delivered benefits in the areas of scheduling and operating the flying programme, which previously had been very labour intensive.

The best way to look at how the new system improved upon the old is by looking at the savings made. Comparing the year the new system was introduced with the previous year shows that the new system contributed an extra 1–2 per cent to the profit of the airline.

The on-the-day decision-making tools are a very important part of the software. These are used for deciding what to do if aircraft have to be diverted, are delayed on take-off or affected by an air traffic control problem. The task performed by the software is to make the best decision, taking all the factors into consideration, to maximise profit and to minimise customer inconvenience.

Finance

The financial system was developed by Britannia in-house. The key element in this system is a 'direct operating cost' system which is based on a large **database** with information about the tariffs charged at all the airports Britannia uses. This tariff information includes everything from parking an aircraft overnight to loading it with breakfasts for passengers. The system checks the invoices which arrive from the airports used against the main database and makes sure that the costs are correct. Invoice errors are picked up which might previously have gone undetected. This saves Britannia a lot of money and adds an extra 1 per cent to the profit. Electronic data interchange (EDI) is also used to exchange information with the suppliers.

The new system supplies important management information and it is possible to segment different areas of the business and look at their contributions to costs and overall profit. It can also be used to determine the holiday routes that are the most profitable.

Engineering

Using the engineering system, aircraft maintenance work is carefully scheduled so that there is minimal time wasted between the completion of one task and the start of the next. It is anticipated that in the future this new system could save about 1.5 per cent on maintenance costs.

Activity 1.8

Read the Britannia Airways case study carefully.

1 There was a reference in the case study to a system called EDI (electronic data interchange). Find out what this system is, how it works and why so many large companies now find it necessary to use it. Produce a document outlining your findings.
2 Many of the benefits of the new system have been identified in the case study. Produce a list of the main benefits.
3 As you can see from the text, it is very important for Britannia to know exactly how much everything costs. Why do you think this is?
4 Here is a list of systems, some of which are commercial and the rest industrial. Your task is to classify them under each heading.
   - Cabin temperature control
   - Route information displayed for the benefit of passengers using the plane's navigation computer
   - The aircraft's automatic pilot computer
   - The small computers used by the air stewards/stewardesses for recording drink and duty-free purchases
   - Crew rostering
   - Procurement (i.e. the purchasing of supplies and services)
   - Cabin air-conditioning system
   - Engineering maintenance scheduling
   - Air traffic control.

London Transport case study

London Transport used to run the bus services throughout the city, but since privatisation the bus services have been run by private operators, although London Transport still oversees the whole operation and makes sure the public receives a high quality service.

A new system is being developed by London Transport which will monitor the positions of all the buses and relay their expected times of arrival at the bus stops. People standing at the bus stops will therefore know exactly how long they will have to wait. Although this system is only working on a small number of routes at the moment, London Transport hopes to apply it to all the 6500 buses running along the 3000 kilometres of the capital's roads within the next few years.

The system is set to work as follows (see Figure 1.3). Buses on a certain route are pinpointed to within 10 metres using microwave transmitters and receivers attached to lamp-posts situated at various places along the route. There is also some hardware on the bus itself. On each bus there is a microwave transponder, **modem** and odometer (a device used to measure the distance the bus has travelled by measuring the number of

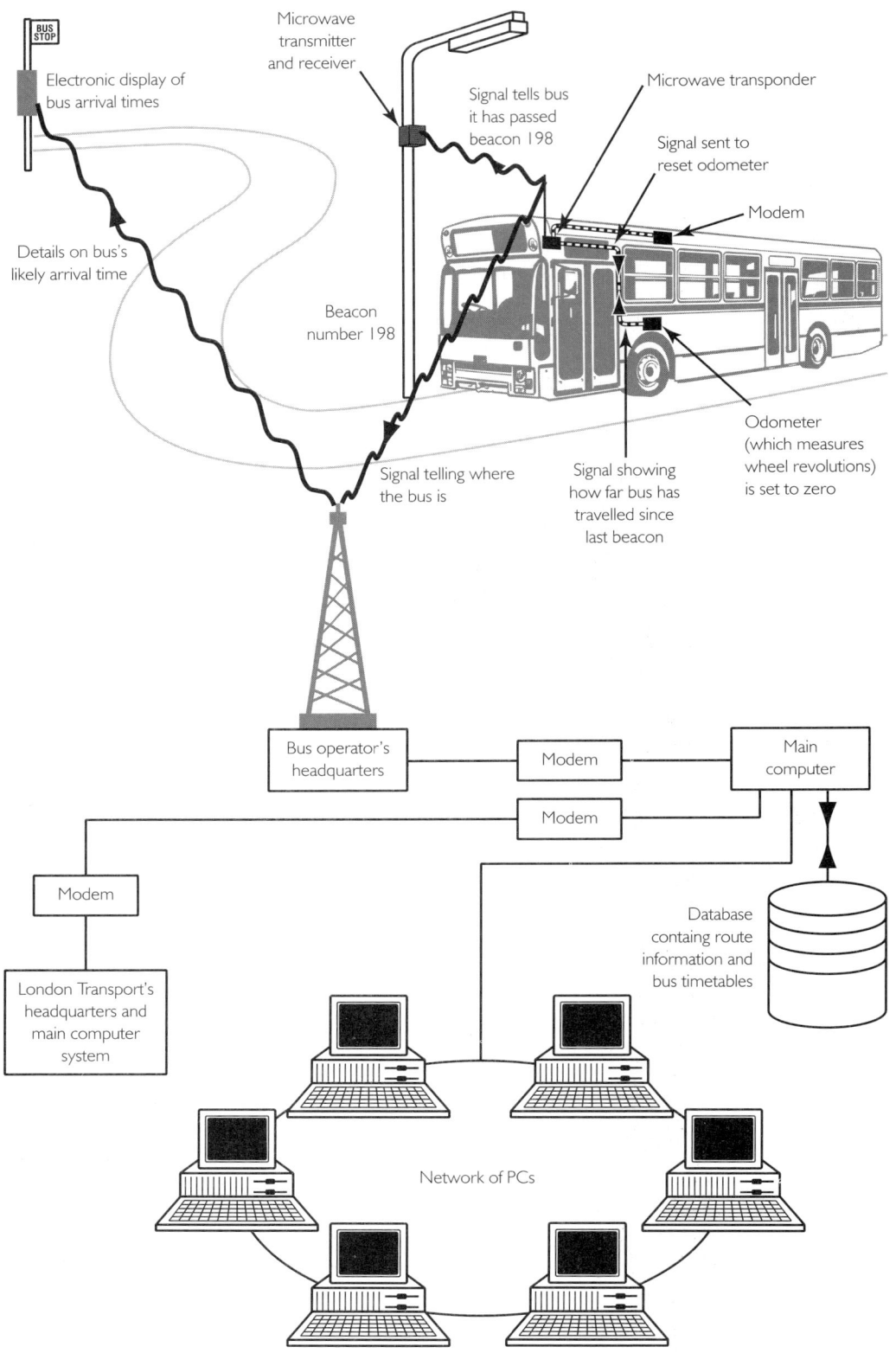

Electronic display of
bus arrival times

Microwave
transmitter
and receiver

Signal tells bus
it has passed
beacon 198

Microwave transponder

Signal sent to
reset odometer

Modem

Details on bus's
likely arrival time

Beacon
number 198

Odometer
(which measures
wheel revolutions)
is set to zero

Signal telling where
the bus is

Signal showing
how far bus has
travelled since
last beacon

Bus operator's
headquarters

Modem

Main
computer

Modem

Modem

Database
containing route
information and
bus timetables

London Transport's
headquarters and
main computer
system

Network of PCs

Figure 1.3 System for monitoring the buses

revolutions of the wheels). Transponders are used to feed back the position of the bus to the computer centre. 'Transponder' is another name for 'transmitting responder': a transponder means that it not only sends out signals but is also capable of receiving them. As the bus passes a microwave beacon attached to a lamp-post it picks up the identity of the beacon that it has just passed and resets the odometer. The modem is used to transmit the information (i.e. the bus's position), using the radio, back to the central computer system.

Here the data is received and analysed and compared against a database containing information about routes and timetables. Using the data from this database the computer can work out when the bus is due at any of the stops along its route and can relay this information back to the electronic timetable which is at every bus stop. By looking at this timetable, waiting passengers can see that there is a bus on its way and are given an accurate time of arrival.

In addition to the equipment on the buses and at the roadside, the computers at the London Transport Operations Centre use a **network** of PCs with an **operating system** called **UNIX**. This network is also connected to the networks of the individual private bus operators.

One important feature of the system is that it doesn't just rely on the data from the stored timetable to work out the likely time the buses will take to travel from one beacon to another. For instance, if there are roadworks or a diversion, the system uses some of the timings from previous buses which have travelled the same route.

Because the private operators of each bus service are run on a franchise basis, the contracts are frequently reviewed and only those operators that provide a high level of service and customer satisfaction have their contracts renewed. Using the new system, London Transport can immediately see which operators are the most efficient.

Activity 1.9

1 Identify the main advantages of the new system.
2 Both the bus operators and London Transport use networks. What are the main advantages of using a network?

H P Bulmer case study

H P Bulmer is a medium-sized British company based in Hereford and has been involved in cider-making for over 100 years. Cider is an alcoholic drink made from apples; its consumption in the UK is growing at a rate of 8 per cent. Currently, around 450 million litres per year are consumed. The brands produced by the company include Woodpecker, Strongbow and Scrumpy Jack (Figure 1.4). Around 900 staff are employed, with about 500 using PCs and 50 using terminals. There are around 28 permanent IT staff and 7 employed on a contract basis, with the majority of these involved in systems development.

The main activities of the company can be summarised as follows:
- manufacturing (making the cider by the fermentation of apples);
- trading and marketing (dealing with customers who buy the cider and suppliers who supply bottles, labels, equipment, etc.);
- finance (payment of wages, accounts, etc.);
- distribution (stock control, dispatch, delivery, etc.).

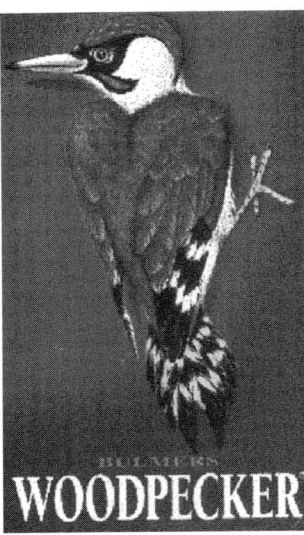

Figure 1.4 Three of the ciders produced by H P Bulmer

One of the problems that Bulmer had with its old systems was that a large number of applications had evolved separately in different areas of the business and this meant that the data from the different areas was not consistent. For instance, instead of a single customer file, there were three: one for order entry, one for invoicing and another for sales outlets (pubs, off-licences, etc.). This meant that information obtained about customers depended on which of the customer files was being used. When the company wanted to produce sales analyses, conflicting results were obtained. It is for this reason that the company decided to rationalise and centralise its customer and product information.

The IT Director had to develop a new system which was controlled centrally but with clear ownership of each application by the department concerned. **Steering groups** and working parties were set up consisting of members of staff from all the departments involved. Agreement was reached on all the definitions and concepts used so that everyone knew they were talking about the same thing. All the data for the system is kept in an **Oracle data dictionary** and the systems development and support teams all use computer-aided system engineering (**CASE**) design tools. CASE involves combining a variety of software tools to assist computer systems development staff produce and maintain high quality systems. Oracle, which should not be confused with the teletext service, is a relational database management system suitable for large, **multi-user** systems.

Within the IT department there are three systems development teams, with each team developing a group of associated applications. These teams cover between them the four core business areas mentioned above. Each team reports to the IT Director as well as to the head of the user department. The budgeting and delivery of the systems is the responsibility of the project sponsor, who will be a senior director of the company.

The main objectives for the new systems include:
- efficient, auditable sales order processing;
- accurate monitoring of revenue generation;
- efficient distribution;
- exploitation of opportunities in the marketplace.

The distribution management system

The distribution management system (DMS) covers sales order processing, warehouse management and distribution. Although the initial development costs were £2 million, the system is already making savings of £400 000 per year.

The distribution operation is large, with over 400 product lines being delivered to the main brewers, the 'big six' supermarkets and outlets such as the smaller off-licences. During the heavy trading periods, the company is involved in the delivery of over 3000 pallets a day on 130 trucks.

Warehouse control

Facilities for controlling the goods in the warehouses are available at the Hereford factory as well as at the depots throughout the country. The system handles stock location and enables the staff to order replacement stock and to obtain accurate, up-to-date information on any items of stock in any of the warehouses. The system also helps with planning the routes that the delivery lorries have to take and their stops along the way.

Customer service

All the telesales staff are located at the Hereford head office. Their job is to take orders, confirm the availability of the goods and confirm delivery dates over the telephone (see Figure 1.5). At the busiest times telesales staff can take an average of over 1000 orders per day, ranging from a single line to several pages. On receipt of an order the order details are automatically passed to the warehouse where a picking list is produced, along with the location numbers of the positions in the warehouse where the goods are stored. A place in the warehouse is also assigned to the pallet on which the goods are placed. Once the goods have been placed ready for dispatch a dispatch note is produced.

Figure 1.5 Inputting telesales orders

Using the new system has resulted in many benefits besides the obvious financial ones. It is now possible to track all stock movements, and an accurate dispatch note can be produced. Under the old system, the dispatch note was printed before the stock was picked, so sometimes it needed to be amended by hand because some of the order was unavailable. Management information about orders is now vastly improved, and customers are more satisfied with the service they receive.

Profitability management system

An account manager is responsible for the sales and servicing of a group of major customers. In order to assess its sales success under the old system, Bulmer looked only at the volume of cider it managed to sell. However, this was misleading since it did not take into account the profitability of the sales: after all, sales could easily be increased by negotiating a price at which the company is making very little profit. Now the system assesses the account managers on their sales by taking into account how much they have spent on marketing, advertising, special promotions and discounts.

Weekly sales report

A sales report lands on the desk of each director and senior manager every week, and is the most important piece of management information they receive. Basically it presents the sales of each product and expresses them as a percentage of the budget figure.

Electronic data interchange (EDI)

There is now a move away from using paper to transfer information between Bulmer and its main customers. Instead, data is transferred electronically. This is how Bulmer and one of the large supermarket chains plan to use EDI to cut out the use of paper (see Figure 1.6):

- prices for the goods are agreed between Bulmer and the supermarket chain;
- Bulmer enters the agreed price on the system;
- this price file is sent electronically to the supermarket head office;
- there is confirmation that the retailer has received this file;
- the retailer can then place an EDI order;
- Bulmer load the vehicles with the pallets containing the order, and as each pallet is loaded a barcode on the side of the pallet is scanned and the information used to build up a delivery note;
- the delivery note is then sent electronically to the retailer;
- goods are delivered to the retailer;
- the retailer confirms delivery and confirmation is sent using EDI to Bulmer;
- when this confirmation is received, Bulmer automatically issues an invoice;
- the invoice is automatically paid and money is transferred from the retailer's bank account to the Bulmer bank account.

The hardware

PCs are used throughout Bulmer and these are usually either **Pentium** or 486 machines running **Windows 3.1** software. Bulmer will upgrade its systems in future, but there are costs associated with this, so the company prefers to make sure that staff are proficient in using the present software.

Running the various networks are four Data General Aviion UNIX **servers**, two DEC ALPHA UNIX servers and seven PC servers.

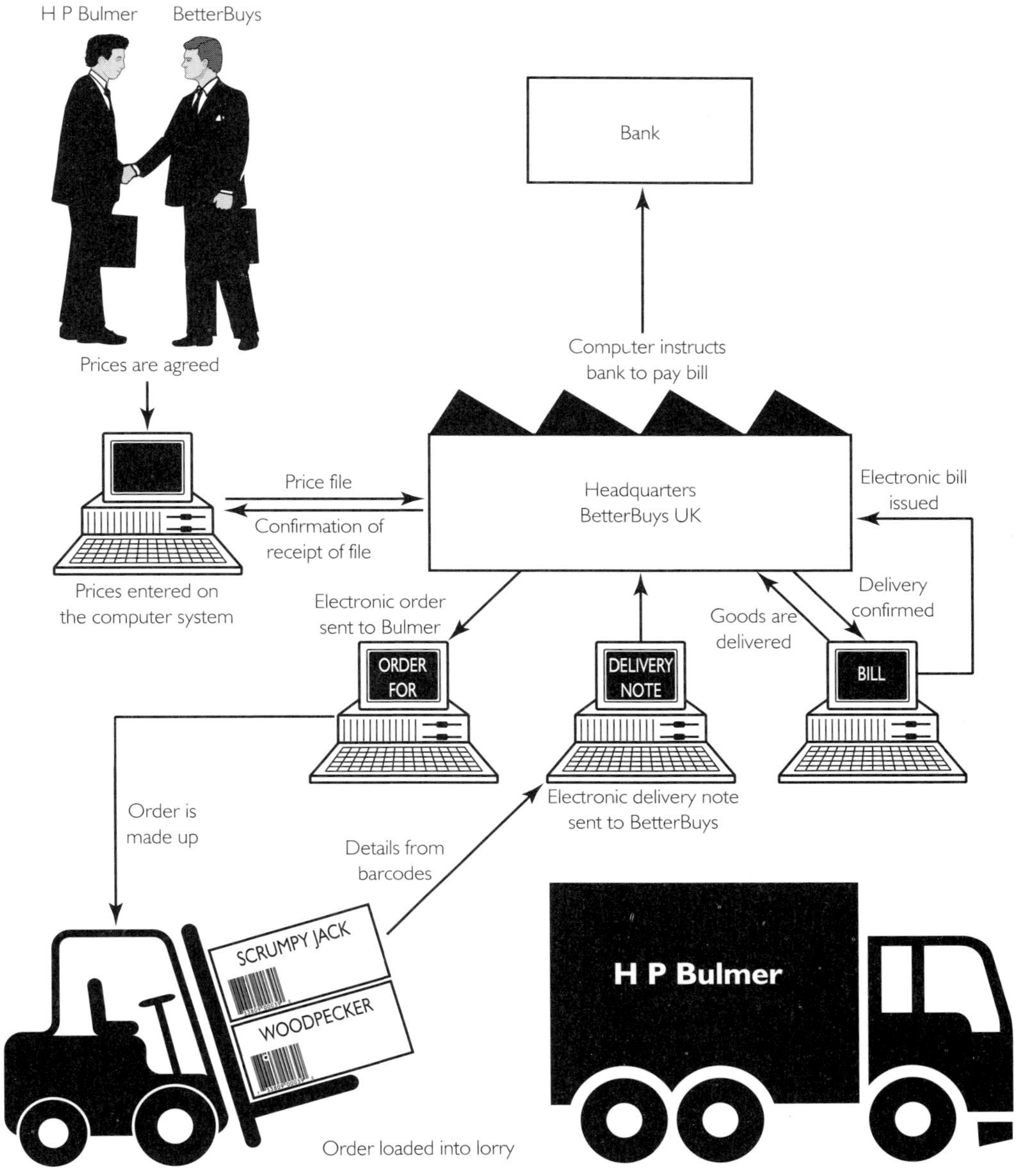

H P Bulmer   BetterBuys

Bank

Prices are agreed

Computer instructs
bank to pay bill

Price file

Confirmation of
receipt of file

Headquarters
BetterBuys UK

Electronic bill
issued

Prices entered on
the computer system

Electronic order
sent to Bulmer

Delivery
confirmed

Goods are
delivered

ORDER
FOR

DELIVERY
NOTE

BILL

Order is
made up

Electronic delivery note
sent to BetterBuys

Details from
barcodes

SCRUMPY JACK

WOODPECKER

H P Bulmer

*Figure 1.6 How
EDI is likely to
work*

Order loaded into lorry

Activity 1.10

When you are using a computer at home it is natural to want the most up-to-date versions of both hardware and software. However, things are not that simple when you want to upgrade a large number of machines and install the latest software. Bearing in mind that Bulmer has 500 PCs, the cost of the upgrades would be substantial.

1 Identify, apart from the cost, what other factors are likely to make Bulmer retain its existing hardware and software rather than upgrade whenever there is a new hardware development or whenever new software is released.

2 You may think that Bulmer could buy new software for only a proportion of its machines. What might be the disadvantages of such an approach?

Bulmer and the Internet

Bulmer has its own **Web page** on the Internet and it plans to make more use of it in the future. Its Web page can be located at http//www.bulmer.com. Bulmer uses the Internet mainly for marketing, and also for e-mail to and from its customers. At present there are 120 users within the company of the software **Netscape Navigator**.

The keg information system

Bulmer sells draught cider through tens of thousands of pubs, wine bars and restaurants throughout the UK. The keg technicians are responsible for installing and repairing the equipment needed to dispense the draught cider at the bar. This equipment includes the pump you see on the top of the bar, the cooler unit and all the pipework which goes to the aluminium barrel, called a keg.

When something goes wrong with the equipment or a new customer needs the equipment installing, a telephone call is made to head office where the scheduling is organised. The schedules for each of the 19 technicians scattered throughout the UK are transferred overnight to the technicians' hand-held terminals.

During the day the technicians record what they have done that day using their hand-held terminals, and this information is relayed back over the telephone lines to Bulmer's head office where the central computer files are updated. Using this system, the technicians are able to deal with more calls each day than under earlier systems, and the staff involved in coordinating this activity can be engaged in another task. A future development might be to give technicians portable modems in their cars so that the files can be updated in real time. If any problems arise in the course of a day, then the technicians can be alerted and the one closest to the location of the problem can deal with it as soon as their schedule permits.

Process control

The cider-making process at Bulmer's Hereford cider mill was previously carried out by the traditional methods of the nineteenth century which had changed little since Percy Bulmer founded the business in 1887. Today, the old equipment has been replaced by the latest computer-controlled technology. Cider maker Jonathan Blair now has a computer terminal to assist him in the art of cider-making (see Figure 1.7).

In 1994 the company invested £20 million in a brand new cider-making plant, making it the most modern cider-making plant in the world. All the processes such as fermentation, microfiltration (to remove the yeast and make the cider clear) and the movement of the cider around the plant, are controlled by computer. Figure 1.8 shows a production worker checking the flow of cider on the computer, and Figures 1.9 and 1.10 show the inside of the fermentation hall and a view of the 50-foot-high fermentation vessels from the outside. Overlooking the hall is a control room where a single person can run several processes using a computer screen.

In order that the changeover to the new equipment went as smoothly as possible, the staff took part in hands-on **simulation** courses. Here they could use computers to simulate control of the new system. This meant that any mistakes did not matter, whereas if they happened using the actual equipment they could ruin, say, a 230 000-litre batch of cider. The use of the new equipment allows Bulmer to produce a consistent, high quality product at a lower cost.

Figure 1.7 Jonathan Blair

Figure 1.10 Fermentation vessels

Figure 1.8 Cider production worker checking flow

Figure 1.9 Fermentation tank

Activity 1.11

1 Bulmer has listed the four main areas of its business as:
   a manufacturing
   b trading and marketing
   c finance
   d distribution.
   Using both business studies textbooks and information contained in the case study to help you, write a series of short paragraphs outlining what tasks would be performed in each of the above areas.

2 Bulmer identified certain problems with the old systems. Identify which systems they were and how the new system is an improvement.

3 There are certain terms used in the case study which were not explained in the text. Give a brief explanation of the following terms:
   a Oracle
   b data dictionary
   c CASE
   d UNIX
   e server.

4 Bulmer hopes to use electronic data interchange (EDI) with all its major customers. EDI was mentioned in the case study. Produce a diagram on computer, using suitable software, to explain how this works.

Sefton traffic control system case study

Urban traffic control systems are a feature of all towns and cities. They ensure that the traffic runs smoothly during the morning and evening rush hours and at other times during the day. The Metropolitan Borough of Sefton was the first local authority to install a computerised system. In this case study we will look at how IT is used in the traffic control department.

The traffic control system

The aims of the traffic control system are:
- to improve the traffic flow;
- to improve driver and pedestrian safety by reducing frustration;
- to make sure that any delays in a journey are kept to a minimum;
- to reduce the risk to the environment caused by fumes from waiting traffic;
- to reduce the use of fossil fuels.

Most urban traffic systems need to be able to cope with a huge increase in traffic flow into a town centre in the morning and the corresponding reversed flow during the early evening. Traffic lights that are on a set sequence throughout the day would not be able to cope with this increased traffic flow and serious delays would result. In the early days of traffic control, the traffic lights would be switched off at busy junctions during the rush hour and a police officer would take over. He or she could take account of the increased traffic flow in a certain direction and allow this traffic more time to go through the junction. This job required a great deal of concentration and was considered to be a waste of valuable police time. It is not surprising, therefore, that the next stage was to keep the lights switched on but to vary the sequencing manually to account for variations in the traffic flow. This was achieved by cabling the traffic lights up to a control room and having a camera situated above the junction to allow the operator to see the traffic. Since an operator was needed for each junction, this limited the system to only the busiest junctions and did not solve the problem elsewhere.

The next stage was the development of a computer-controlled system. In this system the traffic flow is assessed on the basis of the quantity of vehicles within the whole area, and using this information the system can detect in which direction most of the traffic is flowing. It can then make sure that vehicles on main routes into a town are given more time on green lights than usual so that the traffic in this direction flows more smoothly. In the evening this situation can be reversed.

The system is a real-time system and the data on the number of cars passing through a junction is obtained by underground detector cables that are set into the road surface before the junction.

Remote control systems

Remote control systems rely on communication lines being set up between the traffic signals and a central computer situated in the traffic control centre. Basically there are two types of system that can be used and these are as follows:

Urban traffic control (UTC) fixed time (FT)

With fixed time plans the flow at junctions is controlled to a timing plan based on historic traffic count information. The UTC computer sends a series of controlling signals via telephone lines to the traffic lights at each junction. Each light sequence is then driven for a number of seconds. The 'green time' for each approach to a junction does not vary during this period unless the plan being used is replaced.

Different plans are usually used for different times of the day, such as the morning and evening peak periods. Plans can be written so that the sequence of lights for the main through stages at each junction allows the traffic to flow at a constant speed without too many interruptions. Fixed time plans are normally applied only during peak periods.

Split cycle and offset optimisation technique (SCOOT)

The SCOOT urban traffic control system, used by most of the local authorities in the UK including the Metropolitan Borough of Sefton, does away with signal plans, which involve having to work out the sequencing of traffic lights on the basis of vehicle counts, since these tend to be expensive to set up and to keep up to date. Where traffic signals are fairly close together, they need to be synchronised to facilitate the flow of traffic through them. It is quite easy to set up signal plans so that, say, a green signal is obtained at each set of lights on a particular route, but it is difficult to coordinate the signals over a series of conflicting routes.

This is the purpose of the SCOOT system, which was set up by the Transport and Road Research Laboratory in collaboration with a number of private companies. The SCOOT system uses computerised simulations. Sensors situated near junctions and crossings throughout the borough provide the inputs to the system. These sensors are operated in real time so the computer is always kept up to date with the latest traffic information. The data is sent using either wire-based cables or fibre optic links (i.e. the existing telecommunications cables). Once the computer has analysed the data, it can then amend the traffic signal timings and the offset between the signals. The 'offset' is the phasing between one traffic signal and the next along a road. Figure 1.11 shows how the offset works.

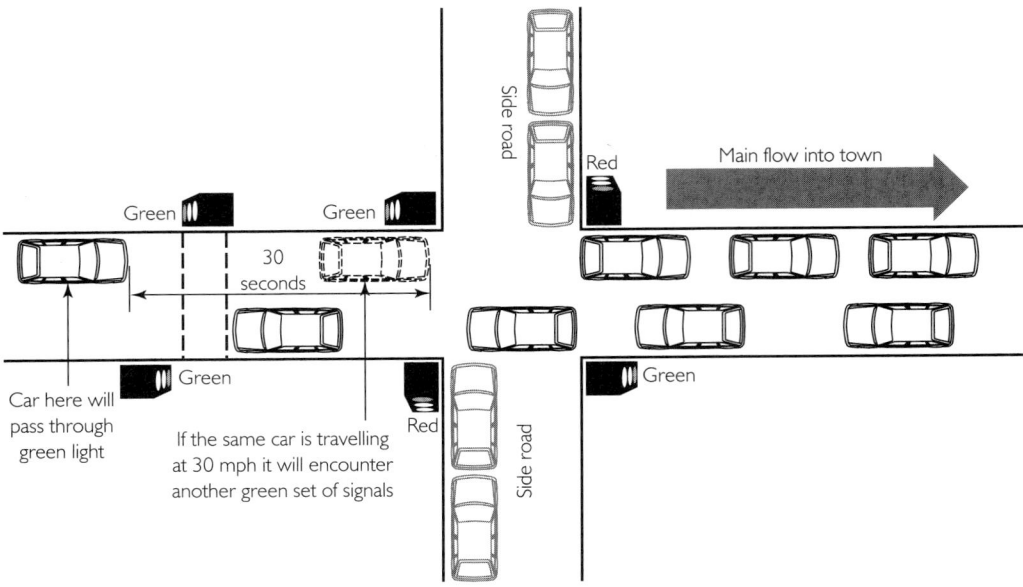

Figure 1.11 Traffic signals are offset so that any car travelling along a main route into town will encounter mainly green lights. This keeps the traffic moving during peak periods.

SCOOT optimises traffic control in three ways:

1 Split optimiser

During any particular cycle time at a junction, each stage will receive a green signal, and the length of time that it is green is a proportion of the total cycle time. The length of the green period, called the 'green split', is constantly varied by SCOOT depending on the current demand at each approach.

2 Cycle optimiser

The cycle time at each junction is also being continually adjusted. At low flow periods, SCOOT reduces the cycle time to around 28–48 seconds, depending on the number of stages, while during the peak periods the cycle time may rise to 120 seconds to cope with the high traffic volume. Additionally, a small junction located between two large junctions may not require a cycle time as high as the other two, so in this case the junction will be made to double cycle, i.e. while the two larger junctions are cycling at 120 seconds the small junction may cycle at 60 seconds.

3 Offset optimiser

The third optimiser attempts to link each set of signals along a particular route to provide a progression, or 'green wave', for traffic heading in the direction of the major flow.

Figure 1.12 shows the flow of information in the SCOOT-based urban traffic control system.

In Sefton, the borough is divided into regions for SCOOT. Figure 1.13 represents a region and shows the numbered sets of traffic signals and the lettered flows of traffic.

In an emergency, another traffic control system can be used. The emergency vehicle priority system enables fire engines, ambulances and police vehicles to obtain an uninterrupted path through a system of linked traffic lights by giving a green signal to an emergency vehicle as it reaches each light along its route.

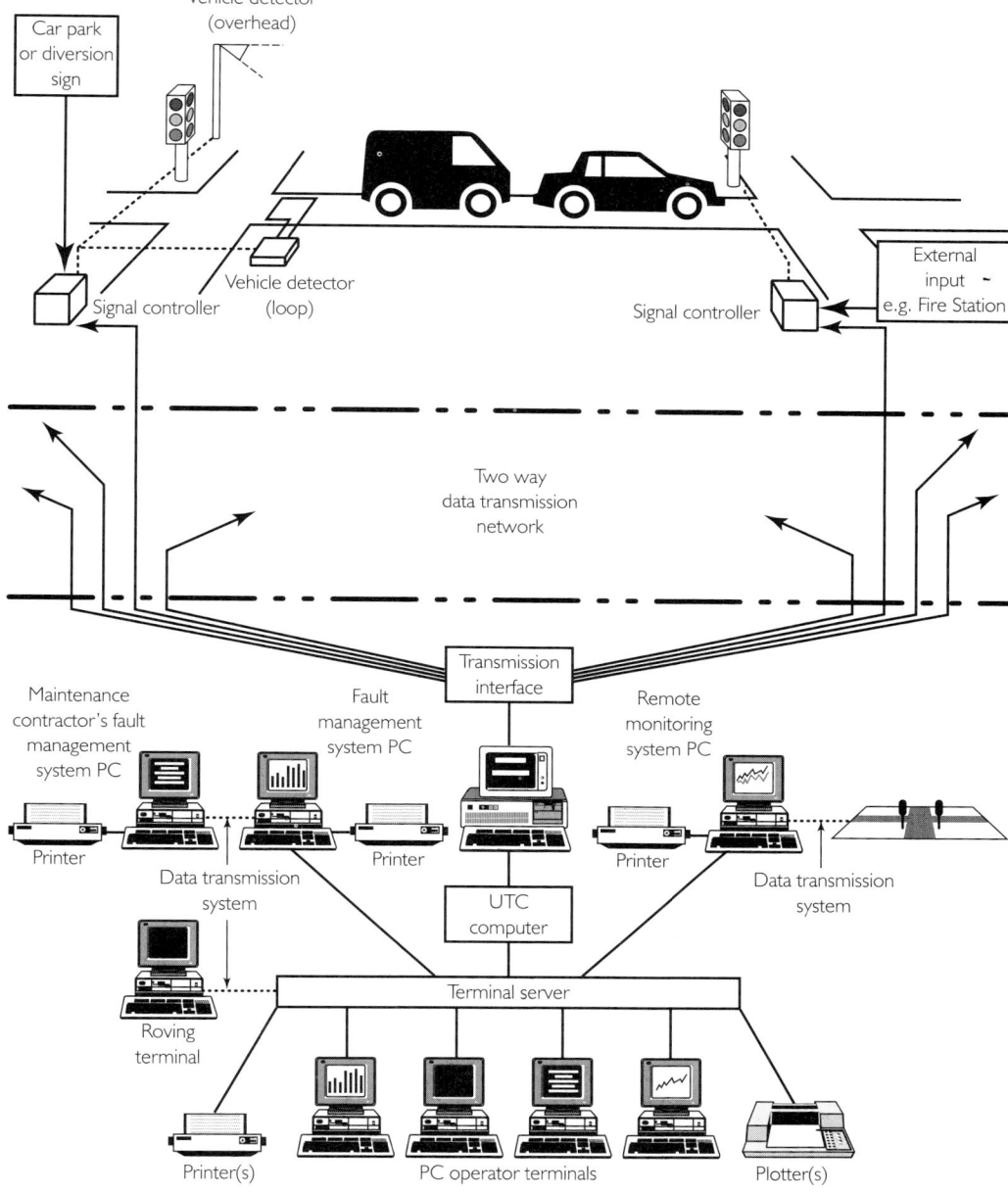

Figure 1.12 The flow of information in a SCOOT-based urban traffic control system

Local control systems

Local control involves using a system built into the traffic signal controller to react to traffic flow in the absence of input from a central SCOOT/UTC computer. There are three main methods of local control:

1 Vehicle activation system

In this system, a vehicle approaching a junction passes over a series of loops of wire (detector loops) set into the road, usually within 40 metres of the junction. These detect the vehicle and pass a demand signal to the controller. Another method uses an infrared beam to detect the presence of a vehicle; the beam is transmitted and received by a small box on the top of the traffic lights. Provided that there is no demand present on

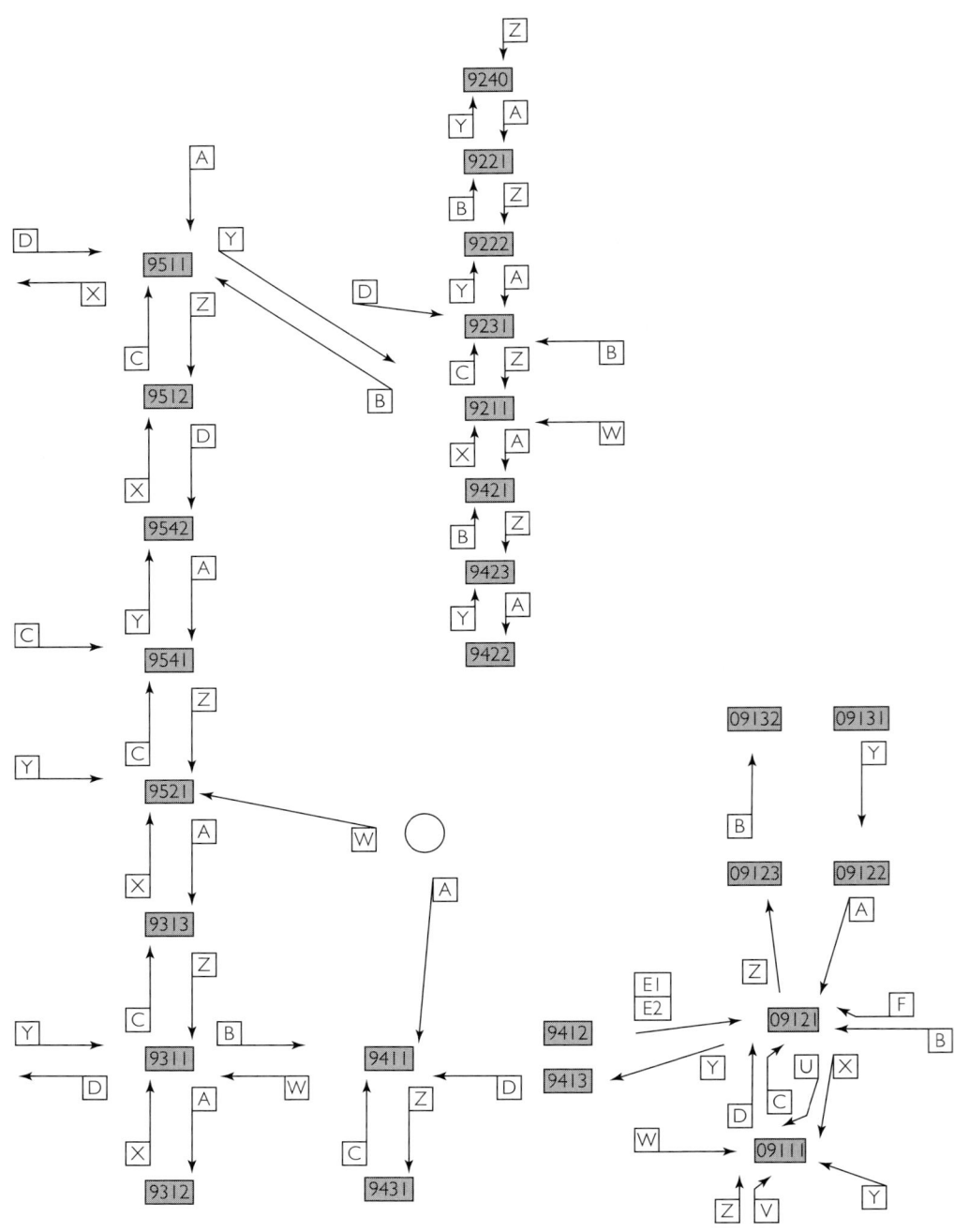

Figure 1.13 SCOOT region 9 – Bootle area. You can see here a printout of what appears on the screen in the control centre. The various numbered junctions and lights (lettered) are illustrated. The arrows show the directions of the traffic flow at each of the lights.

conflicting stages of the route, or a conflicting stage has reached its maximum green time, the signals will change to satisfy the new demand. This stage will remain on green until either the maximum green time is reached, or there is a gap in the approaching traffic of around two seconds over all the loops on the approach. This type of system is most suitable for controlling junctions that are not close to other junctions.

2 Fixed time (FT)

Fixed time is similar to UTC FT control and is generally used only as a fall-back if the detector loops fail, to ensure that all stages receive a green signal.

3 Microprocessor optimised vehicle actuation (MOVA)

MOVA is a more up-to-date method of controlling remote junctions; in some ways it resembles a mini SCOOT system, but is more responsive. This system can cope with light or heavy traffic flows, including complete junction saturation. (Junctions are designed to be able to cope with a certain amount of traffic flow up to a figure called the complete junction saturation; beyond this there are likely to be serious delays.)

With MOVA, old speed discrimination systems, which attempted to prevent the signals from changing when a fast vehicle was detected, can be eliminated: MOVA always knows the exact position of every vehicle on each approach and will generally not allow the signals to change when a vehicle is in the 'amber zone'. This is the area where drivers may decide not to stop as the signals change to red.

In addition to controlling traffic, both SCOOT/UTC and MOVA can store traffic count information for later retrieval.

Weather forecasting

The traffic control centre also has several remote weather stations which collect data about the weather and relay it back to the centre using modems and telephone lines. The physical quantities measured by the system include:
- wind speed
- humidity
- air temperature
- ground temperature.

The data from the weather station is passed to the meteorological office for the production of weather forecasts, but it can also be used to predict the likelihood of black ice on road surfaces. When there is a possibility of black ice forming overnight, an ice alert goes out and the gritting teams, who put salt and grit on the road, are sent out.

There is another important sensor which measures the amount of salt on the road surfaces. For instance, if a road had been gritted the previous night and it had not rained or snowed, then there might well be enough salt left on the road to make further gritting unnecessary. The whole system saves both on the overtime money paid to the gritting teams and the cost of the grit and salt used.

Pollution monitoring

The Metropolitan Borough of Sefton has three remote air pollution monitoring devices which monitor two polluting gases (nitrogen monoxide and sulphur dioxide). These are situated at the busiest junctions in the borough. The data from these is used to monitor the air quality and it is also used by the meteorological office to record air quality information for the region as a whole. Again, modems and telephone cables are used to transfer the data to the borough's technical services department.

Vehicle speeding systems

These systems are used for sections of road where speeding is a problem. They use radar detectors that are fixed in position (unlike police radar traps), and an illuminated sign tells drivers to slow down if they are exceeding the speed limit. If a car passes through the next radar detector and is still travelling over the speed limit a camera is activated and a photograph taken of the vehicle with the speed superimposed on it. The film is developed by the police. Then, with the vehicle's registration number as the search criterion, the **Police National Computer** (**PNC**) can find the registered owner. The police can then establish who was driving the vehicle at the time and take the appropriate action.

Car park management systems

These systems provide a means of directing vehicles around a network to car parks with available spaces. Special signs indicate how many spaces are left in each car park. These signs are driven by a central computer which uses information on how many cars have entered each car park and how many have left. Figure 1.14 shows one of the signs used by the car park management system, which directs vehicles into city centre car parks where there are spaces available. The signs, which operate in real time, are linked to the SCOOT system.

Figure 1.14 Car park management systems can be used to direct vehicles to car parks with spaces. Such systems can be linked to SCOOT.

Remote monitoring

All the traffic control systems use remote monitoring, which means that there are cable or telephone links between the controllers for the traffic lights, pelican crossings, etc. and the control centre. All the equipment within the system is self-checking to make sure it is working correctly. If there is a fault in an item of equipment, it automatically reports the fault back to the control centre. In this way the system does not need to rely on members of the public reporting faults, and there is no need to employ staff to check that the equipment is working properly. If a fault occurs in equipment on a main road, it is displayed on a large map in the control room. This has green lights to show that the signals are working correctly; if a particular signal is faulty a red light comes on.

Activities 1.12

Task 1

The Metropolitan Borough of Sefton's traffic control system is an industrial system. Produce a report covering all the criteria for analysis and evaluation for this system.

Task 2

If you were to construct a model of the traffic flow at a junction which is controlled by traffic signals, it would be necessary to understand first how traffic signals operate.

Look at a set of traffic lights (it is best to choose a simple junction such as a T-junction) and carry out the following:

1 Draw a set of diagrams to show the light sequences.
2 Using a watch which shows seconds, determine the length of each light sequence and then fill in tables like the one here.

Light sequence	Time (seconds)
Red	
Red and amber	
Green	
Amber	

3 Work out the total time for the complete sequence and draw a labelled pie diagram showing the proportion of the total time taken up by each light sequence.
4 Perform steps 2 and 3 for each set of lights at the junction.

Assignment A1.1

This assignment develops knowledge and understanding of the following element:

1.1 Investigate industrial and commercial information technology systems

It supports the development of the following key skills:
Communication 3.2, 3.3 and 3.4
Information technology 3.1, 3.2 and 3.3

Task 1

The following is a list of the range of commercial systems:
- booking systems
- electronic funds transfer (EFT)
- electronic point of sale (EPOS)
- stock control

- order processing
- payroll processing.

Read through the case studies. Identify an example of each system in the list above and give a short explanation of its use.

Task 2

Identify two of the systems you looked at in Task 1 and analyse each of them in terms of the criteria for analysis identified in this chapter. Note that not all the criteria may be applicable to the particular system you are looking at.

Task 3

Choose two of the systems you looked at in Task 1 and evaluate them using the criteria for evaluation identified in this chapter.

Task 4

Some systems have an impact on the environment. For example, they may affect travel, and pollution and radiation levels. Sometimes they can be used to obtain better information about environmental conditions.

There are two systems in the H P Bulmer case study which could have an environmental impact. Identify the two systems, saying what they are and how they affect the environment.

Assignment A1.2

This assignment develops knowledge and understanding of the following element:
1.1 Investigate industrial and commercial information technology systems

It supports the development of the following key skills:
Communication 3.2, 3.3 and 3.4
Information technology 3.1, 3.2, 3.3

Task 1

For this task you are required to research two commercial information technology systems and to present your findings as a report. The two systems you choose can be from the same organisation. You are not required to look at the whole business or organisation, since it will probably consist of many systems. Just pick out two of the systems used and investigate them further.

Here are some organisations that use commercial systems:

- banks
- building societies
- insurance companies
- hotels
- video libraries
- retailers (i.e. shops)
- travel agents
- schools and colleges.

You could base your research on an organisation where you have a part-time job or have worked in the past. Alternatively, you could try asking relatives and friends about the organisations where they work.

Before you embark on the research, you should tell your tutor which systems you are investigating so that he or she can make sure they are suitable.

You should submit a report (typically 500 words) on each commercial system, covering all the criteria for analysis and evaluation that are relevant to the system.

Task 2

Repeat Task 1, but this time look at two industrial IT systems.

Sample unit test

1 Britannia Airways use a variety of IT systems. Which one of the following systems is *not* commercial?
   a decision-making system used when aircraft are diverted
   b crew rostering system (i.e. organising the crews for the aircraft)
   c ordering system for the purchase of duty free goods
   d system for the control of cabin temperature and pressure

2 Which one of the following is an industrial control system?
   a system for controlling the thickness of paper in a paper mill
   b stock control system in a warehouse
   c system for controlling expenses claimed by staff
   d project control system used when developing a new system

3 Which one of these is a commercial control system?
   a environmental control in a greenhouse for growing plants
   b traffic control system
   c pollution monitoring control system
   d stock control system in a supermarket

4 Which one of the following systems would a supermarket most likely use for paying its staff?
   a EFTPOS
   b EDI
   c BACS
   d POS

5 One of the following is *not* an environmental control system. Which one is it?
   a air-conditioning system in a car
   b pollution control system used by a chemical factory
   c fog warning system used to control displays warning of adverse weather conditions on motorways
   d paint-spraying system used in a car factory

Questions 6 and 7 are based on the following information:
   You are investigating a stock control system used by a supermarket.

6 Which statement tells you about the hardware?
   a there are ten POS terminals
   b all the goods are barcoded
   c the system automatically re-orders goods when stocks are low
   d staff find the system user-friendly

7 Which statement tells you about the software?
  a the software runs on a UNIX platform
  b communication lines connect the system to head office
  c the POS terminals can be operated manually if needed
  d the system uses a card reader to read the magnetic strip on a debit card

8 A cider manufacturer uses process control when making cider. The main advantage in using process control is that:
  a invoices are processed faster
  b the quality of the product is more easily controlled
  c less expensive equipment is used
  d more staff can be involved in the cider-making

9 Which one of the following is *not* an advantage of a traffic control system, as used in many large cities?
  a it improves traffic flow and decreases journey time
  b it cuts down on pollution caused by stationary cars
  c it reduces accidents due to driver frustration
  d it keeps large lorries out of city centres

10 Raw facts and figures, before they are processed by a computer, are referred to as:
  a information
  b records
  c details
  d data

11 All systems have their limitations. A limitation of an order processing system might be:
  a it is possible to see if the goods ordered are in stock
  b it makes sure that only customers with a good credit record are allowed goods on credit
  c it is capable of dealing with only 10 000 orders at a time
  d new customers are automatically given a unique customer number

12 Which one of the following systems does *not* make use of electronic funds transfer?
  a EFTPOS
  b BACS
  c EDI
  d EPOS

13 Which one of the following statements does *not* refer to the electronic data interchange system (EDI) used by many large companies?
  a all the information is passed using electronic signals
  b paperwork is eliminated
  c invoices are checked against orders automatically
  d funds have to be transferred from one account to another using cheques

14 You are evaluating a booking system and decide that the possibility of conducting business over the Internet needs to be investigated. Which aspect of the system are you looking at?
  a environmental issues
  b disadvantages of the system

    c potential improvements to the system

    d advantages of the system

15 Many large supermarkets use sales-based ordering. Which of the following statements best describes this system?

    a it allows only old stock items to be sold

    b orders are based upon sales information from point-of-sale terminals

    c orders for goods not in stock can be made using a point-of-sale terminal

    d customers can place orders for goods at a terminal

16 Which is the most appropriate answer to the following?

    An urban traffic control system can help the environment by:

    a using less electricity to power the traffic lights

    b allowing emergency vehicles a clear path through the lights

    c preventing accidents caused by faulty lights

    d reducing the amount of fuel used by vehicles

2 Investigating and configuring a system

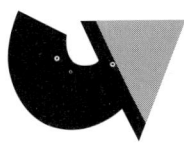

The components of an IT system

There are two parts to all computer systems: hardware and the software. Hardware is the name given to those parts of the computer that you can touch or handle, and to the peripheral devices that make up the system. **Software** is the name given to the programs that allow you to use the hardware. Without software, hardware is useless. Software is made up of a series of instructions that have been written in a computer language.

To understand the difference between hardware and software, think of a tape recorder and a blank tape. The tape recorder and the tape are the hardware: we can actually touch them. If we recorded some music onto the tape, then the music would be the software.

The components of an information system include the hardware, software, information, staff and accommodation which together enable information technology operations.

Types of hardware

Most information technology systems consist of the following components:

Main processor unit

The main processor unit is a hardware device that is used to process instructions and output information. You can find it in any 'intelligent' device (i.e. a device that is able to control the way it works), such as a washing machine, camera, toaster, burglar alarm and heating system control unit. In other words, any modern device which needs to be controlled in some way will probably incorporate a processor.

The main processor of a computer is often called the central processing unit (CPU). Its main operation is acting on instructions and this includes sorting them, filtering them and performing mathematical operations on them. It is called the main processor because many computers now have more than one processor. With PCs, the main processor unit is normally taken to mean all the components inside the casing, excluding the power supply and the storage devices such as hard and floppy disk drives and CD-ROM units. A typical PC main processor unit would include the following components:

- central processing unit (CPU);
- motherboard (the board where all the built-in electronics are situated);
- controller boards (e.g. video and disk drive controllers) which are attached to the motherboard);
- additional special processors (e.g. maths coprocessors) which are usually located on the motherboard;
- input and output ports (serial, parallel, etc.).

Activity 2.1

PCs are usually available in four types of casing: desktop, mini-tower, midi-tower and tower (Figure 2.1). There are also two types of casing for portable PCs: laptop and notebook.

Imagine you are going to equip 40 users in a company with stand-alone machines (i.e. the machines would not be connected together on a network). Write a list of questions you could ask the users to help them decide which type of casing their PCs should have.

Microprocessor

A microprocessor controls most of the core functions of a computer and consists of the CPU, bus (address, data and control), memory (ROM and RAM) and input/output units. These are all covered in detail in the next chapter, and there are definitions of these terms in the glossary at the back of the book.

Control devices

The **control devices** connected within the main processor housing include the disk controller, video card, input/output cards and serial and parallel output cards. Serial

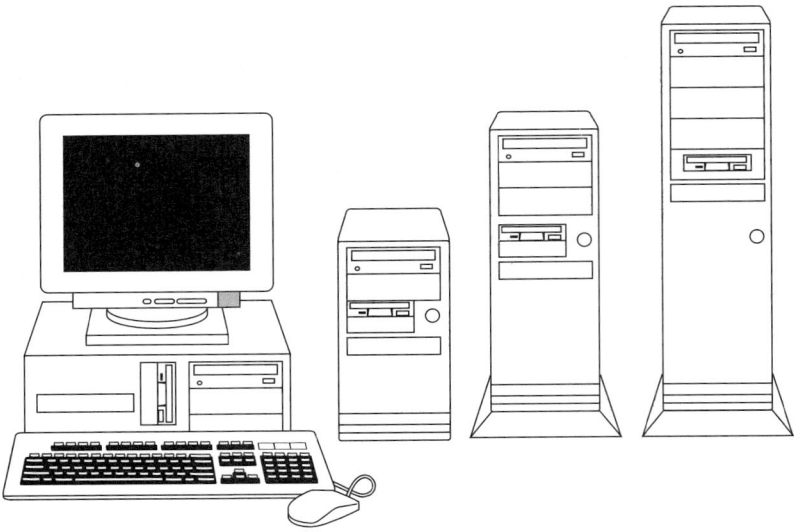

Figure 2.1 Desktop, mini-tower, midi-tower and tower PCs

output cards allow one electronic signal at a time to pass through a wire into an output device. Parallel output cards allow a group of signals to pass at the same time through a series of wires to an output device.

Input devices

Input devices are used to get data into a computer system and act as an interface between the computer system and the outside world. The ideal input device would collect all the required data accurately, without human intervention and be relatively cheap. The input device chosen is usually a compromise, and many systems use more than one device. For instance, a home computer may use a mouse, a joystick and a keyboard.

There are many different input devices and each has its advantages and disadvantages. The most popular ones are:
- keyboard
- mouse
- trackball
- joystick
- light pen
- touch screen
- graphics tablet
- magnetic strip reader
- barcode reader
- optical character reader
- optical mark reader
- punched card reader
- magnetic-ink character reader
- scanner
- video camera
- digital still camera
- microphone.

Storage devices

Computers store data either in chips inside the computer (primary storage) or on other media such as magnetic disk, tape or strip (backing store or secondary storage). Primary storage includes ROM (read-only memory) and RAM (random access memory). Data stored in these chips is immediately accessible to the central processing unit, unlike data stored on secondary storage where there is a delay while the data is loaded into memory from the storage medium.

Examples of storage devices include RAM, ROM, magnetic disk, CD-ROM, rewriteable CD, magnetic tape and magnetic card/strip.

Output devices

Output devices are used to show the results from a data processing system, often in the form of hard copy (another name for a printout) or a screen display. Data can be passed readily from one computer to another as electronic signals, so the output data from one computer can be the input data for another.

Here is a list of the main output devices:
- monitor or visual display unit (VDU)
- graphical display unit
- laser printer (black and white or colour)
- ink-jet printer
- dot matrix printer
- plotter
- speakers for voice output or sound.

In control applications the output could be used to control an electric motor, switch on a heater or control the movement of a robot arm.

Activity 2.2

For this activity, you are required to research input and output devices. Some of the devices are used with PC systems whereas others are more specialised and are used only for certain applications.

For each of the input and output devices listed above, produce a set of notes covering the following:
- examples of applications to which the device is most suited;
- a brief description of what the device does;
- some indication of the cost of the device (if the device is very specialised then it may prove difficult to find out the price; in these cases say that the price is unknown);
- the advantages and disadvantages of the device when compared with other similar devices.

Include a diagram or picture of each device. You could draw these yourself, cut out pictures from computer magazines or photocopy them.

Purposes of hardware

In this section we will look at the purposes of the various hardware components of an information technology system.

Data capture

Getting the information from the outside world into a form which can be processed by a computer is called data capture and the devices used to do this are called input devices. The methods of data capture can be divided into manual and automated.

Manual methods of data capture

The most popular manual method of data capture is to input the data using a keyboard and then to store it on disk. This method of data capture is known as key-to-disk. Although there are many advantages in using this method, the main disadvantages are that it is restricted to the speed of the typist so it is very slow, and typing mistakes can occur that may go undetected. It is for these reasons that other, automatic methods of data capture have been developed, though these tend to be restricted to high-volume work where the time and hence cost savings are more crucial.

Automated methods of data capture

Automated methods, once set up, do not need any human intervention and the data collection is performed automatically. They are usually used where a high volume of input is needed in a short space of time, and include optical mark reading, barcoding, magnetic-ink character recognition and optical character recognition.

The various methods of data capture are discussed in more detail in Chapter 6.

Data logging

Data logging is a way of collecting measurements of physical quantities such as temperature, pressure, depth, etc. over a period of time without human intervention. Data loggers have their own processors and storage and are set to take measurements at regular intervals over a certain period of time. Both of these inputs, i.e.how often readings are taken and the period of time over which logging takes place, may be varied. The data logger can store the data at a remote location and then be connected to the main computer. The data can then be analysed and, if necessary, transferred to a package such as a spreadsheet to be displayed graphically.

Sensed data

Sometimes data is input to a system as a series of electrical signals. For instance, in voice recognition systems, a person's voice is converted by a microphone into electrical signals which are then input automatically to the computer where they are analysed and eventually acted upon. Voice recognition systems can be used, for example, by solicitors to dictate letters straight into a **wordprocessing** system without the need for any typing.

Sensed data is also used in control applications where sensors detect a certain physical property and feed the data in the form of electrical signals back to the computer where it can be acted upon. For example, in a central heating system, a temperature sensor called a thermistor samples the room temperature at predetermined intervals and feeds the data back to the microprocessor. If the temperature is too low the microprocessor will switch the heating on and if it is too high it will switch the heating off. In this way the temperature of the room is kept constant.

Processing

Processing means doing something with the raw data to produce some form of useful output. Processing is performed by the processor following a set of instructions called a program.

Storage

The data to be processed, and the set of instructions for carrying out the processing, have to be stored somewhere until they are needed. Primary storage is storage that is immediately available and includes ROM (read-only memory) and RAM (random access memory). Both of these forms of primary storage are on microchips. Secondary storage takes some time to be loaded and includes magnetic disk, magnetic tape and CD-ROM.

Storage can be divided into two types: permanent and temporary. Temporary storage is provided by RAM and the contents are lost when the power supply is turned off. ROM provides permanent storage, and the contents remain when the power supply is turned off.

Output

There is a variety of ways to output the information obtained from data processing, the most common being the VDU (visual display unit) and the printer. Other less well-known methods include the sound output from the speakers of a multimedia application or a voice mail system.

Screen output is ideal for temporary information such as enquiries at an information desk, whereas printed output is needed if the information has to be sent through the post or used for future reference. Many companies now use e-mail and document imaging systems which cut out the need for printouts, and many offices are now almost paperless. However, it is unlikely that the need for paper will be completely eliminated since companies often need to communicate with people who do not have sophisticated computer systems, and important documents are still usually printed out and stored in the filing system.

Computer output can be in the form of electronic signals, which are then used to provide some sort of control. For instance, in the computer-controlled antilocking braking system called ABS, the sensors pick up the rotational speed of each of the wheels and, if one of the wheels is in danger of locking, this information is sent back to the computer which automatically adjusts the braking force on that wheel. Cars with ABS are safer because the braking is more controlled and they are therefore less likely to go into a skid.

System specifications

Imagine you are selecting a multimedia system for home use, and a company is going to make it up for you from the various components. Before it starts the company will ask you what you require. In other words, it will ask you for a system specification. Usually the user would say what applications he or she is running or what software is likely to be used and this in turn will usually determine the minimum specification for the system. A typical system specification would include the following:

Microprocessor type
Companies such as Intel, Cyrix and Motorola make a range of microprocessors. Typical microprocessors used in microcomputers include the Intel 486 and Pentium, and the Motorola PowerPC 604.

Number of microprocessors
Some computers or microprocessor-controlled devices contain more than one chip.

Processor speed

For a given microprocessor, the speed with which it processes instructions is called the clock speed. Clock speed is measured in megahertz. Typical modern microprocessors have speeds ranging from 120 MHz up to 300 MHz. Each new generation of micro-processors has faster clock speeds.

Cache

A cache consists of high-speed memory in a computer where data can be held temporarily rather than in slower memory or on a much slower hard disk drive. Its effect is to speed up the computer. Only a relatively small amount of cache memory is needed for it to have a dramatic effect in speeding up a computer. Typical sizes of cache memory are 256 KB (kilobytes) or 512 KB.

Primary storage

Primary storage uses RAM and ROM and was defined earlier in this chapter (page 41).

Secondary storage

Secondary storage devices include floppy disk drives, hard disk drives, and rewriteable CD-ROM. Again, secondary storage was defined earlier in this chapter (page 41).

Devices

A device is any piece of equipment that is able to send or receive data, for example for data capture, data display and control.

Performance

The system specifications are important because they determine the overall performance of an information technology system. The following factors all affect system performance.

Speed

The speed of a system, i.e. the time it takes to complete a task, is not just a question of the speed of the processor. For instance, if a 200 MHz Pentium-based computer and a 100 MHz 486 DX4 were used to perform the same task, the Pentium computer would be faster, but if a complicated architectural drawing were being printed using a pen plotter and several different colours, then the time to complete the drawing would be determined primarily by the plotter rather than the processor.

Another factor which affects the time to complete a computer-based task is how long it takes to input the data for processing. If a keyboard is used, the rate of input is restricted to somewhere between 35 and 50 words per minute. If a task needs to access data on magnetic disk, but the disk drive is large and the access time is high, this can slow down the whole job. Obviously, the speed of any system can be increased by using appropriate technology, but the advantage of doing so needs to be weighed against the extra cost incurred.

Parallel processing

Parallel processing means that a computer is able to work on two or more parts of a program at the same time, thus increasing the overall speed of execution of the program. To do this, special computer instructions are needed, and the computer has to have two or more interconnected microprocessors, each of which carries out part of the task. Apart from a few expensive, specialist computers, PCs have only one microprocessor and are therefore able to work only on one part of a program at a time. Computers that are able to support true high speed parallel processing are called supercomputers, and it is common for them to have hundreds of thousands of microprocessors which are able to access the data through a shared memory. Intel, which manufactures the Pentium chip, claims that this chip is able to perform some limited parallel processing.

Quality

The quality of components can vary considerably, and price is usually reflected in performance. For example, if a cheap motherboard has been used there may be no room on it for later expansion. Many computer systems are built up from components obtained from different manufacturers, and comparisons can be obtained between, for example, different makes of chip or other components from most computer magazines.

The quality of monitors can vary widely so it is always best to see a monitor working before buying one. Cheap monitors do not have as stable a picture as higher quality ones, and can cause headaches and fatigue when used for long periods. Keyboards also vary in quality. Cheap keyboards do not have a positive 'feel' when the keys are depressed and can feel a bit 'spongy'. This can result in more typing mistakes and a slower typing speed.

Monitors (sometimes called **VDUs**) come in different sizes, with the 14-inch screen size being the cheapest and therefore the most popular. However, with Windows software, a 14-inch screen can look cluttered with all the toolbars and icons, so a larger screen is preferable. Screen sizes of 15 inches, 17 inches and 21 inches are widely available. A 15-inch screen is usually only slightly more expensive than a similar 14-inch screen. Screens larger than this are considerably more expensive and are usually used by people who need to display a lot of information on their screens such as designers, architects and engineers.

Activity 2.3

Produce a comparative study on monitors, including their prices, and present your findings in the form of a brief report. You may find the following sources of information useful:

- computer magazines such as *Computer Shopper* and *Personal Computer World*;
- computer magazines and monitor manufacturers on the Internet;
- computer shops – look at the different monitors available and make up your own mind about their picture quality.

You will be able to use the information gained from this activity to help you complete Assignment A2.1.

Efficiency

When designing a system it is important to make sure that the various components are compatible and that they are well matched for their speeds, otherwise the whole system could be slowed down by a single component.

Activity 2.4

There are many specialist words and phrases used in computing that can be confusing to someone who is not familiar with them. Computer dictionaries can be helpful, but often include terms in the definitions that also need explaining. This means you may need to look up several words before working out the meaning of the term you were originally interested in. Sometimes you may even have to consult several dictionaries to obtain a satisfactory definition.

Look up and provide an explanation of the following terms and phrases that are used when describing system specifications:

- SRAM
- DRAM
- EPROM
- BIOS
- SVGA
- cache
- future proof
- 3D graphics controller
- SIMM.

Types of software

Software is the general name given to the programs that can be run on computer hardware. There are several categories of software:

- operating systems software
- user interface systems software
- network operating systems software
- communications software
- programming languages, which can be used to write applications software
- applications software.

Other categories of software, such as games, also exist, but are outside the scope of this book.

Operating systems software

Operating systems software is a suite of programs that controls the hardware directly, including inputs, outputs, memory and storage. It is also used to run the applications programs (see Figure 2.2). The main operating systems in use include Windows 95 (see Figure 2.3) (not Windows 3.1 because this can be run only after the operating system MS-DOS has been loaded), UNIX, **OS/2**, **MS-DOS (Microsoft Disk Operating System)** and the Macintosh operating system.

User interface systems software

Interface systems software controls the information presented on the screen which helps the user to learn and eventually use the applications software. The original systems software used command lines, where the user had to construct a command in a certain way for the instruction to be carried out. MS-DOS uses command lines, so, for

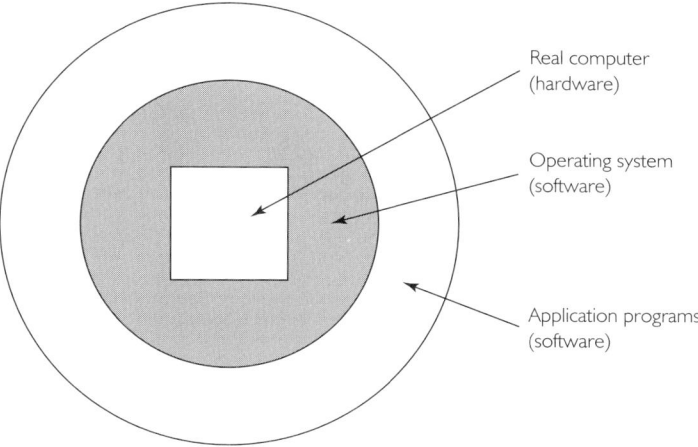

Figure 2.2 The operating system 'sits' between the hardware and the applications programs

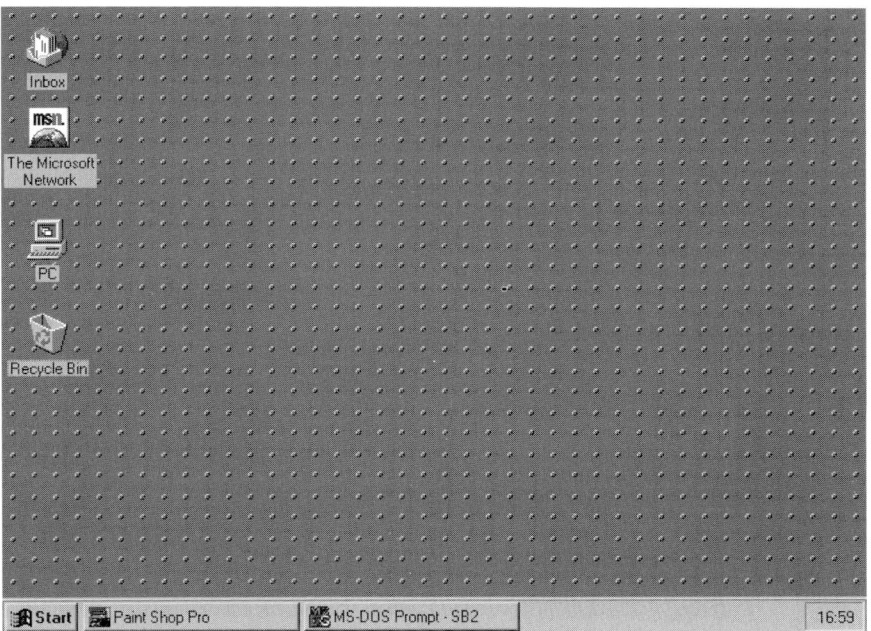

Figure 2.3 The opening screen from the Windows 95 operating system

example, to format a **floppy disk** in drive a, you use the command C:\>format a: .

Now, we have moved away from command line systems towards graphic user interfaces (GUIs) which are much easier for both beginners and experts to use. All the applications packages that use the same GUI have the same 'look' to them, so once you have used one application, others are much easier to learn and use.

Windows 3.1 is a GUI but it cannot be classed as an operating system because it cannot be run without MS-DOS being loaded first.

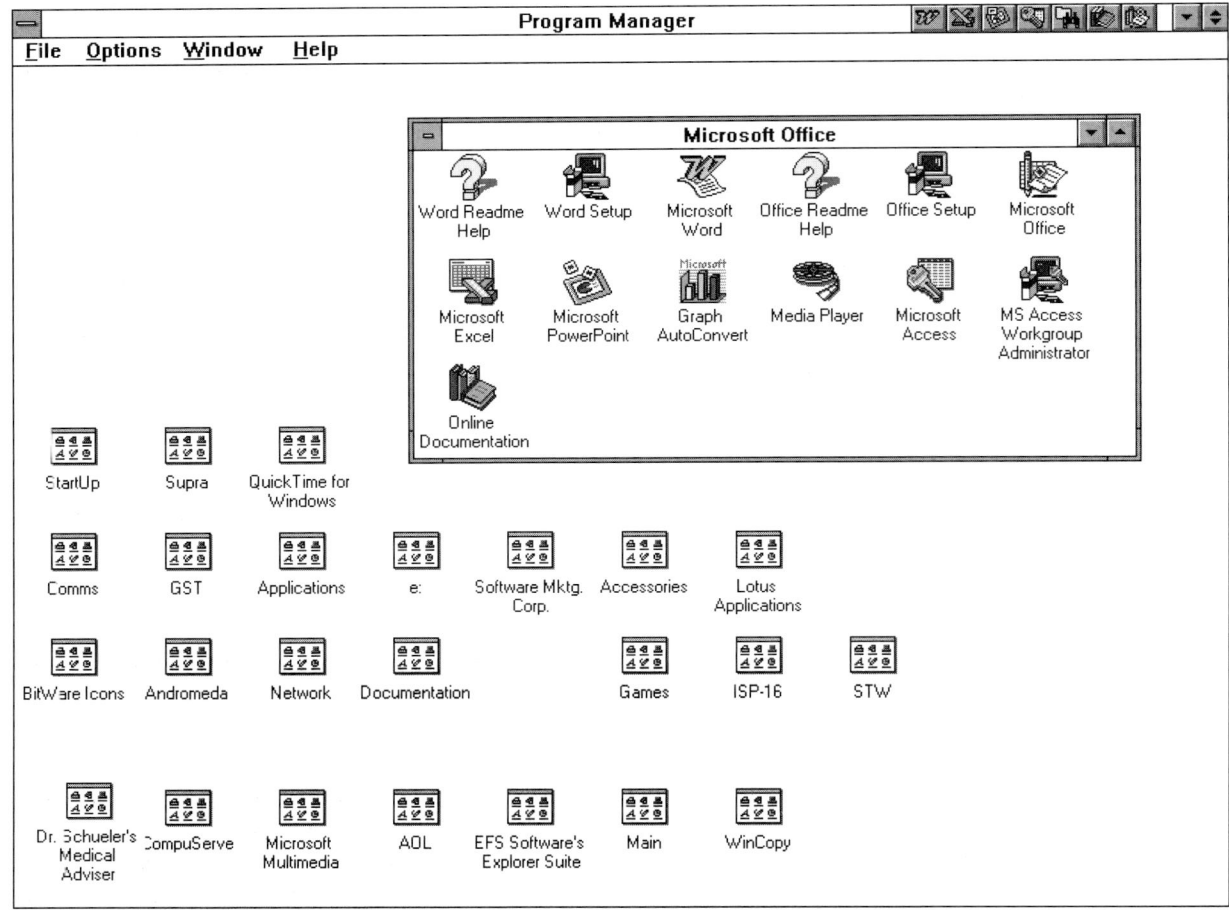

Figure 2.4 The opening screen from Windows 3.1. Notice the icons for the various applications that can be selected using the mouse.

Network operating systems software

On a local area network (LAN), terminals or workstations connected to a central computer called a file server, on which the files are stored, are located within a single building. The network operating systems software consists of the file server software and workstation software that enables communication between the two. Windows NT, UNIX and Novell are all examples of popular network operating systems.

Communications software

Communications software is used to facilitate the transfer of data from one computer to another. It is often provided when you buy a modem, or it can be bought separately. Modems are used to convert the data from a computer into a form that can be passed along a telephone line. Sometimes, service providers such as CompuServe or AOL (America On Line), provide subscribers with communications software which enables data to be transferred using their access system. For a certain fee (usually paid monthly), subscribers gain access to their **on-line** database of services and have access to the Internet.

Programming language software

To produce applications software, a program or series of programs needs to be written. There are many different programming languages available, and each has its advantages and disadvantages. Programming languages are dealt with in detail in Chapters 11 and 12.

Applications software

Applications software is the general name given to any software which performs a specific task for the user (as opposed to software which controls the running of the computer). This software includes wordprocessors, spreadsheets, databases, drawing packages and so on.

Purposes of software

Software is produced for a variety of purposes and the main ones are outlined below.

System initiation

System initiation is when the system prepares itself to do a job. For instance, when the power is switched on the computer initialises itself by loading the files it needs in order to be able to run the user's choice of applications program.

User interaction

Interaction with a computer used to be complicated, with the user having to remember a series of commands and instructions that had to be entered correctly for the computer to work. Learning how to use a single piece of software was difficult and took a long time, and if you changed software you had to learn a completely new set of commands.

Most modern software is developed to operate in a way that is easy to understand and to use. For example, all Windows-based software has a similar interface and 'feel' to it, so the skills developed to use one software package can be readily transferred to another.

Suites of software incorporating wordprocessor, spreadsheet, database and presentation graphics software produced by the same software manufacturer share the same 'look' and 'feel' which makes them much easier to learn and to use. Examples of this type of software include Lotus SmartSuite and Microsoft Office. Another advantage of these suites is that data can be passed from one module to another.

Activity 2.4

Compare and contrast two software packages which are used to perform similar tasks (e.g. two wordprocessing packages) in terms of the following:
- ease of use;
- availability of features;
- ability to translate from one file format to another;
- widespread usage (important if you need to give disks of your documents to someone else);
- speed of operation;
- screen design;
- help screens and menus.

Workgroup sharing

A workgroup is a group of connected computers that have been organised for a particular purpose. For example, a workgroup could be set up in the sales department of a company so that the work can be shared around. A workgroup could also be based on a project. For instance, a company which publishes a magazine might have several users connected together who need to communicate with each other. Sometimes workgroups are set up simply to share resources like printers, scanners and hard drives. Using the workgroup software and the appropriate cabling between machines, all the members of the group are able to access shared resources.

The graphic user interface Windows 3.11 and the operating system Windows 95 both enable workgroups to be set up between several PCs.

Communicating

Communications software controls the passage of data from one computer to another or from one terminal to another over a network. Usually, some communications software is provided when you purchase a modem but you can also buy it separately. Communications software usually comes with special facilities such as fax, voice mail and e-mail.

Production of software

There are many software programs available, called software development tools, whose purpose is to aid the production of new software. To enable a computer to perform a useful task, it is necessary to give it a series of instructions in a form that it can understand. These instructions, arranged in a logical order, are called a program and the person who writes them is called a programmer. There are various languages available to the programmer, and the choice of language is usually determined by the nature of the program and the programmer's ability in each language. As well as writing new software, the programmer spends a lot of time modifying existing program instructions, called the program code.

File management

The hard drive capacity on the average computer is now huge, and the problems involved in dealing with day-to-day file operations are immense. Searching for a particular file you remember creating three years ago amongst 3000 other files can be very time consuming. File management is a feature of most modern systems, allowing you to perform simple file operations such as append (add a bit on to an existing file), delete and copy.

Processing

Processing means using software to carry out a task on data that has been input. In a spreadsheet, this could include entering a column of numbers using the keyboard and using the software to add them up and produce a total. These numbers could then be processed and an appropriate graph produced which could then be brought (imported) into a wordprocessing package.

Wordprocessing software, as the name suggests, processes words in some way. For example, the spacing between the words can be adjusted so that the right or left margins, or both, are kept straight. There are four categories of data which can be processed, and these are shown in the following table.

Data type	Most appropriate software to use
Documents	Wordprocessing, desktop publishing (DTP)
Numerical data	Spreadsheets, statistical packages
Graphics	Presentation graphics, spreadsheets, drawing, paint
Structured data	Database

With modern software there is no longer any clear division between some applications, so for example many wordprocessors will have features that only DTP or graphics packages would have had a few years ago.

Modelling

Modelling means producing a series of mathematical equations which can be used to mimic a real situation. When values are put into the **model** and the model is exercised in some way, we are said to be performing a simulation. There are many types of specialist modelling software, from games to flight simulators. In the traffic control systems looked at in the previous chapter, equations are used to describe the flow of traffic at junctions, and the output from the model is used to issue controls to the traffic signals to ensure that the traffic flows smoothly. Spreadsheets can be used to construct simple models, and these are looked at in detail in Chapter 4.

Controlling

Most electronic devices which need to be controlled in some way are now controlled using a microprocessor or computer. Numerous household devices such as toasters, central heating thermostats, burglar alarms, cameras, washing machines and cookers now contain microprocessor control. All of these require software to be written in order to supply the control instructions.

Expert systems

Expert systems are computer programs that use **artificial intelligence** to make decisions based on data supplied in the form of answers to questions. The software usually consists of a huge database of knowledge about a specific subject, and a set of rules on which to base its decisions. Like a human expert, the software can 'learn' by its mistakes and thus build up its knowledge database. Expert systems are used in medicine for making diagnoses and in geology for predicting the presence of oil or certain minerals from seismic data.

Assignment A2.1

This assignment develops knowledge and understanding of the following element:
1.2 Investigate components of an information technology system

It supports the development of the following key skills:
Communication 3.2 and 3.3
Information technology 3.1, 3.2 and 3.3

Your friends decide to buy a PC system which they hope to use for the work they do at home (they are both teachers – one teaches all subjects in a junior school and the other teaches physics in a secondary school). Their daughter, who is taking her GCSEs, will also use the computer. Ideally they want a system that will last them several years, and they intend to use it for running multimedia software, wordprocessing, desktop publishing and games software. They would like to learn more about the Internet so they will need a modem included as part of their system. They don't know much about computers but have seen an advertisement in a magazine. The advert outlines the following system specifications:

- Intel 200 MHz Pentium processor
- 32 MB EDO RAM expandable to 128 MB
- 512 kB pipeline burst cache
- 2 GB enhanced IDE hard disk
- 8-speed IDE CD-ROM drive
- 64-bit stereo sound card
- powerful 70 W stereo speaker system
- 1.44 MB floppy drive
- midi-tower case
- high performance graphics card with 2 MB dedicated SDRAM
- 15-inch SVGA colour monitor
- Windows 95 keyboard
- Microsoft-compatible mouse
- Microsoft Windows 95 with manuals and CD
- 28.8 external fax/data modem.

Task 1
Your friends have sent you the following note:

Dear ....

Please find enclosed an advert for the system we are thinking of buying. This system has been recommended by a friend, but the system specification, as we think it's called, means nothing to us and we were wondering what it all means. Could you put it into English that a non-technical person could understand? For instance, what is a cache and what effect does it have on the performance of the overall system?

Write a reply to the above note explaining what each item in the system specification means and its relevance to the system performance.

Task 2

Your friends have heard of the following software packages:

- Windows 3.1
- Windows 95
- MS-DOS.

Two of them are classed as operating systems while the other may be considered to be a user interface. A user interface is used to improve the ease with which users can interact with another system.

Investigate and produce a brief report on each of the software packages listed above, comparing and contrasting their use. You should also mention their main strengths and weaknesses.

Task 3

Your friends' neighbour, who lectures in IT at the local college, has suggested that they build their own system from the various components. He says that the main advantages in doing this are that, first, it will be cheaper, and second, they can make sure that all the components are of the highest quality.

Your friends have asked you to investigate this possibility, pricing all the components they would need and to present the details in the form of a spreadsheet. To do this you will need to carry out some research to determine the components they would need, which components to choose from a range to ensure good quality and price, and where you would buy them from.

As well as the spreadsheet showing the components and their prices, produce a short wordprocessed recommendation saying how easy or difficult it would be for your friends to build their own computer and whether or not you think it is a good idea.

Components of a microprocessor system

The components that make up a microprocessor system include:

- central processing unit (CPU)
- memory (ROM and RAM)
- buses (address, data and control)
- input/output (I/O).

Central processing unit (CPU)

The **central processing unit** is the single electronic chip that contains:

- the **arithmetic and logic unit** (ALU), which carries out calculations and comparisons of data;
- the memory registers, which are used in decoding and carrying out program instructions;
- the **control unit**, which controls the computer by sending out three types of signals along sets of wires known as buses (see page 54).

Some of the more powerful computers are capable of performing parallel processing, which means they are able to process two or more parts of a program simultaneously. In order to do this they must have two or more interconnected microprocessors. Some supercomputers have as many as 256 000 microprocessors!

Memory

Memory is used to hold programs and data which may need to be accessed immediately by the central processing unit. There are two types of memory – random access memory (RAM) where data can be written to or read from, and read-only memory (ROM), where data can only be read from.

Buses

A **bus** is an electronic transportation system which passes data to and from its different locations within a computer system. A single wire is used for each bit of data transferred as a single unit. A computer that is able to transfer 32 bits at a time will have a bus with 32 wires so that all the bits can be transferred in parallel.

There are three types of bus: data, address and control (see Figure 2.5).

1 Data bus

A data bus transfers data to and from the memory locations, so the number of wires in it will greatly influence the speed of the computer. Where several devices are connected to a data bus, they must all take their turn in using it.

2 Address bus

An **address** bus carries binary signals (groups of 1s and 0s) for selecting the memory storage locations to be used when data is read from or written to the memory.

3 Control bus

A control bus carries the signals that tell the devices when they may use the bus and sets up the circuits on the bus for data toward or away from the memory. Because the data and address buses are shared by all of the system components, it is necessary to synchronise their actions.

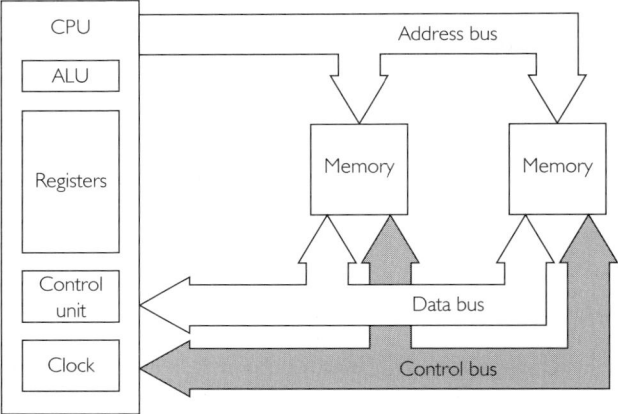

Figure 2.5 How the three buses are used, with each carrying a particular type of information

Input/output controller

The input/output (I/O) controller is the link between a microprocessor and its surrounding components, allowing communication with any device connected to it. Devices that are connected to the microprocessor may also be controlled by it. For example, a printer is linked to a CPU and can be turned on and off by it as required. The

input/output controller can be a card which is slotted into the motherboard, or it may be built into the motherboard. The main purpose of the controller is to translate the signals that pass along the system bus, and the signals that the input and output ports use. The system bus is a series of wires along which the data and control signals are able to pass, and a port is a connector – usually on the side or the back of a computer – to which input devices (e.g. a keyboard or mouse) and output devices (e.g. speakers, printers, etc.) can be connected.

Activity 2.5

Almost every device which needs to be controlled in some way now makes use of a microprocessor in its construction. Produce a list of at least 20 devices which incorporate a microprocessor. Pick three devices from your list and explain the tasks the microprocessor performs in them.

Functions of the components

This section examines in more detail the function of the components mentioned in the section above.

Instructions

For any microprocessor system to do a useful job, it must first be given a series of instructions in the form of a program. Programs consist of sets of instructions, arranged in a logical order, that are written in a particular computer language, the choice of which depends upon the nature of the program. These instructions are ultimately converted into binary code (a series of 1s and 0s).

Instructions can be given directly to a computer by using machine code, but writing programs in machine code is time consuming and difficult. Two other approaches to writing programs are usually used instead. The first option is to use an assembly language to write the program; assembly languages are easier to write in than machine code. Another program, called an assembler, is then used to convert the assembly language instructions into machine code. Although assembly languages are simpler than machine code, they still demand a high level of skill and knowledge. An easier approach to writing a computer program is to use a high-level language. Program instructions written in a high-level language are converted into machine code by yet another program, called a compiler.

There are many different manufacturers of microprocessors and each type will have its own set of instructions so this makes it more difficult for programmers to program them using machine code.

Calculations

Calculations are performed by the arithmetic and logic unit (ALU) of the CPU. The numbers used in the calculations are obtained either from the memory locations where they are stored or from an I/O port if they are input from an external device such as a keyboard or disk drive. Once the required calculations have been done, either the results can be output to the I/O port where they are sent to an output device such as a printer or monitor, or they can be stored for further use in the computer's memory.

Data flow

The storage spaces in the main memory, the CPU and the input/output controller are called registers. Data flow is the movement of data along a data bus, which is a multi-stranded wire, between the registers in these different components of a computer.

Storage

In a microprocessor, data can be stored in the memory or in the CPU.

Characteristics of memory

There are various memory locations in random access memory (RAM) where coded data and instructions can be stored. Each byte of data contains one character (letter, number, punctuation mark, etc.) and is stored in RAM at an address with a specific address number. The computer uses this address number to locate the data. The reason that this type of memory is called 'random access' is that the computer is able to move to any address in the memory to retrieve the contents with equal speed.

ROM (read-only memory) is slower than RAM and is used to hold data and instructions that the computer needs in order to boot up. 'Booting up' is a term used in computing to describe the process of the computer starting itself up when the power is switched on. The contents of ROM are stored in the electronic circuitry of the chip and are not erased when the power is turned off, and for this reason ROM is often called non-volatile memory. RAM's contents are erased when power is lost, and this type of memory is therefore called volatile memory.

Data stored in RAM can be read from the memory as well as written to the memory (called read/write memory), whereas data stored in ROM can only be read (called read-only).

Elements of the central processing unit

In this section we will look at the main elements of the CPU and investigate how the data, instructions and control signals are used.

Program counter

The program counter is part of the control unit of the CPU, and its purpose is to store the memory address of the next instruction to be executed. In other words, it helps the computer to keep track of each instruction so that it knows which instruction should be executed next.

Registers

A register is a memory location within a CPU used to store values and memory addresses while the CPU performs logical and arithmetic operations on them. The more registers a computer contains, the greater the amount of information it can deal with at one time.

There are three types of register: the memory buffer register, the memory address register and the current instruction register (see Figure 2.6).

1 Memory buffer register (MBR)

The memory buffer register (sometimes called the memory data register) is a place in the memory through which the data must pass when it is being moved between the memory locations, the data bus and the memory address register.

2 Memory address register (MAR)

This part of the memory is responsible for giving the address of the memory location where data is either put into the memory or taken from it.

3 Current instruction register (CIR)

The current instruction register contains the instruction that is currently being executed and is also responsible for decoding that instruction.

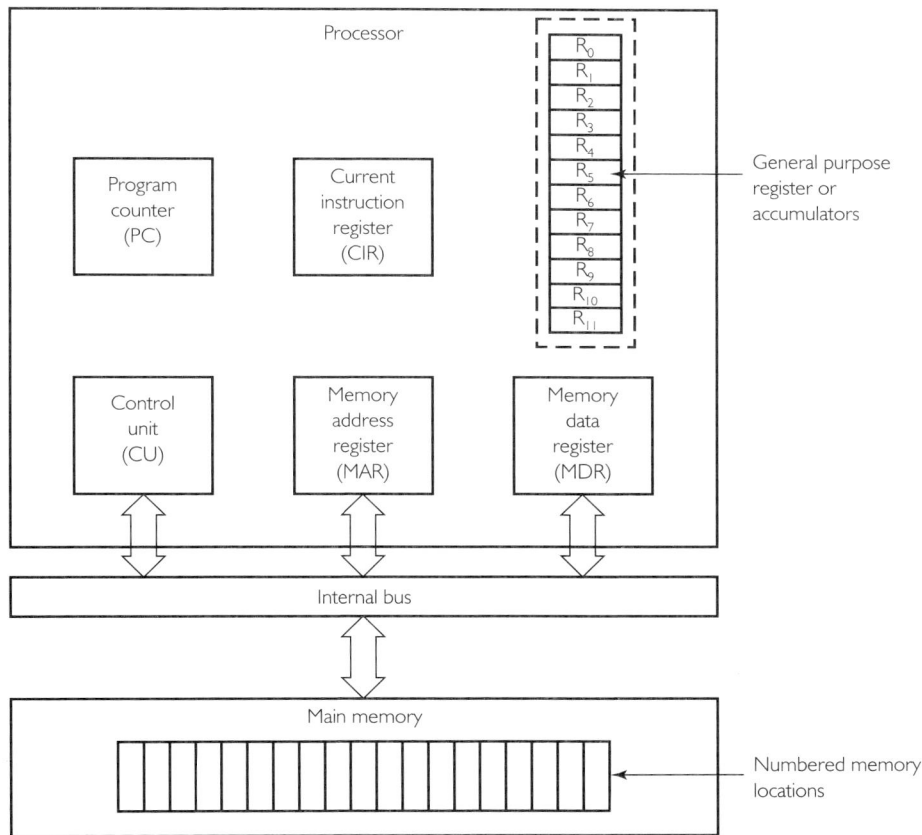

Figure 2.6 The components of the processor and the main memory

The machine instruction cycle

In this section we will look at the purpose of the registers and at the way the computer runs a program. To run any program, all computers follow a cycle of events called either the **fetch/execute cycle** or the machine instruction cycle.

Stages in the machine instruction cycle

The stages in the machine instruction cycle are given on page 59 (see also Figure 2.7).

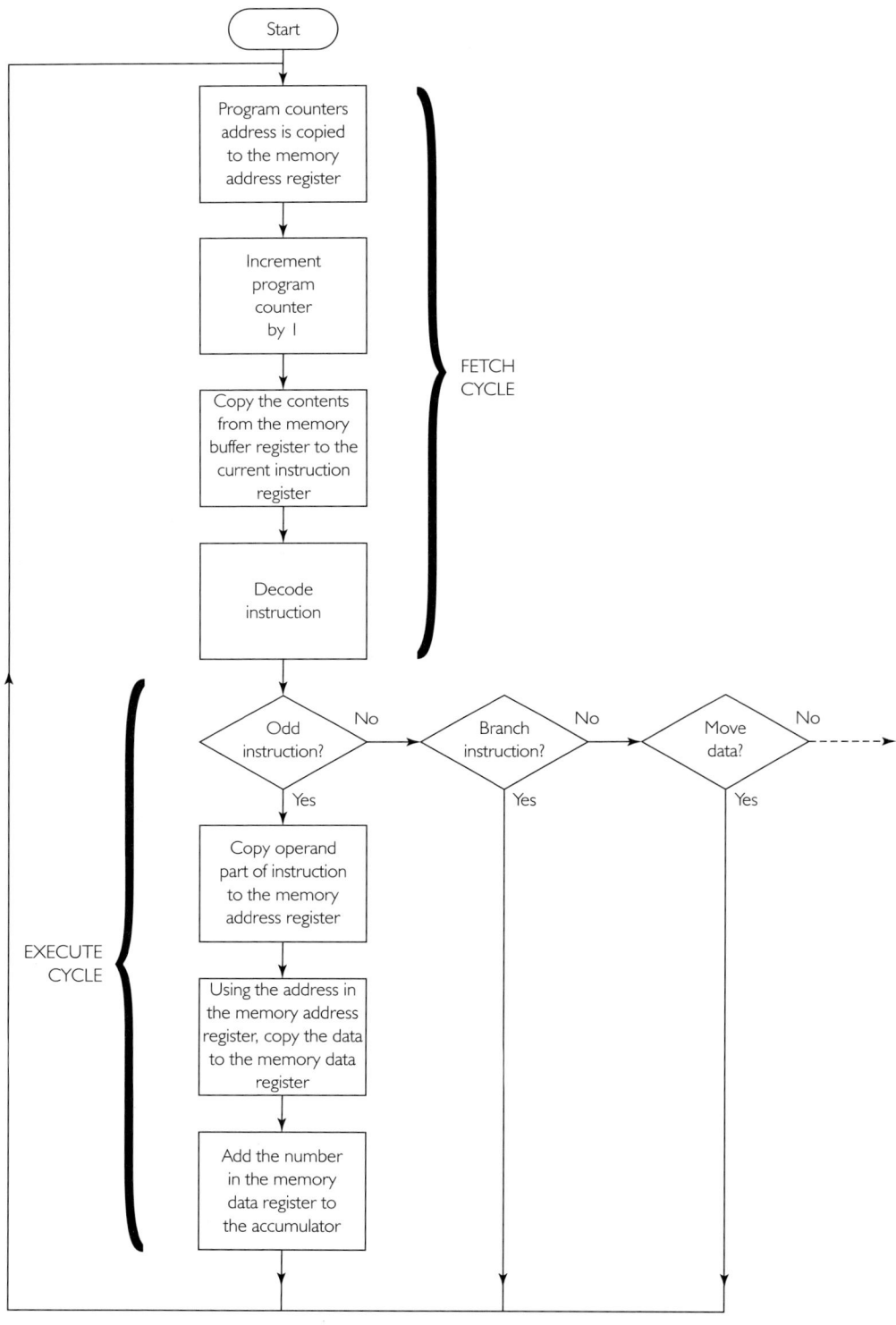

Figure 2.7 The stages in the fetch/execute cycle

1 Fetch the next instruction.
2 Decode the instruction.
3 Carry out (i.e. execute) the instruction.
4 Start the cycle again by going back to stage 1.

We will now look at what goes on during each of these stages.

1 Fetch the next instruction.

The control unit issues a control signal to tell the program counter to copy its address and then pass it to the address bus. It can then be passed along the address bus to the memory address register. Once this is done, the program counter is incremented by one (i.e. it goes up by one) so that it knows that on the following cycle it must use the next program counter address.

A control signal from the control unit is issued to the memory address register telling it to copy the data in it to the memory buffer register. A signal then instructs the memory buffer register to use the data bus to transfer the data to the current instruction register.

2 Decode the instruction.

The instruction in the current instruction register is then looked at to see what type of instruction it is, and also the addresses of the data which needs to have the operations performed on it. This process is called decoding the instruction.

3 Execute the instruction.

Once the instruction has been decoded the computer will know what operations need to be performed. The types of operation include:

- performing arithmetic or logic operations on the data;
- moving the data to another location in the memory;
- branching to another part of the program and at the same time changing the address in the program counter so that the program counter is able to keep track of the next instruction to be fetched.

4 Go to stage 1 and start the cycle again.

Assignment A2.2

This assignment develops knowledge and understanding of the following element:
1.3 Investigate the operation of a microprocessor system

It supports the development of the following key skills:
Communication 3.2, 3.3 and 3.4
Information technology 3.1, 3.2 and 3.3

Task 1
Using graphics, CAD or any other software, produce a block diagram showing the main components of a microprocessor system.

Task 2

Your tutor has problems explaining the following:

- the function (i.e. what it does) of each of the components in a microprocessor system;
- the main characteristics of the memory;
- the main elements of the central processing unit.

Without copying information from books (though you can still use them for reference), explain in your own words each of the above.

Task 3

The stages in the machine instruction cycle could be illustrated using a series of diagrams. Produce either a series of diagrams or a slide show on a computer to illustrate the stages. In addition, produce a handout to be given to students which shows the same diagrams but with some brief text explaining the cycle.

Installing and configuring a stand-alone system

To get the hardware to do a useful job it is first necessary to install both the systems and applications programs and then to get them to work with the hardware by configuring the system. A stand-alone computer system means one which is not connected to a network or other communications device.

Connecting the hardware components

When you buy a computer you usually have to unpack the components and then connect them. Because you need to do this every time you transport a computer or buy a new one you need to know how to connect the components in the correct way.

On a basic (non-multimedia) system, the hardware will, as a minimum, consist of the following components:

- main processor unit
- keyboard
- mouse
- VDU
- printer
- ports (serial and parallel)
- connection cables (power and data).

Activity 2.6

A friend borrowed your computer system, which has the basic components listed above, and to get it into her car she had to disconnect all the components. She has telephoned saying that she doesn't know how to connect it up again since there is no manual. She has asked you to fax her some instructions to help her.

Produce a series of instructions accompanied by diagrams that your friend could use to connect up the computer. It would be a good idea to study the different leads and connectors at the back of the machine so she can be told exactly what goes where.

Configuring the system

When you first buy a system it will probably come preconfigured, which means that it will have been set up to use whatever optional equipment (e.g. disk drives, memory, sound card, display adapter) that was originally installed. However, if you plan to change any part of the system, for instance to install some extra memory or add a peripheral device such as a scanner or modem, then you will probably need to reconfigure the system. (Peripheral devices are devices that are connected to and under control of the central processing unit.) Reconfiguring a modern Windows-based PC is much easier than it was in the past, when extra instructions had to be included and some existing ones changed in a file called the config.sys file. Most hardware devices now come with special software, called installation programs, whose purpose is to reconfigure the system automatically, and most users aren't even aware that it has been done.

If you have DOS on your computer you may like to look at the config.sys program by entering the directory where DOS is to be found and then issuing the command 'Type config.sys'. Remember not to change anything without doing a printout of the original file first. Figure 2.8 shows the instructions in a typical config.sys file.

```
DEVICE=C:\SUPRA\DWCFGMG.SYS
DEVICE=C:\DOS\HIMEM.SYS
DEVICE=C:\DOS\EMM386.EXE NOEMS HIGHSCAN I=B000-B7FF WIN=B500-B7FF WIN=F400-F7F
BUFFERS=20
FILES=30
DOS=UMB
LASTDRIVE=E
FCBS=4,0
DEVICEHIGH/L:1,12048=C:\DOS\SETVER.EXE
DOS=HIGH
COUNTRY=044,,C:\DOS\COUNTRY.SYS
DEVICEHIGH /L:1,4560 =C:\WINDOWS\IFSHLP.SYS
STACKS=9,256
DEVICE=C:\ISP16\CDSETUP.SYS/T:S/P:340
DEVICEHIGH /L:2,38208 =C:\ISP16\SLCD.SYS/D:MSCD_000/B:340
```

Figure 2.8 The instructions in a typical config.sys file

For Element 2.4 you will need to be able to configure a typical system, and in particular be able to:
- configure the display
- configure the memory
- configure devices
- set the date and time.

Your tutor will be able to show you how to do each of the above.

Plug and play

The Macintosh operating system has had a simple intuitive system for installing new peripherals for a number of years. The operating system Windows 95 now provides similar ease of installation with 'plug and play', which means that if you want to add new peripherals such as graphics adapters, CD-ROM drives, sound cards or new hard drives, the operating system will automatically detect them and then reconfigure the system so that the new devices can be used immediately.

Installation

Installing new operating systems or applications software is a lot easier than it used to be and demands little specialist knowledge. Most operating systems and applications programs can be installed automatically since most software comes with an installation program which takes the user through the installation process with a series of questions and options. The user does, though, need to have enough technical knowledge to understand and respond appropriately to the options offered. If the installation is being done from floppy disks, the user's main task is to feed the correct disks into the disk drive when requested. As software programs have grown in size, more and more floppy disks have been needed for installation, so it is now common for a CD-ROM to be used instead of disks. CD-ROMs typically have 650 MB of capacity; a single CD-ROM can easily store all the data needed for a typical applications program. Problems do, though, still occur with program installation: there are so many different programs and versions of them, and so many different hardware configurations, that occasional difficulties are inevitable. It is when these difficulties arise that experience and expertise are needed.

Creating directories

To make it easier to keep track of files on a disk, directories are used and files are stored within these directories. (On Macintosh computers, the word 'folder' is used instead of 'directory'.) All disks have at least one **directory**, and this is called the root directory. It would be possible (within limits) to store every file in the root directory, but this would make it difficult for the user to know which files went with which programs. In any one directory, no two files can have the same name and if all the files on a computer were in a single directory, conflicts would arise if two programs tried to create files with the same name. Directories other than the root directory are therefore created into which groups of files with similar properties can be placed.

Directories can be further split into subdirectories. Directories and subdirectories are given names which need to be chosen carefully to avoid any conflicts.

Installing software in a subdirectory

Software which runs under the DOS operating system needs to be installed into certain directories, and these directories need to be created before the data can be copied into them. To do this you need to know quite a lot about the DOS commands. In particular, you need to understand how to:

- change between different disk drives;
- list all the files in a directory;
- create a new directory;
- move to a new directory;
- copy all the files from a floppy disk to a named directory/subdirectory;
- delete a file from a directory;
- delete all the files from a directory/subdirectory;
- remove a directory/subdirectory;
- copy the entire contents of a directory/subdirectory on the hard disk to a floppy disk.

In Windows you can use the File Manager to create directories, select files and groups of files with certain properties, delete files and copy files. On-line help is available if you encounter any difficulties.

Setting defaults

A **default** is a predetermined setting. You can usually either accept a default setting established by a program or operating system or change it to suit your personal preference. For example, in most wordprocessing packages there is a default template which you can either use or, if you don't like it, change to a different default template. Also, when setting up some wordprocessing software, you may need to specify the type of printer from a list. This printer then becomes the default printer. The software automatically assumes that the default printer is the one being used unless it is told otherwise.

Installing device drivers

A device driver is a special file which instructs the computer how to use a device like a mouse or a printer. A mouse driver makes the mouse pointer appear on the screen and then translates the mouse-clicks into action.

Testing the system

On adding new software, new hardware or both, you need to make sure that they all work together properly, and to do this a series of system tests can be performed.

Powering up

When the computer is first switched on it takes some time for it to self-check before the operating system is automatically loaded from disk. This self-check is performed as soon as the power is switched on, and consists of a set of operations designed to make sure that all the components are working correctly. If they are not, the operator is alerted, usually in the form of a few 'beeps' and a brief message on the screen. It is usually quite simple to correct many faults, which are often nothing more than a loose keyboard or mouse connector at the back of the machine.

When the power is switched on, some instructions stored in ROM are obeyed and the computer performs its self-test routine. It checks the memory by storing a value in each memory location and then reading it to check that it is the same. It also checks for the presence of essential hardware such as disk drives, monitor, keyboard and mouse. The computer's configuration settings are stored in a type of chip called **CMOS RAM**, which has a low power consumption and can therefore be powered by a small rechargeable battery. Because the contents of the chip are maintained even when the power supply is switched off, the computer is able to remember that it has certain devices connected to it. During the self-test routine, the computer checks this configuration against the actual hardware connected to see if the system is the same as when it was last used.

Accessing software

Once the computer has self-checked it will then load the operating system. When this has been completed successfully it is possible to load the applications software and start using the computer.

Entering data

Software can be tested by running it and then checking that the results are correct. If you are running payroll software, for example, you could enter last month's payroll data and check that the results generated are the same as when the task is performed manually.

Saving data

To check that a system and program are working as expected, data can be entered and saved. The data can then be reloaded into the system from disk to check that it has been saved correctly.

Printing

To make sure that the correct printer driver has been installed successfully, it is necessary to print out some results. If strange symbols appear it usually means that the wrong printer driver has been installed and does not understand the data signals being sent to it by the computer. You need to make sure that the printer can deal with the various fonts supported by the software. Fonts, such as Times and Helvetica, are the different styles in which characters are printed (see also page 76). Most computer systems and programs now provide a range of fonts. Some fonts, such as TrueType fonts and Postscript fonts, appear on the screen exactly as they will be printed; others look different. Some fonts can only be printed out using a special output device such as a plotter.

Assignment A2.3

This assignment develops knowledge and understanding of the following element:
1.4: Install and configure a stand-alone computer system

It supports the development of the following key skills:
Communication 3.2, 3.3 and 3.4
Information technology 3.1, 3.2 and 3.3

This is a mainly practical assignment to make sure that you are able to connect up the typical components of a microprocessor system correctly.

Task 1
For this task you are required to connect up a basic computer system. Use a table like the one at the top of page 65 to keep track of the tasks you carry out. This will allow your tutor to check that each operation has been completed successfully.

Task 2
For this task you will be given a system specification, and you will then have to install the applications software on the hardware which you set up in Task 1. Your tutor will give you the software and brief details of the directory/folder the files need to be loaded into.

Use a table like this to keep track of tasks while you are connecting up a basic computer system

Task	Completed by student	Checked by tutor
1 Correctly site system unit.		
2 Connect keyboard to port on system unit.		
3 Connect mouse to port on system unit.		
4 Connect data cable from monitor to system unit.		
5 Connect power cable from monitor to system unit.		
6 Connect data cable from printer to system unit.		
7 Connect cable from system unit to power supply (first making sure that the switches are all off).		
8 Connect the power supply cable from the printer to the power supply.		
9 Switch on the power supply to the system unit, monitor and printer and check that all indicator lights are on.		

Task 3

The applications software you installed in Task 2 will need to be configured so that it can make use of the hardware that is connected to the system. Configure your system for the printer, monitor and mouse that you are using.

Your tutor has informed you that the time and date settings need correcting. Perform this task and then show your tutor.

Task 4

For this task you need to test the software fully by using it and performing as many operations as you can using as many of the software functions as possible. Make sure that you also test the printing using different fonts and font sizes.

Task 5

Once you have set up and used the system, any shortcomings and possible improvements in the system specification should become apparent. Produce a brief report reviewing the system and making recommendations for improving the specification.

Sample unit test

1 A clipart collection consists of 10 000 pictures which will never need to be changed. The collection takes up 300 megabytes of storage space. Which is the most appropriate storage medium?
   a floppy disk
   b RAM
   c ROM
   d CD-ROM

2 Which one of the following components is *not* found inside the main processor unit?
   a input and output ports
   b the motherboard
   c the CD-ROM unit
   d the video and disk drive controllers

3 One of the following devices is *not* an input device. Which one is it?
  a a keyboard
  b a mouse
  c a graphics tablet
  d a VDU

4 Multiple choice questions are often marked automatically by a special input device connected to a computer. This is an example of:
  a automatic data capture
  b sensed data
  c data logging
  d manual data capture

5 One of the following is an example of primary storage; the rest are examples of secondary storage. Which one is an example of primary storage?
  a ROM
  b floppy disk
  c hard disk
  d CD-ROM

6 Software enabling a PC to be connected to the Internet is called:
  a user interaction software
  b programming language software
  c communications software
  d file management software

7 A Pentium 266 MHz computer is better than a Pentium 200 MHz computer because:
  a it has a higher clock speed and therefore works faster
  b it has a larger magnetic hard disk
  c it has a larger memory and can store bigger chunks of data
  d it has a larger VDU so there is less strain on the user's eyes

8 Buses are the electronic transportation system used to carry data and instructions from one part of the CPU to another. There are three such buses; what is the one used to select the memory storage location when either writing to the memory or reading from it called?
  a the data bus
  b the control bus
  c the input bus
  d the address bus

Questions 9–12 refer to Figure 2.9.

9 The purpose of the program counter in the main processor is:
  a to store the memory location of the next instruction to be executed
  b to store the memory location of the current instruction being executed
  c to count the number of lines in a program so the computer knows how much memory is needed by the program
  d to repeat part of the program a set number of times

10 The current instruction register is responsible for:
  a passing data from one part of the processor to another
  b decoding instructions

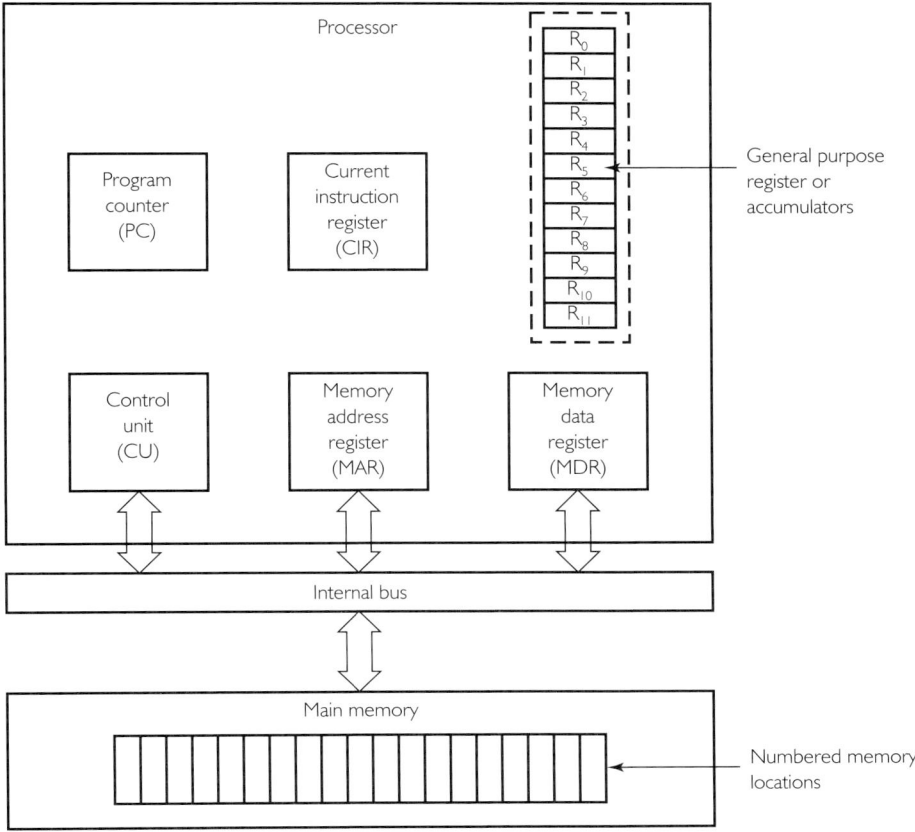

Figure 2.9

c giving the address of the memory location where data is either put or taken from

d supplying the link between the microprocessor and its surrounding components

11 Here is a list of the stages in the machine instruction cycle:

1 Execute the instruction
2 Decode the instruction
3 Start the cycle again
4 Fetch the next instruction

The above steps are not in the correct order. The correct order would be:

a 1, 3, 4, 2
b 4, 2, 1, 3
c 1, 2, 4, 3
d 4, 1, 2, 3

12 A new printer has been attached to your wordprocessor, but the output it produces is not correct. What needs altering?

a the correct printer driver needs to be installed
b the printer needs to be switched to on-line
c the printer needs to be set to receive ASCII text
d the printer toner cartridge needs replacing

13 Which one of the following is *not* normally classed as an operating system?
  a MS-DOS
  b Windows 95
  c Windows 3.1
  d UNIX

14 Plug and play is a feature of the latest operating systems. What does it do?
  a it enables you to get straight to your games programs
  b it allows you to connect peripherals which the computer is immediately able to recognise and use
  c it allows a joystick to be used as an input device
  d it allows more than one person to use the computer

15 The majority of operating systems now make use of a GUI (graphic user interface). What is the main advantage of a GUI?
  a it speeds up processing
  b it makes it easier for people to use the computer
  c it can be used with very little memory
  d it makes the hardware cheaper

16 A kitchen company makes use of computers to produce 3D views of new kitchen designs. What type of software package is it most likely to use?
  a CAD
  b presentation graphics
  c wordprocessor
  d spreadsheet

17 What is a default drive?
  a the drive being used for back-up
  b the drive which is used unless the computer is instructed otherwise
  c the drive used for the floppy disk
  d the drive you will need to use

18 You notice that the date on your printouts is wrong. What needs to be done to put it right?
  a change the date in the wordprocessing software
  b alter the clock setting in the operating system
  c store the date in the calendar database
  d send the computer back for repair

19 Which of the following is normally stored in ROM?
  a the user's data
  b application program instructions
  c the systems software needed to boot up the computer
  d multimedia applications

20 Expert systems are:
  a programs which make use of artificial intelligence to make decisions
  b systems which can be used only by experienced users
  c systems which make use of communications software
  d any system used by a doctor

21 Software used to simulate rush hour traffic is called:
  a database software
  b controlling software

c simulation software

d communications software

22 Which of the following stores can be considered to be volatile?

a ROM

b RAM

c floppy disk

d hard disk

23 A shop uses multi-part stationery to enable the various parts to be sent to different places. The type of printer which would be used for this is:

a a laser printer

b an ink-jet printer

c an impact printer

d a graph plotter

24 The simplest modelling software is:

a wordprocessing software

b spreadsheet software

c database software

d presentation graphics software

3 Commercial documents, presentation and technical graphics

What is covered in this chapter

In this chapter we will look at the processing of commercial documents and the use of graphics and technical drawings by organisations. To produce these documents, we usually use general purpose applications software such as wordprocessors, desktop publishing, presentation graphics, drawing and computer-aided design (CAD) packages. Aspects to be taken into account when preparing documents or drawings are given below.

Element 2.1: Process commercial documents

- Specifications
- Commercial documents
- Page attributes
- Page layout
- Editing documents
- Software tools
- Accuracy checks
- Security checks

Element 2.2: Process presentational and technical graphic designs

- Using the computer to draw
- Graphic design software
- Components
- Presentational graphics
- Technical drawings
- Design specifications
- H P Bulmer sells itself: a case study
- Terry & Partners case study

Resources you will need for your portfolio for Elements 2.1 and 2.2

- Your written answers to the activities and assignments in this chapter.

Commercial documents

This section covers the design and creation of commercial documents.

There is a variety of commercial documents, some of which are only used internally, others which are passed to outside bodies. Many companies use the latest technology, so, although the content of documents may be the same as they were in the past, they may be produced on the computer and transferred to the recipients by e-mail. The trend towards the paperless office continues and many companies are almost at the stage when all their correspondence is stored and dealt with on computer.

The main documents used between organisations are as follows:

Agenda

An agenda is a document prepared before a meeting outlining what is to be covered and thus enabling people who will be attending the meeting to prepare for it in advance. An agenda usually deals with the topics in the order in which they will be covered. It usually contains the following items, though not necessarily in the order shown.

1 **Apologies for absence:** members unable to attend should have given their apologies in advance along with reasons for non-attendance.
2 **Minutes of the last meeting:** this is to refresh members' memories of what was said and decided at the last meeting and usually consists of just a summary. Provided that there are no objections members will agree that the minutes are a correct reflection of the previous meeting.
3 **Matters arising from the minutes of the last meeting:** these are all the items that need to be discussed at this meeting, having arisen from the last meeting.
4 **New business:** a list of all the items of new business that the members need to discuss.
5 **Any other business (AOB):** usually matters arising at the last minute or after the agenda was set, and which need discussing.
6 **Date of the next meeting:** this is important, since agreement can be reached while everyone is present.

Business letter

Business letters are usually written on high quality, company-headed paper because they need to present the image of a successful, well-run organisation. As the use of electronic mail becomes more widespread, fewer letters will be sent between large organisations, but it is hard to see a future entirely without the mail service as we know it, because not everyone has the equipment to send and receive electronic mail.

Invoice

When a supplier sends goods which have been ordered they also send a document, called an invoice, either with the goods or separately by post. The invoice acts as a demand for payment. Invoices should be checked against the original order on receipt, since many invoices contain mistakes (usually to the purchaser's disadvantage!). Many larger companies now deal with invoices electronically, using a system called EDI (electronic data interchange). EDI was mentioned in some of the case studies in Chapter 1.

Activity 3.1

You have been asked to investigate what should be included on a typical invoice. Research the construction of invoices by looking at as many invoices as you can find. Are any clearer than others and what factors enhance their appearance? Produce a brief list of hints for someone who is about to embark on the process of producing a design for an invoice. You can choose any organisation you like. Produce your final invoice and incorporate clip art into the design. Show your design to your tutor who will make sure there are no important omissions.

Memorandum (memo)

Memos are only used internally and are short messages which focus on a small number of points. Many companies now use e-mail for company memos since this saves paper and storage space and is quicker, particularly if a memo needs to reach many people in the organisation. The main disadvantage with e-mail is that recipients do not check it often enough and that you are never really sure whether they have received it. If you are sending e-mail using the Internet, users other than the recipient can read it and it could even be altered. The quantity of of 'junk' e-mail which users receive can also lead to important messages not being noted and read.

Minutes

Minutes are a detailed account of who said what during a meeting and what was eventually agreed. A secretary will often take the minutes in shorthand and from this summarise the main points and present them at the next meeting where they will be agreed as a true reflection of what took place.

Report

Reports contain feedback from a 'finding out' exercise. For instance, a manager might ask you to look at the buildings and office equipment to make sure that your company is complying with the Health and Safety at Work Act. After completing your research you would provide your boss with a summary of the main points arising from your investigation, and it is this that would constitute a report.

Newsletter

Some firms, usually the larger ones, produce their own newsletters which are used to foster an involvement in the company. New developments/investment, new promotions, sports fixtures and results, results of exams taken by staff along with the usual births, marriages and deaths, feature in most newsletters, such as the one shown in Figure 3.1.

Figure 3.1 A newsletter from the cider producer H P Bulmer

Specifications

Many organisations have a corporate style specification for commercial documents which ensures that documents look the same when produced in different areas by various authors. Such a specification also ensures that all documents have a professional appearance.

The corporate or 'house' style is designed to ensure that the information is presented clearly and that it is easy to assimilate. Consideration is also given to the use of company logos, creating an image of the company which improves awareness and provides positive publicity.

Templates

To avoid time and effort planning such documents, each time one is needed a **template** can be used, which provides a framework on which to build. A template is a blueprint for the text, graphics and formatting and it ensures that all documents of a particular type look the same. It is common for members of an organisation to be given templates, one for each type of document, to ensure a common or corporate style. The template is an electronic file which holds the basic outline of the document. The user needs only to input the variable data, since formatting, font size, etc. will already be included. The main advantage of using templates is consistency of style, irrespective of author.

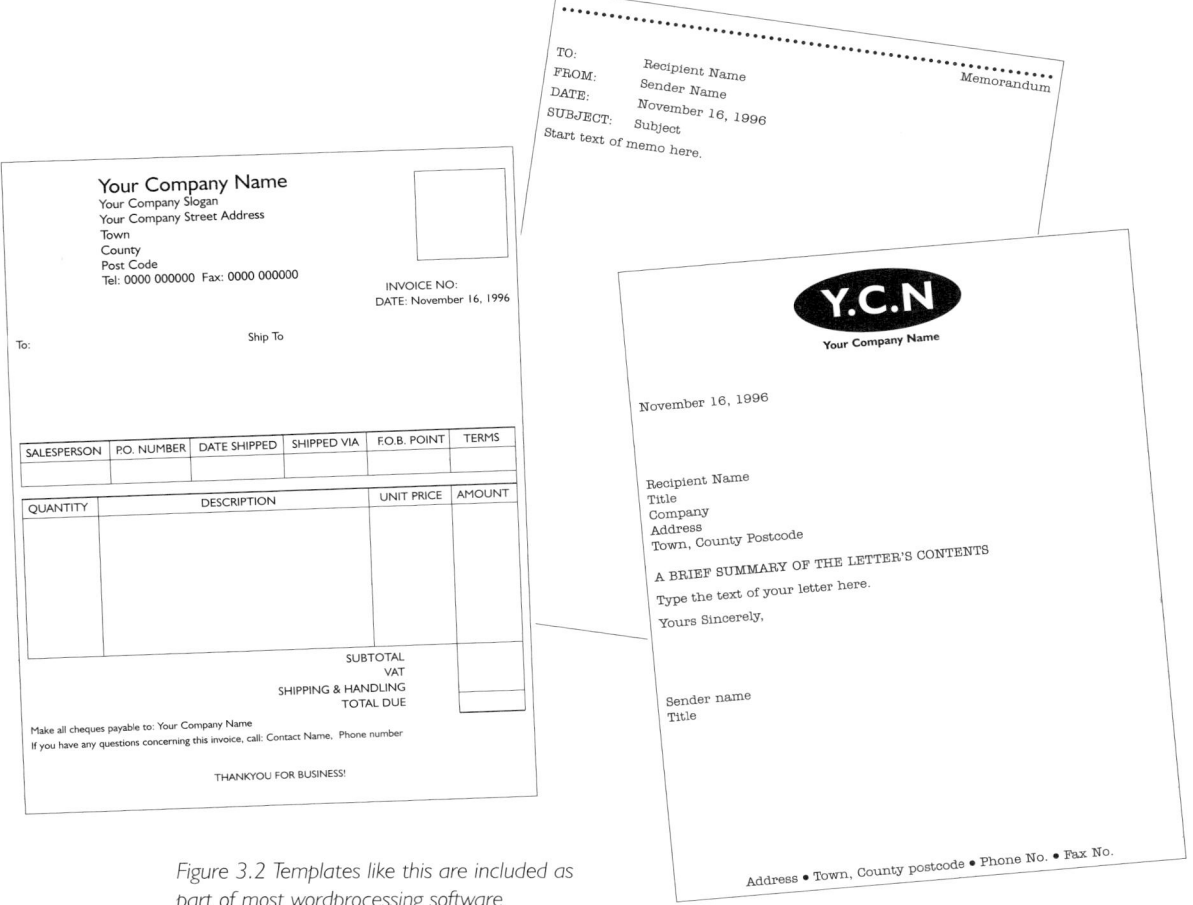

Figure 3.2 Templates like this are included as part of most wordprocessing software

Most wordprocessing software has template facilities so all you need do is 'fill in the blanks'. Each time you want a similar document, simply open the template, fill in the blanks, save the document (under a different name to that of the template) and then print it out.

Activity 3.2

Investigate the availability of templates (sometimes called style sheets) within your wordprocessing package. Print out the most useful templates and then try putting in the variable data and print out some examples of your work. How easy are they to use and adapt? Produce a brief report outlining your findings.

Specifications for a document or template will usually include the following types of information.

Type of document

The types of document likely to be met with are discussed in the first section of this chapter, headed 'Commercial documents' (page 70).

Purpose

The purpose to which the document is to be put must be borne in mind when determining content and presentation. A sales promotion document sent out to thousands of customers obviously needs to be presented more carefully than an internal memo reminding staff of a meeting.

Page attributes

Page attributes include the following:

Paper size

Most wordprocessors have a default paper size, usually A4 (297 × 210 mm), and this is the size assumed unless it is changed in the 'page setup' menu of the program. Other paper sizes may be used, such as 'legal' (which has the same width as A4 but is slightly longer) and most wordprocessors will allow you to adjust the page size to any value within limits. Before deciding on the paper size it is important to consider the use to which the final document will be put and adjust the paper size accordingly. Unless it is the default size (the size for which the printer and software are set up), once you have put paper into the printer, you need either to alter the paper size setting using the wordprocessing software or alter the setting on the printer. Sometimes both are necessary.

Orientation

There are two ways in which a page can be printed onto paper. With portrait orientation the height is greater than the width; with landscape orientation the page is turned sideways so that the width of the page is greater than its height. Portrait orientation is much more common and is used for most business documents such as letters, memos and reports; this book is portrait format. However, landscape format can be useful for charts, spreadsheets and notices.

Figure 3.3 shows the page setup selection menu from Microsoft Word.

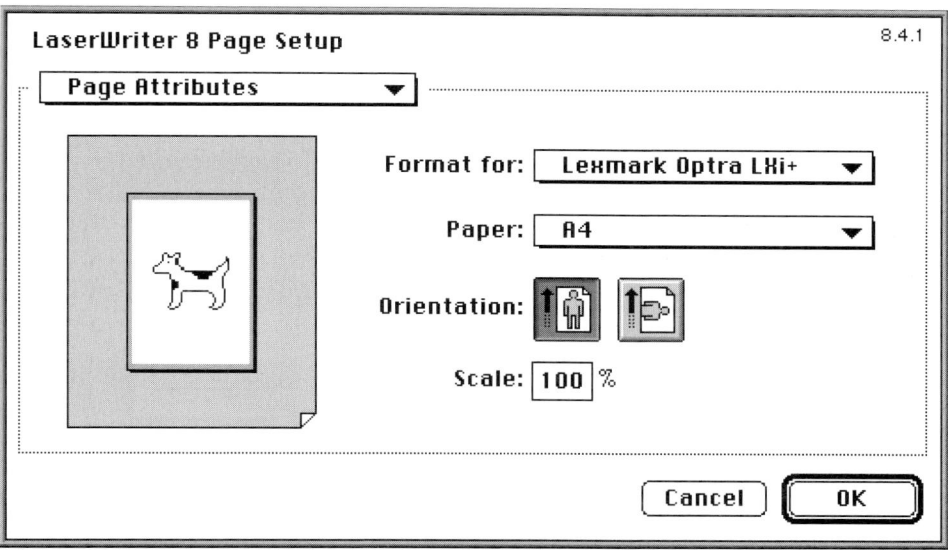

Figure 3.3 The page setup menu in Microsoft Word on a Macintosh computer

Widows and orphans

An orphan is the name given to the first line of a paragraph when it is separated from the rest of the paragraph by a page break. The orphan line appears as the last line at the end of one page, with the rest of the paragraph at the top of the next page. This looks untidy and many modern wordprocessors have a facility which prevents this from happening.

A widow is when the last line of a paragraph appears printed by itself at the top of a page and again this can ruin the appearance (and readability) of a document. Again, modern wordprocessors can prevent it from happening.

Page layout

The following issues need to be considered when organising page layout.

Margins

Margins mark the boundary of the text itself and therefore determine the amount of blank space left at the sides, top and bottom of the page. It is important to leave plenty of space at the sides in case the printed pages are to be bound in some way, since the binding may occupy considerable space and this could encroach upon the text. Also, if the text is too near the sides of the paper, parts of the lines could be cut off when pages are photocopied.

Figure 3.4 shows the menu for changing the margins in Microsoft Word.

Justification

Most wordprocessors are preset to align the text flush with the left margin while leaving the right margin ragged. There may also be the option of centring the text or having only the right margin aligned (this is useful for addresses). If both the left and right margins are lined up, the text is said to be fully justified.

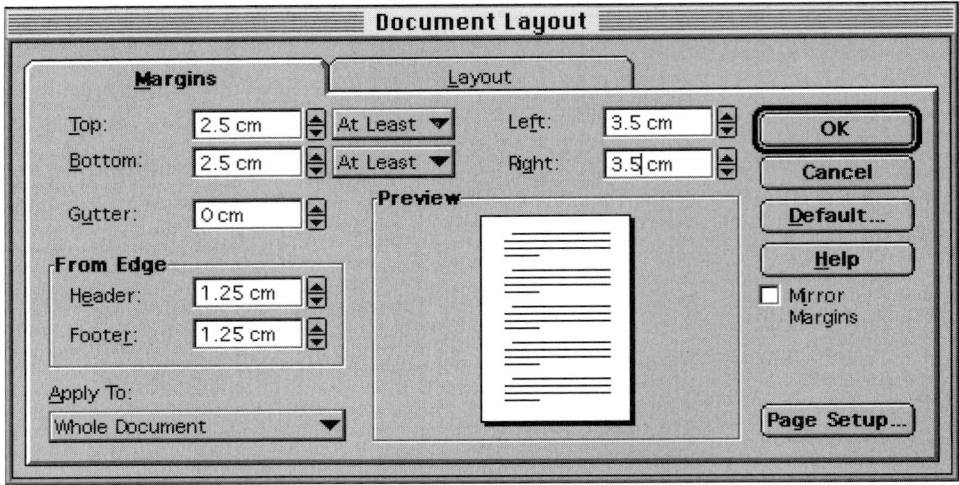

Figure 3.4 Changing the margins in Microsoft Word

Indents

Indents are sometimes used when starting a new paragraph and this involves starting the first word of the paragraph a few characters to the right of the usual margin. This type of indent is referred to as a first line indent. Other types of indents include hanging indents where the first line keeps the usual margin but following lines are indented, and paragraph indents, where the whole paragraph is indented from the left margin.

Tabulations

Most packages have default tab positions and, if these are not suitable, tab functions can be set manually in advance. You can move text to the preset positions simply by pressing the Tab key rather than by pressing the space bar repeatedly and hoping that you can align text accurately. Tabs can be useful when arranging columns of text or numbers so that they are kept in a straight vertical line.

Line spacing

Most documents are typed with single line spacing which has no blank lines between the lines of typed text. Double spacing is often used if a document needs to be sent for another person's comments or for editing, as this leaves a line of space between each line of text for the reader to insert comments. Most modern wordprocessing packages allow you to specify the exact spacing between lines of text. The spacing is sometimes called leading (pronounced 'ledding').

Fonts

Fonts are collections of letters, numbers, symbols and punctuation marks of common design. Fonts and their sizes can be selected using the applications software but they will only be printed out if the printer is enabled to print them. Otherwise a default font can be used instead.

Changing fonts can make the design of a poster more interesting, but care should be taken not to use too many fonts in business documents. With these it is probably best to use no more than two fonts, making the documents more interesting and readable by using different sizes, bold, underlining or italics.

Activity 3.3

Experiment with the font and font size facilities offered by your wordprocessor. See if your printer supports all the fonts, and produce a small booklet that you can refer to in the future, showing the different fonts and font sizes.

Page numbering

Once a document exceeds two pages in length it becomes a good idea to number the pages. A user may need to refer to information contained on a certain page, and page numbering is the only practical option. Also, if a page is missing the reader will probably notice if pages are numbered.

Headers and footers

Headers and footers are text which is repeated at the top of every page (in the case of headers) and the bottom of every page (in the case of footers). Headers and footers are often used for easy reference to the title of the document, section in which the page falls, author's name, date or version of document. The headers at the top of this and the facing page show one common usage in books and larger documents.

Column layout

It is possible to alter the way a document looks by formatting all or part of it in newspaper-style columns. In this style, text flows from the bottom of one column to the top of the next column. This format is handy when producing newsletters, brochures, magazines, etc. Most popular wordprocessors now have this facility which used to be available only on DTP packages; it is usual to allow one, two or three columns. Figure 3.5 shows examples of the possible arrangements.

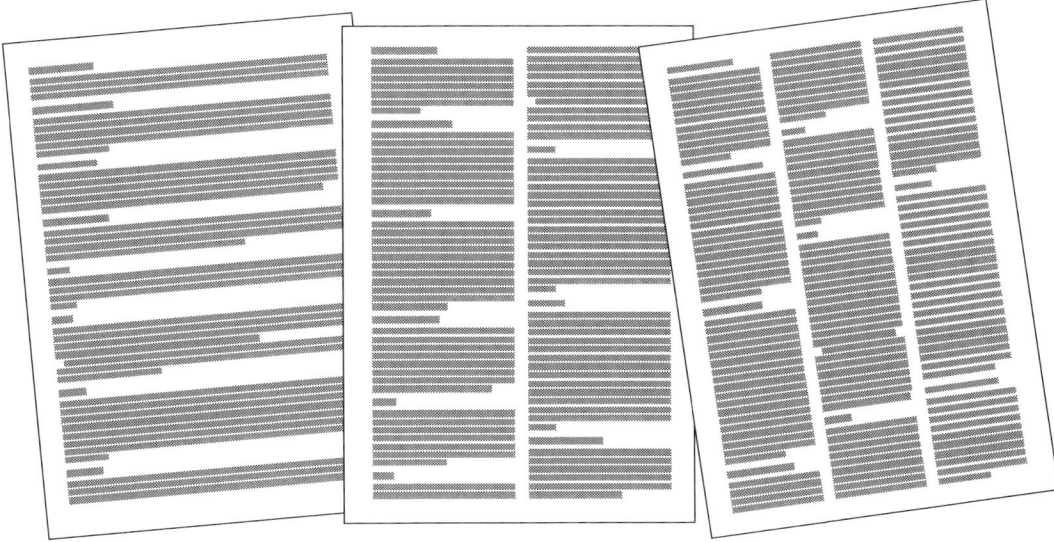

Figure 3.5 You can choose different numbers of columns for your documents

Document notes

Sometimes a reference needs to be made to something contained in the body of the text. A number or symbol is used and this indicates the footnote to which it refers. A footnote is a note, comment or reference at the end of a page. Footnotes can be used for references in academic works, cases in legal documents, translations or personal observations.

Activity 3.4

Produce a copy of your timetable using appropriate software facilities.

Data

Data is raw facts and figures. As part of your portfolio you will need to produce evidence that you have entered and edited various types of data into a computer. The majority of computer data takes the form of text, but data can also be graphics, tables or simply the format of a particular document.

Text

Most of the data stored and processed by computers consists of text which has either been entered via a keyboard or scanned-in using optical character recognition (OCR) software. Data in text format is readily transferable from one program to another by converting it to a standard format such as **ASCII** (American Standard Code for Information Interchange).

Most wordprocessors are able to open documents that have been created on other wordprocessors; if the software is not available within the wordprocessing package you are using, it can sometimes be bought separately.

Tables

There are many instances where it is useful to present data in table format and most wordprocessors have a 'table' facility. Some are able to offer a series of previously stored table formats from which you are able to choose. For wordprocessors without a table facility, it is necessary to produce tables using spreadsheet software and then import the spreadsheet table into the wordprocessed document. Sometimes, if the information needs to be presented in a large table, it may be more appropriate to use spreadsheet software in any case, especially if calculations need to be made. Although many wordprocessors are able to perform calculations, the range of calculations can be very limited.

Graphics

Graphics are pictures, diagrams or charts included in documents to present data pictorially (for example as graphs) or simply to enhance the appearance of the document. Graphics can be created using a special graphics package or drawn using facilities within a wordprocessing package. As most people are not skilled artists there is a range of predrawn pictures available in most wordprocessing packages and these are referred to as **clipart**. Once you have exhausted the supply of clipart included with your wordprocessor you can buy disks or CD-ROMs containing clipart images.

Activity 3.5

Do some research on typical documents. Look at business letters, business cards, advertisements, invoices, statements, etc. You need to look at these documents from the point of view of page attributes and layout. Try to look for any features that you think work well. Produce a report on your findings.

Editing documents

Documents may contain a combination of text, tables and graphics. Occasionally you will want to make changes to them and this process is called editing. Editing facilities are offered by all applications programs and it is important to know how to use them.

Text editing

Delete

There is a variety of ways to delete text. The backspace key can be used to delete the character to the left of the cursor while the delete key is used to delete the character on which the cursor lies. If a large amount of text needs to be deleted, the best method is to mark the text and delete the marked block in one go.

Insert

It is useful to be able to insert letters, words, paragraphs and even pages at any point in a document and this can be done by moving the cursor to the relevant position and simply typing in the text (make sure the 'insert mode' has been selected first, otherwise you will write over what is already there).

Activity 3.6

Use a wordprocessing package to import data from one file into another. If necessary consult your tutor or a guide book to find out how it is done in your particular package.

Move

Sometimes it is necessary to put text which has been typed in one order into a completely different order and this can be done by moving blocks of text that have previously been marked. Depending on which type of wordprocessor is used, you can cut text to place it in the clipboard; the text can then be pasted in the required position.

Copy

Text may need to be copied, because it is used again within the same document, or it may need to be repeated in a second document.

Sometimes it is necessary for a complete file to be inserted into another. For example, you may need a list of conditions of contract to be placed at the bottom of a document. This list could be saved as a separate file and then inserted by copying it into another document such as a letter.

Enhancing text

Text can be made more attractive and easier to read by means of various enhancing techniques. For example, it is possible to alter the size or style of a font, or make the text bold, italic or underlined. This book uses all the features mentioned and incorporates two main different fonts; look through and see if you can identify the various techniques.

Graphics

A graphic is usually a photograph or a drawing, but it can also be a piece of text which has been stored as a complete entity (as a picture), not as a series of letters. Graphics can be edited in the following ways:

Size

The graphic will have been saved as a certain size but the size can be adjusted to fit any space available. This process is called sizing.

Rotate

To produce a more eye-catching display or fit the available space, you may want to rotate a graphic through a specific angle.

Copy

An invitation to a Christmas party could be set on a background graphic of multiple Santa images. The quickest way to do this would be to import one Santa image and copy it to place the graphic in a number of positions.

Move

If a graphic is in the wrong position it is fairly simple to select it and then move it to a new position on the screen.

Manipulate

There is a variety of ways in which several of the above functions can be used to manipulate the image in some way. For instance, with presentation graphics software, you can increase the impact of text by moving it across the screen and at the same time making it increase in size.

Tables

Most wordprocessing packages provide preset table formats, but you may still have to edit them in order to get what you want. Spreadsheets are ideal for the presentation of tabular material. In addition to enhancing/editing text within cells, editing a table can involve inserting and deleting rows, columns and items.

Software tools

Software tools usually come as part of a software application. Tools are used within the software to carry out a particular job more efficiently.

Search

The **search** facility can be used to find a particular word or phrase in a document and it is particularly useful in long documents. You can also use the search facility for finding a particular document by examining the document description.

Search and replace

'Search and replace' allows a wordprocessor or other application to search for the occurrence of a word (or other set of characters) and then replace it with another. For example, if a letter contained a person's name such as Mr Jones, it could be replaced throughout by Mr Smith. You can either replace all the occurrences automatically or have a prompt for each occurrence of an item, and decide whether to replace it or not.

Mail merge

'**Mail merge**' is the name given to the process of combining variable data such as names and addresses in a secondary file with a master file, to produce multiple documents, each containing the same master information but addressed differently. This is especially useful if the same letter needs to be sent to many people (see page 353).

Accuracy checks

It is very important to check that documents are correct before they are printed and distributed. The following checks help prevent incorrect documents from being produced.

Spell check

Documents can be checked for accuracy by performing a spell check. Spell checking is a facility offered by wordprocessors and some DTP and graphics packages. The feature checks every word in a document for the correct spelling and gives possible corrections for words that it does not recognise. It can also check for words that may have been typed twice by mistake (such as 'the the') and make sure that new sentences start with a capital letter.

Even after spell checking, documents still need to be read carefully to make sure that the text makes sense, and to check for words that, although corrupted, can still be recognised as correctly spelt.

Proofreading

Proofreading means visually checking a document for spelling, grammar, punctuation, layout and style, including the positioning of tables and graphs. There are special universally recognised marks which are used to indicate the corrections required.

Security checks

Computer security is concerned with taking care of the hardware, software and, most importantly, the data. The cost of creating the data again from scratch can often far outweigh the cost of any hardware or programs lost. Apart from theft, probably the most important threat to data comes from viruses, which are mischievous programs designed to damage data, introduce annoying messages, or sometimes both. In the past viruses only infected programs, but there are now many viruses which can cause damage to your data. The risk of viruses must be taken seriously and all computers should have antivirus software installed, which is used to scan the computer's memory and disks for viruses and destroy them. Security aspects will be dealt with in greater detail in Chapter 6.

Confidentiality

Many documents are confidential to the originator and the recipient; examples are references for employees, medical records in a hospital and social worker reports. Other documents, such as monthly sales figures, new brand promotions, etc. are of use to competitors and so need to remain within an organisation. In this section we look at the security issues when processing commercial documents.

Many of the documents produced by organisations are confidential and it is important that only certain staff are allowed to see them. Some documents may be of interest to outside bodies and must be kept securely within an organisation. It is worth remembering that documents are vulnerable on and off the computer and there is little point in ensuring data security on the computer if printed copies of confidential documents are left on a desk for anyone to read or steal.

Passwords

Passwords are used to prevent unauthorised access to documents held as computer files and these passwords should be changed on a regular basis. More details on passwords will be given in a later chapter.

Non-disclosure

Although passwords prevent unauthorised access, some staff may still need to access confidential data and may pass on the information they have seen. The only real way of reducing the risk of this is to make staff aware of the consequences of such action. Most organisations put non-disclosure agreements in their staff contracts of employment, which prevent staff from disclosing any information gained in the course of their employment to any outside organisation. Public service employees are often made to sign the Official Secrets Act as part of their conditions of employment and this makes it a criminal offence to pass on information, with penalties as severe as a prison sentence.

Regular file saving

Some software saves data automatically after a certain period; the time between the saves can often be altered to suit the user. Regular file saving ensures that work is not lost if a problem occurs with the computer or its power supply.

Back-up

Most wordprocessors can automatically produce a **back-up file** in addition to the original document. They usually have a different file extension, so in Microsoft Word, for example, back-up files have a .BK! extension while the original documents have the .DOC extension.

Some wordprocessors automatically create a temporary back-up file while you are working thus allowing the last version of the document to be recovered in the event of a system crash.

It is important that you get into the habit of making regular back-up copies of your files and keeping the back-up disks separate from the computer. It is best to keep a series of disks and rotate them as the back-up copies for your most important files. The reason behind this is that some viruses now attack data and you do not always know if your disk is infected, so any back-up copy could also be infected. If your original disk and first back-up become infected, you could still have uncorrupted files on a second back-up disk, although you may lose work done between the first and second back-ups.

Retain source documentation

A **source document** is the original document used when preparing a new document on a computer. For example, if you are writing up an assignment, you may have decided to first write out a rough version on a piece of paper. This could then be used as a rough from which the final version is typed into the computer. In this case the rough version would be considered to be the source document.

If the document held on the computer was lost or corrupted, provided that the rough had been kept, you would have the source document from which to work again.

Theft of hardware and software

Equipment theft

Theft of computer equipment can obviously result in the loss of any documents the equipment contains and possibly the loss of back-ups if these were stored close by. There are many ways in which equipment can be secured against theft, and these will be looked at in Chapter 6.

Software/data theft

Software is owned by the developer. To use it without a proper licence, is theft. Organisations have to make sure that they are not party to software theft by checking that their employees' hard disks do not contain unauthorised software. If networks are used, an organisation needs to make sure that it has the correct number of licences for the number of users to whom the software is available.

Copyright

If work is prepared in an organisation's time, copyright to any new software or data prepared belongs to that organisation. It is also illegal to copy data or software without the owner's authorisation. Copyright is covered by the Copyright, Designs and Patents Act 1989 and further information about the implications of this act are covered in Chapter 6.

Assignment A3.1

This assignment develops knowledge and understanding of the following element:
2.1 Process commercial documents

It supports the development of the following key skills:
Communication 3.2, 3.3 and 3.4
Information technology 3.1, 3.2 and 3.3

For this assignment you have to create a set of corporate document styles for a fictitious business of your own choice. The general appearance of the documents should be in keeping with the image of the type of business you have chosen.

Task 1
Most organisations have a company logo. Before you attempt this task try to find out from business studies books how real companies decide on their corporate image and in particular on their logos. Design a logo for your organisation using suitable software. This logo needs to be saved as a separate file ready to be imported into the documents created in Tasks 1 and 2 as required.

Print out any of the rough logos and explain why they were rejected. Also print your logo and say why you preferred this one to the others.

Since this logo needs to appear on all company documents it needs to be imported into the documents you have already set up. Produce printouts to show that you have successfully imported, moved, sized, saved and eventually printed four different documents incorporating the logo you have designed.

Task 2

Design four templates with appropriate page attributes and layouts for four different documents from the following list:

- business letters
- faxes
- memos
- invoices
- delivery notes
- statements
- visiting cards
- special promotion/marketing advert.

Task 3

Choose four of the documents from the above list and incorporate at least two types of data (text, tables and graphics) into each document. One of the documents should be at least three pages in length. At least one of the documents must include columns and document notes.

It is left to you to make sure that the content of the documents is appropriate to your fictitious business.

Task 4

Tables are often used in business to hold details such as price lists, delivery charges and loan payment rates. Produce a table containing information that might be used in your chosen business. If necessary, import this table into your document, making sure that you use the company logo. Print your result.

Task 5

So that your final documents are free from mistakes, all documents should be proofread and spell checked before they are saved and printed.

Using the computer to draw

The saying goes that 'a picture is worth a thousand words' and it is hard to imagine trying to fix a car engine, or explaining how to put together self-assembly furniture without the use of pictures. Whether is it for putting ideas across using presentation graphics or producing technical diagrams from which engineers can construct components, the production of a diagram using a computer is an important use of information technology.

Graphics can be 'presentational' or 'technical'. These two types serve very different purposes and tend to be produced with different types of software. Presentational graphics are used to enhance the printed page, making the content more eye-catching in some way. They are used to add interest to wordprocessed documents, and presentation slides are often employed in commerce for marketing and promotional leaflets. Presentational graphics software is specialist software used to help design, produce and manipulate all the components of presentational graphics.

Technical graphics include maps, designs and technical drawings. The latter are often produced with computer-aided design (CAD) packages. The emphasis with these is on accuracy and clarity, rather than necessarily on an attractive appearance. More generally, designs and technical illustrations are produced with specialised drawing packages, such as Adobe Illustrator, which was used to produce many of the diagrams in this book.

Graphic design software

Graphic design software broadly generates two types of image: bit-mapped images and vector images. Presentation graphics programs such as Microsoft PowerPoint and painting and image manipulation programs such as Adobe Photoshop store their images in bit-mapped form. Drawing programs such as CorelDRAW! and Macromedia FreeHand save their files in vector format.

Bit-map graphics

With black and white **bit-mapped graphics**, each **pixel** (dot of black or white) is stored as a bit of information. Images are not, of course, always made up of black and white elements: many images have shades of grey in them (grey-scale images), while others consist of many colours. For grey-scale and coloured images, each grey or coloured pixel is made up from several bits. The position of each pixel is mapped out and stored as a series of bits in a file: hence the name '**bit-map**'. The main disadvantage of bit-mapped graphics is that the number of pixels is set when the file is created. Therefore if the image is enlarged the pixels must move further apart, so the image loses clarity. In a similar way, you may have noticed that a television with a large screen will generally have a less sharp picture than one with a small screen. This is because the number of pixels used to make up the picture is the same, but they are further apart on the larger screen. Photographs or drawings are often scanned into computers. These images are stored as bit-map files and may subsequently be manipulated with graphics, DTP or wordprocessing software.

Vector graphics

With **vector graphics**, the information defining an image is stored as a series of equations within the computer. These graphics are defined in vector format so, for example, an individual straight line or a triangle would be defined by reference to starting points, lengths and directions. The user does not need to be aware of how these graphics are constructed within the computer, but needs to know only how to create and use such images. A vector graphic might be created out of dozens, hundreds or even thousands of individual lines, boxes and curves. Any text which is added to the graphic can be stored either in text format or in vector graphic format. The quality of a vector graphic is independent of its size: it can be enlarged or reduced and the image quality will depend on the quality of the output device, not upon how much the image has been enlarged.

Components of graphics and drawings

The components of the various types of graphics include the following:

Lines

Most of the simpler graphics images consist of combinations of lines which can be straight, curved, freehand or part of a circle (called an arc).

Shapes

All packages provide a range of shapes that can be manipulated and sized, by using a combination of a mouse and keyboard. Shapes available include rectangles, circles, ovals and polygons. Both lines and shapes can also be drawn freehand.

Colour and shade

Lines and shading can be coloured to make a design or diagram more appealing. However, the use of colour greatly increases the size of the file needed to store the graphic. Colour ink-jet printers are quite cheap, and posters, leaflets and other promotional material certainly look much better in colour.

Text

There are three main elements to consider with text: font, size and colour. The way in which fonts are used needs to be thought through carefully. For example, if you are preparing an illustration for use on a poster, you need to ensure that the text is large enough and you need to resist the temptation to have too much text on the illustration.

Attributes

Some of the components mentioned previously can have their attributes changed. For example, lines can be dotted, dashed or have arrows on them. You can also alter the thicknesses of lines. Shapes can be 'flood-filled' where the inside of the shape is coloured or patterned. A 'paint spray' can be used to provide shadings in a similar way to that produced by an artist working with an airbrush. Where a 'paintbrush' is used you can alter the shape of the brush to produce different painting effects. Many packages now have huge numbers of features that are worth exploring in detail.

Activity 3.7

You have been asked to produce a short set of notes which will help a person new to graphics packages to use the package you have chosen. You will need to describe the main components of the package and show how it can be used to construct a diagram of your choice. You should illustrate your notes with examples.

Presentational graphics

Presentational graphics packages are used to create artwork and pictures, perhaps for use in a slide presentation or, increasingly, for an illustration that is to be presented in electronic format. Such material is mainly created and stored as bit-map images.

Charts

There is a variety of charts that can be produced and they broadly fit into the following categories.

Text charts

These make useful handouts or slides in a presentation when the concepts can be conveyed better in words than in pictures. Text charts are ideal for making comparisons or for presenting the benefits and drawbacks of a particular issue. When text is used in this way it is often a good idea to present information as a bulleted list.

Graph charts

These are used mainly for numerical information. Rather than just listing series of numbers it is better to make them visually appealing by presenting the information as bar charts, pie charts, etc. You can make comparisons by placing charts alongside each other: you might, for example, compare the monthly sales figures over one year with those for the next year.

Many spreadsheet packages have a graphics facility. The user simply enters the numbers and selects the appropriate type of chart; the graph is then produced automatically.

Figure 3.6 shows pie charts that illustrate the turnover profile over two years.

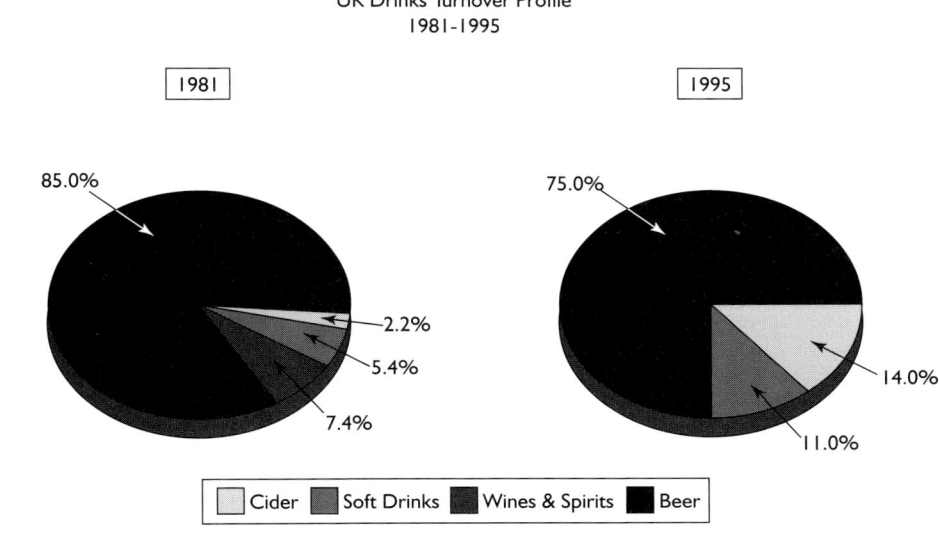

Figure 3.6

Slide shows

With presentation graphics, it is possible to develop a slide show that consists of a series of slides presented on a computer screen one after the other. The software also enables you to print charts onto transparencies or slide film (the latter needs special equipment) and then make a presentation using an overhead or slide projector. You can, of course, also print the slides onto paper for use in handouts. With a colour printer you can make the slides very eye-catching.

Pictures

Slides developed using presentation graphics packages are often images such as photographs that have been scanned in, clipart, company logos, graphs, charts, etc.

Technical drawings

Technical drawings are produced using vector-based software. Such drawings range from simple technical diagrams, such as flow charts, through to complex three-dimensional drawings of, say, cars and buildings. Computer-aided design (CAD) software is used to produce engineering drawings and architectural drawings.

Technical drawings can be categorised as follows:

Layout drawings

These are drawings produced using vector-based software which show the plan view of something, that is, as if you were looking down on it from directly above.

Figure 3.7 shows a series of possible plans for a bathroom. These plans have been produced using a computer-aided design package called AutoCAD. Producing drawings or plans on a computer is efficient because you can quickly modify drawings or plans to produce a range of alternatives then select the one you think most suitable. If you look at the different designs for the bathroom, some are much better than others.

Product design

Technical drawings are used in product design to show how a particular object should appear when manufactured. Such drawings usually define the dimensions of the product, the materials from which it is to be constructed and other detailed specifications.

Figure 3.8 shows the nozzle of a fire hose which has been designed using a CAD package. Notice how the software can generate isometric or perspective drawings from the original two-dimensional drawing.

Block schematic

Block schematic drawings are created using vector-based drawing software. They represent in simple terms any system flow or organisation. Such diagrams often consist of various types of labelled box, with arrows showing flows of information, or activity. Such diagrams can be used to describe the operation of a control system, the functions of an organisation, or the operation of a microprocessor.

Design specifications

Before producing a particular graphic it is necessary first to consider the required features of the design. Those without the necessary skills and time will need to instruct a designer to produce the design. To develop a design, the artist will need to be provided with a design specification. A design specification could include the following:

Graphic type

Whether bit-mapped or vector graphics are to be used should be part of the design specification.

Purpose and context

It is easy to get carried away when preparing illustrations and designs using a computer, using all the features of the package and spending too long on the job. You need

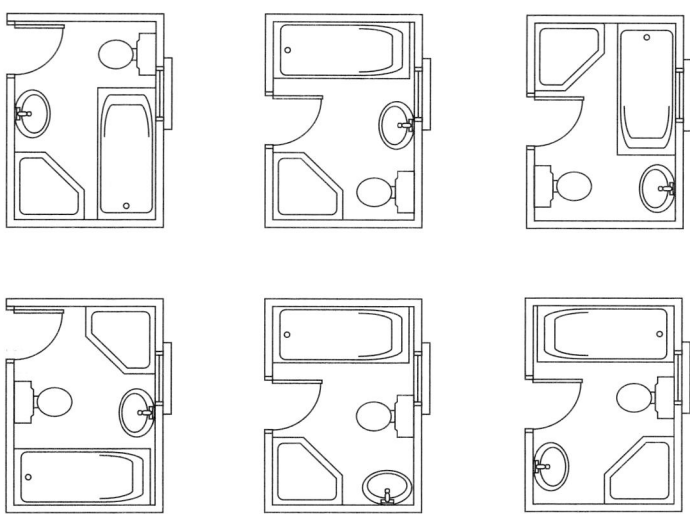

Figure 3.7 Bathroom plans produced using AutoCAD

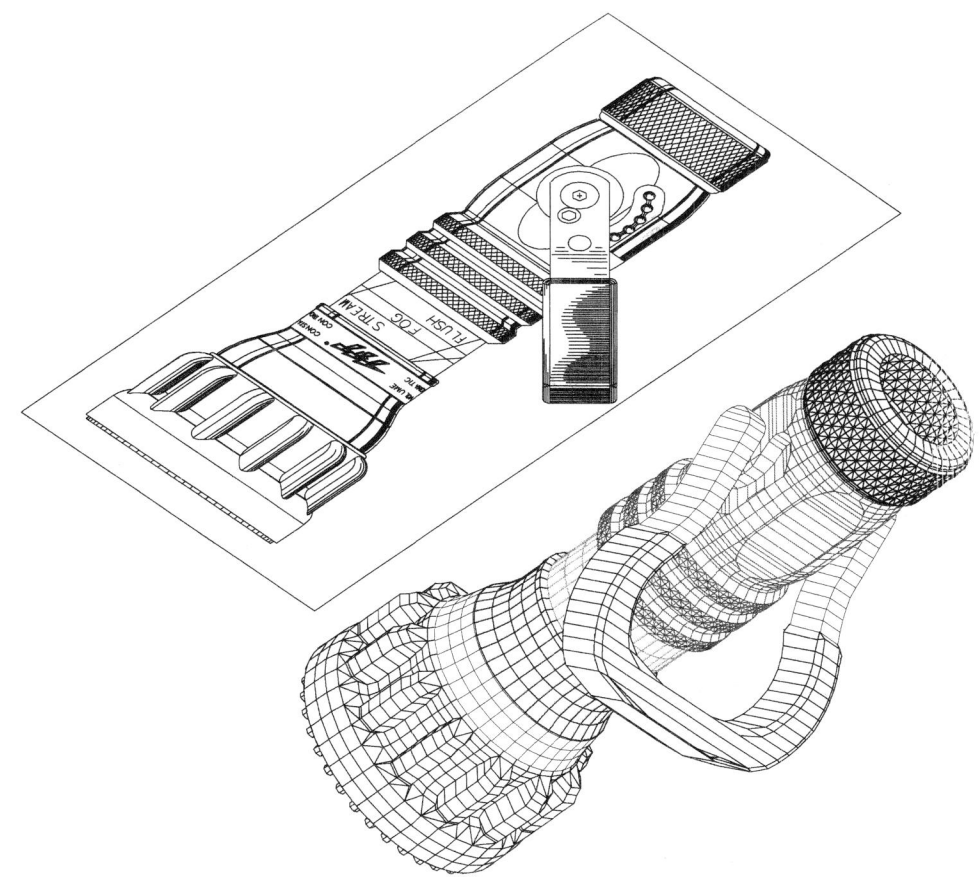

Figure 3.8 Using CAD to design the nozzle of a fire hose

to consider the purpose of the graphic and bear this in mind when allocating time. You should not need to spend as much time preparing a series of slides showing sales target graphs for an internal meeting as you would preparing graphics for sales staff to show to prospective customers. Some graphics, such as company logos, go through several drafts to get them right, since they will appear on company documentation for many years.

Another consideration is the context in which the graphic will be used: is it to be used for publicity, design layout or information presentation? You also need to take into account the likely technical or specialist level of the audience. One graphic could be used to show members of the public how to assemble an exercise bike while another diagram of the same bike could be for use by service engineers.

Content

The content part of the design specification should give an idea of what the graphic must contain. The specification for a company logo, for instance, might need to incorporate either the company name or sometimes the product or service that the company provides. H P Bulmer, the cider maker, uses the logo in Figure 3.9, which, as you can see, gives an idea of the raw material (the apple) as well as the company (the letter B).

Dimensions

In computer-aided design (CAD) work, a product design can sometimes be printed out lifesize. In such a case an engineer can take measurements for manufacture directly off the diagram, so it is very important that the diagram is accurately drawn to certain tolerances. Tolerances are the margins for error in measurements.

Most technical drawings are accurately drawn to a certain scale, so dimensions can still be taken off the printed plan. For example, CAD could be used by a housing developer to plan the position of houses, roads, etc. All relevant measurements and tolerances appear as labels on the diagram, and these can be used to mark out the site.

Image

You could decide a logo should always be the same size on company documents, so this size should be given and used as part of the design specification.

Information about the image should also include the colour and shading used.

Page attributes

Page attributes are similar to those included in the processing of commercial documents earlier in this chapter. To recap, they include the size of the page, the orientation of the page (landscape or portrait), the margins used and any special paper features such as colour, quality, existing pattern, etc.

H P Bulmer sells itself: a case study

H P Bulmer is the UK's largest cider producer. Company presentations are regularly given to the City, potential and existing customers as well as to the company's own staff. To meet the wide range of presentation demands, Bulmer has developed a system for producing presentations. Because of the high costs involved in sending presentation material to outside agencies the company is now able to produce the material itself. The reputation of a company rests on how others see it, so good presentations are vital.

Figure 3.9

Bulmer now has a presentation graphics unit with equipment for scanning in photographs, usually of the company's products but sometimes of the various processes and equipment used in cider-making. A high specification PC is used to prepare material on a 37-inch screen and this is then printed on a colour laser printer. Staff in other departments are also able to produce work on their own PCs using a package called Freelance and then use the network to transfer their work to the presentation graphics department for colour laser printing. As well as providing colour output on paper, the unit also produces acetates for overhead projectors and 35 mm slides. The unit can also produce slides for use on an liquid crystal display (LCD) projector which is used in larger presentations to project a computer screen onto a large white screen.

The department is staffed by two graphics analysts who work on their own projects as well as checking on the material from other departments to ensure that it is of a high standard.

The cost of sending the material to an outside agency used to be around £200 000 per year: doing the task within the company has reduced the cost to about £70 000 per year.

Assignment A3.2

This assignment develops knowledge and understanding of the following element:
2.2 : Process presentational and technical graphic designs

It supports the development of the following key skills:
Communication 3.2, 3.3 and 3.4
Information technology 3.1, 3.2 and 3.3
Application of number 3.3

H P Bulmer, the cider manufacturing company you have already met in Chapter 1, has its own presentation graphics department. You have just started working in this department as a trainee analyst and have been given the following task.

The task is to produce presentation graphics to illustrate the information shown in the table below which describes how the cider market has grown over eight years. As well as showing the growth of cider sales overall it also shows the market share between draught cider (cider from pumps on the bar top) and packaged cider (bottles, cans, flagons, etc.).

The title of your graph/graphs should be 'Cider market growth'.

Year	Draught (M galls)	Packaged (M Galls)	Total cider (M galls)
1988	28.7	36.3	65.0
1989	26.6	34.6	61.2
1990	30.4	39.2	69.6
1991	31.9	44.6	76.4
1992	30.8	45.0	75.8
1993	32.9	52.3	85.2
1994	33.9	58.0	92.0
1995	36.2	63.4	99.6
1996	38.6	76.1	114.8

Task 1

Using the information in the table, plot the three sets of data using a single set of axes. The 'time' axis (the one for the years) should be horizontal while the vertical axis should be used for 'volume of cider'. You can use either spreadsheet or presentation graphics software. If you are unable to plot the three sets of data on the same set of axes, you should draw three separate graphs with suitable labels. Remember to label the axes and add a legend to distinguish between the lines. Save your graphs and print them out.

Task 2

You have now been asked to draw some conclusions about the graphs you produced, in particular to comment on the following:

- What are the long-term trends in each of the three graphs and what fine detail do they show?
- Are there any differences in the growth of popularity of packaged as against draught cider?
- Are there any pairs of years between which the growth has been more substantial than others?

You have been asked to present your findings on an overhead projector acetate. You should use a bulleted list and the guidelines opposite given to you by the analyst.

The analyst has also suggested that you use some bit-map images of the company logo and/or some scanned images of the company's products, such as labels from their main brands (see Figure 1.4 on page 20). She has included some of the images for you to scan. You can, if you like, get some labels off bottles and try to scan your own in; remember that the cider must be a Bulmer product. (When you have finished be careful disposing of the bottle contents!) You may need to alter the size and positions of the images.

Guidelines for overhead projector presentation

Simplicity

Keep the information on the slide simple. Research has shown that there should be no more than six words per line and six lines per slide. The tendency is to put too much detail on the slides and use them as notes rather than as a presentation of the main points.

Brevity

In a presentation most listeners can retain only between three and five brief points. Any more could bore or confuse your audience.

Language

Keep the language simple and avoid the use of any specialist jargon which might be known only to a few of the audience.

Notes

Do not use the graphics for notes. People do not want to see reams of text and if notes are needed it is best if you give them copies after the presentation so that they can refer back to them.

Graphics charts

Try to present numerical information in a more interesting way than just a list. Use bar, pie, line and other charts to help get the figures across to your audience.

Fonts

Don't mix too many fonts on the same diagram and do not overuse upper case (capital letters). Use both upper and lower case letters.

When you are happy with your slide, save and print it. If you worked for Bulmer you would have the luxury of outputting your acetate using colour on a colour laser printer; since this is not possible you should show your tutor the graphic on screen to demonstrate how you have used colour.

Terry & Partners case study

Terry & Partners is an engineering consultancy that provides professional advice on all aspects of electrical and mechanical systems. The company produces design solutions for air-conditioning, heating, power generation, power distribution, lighting, fire protection, communications, lifts and escalators, energy conservation, planned maintenance and noise control.

The staffing at Terry & Partners is as follows: there are two partners and two associate partners, three engineers and three computer-aided design (CAD) operators. There are three staff in administration, two of whom perform mainly secretarial duties while the other deals primarily with the accounts. The secretarial staff use PCs and have just changed to the office suite, Microsoft Office. The accounts are now being transferred to computer and will be processed using the package Sage Accountant Plus. Wages are also processed on the computer using the package Sage Instant Payroll.

Normally, architects design a building and supply the plans to Terry & Partners who then plan and design the services, such as central heating, power points, air-conditioning and hot and cold water supplies. Sometimes architects submit a plan on paper from which Terry & Partners can work; sometimes a disk is provided by the architects if they are using a package that can be imported into the AutoCAD software that the practice uses. The latter saves the time involved in drawing the building outline onto CAD.

Figure 3.10 shows the ventilation plan for the new ophthalmic ward in a hospital. This plan shows the ventilation ducts and was drawn to scale using CAD software by Terry & Partners.

Sometimes Terry & Partners has to make some special calculations for which a calculations package is used. For instance, a heating system is being planned which needs to be able to cope with the heat losses through walls, windows, ceilings and floors, and these heat losses depend on the construction materials and dimensions. Using the calculations package, the engineers can work out the sizes of radiators that should be installed in each room; calculations can be done quickly and arithmetic errors eliminated. Because no great computing power is needed for these calculations, the company makes use of an older 386 PC which is now too slow for the latest CAD software.

Many advanced features are now available with AutoCAD. For example, you can draw a line and turn it automatically into a cavity wall showing the inner and outer leaves. Floors and ceilings can be added and there are even predrawn shapes for sanitary ware such as toilets and washbasins. A different range of specialist features is available for mechanical and electrical engineering users.

The main advantages of using a CAD package rather than producing drawings by hand are:

- CAD ensures consistent quality of drawings.
- With CAD, alterations are readily made without the need for redrawing.

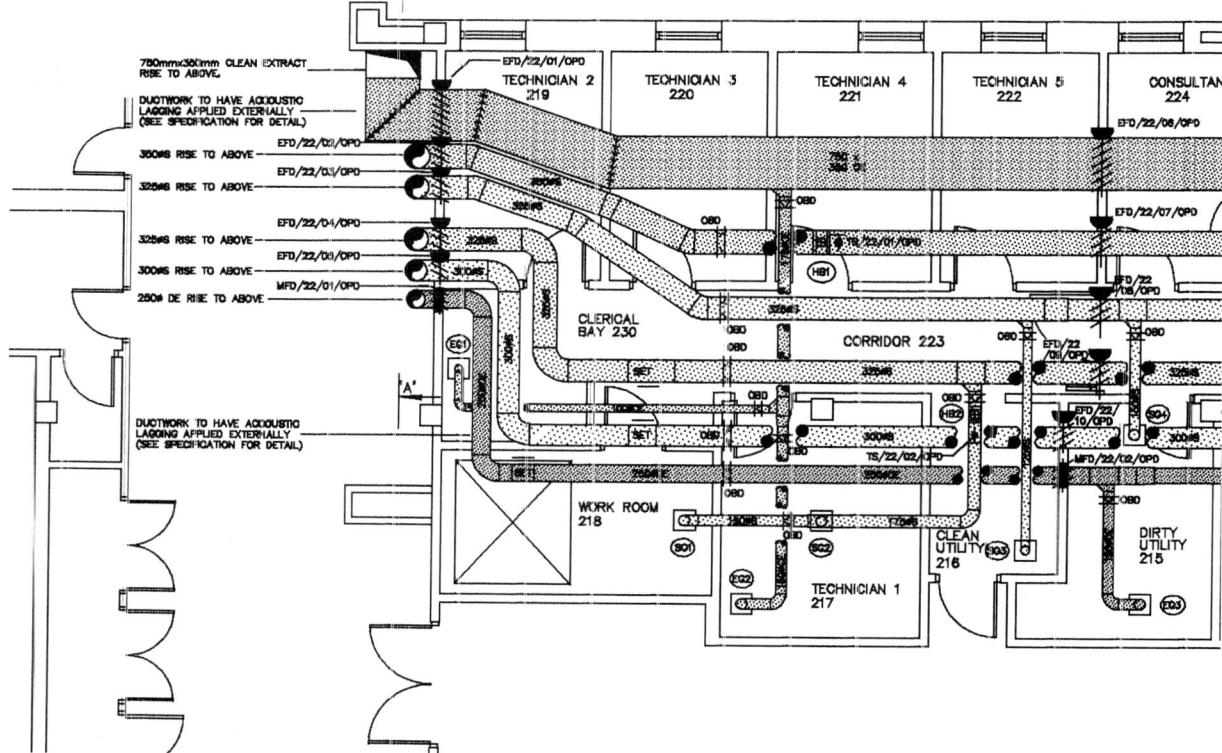

Figure 3.10 Part of a ventilation plan drawn using CAD software by Terry & Partners

- CAD diagrams can be multilayered so that each aspect of the drawing (e.g. heating) can be displayed separately, or combined with other interacting systems. Some diagrams can have ten or more layers.
- Many multi-storey buildings have the same basic plan for each floor. By copying the outline for each floor and any services that are the same on all floors a lot of time can be saved using CAD.
- When a project is completed drawings can be kept on disk and stored for reference, saving valuable space.

Because there is so much detail on each diagram, plans have to be produced at a large scale (typically 1:50) and this means that a special plotter is needed to produce print-outs. These **drum plotters** use an ink-jet technique to spray the image onto the paper as it is moved up and down over the drum.

Pentium-based computers are currently used as stand-alone machines; these have clock speeds of 133 MHz. Either 15- or 17-inch monitors are generally used for this kind of work. Special graphics tablets are also used as input devices and these have software-specific functions on them. Since often-used functions are placed on the tablet the screen need not be cluttered up with toolbars, and this leaves more room for the actual drawing.

Figure 3.11 shows the layout of a **graphics tablet** used by Terry & Partners.

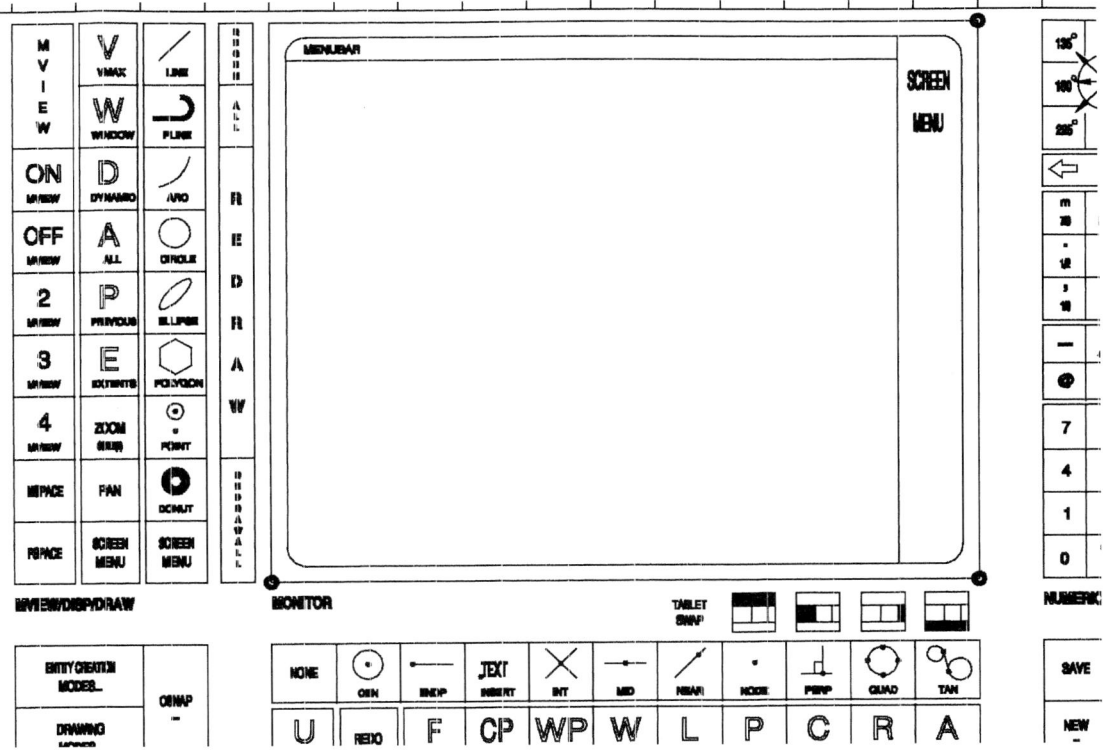

Figure 3.11 Part of one of the graphics tablets used by Terry & Partners

Tower computer systems are used because this leaves space on the desk for the paper plans being transferred, the graphics tablet and keyboard. So that the computers are fast enough to process the images quickly, 16 MB of memory are needed.

Using a CAD package it is possible to generate an isometric or perspective drawing (one that simulates 3D) from a two-dimensional plan. Taking this one stage further, it is now possible to generate from detailed two-dimensional drawings a whole series of images from different internal or external viewpoints. This allows a notional figure moving from one room to another to see a representation of exactly what the whole building would look like when viewed in reality, from outside or inside.

AutoCAD uses vector graphics because of its capacity for resizing, but Terry & Partners incorporates its logo, which is stored as a bit-map file. Figure 3.12 shows the logo.

Because it often receives drawings on disk from outside organisations, the company has to be careful that no viruses are introduced and that all disks are scanned before use using the latest virus checker.

Figure 3.12 The Terry & Partners logo

Assignment A3.3

This assignment develops knowledge and understanding of the following element:
2.2: Process presentational and technical graphic designs

It supports the development of the following key skills:
Communication 3.2, 3.3 and 3.4
Information technology 3.1, 3.2 and 3.3

Task 1
Terry & Partners frequently has to tender for work on large contracts. Basically this means that the company has to submit details of the services that it would provide, some examples of jobs it has completed in the past, and a quote (a price) for the job.

The company usually sends a brochure with the tender and this includes some photographs, but it would like to incorporate some suitable drawings or graphics to liven up one page in particular. Here is the section of text which needs enlivening:

> Terry & Partners is an independent multi-disciplinary building services consultancy, formed in 1976 to provide a complete professional service in environmental engineering. The practice is experienced in every aspect of mechanical and electrical systems and is able to offer the correct design solutions for all engineering services, including air-conditioning, heating, ventilation, plumbing, water services and treatment, power generation and distribution, lighting, fire protection, communications, lifts and escalators, energy conservation, planned maintenance and noise control.
>
> The Partnership has gained several major civic awards after involvement in prestigious projects such as universities, colleges, civic buildings, hospitals, swimming pools, sports centres, commercial and industrial developments, sheltered housing, churches and listed buildings.

You are required to produce a selection of bit-map and vector graphics, from which Terry & Partners can choose to accompany the text above.

Task 2

It has been suggested that when staff from Terry & Partners go to meet architects, surveyors, clients, etc. to discuss a tender, they could use a laptop computer with presentation graphics software, and produce details of their services as a slide show presentation rather than using brochures to market their services.

You are required to produce a slide show presentation outlining the services Terry & Partners offers (you can take the factual material from the case study and the section of text in the box above).

Present the information as effectively as possible and make use of any graphics as appropriate.

Task 3

For this task your are required to familiarise yourself with a technical drawing package and use it to produce two simple technical drawings. You may choose any two from the following list.

- A three-dimensional model (see Element 2.3 in Chapter 4). This could be any three-dimensional representation of a building or object.
- A block schematic diagram of a microprocessor or central processing unit (see Elements 1.2 and 1.3 in Chapter 2.).
- A block schematic diagram for control systems (see Element 2.4 in Chapter 4).
- The production of a data flow diagram or flow chart (see Elements 5.1 and 5.2 in Chapters 9 and 10).

Produce the final copy and any intermediate drafts of your diagrams as evidence for your portfolio. For each of the diagrams you should name the package used and also mention which components were used and how they were incorporated into your drawing using the package.

Sample unit test

1 What is the name for a document used to inform people of a meeting and outline the topics which are to be discussed?
   a invoice
   b agenda
   c business letter
   d memo

2 A detailed account of what was discussed at a meeting and what action is to be taken is called:
   a the minutes
   b a report
   c a memo
   d a newsletter

3 To shorten the time taken to prepare commercial documents, a file can be set up using wordprocessing software in which the user just fills in the variable information. Such an electronic file is called a:
   a specification
   b mail merge
   c search and replace
   d template

4 Which one of the following is *not* a page attribute?
   a paper size
   b orientation (landscape or portrait)
   c scale
   d font

5 A piece of text placed at the top of every page of a document is called a:
   a footer
   b header
   c font
   d tabulation

6 A photograph is to be scanned into a computer using a flat-bed scanner. The most appropriate graphic type for storing the picture would be:
   a a bit-map graphic
   b a vector graphic
   c a wordprocessed document
   d a text file

7 A company wishes to present a comparison of last year's sales figures for a particular product with this year's figures. It decides to use a series of slides placed on an overhead projector. Which type of package would be best suited for the production of the slides?
   a CAD software
   b presentation graphics
   c wordprocessing software
   d desktop publishing

8 CAD is used for producing plans and drawings by a firm of architects. Which one of the following is *not* a good reason for using CAD?

  a CAD produces consistent high quality drawings

  b alterations can be made easily without the need for redrawing

  c CAD files on disk take up less space than drawings kept on paper

  d CAD hardware and software is cheap

9 When using CAD software, drawings sometimes need to be rescaled in order to show fine detail. Which is the best type of software to use for this?

  a bit-mapped graphics

  b presentation graphics

  c a paint package

  d vector graphics

Figure 3.13

10 Figure 3.13 shows a graphic that has been scanned into a computer. Which one of the following best describes this graphic?

  a a bit-map with portrait orientation

  b a vector with landscape orientation

  c a bit-map with landscape orientation

  d a vector with portrait orientation

11 An electrical engineer is using CAD software to prepare a detailed plan showing part of a transformer. The technical drawing which is produced *must* include the following:

  a the designer's name

  b the sizes and tolerances

  c the software used to produce the drawing

  d a copyright notice

12 Data is valuable and needs to be protected against accidental loss. Which one of the following is *not* a way of minimising the damage caused by such a loss?
   a allowing the software to automatically take back-up copies
   b keeping regular back-ups on floppy disks
   c retaining the original source documents
   d making sure all software is protected by passwords

13 Figure 3.14 shows a graphic before and after editing. What is the name given to the editing process which has been used?
   a rotation
   b copying
   c sizing
   d cropping

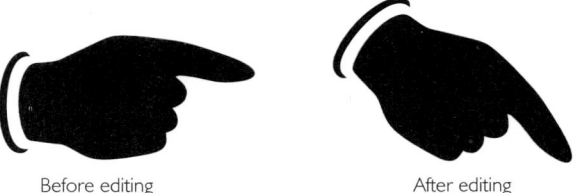

Figure 3.14   Before editing   After editing

14 Software tools are provided as part of a package to make certain repetitive tasks easier. Which of the following software tools would you *not* find as part of a wordprocessing package?
   a mail merge
   b search and replace
   c search
   d saving documents

15 A document showing the amount of money owed for goods purchased by a customer is called:
   a an invoice
   b a memo
   c an agenda
   d a business letter

16 Which one of the following would *not* be used as an accuracy check before printing out a wordprocessed document?
   a proofreading
   b using a spell checker
   c using a grammar checker
   d search and replace

17 Certain people have access to very private and confidential information during the course of their work. To prevent these people revealing this information to other staff they may be asked to sign:
   a an invoice
   b a password document
   c a non-disclosure agreement
   d a memo

18 When designing a graphic it is usual to work to a design specification. Which one of the following would be included as part of a design specification?
   a whether bit-mapped or vector graphics are to be used
   b a list of the formulae used
   c the size of the VDU used when designing the graphic
   d the type of printer on which it should be printed out

4 Computer models and control systems

What is covered in this chapter

Element 2.3: Model data

- Purposes of computer models
- Types of computer model
- Data parameters
- Rules of operation
- Reports
- Effectiveness of computer models
- Suggestions for improvement of computer models
- Examples of real-life simulations
- Creating spreadsheet models

Element 2.4: Develop a control system

- Types of control system
- Components of control systems
- Specification for a control system
- Schematic diagrams
- Control procedures
- Testing a process control system
- Effectiveness of a control system
- Suggestions for improvement
- Examples of control systems
- Airbus Industrie case study
- W H Smith Business Supplies case study

Resources you will need for your portfolio for Elements 2.3 and 2.4
- Your written answers to the activities and assignments in this chapter.

Purposes of computer models

Modelling and simulation are used in many business situations to mimic reality and to see the consequences of various courses of action without risking any damaging consequences.

For instance, project management software allows the manager of a large project consisting of many tasks performed by many different people, to create a model or simulation of the project. Most people are good at organising a small number of tasks but as the number of tasks increases the management of a project becomes more difficult. Using a model, the project manager can see the way that each of the tasks contributes to the time taken to complete the whole project. The project manager can then alter the order of the tasks to see the effect this has on the duration of the whole project. The model can then be used to produce a series of graphs and charts which enable the project manager to understand the project better.

There are many reasons why computer models are used, but they usually fall into one or more of the following categories.

To compress time

In many cases it may not be possible or desirable to wait for an actual event to occur. For instance, a weather forecast is a model of future weather based on current physical quantities such as air pressure, humidity, temperature, wind speed, satellite pictures, etc. With a powerful computer, millions of calculations can be performed on these data and a computer prediction or weather forecast can be made. This forecast needs to be made quickly, so that weather changes can be predicted well ahead of when they actually occur. Although the equations on which such models are based work effectively most of the time, there are some situations in which forecasts are not accurate. It is hard to design any model to behave exactly as the real thing does.

Models can also be built using spreadsheet software to forecast the results of inflation on the value of money and an example of this type of model is given later in this chapter. Models can also be used to investigate the results of breeding plants or animals, or to construct predator/prey models, where a predator may be introduced to control a pest. Just such a model will be constructed later in the chapter.

To produce a cost saving

To see how a particular car behaves aerodynamically, a scaled down model can be built and tested in a wind tunnel. A computer model will often be much more convenient and cheaper than constructing physical models. The model would be based on thousands of equations derived from the behaviour of real cars. A computer simulation is developed, where the model is tested in a variety of conditions, such as at different speeds and with differing crosswinds. Once an initial model of aerodynamic behaviour has been constructed, engineers can alter the design of the car using the computers on their desks and see how design changes affect the aerodynamics.

Although actual cars are used to investigate the effect of air bags or side impact bars during a crash, this is expensive and time consuming. Computer models are therefore also used to test the effect of design changes and safety features.

Modelling a supermarket car park can reveal whether sufficient cars can be accommodated and whether changes to the parking pattern can increase the capacity of the car park. Large articulated delivery vehicles need enough room in order to turn around, and turning arcs can also be checked with a computer model. Such models can help avoid expensive mistakes.

Because it is safer to use a model

When bridges, buildings or other structures are being designed it is necessary to know how they will react to the various stresses and strains they may encounter. It is expensive, difficult and dangerous to carry out destructive tests on real structures, so computer models are often used instead.

The Nuclear Test Ban Treaty, signed by all the major world powers, prohibits the testing of nuclear weapons. However, the ban does not relate to the possession of nuclear weapons. Many existing weapons are old and since it is no longer possible to test them to see if they would still work, computer simulations are used to test their viability. In such simulations, the various external parameters that affect the model can be altered and the behaviour of the model tested. If the model is accurate, it will reflect the behaviour of the real thing. For example, corrosion can be programmed into the simulation. To see how accurate the computer simulation is, some parts of the system will still need to be tested. For example, the conventional explosion which is used to set off the nuclear reaction may still be detonated and the blast examined in detail.

Simulations are particularly important here because, with conventional weapons which are used in considerable numbers, a small failure rate is tolerable but with nuclear weapons each warhead is likely to be of strategic importance, and must be relied upon to work.

It is more convenient to use a model

Models are created by many businesses and are often used to predict the way in which they will develop. You will see some examples of these models later in this chapter.

If you wanted to learn how to fly a plane, build and run a theme park, manage a premier league football team, design a garden, drive a Formula One racing car or even rule an empire, then you can do any of these from the comfort of your own home provided you have a computer and suitable software! Some models are written for specific applications but many can be created using ordinary spreadsheet software, as we shall see later.

To perform hypothesis testing

Any company involved in selling either a product or a service will want to know its break-even position. This is the income that it needs in order to cover its costs; i.e at the break-even position, the company would make neither a profit nor a loss. Consider a company running coach tours around Scotland: for such an operation the company needs to know how many seats have to be sold to pay for the cost of running the coaches and for the overheads of the company. Once it knows this, it can tell how many more seats need to be sold in order to make a reasonable profit.

A company making sweets might use a spreadsheet model to work out the cost of producing a certain type of sweet. If the price of any of the ingredients or any of the other costs (such as rent or the price of fuel) were to change then the company could immediately see the effect this would have on profits. Knowing this, it could then decide whether to pass the increased costs (or savings) on to the customer or whether to absorb the effect and perhaps adjust the price of the sweets at a later date. The model enables the company to experiment with costs, prices and likely sales and so make an informed decision.

'What if' queries

Models may be either specifically written for a particular application or developed using ordinary spreadsheet software. Spreadsheet software will provide quick answers to 'what if' queries. If the contents of any cell or cells are altered a spreadsheet automatically recalculates all the other cells that in any way depend on the changed cell or cells. The speed and ease of this process encourages the user to test the validity of budgets, forecasts and projections by seeing what happens to, say, the overall profit, if certain conditions change.

Take the following example of a fruit seller. The price of oil can affect the price of an apple. How can this be? Look at Figure 4.1 which shows the link from the price of oil to the price of fruit. All these changes could be recorded on a spreadsheet.

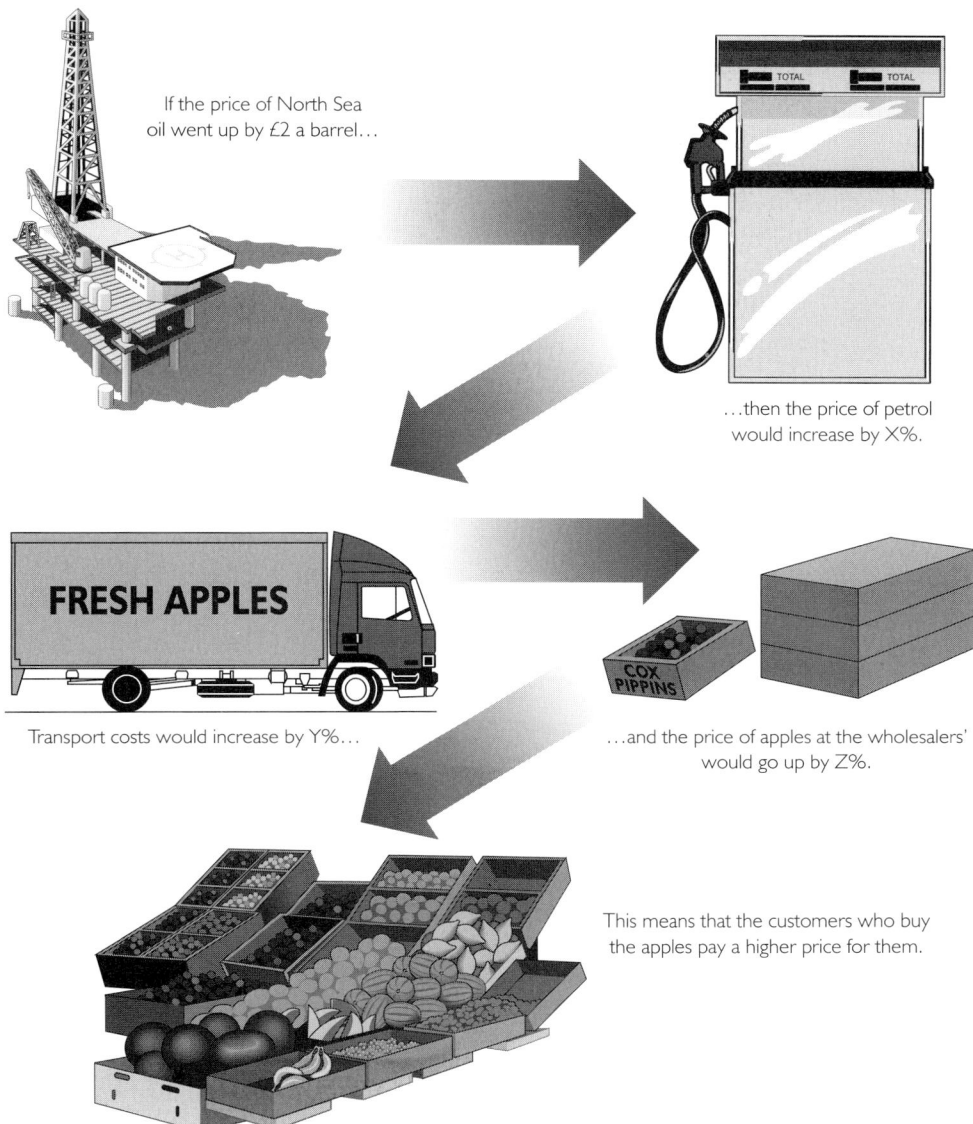

If the price of North Sea oil went up by £2 a barrel…

…then the price of petrol would increase by X%.

Transport costs would increase by Y%…

…and the price of apples at the wholesalers' would go up by Z%.

This means that the customers who buy the apples pay a higher price for them.

Figure 4.1 How oil prices can affect the price of apples

Types of computer model

A computer model is a software representation of a real situation or system which can be used for analysis of its operation. In other words it is a simplified version of a real process. There are different types of model and in this section we will look at each of them.

Simulations

The words 'simulation' and 'modelling' are often used interchangeably, although there is a subtle difference. When most people think of building a model they think of building a physical model of a car, aircraft or building. These models are visual representations of the real thing. So we can say that a computer model represents many aspects of a real-world object or situation. The more sophisticated a model becomes, the more closely it mimics the real thing. A computer model does not, of course, have to be a model of a physical object. As mentioned above, businesses develop financial models for budgeting and business planning.

Doing something with a model that has been created is called 'simulation'. For example you may build a model of a plane and then test its aerodynamics in a wind tunnel. In this case only the testing part would be the simulation.

To build a computer model it is necessary to generate a set of equations which describe some aspect or aspects of the real thing. Computer simulations involve feeding values into the model to see how it reacts to them. In some simulations initial values are fed into the model to see how it reacts over a period of time; other simulations involve constantly interacting with the model, such as in a flight simulator.

Flight simulators

It is very expensive to use aircraft for the training of pilots. Clearly much of a pilot's training has to be done in real aircraft, but considerable use is also made of flight simulators. As well as being used for normal flying training, simulators can be used to create dangerous flying conditions, some of which a pilot would be less likely to experience in everyday flying. It is possible to simulate ice on the runway, thick fog or landing with only one of four engines working. Such training gives pilots valuable experience and really tests their abilities.

Figure 4.2 Flight simulators enable pilots to experience turbulence, snowstorms, thunderstorms, fog and air pockets as well as landing at different airports throughout the world, without leaving the ground

In Figure 4.2 you can see that the flight simulator consists of a windowless capsule. The hydraulically controlled struts (i.e. the legs) when acting in combination can propel the machine in all directions, simulating the pitch and roll of a real plane. Helicopter simulators include a vibrating pilot's seat to add reality and in fighter plane simulators the seat has air pumped into it to simulate the g-force experienced when the pilot performs tight turns.

The scene 'out of the windows' is as realistic as the behaviour of the plane. When a particular airport is chosen, the surroundings look identical to the real location.

Predictive models

A predictive model uses the results of past experience to predict how a particular situation is likely to develop. For instance, a marketing model may be set up based on past experience so that, if the price of goods rises, the likely effect on sales can be assessed. Many of the models used in business, such as cashflow analysis, budget forecasts, etc., are predictive models which are created using spreadsheet software. A weather forecast is a predictive model since it is based on the weather conditions at the time of forecast.

Gaming

Games are really simulations of a real or fantasy world. For instance the following quotation is from an advert for a game called SIM Farm:

> You own a plot of good farmland. Do you want a small family farm or an agricultural profit centre? Do you want to produce food for the local town or feed the world's hungry masses? Do you use the latest chemical fertilisers or run an organic farm? It's up to you.
>
> Plough your fields, sow your seeds, harvest your crops and sell them at market. Easy? Sure, except for soil depletion, crop rotation, changing markets and diminishing farmland — not to mention pests, droughts, dust storms and other disasters!

In a football game you are simulating the playing characteristics of real players. You may also have come across a game called Themepark, where the object of the game is to run a real theme park. You have to build rides and all the other facilities in the theme park and the more interesting you make your park, then the more people you will get through the gates and the more profit you will make. You have to make decisions throughout the game, just as in a real business.

Many board games such as Monopoly and Cluedo are also simulations and there are computer versions of these available.

Three-dimensional representation

In a three-dimensional representation, a two-dimensional model is constructed, which is drawn as a series of plans and elevations using drawing software. Then the views are used to construct a three-dimensional model of the building or object. This view can be taken at any angle and it may be incorporated into a view containing the existing buildings to see the visual impact the new development makes.

Three-dimensional models are also used, for example, by companies who supply fitted kitchens so that customers can see what the fittings will look like in their own rooms.

Virtual reality (the ultimate representation of 3D)

You have probably seen the equipment needed for experiencing virtual reality: the helmet, gloves and wristband. The whole idea of **virtual reality** is to go beyond visual simulation and immerse the subject in a virtual reality world of images, touch and sound.

No matter how realistic the 3D graphics are, a simulation can never be like the real thing because you are still looking at a computer screen from the outside. Virtual reality seeks to bring the viewer into the screen by the creation of a virtual world where he or she can interact as in the real world. For example, it may be possible to walk through a building and view a changing scene exactly as one would if walking through the actual building.

Uses of virtual reality

As the cost of the necessary equipment falls, the number of applications for virtual reality grows and many large companies are now using its power in a wide variety of areas.

- In medicine, special hand controllers are used to record every movement a surgeon makes when performing an operation and any mistakes made can be detected and played back.
- Britannia Airways (the charter airline you met in the first chapter) uses virtual reality to plan the cabins of the aeroplanes and it has also been used to visualise the fabric for the seats and the colour schemes used.
- Virtual reality has also been successfully used by psychiatrists to help people with certain phobias, such as the fear of open spaces and of spiders.
- Soon you will be able to go into any furniture shop and, before you buy, see what the furniture will look like in your room and with your own decor.
- Virtual reality technology is allowing 2500 staff at Barclaycard to design their office environment before it is built. Virtual reality allows the staff to walk into their virtual offices and see the effects of different colour schemes, different widths of walkways, etc. before final plans are drawn up.

Activity 4.1

Assign each of the following types of computer model to the most appropriate of the following categories: simulation, prediction, gaming, three-dimensional representation.

- Working out cashflow for a proposed new business.
- Training air stewards/stewardesses on emergency procedures.
- Learning how to drive a Formula One racing car.
- Planning the design of built-in bedroom furniture.
- Putting an imaginary shop front on an established street to try to win planning consent.
- Producing a model to show the likely climatic changes 200 years from now.
- Being able to say when a hurricane is likely to occur.
- Working out the likely next three years' profits for a company using a spreadsheet.
- Using a spreadsheet to anticipate future demand for a particular product.
- Training inexperienced pilots to land on an aircraft carrier.
- Using data from sensors along with a computer model to forecast earthquakes.
- Working out the quantity of a new product that needs be sold before break-even is achieved.

Data parameters

When designing a model there are many things to be considered before putting the data into the model. Most of these concern either the data itself or something that is done with the data once it has been input.

Input values

The input values are the quantities that are not preset within the model. They are input to the model either through a keyboard or by direct input from data sensors. For instance, when a weather forecast is to be produced the data is obtained from thousands of sensors which all relay their data by radio to one of the largest computers in the world. Here, the data is fed into the model and the weather prediction for the next day or so is built up.

Sometimes the data from another package, such as a database, is imported directly into a spreadsheet.

When data is input to a spreadsheet model using a keyboard, the numbers need to be in the appropriate format for the rest of the model.

Constraints

A constraint is something that is imposed on a system and needs to be taken into account when constructing the model. If we were organising a pop concert and wanted a model to predict the likely profit, the number of seats in the stadium would be one constraint since we could not sell more tickets than we had seats. The more complicated a model becomes, the greater the number of constraints needed.

Variables

Variables are the quantities that we put into a model when constructing 'what if' queries. Such variables include physical response time, speed, cost, time, dimension, scale and position.

For a model to work, some of the data needs to be supplied either automatically or by input through a keyboard. With a model describing the aerodynamics of a car, information such as the speed of the car, wind speed and direction, density of the air, air pressure, road conditions, etc. needs to be supplied to the model. These quantities can then be varied and their effect on the aerodynamic properties of the car observed.

Calculations using operators

Once data has been input to a model, the data may be subjected to a range of different types of **operators**:
- arithmetic $(+, -, \times, \div, \sqrt{}, \text{etc.})$
- relational $(=, <, >, \text{IF})$
- logical (AND, OR, NOT).

You will need to familiarise yourself with how these work in the particular package you are using.

Relational operators

If, for instance, you wanted to use a spreadsheet to make the following decision a relational operator could be used:

If an invoice total exceeds £1000 then a discount of 5 per cent of the invoice total is given.

If the invoice total is in cell C4, then to calculate the discount we can use the following:
=IF(C4>1000, C4*0.05,0)

which would put the answer (the amount of discount) in the cell where the formula is located. If the invoice total were less than £1000, a figure of zero discount would be shown in the cell.

Logical operators

Apart from their use when making up search criteria with databases, logical operators (AND, OR and NOT) can also be used in spreadsheets for making decisions based on the values of certain cells. For example, if cells C2 and D2 contain totals which for a 5 per cent discount to be given both must exceed 1000, then we can apply the discount to the total contained in another cell (say D8) by using the following construct:
=IF(C2 AND D2 > 1000, D8*0.95)

Activity 4.2

Think of any simulations games you have played and give a brief description of a game and its objectives. Consider the game carefully and outline the variables used.

Rules of operation

All models must be based on certain rules of operation and these rules need to be carefully formulated to make a model mimic the real situation as accurately as possible. When designing any model it is necessary to give some thought to the following:

Formulae

If you are constructing a model using spreadsheet software it is important to establish mathematical relationships between variables and constants located in cells in the worksheet and this is done by using formulae. A formula in one cell could reference a value in another, thus making it easy to find the sum of a list of numbers, to calculate interest rates or to make financial predictions. All spreadsheets are able to perform a variety of arithmetic operations from the simple (addition, subtraction, multiplication and division) to more complex operations that calculate statistical derivatives such as mean and standard deviation, or business calculations such as working out monthly payments for loans.

When constructing formulae it is important to bear in mind the order in which the operations should be performed, which is as follows:

1 **Brackets:** any operations in brackets should be performed first and when there is more than one set within the same calculation, the inner ones are worked out first then the next set, until the outermost brackets are reached.
2 **Powers:** squares, square roots, cubes, etc.
3 **Multiplication and division:** if both are present in the same calculation it does not matter in which order they are performed.
4 **Addition and subtraction:** if both are present in the same calculation it does not matter in which order they are performed.

Cell referencing

There are two ways of referring to another **cell** in a spreadsheet: **relative referencing** or **absolute referencing**. This is particularly important when you copy or move cells. An absolute reference always refers to the same cell in a spreadsheet. By contrast a relative reference refers to a cell which is a certain number of columns and rows away from the current cell. This means that when the current cell is moved or copied to a new position, the cell to which the reference is made will also change position. This is best seen by referring to Figures 4.3 and 4.4.

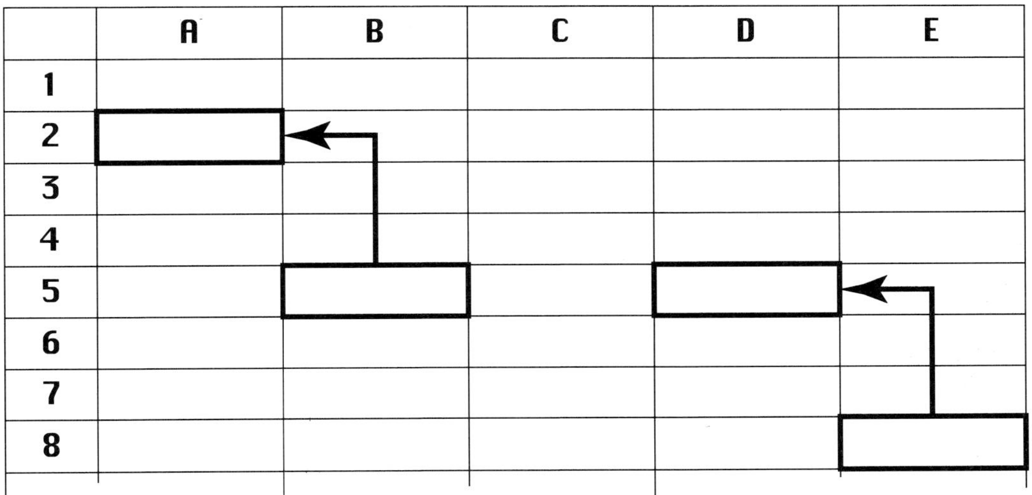

Cell B5 contains a relative reference to cell A2. If the contents of cell B5 are copied to E8 then cell E8 will refer to cell D5.

Figure 4.3

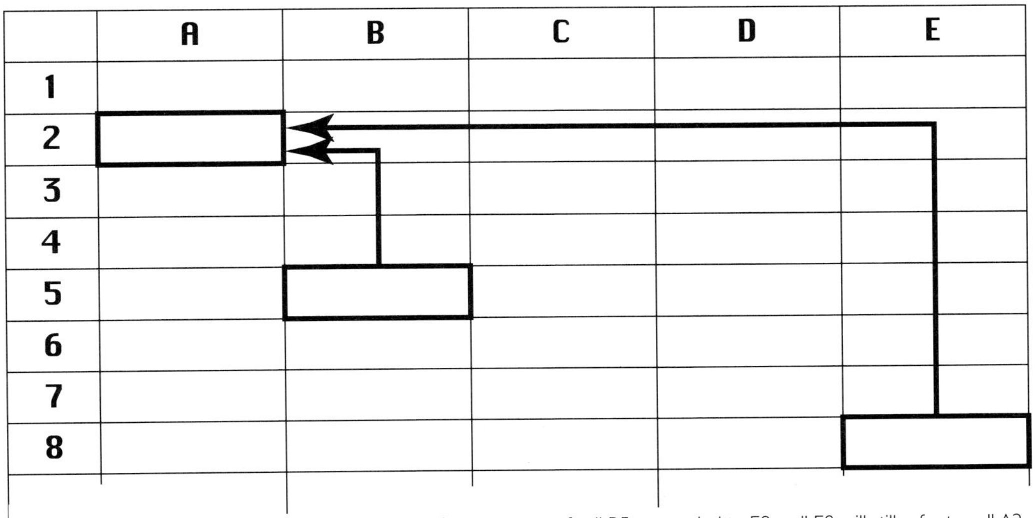

If cell B5 had an absolute reference to cell A2, then if the contents of cell B5 are copied to E8, cell E8 will still refer to cell A2.

Figure 4.4

You need do nothing to specify relative cell references since they are the default. Relative cell references are useful, because the spreadsheet can adjust the formulae automatically when they are copied to other cells.

If you need to refer to a particular value in a certain cell (such as an interest rate, VAT rate, etc.) you must make any reference to it absolute and this is usually done by putting a dollar sign in front of the column and row numbers. For example, the relative cell reference C4 could be converted to an absolute cell reference by inserting the dollar sign thus: C4.

Results of actions

Altering a model's variables can change many quantities including the final result. Results in any model need to be clearly identified and shown as either a text message or a numerical value. Alternatively, results can be displayed as pictures or charts if appropriate.

Relationships

When a model is being constructed, the relationships between quantities need to be established. For example, a model describing braking distance for a car under different conditions needs to estimate the relationship between the braking distance and the amount of tread remaining on the tyres. Since all models depend on mathematical relationships, it is necessary to construct an equation which describes the variation mathematically.

Effect of variable changes

Looking at the braking model again, we would need to identify all the variables and decide which are important. They can then be varied to see what effect they have on the distance.

Method of operation

The method of operation is a brief description, explaining in broad terms the principles behind the construction of a model.

Assumptions made

Sometimes, especially in the early stages of developing a model, it is important to keep things simple, so some assumptions are normally made. For instance, when constructing the braking model, it could be assumed that road conditions are always perfect. On further refinement of the model the number of assumptions can be reduced and the model altered so that it behaves more like the real thing. With our braking model we might try allowing for the condition of the road surface (e.g. wet, icy, with loose road chippings, etc.).

Input and output methods

Most spreadsheet models use keyed data, but in many industrial systems the input is a series of electrical signals obtained from sensors.

Output is usually on either a display screen or as a printout.

Reports

Reports are used to show the output value or values from a model and these may be presented as text, a series of pictures or charts. A look at the traffic control system in Chapter 1 shows that this system was based on a model and the results were displayed pictorially in what looks like a horizontal bar chart. The results from a spreadsheet model are often displayed in the form of a series of graphs such as pie charts or bar charts.

Sometimes, the results need to be summarised, so that they can be outlined in what is called an abstract. An abstract simply separates the main points from the whole body of information.

Effectiveness of computer models

The effectiveness of a model or simulation can best be judged in terms of the following:

Comparative cost

Comparative cost means comparing the costs of alternative approaches to the problem with the costs of the computer model or simulation approach. For instance, a flight simulator can be used to train a pilot rather than using an actual, empty aircraft. Airlines usually hire time on a simulator, so it is relatively easy to find the difference in the cost between the two methods. Flight simulators are much cheaper because of the very large costs involved in flying aircraft without passengers to offset fuel and airport costs.

For models created using standard spreadsheet software, the cost of the software can usually be recovered many times over from the cost savings the model brings.

Speed of response

Spreadsheet models, once they have been set up, provide quick answers when rapid decisions are needed. For instance, if several investment opportunities are on offer, each with different rates of return over different time periods, then it is relatively easy to determine which one would be best using a spreadsheet model.

Accuracy of a model

The accuracy of any model depends on the care taken when the model is set up, which in turn depends on the rules of operation. Once the framework of the model has been created, the user simply inserts the variable data, leaving less room for error than when performing a similar exercises by hand with the possible introduction of calculation errors. Repeated re-calculations are tedious when carried out manually and this may give rise to more arithmetical mistakes than performing the same tasks using a spreadsheet.

Comparison with alternatives

In judging models, we usually look at how a model is an improvement on the previous way a job was done.

Efficiency

Efficiency is often improved by using models, because they usually save time and money, improve accuracy and provide important information on which management or business decisions can be based.

Suggestions for improvement of computer models

To test a model, data is input to the model from a real situation and the results obtained compared with what actually happened. The success of any model can be measured by the reliability of its results.

It is hard to develop a model which works from the outset, since assumptions need to be made and the model simplified to begin with by disregarding some variables. Most models go through a process of refinement, with the user constantly evaluating and testing the model to see if there are any ways in which the model can be altered to reflect the real situation more closely. Obviously, there comes a point where the developer has to stop and accept that perfection is impossible to achieve.

When a model needs further refinement, the refinements may be made either to the data parameters or to the rules of operation, or, indeed, to both.

Examples of real-life simulations

In this section we will look at real-life simulations and models in a series of case studies.

Case study: Tesco, using simulation for staff training

When new credit and debit cards were introduced, the retailer Tesco found it necessary to retrain all petrol station staff in a 14-week period. Some 5600 hours of training were needed without disrupting the normal operation of the petrol stations. To do this, Tesco connected a normal PC to a point-of-sale terminal (till) in order to use simulations on the PC to run and monitor exercises for the staff. By using the actual equipment to simulate real-life situations like this the training did not need to be supervised, since the PC could play both the part of tutor and petrol pump controller. The lessons and practice exercises took about four hours to complete. Using computer simulations in this way saved the company around £250 000 compared with traditional training methods.

Activity 4.3

This activity is based on the brief case study outlined above.

1 Identify the purpose or purposes of the Tesco training computer model from the following list: compress time, cost saving, safety, convenience, hypothesis testing. Explain the reason behind your answer.

2 Explain how Tesco could review the effectiveness of the model.

Case study: The Treasury economic model

If you were the Chancellor of the Exchequer in a position to pull the economic strings of the country, you might want to see the likely effects of tampering with things like interest rates or the rates of income tax using a computer model rather than the economy itself. As Chancellor there are many changes you could make, such as alterations in the basic rate of income tax, interest rates, VAT, National Insurance contributions, etc. If, for example, the Government decided that it would like to introduce a minimum wage, it would be wise first to determine the likely consequences of such an action. For instance, would inflation rise as more money was pumped into the economy or would unemployment increase because companies could no longer afford the higher wages? To make such decisions the Government needs an economic model.

The Treasury's economic model is used to set up a 'pretend economy' on which various courses of action can be tested by altering the variables in the model and observing the results. For any simulation to be successful it needs to be based on an accurate model. Producing an accurate model is where the problems start, since different people have different views on how the equations should be set up and used. For this reason it is possible for different economists to produce different models which in turn produce different results from the same variables. The main problem lies in deciding on definitions to be used when formulating the equations. For instance, one of the equations we might use in such a model is:

unemployment = labour supply − employment

This equation is easy to understand and it defines unemployment as people available for work who are not in work. But what does 'available for work' mean, and do a little part-time or unpaid work constitute 'out of work'? There are still other equations whose formation depends on which economic theory you think is right.

Despite the difficulties, the Treasury uses a model which has been developed by a team of top economists and has around 400 variables. It is this model which is used by the Government and many large businesses to simulate the UK economy.

Activity 4.4

Explain what is meant by the rules of operation of a model.

Why is it not possible to develop a perfect model of the economy which everyone could use?

Case study: Customer account profitability model

Many suppliers such as H P Bulmer, Heinz and Mars use models to work out the profitability of supplying certain products to each of the large supermarket chains. Since these shops negotiate hard with their suppliers to get the best deal, suppliers must continuously check that this trading relationship is still profitable. To do this they use a model which is set up for each supermarket chain, with data for each of the products supplied. The supplier could increase sales to the shops by selling goods so cheaply that they are effectively giving the goods away. The supplier needs to know the real profit obtained from a particular deal, taking into consideration discounts, cost of production, administration and delivery, etc.

The model uses the 'gross sales value', which is the volume of goods multiplied by the cost for each of the volumes. So, for a case of 24 × 500 ml cans of lager, this would be the number of cases multiplied by the cost of each case (note that at this stage no discounts are given). From this amount the deductions are taken and you can see these

CUSTOMER ACCOUNT PROFITABILITY				
BetterBuys Ltd				
Product X and Product Y				
4 week sales				
	Product X	%	Product Y	%
	£	of GSV	£	of GSV
GROSS SALES VALUE	12,123.00	100.00	10,098.00	100.00
TOTAL TRADING DISCOUNTS	2,210.63	18.24		
Short term discounts	1,200.65	9.90	890.76	
Long term discounts	1,009.98	8.33	1,009.98	
NET SALES INVOICED VALUE	9,912.37	81.76		
TOTAL COST OF PRODUCING	4,899.65	40.42	4,002.50	
GROSS CUSTOMER CONTRIBUTION				
BEFORE OVERRIDERS	5,012.72	41.35		
OVERRIDERS	125.34	1.03	130.00	
GROSS CUSTOMER CONTRIBUTION				
AFTER OVERRIDERS	4,887.38	40.31		
TOTAL PROMOTIONAL COSTS	1,429.85	11.79		
Advertising allowances	406.98	3.36	560.10	
Coupon redemptions	230.76	1.90	38.00	
Consumer multiple purchase offers	598.90	4.94	789.03	
Coupon manufacture	126.12	1.04	176.95	
Point of sale material	67.09	0.55	109.00	
CUSTOMER CONTRIBUTION AFTER				
PROMOTIONAL COSTS	3,457.53	28.52		
TOTAL COST OF DISTRIBUTING	342.48	2.83		
Total warehouse costs	134.98	1.11	159.00	
Total transportation costs	207.50	1.71	266.76	
CUSTOMER DELIVERED CONTRIBUTION	3,115.05	25.70		
COST OF FINANCING	470.39	3.88		
Cost of credit	120.39	0.99	134.72	
Settlement discount	350.00	2.89	124.54	
CUSTOMER CONTRIBUTION				
AFTER FINANCING COSTS	2,644.66	21.82		
TOTAL SPECIFIC SELLING & SUPPORT				
COSTS	505.66	4.17		
Selling staff costs	75.00	0.62	89.00	
Costs of order processing	190.00	1.57	218.87	
Cost of invoice processing	172.75	1.42	~189.65	
Cost of query management	67.91	0.56	70.00	
NET CUSTOMER CONTRIBUTION	2,139.0^0	17.64		

Figure 4.5 Diagram of the spreadsheet showing the account profitability model

listed in the spreadsheet in Figure 4.5. Notice the way that the lists of items are constructed, with the total at the top and the description in capital letters. Check the numbers yourself to see where they all come from.

The spreadsheet shown in Figure 4.5 illustrates the costs involved when the supplier sells Product X and Product Y to a retail chain called BetterBuys over a four-week period. The final figure, called the 'net customer contribution', gives a measure of the financial benefit of the supplier dealing with BetterBuys.

Activity 4.5

These tasks are based on the customer account profitability model outlined in the case study above.

Task I

Look carefully at the spreadsheet in Figure 4.5. The figures for Product X have been input and the totals and various figures filled in. Formulae have been used to calculate these totals. The second column, % of GSV, shows the percentage of gross sales value represented by each figure in the column to the right.

1 Input the spreadsheet on your computer exactly as it appears here. When you have done this, check it carefully and correct any mistakes. Save your work before proceeding.
2 Put in formulae to complete both columns for Product Y. You should make sure that the format of the numbers is the same as that for the first column (i.e. commas in large numbers and two decimal places).
3 Save your work and produce a printout.

Task 2

One of the large food chains wants to double the short- and long-term discounts but the sales manager has negotiated with the company to cut by 60 per cent the costs of consumer multiple purchase offers, coupon redemptions and coupon manufacture. Make these changes, and save and print the spreadsheet. Write down the net customer contribution now for Products X and Y.

As you can see, making such a model means that the sales manager can use a laptop computer with spreadsheet software to see immediately the results on the profits obtained from each product of any concessions given to customers.

Task 3

The sales manager has suggested that the spreadsheet model would be even more useful if another two columns were added containing the total figures for X and Y together and the percentage figures for X and Y together. Make these additions on your spreadsheet, and save and print the worksheet.

Creating spreadsheet models

This section shows you how to go about creating your own models. It looks at different types of model and how to use them to perform simulations.

Modelling a supermarket queue

If you were considering opening a new supermarket you might have to decide how many point-of-sale terminals or checkouts to use. Rather than installing too many or too few it would be better to create a model of a supermarket queue and see the effect of varying the numbers of checkouts. We call exercising the model in this way a simulation.

Data parameters

First we need to consider the inputs to the system. Because we intend to use spreadsheet software, all the inputs will be via the keyboard. The inputs to the system include:

- how many people are waiting to be served;
- how many point-of-sale (POS) terminals or tills there are;
- how long each person takes to be served. This will have to be an average time, since the time depends on the number of items each person is buying, the speed of the operator, whether there are any queries and the method of payment used (e.g. credit card, debit card, cheque or cash). An average value could be obtained by visiting similar supermarkets and buying different amounts of shopping, using different methods of payment each time and timing the whole transaction. Alternatively, queues at another branch could be observed and timed.

To create a simple model it is necessary to understand the way a queue starts. Initially it is best to construct the simplest model possible and then to refine it after further investigation. Try not to introduce too many complications at this stage. Make some assumptions and write them down.

Now we look at any constraints imposed on the system. These could be:

- the maximum number of POS terminals the supermarket could afford to buy;
- the number of staff available to operate the POS terminals;
- the size of the supermarket: physical space will limit the number of POS terminals.

Variables

Next we can look at the variables. Variables are those items of data that we intend to vary in some way. In this model we might choose to use the following variables:

- the number of shoppers waiting to be served;
- the number of point-of-sale terminals;
- the average time for a shopper to pass through the checkout.

Calculations

Consider which calculations are needed. Sometimes it is best to look at what you would do if you were doing the task using pen, paper and calculator. If you feel confident about the equations needed and how to construct the model, you could try designing it straight onto the spreadsheet, but you will need to know enough about the software to be able to swap things around later if you need to.

In this case we can have a heading and divide the spreadsheet into two parts: one for inputs and the other for outputs. Calculations are performed on the inputs to produce the outputs. Figure 4.6 shows the design.

Rules of operation

We now need to consider the rules of operation that we came across earlier in this chapter.

Formulae and relationships

Suppose that there are 40 shoppers waiting to pay for goods and 20 checkouts. Let us also assume that, on average, it takes a shopper two minutes to pass through a checkout. We will have to assume that the shoppers will distribute themselves equally in the queues.

	A	B	C	D	E	F	G
1							
2							
3			Model of a supermarket queue				
4							
5	Inputs						
6	Number of shoppers waiting						
7	Number of tills						
8	Time for a shopper to pass through a checkout						
9							
10							
11							
12	Outputs						
13	Average number of shoppers in each queue						
14	Time the last person in the queue has to wait						
15							
16							

Figure 4.6 Design of the model

We can then calculate the average number of shoppers in each queue using the formula:

$$\text{average number of shoppers in each queue} = \frac{\text{number of shoppers waiting}}{\text{number of tills}}$$

Using our figures:

average number of shoppers in each queue = 40/20 = 2

Now, the last shopper in one of these queues will have to wait a time which is given by the formula:

$$\begin{array}{c}\text{time last person in}\\\text{queue has to wait}\end{array} = \begin{array}{c}\text{average time for a person to go}\\\text{through the checkout in minutes}\end{array} \times \begin{array}{c}\text{average number of shoppers}\\\text{waiting in each queue}\end{array}$$

Using our figures we get:

time last person in each queue has to wait = 2 × 2 = 4 min

The beauty of using a spreadsheet is in the ease with which we can carry out the calculations, but we must make sure that we link the outputs to the inputs using formulae.

Activity 4.6

Figure 4.7 shows the formulae that have to be used in the model described above. Set up the spreadsheet and print it out showing any formulae placed in each cell. Then perform a simulation by entering numbers to see what happens.

Cell references

In this simple model there is no copying of formulae so we need not worry about relative or absolute cell referencing.

Results of actions

The results of altering the variables are displayed at a certain place on the spreadsheet. These results are the output from the model and can be presented numerically or in the form of graphs.

Effect of variable changes

Figure 4.8 shows the effect of altering the inputs to the system.

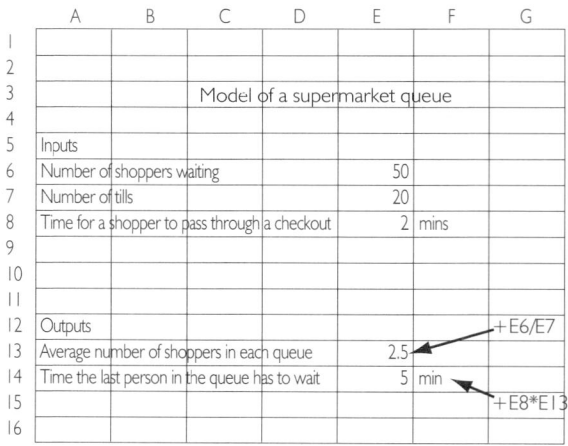

Figure 4.7 *Spreadsheet showing the inputs, outputs and the formulae used to calculate the outputs*

	A	B	C	D	E	F	G
1							
2							
3			Model of a supermarket queue				
4							
5	Inputs						
6	Number of shoppers waiting				50		
7	Number of tills				20		
8	Time for a shopper to pass through a checkout				2	min	
9							
10							
11							
12	Outputs						
13	Average number of shoppers in each queue				5		
14	Time the last person in the queue has to wait				10	min	
15							
16							

Figure 4.8 *Spreadsheet showing the effect of altering the number of tills*

Activity 4.7

Try to use the model you have created to explore the effect of changing the variables and rules and to test hypotheses.

Assumptions made

We have made several assumptions. We have assumed that people distribute themselves equally in each queue. We have also assumed that people stay in the queue and do not jump from one queue to another. We also make the assumption that each person waits the same amount of time, called the average time, to be served.

Input and output methods

As with most models that use spreadsheet software, the input method is via the keyboard and the output is either displayed on the screen or printed out.

Effectiveness of the model
Here we must look carefully at our model. Maybe we could have improved it. We must decide whether we are happy with the model, if any improvements could be made to it and whether it solves the problem that we started with.

Suggestions for improvement
If the model is good, no improvement is needed, but a model usually becomes more realistic as more time is spent on its development. Obviously it is possible to go on for-ever making changes, trying to improve things, but there has to be a point where this stops. Perfection is impossible, especially if human behaviour needs to be taken into account. For instance, it would be hard to allow for people changing queues.

Activity 4.8

Task 1
One of the assumptions used in the model is that queues consist of equal numbers of people. Is this always so? If not, why not? What changes could be made in the model to reflect this?

Task 2
Can you produce a better model of a supermarket queue than this? Remember that the one described is only an initial model. See what you can do!

A predator/prey model

Suppose we wanted to protect vegetables in a greenhouse against greenfly attack. Apart from using pesticides, an organic, natural method of control could be used by intro-ducing ladybirds, which are predators of the greenfly. To find the optimum number of ladybirds to introduce, we must understand something about how the ladybird and the greenfly reproduce. With no control over their numbers, greenfly multiply at an alarm-ing rate and will eventually destroy all of a crop. It is hard to eliminate all greenfly and if we did so the ladybirds would all starve to death anyway. The optimum state is when the population of the greenfly has reached an 'equilibrium state'; that is the numbers of greenfly are constant. When this occurs ladybirds will also be in equilibrium and will have enough to eat, and the damage to the crop will be restricted.

A real-life scientific study on the numbers of predators/prey could be undertaken over a long period of time. Alternatively, we can compress the time scale using a model. Once we have set up the model we can make alterations to the variables, such as initial numbers of prey and predators, and observe the results almost immediately.

Inputs
When setting up this model you will need to decide on the inputs to the system. There are two kinds of input: those for the predators (ladybirds) and those for the prey (greenfly).

Inputs for the predators
- The number of ladybirds at the start of the year.
- Breeding rate (the factor by which they increase each month).
- The number of greenfly each ladybird eats each month.

Inputs for the prey
- The number of greenfly at the start of the year.
- Breeding rate (the factor by which they increase each month).

Spreadsheet design

We will use three columns:

Start of month	Number of ladybirds	Number of greenfly

Let us first look at the situation for the first month, January. The situation will be as follows:

Start of month	Number of ladybirds	Number of greenfly
Jan	10	100

At the start of February, the following will happen. The number of ladybirds will increase by a factor of 1.5 to 15. The greenfly will breed and increase their population by a factor of 4, making 400. However, during January some of them will be eaten. If we assume that the 10 ladybirds at the start each eat 30 greenfly in the month, then 300 greenfly will be eaten, leaving 100. So, at the start of February there will be 15 ladybirds and 100 greenfly. This position is shown in the next table:

Start of month	Number of ladybirds	Number of greenfly
Jan	10	100
Feb	15	100

Activity 4.9

Carry this model forward for the whole twelve months. Perform this task using a spreadsheet and make sure that you link the cells using formulae.

Suggestions for improvement

The above model is too simple. It does not take into account:

- that the breeding rate of ladybirds and greenfly is not constant throughout the year: the rate will increase in the warmer months and we really need to alter the breeding rates accordingly;
- the fact that, if there is not enough food for the ladybirds to eat, they will die;
- that we also need to incorporate a death rate for the ladybirds into our model. To make it simpler, we can assume that the greenfly will remain alive until they get eaten by the ladybirds.

Activity 4.10

Consider the above problems and make specific suggestions about how you think the model could be improved. Produce a revised model including your improvements.

Modelling inflation

Suppose you are planning for the future and would like some income for when you stop working: a pension. A pension is a sum of money paid each week after you retire from work. Sooner or later everyone has to think about this, but how much money will be needed? Suppose you are earning £275 per week now. What will this be just before you retire? The answer is that we just do not know. However, in arranging a pension, we need to have some idea of the amount needed.

A model will help. The object of the model is to determine how much a 23-year-old person who earns £275 per week in 1997 would be earning in 2038, the year before they are due to retire.

There are various constraints to our model:

- No one knows what the percentage rate of inflation will be. We could look at past rates over, say, the last 20 years and use an average value (you should be able to get these figures from the library or from an economics tutor), or you could use some other figure.
- To make things simpler, we can assume that the person is not promoted and that his or her wage increases only in line with inflation. When you are used to the model you might try increasing the wage, assuming a promotion.
- The individual concerned may do better than the rate of inflation. Wages in some occupations have increased faster over the last 20 years than in others. Is it possible to take this into account?

Activity 4.11

First of all calculate the first five years' income manually, assuming that inflation stays at a rate of 5 per cent per year. Before you attempt this, let us look at how this is done for the first couple of years.

Fill in a table like this:

End of year	Wage

To work out how £275 needs to change to keep pace with inflation we perform the following calculation:

Find 5 per cent of 275 using:
$5/100 \times 275 = £13.75$

This is the amount by which the weekly wage needs to grow at the end of the first year. So, the new weekly wage at the end of year 1 is:
$275 + 13.75 = £288.75$

You can add these figures to the table like this:

End of year	Wage
1	£288.75

For year 2 the process is repeated using this new wage like this:
5 per cent of $288.75 = 5/100 \times 288.75 = £14.44$

Hence, weekly wage at the end of year 2 is $288.75 + 14.44 = £303.19$

You can start to build up the table like this:

End of year	Wage
1	£288.75
2	£303.19

Task 1

Now complete the table for the first five years, repeating the processes outlined above. Really good mathematicians will be able to do these calculations a quicker way than that shown above. If you want to know more, ask your mathematics tutor.

Task 2

For this type of repetitive calculation a spreadsheet is ideal. Prepare a model using a spreadsheet and find out how much the person will be earning in 2036 if wages just keep pace with inflation.

Task 3

Try to refine your model so that it better reflects reality. For instance, collect some inflation figures and see if 5 per cent seems about right.

Break-even analysis

Break-even analysis is a technique used to determine how many of a particular product a company needs to sell in order to break even.

CompuBeat is a new company intending to manufacture small loudspeakers. It hopes to sell to customers wanting speakers for their personal stereos/CDs or for multimedia applications. The directors of CompuBeat realise that business will be hard to start with, so as part of their business plan they need to find out how many speakers they must sell to break even.

When a business is started, money is paid out for equipment, parts, premises, etc. before any products are made. So initially money is going out of the business but none is coming in. As the product is made and sold, money starts coming back into the business. Eventually, when a certain number of loudspeakers has been sold, the company will break even. This point, called the break-even point, occurs when the money which has come in from the sale of the loudspeakers balances the money that has been paid out. In other words, at this point neither profit nor loss has been made. Once past this point, the sale of the speakers should start to produce a profit.

Break-even analysis is important when starting a business since banks who lend the money to start up the company will want to know when the borrower should start making a profit to repay the debt.

To produce the break-even analysis model for CompuBeat, the fixed and the variable costs need to be assessed. The company accountant reports the following information.

Fixed costs

These are any costs that do not depend on the number of loudspeakers sold. They include rent of buildings, rates, salaries and some finance costs. It is important to note that fixed costs do not stay fixed forever. They are only fixed over the short term and over a certain range of products.

Variable costs

Variable costs are the costs that depend on the number of speakers produced. So, the cost of the parts which make up the speakers and the electricity used in production, would be classed as variable costs.

CompuBeat has worked out the following figures:

- fixed costs = £1000
- variable costs = £12.50 per speaker
- selling price per speaker = £18.00.

Sales revenue is the money that comes in when a number of speakers is sold. So:

total cost of producing speakers = variable costs + fixed costs
variable costs = variable costs per speaker × number of speakers
sales revenue = selling price per speaker × number of speakers

Using spreadsheet software we can now produce a table with the column headings shown below.

Number of speakers	Variable costs	Fixed costs	Total cost	Sales revenue

A series of tasks will determine the break-even point.

First attempt

The first attempt is used to obtain a rough range within which the break-even point may lie.

Activity 4.12

Initially, try numbers of speakers from 50 to 500 in steps of 50. Make sure that you key in the all the information except that in the columns for variable costs, total costs and sales revenue. You should work these out using suitable formulae and then copy them down the relevant columns.

Check that your final model looks like the one in Figure 4.9.

The break-even point occurs where the sales revenue and the total costs are equal. As you can see, there is no such value on our spreadsheet so we look for the point where the sales revenue goes from being smaller than the total costs to where it is greater. Looking at the spreadsheet, this occurs between sales of 150 and 200 speakers. This region must be investigated in greater detail to get a more accurate picture. A second spreadsheet is therefore produced covering just this area.

Second attempt

Activity 4.13

Produce a second spreadsheet by altering the first one; use steps of ten from 150 speakers to 250 speakers. Check with Figure 4.10 that you get the same values.

This second attempt should reveal that the break-even point lies somewhere between 180 and 190 speakers.

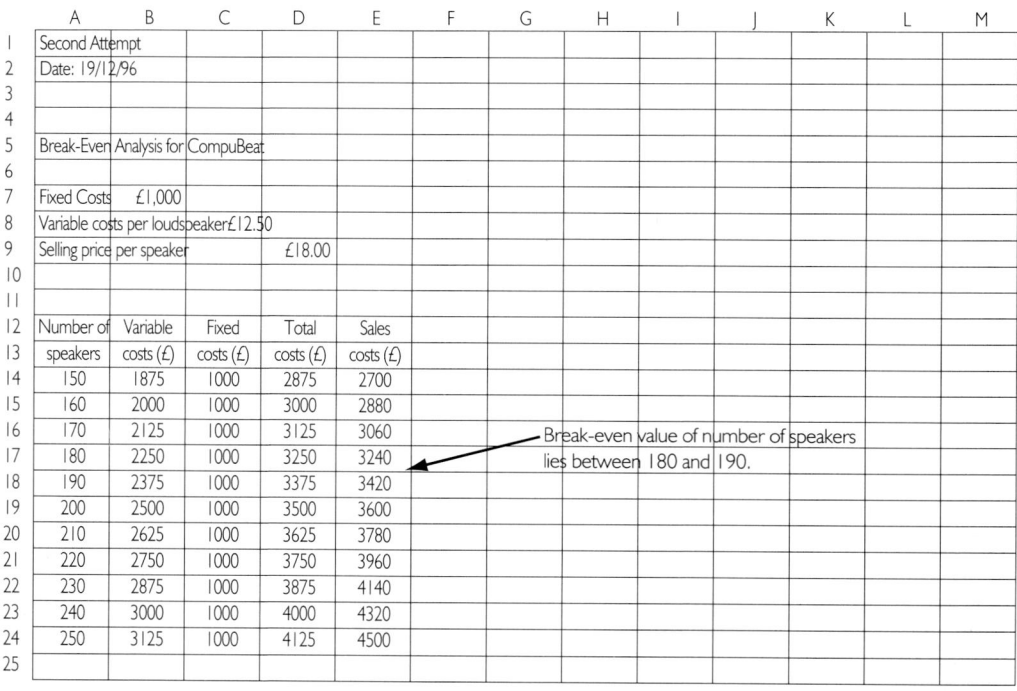

	A	B	C	D	E	F	G	H	I	J	K	L	M
1	First Attempt												
2	Date: 19/12/96												
3													
4													
5	Break-Even Analysis for CompuBeat												
6													
7	Fixed Costs	£1,000											
8	Variable costs per loudspeaker£12.50												
9	Selling price per speaker			£18.00									
10													
11													
12	Number of	Variable	Fixed	Total	Sales								
13	speakers	costs (£)	costs (£)	costs (£)	costs (£)								
14	50	625	1000	1625	900								
15	100	1250	1000	2250	1800								
16	150	1875	1000	2875	2700								
17	200	2500	1000	3500	3600								
18	250	3125	1000	4125	4500								
19	300	3750	1000	4750	5400								
20	350	4375	1000	5375	6300								
21	400	5000	1000	6000	7200								
22	450	5625	1000	6625	8100								
23	500	6250	1000	7250	9000								
24													
25													

Somewhere between these two values the sales revenue will equal the total costs. The number of speakers for which this occurs will be the break-even value.

Figure 4.9 First attempt at finding the break-even point

	A	B	C	D	E	F	G	H	I	J	K	L	M
1	Second Attempt												
2	Date: 19/12/96												
3													
4													
5	Break-Even Analysis for CompuBeat												
6													
7	Fixed Costs	£1,000											
8	Variable costs per loudspeaker£12.50												
9	Selling price per speaker			£18.00									
10													
11													
12	Number of	Variable	Fixed	Total	Sales								
13	speakers	costs (£)	costs (£)	costs (£)	costs (£)								
14	150	1875	1000	2875	2700								
15	160	2000	1000	3000	2880								
16	170	2125	1000	3125	3060								
17	180	2250	1000	3250	3240								
18	190	2375	1000	3375	3420								
19	200	2500	1000	3500	3600								
20	210	2625	1000	3625	3780								
21	220	2750	1000	3750	3960								
22	230	2875	1000	3875	4140								
23	240	3000	1000	4000	4320								
24	250	3125	1000	4125	4500								
25													

Break-even value of number of speakers lies between 180 and 190.

Figure 4.10 Second attempt at finding the break-even point

Third attempt

Activity 4.14

Now repeat the process from 180 to 190 speakers in steps of one.
1 What value do you get for break even?
2 What should you do if it is not a whole number?

Check that your spreadsheet looks like the one in Figure 4.11.

	A	B	C	D	E	F	G	H	I	J	K	L	M
1	Third Attempt												
2	Date: 19/12/96												
3													
4													
5	Break-Even Analysis for CompuBeat												
6													
7	Fixed Costs	£1,000											
8	Variable costs per loudspeaker	£12.50											
9	Selling price per speaker			£18.00									
10													
11													
12	Number of	Variable	Fixed	Total	Sales								
13	speakers	costs (£)	costs (£)	costs (£)	costs (£)								
14	180	2250.00	1000	3250.00	3240								
15	181	2262.50	1000	3262.50	3258								
16	182	2275.00	1000	3275.00	3276								
17	183	2287.50	1000	3287.50	3294								
18	184	2300.00	1000	3300.00	3312								
19	185	2312.50	1000	3312.50	3330								
20	186	2325.00	1000	3325.00	3348								
21	187	2337.50	1000	3337.50	3366								
22	188	2350.00	1000	3350.00	3384								
23	189	2362.50	1000	3362.50	3402								
24	190	2375.00	1000	3375.00	3420								
25													

Figure 4.11 Third attempt at finding the break-even point

Finding the break-even point graphically

We can find the break-even point graphically by plotting the sales revenue and total costs against the number of speakers sold. You can do this either using graph paper or using a computer to draw a two-line graph like the one shown in Figure 4.12. The break-even point is where the two straight lines cross. The number of speakers sold to break even can be read from the graph.

Activity 4.15

Suzanne is 25 and lives at home with her parents. She is bored with her present job working in an office and would like a challenge. Her present job brings her in £150 per week.

She has just seen an advertisement in her local newspaper advertising a training course to become a driving instructor. Tuition fees and final examination are £1300. She can drive but does not have her own car. She therefore needs to buy a car with dual controls. Suzanne sees a car she likes and with the dual controls it will cost her £8000.

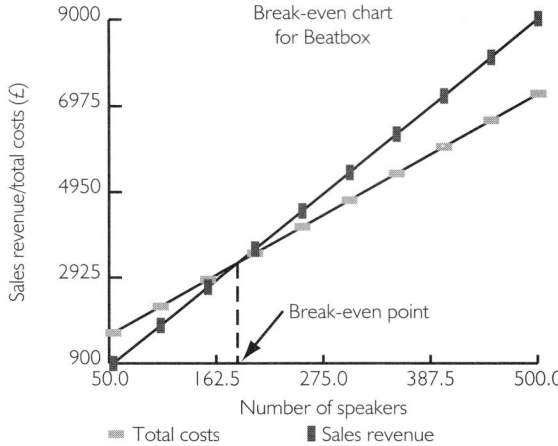

Figure 4.12 Finding the break-even point graphically

In order to get established Suzanne reckons she will need to undercut the fees charged by the other driving schools. She therefore decides to charge £12 per hour. To attract customers she decides to advertise in the local paper and this will cost £30 per week. Also, her mother, who is at home all day, will answer the phone calls and make bookings and Suzanne will give her mother £20 per week for doing this.

Before giving her job up and going ahead with the venture she must work out how many hours she would need to work each week just to break even. With this in mind she summarises her fixed and variable costs as the following figures show:

Fixed costs
- Advertising: £30.00 per week.
- Payment to her mother: £20.00 per week.
- Borrowing to buy the car and pay for tuition fees for her course: £40.00 per week.
- Depreciation of the car: £80.00 per week.

Variable costs
The only variable costs will be the running costs of the car. These include petrol, repairs, etc. She works out these variable costs to be 20p per mile.

On average, in a one hour lesson she reckons that she will travel about 15 miles. Hence, the variable costs for one lesson will be 15 × 20p = £3.00

Suzanne has asked for your help in making her decision. You have your own computer and have told her that you will help, using spreadsheet software.

Task 1
Set up a model of the business and use your model to determine the number of lessons Suzanne would need each week to break even.

Task 2
Suggest some improvements she might make and show them as printouts.

Task 3
Write a brief report on the proposed business. On the basis of your figures, do you think she should quit her job or stick with it?

Assignment A4.1

This assignment develops knowledge and understanding of the following element:
2.3 Model data

It supports the development of the following key skills:
Communication 3.2 and 3.3
Information technology 3.1, 3.2, 3.3 and 3.4
Application of number 3.1, 3.2 and 3.3

To provide the evidence to meet the performance criteria for this unit you are required to produce two computer models, one of which must be a predictive model.

Apart from this proviso there is no further restriction on the type of model. You may use pre-written and designed software or a spreadsheet. You will probably choose to use a spreadsheet since the software is widely available and you are likely to be familiar with its use.

Task 1
For each of the two models defined above:
1 Explain the purpose of the computer model in terms of the items in the range covered under the chapter heading. Basically you need to explain why you are choosing to use a model rather than other possible methods.
2 Specify three data parameters and four rules of operation.
3 Review the effectiveness of the model and make suggestions for further improvement.

The points listed above are effectively the documentation for the model. It is particularly appropriate as the person using the model may not necessarily be the person who created it in the first place. For this reason it is important to be able to explain to another person how the model works.

Task 2
Produce evidence of the outputs relating to your models. Screendumps can be included, along with printouts of the spreadsheets. Each time you change something, produce another printout to show the development.

You must make sure that the output provides evidence that you have:
- undertaken at least three 'what if' queries;
- tested the system for effectiveness.

Ideas for your models
You are free to choose any model you want but it is best to discuss it first with your tutor, who will be able to advise you on whether your choice of model is realistic, bearing in mind the time available and your knowledge of the software.

As one of the models you might like to further develop an idea introduced earlier in the chapter, i.e. modelling a supermarket queue, a predator/prey model, modelling inflation or break-even analysis. Other ideas are provided in the next section.

Types of control system

When they think of information technology systems, many people think of business systems used in offices for administrative purposes. There is, however, a huge number of applications in which computers or microprocessors are used to control things. In this section we will look at some of the applications and also at the theory behind building a **control system**.

Environmental control

When raising plants or animals indoors it is necessary to provide a certain environment which often has to be kept fairly constant. Computers can be used to do this. Better environmental control means that the plants or animals should grow better. Environmental control is used in greenhouses to provide ideal conditions for the crops or young plants being grown.

In a greenhouse, the following parameters may be controlled:

- humidity (the amount of moisture in the air)
- temperature
- light.

Sensors are used to measure the above quantities and the sensors send electronic signals to the microprocessor unit or computer. If humidity inside the greenhouse falls, the windows of the greenhouse close and a pump switches on a fine mist of water, thus increasing the humidity. Once the sensor reports an ideal value has been reached the pump is switched off and the windows re-open as necessary. If humidity rises to much, as it can after the plants have been watered, the sensor detects this and feeds a signal to the computer, which then issues a control signal to the window motor to open the windows, ventilating the greenhouse and drying out the air.

Temperature can be controlled in the following way. A temperature sensor, called a thermistor, continually monitors the temperature in the greenhouse and when it falls below a certain level the computer turns on a heater. This stays on until a set temperature is reached. If the temperature in the greenhouse rises above a certain value the computer opens a window, which stays open until the temperature falls sufficiently. In this way temperature and humidity can be kept between certain predefined values.

Flood warning control

Where there is low-lying land near to a large river there is always a danger that, after prolonged heavy rain, the river could burst its banks and cause flooding. Flooding can cost insurance companies hundreds of thousands of pounds as householders and businesses put in claims for damage caused. If it is known that flooding is imminent, remedial action can be taken to divert the water or to use sand bags to build up the banks or directly protect property. The problem is that a river can burst its banks at any time of the day or night, not just during working hours! It is not feasible for river levels to be continuously monitored by staff. Instead sensors are used which detect the water level. Radio links send data from the sensors to the main computer and if there is a danger of flooding, the emergency services are alerted and a flood warning issued.

Process production control

Control systems are used to control processes in many factories. For instance, in steel mills, rather than keep a whole range of steel sizes and shapes in a warehouse it is much more efficient to input the customer's order and let the computer control the equipment which rolls or draws the steel into the correct shapes. In this way, it is possible not only to avoid having to keep too much money tied up in stock, which takes up space, but companies can also reduce the number of staff needed to manage the warehouse.

Figure 4.13 shows a process control system which is dictated by the customers' orders.

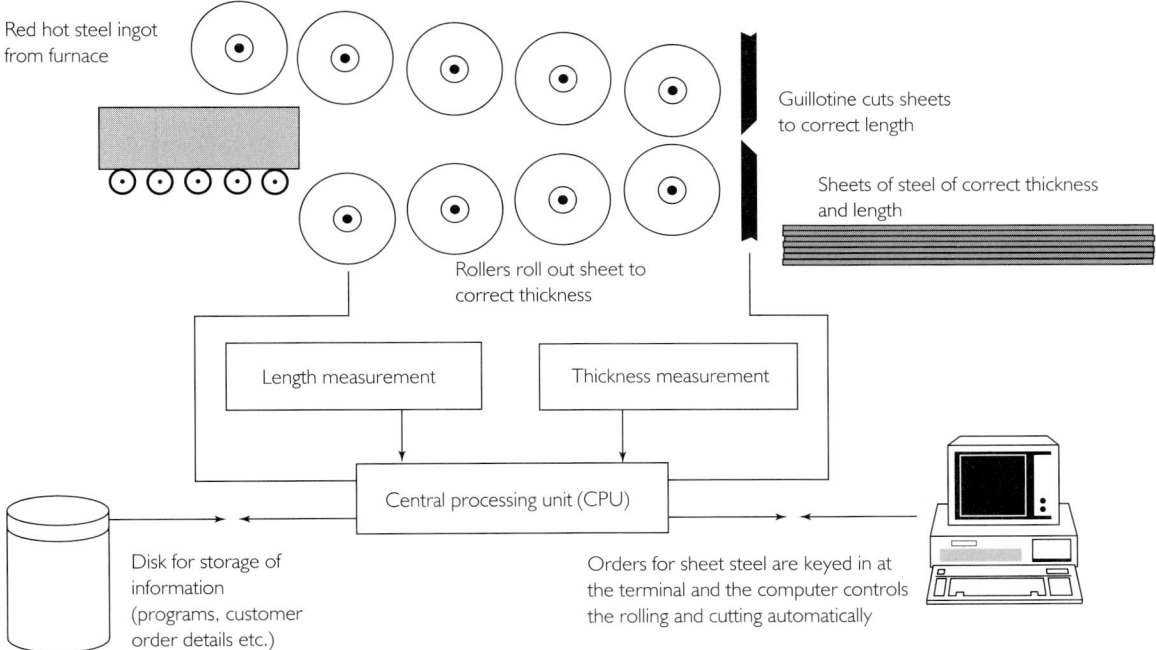

Figure 4.13 In some modern steel works computers control the manufacture of steel bars and cutting them to the correct size according to customers' orders

Looked at in a different way, a process production control system does have the serious disadvantage that it eliminates jobs based in the warehouse and in stock control.

Quality control systems

Checking that goods or materials are of the required quality can be repetitive and tedious, so it is not surprising that much of this work is now performed automatically, using computer-controlled equipment. As an example, the water companies have to ensure the quality of water they supply to customers, by analysing samples daily. To do this, water from tens of thousands of sample bottles each day is taken and analysed using a robot arm which takes a sample from each bottle and transfers it to a machine which automatically analyses the chemicals in the water.

At the Toyota plant in Derbyshire, robots check cars to an accuracy of 0.1 mm. Within a minute of a body shell appearing on the production line, two robots measure it from end to end. Further down the production line, however, the paintwork is checked by eye. The robots do the jobs that are too monotonous, strenuous and time consuming for a human. So why cannot a robot check the paintwork? The reason is that with current technology it would take too long and a robot would not be able to spot imperfections as well as the human eye.

Security control systems

Control systems are used extensively in security. One example is in airports, at luggage check-ins, where luggage travels along conveyor belts which eventually take it to bays where the aircraft are located. Before reaching these points luggage goes though checks similar to those made on hand luggage and is scanned automatically by X-ray machines. If the computer which controls the system finds anything with which it is unfamiliar the case is is re-routed to a certain area where it can be examined more closely by a human operator, who may ask the owner to open the case so that it can be searched.

Transport systems

There is a variety of transport systems which make use of computer control. Traffic lights are by far the most familiar, although car parking, speeding, red-light camera systems and motorway fog warning systems are also examples. The case study in Chapter 1 on the traffic control systems used by the Metropolitan Borough of Sefton should be referred to for further information. Chapter 1 also contains a case study on how London Transport is able to monitor traffic throughout the capital.

Robot production systems

Robots are used in factories because they can reduce labour costs and improve the quality of the finished product. An industrial robot can be defined as 'a reprogrammable, multi-functional manipulator designed to move material, parts, tools or specialised devices through various programmed motions for the performance of a variety of tasks.'

This explains why the equipment used in a factory to make motor cars may be called a robot whereas a domestic washing machine is not, despite its microprocessor control. An industrial robot can be used in different ways: it could, for example, be used to spray-paint or for welding body panels. A washing machine, although it has different preset programs, is restricted to washing clothes.

An industrial robot can be considered to consist of three parts.

1 **The manipulator:** this is the moving part which in Figure 4.14 resembles a moving arm on a stand. Various tools can be placed in the 'hand'.
2 **The power supply:** for robots that need a lot of strength, power will be provided via a compressor which works a hydraulic system. For lightweight robots which use stepper motors (motors which can be turned through a set angle) the power supply will be electrical.
3 **The controlling computer:** this controls the other elements. A computer is a very low current device so it needs something called an interface in order to protect it from the much higher currents used for motors and solenoids when they are connected. These interfaces also allow analogue-to-digital and digital-to-analogue conversion.

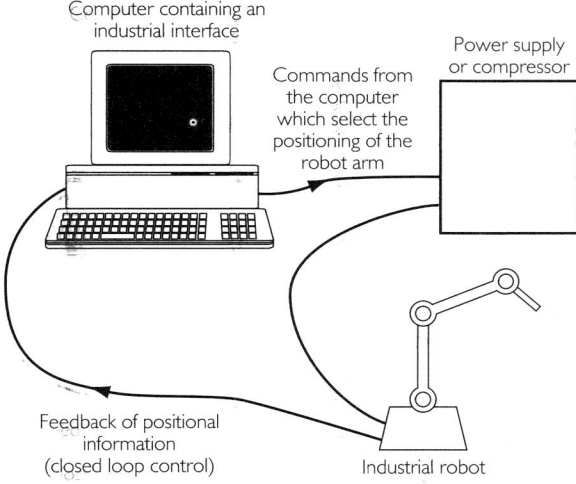

Computer containing an industrial interface

Commands from the computer which select the positioning of the robot arm

Power supply or compressor

Feedback of positional information (closed loop control)

Industrial robot

Figure 4.14 A robot arm being controlled by a microcomputer

Components of control systems

There are various components which form the building blocks of any control system; in this section we will look at each of them and the part that they play in the whole system.

Automatic data capture using signals

Not all data has to be entered using a keyboard or using special forms. Some data can enter a computer directly in the form of electronic signals. This data usually comes from sensors which produce a signal that depends on a physical property. For instance, components passing along a production line break a beam of light as they pass. A sensor detects that the light is absent when each component passes and a signal is sent to the computer which enables it to count the components. Because the sensor receives data from the outside world it is considered to be an input device.

When local authorities wanted to monitor traffic flow along a certain road it was usual to employ people (usually students) to stand beside the road observing and recording the traffic. With the increased traffic we now have, this would not be feasible. Instead a pressure sensor is used which records a pulse every time a vehicle passes over it. You may have seen these: they look like thick black wires running across the road and there is sometimes a box at the side of the road to house the recording system. A diagram of this arrangement is shown in Figure 4.15. Traffic control systems were dealt with in a case study in Chapter 1.

Using sensors for control

You may have been in a queue at traffic lights and thought you would not get through before the lights changed to red, yet managed to do so. This may have been because the lights were computer controlled. With such a system, if sensors in the road detect a build up of traffic on one side of the lights only, the system allows the lights to stay longer on green for the side with the build up. Traffic runs more smoothly in many of our cities thanks to sensors that are continually monitoring the situation and relaying data back to a central computer which alters the sequencing of the lights.

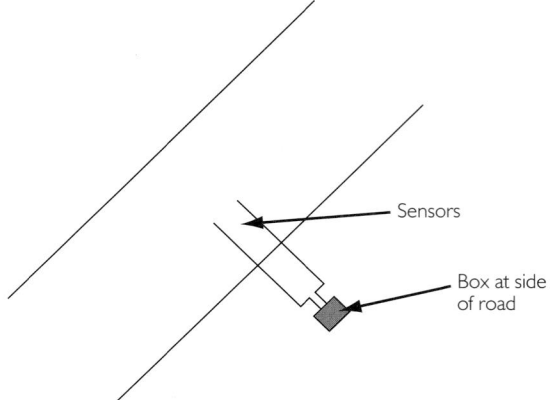

Figure 4.15

Activity 4.16

There are many different environmental control systems in use including the following:

- air-conditioning in buildings and cars
- black ice and fog alert systems on motorways.

Research either one of these systems and find out the basic principles of its operation.

Types of sensors

Sensors are used to detect various physical quantities such as temperature, pressure, sound, light, etc. A range of sensors is shown in Figure 4.16. The sensors are connected to a computer using a special interface, and with special software physical quantities can be displayed on screen in a variety of different ways.

Mercury tilt switch
If a mercury tilt switch is tilted or moved a blob of mercury touches the contacts and completes a circuit. It can be used in pinball machines to detect tilting. It can also be used as an alarm for vending machines.

Light sensor
Light sensors have many uses. They can, for instance, be used to detect low light levels so that street lighting is turned on. They can also be used to detect the light reflected from barcodes.

Push switch
A push switch is the type of switch you might find turning on the interior light inside a car when the door is opened. These switches are also used to detect when fridge doors are opened so that interior lights are switched on.
   Very small switches are available and these are called microswitches.

Temperature sensor
One of the most common sensors, temperature sensors, are used in central heating systems to keep house temperatures constant. There are many different temperature sensors suited to different ranges of temperatures, accuracy and cost.

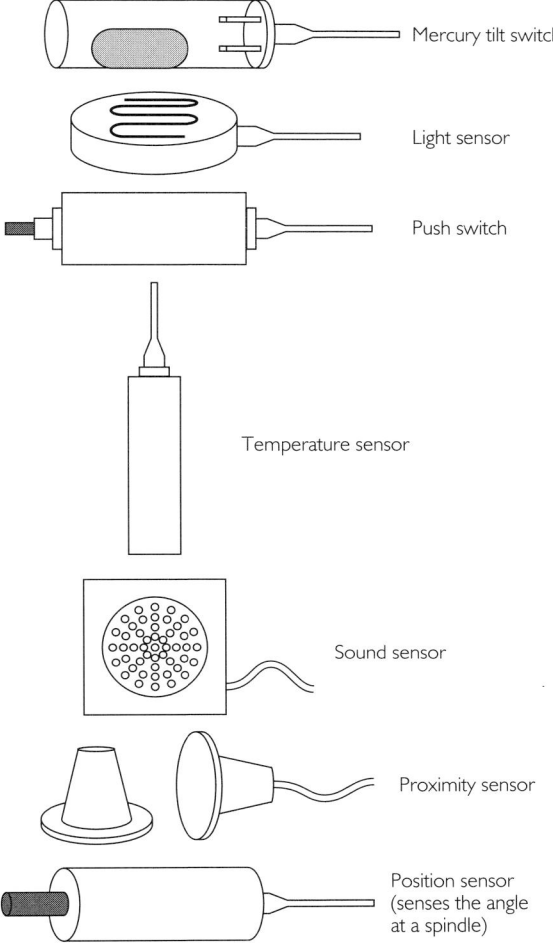

Mercury tilt switch

Light sensor

Push switch

Temperature sensor

Sound sensor

Proximity sensor

Position sensor
(senses the angle
at a spindle)

Figure 4.16 A selection of sensors

Sound sensor

Sound sensors are used, for example, by environmental health officers to record the level of sound coming from shops, clubs, houses, etc.

Proximity sensor

There are several different types of **proximity sensor**. A gas proximity detector consists of a gas emitter and a pressure sensor. The gas emitter pumps gas into an open chamber while ambient pressure is measured. If an object is near the mouth of the chamber, a change in pressure will be measured.

Another type of proximity detector uses a transmitter to emit an ultrasound (very high frequency sound) signal which bounces off any object present; the reflected signal is picked up by a receiver. The system measures the time between when the signal is sent and its return; the time difference is a measure of how far away the object is from the sensor.

Contact sensor

One type of contact sensor comes in two parts. If the parts of the sensor are physically separated a signal is activated. You often see these on windows: if the window is opened the two halves of the sensor are separated and an alarm is activated.

Position sensor

This sensor detects the angle of, for instance, a spindle. It can be used to feed back the position of a robot arm.

pH sensor

This chemical sensor is used to find out how basic or acidic a solution is.

Humidity sensor

A humidity sensor is designed to determine the amount of moisture present (usually either in the air or in soil).

Video sensor

The **video sensor** takes in a whole picture using a video camera which it then stores. Once stored, the picture can be examined and compared with previously stored pictures. Systems that make use of this device operate at all the major ports, recognising registration plates on cars. Registration plates are recorded by cameras and examined against those pre-stored by the computer. Police and security services are thus able to keep suspect vehicles under surveillance.

Video sensors are also used on robots to given them 'simple sight'. Often, more than one camera is used to give the robot depth of vision which means it is able to judge distances in much the same way as humans can, using two eyes. Such robots are used by all the major car manufacturers for positioning and fixing car windscreens. To perform this action the robot is 'taught' to use the picture from the camera to recognise the outline of a car body into which the windscreen needs fitting. As the robot moves the windscreen closer, changes in the picture are fed back to the computer, which acts on this information by making small adjustments to the position of the screen until the correct picture is received.

Processors

The processor is the name given to the chip that performs the arithmetic and logic operations; it can be a whole computer or just a microprocessor. The processor contains a stored program that specifies such things as the sensing rate, and what to do in certain situations. It also turns the output devices on or off, based on the information it receives from the sensors. Another task performed by the processor is to take an input quantity, make a slight adjustment to the output by activating the output device and then feed back part of the output signal, via a sensor. This part of the output signal is then compared with the input signal to see what adjustment needs to be made in order to match the two signals (i.e. make them both the same). This 'feedback' system, as it is called, enables the system to monitor the changes it makes.

Process control procedure

A control procedure is a program created to operate a process control system. The procedure is designed to read input data, process the data and send output signals according to preset rules. For example, such a program might read a light level, compare it with a limit set, and then adjust the output if necessary.

Output devices
Actuators

Actuators are hardware devices, such as motors, which react according to signals given to them by a computer. A motor used to open a window in a greenhouse when it gets too hot can be described as an actuator.

Stepper motor

A stepper motor, as the name suggests, is a motor which turns in a series of small steps. They generally look fatter than ordinary motors and have several more wires coming out of them.

Figure 4.17 shows a typical stepper motor. The rotor may be turned through a certain angle from, say, position 1,1 to 2,2 and so on. Pulses sent from the computer instruct the motor to turn through the required angle. Stepper motors can be speeded up or slowed down and can also be operated in both directions. To connect the motor to a computer we use a buffer. Stepper motors are used in robot arms.

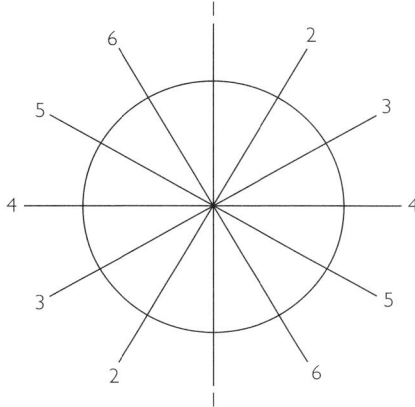

Figure 4.17 A stepper motor

Loudspeakers

Loudspeakers convert electrical signals into sound signals and are often the output device from a control systems where an alarm signal is needed.

Heater

Heaters are used as output devices in many control systems, the commonest being that of controlling the temperature of an environment. Because the amount of electricity used by a heater is so large, it cannot be connected in the same electronic circuit as the electronic components, which could easily be damaged or destroyed by the large current. Instead a relay is inserted which uses the small current in the circuit containing the electronic devices to switch the high-current circuit containing the heater.

Light

Indicator lights are frequently used as output devices. One example is with security systems where an infrared transmitter/receiver is used to detect the presence of a person near a building and this switches on a bright floodlight.

Lights are frequently used as indicators to show that a particular process is taking place or has finished.

Fans

Fans are often used as one of the output devices in an environmental control system to move the air around, thus providing ventilation.

Interconnecting devices

In some situations, the computer and sensors are separated from each other, so special devices are needed to enable them to communicate. Such systems make use of remote sensing. Electronic signals from remote sensors can be passed through telephone wires or using radio or satellite transmission to a computer, which may be in another part of the country or even the world. This system is ideal for use where temperature, pressure and wind speed may be detected at thousands of remote weather stations which send the data to a central computer.

The Environment Agency also uses remote sensing to detect when a river is likely to burst its banks, so that a flood warning can be issued. It also uses sensors to monitor the quality of water in our rivers and to give a pollution alert should the quality deteriorate.

Remote sensing is used by London Transport for monitoring the progress of buses under its control. This system is looked at in detail in the case study in Chapter 1.

Activity 4.17

Consider the 'sensors' you use when catching a ball thrown to you. Describe briefly the problems you might have trying to build a robot that could catch a ball. Assume that the throw is not always accurate so that the ball does not always land in the same place.

Specification for a control system

The specification for a control system is an outline of what the control system must be able to do. The control system is designed to meet this specification.

The specification includes such things as:

Input

The input is the method used to provide the system with the necessary inputs; some of the data might be input using a keyboard while other data might be obtained automatically using sensors.

Tolerances

Suppose that, to secure a high product yield during a chemical reaction, the temperature of the reaction mixture needs to be kept at 70°C. This may seem a reasonable requirement, yet to maintain a precise temperature is almost impossible. It is possible, however, to keep the reaction mixture at an average temperature which moves around this average by a certain set amount. This amount is called the tolerance of the system. Taking the above example, using a thermostat and a heater we might be able to keep the temperature at 70°C ± 2°C, thus giving a maximum temperature of 72°C and a minimum temperature of 68°C.

Response

A response is an action that is taken by a system when the tolerances of the system are exceeded. For instance, a heating system thermostat which is used to keep a room at 25°C ± 2°C should keep the temperature between 23°C and 27°C. However, if someone were to leave an outside door open, the room temperature would fall rapidly, reaching well below the temperature for the heater to be turned on. Clearly, such a system would have difficulty trying to respond to such a rapid variation although after a period the required minimum temperature will be restored. The response is a good measure of how well the control system works. If the system works well, then the tolerances will be closely adhered to.

Costs

The smaller the tolerances, the more rapid the response needed and the more sophisticated the whole system, therefore the greater its cost. Generally, electronic sensors are able to react more quickly to changes in the property they are measuring than mechanical ones. Rapid, electronic sensors such as this are often very expensive; however, such sensors are much more reliable than mechanical sensors which contain moving parts that can wear or go wrong.

There are many ways in which a quantity such as temperature can be measured. Any of the following devices can be used:

- a bimetallic strip (the amount by which it bends is a measure of temperature);
- a thermocouple (two different metals welded together which give a small voltage dependent on temperature);
- a thermistor (a semiconductor whose resistance varies with temperature);
- a resistance thermometer (a piece of wire whose resistance varies with temperature).

There are many factors to consider. For instance, the choice would be determined by the temperature to be measured: you would not use the same sensor to measure the temperature of the human body that you would use for measuring the temperature inside a furnace. Sometimes, the speed of response needs to be high to cope with rapidly changing temperatures; and it is best if the output can be logged and a graph produced automatically.

Cost is usually a secondary consideration, but can enter into the choice if there are two or more suitable sensors to choose from.

Output

Ideally the output from a control system needs to maintain a certain value which is called the set point. If, for example, a heater is to keep a vat of chemicals at 100°C, then this temperature would be the set point, and the output would be the power supplied by the heater to produce the required temperature.

Type of feedback

Feedback is an important principle in all control systems and is the process by which part of the output is fed back to the input in order to regulate the operation of the system in some way. When the feedback signal reinforces the trend of the system, it is called positive feedback; when it opposes the trend of the system it is called negative feedback. Positive feedback results in increased output, whereas negative feedback results in reduced output.

Negative feedback is frequently used to stabilise systems and is used to maintain output near to a desired value. As such, it is an essential part of automation and process control.

Schematic diagrams

A schematic diagram is a picture showing a brief outline of a system with the components usually represented as shapes (rectangles, circles, etc.) rather than as their true shapes. For a control system (like the one shown in Figure 4.18), the schematic diagram needs to include the following:

- environment definition (a statement or title explaining what it is the system is designed to do)
- sensors

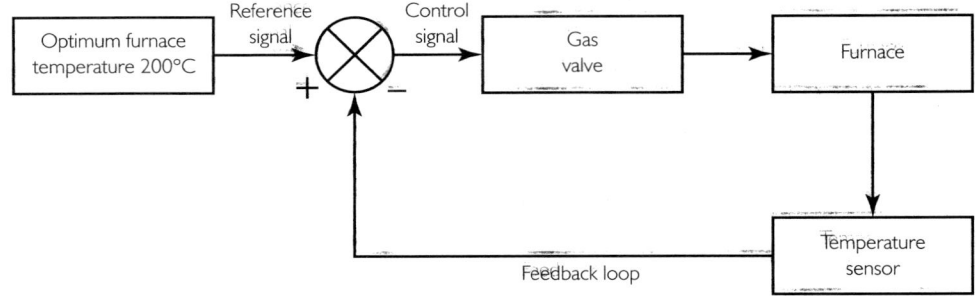

Figure 4.18 A schematic diagram for a gas furnace temperature control system

- processor
- output device
- feedback.

Control procedures

As mentioned earlier, the control procedure is a set of instructions; an algorithm or procedure for the operation of the process control system. Process control procedures consist of the following building blocks.

Input
There are many different variables involved in industrial processes, such as fluid pressure, temperature, flow rate, etc. These variables must be converted into electronic signals which can be used as input to the controller; part of the signal might be used as a feedback signal.

Feedback
The way in which feedback works is detailed on page 139.

Decision
Decisions are made by the controller or processor. A decision is made when the variable value is compared with the desired value and the difference, called the error signal, generated. The system then produces a feedback signal that will reduce the error towards zero.

Process
The feedback signal is used to alter the process that is being controlled. An example of this is in controlling the opening and closing of a valve. The feedback signal determines the correct opening of the valve.

Output device
There is a wide range of output devices. In industrial process control systems output devices may include valve actuators or the movement of heavy machinery using hydraulics, as well as more familiar output devices such as electric motors, heaters, etc.

Testing a process control system

Once an industrial control system has been developed it needs to be tested to make sure that it works according to the original specifications. If the system does not work as the specification demands it will be necessary to make certain adjustments to either (or both) the control procedure or the sensitivity of the sensors.

If these adjustments do not remedy the situation it may be necessary to consider using different sensors.

Activity 4.18

The human body has a control system which keeps the body at a more or less constant temperature.
1 What is this temperature?
2 Explain the process by which the temperature of the human body is kept constant. Think about what happens when you are cold as well as hot.

A dog has a different mechanism by which its temperature is controlled. Explain the mechanism by which a dog's temperature is controlled.

Effectiveness of a control system

As with a model or simulation, the effectiveness of a process control system can be judged by considering the following:
- comparative cost
- speed of response
- accuracy
- comparison with alternatives
- efficiency.

For more details, look at the same section in the first part of this chapter which covered models.

Suggestions for improvement

Any system can be improved by the use of more advanced technology, more time and more money. At the end of the development of a control system it is important to test the system, see if there is any room for improvement and make the necessary adjustments. Improvements frequently fall under the following headings.

Change in feedback
There are two main feedback methods: positive and negative. In addition, there are many different ways in which the feedback signal can be compared with the input or reference signal and different methods may be tried.

Use of different devices
Sometimes, more accurate control can be achieved by using different input or output devices. For example, a proximity sensor can detect whether or not something is near but a video sensor is a better choice if accurate positioning is needed; it will, however, be a lot more expensive.

Alteration of sensitivity

The specification obtained from suppliers will outline the capabilities of particular sensors. The required level of sensitivity can be obtained by selecting an appropriate sensor.

Modification to the software

If you have written software specifically for a task it will be possible to alter it in some way by, for example, adjusting the frequency at which the sensors take readings, or by altering the output.

Examples of control systems

In this section we will look at a variety of simple and more complicated controlled systems and also at some case studies where a variety of systems is in use.

Control systems used in video recorders

A video recorder contains many control systems. There are, for example, sensors used to detect the end of the tape and stop it from moving once the end is reached, thus preventing physical damage to the tape. The mechanism works via a light bulb on one side of the tape and a light sensor on the other, with the tape in between. A segment at each end of the tape is transparent, rather than the brown colour of the magnetised sections. Light cannot pass through the brown section so the sensor detects no light until the clear section is reached when the light from the bulb reaches the sensor and the motors rotating the tape are instructed to stop. Figure 4.19 shows the arrangement.

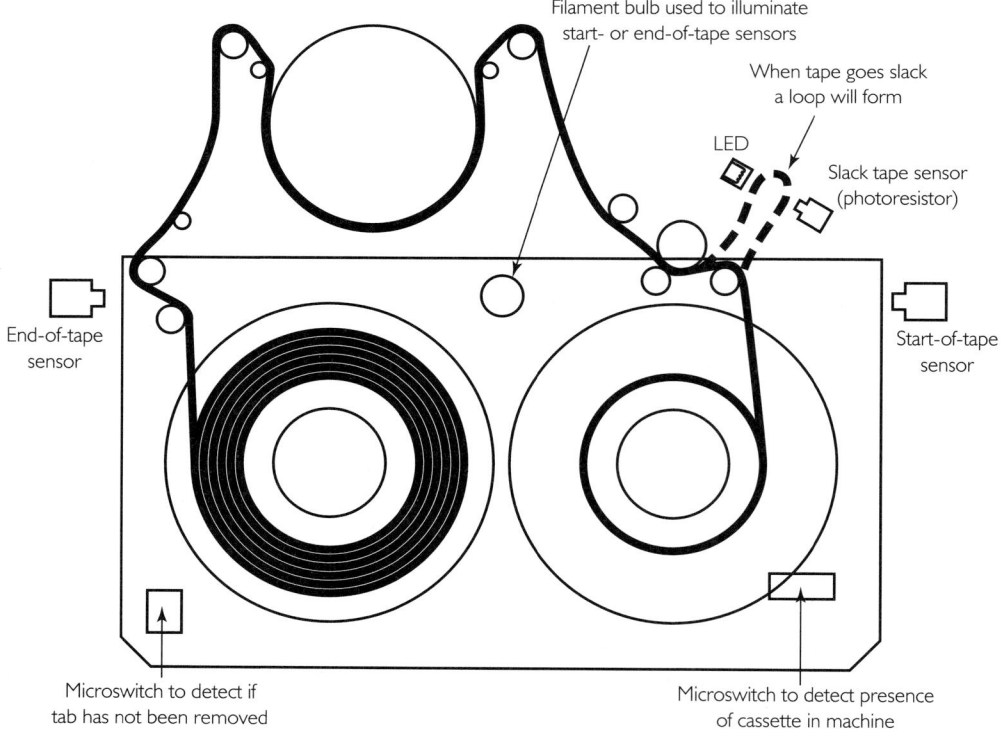

Figure 4.19 The various control systems in a video cassette recorder (VCR)

Another sensor, called a slack sensor, is used to detect whether the tape has gone slack, usually meaning either that the tape has broken or that there is something wrong with the tape transport mechanism. Either way the tape must be stopped immediately to prevent further damage to the tape, machine or both. The slack sensor works by using a light emitting diode (LED) which shines on the surface of a phototransistor (a sensor used to detect light); if a loop of tape comes between them, light will not be detected by the phototransistor and the video recorder stops. Some older video recorders use a different system for detecting slack and use instead an arm containing a bar magnet. When the tape goes slack, the arm moves down and the pivot action moves the magnet near to a reed switch which turns off the tape drive. Figure 4.20 shows this older method.

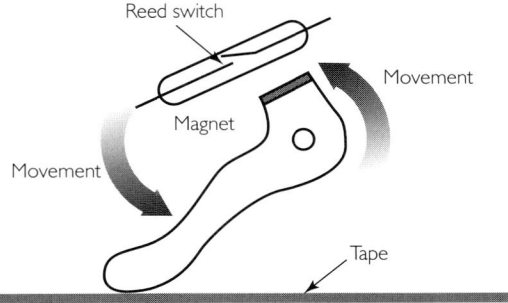

Figure 4.20 An older method for the detecting slack in the tape

Other sensors include microswitches (a form of proximity sensor) which detect the presence of a video cassette in the recorder and prevent the recorder from starting without a video inserted. Another such switch senses whether the video cassette has had its tab removed to prevent the tape being recorded over.

Airbus Industrie case study

Airbus Industrie is a company set up jointly by aircraft manufacturers in different European countries, with Britain, France, Germany and Spain the major partners and The Netherlands and Belgium as minor partners.

In this case study we will not be looking at the partnership itself but at the final product: the aircraft that the company produces. Passenger aircraft produced by Airbus are among the most up-to-date passenger aircraft in the world, incorporating all the latest computer control technology to eliminate pilot error (which is known to be the cause of around 75 per cent of all accidents).

There are seven airliners in the current range, the smallest being the A319 with around 124 seats and the largest the A340, which has 232 seats (Figure 4.21).

Fly-by-wire systems

In older aircraft the pilot would use a variety of controls, such as the joystick and thrust levers, the movement of which was transferred through a variety of mechanical linkages, levers and hydraulics to the parts of the plane that actually move, such as the control surfaces on the wings and tail. The pilot was solely in control of the settings to be made, and this could cause problems because so much depended on the skill of the pilot.

Figure 4.21 The Airbus A340, a four-engined, long haul passenger airliner

Figure 4.22 shows the moving surfaces on the wings and tail, the hydraulic jacks which move these surfaces and the wires along which the electronic signals are sent to control the jacks.

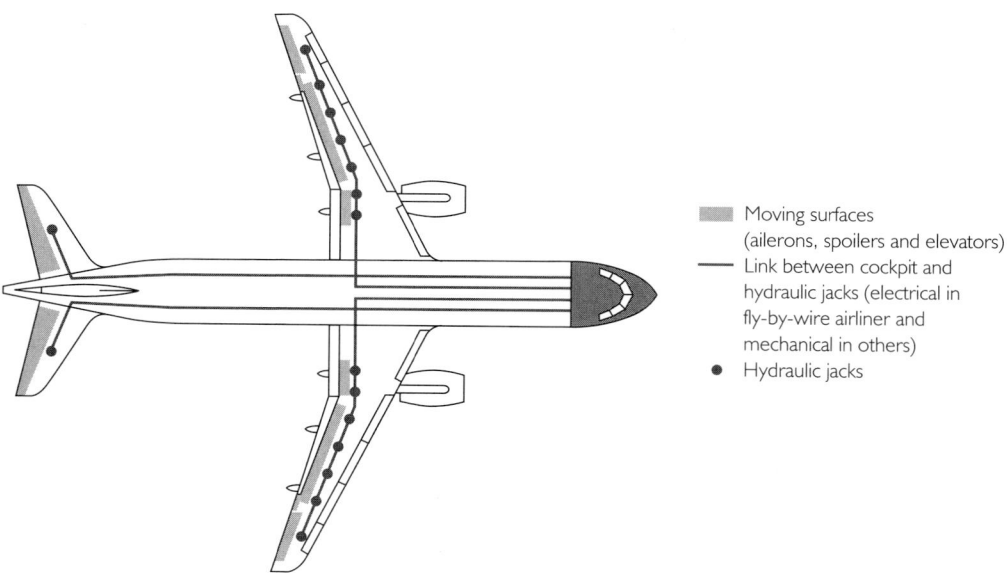

Moving surfaces
(ailerons, spoilers and elevators)
Link between cockpit and
hydraulic jacks (electrical in
fly-by-wire airliner and
mechanical in others)
Hydraulic jacks

Figure 4.22 Diagram of a typical plane showing the moving surfaces on the wings and tail

Fly-by-wire uses control from the pilot, but in this case it is sensed electronically and fed along wires to a computer where the signals from the pilot are mixed with stabilising signals from motion sensors. It is this mixed output signal that passes to actuators which work the moving parts on the wings, tail, etc. While computer and pilot normally act in partnership, if necessary the plane could take off and land entirely by computer.

The safety of such an aircraft, its crew and passengers, now relies entirely on the electronic fly-by-wire system.

For safety reasons there are two pilots on all but the smallest passenger aircraft. Pilot and co-pilot each have a set of controls and can take over control at any time, since the two sets of controls are mechanically linked. With a mechanical system, in theory, if the captain were to decide that the plane should turn one way but the co-pilot thought that it should turn the other way, then the person with the stronger pull on the controls would win. (In practice, of course, procedures do not allow this to happen.) With the fly-by-wire system, the system would decide which pilot had given it the most sensible command and take that course. One of the best features of this system is that the computer system will ignore any dangerous demands made by the pilot which might, for instance, cause the aircraft to stall or put too great a strain on the structure of the plane.

The fly-by-wire system has changed the whole appearance of the flight deck, because so many of the dials on older systems have now been replaced by output on computer screens.

The Airbus 320 has five fly-by-wire computers, but the aircraft can be flown perfectly with just one of these working. As soon as one system fails the next one takes over and so on. Each of the fly-by-wire computers is actually two computers in one, with each continually monitoring the other. Another safety feature is that all the components that make up the computers are designed and manufactured by different manufacturers and are even programmed using different programming languages, so that it is practically impossible for the same fault to affect all the computers at once.

If all the fly-by-wire computers were to fail, the pilot could still fly the plane, albeit with difficulty, using back up mechanical controls which act via the trim surfaces.

Disadvantages of mechanical control

Most mechanical systems are duplicated for safety reasons and this means that the whole arrangement is heavy and difficult to maintain.

Advantages of fly-by-wire

All aircraft have their limitations. If they are flown too slowly they can stall and if they fly too fast then the stresses will be too great and the plane could break up. Although these extremes will not be encountered in normal operation, they could still happen with pilot error. The fly-by-wire system prevents such manoeuvres since if they are attempted, then the computer will detect potentially dangerous commands and prevent them from being obeyed.

Because the fly-by-wire controls are electrical they have fewer moving parts and are simpler, lighter and easier to maintain.

Disadvantages of fly-by-wire

- Fly-by-wire is more complex and therefore expensive to service.
- It will not allow safety limits to be exceeded, even in emergencies when the pilot needs to take drastic action to avoid a crash.
- There is no conclusive evidence, even after the ten years that fly-by-wire has been in use, that it makes planes significantly safer.

Activity 4.19

Explain how the control systems used in fly-by-wire aircraft make them safer than conventionally controlled aircraft.

Computer control in Formula One

Formula One (F1) car racing attracts a huge amount of money each year so it is not surprising that much of this is spent on information technology. Digital sensors are placed around each car and these continuously relay data about engine revolutions, oil temperature, gearbox information, suspension characteristics, etc. Radio signals are used to transmit this data to computers in the pits. The computer system in many F1 cars is so advanced that it could, in theory, drive a car at high speed around the track; the driver is needed only to keep the car clear of other competitors.

Features on some Formula One racing cars include:

Active suspension

Active suspension uses sensors to measure the position of a car on its suspension when on the straight or cornering. It can use the speed of the car and information about the corner being taken to adjust the hydraulics in the suspension unit. In simple terms, this determines the height of the car above the ground. On a straight the suspension alters so that the car is low, thus reducing air drag. When the car is going around corners the suspension is raised to increase the grip on the track.

Computer-controlled gear boxes

Computers are used to tell the driver the optimum time to change gear, based on the data received from sensors which detect the engine speed, the speed of the car and its position on the track.

Traction control

Traction control is used to make sure that cars do not skid because the power from the wheels is too great for the grip of the tyres on the road. Sensors are used to detect the power and the grip and if there is a risk of skidding the power is reduced until grip is established.

Launch control

Launch control uses data on the grip of the tyres and the power transmitted to the wheels from the engine to ensure a car gets away quickly from the starting grid.

W H Smith Business Supplies case study

W H Smith is a familiar name, with shops on nearly every high street in Britain. There is, however, another important part of the business, called W H Smith Business Supplies, which is the UK's largest direct supplier of business stationery. The whole business is centred around giving customers a next day delivery service and to do this the company has invested large amounts of money in using very sophisticated computers and computer-controlled equipment. The business operates from a huge warehouse using fully automated put-away systems which automatically place stock in designated places as it arrives from suppliers. There are 12 000 pallets and 1000 metres of computer-controlled carton and pallet conveying, and the whole system is the most automated in the UK.

The system at work looks like something out of a science fiction film with all the tasks performed automatically. Thousands of boxes and pallets move along conveyor belts while automatic cranes deliver or retrieve the pallets. Robotic arms are used to remove individual boxes from the line.

The warehouse control system (WCS) is able to identify at any time the exact location of any item whether in store, somewhere along the picking process or waiting to be dispatched.

The whole warehouse control system links to the ordering and stock control systems. The WCS knows the size, shape and weight of every article in stock, how many are held in stock and where each is located in the warehouse. The size, shape and weight of each item is important because, with this information, the computer can decide what size carton is needed to pack the various items making up a mixed order. It even knows how much space to allocate in the delivery vehicle and also how to load the vehicle so that goods delivered first are nearest the door.

Bulk stock is stored on shelves right up to the ceiling in about 4000 storage locations. A combination of manned and unmanned cranes put away stock when it arrives and also retrieve goods when needed. Some of the unmanned cranes travel quite fast at speeds of around 50 km/h in confined areas so staff are not allowed in such areas because of the obvious danger.

The main picking operation, where individual orders are made up, is situated in a low bay area where 'full cases' of products are picked. In this area, full cases (usually of rapid turnover products such as photocopying paper, envelopes, etc.) are labelled with the customers' names and addresses and sent to the dispatch sorter which unites them with the other parts of each customer's order. There is another area for dealing with 'split cases' where a customer has not ordered a complete case of an item. At this site, one of the three sized cartons is automatically erected according to WCS instructions and this is conveyed to one of a number of picking stations where individual items are added to the carton. This part of the order then joins the full case part of the order at the dispatch sorter. A picking list of goods is printed and added to the carton along with an advice note for the customer.

The whole warehouse system is geared to next day delivery. At present the system deals with 3000 orders per day, requiring 16 000 picks. The range of items picked is huge, from office desks to printers, pens and pencils.

Activity 4.20

1 Explain why you think W H Smith feels that it needs to have such a heavily automated system in place rather than perform all the tasks manually.
2 All the goods are measured and weighed. Explain why this is so important.
3 Frozen-food warehouses are often very similar to the above example, with few or no staff working in them. What are the main advantages of such a system in a frozen-food warehouse?

Assignment A4.2

This assignment develops knowledge and understanding of the following element:
2.4 Develop a control system

It supports the development of the following key skills:
Communication 3.2 and 3.3
Information technology 3.1, 3.2, 3.3 and 3.4

For this assignment you are required to develop a control system and procedure either using the actual components connected to the computer or by making use of special software that allows you to simulate a control system. You should consult your tutor who will advise you on the resources available.

Your tutor will give you the control system specification which you should study carefully before attempting the rest of the assignment.

Your control system should be reasonably sophisticated and include a minimum of two sensors and two types of output device.

You should provide the following evidence as part of your portfolio:
- a schematic diagram;
- an outline of what the system is designed to do;
- a specification for the system;
- a list of the components which meet the specification used in the system along with reasons for their choice;
- evidence that the system has been thoroughly tested;
- suggestions for possible improvements in the system.

Assignment A4.3

This assignment develops knowledge and understanding of the following element:
2.4 Develop a control system

It supports the development of the following key skills:
Communication 3.2, 3.3 and 3.4
Information technology 3.1, 3.2, 3.3 and 3.4

There is a variety of different control systems which broadly fall into the following categories:
- environmental control
- process production control
- quality control
- security
- transport
- robotic production systems.

For this assignment you are required to research six systems, one for each of the categories. For each system you are required to find out the following:

- a broad outline of what the system does;
- the types of sensors used by the system;
- a brief description of the control procedure (this could be a description or by using pseudocode);
- a comparison of the effectiveness of the system with alternative methods of control.

You are free to choose your own systems using any research material (the Internet, CD-ROMs, specialist books and magazines).

If you have trouble finding suitable systems to investigate, here are a few to help you.

- television remote controls
- automatic door opening systems
- rail ticket machines
- drinks machines
- garage door opening systems
- car park systems
- security alarm systems
- central heating systems
- greenhouse environment control systems.

Sample unit test

Questions 1–4 refer to the following list of reasons for producing models:

- **a** it is cheaper
- **b** it can be done in a shorter time period
- **c** it is safer to use a model
- **d** it is more convenient to use a model

1 Flight simulators are used to train pilots to deal with emergency situations. What is the main reason for this?

2 The aerodynamics of a new car can be tested in an air tunnel. Alternatively, computer models can be constructed. What is the main reason for this?

3 Weather forecasts are produced by first constructing a model of the weather based on data obtained from many weather stations. Why is a model used in this situation?

4 Many company managers and directors use computer models to simulate the running of their business. What is the main reason for this?

5 Which one of the following may *not* be used as a criterion when assessing the effectiveness of a computer model?
- **a** the cost of the model compared with other alternatives
- **b** the speed of the model compared with other alternatives
- **c** the accuracy of the model compared with other alternatives
- **d** the choice of software used

6 Which one of the following is *not* an example of environmental control?
- **a** a system which monitors and controls the humidity (moisture content) of the air in an art gallery containing expensive works of art
- **b** an air-conditioning system used in an office

    c a system used to maintain the ideal growing conditions for plants in a greenhouse

    d a system called ABS used by cars to control the braking process

7 A system used to monitor the weight of the crisps placed in packets in a factory is an example of:

    a a quality control system

    b a process production control system

    c a security control system

    d a robot production system

8 Street lights come on automatically when the light level falls below a certain value. What would be the most appropriate sensor to use in the lights?

    a a light sensor

    b a video sensor

    c a pH sensor

    d a position sensor

9 Which one of the following may *not* be considered to be an output device?

    a stepper motor

    b loudspeaker

    c electric motor

    d push switch

Questions 10–12 refer to the information in Figure 4.23.

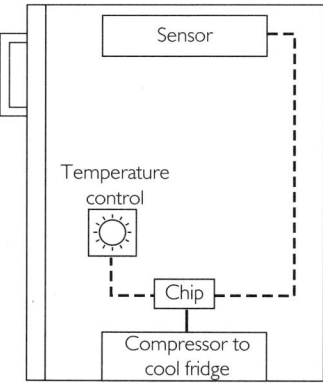

Figure 4.23

10 The quantity measured by the sensor is:

    a pressure

    b light

    c temperature

    d ice

11 When the door of the refrigerator is opened, a light comes on. What input device causes this to happen?

    a a temperature sensor

    b a light sensor

    c a push switch

    d a humidity sensor

12 The refrigerator makes use of feedback. The purpose of feedback is to:
  a reduce the amount of energy used by the refrigerator
  b inform the chip when the door is opened
  c send temperature data from the sensor back to the chip so that the compressor can be turned on or off
  d allow the chip to alter the temperature control

Questions 13–16 relate to the information below.
  A small computer shop sets up the spreadsheet In Figure 4.24. The user has to input the sales of various types of computer for the particular week shown.

	A	B	C	D	E	F
1	Sales for week ending 19/12/97					
2		Sales	Unit price	VAT	Price inc. VAT	Total value of sales
3	Pentium 166	12	£799	£139.83	£938.83	£11,265.96
4	Pentium 200	8	£999	£174.83	£1,173.83	£9,390.64
5	Pentium Pro 200	10	£1,200	£210	£1,410.00	£14,100.00
6	Pentium Pro II 233	7	£1,499	£262.33	£1,761.33	£12,329.31
7						
8	Rate of VAT	17.50%				£47,085.91
9						

Figure 4.24

13 Which one of the following is the main purpose of the spreadsheet?
  a to enable the manager of the shop to produce invoices for customers
  b to see the effect of changes made to the VAT rate
  c to enable the manager to see the sales values of Pentiums for that week
  d to provide a prediction for the following week's sales

14 The VAT rate contained in cell B8 is best described as a:
  a variable
  b constant
  c operator
  d formula

15 In the Budget, the Chancellor decides to increase the rate of VAT to 20%. The number in cell B8 is altered to take account of this change. Which of the following happens?
  a the data in all the columns changes
  b the data in only columns D, E and F changes
  c the data in only columns E and F changes
  d only the contents of cell B8 change

16 In which cells will there be a formula which uses the arithmetic operator * (multiplication)?
  a D3 and F3
  b B3 and C3
  c C3 and D3
  d C3 and E3

17 A warehouse system uses a weight-checking system to make sure that robots have packed all the ordered goods in a parcel. In which ways should the system be tested?

1 with an underweight parcel
2 with a parcel having the correct weight
3 with an overweight parcel

   a 1 and 2 only
   b 2 and 3 only
   c 1 and 3 only
   d 1, 2 and 3

18 Flight simulation software can be used to help train airline pilots because:
   a a simulation is better than the real thing
   b it is safer and cheaper to use a flight simulator
   c pilots need to be familiar with the use of computers
   d using a fly-by-wire system, the pilot no longer flies the plane

19 The diagram in Figure 4.25 shows boxes in a parcel distribution centre. They can take one of two paths to two different delivery bays where they will be put on lorries going to different parts of the country. What is the purpose of the barcode reader?
   a to provide feedback
   b as an output device
   c as an input device
   d as a processor used to decide which route to take

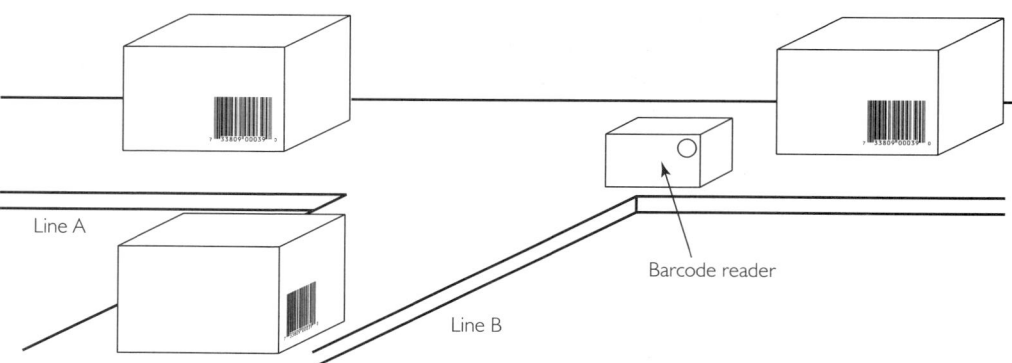

Line A

Barcode reader

Line B

Figure 4.25

Questions 20–22 refer to the diagram shown in Figure 4.26.

20 The greenhouse shown in Figure 4.26 maintains steady conditions which are essential for optimising the growth of young plants. Such a system uses which type of control?
   a stock control
   b environmental control
   c quality control
   d project control

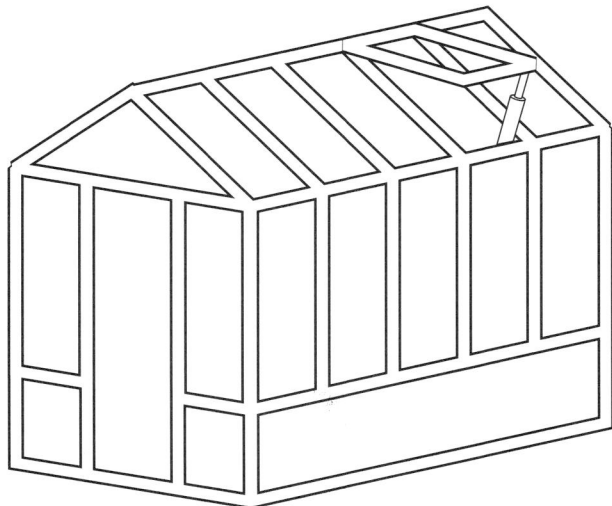

Figure 4.26

21 Which of the following sensors are most likely to be used as input devices in the greenhouse?

   a temperature and humidity

   b light and sound

   c proximity and temperature

   d position and humidity

22 When the temperature inside the greenhouse is too high a vent is opened. If the air or soil is too dry then an automatic sprinkler system starts up. If the moisture content is too high, then a vent will open to ventilate and dry the air. Which output devices will be needed to do the above?

   a actuators

   b heaters

   c lamps

   d fans

23 When you change the default drive of your computer from the hard drive to the floppy drive and there is no disk in the drive, an error is reported. This is an example of:

   a processing

   b feedback

   c fly-by-wire

   d a thermocouple

Questions 24 and 25 refer to the information in Figure 4.27.

24 Which one of the following is the purpose of the electronic scales shown in Figure 4.27?

   a quality control

   b temperature measurement

   c counting system

   d humidity measurement

(RSA, June 1996)

25 Which one of the following is the purpose of the infrared transmitter and reflector system?
   a quality control
   b temperature measurement
   c counting system
   d humidity measurement   *(RSA, June 1996)*

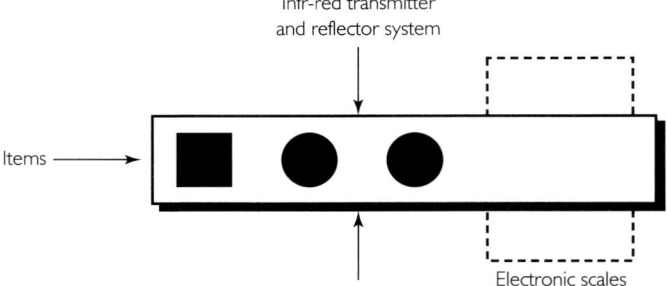

Figure 4.27

Questions 26 and 27 refer to the information in Figure 4.28.

26 Which one of the following is the feedback loop?
   a W
   b X
   c Y
   d Z   *(RSA, June 1996)*

27 Which one of the following is the reference signal?
   a W
   b X
   c Y
   d Z   *(RSA, June 1996)*

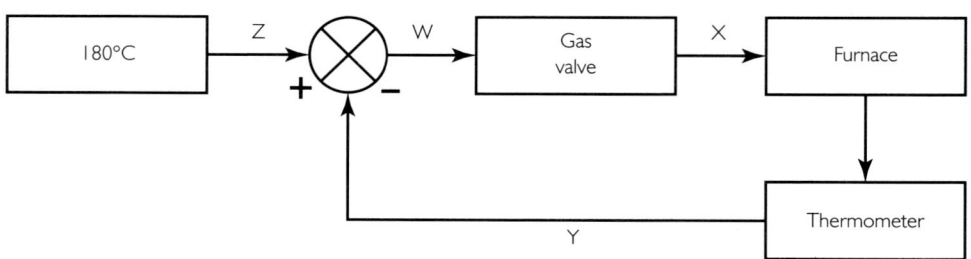

Figure 4.28

28 Only people aged 16 to 21 are to be interviewed in a market research survey. Which one of the following data parameters does this determine?
   a input values
   b formulae
   c constraints
   d variables   *(RSA, June 1996)*

29 A predictive model is required to calculate profit margins for a company financial forecast. Which one of the following data parameters performs the calculations?
  a input values
  b formulae
  c constraints
  d variables   *(RSA, June 1996)*

30 A spreadsheet can be used in financial management to model cashflow, and perform 'what if' projections. Which one of the following does a 'what if' projection provide?
  a a list of variables used
  b the effect of variable changes
  c a record of past expenditure
  d a report of constraints used   *(RSA, June 1996)*

31 Which one of the following could be determined using the information shown in Figure 4.29?
  a lifespan
  b effectiveness
  c dimensions
  d flexibility   *(RSA, June 1996)*

Price	Accuracy	Efficiency	Speed
£325	+/- 0.5%	1mA	0.5 s FSD

Figure 4.29 Product specifications of a prototype pressure sensor, in comparison with alternative sensors, when installed in a chemical reaction bath

32 Which one of the following types of information technology model would be chosen by a hydroelectric power company wanting to forecast upstream water pressure?
  a analytical
  b simulation
  c prediction
  d gaming   *(RSA, June 1996)*

33 In order to keep an office at a nearly constant temperature, a certain measurement and control device is used. Which one of the following devices would be the most suitable?
  a a thermometer
  b a thermostat
  c a solar cell
  d a light-emitting diode

34 Some garages have doors that open and shut automatically. Which one of the following measurement and control devices would be best suited for this purpose?
  a an infrared transmitter/receiver
  b a light beam and light sensor
  c a solar cell
  d a sound sensor

35 Which one of the following would *not* be a suitable application of virtual reality?

   a kitchen design, allowing customers to see what the units, wall tiles, etc. would look like in their own kitchen

   b seeing what a new shop front would look like in a high street

   c teaching aircraft engineers how to dismantle a jet engine

   d working out the quantity of a new product that needs to be sold before break-even is achieved

36 A robot is used in a warehouse for transporting goods from one place to another. Sometimes boxes can fall into the path of the robot and the robot needs to be able to sense this to avoid a collision. Which one of the following sensors is the most suitable for this purpose?

   a a contact sensor

   b a proximity sensor

   c a position sensor

   d a humidity sensor

5 The flow of information in organisations

What is covered in this chapter

Element 3.1: Investigate the flow of information in organisations

- Types of organisation
- Ways in which organisations are structured
- Forms of information
- Types of information
- Functions within organisations

Resources you will need for your portfolio for Elements 3.1

- Your written answers to the activities and assignments in this chapter.

To appreciate the relevance and use of information technology it is essential to understand the concept of an organisation and its operation. It is also important to look at the various functions within an organisation and any external factors that influence the way the organisation is set up or run. It is possible to look at the information flow between functions, both within the organisation and to and from external bodies.

Types of organisation

Organisations can be grouped under three headings: commercial, industrial and public.

Commercial organisations

The prime function of a commercial organisation is the purchase and sale of goods and services. A shop, for instance, buys goods from its suppliers, adds its profit and sells the goods on to the public. Some shops do not deal with a manufacturer direct but instead buy through a wholesaler. The wholesaler, like the shop, adds its profit to the goods it buys before selling them on to the wholesaler and so is also a commercial organisation.

Commercial organisations are not just those organisations that sell goods for profit. Many commercial organisations sell a service. For instance, a private nursing home sells care facilities, food and accommodation to its residents. A bank will sell banking facilities to its customers. The banks' profits are obtained from the bank charges, loan and overdraft interest that they levy on their customers.

Industrial organisations

The prime function of a commercial organisation is the manufacture of products, the processing of raw materials or construction. So the main feature of such an organisation is that it makes something from something else.

For example, Imperial Chemical Industries (ICI) mines rock salt in Cheshire. The raw material is processed by having all the rock and sand removed from it before being sold to customers for a variety of uses. ICI is therefore an industrial organisation. Salt is also used by ICI in the manufacture of sodium hydroxide, another important chemical. Sodium hydroxide is bought from ICI by Unilever and used along with oil or fat to produce soap. Unilever, which makes soap, is another industrial organisation.

Many industrial organisations make things up from components supplied from other industrial organisations. Car manufacturers such as Ford, household appliance manufacturers such as Hotpoint and computer manufacturers such as IBM are all examples of industrial organisations.

Public service organisations

The prime aim of public service organisations is to provide services and goods from public funds. They do not have making a profit as a primary aim, although many of them do aim to be profitable. However, their main aim is to obtain the maximum benefits for the public they serve. This means that they are under constant pressure to keep their costs down while providing a good service. Like other kinds of organisation, they have turned to information technology to help them perform their work in the most efficient manner.

Activities 5.1

Task 1

Each of the following organisations can be classed as commercial, industrial or public service. Construct a table with a column for each of the three classes. Then fill in the table by putting each of the organisations in the correct column.

- oil company
- building society
- stockbroker
- local area health authority
- college
- dating agency
- computer manufacturer
- supermarket
- garage
- private nursing home
- quarry
- coal mine
- bank
- Department of Social Security
- car manufacturer
- council tax department
- insurance company
- insurance broker

Task 2

Draw a similar table to that drawn in Task 1, and this time place each of the following organisations into the most appropriate column.

- Sainsburys
- H P Bulmer (cider-makers)
- Liverpool Area Health Authority
- Driver and Vehicle Licensing Authority (DVLA)
- Esso (an oil company)
- The Ford Motor Company
- Manchester Airport
- Halifax PLC
- British Airways
- Metropolitan Borough of Sefton Education Department
- IBM (a computer manufacturer)
- GLAXO (a pharmaceuticals company)
- City of Liverpool Community College (a college of further education)
- Direct Line Insurance
- Imperial Chemical Industries (ICI)

Ways in which organisations are structured

Organisations can also be classified in another way, according to how they are structured. There are two basic groups: hierarchical organisations and flat organisations.

Hierarchical organisations

Some organisations have many levels and grades of staff with a tree-like management structure and strong patterns of vertical communication. This means that there are many different grades of staff between people lower down the organisation and the person at the top. This kind of structure can be represented as a triangle, with a greater number of staff in the lower tiers and gradually fewer towards the top, more senior, posts. Large traditional types of company tend to have this structure, as do many government departments. Hierarchical organisations suffer from problems with bureaucracy, as information needs to be directed through the correct channels before appropriate action is taken.

The main features of such a structure are as follows:

- At each level there are several staff responsible to a person at the next level up. The process is repeated until the top of the organisation is reached.
- In a limited company the person at the top is the Managing Director who is ultimately responsible for the whole organisation.
- As the levels within the organisation are ascended, the number of people at each level decreases and this gives the organisation a pyramidal structure.

Flat organisations

In an organisation with a flat structure there are fewer levels or grades of staff and much more emphasis on communication across the organisation. This is more likely to be the structure of a small business where everyone knows each other and works together more as a team.

Examples of flat organisations would include shops and small family-run businesses. The main advantage with the flat organisation structure is that staff are able to work more on their own initiative and this brings flexibility and more creativity to their jobs.

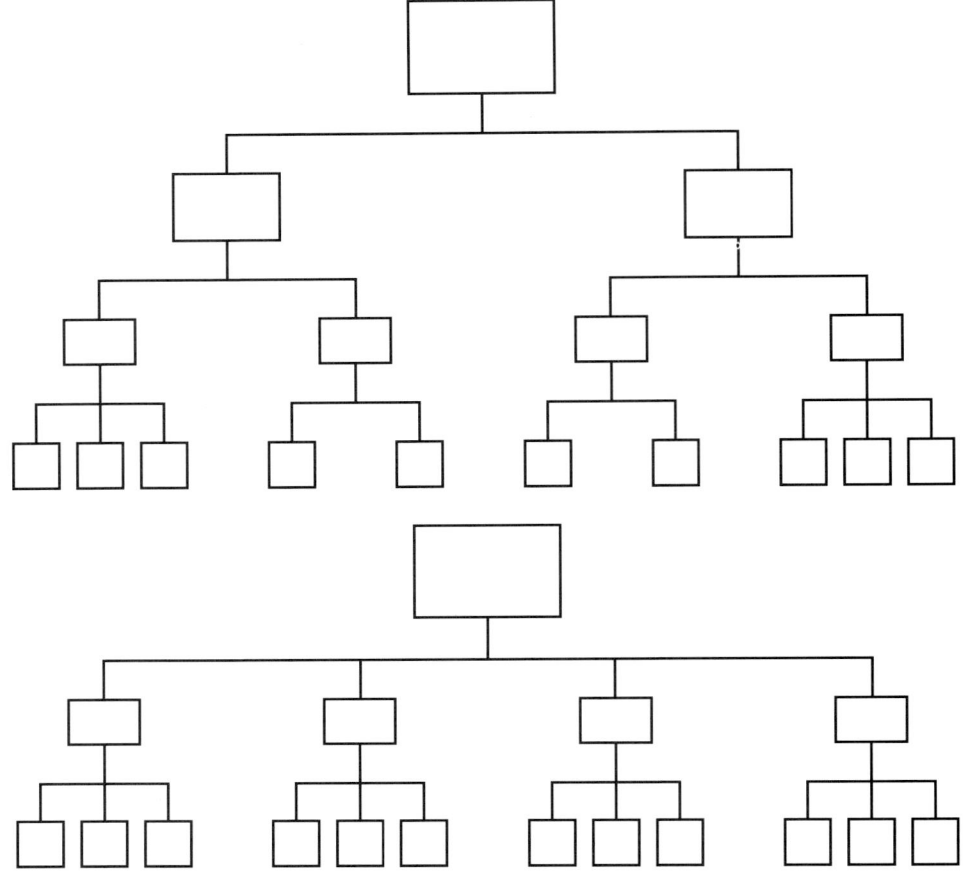

Figure 5.1 The two types of organisational structure

Drawing organisation charts

An organisation chart is a diagrammatic illustration of the structure of an organisation. Such charts show the organisation, functions, activities, posts, lines of responsibility, levels of authority, accountability, lines of communication and span of control. Some organisation charts refer to particular people and others refer to particular functions or activities within an organisation. Organisation charts can also do both, showing a name alongside a particular post. By looking at such a chart it is easy to determine a particular person's position within the organisation, who they are directly accountable to (i.e. their immediate boss), and which staff are at the same level. You can also see whether they too are responsible for a group of staff.

Organisation charts are useful aids for systems analysis: like most diagrams they present the information more concisely than is possible in words.

The steps to be taken when drawing an organisation chart are as follows:

1 Find out the name of each job and to whom the job holder reports (i.e. who their boss is). In some organisation charts you can attach a person's name to each of the jobs shown, but this has the disadvantage that staff frequently change, so in large organisations the chart will require frequent updating.

2 From the information gained in step 1, complete a table similar to the one shown on the next page.

Name of post	Responsible to

3 The person who reports to no one is obviously the boss or the person in charge of the organisation. Place a box with the name of this post (and the name of the person if required) at the top of the page.

4 Find out from the table in step 2, the names of the posts who report to the person in step 3 and add them one level lower down.

Example
Look at the table below and the organisation chart that was constructed using it.

Name of post	Responsible to
Costing Supervisor	Chief Accountant
Managing Director	
Chief Accountant	Financial Director
Management Information Services Manager	Financial Director
Production Supervisor	Production Manager
Sales and Marketing Director	Managing Director
Transport Manager	Production Director
Office Manager	Chief Administrator
Senior Wages Clerk	Chief Accountant
Head of Planning	Production Director
Sales Engineer	Head of Marketing
Sales and Marketing Manager	Head of Marketing
Chief Administrator	Financial Director
Production Director	Managing Director
Production Manager	Production Director
Head of Marketing	Sales and Marketing Director
Financial Director	Managing Director
Sales Admin Supervisor	Sales and Marketing Manager and Sales Engineer

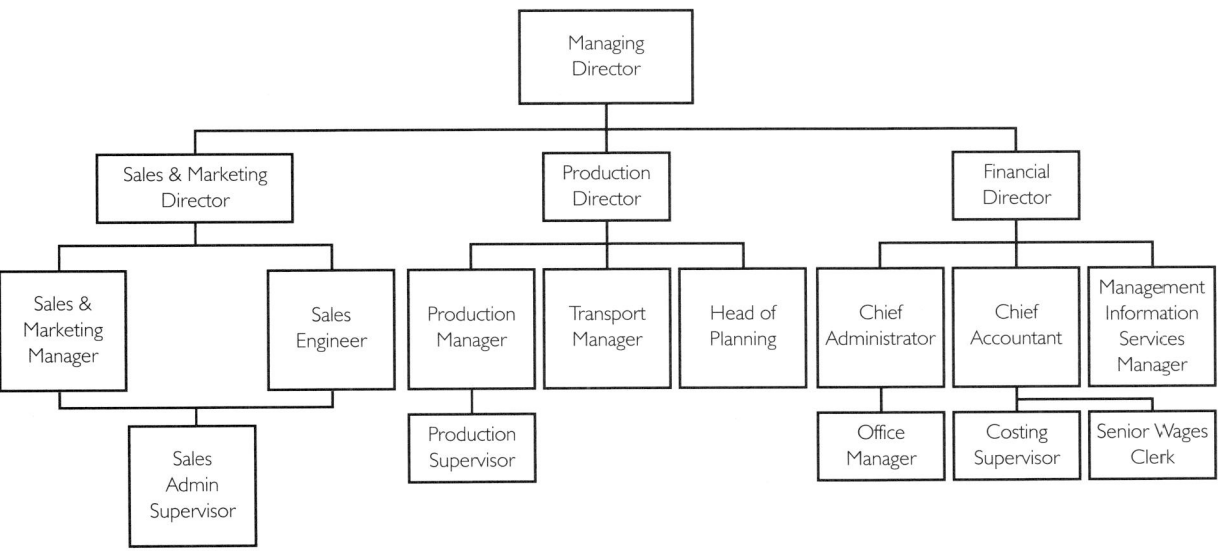

Figure 5.2 Example of an organisation chart

Activity 5.2

Using the following table, produce an organisation chart to show the relationships of the various members of the senior management team in the computing department at Tesco.

Choose suitable software and explain reasons for your choice. You may find that a graphics package such as Powerpoint (in the Microsoft Office suite of programs) has a special template for the production of organisation charts.

Position	Reports to
Retail New Technology Manager	Divisional Director, Computer Systems Development
Divisional Director, Computer Systems Development	Director of Computing
Retail Systems Manager	Divisional Director, Computer Systems Manager
Project support Manager	Divisional Director, Computer Services
Technical support Manager	Divisional Director, Computer Services
Commercial and Estates Manager	Divisional Director, Computer Systems Development
Service Initiatives Manager	Divisional Director, Computer Services
Operations Manager	Divisional Director, Computer Services
Contracts Manager	Divisional Director, Computer Services
Finance and Personal Systems Manager	Divisional Director, Computer Systems Development
Project Support Manager	Divisional Director, Computer Systems Development
Stock Control and Distribution Manager	Divisional Director, Computer Systems Development
Divisional Director, Computer Services	Director of Computing

Forms of information

Information comes into an organisation and flows around it in a variety of forms. These may be summarised as verbal, written and electronic.

Verbal information

Verbal information would include 'face-to-face' and telephone conversations either in real time or recorded using an answering machine; it would also include using the voice mail facility which is available on newer PCs. Although verbal information is usually obtained quickly it often needs to be backed up by some form of documentation. For example, if you want to book a last-minute holiday, you can look at teletext on the television, select one of the many holiday companies offering last minute deals and ring them up to check availability. You can then book, quoting your credit card details over the phone, but the company you choose will still send you a receipt and, if there is time, tickets. The strength of this system is the fact that it is fast, but misunderstandings can take place and, unless the telephone conversations are recorded (which they frequently are), there is little evidence to back up either side in a dispute.

This type of system is very popular now and is used by many catalogue, direct insurance, direct holiday and direct mortgage/banking companies.

Documentary information

Under this heading we will be talking only about paper documents; 'documents' passed in electronic form will be dealt with below. Most companies try to reduce the amount of paperwork to a minimum but it is very difficult to eliminate it completely, as customers' suppliers and other outside agencies may have no facilities for dealing with electronic mail (e-mail), EDI (electronic data interchange), etc.

Paper documents (letters, brochures, price lists, memorandums, contracts, invoices, etc.) are used throughout society as the main medium for the transmission of business information between organisations and between organisations and the public.

Electronic information

Information can be passed from one place to another in electronic form. For instance, a stock list can be sent on disk to all the branches of a shop. A more streamlined way would be to transfer the data over the telephone lines electronically, using computers and modems. Many organisations now network their computers so that the need to transfer data via floppy disks is avoided. Nearly all networks have an e-mail facility and this is used to send documents in electronic form around a company. Widespread use of e-mail for external mail is restricted because not everyone is a subscriber to e-mail systems. Electronic data interchange (EDI) allows companies to place orders and make payments to their suppliers, without the need for any paperwork to be produced.

Activity 5.3

Which form of information (verbal, documentary, electronic) best describes each of the following?
- a telephone conversation
- a pick list to be given to warehouse staff
- a memo sent using e-mail
- payment made for goods using a debit card such as Switch
- an answerphone message
- a curriculum vitae (CV) sent using e-mail to a potential employer
- invitations to a party sent by post
- a voice mail message
- a discussion at a meeting
- minutes of a meeting written in shorthand
- a requisition slip
- the winning lottery numbers obtained from the TV using teletext.

Types of information

The types of information used within a company depend ultimately on the nature of the business, but most businesses use at least some of the following types of information.

Sales information

Most companies have a sales department where either goods or services are sold and records kept of these sales. In many cases, customers will be given credit so there is a certain period between the receipt of goods or services and having to pay for them. The value of goods a customer is allowed to receive without prior payment is called that customer's credit limit. When customers place orders they can do so in a variety of ways. Sometimes they use their own order forms; at other times they use one provided by the supplier. In many cases orders are made over the telephone or even using the Internet. Some companies use a service called EDI through which one computer places orders directly to another computer with no corresponding paperwork.

A sale usually takes place as follows:

1 the customer places an order for goods or services;
2 the goods or services are supplied;
3 the customer is invoiced (an invoice is a request for payment);
4 the customer makes payment.

In a perfect world, once an invoice is received, the customer will make payment for the correct amount without further requests. It is, however, often necessary to generate further requests for payment. The letters generated by the system become more severe and threatening as more time elapses. Take, for example, an electricity bill: the first bill is usually printed blue, the second one red and there are a couple more after this before the supply is cut off. In addition to non-payment, all sorts of other problems can occur. For instance customers can send the wrong amount or they may send goods back and require refunds.

Sometimes, if an order is made and no invoice produced, a receipt is given to record the transaction. This is often the situation where goods are ordered over the telephone using a credit card. Another example of this is when a purchase is made from a 'catalogue shop' such as Index or Argos. With this system the the customer looks through a catalogue and writes down the catalogue number and price of the goods. This is taken to the point-of-sale terminal where the details are entered, payment is made and a receipt issued. Finally the receipt is presented at a storage area where the goods are collected.

Activity 5.4

Investigate two different systems for dealing with sales of goods or services with which you come into contact in your everyday life. In particular you may like to base your investigations on the following systems.
- the system used by a retailer who uses a catalogue to advertise goods, such as Index or Argos;
- the system used for payment of petrol at a petrol station;
- the system used for booking a holiday at a travel agent;
- the system used when buying a ticket at a railway station;
- the system used for buying a meal at a self-service 'burger bar' restaurant.

In your investigation you need to consider the following:
- the forms of information used in the system (verbal, documents and electronic);
- how information is passed from one place to another. (You could draw a simple diagram to show this along with a brief explanation of your drawing.)

Purchase information

Some organisations, such as retailers, purchase goods from suppliers to which they add their profit when re-selling to someone else. All companies must purchase goods or services from other organisations, if only basic services such as water, electricity and gas. In addition nearly all companies buy stationery, office furniture, cleaning and toilet supplies and so on. In companies purchasing departments can be huge. Take for example all the equipment and services needed by the armed services. A whole civil service department deals with this. Manufacturing companies usually have their own purchasing departments where raw materials are ordered.

As well as making sure that orders go out, it is also necessary to keep track of goods received and to check invoices for these against the original orders before payments are made. It is quite common in industry for an order to be only partly fulfilled, and this makes keeping track of the purchases more complicated.

Market information

It is important for companies to match the supply of goods with the demand for them. For instance, a car manufacturer needs to know how many cars have been sold at certain times of the year in previous years so that the production can be matched to likely demand.

Marketing information is used to plan marketing initiatives which increase consumer awareness, increase the company's market share, devise new pricing strategies and direct development of new products.

Market information also includes details about competitors and their products. It is useful to know whether rivals are offering special promotions (such as 'buy one get one free') since companies may do this to encourage customers to buy their products. Such offers are often used as a way of increasing brand awareness and may increase a company's share of the market. Companies may react to market information and decide to reduce the prices of their products in a similar way to their competitors, or offer a special deal, to ensure that they maintain their market share.

It is also important to make sure that the goods or services provided are what customers actually want. Market information includes details of customer opinions obtained by talking to customers and/or getting them to complete questionnaires. Such information can be processed by computer to give valuable market knowledge.

Sources of market information include such things as the volume of sales for a certain item over a period of time or the motives and attitudes of consumers and why they behave in certain ways.

Design specification

A design specification is a document which specifies the preset company rules and statutory regulations that govern the manufacture of the goods being produced. It also ensures that the goods are manufactured in accordance with the customer's wishes. It is hard to generalise about what should be present in a design specification since its details depend on the nature of the goods being made. It would usually involve the following information: materials from which the goods are to be made, tolerances, special finishes, sizes and colours.

Operational information

Operational information relates to the internal workings of an organisation. Examples of operational information include such things as instructions, decisions, responsibilities, holiday dates and times of opening.

Customer information

Most organisations hold information about their customers, including some or all of the following:

- name of company
- invoice address
- delivery address
- contact name (often this is someone in the purchasing department)
- credit limit
- average value of order
- main products ordered.

Supplier information

Organisations also need information to place orders with their suppliers:
- name of supplier
- invoice address
- delivery address
- contact name (usually this is someone in the sales department)
- credit limit.

Activity 5.5

An organisation uses many different documents to cope with the day-to-day running of the business. Your task is to identify the different situations which could give rise to each of the following documents:
- quotations
- requisitions
- invoices
- orders
- statements
- delivery notes
- credit notes
- expense claim forms.

Functions within organisations

The functions within an organisation relate to broad areas of activity which must be carried out in order to achieve the objectives of the organisation. A study of any organisation will reveal that it is divided into certain functions such as finance, marketing, personnel, operations, purchasing, design and sales.

Functions can be classed as either internal or external.

Internal functions

Internal functions are distinct areas into which an organisation can be divided. These functions obviously vary depending on the type of organisation, with some functions appearing only in certain organisations.

Finance

The finance department (sometimes called the accounts department) is responsible for all financial records. This involves logging all money coming into and going out of a business, either manually or by computer. The finance function also covers the payment of wages and pension contributions, the collection of tax and National Insurance contributions and making sure that legal requirements for collection are adhered to. Finance departments also set up departmental budgets and make sure that managers do not overspend.

Marketing

The marketing function is the process of identifying, anticipating and satisfying customer requirements profitably. Marketing does not apply just to goods: it is equally relevant to services, so, for instance, your school or college will need to do a certain amount of marketing to attract students. Large companies have a separate marketing function but in smaller ones its role tends to merge with the sales function.

Personnel

Only large organisations have a separate personnel department; smaller ones tend to leave this function to individual managers rather than employing specially qualified personnel staff. The main tasks undertaken within the personnel function are the recruitment of staff, dealing with industrial relations and staff training.

Operations

Operations may be thought of as the production function in a manufacturing company. Some organisations do not have an end product, but instead provide a service. In this case the day-to-day task of providing the service is akin to the 'production' part of the business. Either way, this part is sometimes referred to as the operations function. Types of businesses which would have large operations departments include building societies and travel agents.

Purchasing

Manufacturing companies buy raw materials and components which are then processed in some way to produce finished goods. The purchasing function is a crucial one in many manufacturing companies, since the lack of one type of component could hold up a whole production line. To remain competitive, it is important for all organisations to ensure that they are buying the highest possible quality components at the cheapest possible price and to make sure that the timescale for delivery is suitable.

Whether or not they are involved in manufacturing, all organisations have a purchasing function even if it is just essential services (gas, electricity, telephone), car rental, office equipment, stationery or office space that they are buying. There needs to be a system in place for dealing with this.

Basically, the purchasing function can be broken down into the following tasks:
- finding a suitable supplier;
- establishing payment and discounts and negotiating delivery schedules/dates;
- placing an order;
- taking delivery of the order or chasing up delivery;
- checking that the goods received are the same as those ordered;
- paying the invoice.

Design

Not all organisations have a design function. If required, product design, the production of plans and drawings and the preparation of scale models are tasks that can be performed by a design department or contracted to an outside organisation. Often CAD (computer-aided design) software is used to help with design and it is possible using this software to view a two-dimensional plan in perspective without redrawing it.

Sales

The sales function of a business is the most important function, since it secures income to drive the rest of the business. The sales function aims at persuading customers to buy products or services and this involves coordinating travelling representatives, telephone sales, preparing and sending mailshots, etc. It also involves interaction with the marketing function.

External functions

There are also several external functions/entities that influence the administration of an organisation and these are dealt with below.

Supplier/customer functions

Sometimes customers or suppliers determine the administration procedures adopted by an organisation. For example, suppliers of parts for military aircraft may have to get staff to sign the Official Secrets Act as a condition of their contracts.

Legal and statutory bodies

There are various legal and statutory bodies which influence the way in which administration procedures are performed. Health and safety at work regulations govern the working environment and some working patterns. There are income tax, VAT and National Insurance requirements for ensuring that correct deductions are made and passed on to the Inland Revenue and Customs and Excise. In addition to these there are certain obligations that apply to limited companies under company law.

Activity 5.6

There are many external organisations that can affect the way a business is run.

Find out what the following organisations do, and say how they can influence the running of a business:

- Health and Safety Executive
- HM Customs and Excise
- Trading Standards Department
- Environmental Control Department of a local council.

Constructing information flow diagrams

Information flow diagrams show how information flows between the functions within an organisation and between the internal and external functions.

Consider a mail order company which supplies goods that have been bought from a series of suppliers and are then advertised and sold through a catalogue.

For the sake of simplicity we will assume the following list of functions:

- sales
- customers
- suppliers
- purchasing
- accounts
- dispatch.

When constructing information flow diagrams it is useful to adopt the following steps:

1 Consider which functional areas you are going to look at. If you are investigating a large organisation it may at first be easier to limit the diagram to a few functional areas, although it is quite difficult to isolate areas in this way. Look at the internal functions first and then see if any of them communicate with external functions in

any way. In our example, both suppliers and customers are external functions, the rest being internal functions.

2 Add lines showing the information flow. Identify and add the type of information that passes between functions and also add the form that this information takes (e.g. documents, verbal or electronic).

3 Don't worry if the design is not right first time. One problem you may encounter after drawing several of these diagrams is that the flow lines start to cross each other and the diagram ends up looking like a plate of spaghetti! If so, redraw the diagram, moving the boxes to try to prevent this.

4 Try not to include too much detail at first. Draw a simple diagram and then redraw it, adding more detail.

Remember that the whole point of an information flow diagram is to be able to identify all the functions and then see the way information flows between them.

Activity 5.7

Investigate the functions and information flows for two of the types of organisation described below. Choose the two with which you are most familiar. Some questions are included to get you to think about the system. You don't have to answer them, but will need to bear the answers in mind when explaining and illustrating the system.

Your college/school library
When a person joins the library, what documentation is produced and how is it stored? When the library buys a new book, what information about the book is needed and how is it stored? When a person who is a member of the library borrows a book, how are the details recorded? What needs to be done when a book is returned? What happens if the book is overdue by several weeks?

A college enrolment system
You are best attempting this one only if you are at a college. Think about what happened when you first came to college. What forms did you fill in? Did you have an interview? Did you receive an acceptance letter? Did you have to turn up at a certain time on a certain day to enrol or was it done by your course tutor? What information needed to be supplied by you in order to enrol? What forms were filled in during the enrolment process and what does the college do with them?

A video library
What information needs to be recorded when a new video is bought and where is it held? What information (e.g. proof of identity, name, etc.) is needed when a person joins the library and in what form and where are these details stored? What information needs to be recorded when a video is hired out and in what form are these details kept? What information is needed when letters are sent out to people who have not returned their videos?

A mail order company
What forms of information (order forms, phone orders, Internet orders, etc.) are used when placing an order? What payment methods are used? What information needs to be included in each order? What are the methods by which a customer may pay for their goods? What information is needed so that the goods may be picked from stock? What documents are sent with the goods if applicable?

Assignment A5.1

This assignment develops knowledge and understanding of the following element:
3.1 Investigate the flow of information in organisations

It supports the development of the following key skills:
Communication 3.2, 3.3 and 3.4
Information technology 3.1, 3.2 and 3.3

For this assignment you will need to perform some research about the types of organisation, the functions they have, the type of information used and the way it flows between functions.

Business studies textbooks will be your main source of reference for this assignment although you could arrange site visits and perform the investigations yourself. Another way of doing this would be to watch one of the many videos available describing real organisations.

Task 1

Research a selection of organisations using business studies books, company reports, the Internet, newspapers or any other source and produce brief notes outlining the activities of these organisations.

In describing these activities you need to find out the following information:
- the name of the organisation;
- a statement of what the organisation does;
- a brief description of the types of task performed by the organisation;
- how many people are employed by the organisation;
- what category (i.e. commercial, industrial, public service) the organisation falls into.

You should choose your organisations so that commercial, industrial and public service organisations are covered.

Organisations may be hierarchical or flat. Explain the difference between these two types and explain how you would determine the difference. Identify each organisation selected as hierarchical or flat.

Task 2

You are required to look in detail at the flow of information and the types of information generated in two organisations of your choice. You could use some of the organisations chosen in Task 1.

In particular, you need to identify the following for two organisations that you have selected:
- the form of the information generated (verbal, document or electronic);
- the types of information generated (sales, purchasing, market information, etc.).

Task 3

Produce some diagrams which can be used to help understand the flow of information to and from the various functions. Your diagrams should be produced using suitable graphics/paint/drawing software.

Try to incorporate suitable clipart into your design but if this is unavailable, simply use blocks showing the functions, with lines between them showing the information flow. Make sure that all your diagrams are given a title and that all the flow lines are suitably labelled.

Task 4

Produce a short report comparing information flow in the two organisations selected. Is the flow more streamlined in one than in the other and in what way? Make sure that:

- all forms of information have been covered for each organisation;
- a total of at least four types of information has been covered for the two organisations combined;
- within the two examples you have investigated the flows between at least three internal and two external functions in total.

Sample unit test

1 Which one of the following is an example of a public service organisation?
 a a local education authority
 b a utility company (gas, electricity or water)
 c a private health insurance company
 d a pharmaceuticals company

2 A company manufactures modems. It decides to carry out a survey to find out which computer magazines are most popular with its customers. This survey is designed to find out:
 a accounts information
 b sales information
 c marketing information
 d operational information

3 When goods are delivered from a factory to a customer, what is the name of the document which normally accompanies the goods and is used by the customer to check that the goods delivered are correct?
 a an invoice
 b a statement
 c a delivery note
 d a stock list

4 Which one of the following is *not* classed as electronic information?
 a an e-mail sent from a branch of a company to its head office
 b electronic data interchange
 c a file containing a list of stock attached to an e-mail
 d a price list sent by post

5 In the sales department of a large company, the sales staff report to the Sales Manager, who in turn reports to the Sales and Marketing Director. What type of organisational structure is this?
 a a flat structure
 b a hierarchical structure

   c a practice structure

   d a responsibility structure

6 In order to build a new part for a jet engine, an engineer must know the exact details of the required part. Which document gives these details?

   a a sales brochure

   b a delivery note

   c a design specification

   d a questionnaire

7 The department of an organisation most likely to be responsible for ordering stationery and supplies would be:

   a the sales department

   b the accounts department

   c the purchasing department

   d the marketing department

8 The main purpose of the marketing department is to:

   a sell goods direct to customers

   b make sure that the company has the right product being sold at the right price

   c purchase goods from suppliers

   d check on a customer's credit worthiness

9 Which one of the following is an external function of a company?

   a the operations function

   b the purchasing function

   c the sales function

   d the supplier function

Questions 10 and 11 refer to the information in Figure 5.3, which shows the information flows when a company sells goods to its customers.

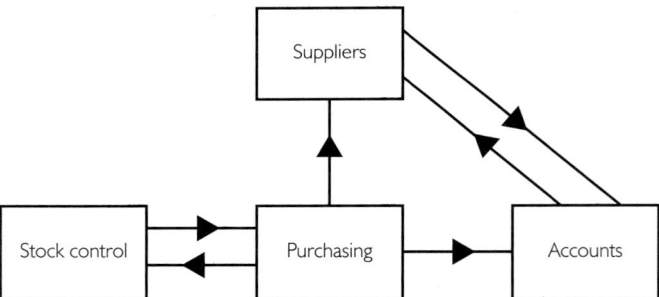

Figure 5.3

10 Which document would the sales department receive from a customer?

   a an order

   b an invoice

   c a purchase order

   d a statement of account

11 Which document would a customer receive from the accounts department?

   a an invoice

   b a purchase order

   c a stock list

   d a list of creditworthy customers

12 Which one of the following is a public service organisation?
   a a tourist information centre
   b a travel agency
   c an airport
   d a holiday operator   *(RSA, June 1996)*

13 Look at Figure 5.4. Which one of the following describes this type of organisational structure?
   a flat
   b hierarchical
   c horizontal
   d vertical   *(RSA, June 1996)*

Figure 5.4

14 Which one of the following is only communicated via a document?
   a an answerphone message
   b a voice mail message
   c a curriculum vitae (CV)
   d an interview   *(RSA, June 1996)*

15 A breakdown of the sales figures for the last five years is an example of:
   a operational information
   b external information
   c market information
   d supplier information   *(RSA, June 1996)*

16 A high street electrical supplier has a timetable of deliveries to local addresses. This is an example of:
   a marketing information
   b operational information
   c supplier information
   d external information   *(RSA, June 1996)*

17 In a public service organisation which two of the following are internal functions?
   1 administration
   2 personnel
   3 production
   4 delivery

   a 1 and 2
   b 2 and 3
   c 3 and 4
   d 1 and 4   *(RSA, June 1996)*

18 The administration department sends a requisition slip for printer paper to the stores. This is an example of:

a an external function

b an internal function

c a personnel function

d a design function

(RSA, June 1996)

Questions 19 and 20 refer to Figure 5.5.

19 Which one of the following represents a cheque paid for goods received?

a P

b Q

c X

d Z

(RSA, June 1996)

20 The purchasing department completes a two-part purchase order form. The top copy goes to the supplier. The second copy (labelled Y) goes to the accounts department. Which one of the following describes the form of information in flow Y?

a document

b verbal

c electronic

d signal

(RSA, June 1996)

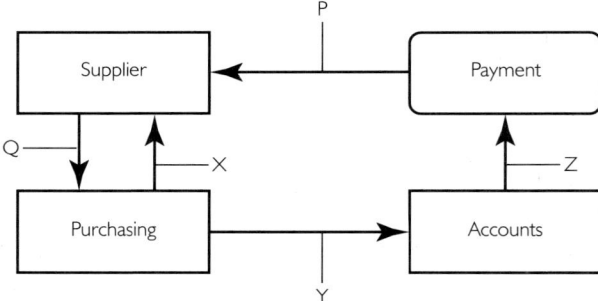

Figure 5.5

6 Investigating data handling systems

The following sections look at the methods of processing and the types of data handling systems. They also look at the methods of **data capture** and the data handling processes used.

It is important that any system has objectives. These objectives should be periodically reviewed to ensure that the system is still meeting them and to identify new objectives. In the following sections we will look at system objectives, and how to review the performance of systems in terms of their objectives in order to recommend improvements.

Methods of processing

There are two main ways of processing data: batch processing and transaction processing. In this section we will look at these two methods along with single-user and multi-user systems, and centralised and distributed systems.

Batch processing

In **batch processing**, jobs are collected over a period of time and at certain intervals, and the whole batch of data is processed in one go. The disadvantage of batch processing is that a batch is only up to date at the end of the processing run; before then it is out of date. The main advantages of batch processing are that it is fast, and that once the input data is batched the process can be performed with little human intervention. In fact, many batch processes are performed at night when the computer is not being used interactively. Figure 6.1 shows the way each job is automatically processed.

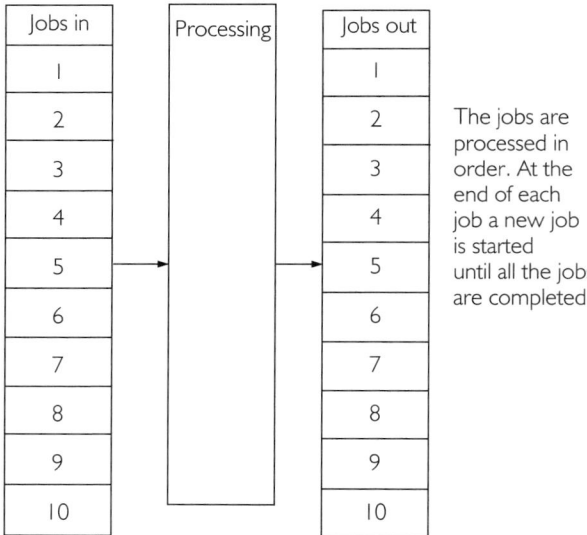

Figure 6.1 Batch processing

Examples of applications suitable for batch processing include:
- cheque clearing in banks;
- stock control in shops;
- producing monthly statements for banks, store cards and credit cards;
- producing gas, electricity, water, telephone and council tax bills;
- marking multiple choice examination papers and processing the results.

Transaction processing

In **transaction processing** the processing is immediate and takes place as soon as the job is received. Transaction processing is also called **real-time** processing, since files are updated while a transaction is being processed. If two people try to alter the same record at the same time, then one of the users will be locked out of the system. This type of system is therefore used with airline booking as it prevents two people from booking the same seat. Most booking systems (travel tickets, concert and theatre tickets) use this type of processing.

As well as batch and transaction processing, data processing can also be classified according to the number of people using a computer. There are two types: single-user and multi-user processing.

Single-user processing

Single-user processing is the most common method of processing since it is used by all stand-alone PCs. Basically, only one user can use the processing facilities at a time.

Multi-user processing

In **multi-user processing** many users are able to access the processing power of the computer at the same time, and this is done through a process called **timesharing**. Each terminal is allocated a small amount of time, known as a **time slice**, to be connected to the processor.

To the user, it appears that they have sole use of the processing facility. Terminals that are used for enquiries while a customer is kept waiting may be allocated a longer time slice than terminals that are only occasionally used by staff. Figure 6.2 shows the concept of timesharing.

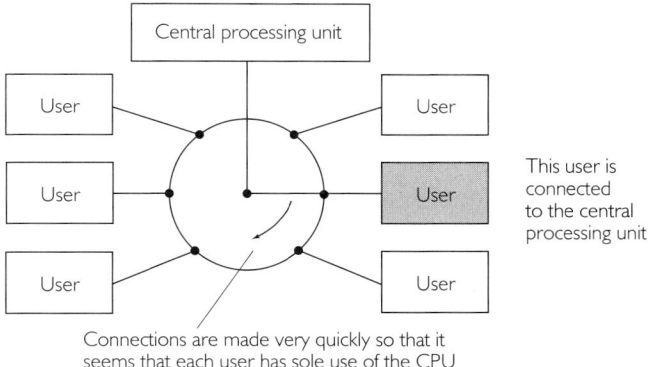

Figure 6.2
Timesharing

Another way of classifying data processing is according to the position (or positions) of the central computer. The two types are centralised systems and distributed systems.

Centralised systems

Centralised systems are those in which data processing is performed at a single site. All the data to be processed is sent to this site. However, with the advent of networks and company **intranets** (see page 256) companies are tending to decentralise their computing facilities.

Distributed systems

Distributed systems are those in which data processing is spread over several connected computer systems that are able to share resources. One of the computers may have information on it pertaining to customers, whereas another may have data concerning sales. Distributed systems are able to combine the data on each computer. Their main advantage is that the workload is spread or 'distributed' over the whole network.

Types of data handling systems

There are many different types of data handling systems but for the GNVQ Advanced IT course you are required to know about certain types in greater depth than others. In particular, you need a good knowledge of the following types of system:
- bookings
- payroll
- ordering
- invoicing
- stock control
- personal records.

Ordering, stock control and invoicing systems are looked at in detail in the case studies in Chapter 1. In the following case study, we will look at a system used by a company to hold personal information about its employees.

Cozy Plastics case study

This case study looks at the personnel system for a small manufacturing company called Cozy Plastics which manufactures plastic buckets and bowls. The company employs about 123 staff and most of these work at the head office/factory although some of the sales staff work from their homes.

The manual system

The manual system has been in use since the company started trading in 1986, and it is now unable to cope with the increasing demands placed on it. The manual system involves storing employee details in a filing cabinet, and the company now feels it is time that the system was computerised. Figure 6.3 shows a typical record from the manual system.

Problems with the existing system
- Updating the manual files involves crossing out information on the cards that is out of date and writing in the new information, if there is enough room. This looks messy and is sometimes confusing.
- With the increasing number of staff over the years, it has become more difficult to keep track of absences due to sicknesses, holidays, etc.
- With the manual system, employees' details are stored in alphabetical order according to surname. Sometimes the company needs to answer questions like 'how many disabled employees are there?' To do this, each record in the file needs to be looked at and a note made of the information for the relevant employees, which is very time consuming.

COZY PLASTICS LTD   PERSONNEL RECORD

SURNAME ~~JOHNSON~~ .... HUGHES ....

FIRST NAMES .SUZANNE ....

TITLE Mr/Mrs/~~Miss~~/~~Ms~~ Mrs

DATE OF BIRTH .19./12./54 ....

SEX: ~~M~~/F

MARITAL STATUS: Single/Married/~~Divorced~~ MARRIED ......

NATIONALITY .BRITISH ....

ADDRESS 3.CHANNEL VIEW ...15 LINTON CLOSE ...16 ELM ROAD .....

.CHANNEL CLOSE .... FORMBY .... CROSBY ....

.BLUNDELLSANDS .... Nr LIVERPOOL .... LIVERPOOL ....

.LIVERPOOL .L23 6TP .... L25 6PX ....

POSTCODE L23 6TP L25 6PX

HOME TEL. NO ~~051-924-8126~~ FORMBY 71854   051-920-5840

NAME OF NEXT OF KIN ~~MRS H JOHNSON~~ .... MR S HUGHES ....

RELATIONSHIP .~~MOTHER~~ .... HUSBAND ...

ADDRESS (if different) ..As above ....

....

WORK TEL. NO. 051-624-2914 .... SOUTHPORT 68857

HOME TEL. NO. ~~051-924-8126~~ FORMBY 71854   051-920-5840

NAME OF EMPLOYER ~~NEETLE SWEETS LTD~~ ... JOHNSON & HUGHES ....

... SWEETS --

STARTING DATE .16/12/83 ....

STARTING SALARY ..£4500 .... per annum

TITLE OF POST .CLERICAL ASSISTANT ....

QUALIFICATIONS 3 O'LEVELS BTEC Business Studies ....

PREVIOUS EXPERIENCE .Secretary for a solicitor for 8 years ....

MEDICAL HISTORY ....

OTHER NOTES ....

....

....

Figure 6.3 A typical employee record from the manual system

- Sometimes a departmental manager borrows a file and the personnel department is then unable to find it.

The main source of data for the personal details file is the application form completed when each employee joins the company. Over the years this data needs updating owing to changes in the employee's circumstances.

Data for other files (i.e. absences and holiday files) comes from forms completed by the employee. Holiday absences are filled in on a form which is sent to the personnel department by the end of each week. It needs signing by both the employee and their immediate superior.

In order to keep the system up to date, a certain amount of file maintenance needs to be done on a weekly basis. The system relies on each employee telling the personnel department of any changes that need to be made to their personal record. Information is collected from the employees on a weekly basis and forms are filled in containing the changes which need to be made to the employee records. Most of the file updating is performed on a Monday.

When a person joins the company, they are given a unique reference number which is also used by the payroll department as the employee's payroll number. This is used to distinguish between employees who have the same name and/or are living at the same address. However, the manual system is in surname order, although a list is kept to cross-reference each surname with its payroll number.

The system is used throughout the week for making enquiries. Here are just a few of the enquiries dealt with:

- a building society requires proof of income for an employee who has applied for a mortgage;
- the works manager requests details about absences of a person who has had a lot of time off recently;
- the directors require a list of employees who have been with the company since it started;
- another company asks for a reference about a past employee who left the company six years ago.

The objectives of the new system

The directors of Cozy Plastics have identified some objectives for the new system. These are the main ones:

- They would like to keep records on each member of staff similar in format to the records contained on the manual system.
- The accounts department uses computers for doing the payroll. The new personnel system must be compatible with the payroll system.
- The system must be able to record absences from work, together with the reason for each absence (e.g. absence due to holidays, sickness, jury service, personal reasons and maternity).
- Details concerning training courses attended and extra qualifications obtained must be recorded on the new system.
- Because of the personal nature of the information kept about its employees and the company's obligations under the Data Protection Act 1984, the new system must incorporate appropriate security measures.
- The system must make routine file maintenance operations as simple as possible.
- The database system must be capable of producing the reports listed on page 190.
- There must be suitable accuracy checks so that the company fulfills the requirements of the Data Protection Act 1984.

Activities 6.1

Cozy Plastics has decided to go ahead with the development of the computerised personnel system. Your task is to help the company find out about the types of system it could use.

A firm of consultants has been employed to develop the system for the company, but the directors of Cozy Plastics need to be sure that the consultants are working in the company's best interests. You have a good idea of what IT is about, and you are going to help the company make up its mind about the system.

The manual files are frequently processed in some way, and this processing falls under the following headings:

- **Searching**: the staff in the personnel section frequently need to locate a particular employee's file, and to search through the file to find something that is included within the records.
- **Sorting**: records are arranged in the file in alphabetical order only, so putting them in any other order using the manual system is a time-consuming task.
- **Updating**: this involves changing the information contained on the cards. When the cards start to look untidy, it is necessary to complete a new card and throw the old one away. This is wasteful and time consuming.

Task 1

There is a variety of processing methods that could be used by Cozy Plastics. Produce a brief report outlining the various methods, and stating which you think the company should adopt.

Task 2

At present Cozy Plastics has the details of its employees recorded on cards. Think carefully about how this information could be used by the company. Write down a list of the information Cozy Plastics might hold about its employees. (You could refer to textbooks on business or personnel studies to see the sort of information that companies hold.)

Task 3

Produce a brief outline, with diagrams, to help explain how the absences file could be used.

Objectives of data handling systems

Any data handling system must have objectives, and the system must be reviewed from time to time to make sure that the original objectives are still being met, and to identify any new objectives in the light of developments in technology. There are many possible objectives of a data handling system, but the commonest ones are outlined below.

Speed

Everybody knows that computers are very powerful, but to make the whole system function at high speed it is necessary to have appropriately trained staff and the correct administrative procedures in place.

Systems used in the dealing rooms of banks for the buying and selling of foreign currency are very time-critical. One company paid over £14 million for a system which gave it a two-second advantage over its competitors, and this enabled the company to react to the market more quickly and hence make greater profits.

Accuracy

'Computers are only as good as the people who operate them' is a phrase used frequently in computing. It is true because the human element always provides the weak link in any computer system, and most errors are introduced during the data entry stage, especially if data is typed in at a keyboard. To introduce a greater degree of accuracy, it is necessary to allow the computer to do as much of the work as possible. This usually involves automatic input methods such as MICR, OMR, barcodes, etc.

Cost

Companies have to make profits in order to survive, and one way of increasing profits without raising the prices of the goods being sold is to reduce the cost of producing them. One way of doing this is to automate some of the processes by using computer control or robots; another is to reduce the administration costs by cutting out the paperwork by using EDI, electronic mail, etc.

Not all organisations make profits – many provide services such as health care, education and so on, but these have only a certain amount of money allocated to them, so it is equally important for non-profit-making organisations to be run as efficiently as possible.

Supporting decision making

One of the main features of computerised data handling systems is that they produce management information which is used by senior staff to aid decision making. Older systems are incapable of providing this information without a great deal of effort. The latest computerised systems are able to provide management information very quickly. It can be presented in an easy-to-understand form using graphs and charts if necessary. The systems that provide this sort of information are called **management information systems (MIS)** and **executive information systems (EIS)**.

Methods of data capture

Data capture involves getting information into a form that can be processed by a computer. There are various methods of data capture, each with their own advantages and disadvantages, and the choice of method depends on many factors. Before looking at the methods available, we will consider what properties the ideal method of data capture would have:
- it would be accurate to ensure the integrity of the data stored;
- it would be fast;
- it would not involve high labour costs – usually this means that the method would need to be automatic;
- the equipment would be cheap to buy.

Unfortunately there is no single method of data capture that satisfies all the above conditions, and the choice of method is usually a compromise. In this section will look at the various methods available so that you are able to choose the most suitable when designing your own systems.

Keyboard entry

Keyboard entry is the most popular method of data capture for small-volume work but it does have severe limitations when it comes to large-volume work.

Advantages of keyboard entry
- No additional equipment is needed since nearly all computers or terminals have keyboards.
- The use of keyboards allows interactive processing, where the data is input and the output is received quickly so that the rest of the input can be altered accordingly. This is ideal for systems such as airline booking where the user inputs the destination and date of travel and the computer tells the operator if a seat is available. If there is, then the seat can be booked by entering the customer's details.
- Many people have been trained to use a keyboard.
- Keyboard entry can take place away from the main computer provided that suitable communication links have been set up.

Disadvantages of keyboard entry
- It is a slow method of data capture, especially for large volumes of data. Typically, a fast typist can type at a maximum of 50 words per minute.

- Because the method relies on humans, errors are often introduced, and careful checking is needed to make sure that incorrect data is not processed.
- For the input of large volumes of data, a large number of typists is needed, and this is very expensive.
- Typing at high speed can cause certain health problems, such as repetitive strain injury (RSI).
- Many people who use PCs have limited keyboard skills, so using this method of data capture is extremely slow.

Using a mouse for data capture

Most people who use computers know that a **mouse** is an input device, but it can also be used as a method of data capture. Commands can be entered using the mouse instead of the keyboard. Many database packages which use Windows enable the user to select fields from lists rather than having to make up the field names and type them in.

Optical mark recognition (OMR)

Nearly everyone will have come across **optical mark recognition** as a method of data capture, since it is the method used to capture National Lottery numbers. When people buy their lottery tickets, they draw a line through their selected numbers, and the terminal reads them and prints out a ticket. When the winning numbers are selected, the central computer automatically knows how many jackpot winners there are and at which terminals the winning tickets were sold. Figure 6.4 shows this and some other OMR applications.

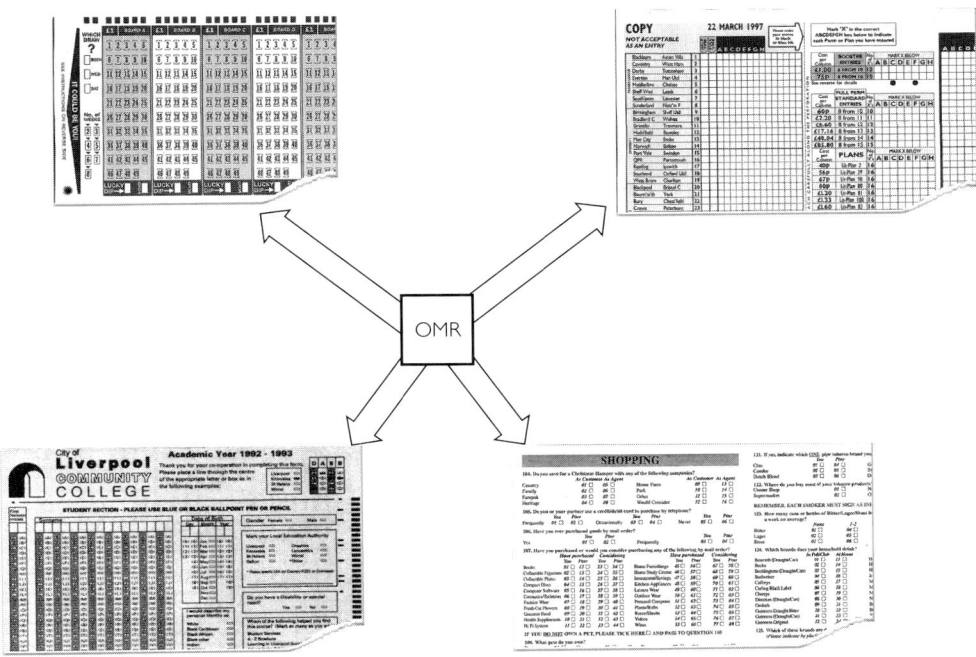

Figure 6.4 A variety of OMR applications

Optical mark readers work by sensing marks made in certain places on a specially designed form. Figure 6.5 shows a typical example of such a form, which is used to collect details of student enrolments. Notice that to collect just a single letter, all 26 letters have to be printed on the form.

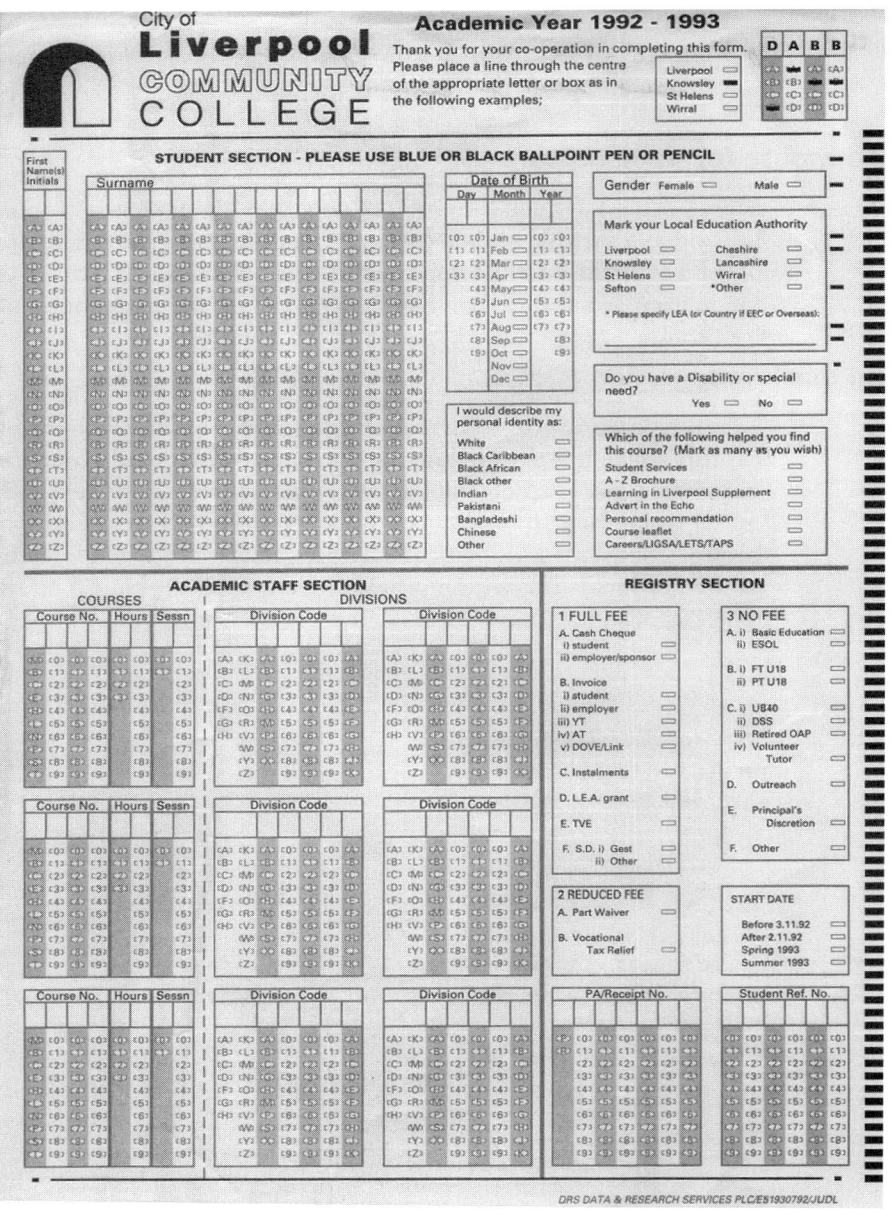

Figure 6.5 A student enrolment form that uses OMR

As well as being used to capture lottery numbers and information from enrolment forms, OMR is also used for marking multiple choice answer sheets, capturing data from questionnaires and checking football pools coupons.

People who have never filled in an OMR form before may not fill them in correctly, so the rejection rate using this method of data capture is quite high – currently around

30 per cent. For instance, in a questionnaire to find out people's opinions of television programmes, the following variations were obtained, despite the correct method of shading being shown in an example:

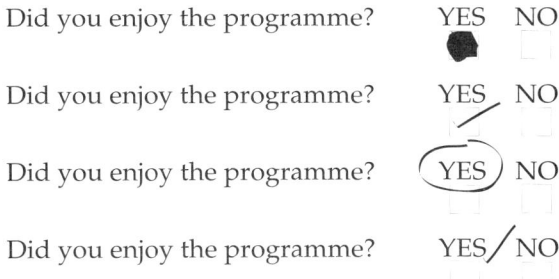

Advantages of OMR
- OMR avoids having to type details in, which is time consuming and could introduce errors.
- It reduces the cost of entering large volumes of data.
- The method is useful when results to tests are needed very quickly, e.g. with an aptitude test for a job.

Disadvantages of OMR
- Very clear instructions are needed on how to fill in the forms, preferably including examples. Even so, a high proportion are filled in incorrectly.
- If the forms are creased or folded then they may be rejected or jam the machine.

Magnetic-ink character recognition (MICR)

Magnetic-ink characters are the strange-looking characters that you see on the bottom of cheques. The characters are printed in magnetic ink, which contains particles of iron that can be magnetised and used to hold numbers such as the bank sort code, the account number and cheque number. Another number needs to be typed in after the cheque has been written, and this is the amount that the cheque has been written for. This is put on the cheque in magnetic ink before the cheque is sent to the clearing house where all bank and building society cheques are cleared. Figure 6.6 shows the magnetic-ink characters on the bottom of a cheque, and what they mean.

Magnetic-ink character recognition uses very expensive equipment and is suitable only for large-scale applications.

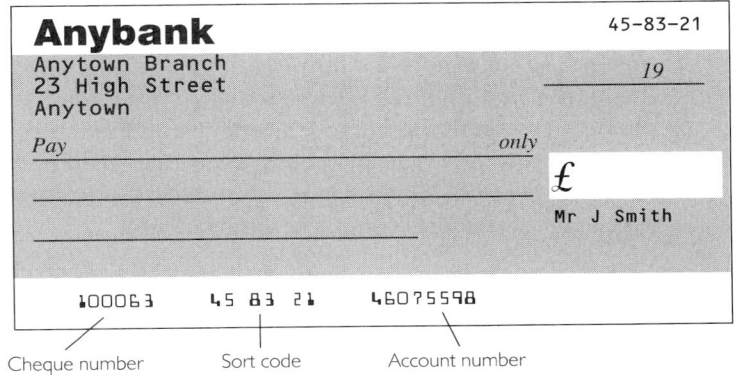

Figure 6.6 A cheque showing the magnetic ink characters

Barcode reading systems

Barcodes consist of a series of black and white lines of varying thickness, and are used to capture numerical information. By using a laser scanner the information coded in the bars is used to enter into a computer a number or series of numbers which is usually printed underneath the barcode. The method was first developed for supermarkets and is now used in all large shops.

Barcode systems are only suitable for reading pre-printed information. You could not, for example, capture student details entered on a form using this method. Although barcodes can be printed by ink-jet or laser printers, special software data would need to be typed into the computer to produce the barcodes, so this method would have no advantage.

The price of barcode readers has come down over the last few years, and for this reason the number of applications of this method has increased. Barcodes are now used in library systems, luggage handling systems at airports and warehouse stock control systems (see Figure 6.7). Barcode systems are now at an advanced stage, and readers are able to read the barcodes at distances of five metres or more.

Figure 6.7 The barcode on a library ticket. The last two digits of the borrower's code number are used as check digits to make sure that the code has been input correctly.

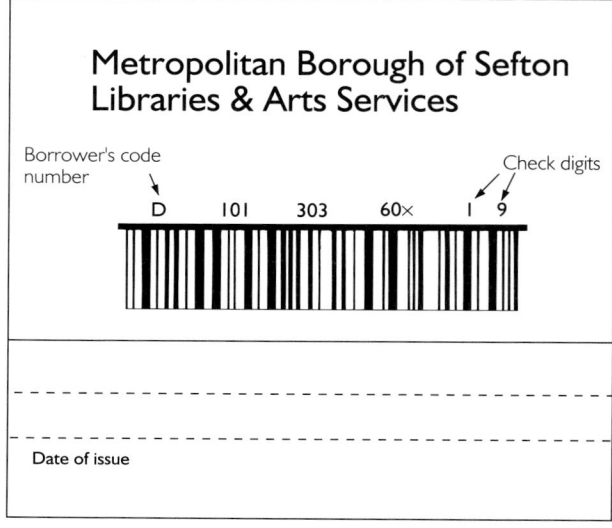

Touch-tone telephones

Modern telephones work by having a different tone for each of the numbered keys pressed, so for example a number five has a slightly different tone from a number six. It is in this way that the numbers dialled are recognised and routed to the correct telephone. Once connected, a touch-tone telephone can be used as a data entry device. For instance, in some home banking systems the customer keys in their identification number using the phone keys. Once connected, the customer can select certain services such as statement requests using the same keypad.

Magnetic strip readers

Magnetic strips are found on all cash and credit cards and the readers can be found inside cash dispensers or at the side of point-of-sale terminals. Information encoded in the strip includes information about credit limits, balances, etc.

Keypad

Keypads are used to input data into computer-controlled lathes and other computerised equipment. Robot arms like the one shown in Figure 6.8 have a keypad for keying in the series of instructions (as a series of numbers) that tells the arm what it has to do.

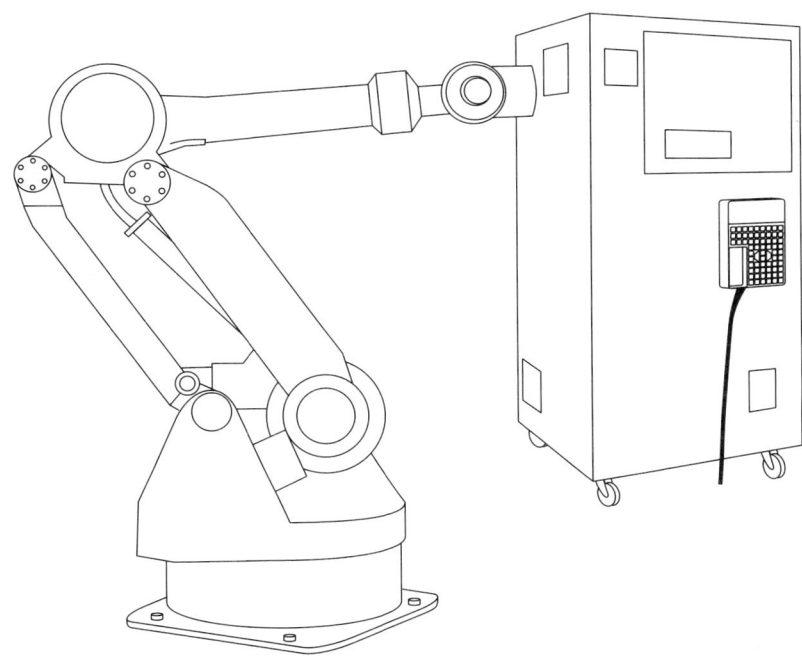

Figure 6.8 Robot arm showing the keypad where the number code that controls it is typed in

Data handling processes

When data has been captured by a computer it is processed in some way, and this processing usually falls into one or more of the categories given below.

Calculating

Calculating is an important process and most applications involve some form of calculation.

Converting files

Often a file in one type of format needs to be changed to another format so that it can be used with a different program from the one used to store it originally. For instance, you may have stored your wordprocessing files in WordPerfect format but decide to change your wordprocessing software to Microsoft Word. In order for the documents in WordPerfect format to be read by Word, they need to be converted. Sometimes the conversion program is part of the wordprocessing software and sometimes it is separate from it.

Database files may need to be converted if the database program is changed, and this avoids having to re-enter huge amounts of data.

Sorting data

Reports are normally sorted into some sort of order since this enables particular items to be located easily. For example, details of outstanding invoices might be presented in any one of the following orders:

- in the order of the amount outstanding;
- in chronological order (date order);
- in alphabetical order according to company surname.

In fact many reports contain data sorted into more than one order, so you could have a list of outstanding invoices in alphabetical order, and in numerical order within this. So first would be all the companies beginning with the letter A, all in numerical order, then companies beginning with B and so on.

Searching for specific data

If there is a large amount of data in a database then it makes sense to use a search condition in order to find data quickly. Searching is also used in wordprocessing for finding all the occurrences of a particular word. Special programs, called search engines, can be used to search through the mass of databases and files held on the Internet.

Selecting data

Selecting involves picking out those items of data that meet certain criteria, for instance those customers who place orders above a certain value each year. Selection also enables summary reports to be produced.

Merging files

Merging involves combining two separate files into one. One file may simply be added onto the end of the other (this is called appending) or it may be placed within the same sequence as the original file.

Grouping data

Grouping involves providing a summary of a particular group of data. For example, data about sales could be grouped according to product.

Assignment A6.1

This assignment develops knowledge and understanding of the following element:
3.2 Investigate data handling systems

It supports the development of the following key skills:
Communication 3.2, 3.3 and 3.4
Information technology 3.1, 3.2 and 3.3

Task 1

In this assignment you will investigate two data handling systems from the following list:

- bookings (holiday, theatre, car rental, air tickets, etc.) system
- stock control system
- mail order system
- medical record system
- school/college student records
- school/college employee records.

Before choosing which two systems to investigate, make sure that you will be able to find out sufficient information about each one.

For each of your chosen systems, explain which method of processing is used and the reason for using that method.

Task 2

Identify the original objectives of each system you investigated in Task 1 and review the performance of each system against these objectives. If the objectives have changed or are no longer being met by the system, identify any recommendations for improving the system.

The next sections look at the various operations performed during data handling. The practical aspects of this topic are dealt with in Chapters 13 and 14, which cover database design.

File maintenance

File maintenance involves keeping a file up to date and includes entering new data, appending new data to an existing file, editing existing data, and deleting old or incorrect data.

Data entry (manual and automated)

Data entry is the process of getting data into a form that can be processed by a computer. In many cases this will involve reading source documents such as order forms, invoices, etc. and typing in the details using a keyboard. This method is gradually being replaced by automated methods which involve the document itself being read by a computer, thus reducing the number of errors and the cost of capturing the data. Automatic forms of data entry include **optical character recognition (OCR)**, optical mark recognition (OMR), barcode reading, magnetic-ink character recognition (MICR) and **voice recognition**.

Amending data

Amending data means making alterations to it. For example, you may need to make the following amendments to a student records database:

- change of surname due to marriage;
- change of address after moving house;
- change of courses undertaken.

Deleting data

Deleting involves the removal of data. An example of this could be when a student moves out of the area and no longer attends the college and their details therefore need to be deleted. Deleting obsolete data is an important part of file maintenance and should be performed on a regular basis. For instance, if you are constantly using your hard drive, it will gradually become cluttered and this will use up valuable space and slow your computer down. You should therefore review the contents of your hard drive regularly and delete the files that are no longer needed.

Appending data to a file

Appending means adding more data to an existing file. When a database is appended, more records are added to the end of it.

Data handling processes

Data handling processes have already been described earlier in this chapter.

Database reports

Database reports no longer consist of the contents of entire databases printed on poor quality paper using a dot matrix printer. Today, successful information systems need to present information in the most effective manner. Only selected information should be supplied, and this should be grouped logically (in alphabetical order, numerical order, date order, etc.). It should be printed using an easy-to-read font and the print should be high quality, which usually means that a laser printer should be used.

Printed information from a computer is usually presented in the form of reports. There are various types of reports, and some reports are combinations of more than one type. The main types are described below.

Operational reports

Operational reports are reports that are needed on a day-to-day basis and that are essential for the successful running of an organisation. They are usually provided at regular intervals and include daily work in progress, weekly sales figures, daily stock reports, lists of debtors, etc.

Summary reports

Summary reports provide a summary of the data held in a database. Nearly all management reports are summary reports because managers do not want to waste time searching through huge volumes of data for the items they are interested in. Examples of summary reports include the sales figures for a certain product, or a list of customers who owe money after a certain date.

Exception reports

To be able to make forecasts, the senior managers of organisations need to know about current trends. Managers tend to be interested in the unusual rather than the usual, so for example they would be more interested in customers whose payments are overdue than those who have paid. Successful information systems should be able to differentiate between normal and exceptional situations, and exceptional reports are usually required by management to help with decision making.

Other examples of exception reports include a list of customers who have exceeded their credit limits, sales which are beyond those forecast, or lists of goods which have been in stock for more than one year.

Data grouping

A data grouping report takes data from a variety of sources and groups it together in a single report. For instance, one of the directors of a company may wish to visit their ten best customers in the North of England. This information could be obtained from the customer file (for their names and addresses) and the sales file (for the sales figures).

Accuracy checks

In order to make sure that the output of a computer is accurate, it is necessary to check that the input data is correct. There are various ways of ensuring the integrity of the data and these can be divided into verification checks and validation checks.

Verification of input data

Verification is the process of checking the input data before it is accepted by the computer for processing. In many cases verification consists of comparing the input with the original document to ensure that the data matches. In other words, the input is proofread. It is important to note that this does not necessarily mean that the input is correct, since all that is being checked is that what is on the source document matches exactly with what has been entered. It could be that the information on the source document, such as an order form, is incorrect: for example a customer might have filled in the order form using an out-of-date copy of a catalogue. The verification check ensures only that no typing errors have been introduced at the keyboard entry stage.

Another method of verification involves two people typing in the same data, and only if the data is identical will it be accepted for further processing. The problem with this is that two people need to be paid for doing the same job, and, although it is unlikely, they may make identical errors that therefore go unnoticed.

Validation of input data

Validation is a check during data entry to make sure that the data being entered is valid. It is impossible to be completely sure that the data is correct since a name could be spelt incorrectly each time and no amount of validation checks would be able to pick it up. However, validation checks can trap some of the likely errors and go some way to making sure that the data is as accurate as it possibly can be. Validation checks are sometimes performed as part of a separate program, although many databases such as Microsoft Access enable you to specify certain characteristics of the data to be entered into each field.

There is a variety of validation checks, including:
- **Range checks**: the input data is compared with pre-stored upper and lower values to make sure that it lies somewhere between the two extremes. If an item of data falls outside the range the user is alerted so that it can be checked.

- **Data type checks**: these make sure that the correct type of data is entered into certain fields. You can specify fields as being numeric, character, date or logical. If you try to enter a letter into a field which has been specified as being numeric, then the program will not accept it. It is important that numeric fields are only specified if they are to contain the sorts of numbers that could have calculations performed on them. So order numbers like 004564, and telephone numbers like 0151-450-9876 should be placed in character fields.
- **Existence checks**: some fields must always be filled in and others are optional – all people have a date of birth but not everyone has a telephone number.
- **Consistency checks**: these check one data item against another to ensure consistency. If a customer orders goods from a catalogue and these details are entered into an order processing system, then the computer could check that the price and catalogue number being entered are consistent with those already stored.

Security checks

In this section we will look at the methods available to ensure the security of data stored on a computer system.

Saving data

There is always a tendency, when working with computers, for people to save their work at the end just before printing. Regular saving at predetermined intervals is an essential security measure to avoid large amounts of work being lost due, for example, to the power going off. Many programs have an 'autosave' facility which saves work automatically, and the time period between saves can be altered if necessary. This facility means that the user no longer has to remember to save.

Regular file saving is essential because:

- power surges cause 'spikes' in the mains power which can result in work being corrupted;
- power cuts cause work to be lost;
- mistakes may be made which cannot be rectified easily: for example if you press a key accidentally and an action is performed that you do not know how to get out of, it may be easier simply to revert back to your back-up copy;
- someone may unplug your computer by accident.

Confidentiality

It is important that access to certain programs and data is restricted to certain personnel, and there are several security checks that can be put in place to achieve this. It is best to select staff carefully and to make sure that they fully appreciate the consequences of any activities they may perform.

Passwords

Most software, particularly spreadsheets and databases, allows users to specify passwords that have to be entered before a person can enter the system and access the data. Many users prefer not to use passwords because they are worried about forgetting them. If they have to write them down, this negates the point of having them in the first place. To keep passwords secure, they should be changed regularly to avoid them being discovered and used by someone else. Figure 6.9 shows some tips for ensuring that passwords are kept confidential.

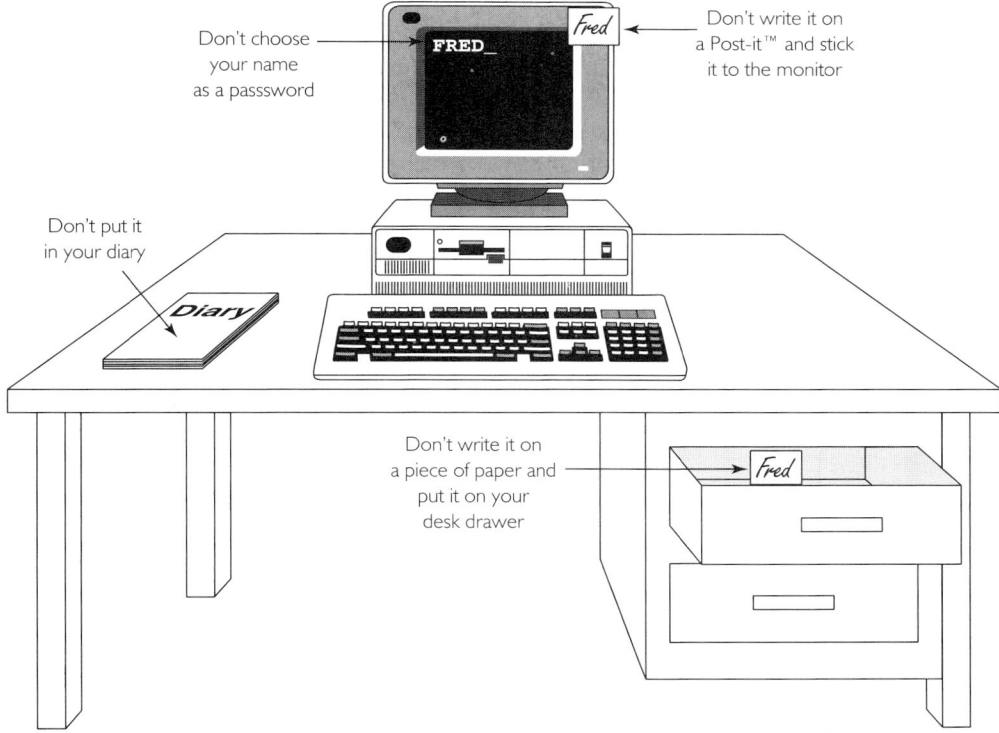

Figure 6.9 Places where not to hide your password and advice about passwords

Non-disclosure

If staff are to use computers, they need to have access to data. It is therefore important to make sure that staff who have access to private and confidential data are chosen carefully, and often non-disclosure agreements are included in their contracts of employment to make sure that they do not disclose to any other person or organisation anything that they may come across in the course of their jobs.

Access rights

Access rights are offered by most local area network software. They enable users to set rights to their directories, subdirectories and even individual files. This means that, for example, the company accounts can be accessed only by certain authorised people such as the company accountant. It is possible to allocate certain users read-only status, which means that they can view the contents of a file but not make any alterations.

Copyright

Copyright ensures that the creators of either a software package or database are protected by law against other people copying their material.

Software piracy

Software piracy involves the illegal copying of computer software and is estimated to cost the software developers around £3000 million per year. In 1992 it was estimated that about 66 per cent of the software used in Europe was illegal.

If a company has developed its own software rather than using an off-the-shelf package, then it will have spent a lot of time and money on its development. Large programs are usually written by a team, with each person writing a particular section or module. The number of man hours taken to write the programs can be huge. For example, suppose that five programmers are working on a project and it takes each programmer 200 hours to complete, then the total number of man hours would be $5 \times 200 = 1000$ man hours. The programs for the Police National Computer have been estimated to have taken around 2000 man years to write and test.

Copyright of data

Data paid for or collected by one organisation may be of value to another organisation and it is for this reason that data may also be copyrighted. An example might be a database containing the names, addresses and telephone numbers of all private and business premises in the country.

The Copyright, Designs and Patents Act 1988

This act makes it a criminal offence to be caught copying or stealing software. Under the act it is an offence to copy or distribute software, or any manuals which come with it, without the permission of or licence from the copyright owner, who is normally the software developer. It is also an offence to run purchased software covered by copyright on two or more machines at the same time, unless the licence specifically allows it.

The act makes it illegal for an organisation to encourage, allow, compel or pressure its employees to make or distribute copies of illegal software for use by the organisation.

The Computer Misuse Act 1990

With the increasing use of computer and communications systems, problems started to arise concerning their misuse. The problems centred on a variety of uses that were not covered by existing laws. Several cases went to court but the courts were unable to convict. One particular case involved a schoolboy who used his computer and a modem at home to hack into the Duke of Edinburgh's electronic mailbox and read his correspondence. Other schoolboy **hackers** were able to get access to the computer systems of stockbrokers, hospitals, oil companies and even the Atomic Energy Authority. The courts were reluctant to use the theft laws, which were not intended to cover these kinds of situations, and advised Parliament that it would need to make new specific laws. This gave rise to the Computer Misuse Act 1990.

The Computer Misuse Act 1990 covers a variety of misuses. These include:

- deliberately planting viruses into a computer system to cause damage to program files and data;
- using computer time to carry out unauthorised work, for instance using a firm's computer to run a friend's payroll;
- copying computer programs illegally (i.e. software **piracy**);
- hacking into someone's system with a view to seeing the information or altering it;
- using a computer for various frauds, for example putting fictitious employees on the payroll program and using false bank accounts opened in their names to steal money.

The maximum penalty for unauthorised access to a computer system is six months imprisonment and a £2000 fine. For the other offences there is a maximum of five years imprisonment and an unlimited fine.

Evaluating the effectiveness of data handling systems

The effectiveness of any information system can be evaluated in terms of the following criteria:
- reliability
- speed
- cost
- benefit
- volume.

The following sections look at the reasons for protecting data held on individuals and organisations; health and safety issues for system users; obligations of system users and security checks.

Reasons for protecting data

There are several reasons why data which refers to individuals or organisations should be kept private. Unfortunately, there are people who would like to get hold of this data, usually for commercial or political gain. The reasons why data should be protected are described below.

Confidentiality

It is important that business transactions and decisions are kept private since disclosure to another company could result in loss of business or money. Although some companies pass on clients' information, they usually ask the clients to say if they do not want the information passed to a third party. There is a law concerning the privacy of information called the Data Protection Act. This act applies only to data held on a computer about living individuals.

Legal reasons

Under the Data Protection Act 1984, individuals are given rights to access the data held about them on computer systems. If this data has been passed to another person and as a result the individual incurs some damage, then they are able to claim compensation through the courts.

Moral reasons

As people become more dependent on computer systems, the designers, makers and operators of these systems have a moral responsibility to make sure that computers are used properly. For example, they must make sure that the data stored or passing along communication lines is secure.

There are many moral issues to be dealt with in computing, and some of them are discussed in the next sections.

Data held on individuals

A wide variety of organisations, both private and public, hold personal information about each one of us. Personal information usually falls into one of the following categories:

Criminal

- details on all suspects, crimes and previously convicted criminals;
- computerised records of all convicted criminals' fingerprints;
- DNA profiles of all criminals;
- criminal details on suspects who may be involved in organised crime.

Educational

- medical details which may affect schooling;
- details of exam results held by examining bodies;
- personal details on school pupils held by the schools information management system (SIMS);
- references for jobs, further education and higher education colleges;
- reports giving details of the performance of students at the end of each term/year.

Medical

- GP records;
- prescription details kept on a card by pharmacies such as Boots;
- hospital records (referral letters from GPs, appointments, treatment details, etc.);
- medical details held by life insurance companies;
- medical details held by solicitors dealing with compensation claims;
- private health insurance details;
- details about employees' medical conditions kept by personnel departments.

Financial

- mortgage details held by a bank or building society;
- loan details kept by a finance company;
- bank account or building society details;
- pension details;
- credit and debit card details.

Employment

- personal details (name, address, illnesses, next of kin, etc.);
- references;
- pension details;
- payroll details;
- tax details.

Examination of the eight data protection principles (see page 198) reveals that data about an individual should be held only for specified and lawful purposes, and the data must be accurate and relevant to those purposes.

Activity 6.2

Task I

Each of the following pieces of information falls into one or more of the above categories. Say which category or categories each one falls into.
1 salary tax code
2 medical history
3 bank account balance
4 GP record
5 job appraisal
6 employer reference

7 social worker report

8 credit limit

9 police record

Task 2

The Data Protection Act 1984 applies to personal data held on computer about living people, though there are some exemptions. Research the extent of these exemptions and produce a report outlining what type of data is exempt and the reasons behind its exemption.

Data held on organisations

Organisations need to hold data in order to operate and only a small amount of the data held would be classed as personal data. The data held by organisations can be placed in the following categories.

Commercial data

Commercial organisations hold data in order to trade and, hopefully, make a profit. Organisations can be divided into those that provide a service and those that sell a product.

Activity 6.3

Classify each of the following commercial organisations according to whether they provide a service or make or supply a product:

1 computer dating agency

2 bank

3 oil company

4 shop

5 building society.

Commercial organisations hold data about their suppliers, customers, costings, sales, orders, budgets, production, etc. Some of this data would be of benefit to a competitor. Take, for example, costings. Suppose company A was in the process of tendering for the resurfacing of a large stretch of motorway for the Highways Department. It would be of benefit to another company, company B, who was also tendering, to know what price company A intended to charge, since company B could then bid slightly lower. Most commercial organisations hold information that would be of great interest to their competitors, so it is not surprising that they take precautions to keep this valuable data secure.

Financial data

Organisations need to keep financial details relating to sales, purchases and general ledgers, cashbooks, cashflow predictions, payroll and final accounts. Again all these details need to be kept secure on a computer and there should be stringent security procedures in place to prevent anyone from tampering with them. Financial records are also required to ensure that the correct income tax and VAT are paid.

Legal data

There is a variety of legal data held by most organisations, and again this information is often confidential. The sort of legal data held includes documents for the registration of the business if it is a limited company, contracts of employment for employees, contracts made between suppliers and purchasers, copies of all the acts pertaining to the business and so on.

The Data Protection Act 1984

The Data Protection Act was made law in 1984 and applies only to the processing of data by computer; other acts cover manual, paper-based systems. ('Processing' is the collection, storing and distribution of information.) The Data Protection Act applies only to personal data about living individuals.

The act places obligations on those people who record and use personal data, and these people are called 'data users'. Data users must be open about the use of the data by telling the Data Protection Registrar (i.e. the person who enforces the act) that they are collecting personal data and how they intend to use it. They must also follow a set of eight principles, called the data protection principles.

The data protection principles

The principles state that:
1 The information to be contained in personal data shall be obtained, and personal data should be processed, fairly and lawfully.
2 Personal data shall be held only for one or more specified and lawful purposes.
3 Personal data held for any purpose or purposes shall not be disclosed in any matter incompatible with that purpose or purposes.
4 Personal data held for any purpose or purposes shall be adequate, relevant and not excessive in relation to that purpose or those purposes.
5 Personal data shall be accurate and, where necessary, kept up to date.
6 Personal data held for any purpose or purposes shall not be kept for longer than is necessary for that purpose or purposes.
7 An individual shall be entitled:
  a at reasonable intervals and without undue delay or expense
    (i) to be informed by any data user whether he holds personal data to which that individual is the subject
    (ii) to have access to any such data held by a data user; and
  b where appropriate, to have such data corrected or erased.
8 Appropriate security measures shall be taken against unauthorised access to, or alteration, disclosure or destruction of, personal data and against accidental loss or destruction of personal data.

Health and safety

There are several health problems which can occur when working with computers for long periods, but if you are aware of them then steps may be taken to prevent them. As more and more computers are used in the workplace, health problems have increased. In this section we will look at the main problems and how to prevent them from occurring.

Eye strain

Most people who use computers have experienced eye strain. It is caused by several factors which include reflections from lights on the screen, concentration on the screen for long periods and shifting focus between the screen and paper. Both keeping focused on the screen and refocusing the eyes lead to eye strain. The early symptoms of eye strain are hazy vision which is usually followed by a headache. When this happens the person needs to rest and lie down if possible.

Preventing and relieving eye strain

There are several ways of preventing eye strain and these include:

Giving your eyes a break

This means taking a break from the computer screen every so often. Experts recommend that a 15-minute break should be taken for every hour of intensive work on the computer. During this break you should try to relax if possible but if there is so much work to do that this is impossible, then you should do some non-computer work in this period.

Refocusing your eyes every so often

This should be done every 10 minutes and it involves looking up from the computer and focusing your eyes on a distant object.

Suitable lighting

You need to make sure that there are no concentrated sources of light such as pendant lights since these will produce reflections on the screen. Instead fluorescent tubes should be used which have plastic covers, called diffusers, which disperse the light and illuminate the work area evenly.

Using a copyholder

Shifting your eyes between paper and the screen can cause eye strain, and if your neck also moves then this can also give rise to neck strain. It is best to use a copyholder which will keep the paper you are working from at the same height as the computer screen and this will mean your eyes will not continually have to refocus.

Adjustable blinds on the windows

A frequent problem is the glare of sunlight on the screen and to get round this you can use adjustable blinds on the windows. Try to avoid using curtains since they cannot be adjusted easily and are not as easy to clean as blinds.

Frequent eye tests

Employees who work with computer screens are required by law to have their eyes tested, at the expense of their employer, every so often, and if glasses need to be worn then the employer should also pay for these.

Radiation

There have been many 'scare stories' in the press about the dangers of electromagnetic radiation given out from computer screens. Many other devices also give out this radiation and most of the research on it is centred around radar installations and electricity power lines which give out quite strong emissions. There have been cases of women who have been using computer screens for long periods having abnormal pregnancies, but there is little real evidence to support a connection between the two. Nevertheless, many employees allow pregnant women to move to a different area which does not use display screens. There are also many products advertised in computer equipment catalogues for devices which can be placed over the screen to reduce radiation. In recent years, several new European and international regulations have been introduced to reduce the amount of radiation emitted by computer screens. All new computer screens must conform to many of these standards.

Repetitive strain injury (RSI)

People who spend long hours keying in at a keyboard can develop a condition called repetitive strain injury (RSI). This condition is caused by the constant pounding that the joints in the fingers, hands and wrists take during this action. When an operator is keying in at high speed, the keys are pressed quite hard and when the key reaches the end of its depression it stops, and a shock wave travels up through the various bones in the hand causing damage to the muscles and tendons in the fingers, wrists, arms and neck. Symptoms of RSI include soreness or tenderness of the fingers, wrists, elbows, arms or neck. If left without treatment it can give rise to a painful condition similar to arthritis which causes long-term disability.

Good keyboard design, a well-positioned keyboard, good typing technique and frequent breaks can help prevent RSI. There are special keyboards and wrist-guards available to ease fatigue, and these are worth using.

Physical stress

Physical stress is a general condition brought about by the body working in the wrong environment or trying to do a task for which it isn't really designed. Physical stress causes direct damage to the body and a doctor can see the damage that has been done. Examples of physical stress include RSI, eye strain, backache, etc. Many employers are aware of these stresses and have tried to improve conditions in the workplace by using ergonomic designs.

Psychological stress

Psychological stress is caused by using inappropriately designed software. An example might be if you change over to a new wordprocessing package and are unable to do a task that before was quite simple. You feel frustrated because you are wasting time and this gets worse if the job is urgent. Losing files or finding there is a virus on your machine which has ruined some data are among the most stressful situations.

What can be done about these problems?

Because of the various health problems that can occur with incorrect computer use, the Government has laid down certain laws which require employers to provide the following:

Inspections
Employers should periodically inspect the workplace environment and the equipment being used to check that it complies with the law. Any shortcomings in the conditions, working practices or equipment should be reported and corrected. Desks, chairs, computers, etc. should be inspected for possible risks to workers' eyesight and to their physical and mental health.

Training
All employees should be trained in the health and safety aspects of their job. They need to be told about the correct posture when using keyboards etc.

Job design
Each employee's job should be designed so that the worker has periodic breaks or changes of activity when using computers.

Eye tests
For computer users there should be regular free eye tests, with free glasses provided if necessary at the employer's expense.

The law also lays down certain minimum requirements for computer systems and furniture. All new and existing equipment should now meet the following requirements:

Display screens
These must be easy to read, have no 'flicker' and be very stable. Brightness, contrast, tilt and swivel must all be adjustable and there must be no reflection off the screen.

Keyboards
These must be separate from the screen and tiltable. Their layout should be easy to use and the surface should be matt in order to avoid glare. There must be sufficient desk space to provide arm and hand support.

Desks
Desks must be large enough to accommodate the computer and any paperwork and must not reflect too much light. An adjustable document holder should be provided so as to avoid uncomfortable head movements.

Chairs
Chairs must be adjustable and comfortable, and allow easy freedom of movement. A footrest must be available on request.

Lights
There should be suitable contrast between the computer screen and the background. There must be no glare or reflections on the computer screen, so point sources of light should be avoided and the windows should have adjustable coverings such as blinds to eliminate reflections caused by sunlight.

Noise
This should not be loud enough to distract attention and disturb speech.

Software
This must be easy to use and should be appropriate to the user's needs and experience. Although software can be used to monitor an employee's performance, this is not allowed without the knowledge of the employee.

Heat, humidity and radiation
Heat and humidity should be kept to optimum levels while radiation emissions should be kept to a minimum.

Other hazards in the workplace

Fire hazards
- **Overloaded power sockets**: never overload power sockets since this is frequently a source of fire. If there are insufficient power sockets then the room should be rewired to cope with the level of power consumption.
- **Large quantities of paper lying around**: fire frequently starts from cigarette ends disposed of in wastepaper bins. There should be a 'no smoking' policy in office areas and bins should be emptied regularly. Paper stores should be separate from the working area.

Obstructions
- **Trailing wires**: these are dangerous, so make sure that wires are long enough to go around the walls of the room or are placed in plastic or rubber trunking.
- **Boxes of paper**: frequently, boxes of paper are left around the work area. As well as constituting a fire hazard, they are frequently the cause of people tripping.

Electrical
- **The wrong-size fuse being used**: fuses are designed so that if a fault occurs and the electrical current starts to rise, the thin piece of wire inside the fuse will melt. The melting fuse cuts off the electricity and prevents damage to the computer equipment. Since computers, scanners, printers, etc. all use different amounts of electricity, you should always make sure that the correct size of fuse is placed in each plug.
- **Bare wires showing**: there should be no bare wires showing from any plugs or sockets.
- **Tampering**: when taking the casing off any piece of equipment, make sure that the equipment is unplugged first.

Other safety aspects
- **Lifting**: any lifting of computers, printers, heavy boxes of printer paper, etc. should always be performed with your knees bent while keeping your back straight. There is a legal obligation on a company to show its employees how to lift properly if that is a requirement of a person's job.
- **First aid**: there must be a qualified first aider available at all times.
- **Fire precautions and emergency evacuation procedures**: these should all be in place and should be practised at regular intervals. Employees must be told not to use lifts during emergencies.

Obligations of system users

As mentioned previously, the confidentiality of data must be ensured, and procedures need to be in place to do this.

Responsible attitudes to private or uncensored materials

There has recently been a lot of concern from governments all around the world over the content of material which people can freely obtain on the Internet. The Internet provides access to an enormous range of information, and this information comes from many different countries worldwide. One problem with the Internet is that all the information is freely available to anyone who is connected. There are sex-orientated news areas to the Internet which contain large amounts of pornographic material. Although this material is illegal in this country, in other countries it is perfectly legal. The Government has the problem of finding a way of allowing users to gain access to the Internet but not to any illegal areas. If access to these areas is restricted on one part of the Internet then the user could simply move to another part to find a way into the material.

There is another problem in restricting access. The Internet is a global system and it is difficult for individual countries to make laws to control it. Another problem with restriction is that it could lead governments to begin attempts to censor, legislate and regulate the Internet for political, cultural and religious reasons. Civil liberty groups are naturally concerned about this aspect of control.

System security methods

In order to ensure the security of commercial and personal data there are various security methods that can be used, and these include the following.

Control of access

Control of access can be divided into two: physical access and logical access.

Physical access controls

Physical access controls usually involve improving the security around the computer system. If the building is secure then the computer system will be secure. To ensure the security of the buildings, some or all of the following need to be investigated:

Access to buildings
The following methods can be used to improve the physical security of the building:
● having fewer entrances to the building and using alarms on the emergency exits;
● using security guards, in uniform, to patrol the buildings (these act as a deterrent);
● making all staff and visitors wear security badges.

Activity 6.4

Write a paragraph on each of the above methods to explain in more detail how each one improves the security of a building.

Automatic access control
Automatic access control means controlling the access to a room automatically so that only allowed personnel are able to enter. Keys are unsuitable because they are easily copied and a lot of time can be spent getting security guards to unlock doors. Automatic access control involves fitting a device on the door so that a code has to be keyed in or a card inserted before the door can be opened. Sometimes the keypads are mechanical, though in newer systems they are electronic and look like the keypad of a calculator. There are other systems that make use of small radio transmitters that look like those used with alarm systems or remote locking systems for cars.

The main advantage to having automatic devices to control access to buildings or computer rooms is that the security guards and receptionists are then able to deal with exceptional rather than routine access.

Activity 6.5

Look through the catalogues of computer equipment suppliers and find out what devices are available to allow authorised entry to rooms but prevent unauthorised entry.

Access to computers
There are various factors to consider when trying to prevent access, either to steal the equipment or data or to gain unauthorised access.
● **Location of computer equipment**: computer equipment should be kept away from visitor areas or areas where the equipment is visible from the street.
● **Fixing microcomputers and other peripherals to the desks**: this deters and prevents

theft. Some systems include a lock, so that the computer can be moved by authorised staff if needed.

- **Holding sensitive data only on removable disks**: sensitive data should be held on removable disks so that they can be locked away when not in use.
- **Locking the computer when not in use**: many computers have a lock on the front of the processor and a key is used to prevent it from being turned on by unauthorised personnel.
- **Borrowing procedures**: the borrowing of computer equipment should not be encouraged. People get used to seeing other people carrying computer equipment out of the building and loading it into their cars. Security guards and staff should challenge anyone carrying equipment and there should be a set procedure for borrowing it.

Logical access controls

Logical access controls are used to prevent unauthorised access to data files and software. There are several logical access controls, including:

Use of passwords

Passwords are used to restrict access to certain files or data. The use of passwords involves entering a string of characters which have to match the password stored by the machine. If the password is too short then it can be easily discovered; if it is too long then the user is more likely to forget it. The ideal length for a password has been found to be around six characters.

Restricting the creation of user identities

It should not be easy to obtain a user identity and therefore to gain access to a computer system. User identities should be carefully monitored by the network manager or system administrator.

Use of encryption techniques

Banks and other financial institutions use **encryption** techniques, where data is coded before being sent via communication lines. A machine at the other end decodes the data. It is also possible to use these techniques to code data onto floppy or hard disks.

Restricting access to the operating system

It is possible to restrict access to certain functions in the operating system. For instance, you could use a menu system so that users never need to access DOS, Windows, etc. This prevents users from doing certain things like copying disks or formatting the hard disk.

Virus checking

What is a virus?

A **virus** is a mischievous program whose purpose is to disrupt the use of computers. Many viruses do little more than display a message (usually insulting!) on the screen, but some are designed to act after a certain period of time and do such things as make the characters start to 'drop off' the screen or even erase the entire contents of a hard disk. As their name suggests, viruses are able to spread from one computer to another by 'infecting' other disks. They do this by copying themselves onto floppies which then become infected. When an infected floppy is transferred to another computer, it copies itself onto the hard drive so that the computer is infected. The process then repeats itself.

Recently, an unemployed 26-year-old man was found guilty of 11 charges following a police inquiry after computers became infected with two destructive viruses called Pathogen and Queeg. A judge sentenced him to 18 months imprisonment, and he became the first person to be convicted under the Computer Misuse Act 1990. The viruses hit many large companies but one company in particular was badly hit and had to close down its international communication network to stop the virus from spreading. As a result of the virus the company lost between £0.25 and £0.5 million.

The viruses disguised themselves so that they hid in different forms as they passed from computer to computer, and this meant that most virus checkers were unable to detect them. The man even wrote a manual which was distributed to other virus writers using the Internet telling them how to write viruses that could remain hidden in the system.

The virus called Pathogen was designed so that when it had become live and infected 32 times, it would cause disruption and damage at a certain time on a Monday evening. In addition to the damage it would also display the message 'Smoke me a kipper, I'll be back for breakfast. Unfortunately some of your data won't.'

Here are the names of some viruses you might encounter:
- Cascade
- Friday 13th
- Ping Pong
- Gen B
- Gen P
- Stoned.

The dangers of viruses

Most people see viruses as troublesome but few would consider that you could be killed by one! This has not happened yet, but there was a life-threatening situation recently when a patient suffered a dangerous reaction to penicillin prescribed by a stand-in doctor. The GP's files had a virus on them which resulted in the erasure of this vital information.

Remember: computers are not limited to the commercial world; hospitals, emergency services, aircraft all use computers. The effect of a virus on one of these systems could be devastating.

Virus detection software

Viruses are a serious threat and therefore should be taken seriously by all computer users. **Virus checking** should be carried out routinely rather than just when problems occur and a virus is suspected. Virus detection software (**antivirus software**) should be installed on the hard disk so that when the computer is booted up it checks the memory and the disk for viruses, and when any floppy disks are inserted into the drive, these are checked as well.

Because new viruses are being developed all the time, and the widespread downloading of Internet files aids the transfer of such viruses, it is essential to make sure that up-to-date virus checkers are used. These can be obtained with quarterly or even monthly updates.

Virus removal

Most viruses, after detection, can be removed without harming the data, but if the virus has already done some damage then it becomes important to make regular back-up copies. The process of removing a virus from a disk is often referred to as 'disinfecting' the disk.

Avoiding viruses

- Software should be bought only from known and reputable suppliers.
- Any software from external sources should be scanned thoroughly using virus detection software.
- Try to avoid using too many different computers, since this will increase the risk of picking up a virus.
- Do not allow people to use boot disks or unauthorised disks, or to play games on a machine.
- Install antivirus software on all machines for checking the memory, the hard disk and any floppies that are inserted for viruses.

Activity 6.6

Schools and colleges always have problems with viruses, mainly because of the large numbers of floppies put into the machines by students every day. Although virus checkers can check most viruses, there are always new strains which are not detected by the older virus checking software.

Produce a small pamphlet to be given to all students when they join a college alerting them to viruses, including what they are, the damage they do and how disks can be checked for viruses using the virus checking software with which you are familiar.

Back-up procedures

Back-up is the creation of copies of programs and data so that should the programs or data be lost, they can be recreated using the back-up copies. Although there are many software utilities (e.g. Norton Utilities) available for the recovery of lost data, these won't be able to recover data from every situation, so there is no substitute for making a back-up copy.

Back-up copies should be kept on a separate disk or tape and stored away from the computer system. If a back-up copy were kept on the same disk as the original, then if this disk were stolen or destroyed by fire the back-up copy would also be lost.

Rules for backing up

- Never keep the back-up disks near the computer. If the computer is stolen, then unless the thieves are ignorant about computers, they will probably take the disks as well. Never keep the disks in the drawer of the desk since this is the first place thieves will look.
- If you hold a lot of data which would be very expensive to recreate, then you should invest in a fire-proof safe to protect your back-ups against theft and fire.
- Keep at least one set of back-up disks in a different place (i.e. at a different site).

Disk failure

It is important to bear in mind that all microcomputers will suffer at least one serious fault during their lifetime. A typical hard disk unit has a mean time between failures of 20 000 to 200 000 hours. This means that if a computer were used for 12 hours a day, 5 days a week and 52 weeks a year, then you could expect its hard disk to break down once in about 6 years. If the computer were being used as the file server (i.e. the computer used to control the network), then it could be switched on 24 hours a day, 365 days a year, and the hard disk could fail on average every 27 months. Couple this with the chance of other components failing and you have a complete computer system which is likely to break down every 14 months.

Back-up copies of the programs and data on the hard disk should be taken at regular intervals. A tape streamer should be used, which looks something like an ordinary tape recorder. Transfer from the hard disk to the tape takes place quickly and you don't have to supervise the computer while it is being backed up. Should the hard disk become damaged, then the reverse transfer is quick.

The grandfather-father-son system (the ancestral file system)

There is always the chance that data held on either a disk or tape master file could be lost. It could be destroyed by an inexperienced user, a power failure, fire or even theft. It might even be deliberately damaged by a disgruntled employee. For most companies, the loss of vital data could prove disastrous. However, using the **grandfather-father-son principle** it is possible to recreate the master file if it is lost.

The principle works like this. Basically three **generations** of files are kept. The oldest master file is called the grandfather file and is kept with its transaction file. These two files are used to produce a new master file called the father file which, with its transaction file, is used to create the most up-to-date file, called the son file. The process is repeated and the son becomes the father and the father becomes the grandfather and so on. Only three generations are needed and the other files can be re-used. Usually this system, also called the ancestral file system, is used for disks, although it can also be used for tapes. Figure 6.10 summarises the principle.

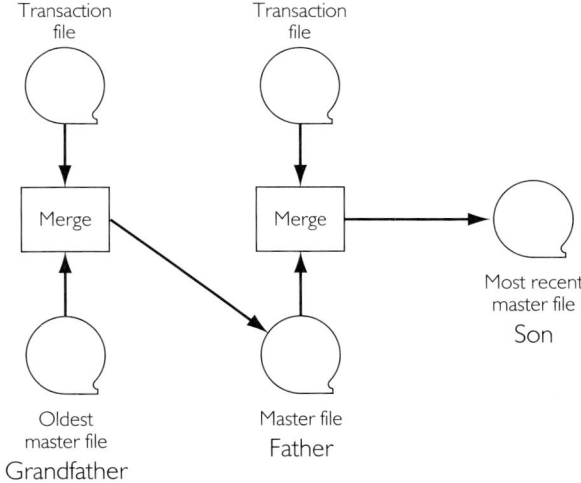

*All these files are kept so that if one or more of
the files are lost they can be recreated*

Figure 6.10 The grandfather-father-son principle

Forced recognition of security

Information technology is used extensively for a wide range of tasks, including operating nuclear power stations, flying planes, and storing and updating medical records, insurance records and even police records. With so much information being held, it is very important that adequate security systems are in place to protect the systems against deliberate, natural or accidental harm.

207

Non-disclosure agreements

Non-disclosure agreements are terms that are placed in a contract of employment which impose certain restrictions on employees even after they no longer work for an organisation. They usually refer to the passing on of valuable business information to a competitor. Sometimes they are used to prevent a person from speaking about their previous employment. Such clauses have been used recently by the royal family to prevent staff from talking to the press.

Official Secrets Act

The Official Secrets Act is used to protect the privacy of information held by the Crown and to protect national security. Civil servants, military personnel, prison warders (in those prisons which have not been privatised) and police officers all have to sign the Official Secrets Act as a condition of their employment. In taking such employment and signing the act, the person is then legally bound to a certain amount of security during the course of their employment.

Audit trails

All computer systems which process transactions involving money need to be audited. An audit is a check to make sure that the results from the computer are correct and that they haven't been interfered with in any way. Auditing prevents fraud and often acts as a deterrent against crime.

Auditing with a paper-based system is easy since it is possible to trace individual transactions through their various stages of processing. So an auditor (the person who performs the audit) can trace an order through the different stages to the point at which payment is made to the supplier.

Many financial transactions which take place using computers do so with little or no paperwork, so the above method cannot be used. Instead, the computer provides what is known as an **audit trail**. An audit trail is a record of the file updating that takes place during a specific transaction. It enables a trace to be kept of all operations on file.

An audit trail allows the auditor to pick a transaction at random, and check that the transaction goes through the correct processes, that any money goes into the correct accounts and that any output or reports produced by the system are correct. It is also possible to pick out a balance or total and then to find out all of the transactions that have been used to calculate it.

Assignment A6.2

This assignment develops knowledge and understanding of the following element:
3.4 Investigate the safety and security requirements for a data handling activity

It supports the development of the following key skills:
Communication 3.2, 3.3 and 3.4
Information technology 3.1, 3.2 and 3.3

You are employed as the data processing manager of a mail order company involved in the sale of the latest fashions direct to the public via a catalogue. Your main duties involve the day-to-day running of the data processing department and making sure everything runs smoothly. You have in your charge 40 staff most of whom use computers all the time or periodically in the course of their work. The majority of these staff enter details of orders, invoices, etc. using keyboards. Much of this work necessitates them having to work at high speed from source documents or customer telephone calls and this means some of them spend long periods at the computer.

A television programme is broadcast one evening which draws attention, in an alarmist way, to the problems which could occur when working for long periods with VDUs and keyboards. Many of the staff watched it and are worried that their work may be affecting their health. The safety and union representative has approached you to allay some of the fears the workforce might have. She has only a superficial knowledge of computers and has come to you for further information, and she would also like to know what steps the company is taking to reduce the risks.

The Managing Director also saw the programme and has heard that the staff are voicing their concern.

Another problem has come to light. The company holds personal information not only on its own employees but also on all of its customers, and this has meant that it has had to register its use of the personal data with the Data Protection Registrar. The Managing Director has decided that many of the staff do not know anything about the Data Protection Act 1984 and the company's obligations under the act.

Task 1

The safety and union representative is concerned about the following problems raised in the programme:

- eye fatigue leading to poor eyesight caused by continually looking at a screen;
- backache caused by incorrect posture;
- the dangerous radiation given out by the screen (particularly the dangers to pregnant women);
- skin rashes;
- stress caused by a large workload.

1 Research each of these problems, making use of information from reliable sources. Plan a presentation outlining the facts relating to each problem and what the company intends to do to reduce the risk of each problem occurring. You should also mention any other problems which you come across during your research.
2 The Managing Director suggests that you find out if there is any equipment which could be bought to help with the problems outlined above. He would also like you to see if a change in working practices would help. Carry out research into the points raised by the Managing Director, and plan a structured presentation.

Task 2

The Managing Director thinks it would be a good idea for you to talk to the staff about the following:

- the Data Protection Act 1984 and the reason for its introduction;
- the eight data protection principles;
- data covered by the act and what exemptions there are;
- the obligations the act places on the company;
- some security guidelines for the staff.

Produce brief notes that could be used as handouts to help reinforce the points made in your talk.

Task 3

You have recently been looking at the contents of the hard drives used by the department and have found some unlicensed software as well as some games. The company intends to bring in a terminal connected to the Internet on which it intends, eventually, to put the entire catalogue so that customers will be able to place their orders direct using a computer.

You are concerned about the following issues and need to mention each one to the staff during a presentation:

- copyright infringement;
- responsible attitudes to uncensored materials available on the Internet;
- the confidentiality of data.

Plan a presentation to cover each of these issues.

Task 4

Staff have lost important and valuable files due to viruses, operator error, etc. Write a brief report about the security methods which could be used routinely by staff to reduce these problems.

Sample unit test

1 The method of processing most suited to clearing bank cheques is:
   a single-user processing
   b batch processing
   c real-time processing
   d transaction processing

2 In a travel agents, where holidays and flights need to be booked on the spot, the most suitable method of processing would be:
   a single-user processing
   b batch processing
   c transaction processing
   d any method of processing

3 A large company uses many terminals which are all connected to a large, central computer where all the processing is carried out. Each terminal in turn is given a certain amount of time connected to the main computer. What is this period of time called?
   a multiplexer
   b transaction
   c time-slice
   d frequency

4 Some organisations prefer, for security reasons, to spread the processing out over several computer systems. Such a system is referred to as:
   a a distributed system
   b a centralised system
   c a single-user system
   d a batch system

5 A video library needs to know which videos are rented out most frequently, so a new system is developed. The main objective of this system is:

a to speed up the system

b to reduce cost

c to support decision making

d to enable a greater degree of accuracy

Questions 6–10 refer to the following information:

An examination board uses computers for marking multiple choice answer sheets, producing lists of candidates, producing the slips that are given to students showing the times of exams, and also for producing mark sheets.

6 What method of data capture is the most appropriate for marking the multiple choice examinations?

a optical mark recognition

b magnetic-ink character recognition

c keyboard entry

d barcode reading

7 All the candidates need to be put into alphabetical order on the mark sheets. This type of processing is an example of:

a calculating results

b sorting information

c converting information

d merging information

8 When the final results are produced, each school and college is given a list of its students. Which best describes this type of report?

a a forecast

b an exception report

c a summary report

d a merged report

9 Two people are used to check the mark sheet against the central database and against the marks on the examination paper so that students are given the correct marks. This checking is an example of:

a validation

b verification

c a range check

d a consistency check

10 It is possible that some of the staff working at the examination board's office know some of the candidates, and they could obtain these candidates' results for them before the official results are published. The best way of preventing this is to:

a use passwords on all computers

b store only each candidate's number with their marks and not their name

c get all the staff to sign a non-disclosure agreement

d deny all the staff access to the computer

11 A doctor's surgery holds confidential medical information on all its patients. What is the *main* reason for keeping this information safe?

a the doctor could be guilty of copyright violation

b patients could gain access to their own medical information

   c the doctor is legally required to protect the data

   d the doctor could be guilty under the Official Secrets Act

12 A bank gives all its customers a credit limit. What type of information is a credit limit?

   a marketing

   b sales

   c financial

   d legal

13 The security of the computers, programs and stored data in an organisation is vital. There are two type of access control: logical and physical. Which one of the following is *not* an example of physical access control?

   a having fewer entrances to buildings

   b making all staff and visitors wear security badges

   c putting all computers on one of the top floors of the building

   d using passwords on all the computers

14 Which one of the following would *not* be part of a validation check?

   a a range check

   b proofreading information on the screen before it is accepted for processing

   c a data type check

   d an existence check

15 Which one of the following is an example of logical access control?

   a fixing computers and their peripherals to desks

   b using encryption techniques with all data

   c locking computers away when they are not being used

   d discouraging staff from taking computers for home use

16 An architect receives plans for a building stored on magnetic disk. Before using these disks it is essential that:

   a they are formatted first

   b they are checked for viruses

   c they are checked for file type

   d a back-up copy of them is made

17 What is the grandfather-father-son principle?

   a a program for tracing your ancestors

   b a tree structure used by a file management program

   c a back-up procedure which keeps the last three generations of files

   d a way of ensuring that only authorised people are able to access data

18 Many financial transactions now take place with little or no accompanying paperwork. To track the transactions which have taken place, it is necessary to:

   a perform an audit trail

   b produce an exception report

   c produce a summary report

   d carry out a range check

19 Static electricity can cause damage to the data stored on magnetic media. To reduce static electricity in a room containing computer equipment it is necessary to:

   a avoid the use of carpets made of artificial fibres

   b make sure that all plugs contain a fuse

c site computer screens away from sunlight
d use wrist-guards

20 A database used by a credit card company holds data about all its customers, including details of customers' credit limits and of the amount of money they owe on their cards. The company needs to search the database to extract details of customers who have exceeded their credit limit. What type of report would be the most appropriate?
a a summary report
b an exception report
c a mail merge
d a report showing every customer

21 Networking software allows users to access only certain files or directories. This is restricting the users':
a privacy
b piracy
c access rights
d non-disclosure

22 People who spend long periods of time keying in data at keyboards may develop a condition called repetitive strain injury (RSI). One of the methods of preventing this is to use:
a a copyholder
b suitable lighting
c a wrist-guard
d adjustable blinds on the windows

23 Which one of the following is *not* a method of preventing viruses?
a avoid using too many different computers
b scan all software and data before it is loaded
c make sure that all software is downloaded off the Internet
d install up-to-date antivirus software

24 A company stores the personnel records of all its employees on computer. Which of the following *must* the company do?
a register the fact that it is holding the data under the Data Protection Act
b sign the Official Secrets Act
c get all staff to sign a non-disclosure agreement
d register with the Copyright, Designs and Patents Act

25 When obtaining money from a cash dispenser, a secret number called the PIN is entered. The input device normally used for this is:
a a keyboard
b a mouse
c a touch screen
d a keypad

26 Bookshops use the International Standard Book Number (ISBN) to identify a book. The ISBN contains a check digit which enables the user to ensure that the number has been entered correctly. The best description of a check digit is:
a a unique number used to identify a book
b a number which is compared with the answer to a calculation involving all the

other numbers in the ISBN to make sure that the ISBN has been entered
correctly

    c a number used to make sure that the ISBN is in the correct range

    d a number used to check if a book is currently in stock

27 The magnetic band on the back of a credit or debit card is read using:

    a a magnetic strip reader

    b a magnetic-ink character reader

    c an optical mark reader

    d a barcode reader

28 'Appending' means:

    a adding extra data to the end of an existing file

    b deleting some of the data at the end of a file

    c altering part of each record stored on a database

    d waiting for changes to be made to a file

29 Which one of the following is *not* considered to be a file maintenance activity?

    a appending

    b deleting

    c amending

    d printing

30 Hacking into someone else's system with a view to looking at the information
stored on it or altering it in any way is an offence under:

    a The Computer Misuse Act 1990

    b The Copyright, Designs and Patents Act 1988

    c The Data Protection Act 1984

    d The Official Secrets Act

31 The data protection principles can be found in:

    a The Computer Misuse Act 1990

    b The Copyright, Designs and Patents Act 1988

    c The Data Protection Act 1984

    d The Official Secrets Act

32 Most people who spend a lot of time looking at a computer screen experience
eye strain. Which one of the following is *not* a way of preventing eye strain?

    a using suitable lighting

    b using a copyholder

    c having frequent eye tests

    d making sure that an anti-radiation screen is fitted to the VDU

33 A document has been set to read-only. This means that:

    a it is impossible to change the document

    b no one can read the document

    c an inexperienced user is prevented from altering the document

    d the document can only be stored on CD-ROM

34 The personnel department of a company keeps copies of the contracts of
employment for all the company's employees. What type of information is a
contract of employment?

    a legal

    b financial

c marketing

d product

35 Which one of the following would be an inappropriate application for batch processing?

   a the production of electricity bills

   b the production of credit card statements

   c the real-time booking of theatre tickets

   d the marking of multiple choice answer sheets

7 Communications

What is covered in this chapter

Element 4.1: Investigate electronic communications

- Introduction to communications systems
- Network services
- System components
- Standards for electronic communication
- Protocol parameters
- Modes of electronic communication

Element 4.2: Use electronic communication to transfer data

- Preparing and connecting hardware for electronic communication
- Accessing software for electronic data transfer
- Interactive electronic data communication
- Maintaining a communications activities log

Resources you will need for your portfolio for Elements 4.1 and 4.2
- Your written answers to the activities and assignments in this chapter.

Introduction to communications systems

In the first part of this chapter we will explain network services used for electronic communication, and describe the system components and standards for electronic communication. We will also explain the purposes of the protocol parameters and modes of electronic communication.

There are three parts to any communications system:

- **A sender of information**: this could be a person sitting at a workstation/terminal or data from an automatic measuring device, for example a traffic flow sensor at a busy junction.
- **A communications link**: in most cases this will be a physical link, a wire or cable along which the data is sent, but it may be a logical link with data received as radio signals.
- **A receiver of information**: this could be another workstation or remote computer.

Network services

A network service links together users in different places. Such networks offer a variety of services, which are outlined below.

Electronic mail

Most networks have electronic mail facilities, whether they are local area networks (LANs), which are based at a single site, or wide area networks (WANs), which are widely dispersed and may be based around many sites.

Electronic mail, or e-mail, enables messages, letters and other documents to be sent from place to place electronically rather than through the conventional postal system (now sometimes called 'snail mail'). With e-mail sent via a **service provider** (such as CompuServe), the sender sends the document to the recipient's e-mail address, which is actually a small area on the service provider's computer, and not directly to the recipient. When the intended recipient logs onto the system they are informed that there is mail waiting for them; they can then either read the mail while logged onto the system or download it onto their own hard drive for reading later.

The use of the Internet has made e-mail facilities available to anyone who has a modem and is connected to the Internet by a service provider such as CompuServe or AOL (America On Line).

Main advantages of e-mail
- E-mail is faster than ordinary mail.
- You do not need to print the mail out, find an envelope, stamp, etc.
- It costs very little to send.
- It is more environmentally friendly since less paper is used and less energy is consumed in delivering the mail from source to destination.

Main disadvantages of e-mail
- People may not read their e-mail regularly or if they are away others may not know how to use their system.
- Not everyone is a subscriber to an e-mail system, so ordinary mail is still needed.

When you are replying to an e-mail message, it is a good idea to copy the incoming text into your reply so that the recipient does not have to search for the original message. Most programs allow this and any copied text is marked by chevrons like this >> to distinguish the original message from the reply.

Activity 7.1

A friend, knowing that you are a bright GNVQ Advanced IT student, has come to you for advice.

Your friend has heard about e-mail and how easy it is to send but does not know much about the ins and outs of the system. He has heard that more documents are sent by e-mail in the USA than by traditional post and is keen to find out if an e-mail system could help him in any way.

You agree to find out more about it. Your friend has a PC but no modem and is not on the Internet. Here are some questions he would like you to answer.

1 What additional hardware and software do I need to send e-mail and how much will it all cost?
2 What is a 'service provider' and how much does one charge?

3 Are there any service providers you can suggest and why are they better than the others?

4 What are the main advantages and disadvantages of e-mail?

5 How simple is it to use?

6 I have only one phone line; will I need to install another?

Conferencing

The introduction of a new digital communications system called ISDN (see Chapter 8) has led to an ever widening use of desktop **video conferencing** systems. Video conferencing enables people to conduct face-to-face meetings with people in another part of a building or even another part of the world, without any participants leaving their desks.

Although video conferencing has been around for some years, any participants needed to use rooms with special equipment from which the conference could be administered. With such systems the conference delegates still had to leave their desks and it was quite expensive to hire the rooms and equipment. The latest desktop systems are able to communicate with these larger systems so everyone does not need to have a desktop system.

Desktop video conferencing systems require, in addition to a PC, a **video compression card**, a **sound card**, a video camera and specialist software.

Advantages of video conferencing include:

- reducing travel and hotel accommodation costs;
- making meetings more productive, since computer and paper documents can be sent rapidly to delegates' screens;
- allowing people who normally work from home (telecommuters) to stay at home yet still take part in meetings;
- suitability for training and customer support since it is possible for demonstrators to show customers and trainees exactly what happens.

There are several main systems which dominate the desktop video conferencing market: Vivo Software Vivo 320, Intel Proshare, PictureTel LIVE PCS 50 and AT&T Visitum 1200.

Activity 7.2

You have been asked to organise a traditional meeting with ten branch managers who are scattered around the country. Write down a list of the things you will need to organise.

Bulletin boards

A **bulletin board service (BBS)** may be best described as an electronic noticeboard. It is provided by a computer which is permanently connected and switched on to a telephone line so users can log into it via their own computers to place notices or access information. Bulletin boards are frequently used to sell services and goods. Chat services, a form of conferencing in which users carry out a typed conversation with any number of other people, are also classed as BBSs. You have probably used such a service if you are connected to the Internet. Many BBSs deal with specialist information and are rather like clubs run by enthusiasts. BBSs are now often called **forums** on the Internet.

File transfer

Electronic mail transfers text from one computer to another, but it is relatively slow, so another method is used for transferring large files. **File transfer** is used to transmit any type of file (computer programs, text files, graphics, etc.) by a process which bunches the data into packages. When a package of data is received the receiving system checks it to make sure that no errors have been introduced during transmission. A message is then returned to the sending system to confirm that the package is OK and that it is ready to receive the next package of data.

There are many technical problems associated with transferring files using modems and communication lines and these will be dealt with later in this chapter.

Interacting with databases

One of the main advantages of a company using a network rather than a series of stand-alone computers is that the users are all able to access the same database thus avoiding the need to duplicate data. This is particularly important with data that is frequently modified or updated, as without a common database different users' versions soon begin to diverge in content. Being able to interact with databases is therefore an important service provided by any network.

Interacting with databases is an essential element of one network service which is growing in popularity: **electronic data interchange (EDI)**, which allows companies to automatically exchange data. Large food retailers use this method for ordering goods automatically from their suppliers. The system performs ordering, checking and making payments, without any paperwork.

Direct interaction (voice, data, video)

Until recently the transfer of data-hungry multimedia applications which use video, sound, voice, etc. was not practical because of the power of the average PC and the slow speed of data transmission. The introduction of high-speed links and the processing power of the latest PCs has now made the transfer of such data possible. Nissan, for instance, uses a network to send a ten-minute video presentation by its chief executive to all its dealers.

Voice messages can be sent via a communications network in which they are transformed into digital form, which can be stored in the same way as e-mail. When logging onto the system the user is informed that there is voice mail waiting and can play this message back.

Fax

A conventional fax (an abbreviation of 'facsimile copy') consists of a fax machine at one end of a line acting as the sender and another at the other end acting as the receiver. The sending machine scans a paper document placed in it and converts the image (text, graphics or both) into digital form which is sent via the modem in the fax along the telephone line to the receiver. The receiving fax uses its modem to convert the digital data back, recreate the image and then print it out.

It is clear that all these functions could be carried out perfectly well by a typical small computer and this is the purpose of the fax modem. A fax modem enables one computer to send a fax directly to another, eliminating the need to scan a hard copy (a printed copy) into a fax machine.

If a fax is sent to the computer on which you are working, the fax modem automatically takes charge, answering the phone and storing on your hard drive the data from the fax transmission. You are then able to view the fax using special software supplied with the fax modem; a hard copy will only be made if you need one. This system saves both time and paper.

Since all fax files are sent in graphic format you cannot simply transfer them to your wordprocessing software. To do this, optical character recognition software will be needed to recognise the shape of each character and convert it into the ASCII code which can be imported into any wordprocessing package.

System components

There are several items of specialist equipment needed when computers are networked. These include the following system components.

Data terminal equipment (DTE)

Data terminal equipment is the component at the end of the communication chain which acts as a terminal on a computer system or network. In most systems this is either a **dumb terminal** or a PC (personal computer). However, it could also be a point-of-sale terminal or a cash dispenser.

Data circuit-terminating equipment (DCE)

Data circuit-terminating equipment is the name given to devices (such as a modem) which pass information to a terminal. Such a device must be capable of establishing a connection, maintaining it during the data transfer and then closing down the connection at the end of transfer. The DCE therefore controls the connection between data terminal equipment and the telephone line.

Modems

Telephone lines were not originally designed to transfer data. They were developed to transfer sound signals from one place to another. In a telephone, the varying frequencies of the human voice are converted into electrical signals which are then passed along the telephone wires to an earpiece that converts the electrical signal back into sound. Sound signals are analogue signals; their waveforms vary continuously with time. Since the electrical signals generated are replicas of the sound, the electrical signals are also analogue.

Analogue signals
Analogue signals have an infinite number of 'in-between positions', whereas digital signals jump from one value to the next. A watch with a dial and hands can show an infinite gradation of times, whereas a digital clock face jumps from one minute (or second) to the next.

Digital signals
Digital signals consist of pulses of voltage or current which represent the information to be processed by a computer. The digital voltages can be 'high' or 'low', the high voltage being used to denote a '1' and the low voltage a '0'. Data is thus represented as binary pulses (1s and 0s) consisting of high and low voltages. It is cheap to produce

electronic circuitry to deal with digital signals, and noise is not too much of a problem with binary signals since if the signal becomes distorted it can usually be regenerated and the noise removed. This is not possible with analogue signals because of the complex nature of the waveform which easily becomes confused with the noise, and thus is continually degraded.

Modems

Modem is an abbreviation for modulator/demodulator and this hardware device is used to convert the digital signals from a computer into an analogue form so that they can be passed along the telephone lines. A second modem then changes the analogue signals back to their digital form at the other end. Most external modems are small boxes with several indicator lights which flash on and off. Internal modems are situated inside a PC and often show what is happening by flashing indicator lights on the screen. Modems plug directly into the telephone socket, although the lead provided is seldom long enough and generally requires an extension. Figure 7.1 shows two modems connected at either end of a telephone line.

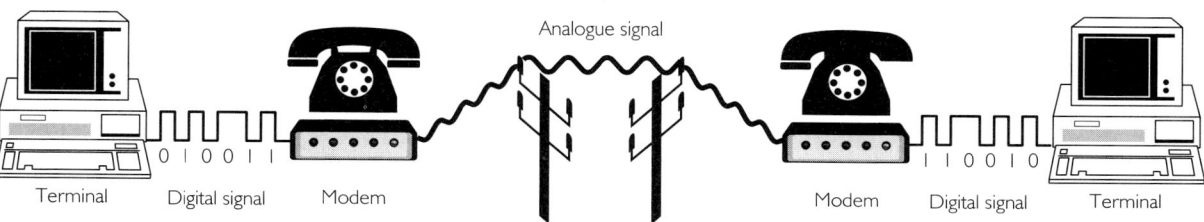

Figure 7.1 Using a telephone line to carry data

Modems determine the speed at which you can interact with other computers over the telephone lines. When a modem makes a connection to another computer it will negotiate with the receiving modem a speed for the transmission and receipt of data. The speed of transmission is important since this determines the time it takes to transfer the data and hence the cost of the phone call, and possibly the on-line charges levied by the service provider. There will be more information on data transmission rates later in this chapter.

Some of the latest modems are able to deal with both voice and data at the same time using a single telephone line with a system called **digital simultaneous voice and data (DSVD)**. This is important during a video conferencing session since it allows participants to speak and exchange data (in the form of an on-screen whiteboard) at the same time.

Connectors

Connectors are used to join the cable to the terminal. Examples of connectors include Centronics parallel, 9 pin D and **null modem** connectors.

Software

All types of computer-based communications systems need software to enable the hardware components to function. All computers require system software (an operating system) to work, and communications systems require some additional software. User interface software and communications software are also needed.

It is important to use communications software that is able to work properly with the modem selected.

Cabling

Cables are an essential part of any network and can contribute substantially to the cost of the whole system. It is very important not to skimp on cabling since it is frequently a cause of network failure. Since trailing wires are dangerous, they must be sunk into channels or passed through hollow plastic conduit. Network cables are frequently placed inside the same hollow plastic channels used to hold telephone wires. There is a wide variety of wire types and choosing the best for an application is discussed in the next chapter.

Standards for electronic communication

Devices connected to communication lines must have certain characteristics in common so that they present electronic signals in a similar way, thus ensuring that devices are able to communicate with each other. In other words, they need to be able to understand each other's signals, and to do this manufacturers need a common standard for electronic communication.

Unfortunately there is a variety of organisations which set (different!) standards for electronic communication. In this book, wherever communications are discussed, the terms used are those defined by the CCITT (the international committee for data communication).

Data representation

Whenever a character (letter, number or symbol) is typed on a keyboard it is converted to binary code (a series of 1s and 0s) and on a network these are transmitted along a wire until the code is received, decoded and converted back to the character again. Most computers represent characters using ASCII code (American Standard Code for Information Interchange) and Figure 7.2 shows the 8-bit code for the 26 letters of the alphabet.

A 0100 0001	B 0100 0010	C 0100 0011	D 0100 0100
E 0100 0101	F 0100 0110	G 0100 0111	H 0100 1000
I 0100 1001	J 0100 1010	K 0100 1011	L 0100 1100
M 0100 1101	N 0100 1110	O 0100 1111	P 0101 0000
Q 0101 0001	R 0101 0010	S 0101 0011	T 0101 0100
U 0101 0101	V 0101 0110	W 0101 0111	X 0101 1000
Y 0101 1001	Z 0101 1010		

Figure 7.2 Representing letters in ASCII

Data circuit connections

The two main standards for data circuit connections are V24, which is the CCITT standard, and RS232C which is the US standard. Both of these standards define the pin connections for each communication device. In fact, the V24 and the RS232C standards can be considered equivalent.

Protocol parameters

When people communicate with each other, a set of rules apply although we are not aware of them. For instance, we wait until another person has finished talking before we speak, and we usually show that we have understood what has been said by nodding occasionally. This may be considered a 'protocol' for conversation.

Similarly, networking is not just a question of connecting computers with wires and then assuming they will be able to understand each other. A set of standards is needed to make sure the computers are communicating with each other in the same way and in an organised fashion. This set of communication standards is the protocol, and it covers the areas set out below.

Transmission rates

The transmission rate is a measure of the number of bits that can be sent along a communication channel by a modem and is measured in bits per second (bit/s). One bit per second is called a baud so the number of bits per second is the same as the baud number.

Transmission rate is an important consideration when buying a modem. Faster modems cost more but this cost may soon be recovered if you consider the quicker data transfer obtained. During transmission you are paying for the phone call and possibly an on-line connection fee; both of these will be reduced with a faster modem.

Modems are available in a range of speeds, typically 9600, 14 400, 28 800 and 33 600 bits/s. However, these are not necessarily the baud rate since many modems are now able to compress data before transmitting it. **Data compression** repackages data to one quarter or even one sixth of its original size, which means that such modems will have **baud rates** four to six times higher than their crude data transmission rate. So, for example, a modem with a transmission rate of 2400 bits/s and a compression ratio of 4:1 would have a baud rate of $4 \times 2400 = 9600$.

Activity 7.3

In this activity, you will produce a comparison between three different modems on which a purchasing decision can be based.

Look through a couple of recent computer magazines for modem adverts. The three modems you choose should operate at different speeds and have different compression ratios. Produce a comparison of the costs of sending different file sizes through telephone lines using each of the modems you have selected. You will need to calculate the time taken to transmit the various quantities of data, research the cost of using the telephone line (BT, Mercury, Cable, etc.) and look into the costs at different times of the day.

Show evidence of your research, including any calculations used, and present your findings clearly in a report.

Flow control

Flow control is a common method used by the receiving computer to issue 'start' and 'stop' commands to the computer sending the data; this prevents data being sent faster than the receiving computer can deal with it. The commands used are sometimes called **XON** and **XOFF** commands. Flow control causes the modem to stop and start the data transmission as required.

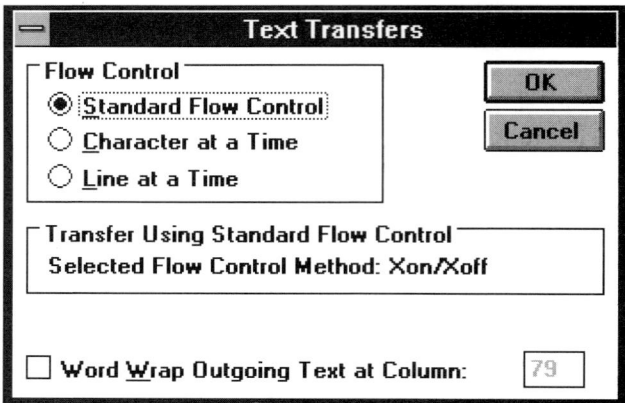

Figure 7.3 A settings menu showing flow control options

Figure 7.3 shows a menu used to select the flow control method.

Number of data bits

Each keyboard character is converted to a series of bits (0s and 1s) which is called a **byte**. A byte may therefore be defined as 'the number of bits used to represent a single character'. Data bit lengths are the number of bits within a byte that carry the actual character. Data bit lengths can be set to 5, 6, 7 or 8 but the most popular lengths by far are either 7 or 8.

Number of start bits

In serial communication where bits are sent one at a time, a **start bit** is included in the stream of data to tell the receiving computer that a byte of data is to follow. The start bit is added to the start of the data stream.

Number of stop bits

A **stop bit** is added to the data stream in serial communication to inform the receiving computer that the transmission of a byte of data is complete.

Parity

In addition to the start and stop bits, another bit is added called the **parity bit** and this is used for error checking. Parity checking works likes this. The computer adds up the number of bits in one byte and if the parity bit is different to the parity setting the computer will report an error. It is possible to use either even or odd parity. Taking odd parity, for instance, suppose we are sending the letter C along a communication line. In ASCII code the series of bits used to represent C is 1000011. Since there are three 1s in this code and odd parity is being used, then a 0 is added to left-hand side of the group of bits so that the total for the byte is odd. If even parity were being used, a 1 would need to be added so that total for the byte would then be an even number.

Modems have a chip inside them to deal with parity checks; the sending modem adds the parity bits and the receiving unit calculates what the parity bit should be. If an error has occurred, transmission parity will no longer be observed, and the corruption is detected. The problem with parity checks is that if more than one error occurs and the errors compensate for each other, parity can still appear to be correct.

In order to use your computer as a terminal it needs to have the same settings as the computer it is connected to (called the host computer). Figure 7.4 shows the screen where the setting can be altered.

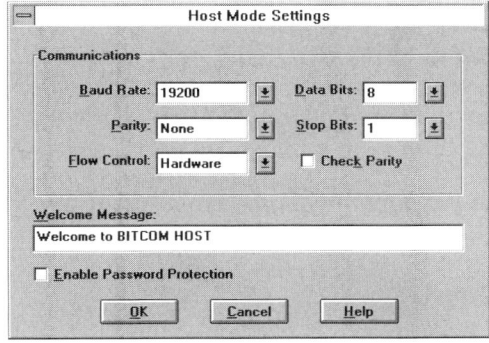

Figure 7.4 The host mode settings menu

Activity 7.4

I If even parity is used to check a group of bits after they have travelled along a communication line, which of the following groups of data are correct? (The parity bit is on the far left.)

a 10000101
b 01101010
c 10001110
d 01100101
e 10101010
f 01101100

2 Another system uses odd parity, and again the left-most bit is the parity bit. Using the same bits as in I above, say which ones are correct by this system.

Modes of electronic communication

Devices can act in a variety of ways or **modes** when receiving data along a communication line. These include terminal modes and transmission modes.

Terminal modes

There are several ways terminals can operate in terminal mode and features of such modes include the following:

Echo
Some terminals (very slow ones by today's standards) cause the characters to appear on the sender's screen when sending or receiving data so the sender is able to check for errors. Duplication of the sent characters in this way is called **echo**.

The idea of echo is for the sender to check that the received characters are correct, and if they are not a control character is sent so the receiving computer knows to ignore the incorrect character. This is a very crude form of error correction and its slowness and the need for manual error checking means that it is seldom used nowadays. With today's high-speed communications links, automatic error checking is necessary.

Wrap

In the context of networks (rather than wordprocessing), **wrap** means that once a certain number of characters has been exceeded on one line, a new line is automatically started. Without this facility it would be necessary to use either the cursor keys or the scroll bar to move horizontally to read the line.

CR/LF

CR/LF is the abbreviation for 'carriage return/line feed'. Carriage return is used to end a line of text and move back to the start of the line; it is activated by pressing 'enter' or 'return' at the end of a line.

Line feed is the command which moves the cursor down to the next line and moves a set of data up as it is received. On a printer, however, the line feed moves the paper. Carriage returns and line feeds are used together to take the cursor to the beginning of the line below. In the terminal preferences screen you can set the inbound and outbound signals separately to CR/LF.

Terminal emulation

Suppose you want to connect your PC to an IBM mainframe computer to access a database. Problems will arise, because IBM computers can communicate only with IBM dumb terminals and the formats used by a PC and an IBM mainframe are very different. The keys that you press on your PC mean something completely different to the IBM mainframe, which has its own character and control codes. If you want your PC to communicate with an IBM mainframe it will need it to behave exactly like an IBM dumb terminal. Software, called a **terminal emulation** program, is used for this purpose.

If, when using a terminal, you can make out what the characters say, but they are surrounded by strange symbols, it is likely that the wrong type of terminal **emulation** is being used. Two things could be done to rectify the situation: either the PC's or the host computer's emulation settings could be changed. In most cases, it will be the terminal's emulation settings that will be adjusted.

Transmission modes

The transmission mode determines whether a signal can be sent in both directions and if so whether the two directions can operate at the same time. There are several transmission modes and these are dealt with below.

Simplex

In **simplex** mode, data is able to travel only in one direction, although in some systems this may be sufficient. For example, for remote weather stations data from the sensors has to travel only in a single direction – from the weather station to the central computer.

Teletext systems, where data is sent using television signals, can be classed as simplex since the data is only sent one way.

Duplex (sometimes called full duplex)

In **duplex** transmission two channels are used at the same time: one to send the signal and one to receive the reply, thus making possible simultaneous two-way communication. A mobile phone uses this type of transmission mode.

Half-duplex

In **half-duplex** mode, two-way transmission is possible because there are two communication lines, but using the equipment available it is possible to send and receive only in one direction at a time. Older walkie-talkie systems used this mode; after talking you would say 'over' and press a switch to let the other person use the communication channel, but in the opposite direction.

Figure 7.5 shows the three modes of transmission outlined above.

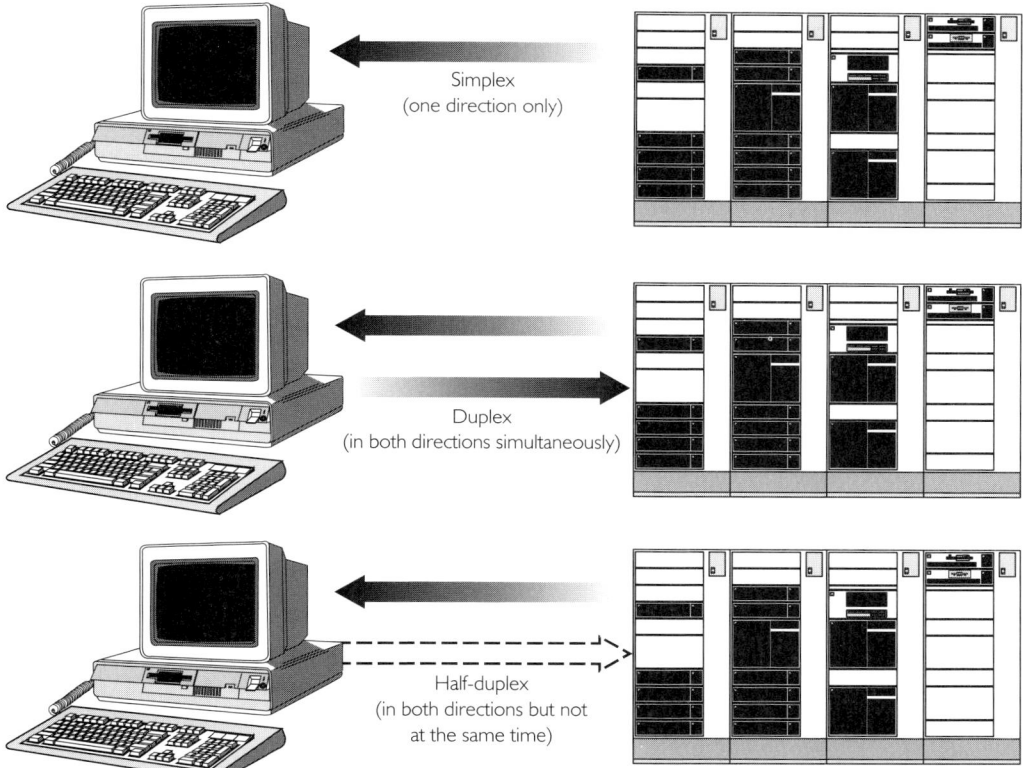

Figure 7.5 The three main transmission modes

Asymmetric duplex

Asymmetric duplex mode operates in a similar manner to duplex mode, except the transmission speed in one direction is different to that in the other.

Serial transmission

With **serial transmission** each character is broken down into its binary code and the resulting series of bits (0s and 1s) sent one after another down the communication line. When they reach the receiving device they are reassembled into the character again. Although serial transmission is slow compared with parallel transmission, it is the method used over all but very short distances.

Handshaking

Handshaking is the name given to the method of controlling the flow of serial communication between two devices so that data is transmitted only when the device at the receiving end is ready. There are two methods in use, the hardware method and the software method. With the hardware method, a separate wire sends a signal to tell the sending device that the receiver is ready; this method is really only suitable when the devices are near enough for a special cable to be used. It is used, for example, when a computer communicates with a serial printer.

Communications systems which make use of a telephone cable have only a single wire so hardware handshaking is not possible. Instead, software handshaking is used, where special control characters let the sending device know when to send data. One software method used is called XON/XOFF and this uses Ctrl+S to pause sending the data and Ctrl+Q to resume transmission.

Parallel transmission

In **parallel transmission**, groups of bits are transmitted side by side at the same time. While this method is faster than serial transmission it is only suitable for transmission over short distances. The number of bits in each group depends on the number of bits used to represent each character, any additional bits needed for control (start and stop bits) and any parity bits. Parallel communication is the method used between disk drive or printers and the CPU and is usually satisfactory provided the length of cable used does not extend beyond about three metres.

Asynchronous transfer mode

If the characters sent along the communication channel can be sent at any time, there needs to be a method of stopping the flow if either side cannot keep up with the speed of transmission. Start and stop bits, mentioned in the previous section, overcome this problem. Although the characters can be sent at any time (hence the name synchro-nous), the bits for each character are transmitted at a constant rate. Because of the extra bits needed for each character this method is slower than the alternative method called **synchronous transmission**.

Asynchronous transfer mode (ATM) uses high-speed packet switching to transmit fixed-length packets of data at speeds of up to 155 megabits per second (Mbits/s). Until recently ATM was available only on expensive, high-speed links between mainframe computers and their terminals but costs have come down to such an extent that they are now within the reach of most LAN users. As well as the high transmission speed, ATM has another advantage in that it is less error prone than synchronous transmission.

Synchronous transfer mode

Synchronous means 'happening at the same time'. With synchronous transfer mode the two computers are synchronised so that they keep exact pace with each other as they send and receive the binary pulses. This type of communication is suitable for high rates of data transfer.

Assignment A7.1

This assignment develops knowledge and understanding of the following element:
4.1 Investigate electronic communications

It supports the development of the following key skills:
Communication 3.1, 3.2, 3.3 and 3.4
Information technology 3.1, 3.2, 3.3 and 3.4

Communications have moved forward in the last couple of years in leaps and bounds and networking is no longer the domain of the network manager. The demand for quick and cheap information has led to a huge growth in the use of networks and the Internet.

Task 1

A radio programme aimed at young people is to have a short slot of about 15 minutes on the latest developments in networks and communications in general. You have been asked to do some research on this area and present your findings in the form of a report, but an experienced writer will actually write the script. When writing your report ensure that you:

- make the report interesting
- explain any specialist jargon
- use language appropriate for a teenager.

Your report is to cover network services which include:

- electronic mail
- conferencing (video and chat)
- bulletin boards
- file transfer
- interacting with databases (you could look at the search programs that seek out data on the Internet)
- direct interaction (voice, video and data).

Task 2

The broadcasting company is to issue a free booklet to accompany the series and you have been asked to provide some information which could be included. The same criteria apply here as for the previous report.

The suitably illustrated booklet should contain the following:

- a description of system components and standards for electronic communications;
- an explanation of the purpose of the protocol parameters and modes of electronic communication.

You need to make sure that the booklet covers all the material in the range for this element.

Preparing and connecting hardware for electronic communication

Networks are as different from one another as the people using them so it is difficult to talk about a typical network. The network you will be using in your college is most likely to be a local area network (LAN) with a way of accessing the Internet, which is itself a wide area network (WAN). Wire links are by far the most common method used to connect together the data terminal equipment, although if you access any of the Internet resources in other countries you will most likely be using satellite links.

Modems are available in two types: internal and external. Internal modems, or card modems as they are often called, fit into one of the expansion slots inside the PC. They are usually cheaper than their external counterparts and have the additional advantage that they do not take up valuable desk space. However, they do need physically inserting into the machine which can deter non-technical users, and they do not have any lights to indicate that they are working.

External modems contain LED displays which let you know when they are working and, more importantly, when they are transmitting or receiving data. They come in a variety of physical sizes, including modems the size of a credit card for connection to laptop machines.

Connecting cables

Connecting cables are commonly used to connect computers and their terminals but there are other methods which do not use cables. Radio signals or microwave links can be used. Sometimes, when data needs to be sent over large distances, satellites are used.

Different types of cables are needed for different networks. Cabling is a hidden cost when networking and it can add considerably to installation costs. The wiring is crucial to any network and is one of the weakest links in a network system, so it is important to use the best possible wiring and not to skimp on cost grounds.

There are various factors to consider when choosing cables:
- Using shorter cable runs will mean that the network will run faster.
- Cheap cable will affect the performance of the system. As always, you get what you pay for!
- Cables should not be left across walkways since people will trip over them; they must be sunk under carpets or, better still, placed inside the trunking which carries the phone lines in most modern offices. There can be considerable costs involved in hiding cables yet still leaving them accessible for maintenance.
- A layout diagram should be drawn and kept, to show how the network has been connected and where the cable runs are.

Unshielded twisted pair wire

Figure 7.6 shows a typical unshielded twisted pair (UTP) wire with its four twisted pairs of insulated, colour-coded wires inside a plastic outer cable. The purpose of the twisting is to cancel out any electrical noise produced between the pairs and also noise from any nearby electric cabling. The advantages and disadvantages of this type of cabling are as follows:

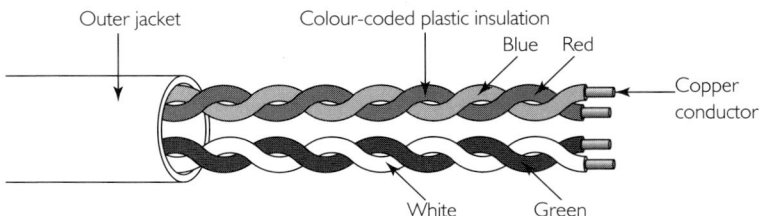

Figure 7.6 Unshielded twisted pair wire

Advantages
- It supports fairly fast data transmission rates.
- It is the cheapest form of cabling.
- Thin wires and small connectors allow it to be easily sunk into trunking.

Disadvantages
- Cable lengths have to be kept short.

Coaxial cable

Coaxial cable gets its name because of the way the two metal conductors share the same central axis along the length of the cable. You will probably have seen cable of this type used to link the aerial socket of your television and the aerial. Figure 7.7 shows a cross-section of such a cable. Coaxial cable is used with Ethernet and ARCnet systems. The advantages and disadvantages of coaxial cable are as follows:

Advantages
- Very fast rates of data transmission can be achieved.
- It is a mid-priced cable.

Disadvantages
- It is thicker than UTP cable and tends to be quite rigid, which can cause problems when bending the cable in a small space, resulting in higher installation costs.
- It is suitable only for medium distances (typically 0.5 km).

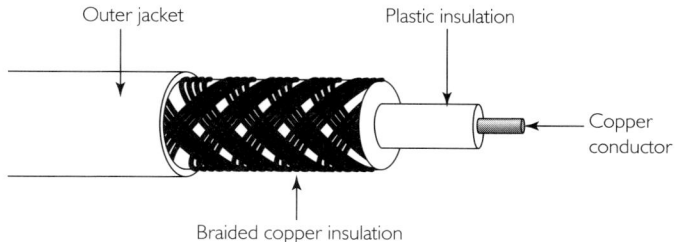

Figure 7.7 Coaxial cable

Shielded twisted pair wire

Shielded twisted pair (STP) cable differs slightly from twisted pair cable as it contains two lots of shielding: a braided copper layer which shields all the wires and a foil layer round each pair of wires. This high degree of shielding offers considerable protection from outside interference and is used primarily in token-ring LAN applications. The advantages and disadvantages are as follows:

Advantages
- Very fast rates of data transmission can be achieved.

Disadvantages
- It is expensive.
- A lot of shielding means the cable is thick and soon fills cable ducts.
- It is generally only suitable for short cable runs.

Figure 7.8 shows shielded twisted pair wire.

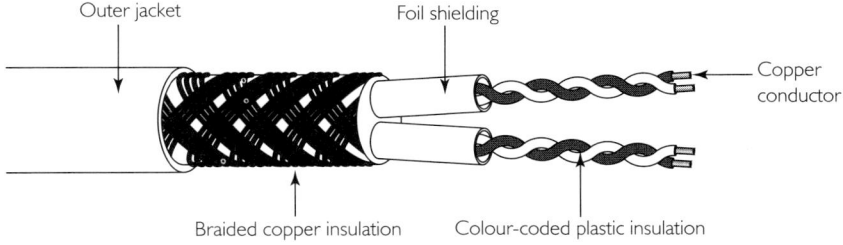

Figure 7.8 Shielded twisted pair wire

Fibre optic cable

Unlike the other cables discussed, fibre optic cable works by transmitting light along its fibres, each fibre conducting messages in one direction only. Two bundles of fibres are thus used, one for forward pulses, the other for return pulses. Because each of the fibres is fragile, they are encased in plastic, and the two bundles placed in a plastic outer cable. In order to use this cabling for networking, special optical connectors are needed connected to laser transmitters which project the signals down the fibres. At the other end of the cable there is an optical receiver which turns the light pulses back into electrical signals. Figure 7.9 shows the construction of a fibre optic cable.

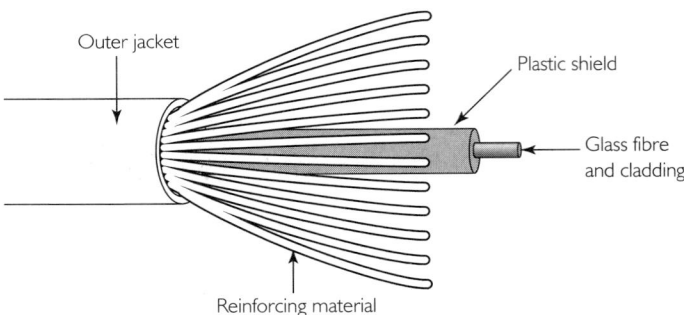

Figure 7.9 Construction of a fibre optic cable

The advantages and disadvantages are as follows:

Advantages
- Because pulses travel at the speed of light this is the fastest possible transmission medium.
- The cables may be very small which makes them easy to lay.
- No electrical signals are used, so this method does not suffer from any outside noise.
- Extremely long cables can be used because light pulses do not degrade very much with distance.
- It is more secure than other cables since fibre optics create no magnetic field which can be tapped into.

Disadvantages
- The extra equipment needed to send and receive optical information, and the technology needed to make the cables, makes this the most expensive transmission medium.

Accessing software for electronic data transfer

As always, the hardware of a network can work only if it has appropriate software to direct it. Software for networks falls into the following categories.

Operating systems software

Most modern operating systems provide some facilities which support networks; Windows 3.1, Windows 95 and UNIX are the most popular. Although the facilities to support networks offered by modern operating systems are excellent, many people prefer to use specialist networking software with its extra facilities. This specialist software, generally called **networking software**, is either an operating system in its own right, or needs an operating system such as UNIX to be loaded before it can be used.

As well as providing the usual services that single-user operating systems provide, operating systems with networking facilities have to be able to accept requests from users to access certain network facilities, such as printers, CD-ROM drives, or files from the file server or from the hard drives of other machines. Such operating system software must make sure that the request is valid (i.e. the terminal making the request is allowed access to the device), check to see if there are any conflicts (two terminals could send a signal to access the same device simultaneously) and then provide the requested service.

Networking software

Networking software may be part of the operating system you are using or special software which you need to buy separately. **Novell's** Netware is the best known and most popular network operating system and has around 70 per cent of the market.

Applications software

Suppose that two users are trying to make alterations to the same record on a centrally held database at the same time. They cannot work simultaneously, so the application allows only one user at a time to make an alteration; it does this by a process called file locking. However, although simultaneous file writing is not allowed, records can still be viewed by many users at the same time. The ability to perform file locking is one main difference between network versions and stand-alone versions of applications programs.

Configuring controls and protocols to match a remote station

In the past, the user had to alter the settings of their computer to match those of the host computer to which they were connecting. Nowadays, however, some communications software performs this task automatically without the user even being aware of it.

Binary transfer

Binary file transfer, as the name suggests, is a method of transferring binary files from a terminal to a remote computer. When performing binary transfers you need to select 'binary transfer' from the settings menu in the communications software. There are two protocols which allow binary transfer: one called XModem/CRC which uses all eight bits as data bits and therefore has no parity, the other called Kermit which transfers either seven or eight bits as data bits. With Kermit the parity option can be set to even or odd for seven data bits, or none if all eight bits are used for data packets.

Modem commands

Modern modems are almost invariably controlled from software so there are no switches on the modem to alter before use. Modem commands are instructions which are issued to configure the modem and enable it to communicate across a network.

Terminal preferences and emulation

When you want your PC to behave as a terminal linked to a remote mainframe computer it has to mimic a dumb terminal. There are no 'frills' when using a dumb terminal and most of the screen appears blank, waiting for either you or the remote computer to make the first move. Before a connection is made, the settings menu appears so that alternative settings to the usual ones can be made. The usual settings assumed by the system are called the default settings.

One setting is the 'terminal preferences' option. Rather than alter many settings each time you want to connect to a remote computer, it is easier to get your PC to behave as if it were a dumb terminal, behaving in the same way as other terminals connected to the same mainframe or mini-computer. To do this it is necessary to choose from the list in the terminal emulation settings the type of terminal your PC is to mimic. The default value is set to the most popular terminal and there are a couple of other settings which can be used if the default terminal proves unsuitable. Figure 7.10 shows the terminal emulation screen.

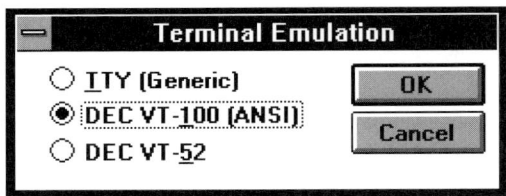

Figure 7.10 Selecting a suitable terminal from the terminal emulation menu

Once a terminal has been chosen it is possible to change the preferences using the 'terminal preferences' menu. Some options are fairly trivial, but others are important, for example the 'number of buffer lines' retains a certain number of lines of text, enabling you to look back at the previous lines of a message. The 'line wrap' means that the text automatically moves to the next line (like word wrap in wordprocessing) and this prevents the text going outside the allocated window on the screen. The CR->CR/LF makes a simple carriage return into a carriage return and line feed. This is only usually applied to the inbound data and you know that it is needed when lines appear superimposed on each other.

In order to see what you are typing at a terminal it is sometimes necessary to turn the local echo on. If, however, the lines appear twice, the local echo must be turned off. A typical terminal preferences menu is shown in Figure 7.11.

Protocols

Protocols can be chosen from a menu similar to the one shown in Figure 7.12 which is the communications window from Windows 3.1.

Data bits, parity and baud rate

You can select from the communications menu the number of data bits in each of the data packets sent between your terminal and the remote computer. Parity can be even, odd or none. If the number of data bits has been set as eight the parity must be set at none. The baud rate of the terminal needs to be matched to the baud rate of the remote computer. Remember, the baud rate is a measure of the speed at which the modem transmits data between the two systems. Many modern modems are able to transfer at a variety of baud rates and will try the highest rate first and then lower rates until connection is achieved. They are able to do this automatically. If your modem cannot do this, you will need to find out the baud rate of the computer to which you are connected and alter the setting of your terminal accordingly. Alternatively you can go through the rates one by one, starting at the highest, until connection is obtained.

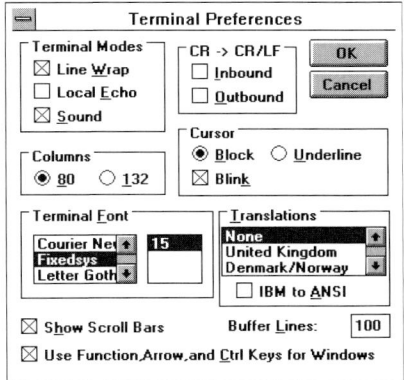

Fig 7.11 The terminal preferences menu

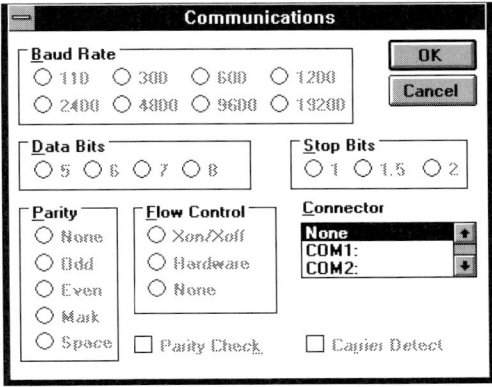

Figure 7.12 Communications window

Flow control

Flow control determines what the terminal should do if the buffer becomes full and is therefore unable to receive more data, at least until the existing data is dealt with. There are two methods of flow control: XON/XOFF or the hardware method. Some computers have no method of control, so flow control will need to be set as 'off'. XON/XOFF is the best method to use at first and will usually be the default setting.

Stop bits

Stop bits can be set to 1, 1.5 or 2 and determine the time interval that elapses between transmitted characters.

Connection port

The connection **port** (commonly called the communications port) is the connection into which the modem is plugged at the back of the computer. There are usually several communications ports, called COM1, COM2, COM3, etc. It is important that the correct port is selected using the communications menu.

Carrier detect

Carrier detect is the name given to the method by which the modem signal is used to detect a carrier signal and so indicate whether the modem is on-line. If this is not selected, the terminal will look at the string of bits given out by the modem (called the **modem response string**) in order to determine whether the modem is connected.

Data file transfer

There is a series of processes which must be performed in sequence to transfer a file from one machine to another. These processes are as follows:

Data file identified

You will often want to transfer a file between two systems using electronic communications. For instance, you may want to transfer a text file or maybe a copy of a program or just a list of data. To transfer the data the name of the required file must be known. It is possible to retain the filename once the file has been transferred or to rename the file.

Destination selected

Each device connected to a network is a node and has a node number. Files are often sent using communication channels, in which case it is necessary to know the telephone number of the host modem or an Internet address. To send a file to another terminal, a print server or file server over the LAN, it is necessary to know the address of the node.

Modern communications software performs many of the tasks automatically so it is often possible to select the destination from a menu or with one of the function keys.

Communications link established

Communications links are established in a variety of ways but all the methods provide a means of letting the user know that the link has been established. Usually this is either a text message or some sort of graphic (traffic lights, bolt of lightning, etc.). If the link is not established the communications software will attempt the connection again, sometimes altering the configurations slightly or trying a different communications port. If there is still no connection after a set period of time (which you can select) the computer will tell you that the connection is unsuccessful.

Activity 7.5

Write down the series of steps needed to access your Internet service provider from the software.

Data transfer undertaken and communications link closed

When you are downloading files off the Internet, your software frequently tells you how long the file transfer is likely to take (at a variety of different modem speeds) so it is possible to work out the cost of the file in terms of on-line and telephone charges.

The system will automatically tell you once transfer is complete so that you may disconnect from the telephone line and avoid any further charges.

Downloading files off the Internet

The Internet contains innumerable files which you could find useful, so it is important to be able to download these to your own computer. Downloading means copying files from a remote source to your own computer. In many ways the process is like copying a file from a floppy disk to a hard drive, except that the drives are in different places and the file is coming to you over the telephone line.

The software you load when you subscribe to an ISP (Internet service provider) will contain a download button to enable you to display a dialogue box asking where on the hard drive you would like the file placed. The file you want to download should be highlighted and appear automatically in this box. Usually a directory or **folder** will be created by the communications software to hold these downloaded files.

When you have decided where the downloaded file is to go, you can commence downloading by clicking on the download button. The estimated time for the download should now be displayed, which is useful as some files can take 20 minutes or more to download and you may switch off thinking that you have lost the communications link!

Compressed files

Many files which you download will be compressed, which means they have been made smaller using a special program. This is useful as they will download faster which in turn costs less. In order to use a compressed file it is necessary first to decompress it. Most ISPs will come with software for doing this and the most common file formats used are PKZIP and PKWARE. These files are easy to spot as they always have the file extension .ZIP. With many service providers, any compressed files which you have downloaded will be decompressed when you sign off. This saves the cost of decompressing the files while still on-line.

Interactive electronic data communication

Interactive communication is used when two operators wish to 'talk' to one another via the keyboard. It involves linking up two computers directly, using a null modem or a public WAN. The chat service provided by ISPs such as CompuServe or AOL can be considered interactive electronic data communication. These services provide a way of chatting to people all around the world, except that instead of talking you type. Although much slower than a normal conversation, you can talk to people anywhere in the world for the price of a local phone call.

Maintaining a communications activities log

This is an automatic log (like a diary) stored on the computer by the communications software which records all activity on the network. It is a little like an itemised phone bill from which it is possible to find out to whom connections have been made and how long each call took. However, the activities log is much more sophisticated than this.

An activities log will normally contain the following information:

- date and time of the communication;
- time taken on-line;
- amount of data transferred;
- names of the files transferred;
- destinations of the files (this is often combined with the names of the files).

If you have an account with an ISP your current statement on-line itemises your sessions. Figure 7.13 shows the structure of an account with AOL (America On Line).

Figure 7.13 Extract from a statement of account from AOL

Time		OnName	Free	Paid	Charge	Credit	Total
29.1.97	16:04	SDoyle6945	0	5	0.15	0.15	
0.00							
29.1.97	15:53	SDoyle6945	6	5	0.15	0.15	
0.00							
28.1.97	22:30	SDoyle6945	2	6	0.19	0.19	
0.00							
28.1.97	22:25	SDoyle6945	1	5	0.15	0.15	
0.00							
28.1.97	22:20	SDoyle6945	0	6	0.19	0.19	

237

Assignment A7.2

This assignment develops knowledge and understanding of the following element:
4.2 Use electronic communication to transfer data

It supports the development of the following key skills:
Communication 3.4
Information technology 3.4

For this assignment you will be required to set up equipment and perform a variety of file operations using the Internet.

Your tutor will give you the components to enable Internet access. You will have to access the installed communications software to perform the following tasks.

Task 1
Assemble the hardware components you have been given according to the instructions your tutor has provided.

Task 2
Switch on the machine, load the operating system and the communications software.

Use the communications software and make any necessary adjustments to the controls and protocols to enable you to access an on-line service. Your tutor will give you information about the services you are to access.

Task 3
For this task you are required to undertake file transfer. Your tutor will tell you the files you need to download and where they can be found.

Provide evidence of successful completion of this task by writing an account of how the task was achieved.

Task 4
Keep a manual communications activities log, showing your various activities using data communications.

Sample unit test

1 Which two of the following are network services used for electronic communications?
   1 file transfer
   2 file structure
   3 file attributes
   4 database interaction
   a 1 and 2
   b 2 and 3
   c 3 and 4
   d 1 and 4

(RSA, June 1996)

2 Which one of the following is a type of conferencing used on an electronic communications network?

  a teleconferencing

  b mail conferencing

  c indirect conferencing

  d destination conferencing   *(RSA, June 1996)*

3 Before transmission, data characters are:

  a increased to ten bits in length

  b sorted into numerical order

  c converted into flow control codes

  d converted using a code   *(RSA, June 1996)*

4 Interactive electronic data communications is used:

  a to establish terminal type

  b to set the correct baud rate

  c to communicate directly 'user to user'

  d to connect data terminal equipment (DTE) to the physical transmission network   *(RSA, June 1996)*

5 Which one of the following items is found in a communications activities log?

  a carrier detect information

  b the terminal emulation log

  c the time taken on-line

  d data terminating equipment log   *(RSA, June 1996)*

6 Figure 7.14 shows the arrangement used when one computer communicates with another using the telephone lines. A special device is needed to change the digital signal from the sender's computer into an analogue signal which may be then passed along the telephone line. The name given to this device, marked by the arrow on the diagram, is:

  a a modem

  b a telephone

  c a terminal

  d a protocol

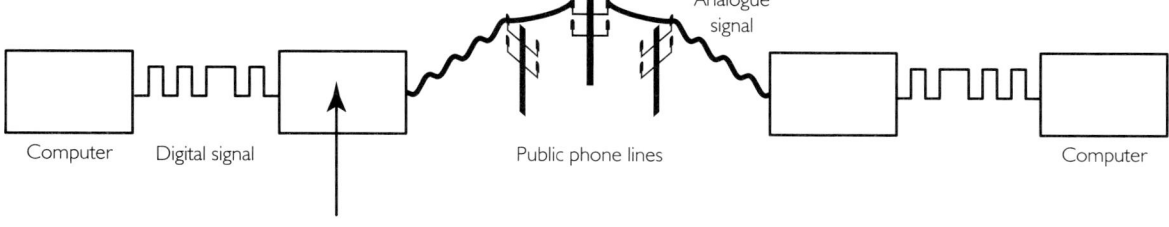

Figure 7.14

7 Before files are transferred using communications lines, they are often compressed first. What is the reason for this?

  a so that they can be stored using less space on the receiver's hard disk

  b so that they cannot be intercepted by hackers as they travel along the line

  c to enable them to be sent using a lower baud rate

  d so that they take less time to transfer and therefore cost less

8 A computer magazine advertises a modem as having a 28.8K. What does this figure measure?

a the speed of data transfer using the modem

b the size of the maximum file which can be sent using the modem

c the size of the memory of the chip inside the modem

d the size of the e-mail file which can be sent using the modem

9 Which one of the following is *not* considered to be data terminal equipment when on a network?

a a point-of-sale terminal

b a cash dispenser

c a dumb terminal

d a modem

10 Which one of the following is *not* an advantage of e-mail compared with the traditional postal system?

a it is faster than ordinary mail

b only people connected to the service can receive mail

c it costs less to send mail

d it is more environmentally friendly because it uses less energy

11 There is a system used by many large companies for ordering goods, checking that the correct goods have been received and making payments for the goods. All this is done without the need for any paperwork. This system is called:

a EDI

b fax

c DCE

d DTE

12 The bit used for error checking when data is transferred along a communications line is called:

a a stop bit

b a start bit

c a parity bit

d a check digit

13 When communicating with a mainframe computer, it is sometimes necessary for a PC connected to it to behave in a similar way to a terminal of the mainframe. This is referred to as:

a echo

b terminal emulation

c CR/LF

d data compression

14 The transmission mode in which data is able to travel in only one direction at a time is called:

a simplex

b full duplex

c half duplex

d handshaking

15 The purpose of two computers agreeing protocols before data transmission is:

a to make sure that the speeds of the modems are set to the same value

b to make sure that both computers are of the same make

c to ensure that data is checked by a virus checker before entering the system

d to make one computer behave as a terminal of a mainframe

16 XON and XOFF are commands used in:

a a method of flow control

b a method of error checking

c a form of parity

d parallel transmission

17 The fastest transmission media is:

a unshielded twisted pair wire

b shielded twisted pair wire

c fibre optic cable

d coaxial cable

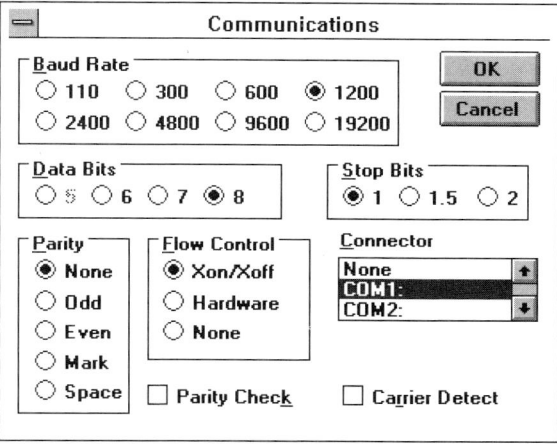

Figure 7.15

18 Figure 7.15 shows the communications window from the operating system Windows 3.1. From the settings you can see that:

a there is even parity checking

b seven data bits are used

c there is a method to ensure that data is not sent to the receiving computer too quickly for it to deal with it

d the fastest rate of data transmission has been chosen

19 A company is to implement team working practices and buys a new computer system so that all team members can access a database. The *best* solution would be for the company to:

a put the database onto the internal office e-mail system

b put the database onto several stand-alone machines

c put the database onto a file server and to install workstations

d put the database onto one machine and allow different users access at different times *(RSA, June 1996)*

20 A parallel communications connection is used between a computer and a printer because the computer system:

a can only send single bits

b is too fast for serial communications

241

c uses simultaneous 8-bit communications

d uses full duplex communications   *(RSA, June 1996)*

21 A message is transmitted as a series of data packets. Which one of the following *best* describes'stop bits'?

    a stop bits are used instead of parity bits

    b stop bits are used between transmitted data packets

    c stop bits are used only at the start of the transmitted message

    d stop bits are used only at the end of the transmitted message   *(RSA, June 1996)*

22 Which two of the following are assumptions that could be made about networks?

    1 fewer users will be able to access a terminal

    2 network software can be shared

    3 network security will have to be considered

    4 network software will run more quickly

    a 1 and 2

    b 2 and 3

    c 3 and 4

    d 1 and 4   *(RSA, June 1996)*

8 Computer networks

Computer networks

In this section we will investigate networks, the components that form networks, network topologies, the benefits of using computer networks, data flow control methods, network management activities and system security methods.

Types of network

All computer networks are either **LAN**s (local area networks) or **WAN**s (wide area networks) and in this section we will look at the differences between them and also the different types of network.

Local area network (LAN)

A LAN consists of computers connected together over a small area, usually a single building or site. The factor which distinguishes a LAN from its big brother, the WAN, is that no third party communication channels are used. All the wires connecting devices are owned by the organisation itself and how devices are connected is an internal matter.

Wide area network (WAN)

A WAN consists of computers connected over a large geographical area and dependent on the use of third party telecommunications equipment, such as telephone, radio or satellite communications links. It is common to find many LANs in different buildings around the country (or the world) connected together to form a WAN.

The backbone of a LAN in a single building is the wiring which links the terminals. All the equipment is owned by one organisation and it is up to that company to install and run the network as it sees fit. If changes need to be made to the network, such as adding new terminals, this is relatively easy and inexpensive.

With a WAN things are not that simple. WANs are much more sophisticated; the operator has to deal with telecommunications companies and does not own all the equipment. For instance, the wires between one LAN and the next are supplied by a telecommunications service provider, each of which has its own rules, regulations and service charges.

The simplest WAN connects two LANs in different buildings, using two modems and software on each machine together with communications link such as the public telephone line. This method is fairly cheap and does not need much extra equipment, but data transfer is slow and the phone bills correspondingly high. The other main disadvantage of using the public telephone lines is that they are not very secure, so there is a risk of unauthorised access by hackers who may see and possibly alter the information.

An alternative is to use a **dedicated leased line**, which is a line rented from the telecommunications service provider, of which you are the sole user. These lines have the advantage that they are fast, reliable and secure but the disadvantage of being expensive; you have to pay for the line itself as well as use of the line.

Broadcast services

Broadcast services are services that use radio links. The commonest broadcast service is that provided by **teletext** where pictures from computers are sent as part of the television signal used to transmit programmes. Teletext is not **interactive**; you cannot send a message back to the computer. The pages of information are sent cyclically so when you select a particular page number you have to wait until that page is reached in the cycle.

Broadcast services also include those networks that have terminals or workstations linked by radio or infrared signals rather than wires. Wireless local area networks allow users to access all office services when they are away from their desks at any time, even from a remote site. There are many situations in which this type of technology is useful. For example, it can be used in hospitals so that doctors and nurses can file information and data about a patient without having to go back to their desks to type in the information. Another use is in checking stock on supermarket shelves which at present is usually input using a hand-held terminal and then downloaded into the main system via a cable. With a wireless system, the terminal can transfer the data directly from shelf to main system.

House of Fraser case study

House of Fraser, the large department store group, is investing in a new radio-based local area network for its stores. It also looked at traditional cable-based networks but the laying of the cable would cost too much since many of the stores have marble or wood floors and these would need to be taken up and replaced. In such stores, the EPOS (electronic point of sale) terminals will all use radio signals to communicate with the main computer. Many of the stores are in older buildings but where newer premises already have cable ducts these will be used to link the LAN using copper cables. However, in both types of store, radio communication will be used for stocktaking, with hand-held terminals relaying stock information to the store's computer.

Private wide area network

A **private wide area network** is a network which uses privately leased or owned lines and may only be accessed if you are a subscriber to the system. One such network is called **JANET** which stands for Joint Academic Network. This is used to join together educational establishments worldwide.

With the growth in the Internet, there are many more private wide area networks. Internet service providers (ISPs) enable anyone with a modem and suitable communications software to access their network and also allow access to the Internet if required. Popular Internet service providers include AOL (America On Line) and CompuServe.

In general, Internet service providers are able to provide the following:
- **Instant messages**: you can hold a conversation interactively by typing messages at the keyboard and receiving others back.
- **Electronic mail (e-mail)**: electronic mail can be sent to other users of the system or anyone connected to the Internet by other service providers.
- **Message boards**: these enable people to exchange messages on a wide variety of topics. This is particularly useful if you have a problem and need advice. You simply post your message on the board and wait for any replies.
- **Directories of members**: these are rather like phone books, but give more information than just an e-mail address. Using this facility you can find people who share the same interests or hobbies as yourself.
- **Software downloads**: many people like to write programs for pleasure and are keen that others should use the results of their efforts. They do this by making their software freely available; the software can be downloaded using the communications line. Some of this software is 'shareware' which means that although you are free to download and evaluate it, if you find it commercially useful you pay a small fee to the developer who will usually then send you documentation or a more complete version. The developer also registers you for further upgrades as and when improvements are made to the program.
- **Members' services**: these enable you to keep track of how much time you have spent on-line and, more importantly, how much time you have to pay for. There are various

help services on offer for new customers. There are services that allow users to control the areas of the service that their children can enter; this is called parental control.

- **Hosted chats**: here you can 'chat' to someone famous. There is usually a list of times when a host will be on-line.
- **Main menu**: here is the place where you can start looking for information under a range of headings. Figure 8.1 shows the main menu from CompuServe.

Figure 8.1 The main menu from the Internet service provider CompuServe

Integrated services digital network (ISDN)

Although all data now seems to be stored in digital form from camera images, music recordings on CD and videos to computer data, the technology used to transmit the data (the telephone system) is over 100 years old and was originally developed for the transmission of voice signals. To transmit data along telephone lines the digital material has to be changed to analogue form and then converted back again at the other end. The problem with this is that the telephone system is not really up to the job. Files are becoming much larger and it is not just textual data which needs to be transferred.

There has been a gradual development in the UK towards a completely digital telephone system; known as **integrated services digital network** (**ISDN**). Many other European countries are also developing ISDN and countries such as America and Japan already have all-digital systems. The main advantage of ISDN is that it delivers data communication at speeds up to eight times faster than a modem, even without compression. If data compression is used, ISDN is able to transmit data at speeds up to 512 000 bits/s (bits per second); without compression a respectable 128 000 can be achieved. Surfing the Internet or transferring multimedia files can be done almost instantly.

Other advantages of ISDN include the facility to conduct 'virtual' meetings using desktop video conferencing and being able to use the telephone as a sophisticated business telephone with a wide range of new facilities. It is now possible to do several things at once on the same line, so you could be transferring a file to another person while holding a conversation with them.

There are two levels of ISDN service available: primary and basic. Primary offers more capacity but at greater expense while the basic service is mainly used by individuals and small businesses. One of the problems with ISDN at the moment is that it can only communicate with ISDN, so if you want to communicate with the Internet using ISDN, then the Internet service provider must also support ISDN connection.

To use ISDN you either need **terminal equipment (TE)** or a **terminal adapter (TA)** in place of a conventional modem. Remember that no modem is needed because ISDN is itself a digital service so there is no need to convert digital signals to analogue, and back again.

Activity 8.1

Task 1

Pettifog & Scrimp, a medium-sized business specialising in the publishing of historical journals, is thinking of converting from the slow world of analogue communications to a fully digital system. The IT manager has asked you, one of the systems developers, to investigate ISDN and report your findings.

Your report should be written in simple, non-computer language with all specialist terms explained, since it will be handed to the board of directors, most of whom have only a limited knowledge of IT.

You will need to include the following information in your report:

- what ISDN is and what is new about it;
- how ISDN works;
- all the advantages of ISDN over the traditional telephone system (make sure the advantages you state are relevant to a publishing company);
- the extra equipment needed to set up the ISDN connection;
- how to obtain ISDN from a telephone company and the costs involved.

Can devices which use analogue signals such as modems, faxes and answering machines still be used with ISDN? Explain your answer.

Task 2

There is the possibility that in the future many of the office staff at Pettifog & Scrimp could work from their own homes. One of the things preventing this from taking place is that many people work together on a project and there is the need for frequent meetings where ideas are discussed. One of the directors sees home working as a possible way of reducing costs, but the need for meetings may involve considerable added costs in respect of travelling expenses and hotel bills.

Write a brief memo to this director outlining the advantages of ISDN for telecommuting and also the use of ISDN for desktop video conferencing.

Public switched telephone network (PSTN)

The public switched telephone network (PSTN) is just another name for the telephone system. It is called 'public switched' because the user determines the number dialled. With communications systems the telephone numbers are stored in the computer and dialling is done automatically by the modem.

There are two types of telephone lines available: the standard telephone line and the dedicated or leased line. The standard line is the one we all use for telephone conversations but it can also be used for transporting data. Dedicated lines are usually used only by larger commercial and public service organisations such as banks, building societies, police, etc. Dedicated lines are faster, less prone to signal problems and also more secure, but the expense of leasing them precludes their use by all but the larger organisations.

Components which form networks

It is always hard to talk about a typical network since networks differ so much, but most will consist of some or all of the following components.

Workstations

A **workstation** is either a stand-alone computer or a dumb terminal connected to a network. If a stand-alone microcomputer is used as a workstation it is necessary to install a network card along with communications software. If a dumb terminal is used, the network card is included in the file server along with the communications software.

Workstation to media connectors

Workstation to media connectors connect the wires between terminals to the input socket situated at the back of a computer. The type of connections used depends on the medium employed. In most cases the medium used will be some type of metal wire, but fibre optic links are also quite common.

Figure 8.2 includes a T-piece connector which connects two network wires to a network interface card via a BNC socket at each end. This type of connector is used mainly with thin cables such as coaxial which is used in token-ring, Ethernet and ARCnet systems.

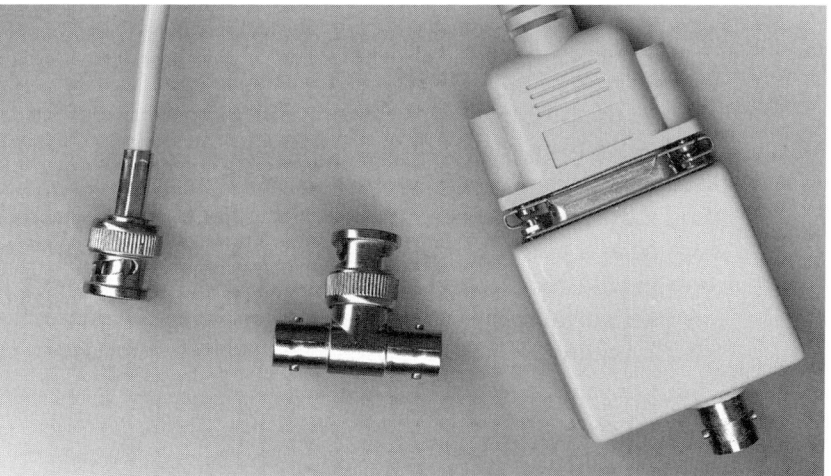

Figure 8.2 Network connectors

Data transmission media

The **data transmission medium** is the material through which data signals are sent. Such materials include metal wire, optical fibre and even air (if radio or microwave transmission is used).

Network cards

In order to use PCs as terminals for a network it is necessary to include inside each PC a piece of hardware called a **network interface card**, sometimes just called a network card. This is a small circuit board that slots into one of the connectors on the main motherboard. Network cards can be bought separately and their main purpose is to reduce the cabling between each terminal to a single wire.

File servers

As the name suggests, a **file server** is a computer used for managing the files on a network. File servers may be 'dedicated' in which case they will only manage files and not be used for anything else. Other file servers might also run programs as well as store files. In a network where the computers connected have different specifications, the computer with the highest specification should be chosen as the file server since the speed of this computer will determine the speed of the whole network.

In some ways a file server can be considered to be a giant hard disk drive to which all the other computers on the network have access.

Printer servers

A **printer server** is the name given to a computer in a network which has a printer or printers connected. The printer server manages printing for all of the network users. Each network user directs print commands to the printer server, which then controls the printers. Such a system has the advantage that individual workstations are then no longer tied up in managing their own printing. On very small networks, the printer server and the file server may be the same computer.

Gateway

A **gateway** is the name given to the facility which enables connection to wide area networks and network facilities. Figure 8.3 shows gateways (indicated by the hexagons) being used to connect a series of star LANs together ('star' is a type of network) over a wide geographical area. Since each star cluster may operate with different equipment and protocols, gateways are needed to convert protocols and allow LANs to communicate with one another.

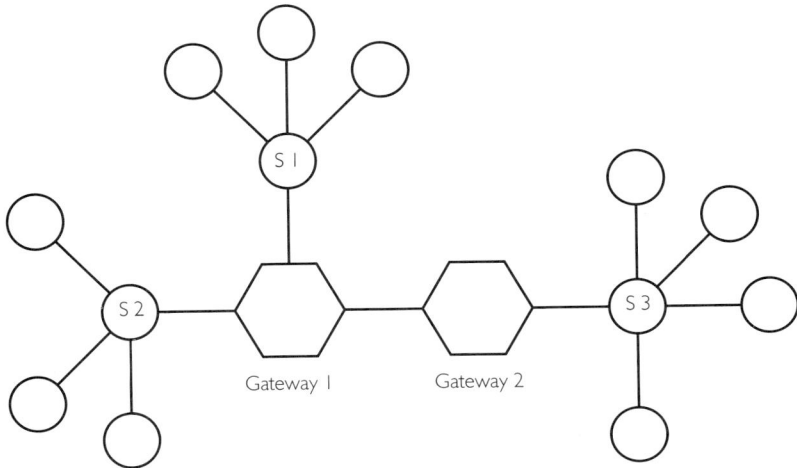

Figure 8.3 Gateways being used to connect a series of star LANs

The connection between one gateway and another may be a telephone line, a microwave link, a satellite link, etc.

Software

The software component of a network will include the operating systems software, networking software and special applications software. These types of software are covered in Chapter 7.

Multiplexers

Suppose we need to connect ten terminals to a single host computer. We could do this using separate connections to the host but this would involve a large amount of cabling and considerable expense. Instead we can use a hardware device called a **multiplexer** which allows simultaneous transmissions of multiple messages through a single communications channel. In practice two multiplexers are used, the one at the host end combining the multiple signals so that they can be sent along a single line, the other to separate the signals on arrival so that they can be sent to separate terminals. Figure 8.4 shows how each terminal needs its own pair of modems and a communications line. With a multiplexer, only one pair of modems and a single line are needed; Figure 8.5 shows this arrangement.

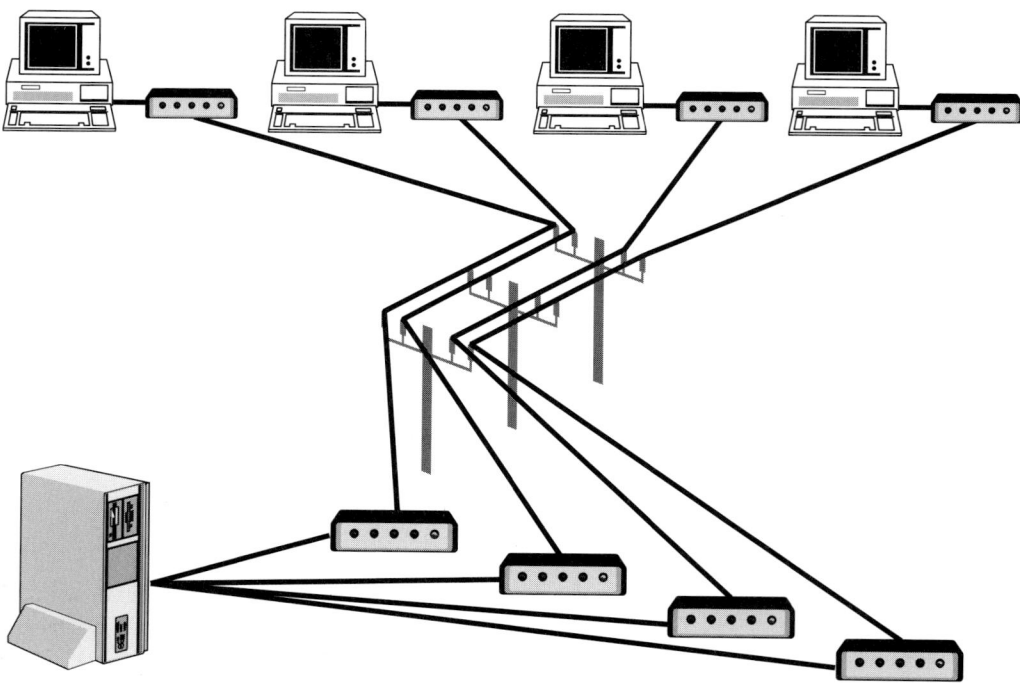

Figure 8.4

Auxiliary storage

Auxiliary storage may be classed as extra storage to the normal storage facilities on the file server. If PCs are used rather than dumb terminals (which do not have any storage capacity of their own), then work can be saved on the hard drive of any PC connected to the network.

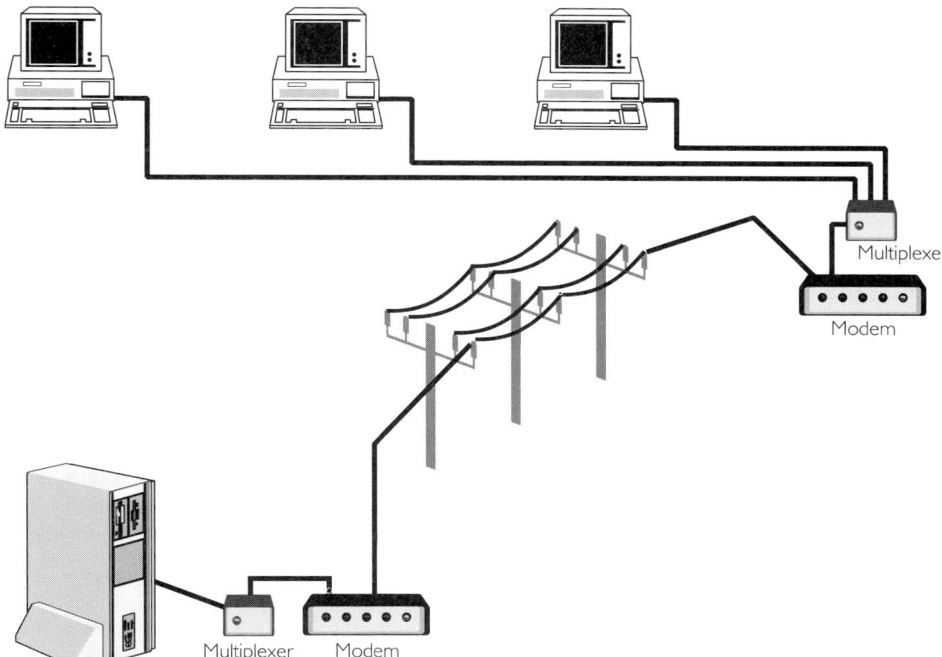

Figure 8.5 With multiplexers, a single wire and a pair of modems can be used for many terminals

Bridges

Bridges are hardware devices used to link together multiple LAN segments to form a single logical LAN. Their purpose is to send packets of data between one segment and the next.

Routers

Routers are hardware devices that decide which path an individual packet of data should take, thus ensuring that it is sent along the backbone in the fastest way.

Hubs or concentrators

Hubs or **concentrators** are hardware devices that enable LANs to be linked to each other and to WANs. The ring or bus topologies of a LAN can be connected to the backbone of a WAN.

The network computer (NetPC)

There has been a new development in computing with the introduction of the **network computer**. One of the main advantages to a business of using network computers is that they reduce costs. Although the hardware is not significantly cheaper the administration and maintenance costs can be much less.

A network computer is a diskless workstation designed to run special networking software written in a language called **Java**; this is either contained in a ROM chip inside the workstation or supplied from a server on the network to which it is connected. Because there is no disk storage in the workstation, all the user's work must be stored on a central server. Applications all need to be written in Java but access to the World Wide Web is easy because the browsers (the special software used to interrogate the Internet) are all written using Java.

One of the problems companies face with ordinary PCs is the users' tendency to modify them in some way, by installing programs or 'customising' the operating system. This all adds to problems when things go wrong. With the network computer the user cannot introduce viruses, alter the software settings in any way or make hardware additions. If a piece of software needs to be upgraded, the copy on the file server is changed and all users will then access this same new version.

Network topologies

Networks consist of stations (CPUs, servers, printers, POS terminals, etc.) connected together by communications channels, which usually means wires but can include fibre optic or radio links. When a network diagram is drawn, lines show the communications channels, and the stations, which are commonly called nodes, are drawn as circles. Networks may have their nodes logically and physically connected in a variety of patterns and these are called **topologies**.

Although other topologies are possible, for the GNVQ Advanced IT course you need only know about four: the ring, bus, mesh and star.

Ring topology

Ring topology is used only with LANs and in this topology the nodes are connected together in a circle, none of the computers having overall control of the network. If you look at Figure 8.6, a diagram of a typical ring network, you will see that for a node to communicate with a non-adjacent node it is necessary for the data signal to pass

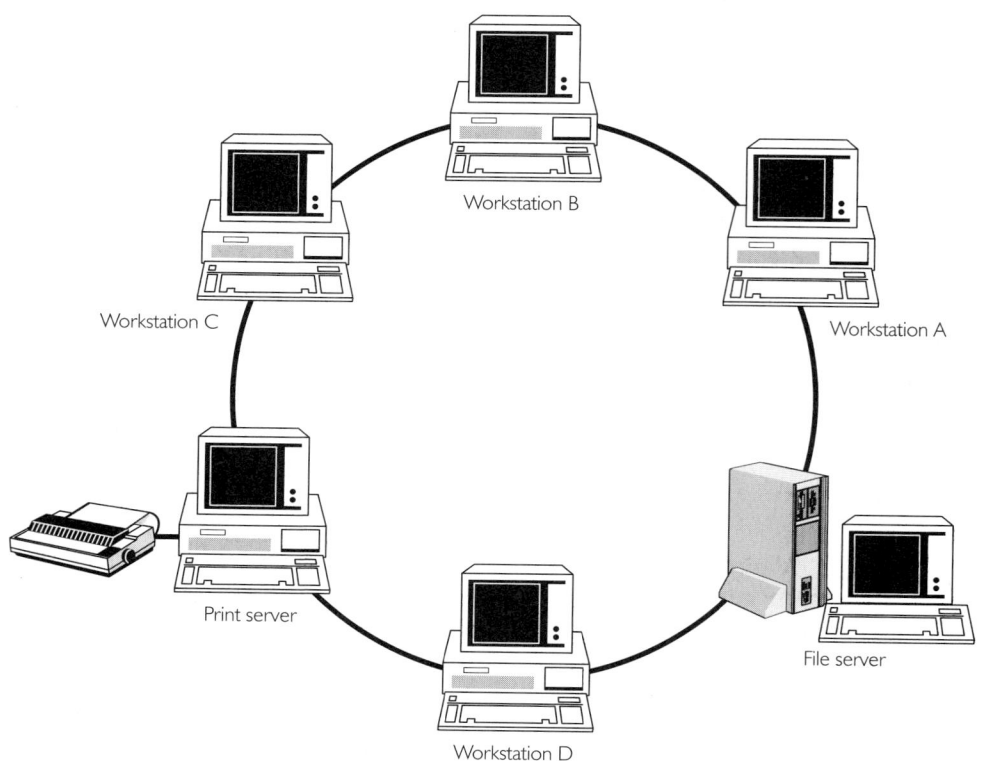

Figure 8.6 A typical ring network

through other nodes. As the data signal passes around the ring it tends to degenerate if the wires between the nodes are long, so special devices called **repeaters** are used to increase signal strength. The use of repeaters in this way increases the possible distance between nodes.

One advantage of the ring topology is that it is easy to identify a problem with either the cable or the data carried.

Bus topology

With the **bus topology**, a message sent from one node to another is also sent to every other node in the network at the same time. It is not necessary for one node to pass the message on to another and one node cannot block the signal to another. There are two main types of bus topology in use: the **linear bus** and **ring bus**. With both of these topologies, there is no central computer controlling the network, so all the nodes are directly connected to a single pathway which carries all the signals. Only one node is able to transmit data on the bus at a time.

Figure 8.7 shows the arrangement of the nodes in the bus topology.

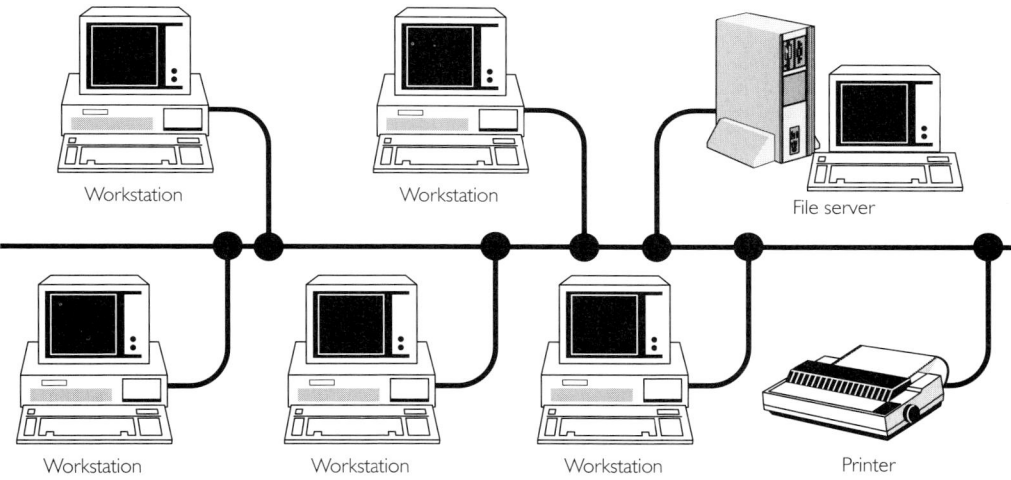

Figure 8.7 A typical bus network

Mesh topology

In the **mesh topology** not all the nodes are linked together so this may be regarded as a partially connected topology. Mesh topology is one of a group called **point-to-point topologies**; using these, messages can be sent from one node to another via a single link or, if there is no single link, by a pathway consisting of several. Figure 8.8 shows a mesh topology. If node A wishes to send a message to node E, since there is no direct link it could be sent to node B which then retransmits it to E. Using this method node B stores the data and examines it to determine the address and network information contained in the package. When it discovers that the package is not meant for it, it will send it on to the next node, which in this case is E.

The main advantage of mesh topology is that if there is a problem with one link between nodes, there is usually another path which can be taken. The possibility of multiple paths is more likely to arise with larger mesh networks because of the greater number of possible paths between nodes.

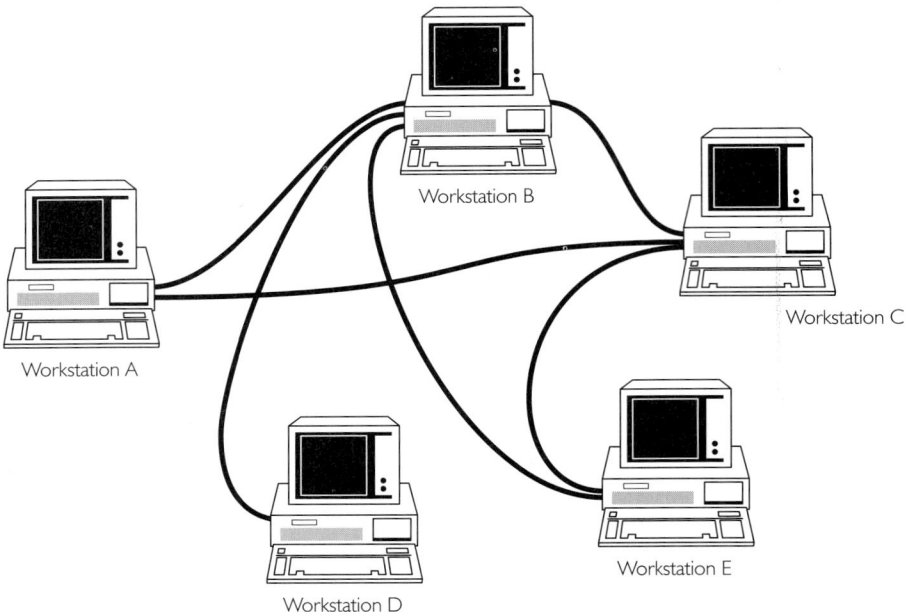

Figure 8.8 *A typical mesh network*

Star topology

The **star topology** shown in Figure 8.9 has one machine at the centre, whose operation controls the whole network. If this machine malfunctions the entire network becomes inoperative. The central machine is called the **hub** node or **central controller** node and as well as controlling data passage between the other nodes it also manages the network file system.

The main advantage of the star topology is that there is no competition for pathways since all nodes have their own line to the central node. This means that data can be passed more quickly than with bus topologies. Another advantage is that if one of the non-controller nodes (i.e. not the central controller node) fails, the remaining links will still work. On the negative side, the operation of the central node is crucial and a large amount of cabling needs to be used to connect up a star, substantially adding to the cost of installation.

Popular networks

In this section we will look at some of the popular types of network and how they operate. There are two main types of small, local area networks in use in offices: peer-to-peer and client/server.

Peer-to-peer

Your peers are people who are of equal status to yourself. In **peer-to-peer** networks each computer is of equal status. This contrasts with client/server architecture where the server is 'king' of the network.

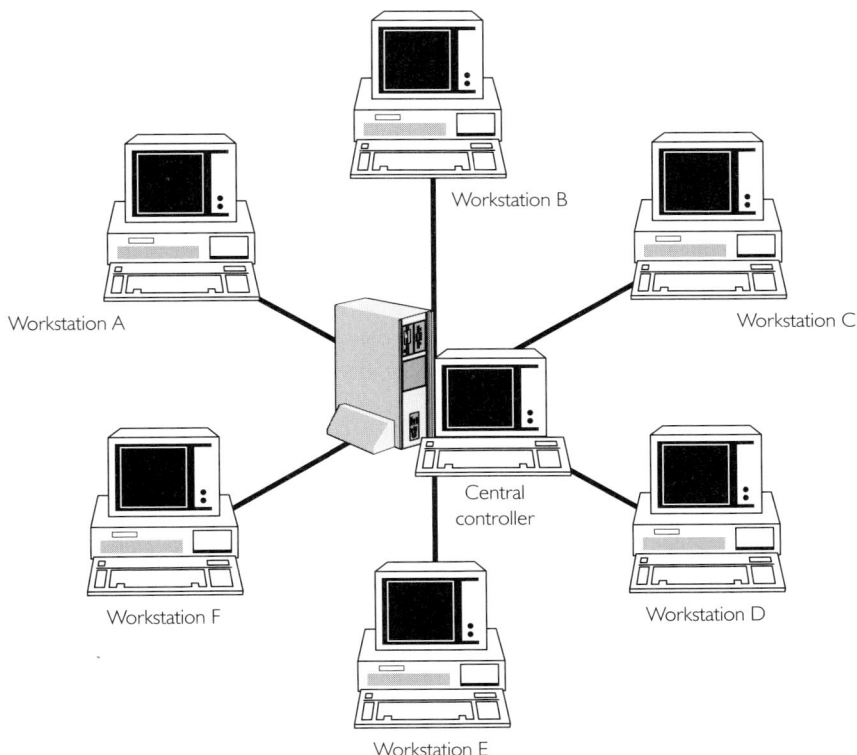

Workstation B

Workstation A

Workstation C

Central
controller

Workstation F

Workstation D

Workstation E

Figure 8.9 A typical star network

The important feature of peer-to-peer networks is that file storage and printing facilities do not come from a single server but from any of the computers connected to the network. Any workstation can use another's resources, such as CD-ROM drives, hard disks, tape streamers, fax, printers, plotters, etc. The main advantage of peer-to-peer architecture is that systems are quite easy to install and economical to run since a powerful server is not needed. They do, however, suffer the disadvantage that they are difficult to administer on a large scale and there is a noticeable decrease in speed if two people are trying to access the same hard disk at the same time.

To run a peer-to-peer network, a network interface card needs to be installed in each machine. The wires at the back of each machine must be attached via T-piece connectors to thin coaxial cable (thin Ethernet) and a suitable network operating system must be in place.

Because of the disadvantages already mentioned, peer-to-peer networks are really only suitable for small networks with fewer than 20 terminals.

Client/server

Client/server architecture employs one more powerful computer, called the server, to look after printing, file maintenance and any other peripherals connected to the network. The less powerful computers, called clients, are connected to the network and can use the services offered by the server.

Client/server architecture is the preferred network option for most large companies because each terminal can access all network facilities without losing any of its own processing power.

255

The main disadvantage of client/server architecture is that the network is entirely dependent on the server for its operation and if the server should break down it will affect every PC to which it is connected. However, if the network is administered properly and the files are regularly backed up there should be no serious problems with this type of architecture.

To run a client/server network a powerful computer is needed to act as the server responsible for storage and distribution of the data around the network. Along with the less powerful client workstations, a special electronic switching box, or hub, is needed to control the flow of data traffic around the network. Another purpose of the hub is to allow the machines on the network to operate without interfering with each other, so if a fault occurs with one client machine the other machines will still operate normally. The main network software for client/server architecture on PCs is Novell Netware.

Intranets

An intranet is a corporate network that is able to run over the Internet. Although a new development, they are set to grow rapidly over the next ten years. An intranet allows companies to assimilate information internally using the same technology as is used on the Internet.

The Internet

The best way to describe the Internet is as a 'network of networks' enabling people to exchange and share data. There is no one person or government involved in the administration of the Internet and to many people this is one of its attractions. There are security problems with viruses, pornography, etc. but for most users the advantage of being able to reach other people all over the world and exchange ideas and information far outweighs the disadvantages.

There are various reasons why people are subscribing to services which enable connection to the Internet. Some like to use the electronic mail service which is both quick and cheap compared with conventional mail services, while others like to access the chat services and bulletin boards where they can communicate with others with similar interests. Another attraction is the vast databases of information available on every topic imaginable.

The main problem for all Internet users is finding the information sought and there are various pieces of software called **search engines** which are used to search the vast databases for references to the required information.

The benefits of computer networks

The main reasons for networking together a group of computers are listed below.

A common pool of data can be shared amongst all the users without any need for duplication

Imagine two people working in an office using **stand-alone** machines and sharing the same client database. They will need identical copies of the same client database and any alterations will have to be notified to the other person and made twice over. This could involve the exchange of files on floppy disk from one machine to another. Increase the number of people sharing the same database and the problems soon start to multiply with some users failing to update, and different versions of the database developing. This is one of the main reasons why most companies use a network. Networking allows access to a shared client database and updating need only be done once and can be done by anyone on the network.

Hardware resources such as laser printers, plotters, scanners, fax machines, etc. can be shared by all the users

Many peripherals are quite expensive and spend much of their time idle, so if there are several users in an office it makes sense to share facilities. As an alternative it is possible to share a printer, for example by having one computer connected to it and other users transferring their work on floppies to this computer for printing. However, if this computer is in use the person sitting at it will face constant interruptions. Another alternative is to use manual switches to make a connection between each computer and the printer, but a lot of cabling is needed to do this. Using a network, all the resources attached to the network can be used by all the users.

Software can be shared

Network versions of popular software are available making it cheaper than buying individual copies for stand-alone machines.

When programs are accessed from a central point, usually the file server, only one network version of the applications software needs to be bought and this is usually much cheaper.

Security is likely to be improved

This is especially so if terminals are used which have no processing power of their own and no disk drives are used. Many large organisations use diskless workstations; this prevents users from stealing company data or software as well as preventing the introduction of viruses via floppy disks.

If all the software is kept on a central computer, it is easier for the company to make sure that its employees are not using any illegal software.

Better backing up facilities

One person, usually the network manager, can be responsible for the periodic back up of data rather than leaving it to individuals. Back-up procedures are more closely controlled and users less likely to lose data.

Improved communication between users

All networks have a facility for electronic mail, which is quick and saves paper. If the network is connected to the Internet, this opens up a whole sphere of worldwide communication.

Central maintenance and support

When upgrades need to be added to software held centrally it can be done on the file server instead of having to load many stand-alone machines. With stand-alone machines it is inevitable that different versions of the same applications programs come to be used within an organisation, and this may lead to non-standard output and serious difficulties with staff using terminals other than their own. All this can be avoided by using a standardised central copy of applications software.

Terry & Partners case study

You came across Terry & Partners in Chapter 3. Look back at the chapter if you need to refresh your memory as to what the company does.

At present the three CAD computers used by Terry & Partners are operated as stand-alone machines. The problem with this is that drawings frequently need to be transferred between the machines and the only way of doing this at present is to transfer files onto floppy disks and then move the disks to one of the other computers. Another disadvantage with the current system is that different versions of drawings can be confused, and it is even possible to end up doing the same alterations twice! This usually happens when someone is absent and another member of staff has to complete their drawings.

A member of the company has suggested that it would be much better if the machines were networked and that an Internet connection would be useful.

Activity 8.2

Task 1
1 What is a network?
2 As far as Terry & Partners is concerned, what are the main advantages in networking its computers?

Task 2
What features of the Internet might Terry & Partners find useful?

Data flow control methods

If two sets of data are sent along the same communication wire, at the same time but in opposite directions, the signals will collide and both sets of data will be corrupted. Worse still, the computers may not know that the data is corrupted and start processing it, producing incorrect results without anyone knowing. It is therefore important that a method is adopted to make sure this does not happen. There are many ways in which the flow of data can be controlled. The main methods of flow control are outlined below.

Reservation

Line **reservation** is the process by which a terminal keeps exclusive use of a communication line while it is sending data to another computer or terminal in a network. There are various mechanisms that terminals can use to achieve this and they are outlined below.

Time slots
One method of line reservation uses **time slots**, where each terminal is given a time slot in which to transmit its data. The slots are managed in a 'round-robin' manner. Since no two time slots coincide there are no problems with collisions, but if there are time slots vacant the whole network can slow down considerably.

Token passing

This form of line reservation is used for networks that have a physical ring or can be managed as a ring, where each message can be sent from one node to another until all the nodes in the network have been traversed. A special message called a **token** is passed from node to node around the ring. When a node wishes to send a message it waits until the token arrives, captures it and transmits the message. After the message has been transmitted, the token is released by the terminal and carries on around the ring until it is captured by another terminal waiting to send a message. Networks which are able to use physical or logical rings for the passing of tokens in this way are called **token-rings**.

One of the main problems with this method is that occasionally the token is lost along the line and it is quite difficult to discover how and where this has occurred and to restart the token. Nevertheless, the method does tolerate broken links and terminals which fail to respond properly, and this makes it useful where reliability, fault tolerance and a high rate of data transfer are needed.

Polling

Polling is used in LANs for controlling communications channel access. It works by the central computer asking or polling each of its workstations to see if they want to send information. Since some workstations will be busier than others, the networking software adjusts how often they are polled and for how long.

The star topology, which uses a central computer to control the network, also employs polling. The purpose of polling within the star topology is to make sure that data is transferred to the central file server in an orderly manner.

The main problem with any system which uses polling is that all terminals are polled in turn, but some will have no data to send, and this wastes time. It is more efficient if the operating system deals immediately with data as it is sent.

Contention

Contention occurs when two data signals from different parts of the system try to share the same path. Contention is more likely to occur on bus and ring topologies where the whole network uses the same media links. In most cases a link which is idle will be used on a 'first come first served' basis.

There is a standard control mechanism for dealing with contention. It involves a terminal 'listening' to see if data is being transmitted. If data is detected it is captured, stored and the destination address of the data checked to see if it is for the terminal at which it has arrived or one of the others. If the address is for another node the data is allowed to pass on. When the data arrives at the correct terminal it is captured, stored and processed. If the terminal detects no transmission of data on the line, it is free to transmit its own data. Despite this, there is still some chance that two terminals may think the line is free and try to transmit their own data simultaneously, with the resulting intermixing and corruption of the two transmissions. Terminals must have a procedure for dealing with these 'collisions', or find a method which will avoid entirely the possibility of collisions.

Collision avoidance/detection

The most common method of dealing with collisions is called **carrier sense multiple access/collision detection (CSMA/CD)**. This is quite a simple method and involves a 'listen-and-wait' scheme. When a collision occurs, each transmitting node waits a random period of time before retransmitting the signal. The use of a random delay makes a repeat collision unlikely, but if it does occur again the process is repeated until both signals are transmitted successfully.

The term 'carrier sense' comes from the fact that a **carrier wave** is combined with the data signal to form what is called a **modulated signal**. If a terminal detects just the carrier signal it knows that the line is free for the transmission of data. If, however, it detects a modulated signal, it knows that the line is being used and it should therefore wait for a random time interval to elapse before re-trying. If, as is likely, the time intervals are different, one node will take control of the link before the other. One disadvantage of this system is that if the links are loaded heavily with data traffic then use of the network becomes very slow.

The CSMA/CD method is most often used with the bus topology, since this type of network tends to have a lighter loading and shorter file transfers.

Network management activities

Many companies are completely dependent on the operation of their networks, and any loss of function, even for just a short period, can cost thousands of pounds in lost business. Just imagine a chain of supermarkets losing use of all point-of-sale terminals connected to a network throughout the country on a Saturday morning. Although these events happen very rarely, when they do they cause complete chaos and at the very least a serious loss of 'quality image'.

All networks need careful management if problems are to be avoided and the job of looking after the network usually belongs to someone called a **network manager** (sometimes **network administrator**).

Checking network activity levels and system reporting

As networks grow in size and become connected to other networks, implementing and managing a network becomes much harder. Naturally, software manufacturers have taken this problem on board and produced a variety of products to make the job easier. This software is collectively called **network management software**.

Simple network management protocol (SNMP) is a set of standards set by the network equipment manufacturers for the operation of all network management software. The purpose of network management software is to gather statistics about the movement of data around the network and watch for any conditions that might exceed the programmed limits.

SNMP uses small programs called agents which are run in the processors of the network devices. Such network devices include network cards, file servers, printer servers, routers and hubs. Agent programs monitor the data flowing to and from the device and send the resulting statistics to the management console program, which runs on the network manager's machine. With this system the network manager can instantly see any problems with the network and take appropriate action. SNMP can even tell the network manager when a network printer is low on paper or toner or when a paper jam occurs.

The main purpose of these agents is therefore to check activity levels in the various devices and to report back on a regular basis, the details being displayed on the management console as graphical maps (or even saved on a database which may be analysed at a later date). Should a problem arise, some management software can automatically dial a pager to alert the network manager, who may be at home but on call.

Security

Security is always important but with networks its importance is paramount since data is widely distributed to many people, so there is a greater possibility of misuse.

The chance of serious virus problems is also greater when using networks because such viruses are able to pass from any one computer to the whole network, causing havoc in the process. If terminals with no storage capacity of their own and no floppy disk drive are used, virus-infected floppy disks cannot easily gain access to the network, making a virus problem much less likely.

Activity 8.3

Your college is having a problem with viruses and despite all users scanning their disks, some of the machines still become infected. Many people only discover a virus on their machine when it is too late and the virus has already done damage. The system manager would like to be able to spot the tell-tale signs before serious consequences have ensued.

You need to research viruses and produce a list of the tell-tale signs or symptoms associated with them. Make your list into a poster to alert users, importing suitable graphics. There are many sites on the Internet which contain useful information for your research.

Avoiding viruses on a network

Here is a set of hints on how to avoid getting viruses onto a network and how to minimise the damage if they do gain access.

- Back-ups should be taken frequently but it is best not to recycle the same tapes or disks too often as this makes it more likely that some of the back-up disks may eventually get a virus.
- Install antivirus software on all machines, including any portables. All disks must be scanned before they are put into a drive.
- Make sure that everyone has a copy of the virus checker.
- All users of the network should be alerted to the virus problem and given appropriate training.
- Have a 'sacrificial machine' which is used to scan all floppies. No irreplaceable material should ever be kept on this machine.
- Always scan disks, even if they come from a manufacturer.
- Many viruses infect executable files (program files) so these files need to be placed in directories to which the user has no access.
- Do not allow users to download files from the Internet or bulletin boards.
- Be careful when using e-mail from sources outside the company.

Storage

Normally each user is allocated a certain amount of space on the hard drive of the file server (if client/server architecture is used). It is important to restrict the amount of disk space allocated to encourage users to perform periodic housekeeping operations, getting rid of files which are no longer needed.

System configuration

The network manager also has the very important task of configuring the system, which entails setting passwords for users (and making sure that they are changed periodically), arranging users' rights (informing the system who should see which files), allowing access to certain servers only and prioritising users when in queues for devices such as printers, plotters, etc.

System security methods

The security of data held on a network is crucial to any organisation. The various considerations are discussed below.

Control of access

Access controls can be divided into two groups: physical and logical.

Physical controls

Physical controls prevent the user from getting near the computer or making it work; one or more of the following methods are usually used:

- controlling access to the room (keypads, special cards);
- controlling access to the building (guards, locks operated by security badges);
- using the locks on computers to prevent them from being switched on;
- locking computers away at night or securing them under steel covers.

These are just a few of the many methods used, and more detail on this can be found in Chapter 6.

Logical controls

Logical controls are used to prevent the user, once logged on, from accessing or changing certain information or damaging important files (whether accidentally or deliberately). Staff need to be able to alter certain files but there should be some mechanism in place to prevent a person who works in sales, for instance, from accessing the payroll system from their terminal.

There are two main types of network security: **user level security** and **share level security**. In user level security, each user is allocated a user name and a password and both have to be entered correctly before access is gained to the network. Once logged onto the network there still need to be further restrictions as to what can be seen or altered. For instance, if you had set up a certain budget spreadsheet, you would have unlimited access to see or change it when you like. If company policy meant that you were the only person allowed to update the spreadsheet, but your boss wanted to see it, this could be allocated to your boss's terminal on a read-only basis. Other users would be denied access altogether through their own terminals.

Share level security means that each resource available on the network is given a password, rather than each user. In some cases two passwords may be used, one for full access and a different one for read-only access. The main problem with this method of security is that in certain types of network, particularly peer-to-peer networks, this can result in a larger number of passwords for each user to memorise. Writing them down on paper or not changing them very often means that users get to know each other's passwords with a consequent breakdown in security.

Some network operating systems give each user the opportunity to create a list of passwords for each resource they are allowed to use. To access this list it is necessary to input correctly both the user name and a password, so this actually uses a combination of both user level and share level security.

Forced recognition of security

Not all users are interested in security or see a need for it, since it presents an added burden to their daily work. In order to make users more aware of the importance of security, clauses can be written into their contracts of employment. For instance, there may be non-disclosure clauses which state that an employee is liable to be dismissed if they disclose their password or any confidential company information to another person, and once this contract is signed the employee is bound by all the clauses and conditions in it. In government departments and the armed forces, staff have to sign the Official Secrets Act which makes it a crime to pass on information to any outside bodies. Many of the staff in private companies working on government contracts may also have to sign the Official Secrets Act.

Activity 8.4

Many companies are completely dependent on their networking facilities and the loss of their networks for just a couple of hours can involve them in expense running into hundreds of thousands of pounds. It is not surprising, therefore, that the job of network manager is crucial in many organisations.

For this activity you will research and produce a report on the post of network manager. Your report should include the following material:

- photocopies or originals of about ten advertisements for the post of network manager/administrator. Attached to each advertisement you should mention the date and origin of the advert (this will usually be a newspaper or magazine but you could find job searching sites on the Internet);
- a brief statement of what a network manager is;
- a list of specific tasks which a network manager does;
- a summary of the personal skills needed for the post;
- a summary of the salaries offered (you will need to bear in mind that networks may be small or large and the salaries will reflect the level of this responsibility).

Use any statistical methods to analyse and present your findings graphically.

The Royal Bank of Scotland and the Internet: a case study

The Royal Bank of Scotland was the first bank to introduce a range of banking services on the Internet. Until recently, many experts thought that security problems would hinder the development of such a service, but the opportunities were so great that ways around these problems have been found. Using the Internet, any customer with a PC and a modem can access full banking services and is able to check the balance of their account, move money from one account to another and even apply for a loan or mortgage, all without queuing at or even visiting a bank.

The bank reckons that around 50 000 of its half a million telephone banking customers have the technology to access the service. Phone-based banking is now very popular with customers unable to get to branches during opening times. These customers prefer to pay for goods either using electronic funds transfer or credit card and use cash dispensers to obtain any cash they need. The use of the Internet is simply an extension of this service. The Royal Bank of Scotland hopes that by conducting routine transactions over the Internet, branch staff will be free to concentrate more on customer-based activities. The 'direct banking by PC' scheme is free for the first six months, but after that there is a small charge made for the service.

Assignment A8.1

This assignment develops knowledge and understanding of the following element:
4.3 Investigate computer networks

It supports the development of the following key skills:
Communication 3.1, 3.2, 3.3 and 3.4
Information technology 3.1, 3.2, 3.3 and 3.4

For this assignment you are required to gather information on a series of networks used by businesses or organisations. Work in pairs for this assignment; it is up to you to make sure that the workload is evenly divided.

Task 1

First find at least five networks used in real businesses or organisations which cover the following:

- local area networks
- wide area networks of the following kinds: broadcast, public switched telephone network, integrated services network, private wide area networks.

You may find that more than one of the above is included within a single network. For instance, in a large company it is common to find several LANs connected to a WAN.

For each network system, you should describe the nature of the organisation or business and briefly mention which components of the network are used and for what purpose.

Task 2

For each network mentioned in Task 1 draw a diagram, explain what topology is used and the reason for its choice.

Task 3

For each of the networks studied in the previous tasks, describe what the benefits have been to the organisation in using the network.

Task 4

There are various flow control methods used to ensure that data is successfully transferred from sender to recipient. Give a brief summary of the types in use.

Task 5

There are various software products available to automate management activities. Investigate these pieces of software, outlining all the main tasks for which they can be used and explain why these tasks are essential to ensure the smooth running of the network.

Task 6

'*Security issues are more important with networks than with stand-alone machines.*'
The above statement is the first sentence in an article in a computer magazine on security issues. Explain what methods can be used to ensure the security of hardware, data and software.

Introduction to using networks

Element 4.4 covers the practicalities of using a network. To meet performance criteria you must have:
- accessed a network in accordance with the organisation's standards;
- undertaken a variety of file processes and file management activities;
- modified other users' access rights to their own files;
- learnt how to send and receive electronic mail;
- learnt how to install new users on the network.

All these tasks are important if you are to use or manage a network successfully.

Accessing a network

All networks have a set procedure which is followed to gain access to the system. The standards are set by the organisation owning the network to ensure that the services are not abused. When accessing and using network services, the following steps are normally involved.

Log-in/log-on procedures

This is where you gain access to the network by supplying two things: a user name and password. The purpose of the procedure is to let the network know who is using it so that it can allocate resources fairly and also to make sure that only authorised personnel have access to the network.

To use the network, you will need to set up a user name and password with either the network manager/administrator or the service provider in the case of the Internet.

Displaying and accessing files/applications

Once logged onto the network, you will be supplied with a list of files or a menu of the options open to you. You will now be able to access files from any of the disk drives connected to the network as well as to save your work on any of the drives. Printers, scanners, etc. will also be available for your use.

Organisation standards

All organisations have a set of standards of behaviour when accessing and using their networks and these are put in place to make life easier for all users. There are various relevant issues regarding user identification, security conventions, copyright requirements, procedural requirements and allocated workspace.

Why have user identification?

Several users may use the same password, so to distinguish between them a user name is needed. In large systems, many people may use the same terminal in the course of a day, so if there is a query it is necessary to identify the member of staff who was using the terminal at the time.

Security conventions

Security conventions are the contractual arrangements under which network access to a computer system is provided. They may involve signing documents, using logical names and passwords and can include physical access restrictions.

Copyright requirements

A clause in the employees' contract of many organisations states that any work that employees do (for instance, developing new systems and programs) automatically belongs to the organisation and not to the individual who did the work. In other words the organisation owns the copyright on any material produced by its employees in company time.

In addition to the above, organisations must also make sure that other organisations' copyright is respected. This is especially important for software available on a network, since just one copy of a software package can be accessed by an unlimited number of users. A site licence will usually specify the number of users allowed. It is illegal to exceed the specified limit and if discovered the company could face a large fine. It is therefore one of the responsibilities of the network manager to make sure that only the number of users specified on the site licence are using the software.

For further information on software theft/piracy see the section on the Copyright, Designs and Patents Act 1988 in Chapter 6.

Activity 8.5

You are required to research software piracy and produce a brief report which includes details of the following:
- the scope of software piracy;
- what software producers such as Corel and Microsoft are doing about the problem;
- what the likely consequences are for companies caught using pirated software or software for which they have no licence;
- how network management software can help by keeping the network manager informed about site licences, number of users, etc;
- information about the organisation called FAST (Federation Against Software Theft): who funds it and what is its purpose?

Procedural requirements

Users in an organisation must obey procedural requirements when using the network. These usually involve the following:
- ensuring proper security of user names and passwords, and that passwords are changed regularly;
- making sure that the correct log-on procedure is used;
- logging off in the correct way (and not just by switching the terminal power supply off!);
- ensuring that each user's own housekeeping is undertaken regularly (e.g. deleting files that are no longer needed);
- reporting immediately to the network supervisor any faults with equipment or software;

- checking data carefully before it is printed out so that resources such as toner and paper are not wasted;
- making sure that no unauthorised software is used or downloaded from other networks (e.g. using the Internet);
- making sure that without prior permission printing facilities are not tied up for long periods making them unavailable to other users.

Allocated workspace

This is the disk space, usually on the server, which has been allocated to each user on the network. Some users such as secretaries may be using the space for memos, letters, reports and spreadsheets, so their space requirements will be fairly modest, while others may be doing CAD work or developing multimedia applications, which would involve the production of large files. Therefore the amount of allocated workspace for each user is varied by the network manager/administrator.

Data file processes

Provided that your access rights allow it (see page 268) you can do anything with your data files on the allocated workspace of a network that you could do on the hard drive of your own stand-alone PC. This includes the file processes 'retrieve', 'amend', 'delete', 'save' and 'protect'.

File management

All networks provide software for file management activities so users can act much as they would with a stand-alone machine. The main file activities are as follows:

Copy
There are many situations where a data file would need to be copied, for instance:

To keep a portable copy of the data
If a PC is being used as a workstation, its floppy disk drive can be used to copy from the user area on the file server to a floppy disk. This may be because a member of staff wants to transfer their current work to their home or portable computer. However, this might not be allowed by some companies, since the transfer of data in this way could be a security risk as files could easily be stolen.

To transfer a copy of the file to someone else on the network
If more than one person is working on a project it is often necessary for the whole task to be assembled by the team leader. To do this, each member of the team can send a copy of their work over the network to the team leader.

Rename
Renaming becomes important when you decide to change a set of filenames which have been adopted without any plan in mind, replacing them with more logical or useful names. This can be done using the rename facility.

Delete
If your allocated space on the file server is not to be used up quickly, it is vital to be systematic in removing files that are no longer needed. This needs to be done on a regular

basis, preferably while you remember what the original file contained. This type of housekeeping is particularly important on a network, where the amount of unwanted data stored by multiple users will very soon reduce access speed over the whole system.

Move

Users frequently need to move single files or groups of files from one directory or folder to another and it is necessary to know how to do this on the network.

Back-up

Most network operating systems back up data automatically, the user having little knowledge that this is taking place. In many cases **disk mirroring** is performed, where two hard disks are used, one of them being an exact copy of the other. In effect one disk is used as the back-up for the other. This sounds ideal, but unfortunately the system is not foolproof since if one disk contains bad sectors the corrupted data can end up being copied to the back-up disk.

List files

All network operating systems allow you to keep track of your files and list them by folder or directory in various orders, such as by date, size or type.

Create directory structure

Just as it is important to keep your files arranged tidily in directories when using a stand-alone machine, so it is important to structure the files in your workspace in a similar manner. This is done on a network by creating directories and subdirectories (sometimes called folders), changing directory names and performing file operations such as copying files from one directory to another.

Modify directory structure

Once a directory structure has been set up, changes or modifications can be made to it even if it already contains files.

Set rights to directory structure

A network manager/administrator can normally access any file on the network and make changes to it since this is a necessary part of the job. Other users will usually have restricted access. Users are given rights to each directory (and accompanying subdirectories) that need to be accessed by them. Often whole categories of staff are given access rights.

Access rights

The various access rights that might be given are as follows:
- **Read**: the user can read all the files in a particular directory.
- **Write**: the user can change the data in a particular file or directory.
- **Create**: the user can create new directory structures and subdirectories.
- **Erase**: the user can erase certain directories and files.
- **Modify**: the user can rename directories or files or change their attributes.
- **Copy**: the user is allowed to copy work from one area to another and might be allowed to copy onto floppies (although this is rare because of the security implications).

By exercising access rights an organisation is able to restrict use of the computer, preventing, for instance, a user in the accounts department from even reading any personnel section files.

Installing new users on the network

When a new user arrives, or a new workstation or terminal is connected to the network, it is necessary to set this user up on the network. To 'install' the new user, several things need to be done:

- gain access to the server;
- create a user name;
- give the user an initial password;
- set initial access rights for the user.

Do-It-All case study

Do-It-All, the retail do-it-yourself chain, has recently decided to replace its point-to-point ICL systems with a local area network serving each store. The LANs consist of Novell servers running Netware 4.1 and network hubs. Each LAN is connected back to the head office via ISDN links.

Clients (workstations and point-of-sale terminals) connected to the LAN in each store generally consist of five PCs acting as tills and three as workstations for administration. Some stores also have extra terminals used by customers for information.

In order to satisfy the performance criteria and cover all the range statements for Element 4.4 you will need to complete both Assignments A8.2 and A8.3.

Assignment A8.2

This assignment develops knowledge and understanding of the following element:
4.4 Use a computer network

It supports the development of the following key skills:
Communication 3.1, 3.2, 3.3 and 3.4
Information technology 3.1, 3.2, 3.3 and 3.4

For this assignment you are required to demonstrate that you are able to use a network to perform a series of tasks. You will need to have a good understanding of networks and how to operate them before attempting it.

Task 1
You are required to demonstrate your ability to do the following:

- log into the network and adhere to the organisation's standards;
- access and display files previously saved on the network;
- display the applications programs available and access a particular package;
- use the chosen package to do a useful task;
- create a file using the chosen package;
- save the file;
- retrieve the file;
- make amendments to the file;
- protect your file.

Record your work in a table like the one below.

Task	Evidence	Date	Verified by tutor

Task 2

For this task you will be playing the part of the network administrator and will be required to do several of the management activities typical of this post. You will need to demonstrate a level of competence to your tutor.

You must demonstrate that you can install a new user on the network. As part of this you will need to prove that you can:
- allocate a user name and give the user a password;
- allocate the user some workspace;
- set initial access rights for the user;
- modify the user's access rights.

Assignment A8.3

This assignment develops knowledge and understanding of the following element:
4.4 Use a computer network

It supports the development of the following key skills:
Communication 3.1, 3.2, 3.3 and 3.4
Information technology 3.1, 3.2, 3.3 and 3.4

For this assignment you are required to use the Internet and perform a research-based evaluation of its use and implications.

Task 1

Access the Internet and download two files which can be used by a tutor for the teaching of a certain subject. It is up to you to find a suitable, useful file and you should provide a brief description for each program, outlining the following:
- where the file was found, its size, whether or not it was compressed and how long it took to download;
- the steps taken to download it;
- the purpose of the program;
- a brief evaluation of the program.

Task 2

For this task you have to send and receive electronic mail using the Internet. You should supply evidence in the form of printouts of your activities.

Task 3

For this task examine the Web sites of various computer companies and produce a comparison of the facilities offered. Produce a two-page report on your two favourite computing Web sites.

Sample unit test

I Which two of the following are hardware components of a computer network?

1 ring
2 token
3 multiplexer
4 file server

a 1 and 2
b 2 and 3
c 3 and 4
d 1 and 4   *(RSA, June 1996)*

2 Which one of the following is required to connect two local area networks (LANs) together?

a a star
b a bridge
c a gateway
d a multiplexer   *(RSA, June 1996)*

3 Figure 8.10 represents:

a a gateway network
b a bridge network
c a ring network
d a mesh network   *(RSA, June 1996)*

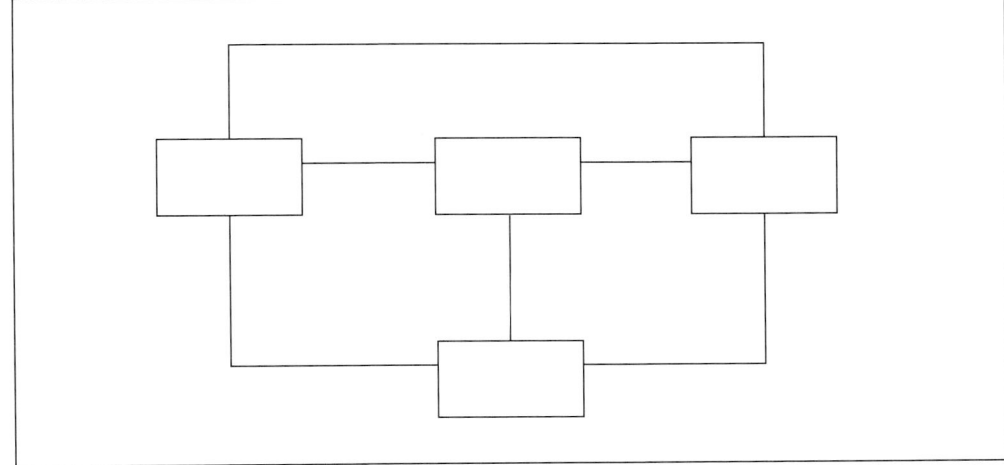

Figure 8.10

4 'Reservation' is:
  a a type of flow control
  b a software back-up technique
  c a type of back-up control
  d a contention technique   *(RSA, June 1996)*

5 The process of protecting a file is:
  a a network access security method
  b the same as backing up a file
  c a file order control technique
  d a method for controlling user access to a file   *(RSA, June 1996)*

6 Which one of the following is a file access right?
  a list
  b move
  c delete
  d retrieve

7 Some police patrol cars have terminals in them which are able to access the Police National Computer. This type of network uses:
  a a local area network
  b a broadcast service
  c fibre optic links
  d a private wide area network

8 The Internet service provider CompuServe is best classed as:
  a a broadcast service
  b a local area network
  c a private wide area network
  d an operating system

9 The main advantage of using a multiplexer is that:
  a each terminal requires its own communications line
  b each terminal can use the same communications line
  c each terminal needs its own modem
  d only one modem is needed

Questions 10–13 share the answer options **a** to **d**:
  Various items of hardware are used in most of the larger networks and these include:
  a bridges
  b routers
  c hubs
  d gateways

10 Which pieces of equipment are used when a person wants to access a wide area network in order to take account of the different sets of protocols?

11 Which pieces of equipment are used to connect multiple local area network segments to form a single logical LAN?

12 Which devices are used to make sure that an individual packet of data goes from one terminal to another by the fastest route?

13 Which devices are used to link LANs to form WANs?

Questions 14–16 refer to the diagrams shown in Figure 8.11.

14 Which one of the diagrams shows a star topology?

15 Which one of the diagrams shows a bus topology?

16 Which one of the diagrams shows a mesh topology?

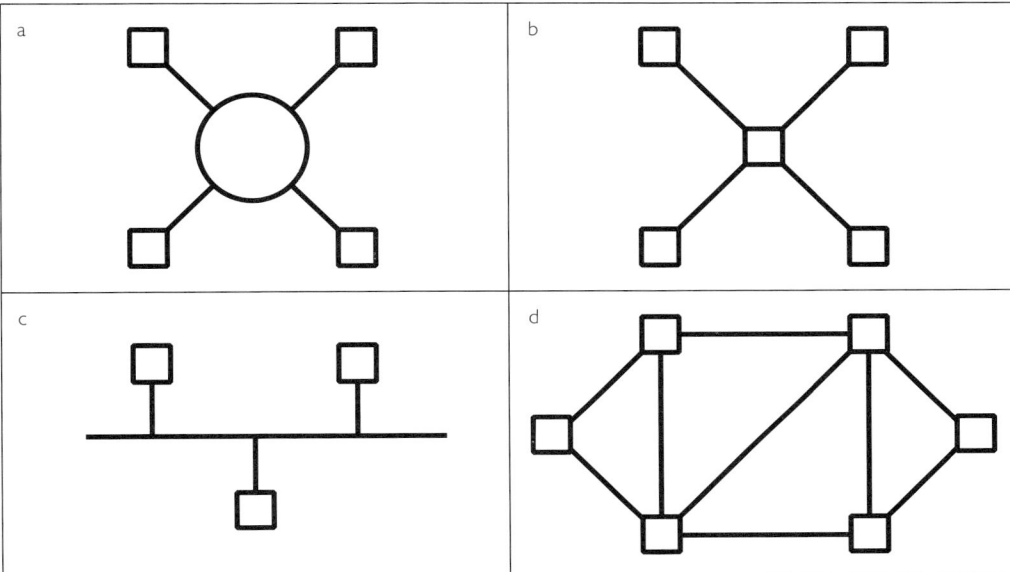

Figure 8.11

17 Which one of the following is *not* a good reason for using a network?
  a all the users can access the same data
  b hardware needs to be shared among the users
  c it offers better security of the computer system
  d it suffers from fewer technical problems than stand-alone machines

18 In some network topologies it is possible for two signals from different parts of the system to try to share the same path. When this occurs, it is called:
  a echo
  b contention
  c polling
  d token passing

19 In a personnel department, staff are able to use a network to access the personnel records. Some of this information, such as staff salaries, comes direct from the payroll file. They are able to see this information but not alter it. What type of access rights should the staff have to the payroll records?
  a read only
  b read/write
  c no access at all
  d unlimited access

20 The type of network where all the computers on the network are of equal status is called:

a client/server

b peer-to-peer

c ISDN

d EDI

21 The purpose of 'reservation' is to:

a enable a terminal to keep exclusive use of a communication line

b book time on a terminal connected to the Internet

c generate a communications log

d back up data automatically at set intervals

22 Which one of the following tasks would be performed by a network manager?

a entering data into a central database

b managing all the staff who use a network

c configuring a system

d writing a network operating system

23 The information service provided by teletext can be considered to be:

a a broadcast service

b an LAN

c a WAN

d an ISDN

24 Which one of the following is *not* a file access right?

a create

b modify

c read

d print

25 Which one of the following is a logical access control?

a the use of passwords

b locking terminals so that they cannot be used

c putting keypads on doors so that only authorised staff can enter a room

d using diskless workstations so that users cannot load their own disks

26 The main purpose of a network interface card is to:

a reduce the amount of wiring needed between terminals

b enable a computer to be used as a stand-alone machine

c enable a terminal to access the Internet

d enable an ordinary PC to be converted into a terminal

27 Which is the hardware device used to increase the strength of a signal as it passes around the wires in a network?

a a multiplexer

b a repeater

c a hub

d a gateway

28 Which of the following network topologies makes use of a central machine that controls the data to the other terminals and also manages the network file system?

a bus

b mesh

   c star

   d ring

29 The main method used for dealing with collisions of data in a network is called:

   a ISDN

   b CSMA/CD

   c contention

   d polling

30 A network system user's file management activities would include:

   a issuing identity cards

   b updating network system security

   c creating a directory structure

   d modifying the system configuration file

9 Principles of systems analysis

What is covered in this chapter

In this chapter we will investigate processing activities and the IT methods used to implement them, the user information needed to initiate a feasibility study, the stages of systems analysis, analysis documentation and the elements of a system specification.

Element 5.1: Investigate principles of systems analysis and specification

- Processing activities
- Information technology methods
- User information
- Introduction to systems analysis
- Stages of systems analysis
- Analysis documentation
- Elements of a system specification

Resources you will need for your portfolio for Element 5.1
- Your written answers to the activities and assignment in this chapter.

Processing activities

Data is only the raw material for data processing; once it has been collected it must be **processed** in some way before useful information can be derived from it (See Figure 9.1).

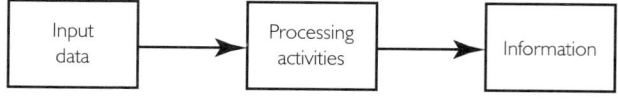

Figure 9.1

'Processing activities' are things that are done to the raw data to produce the final output. They include manipulation, calculation, interrogation and repetition. We will now look at each of these in turn.

Manipulation (sorting, selecting and merging)

Sorting

Sorting the data involves putting it into a certain order, either numerically or alphabetically. Most software packages allow data to be sorted but database software often has a greater choice of ways in which data can be ordered.

Activity 9.1

Consider a manual method of sorting a list of 30 names into alphabetical order according to surname. Write a short description outlining the manual method you would use. Now consider the same problem but this time with 300 names. How would you perform the task now?

Sorting data into order is not as easy as it seems when the number of things to be sorted is large.

Selecting

In many systems (particularly those using Windows) the user is presented with a series of options from which they select. In many cases the user needs only to point the mouse to the item being selected and click the mouse button. In other systems selections are numbered, and the choice is made by typing in the number; a similar system uses the first letter of each selection on the menu, which is entered. Some systems use a highlighted area which is moved from selection to selection until it covers the option required, when selection is made using the enter key.

Selection is used in programming to make decisions based on the input data and this is dealt with in detail in Chapter 11.

Merging

Sometimes the user wants to combine the contents of two files to form a single file. This process is called **merging**.

You can use the merge facility in wordprocessing software to create form letters (letters with blank spaces left in them) then insert individualised information to produce 'personalised' mass mailings. To produce a mail merge it is necessary to set up a data file containing the data to be inserted and a standard form to be used as the template.

Calculating

Calculating involves doing arithmetical or statistical manipulations with the data.

In a payroll program, calculations are performed on the data (the hours worked) and the rate per hour to give the gross pay. Various calculations then follow to deduct tax and National Insurance contributions to produce the final net pay.

Interrogation

Interrogation involves searching for particular data. Although the time taken to search for a file in a single filing cabinet may not seem excessive, searching for such a file when there are hundreds of cabinets is less practical, and could take forever if the file has been put back in the wrong place! Often, more information is needed, which necessitates looking at each file in turn. Suppose a college with a manual filing system needs to produce a list of its disabled students. Students will be filed either in order of their enrolment number or according to surname. To find out, for example, whether or not they are disabled would involve finding and reading the section in each student's file.

By interrogating the student file on a computer database, these details could be obtained very quickly for all the students.

Repetition

A computer can repeat a process any number of times. For instance, once you have typed your work into a wordprocessor, you can print as many copies as you wish. Once the system is set up to deal with a job correctly, repeating the process involves the user in little extra effort.

Activity 9.2

The following is a list of processes used in data processing:
- sorting
- selecting
- calculating
- interrogation
- repetition.

For each of the following, say which of the above is the main process involved.
1 Listing all the files in a directory with the file extension .DOC.
2 Adding up a column of numbers in a spreadsheet.
3 Replicating **absolutely** a cell down a column in a spreadsheet.
4 Producing an alphabetical list from a college class file.
5 Using the search facility on a database to find a particular student's personal details.
6 Printing out an agenda to give to six different people before a meeting.
7 Sending out personalised letters to employees.
8 Replicating **relatively** a formula down a column in a spreadsheet.
9 Making a single document from two separate documents.

Information technology methods

There are several ways in which a computer can be instructed to carry out processing activities. These are called information technology methods.

Programming languages

Programming is often thought to consist solely of writing thousands of lines of computer instructions, in the code of a particular computing language. When this is completed the **programmer** simply 'debugs' (removes the errors from) the code and tests it – all this while sitting at the computer screen. This is far from the truth.

Much work is needed before the code is written, and a programmer employed in a large computer department works from a brief supplied by a systems analyst. Program design and documentation are considered to be as important as the lines of code themselves. A programmer needs always to bear in mind that a program must be easily understood by someone revising it, since programs are more often changed than completely rewritten.

There are various programming languages and the one selected for a particular job depends mainly on the type of task being performed. Like other aspects of computing, programming languages tend to go in and out of fashion. A language popular one year may not be the next, so it is difficult for a programmer to decide in which language to develop their skills.

At present, **C**, **C++**, **Cobol** and **Visual Basic** are the most popular languages for the development of commercial software, for either mainframes or PCs.

Applications software facilities

Applications software is defined as 'software developed to perform a certain task or tasks'. A payroll program would, for example, be classed as applications software.

Applications software might be produced for a general purpose such as wordprocessing, databases, graphics, accounting, stock control, etc. These packages are mass produced and this results in relatively cheap software which has undergone extensive testing to eliminate all the bugs. One of the main disadvantages with **software packages**, as they are called, is that they offer general solutions to problems. In other words, your requirement has to be adjusted to fit the package and this may not always be possible or desirable. Figure 9.2 shows some of the advantages of software packages.

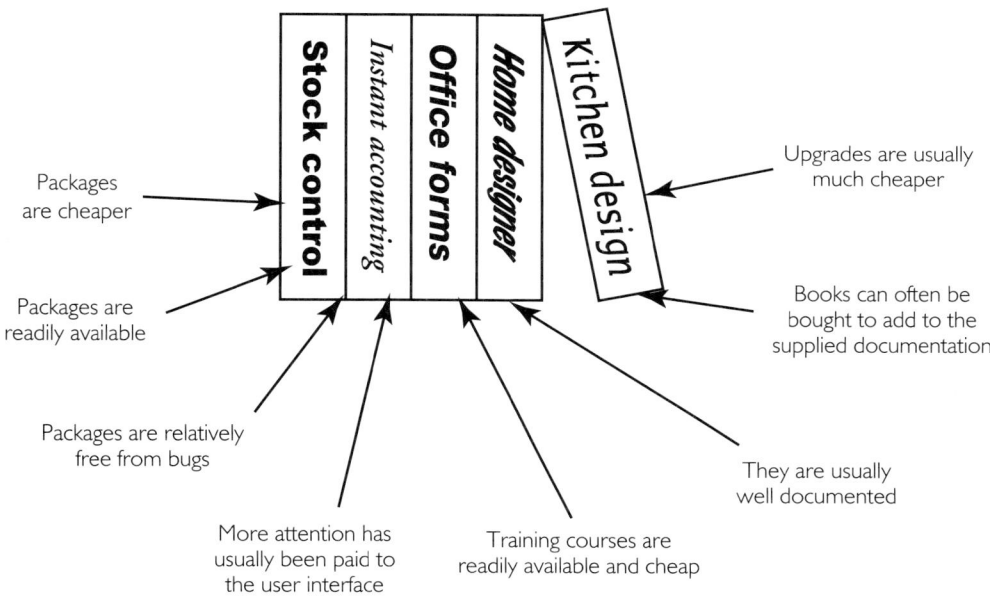

Figure 9.2 Off-the-shelf packages offer several advantages over tailor-made software, but sometimes tailor-made software, although more expensive, is the best solution

If a user has a specific problem which needs solving and it is not a common problem, it may be necessary to develop and write specific software. Such software is referred to as either **tailor-made software** or **bespoke software**. Most companies with large computing departments employ specialist computing staff who will develop their own applications software, although they will still use applications packages (such as wordprocessors) on an individual basis.

Applications generators

Applications generators, sometimes called program generators, are software tools that are sometimes provided as part of a package such as a database package, to help non-programmers develop their own applications. The developer decides in general terms what needs to be done and which files to use, and the applications generator produces the required program code.

Although applications generators can enable inexperienced users to produce simple programs, with more complex programs they become less useful and the talents of an experienced programmer are needed. Nevertheless, applications generators are ideal for simple programs that link several files together.

Report generators

A report in this sense is a tabulated list of data compiled in a specific way. A report generator is an applications generator which produces a report made up from some of the contents of one or more files. Again, the non-specialist can produce these reports from carefully constructed statements. Nearly all database and accounting packages are able to produce such reports.

Data capture

Data capture is the name given to the various methods of entering data into a computer ready for processing. The commonest form of data capture is keyboard entry. Here the data is entered from documents (called source documents) or directly from dictation, by typing into the computer. Transcription errors (misreading the source documents) or simple typing mistakes make keyboard entry more prone to errors than other methods. If possible, other methods of entry should be considered, such as **OCR (optical character recognition)**, **OMR (optical mark recognition)**, MICR (magnetic-ink character recognition) and from **barcodes**. All these methods are more accurate and faster than keyboard entry and (excepting MICR) the cost of the hardware needed has fallen considerably. It is necessary to check that the applications software used and any device for data capture (for example, a barcode reader) will work together.

Activity 9.3

Read the following summary of an article which appeared in the *Financial Times* on 31 May 1994.

> An imaging system has brought about a startling change at Birmingham and Midshires Building Society. Two years ago it took an average of five weeks to process a mortgage application. Now a department of only one fifth its previous size processes applications in three weeks. About 80 per cent of mortgage deals are now offered within this new timescale. More remarkable is the reduction in staffing levels from 150 people processing mortgage applications to a staff of 30 or so.
>
> The advantages to the building society include:
> - a reduction in the number of staff needed to process the mortgage applications;
> - an improvement in the speed of decision making;
> - all the information is to hand so that it is possible to answer broker questions and customers' questions immediately from the screen;
> - using the imaging system along with a database, staff have a lot more information about a customer and how likely they are to be able to meet the mortgage payments, and this has reduced arrears.

You have been asked by the Managing Director of your company to investigate imaging systems and their advantages.

You have spoken to a friend who is used to doing this type of research and she says that you may find the information you need in the library, using the following resources:
- the *Financial Times* CD-ROM
- encyclopaedias on CD-ROM (e.g. Encarta, Grolier, etc.)
- back copies of *Computer Weekly*
- back copies of any of the popular computing magazines
- the Internet.

Produce a report outlining what you have found out.

Macros

A **macro** is a high-level programming tool which can be used to automate a series of tasks or procedures within a program. A macro consists of a series of individual instructions; to start the macro you need only press a couple of keys on the keyboard or click the mouse.

A macro used within a particular applications program, such as the spreadsheet Excel, will run only when the applications software has been loaded; such macros cannot be run on their own.

Some macros can be created by users who know nothing about programming. This type of macro will automatically record your keystrokes (or mouse movements) and selections so they can be automatically 'played back' when you need them simply by activating the macro.

Activity 9.4

Macros can be found as an advanced feature of most software. Using the software manuals or on-line help menus to help you, find out how to write a macro for a task that you find tedious when using your spreadsheet or wordprocessing software.

Produce an easy-to-understand set of instructions which you could give to a friend who needs to perform the same task.

User information

Before a new system is developed, it is necessary for the user to supply information regarding the type of business that they are involved in and the way in which the existing system works. The user is usually asked to describe the following:
- the purpose of the business or system;
- the existing system in terms of input, processing and output;
- their expectations of the new system;
- any constraints to be placed on the new system (timescale, costs, etc.).

Purpose of the business or system

Before beginning systems analysis it is necessary to know a little about the business or organisation for which the work is being done. In many cases the systems analysis may be applied only to one area of the business, but knowledge of how this area fits into the whole system will still be needed.

Description of the present system

Here the user explains briefly how the present system works. At this stage only an overview is needed, but it should still give a rough idea on which further investigation can be based.

Details should include inputs to the system (e.g. the way orders arrive from the customers), the processing that is performed on these inputs and the outputs required from the system.

Expectations of the system

It is important to determine what the user expects from the system, and whether or not this is realistic. The user may know little about computers and have no prior experience of them, and therefore needs some advice as to what they can expect from the system.

Constraints

Most (but not all) problems with existing systems can eventually be solved, provided that there is enough money, time and resources. In reality there are limits to these, called the **constraints** on the system. Figure 9.3 shows some of the constraints which might be supplied by the user to the person developing the system.

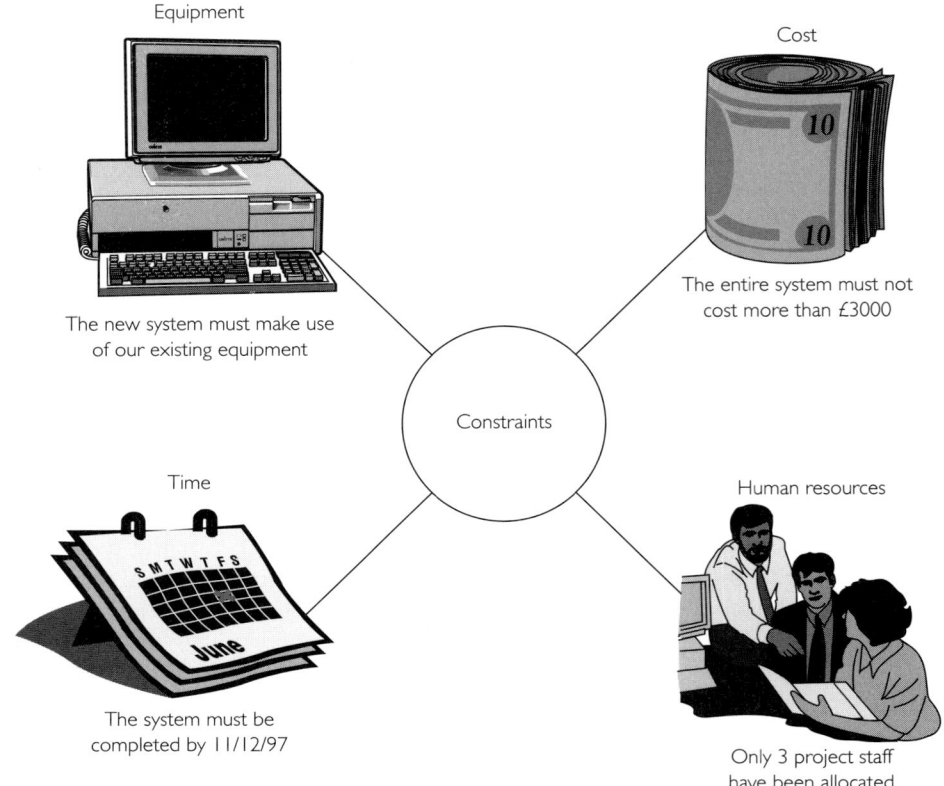

Figure 9.3 System constraints

Cost constraints

There is always a limit to the amount of money which can be spent during the development of a new system and this figure must be made clear at the start of the project, as it will influence the choice of system.

Time constraints

It is best to develop a good working solution as quickly as possible. If a project takes too long to complete the resulting system could be out of date before it is implemented.

Resource constraints

Resource constraints can be divided into human and equipment constraints.

Human resources are people; if there are only a few people working on a project, it will take longer to complete. Remember, some of the people qualified to work on a system may already be committed to other work.

Equipment constraints include hardware and software resources. For instance, a company might want to build a network to allow all staff to access the same data files, but it wants to make use of its old 486 PCs. This is an equipment constraint.

If the envisaged network is large, with many terminals, it would be advisable to appoint a network manager or administrator. If the organisation does not have a suitably qualified person for the post and one could not be appointed, this would represent a human resource constraint.

Introduction to systems analysis

What is a system?

Before looking at the task of analysing a system, called systems analysis, we need first to define what a system is.

A system is a way of doing things. Another way of describing a system would be as a complex whole, the component parts of which are arranged together for a common purpose. In the morning, you will have a system for getting ready to go to college. For instance, do you clean your teeth or have a wash first?

We develop our own systems from habit, without realising it, and we are happy with these systems because we are familiar with them and they work for us. Many business systems evolve in a similar manner. Perhaps the original owner of a business set up a system, and the same system continues to be used even though the business has grown much larger. Sometimes the system cannot cope when certain problems arise, so the system is modified. However, a system which has been developed in such a piecemeal manner is unlikely to be efficient and it is here that systems analysis can help.

Most businesses have various systems to deal with the different functional areas. There need to be systems for paying wages, purchasing raw materials from suppliers, sending goods and so on.

Activity 9.5

Describe your system for getting ready in the morning, from the point of getting out of bed to finishing in the bathroom.

How does your system compare with that of your friends? Would you consider changing your system? Explain why or why not.

Systems often need to interact with each other in some way. With stock control the main objective is to make sure that money is not being tied up in stock which stays on the shelves for months before being sold. This, however, must be balanced with the need to satisfy orders without running out of fast-selling items.

For a company making items from raw materials there needs to be a system for processing orders as they come in and also for processing the payments.

Activity 9.6

You have been asked to research and give a ten-minute careers presentation on jobs in systems analysis and, in particular, the job of a systems analyst.

Investigate some or all of the following:
- typical salaries
- qualifications needed
- personal qualities needed.

What is systems analysis and why is it needed?

There are many reasons why systems analysis is carried out and some of these are described below.

The profit reason

People go into business to make a profit. Profits can be increased by expanding the business, which could mean buying up smaller companies or merging with other companies. Profit can also be generated by increasing the amount of business, either by taking a greater share of the market or perhaps creating a new market. Market share is usually expanded by being more competitive and this is achieved by keeping prices low. To keep prices low costs must be kept down and it is often for this reason that systems analysis is performed.

The efficiency reason

Not all organisations aim to make a profit. Take a school or college, for instance. Such institutions receive funding for the number of pupils or students they attract. This funding has to pay for buildings, maintenance, cleaning staff, teachers or lecturers, library books, computers, etc. For many years the Government has wanted improved efficiency in the way this money is spent. If the costs of the administration can be reduced this will allow more money to be spent directly on the students' resources. For this reason computer systems are now used in the administration of all schools and colleges.

Stages of systems analysis

In this section we will look at the series of activities involved in the whole process of systems analysis.

Sponsor

Systems analysts do not tour the organisation that employs them, actively looking for things to improve. What usually happens is that senior managers or executives suggest to the systems analyst that a particular part of the business is inefficient and needs examination. The senior person who instigates the project is called the **project sponsor**.

Systems development life cycle

The systems development life cycle is a sequence of activities that is performed when a system is analysed, designed and implemented. The reason the process is cyclic is that once the process has been completed and the system is working, it is usual to look critically at the system to see if it can be improved; if so the whole series of steps is repeated.

Figure 9.4 shows the stages involved in the systems development life cycle.

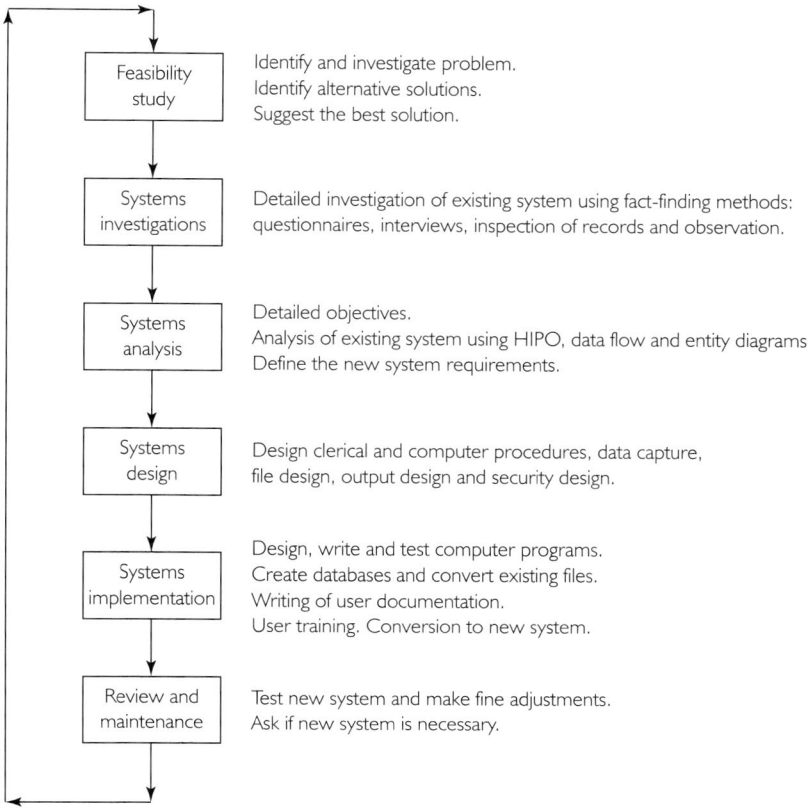

Figure 9.4 The systems development life cycle

Problem statement

Systems development starts with the identification of a problem in the existing system. There is nothing to be gained by changing an existing system if it works perfectly well and the management is satisfied with it. In many cases within a company, different departments use different systems. To develop a new system it is necessary to look in detail at the existing system and identify all its shortcomings. The process of investigating the existing system is called **fact finding**.

After a full fact find you should be able to answer the following questions:

- Is there anything that the existing system does not do or anything extra you would like it to do?
- Could IT be used to improve the timescale for the completion of certain tasks?
- Would it be possible to use new technology to reduce the costs involved when performing certain tasks?

Feasibility study

The **feasibility study** starts with an outline of a problem that needs to be solved using information technology. To identify the problem in the first place, it is necessary to perform a fact find.

Once all the facts have been investigated it is then possible to prepare a feasibility study report. This document looks at the likelihood of achieving the stated aims and objectives at reasonable cost. Since many projects are rejected at this stage it is not worth going into too much detail in such a report. However, the feasibility study report needs to give an idea of the costs and timescale associated with the project as outlined in the **project brief** or **problem statement**. One of the main problems you are likely to face when producing a report is that it can be very difficult to estimate costs and benefits without going so deeply into the system that you incur too much cost and take too long.

The amount of time a feasibility study takes depends on its scope and the experience of the systems analyst.

A feasibility study is also intended to suggest if the project is technically possible and, furthermore, if the organisation has the human resources (staff) with the time and necessary qualifications to successfully complete the project.

Is a feasibility study necessary?

A feasibility study is an optional stage in systems analysis and design. Where there is a clear-cut need for a new system and it is obvious that a certain system is required, then there is no need for this stage, and once analysis is complete the systems design can start. Much of the work involved in a feasibility study will be performed in greater detail during the analysis stage.

Projects are all different, and the following is only a guide to a typical feasibility study.

Objectives

This is a clear statement of what is hoped will be achieved by the project. For instance, an order processing system could have the following objectives:

> 'A new order processing system will enable three quarters of the existing staff to process the orders in around half the present time. The new system must also be able to cope with an expansion in the number orders of around 10 per cent per year over a period of five years.'

Scope

This gives some indication of the amount of detail into which the project will go. For instance, an order processing system could just concentrate on the sales department or it could, in addition, look at how information about credit limits comes from the accounts department.

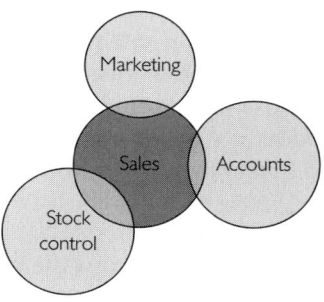

Figure 9.5

It is often difficult to look at part of a complete system in isolation because other parts of the system affect it, even if indirectly. Figure 9.5 shows how the various parts of a typical system overlap.

If we were replacing just part of a system it would be necessary to make sure that links to other parts of the system are not removed. If part of a system is computerised and other parts still manual, links between the computerised and manual parts would need to be considered and a description of any problems envisaged mentioned in this section of the feasibility study.

Outline designs for alternative systems

Once objectives and scope have been agreed, the systems analyst can look at the possible systems that would meet the objectives. Such possibilities might include:

- continuing with the present system;
- continuing with the present system after modification;
- using a combination of a manual and computer system;
- trying to avoid all paperwork;
- using a series of stand-alone computers;
- using a network so that everyone can have access to the same files.

Benefits

To help users and management accept a change in a system it is necessary to convince them that it will be an improvement. They therefore need to be told about the likely benefits, which may include:

- the job can be performed more quickly;
- fewer people are needed in administration and so can be transferred to more productive work, such as creating more sales;
- smaller offices are needed, reducing rental, heating and lighting costs;
- better security of information will be provided;
- customers/clients will be more satisfied with the service, leading to fewer complaints;
- management information can be obtained more quickly (e.g. the value of the sales made one month compared with the same months over previous years);
- it is more environmentally friendly (an electronic mail system would save trees by saving paper);
- it provides more accurate management information.

It is important to note that benefits to the management may not always be benefits to the user.

Costs

It is very hard to anticipate the likely cost of completing a project, but to obtain approval it is important to get some idea of cost. The costs are not simply those of the hardware and software. Here are some of the likely sources of costs:

- **Creating a new working environment:** this might include rewiring, decorating the office, fitting blinds or new carpets.
- **Staffing**: new staff might be required because there is no existing expertise in the area. This might apply if a network manager is required. If fewer staff are needed redundancy needs to be considered.
- **Training**: staff will need to be trained to use the new system either in-house or at a college/private training centre. Either way, training costs need to be taken into account and you must bear in mind that while they are being trained their work still needs to be done, incurring overtime or temporary staff costs.

- **Development costs**: these are the staffing costs involved in developing the new system and should include the wages/consultant fees of the systems analyst. There may be some cost incurred for the conversion of manual files to computer files.
- **Hardware and software**: these are more obvious costs. Remember to include items such as magnetic media and back-up devices such as tape streamers.
- **Costs associated with running the system**: these would include consumables such as pre-printed continuous stationery, printer ribbons, toner cartridges, etc. With wide area networks the costs of data transmission also need to be included.

Activity 9.7

An old-fashioned company has been taken over by a more progressive competitor which has decided on complete computerisation of all the administrative procedures. Write a list of the disadvantages to the staff of this computerisation.

Feasibility report

In the early stages of a systems development project, an estimate of the amount of time, effort and money involved needs to be made, though this can be difficult. There may be serious consequences if the project runs over the allotted time or exceeds its budget.

Once a project has been identified, the person or team responsible for system development has the job of selling the benefits of the proposed system to the management. A summary of all the activities outlined as part of the feasibility study is contained in the feasibility study report. This can be a written report or an oral presentation. A **feasibility report** should contain the following:

- an outline of the problem that needed to be looked at;
- how this part of the business fits in with the rest;
- the scope of the proposed project;
- the name of the project sponsor;
- a statement of the objectives of the proposed system;
- brief details of the alternative systems looked at;
- reasons why the alternative systems were rejected;
- evaluation of the technical, cost and human resource implications for each of the suggested systems (the ones not rejected at the previous stage);
- a draft plan for the implementation of the project within a certain timescale.

Investigation

Investigation takes place throughout all the stages of systems analysis, though the main body of the investigation needs to be performed before the analysis.

In order to improve a system it is essential first to understand how it works. This process is called fact finding and can be performed by various methods, as shown in Figure 9.6.

Interviewing

Interviewing is one of the best ways of finding out how a business operates. It is usually best to start at the top where the interviews will give an overview of the organisation's activities. They will also tell the systems analyst about the overall strategy (staff restructuring, development of new markets) and likely developments (mergers and takeovers) in the future. Lower down the management structure, interviews should reveal the problems experienced in particular departments. These managers will be closer to the information flow in the business, and systems analysts need to find out

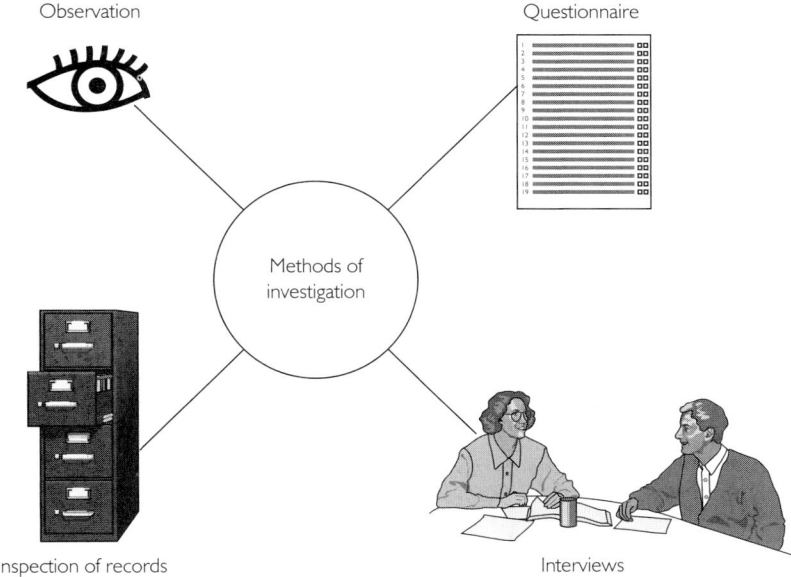

Figure 9.6 Fact-finding methods

about this. At the lower management end a systems analyst will probably get some suggestions as to how the existing system could be improved on a local scale.

At the bottom of an organisation's structure are the operational staff who deal with the day-to-day processing of information. These people often have strong opinions of what should and should not be done, but their experience of the whole organisation is narrow and often restricted to their own jobs. Since the operational staffs' jobs are threatened by the development of any new system, a considerable amount of tact needs to be exercised when interviewing them. The company employs systems analysts to reduce the costs of operating the business and this usually implies job cuts. Although the systems analyst researches and develops the new system, the decision to lay off staff is ultimately a management decision.

Some rules to follow when interviewing

Suppose that you are a systems analyst and need to interview staff. You need to prepare yourself for the interviews. Have a 'crib sheet' of the questions you are going to ask and make sure you are asking questions at a level appropriate to the member of staff being interviewed. It is no use asking a person who processes orders about the future expansion of the company.

Here are some general rules to follow:

- Make sure you structure the questions so that they start off in general, but lead on to more specific, areas.
- Introduce yourself and mention the purpose of the interview.
- The person being interviewed should do most of the talking.
- A record of what the person says should be kept and in many cases it is a good idea to tape record it.
- Before the end of the interview, confirm what has been said. If you are making notes, tell the interviewee that you will send them a copy for checking once the notes have been typed up.
- At the end of the interview thank the person for their time and ask if it would be possible to meet again if the need should arise.

289

Observations

This type of information gathering involves a variety of techniques, from watching a person doing their job (which can evoke hostility) to just looking around a building to get a feel for the organisation.

Activity 9.8

The following document forms part of an observation sheet which could be filled in when making a visit to a company's premises. Your task is to complete the design of the sheet ready for your visit. The document aims to provide a checklist of things to look for during your visit. Your document should be designed and printed out using wordprocessing software.

Observation	Comments
Working environment	All old office furniture and does not comply with EU regulations. New furniture will be needed. Not enough electrical sockets (may need rewire?) Too much light through the windows.
Flow of work	Much of the work comes in the morning. Start of the week much busier than the end.

This may be a good opportunity to learn how to produce tables using your wordprocessor; you will need to produce a variety of information in tabular form in the chapters that follow.

Inspecting records

All organisations still use and generate a fair amount of paper-based documentation. By examining these documents you can get a feel for the way an organisation operates.

Documents can be divided into those giving specific information and those giving general information. A list of documents divided into these two types is shown below.

Specific information	General information
Order forms	Organisation charts
Invoices	CVs of relevant staff
Dispatch notes	Job descriptions
Picking lists for warehouse staff	Policy/procedure manuals
Files	Results of previous feasibility reports

All the above documents provide information about the existing system and should be used in conjunction with other methods of fact finding.

Questionnaires

At first sight, questionnaires seem an ideal way of collecting information about a company. You do not have to spend time interviewing people and a questionnaire sticks to the important points without digressing, which can occur in an interview.

However, questionnaires have drawbacks. Many people forget to fill them in, which can result in an incomplete picture of a system. Respondents may misunderstand some of the questions if the forms are simply posted to them and no personal help offered.

Nevertheless, questionnaires are useful when information needs to be collected from a large number of individuals as they consume a lot less staff time than interviews.

When compiling questionnaires, the following should be borne in mind:

- Make sure that the questions are precisely worded so that the users do not have to interpret the questions.
- It is best for respondents not to have to put their name on their questionnaire as otherwise you may not get honest answers.
- Structure the questionnaire so that general questions are asked first followed by more specific ones. It is also worth dividing up the questionnaire into functional areas, so for example one part could deal with sales order processing, another with stock control. Obviously this approach will vary depending on the type of organisation.
- Avoid 'leading questions' (questions which suggest a preferred answer).
- At the end of the questionnaire, always add the question 'Is there anything I have missed that you think I ought to know about'?

Activity 9.9

Read the following scenario about a business.

> A group of businesswomen have set up a CD music club offering a selection of the best chart-topping CDs along with some 'golden oldies'. At present they have around 8000 members, although this is likely to increase steadily over the next few years as more people find out about the club. The members get five free CDs when they join but have to pay postage and packing on them. Over a two-year period they have to buy a minimum of eight CDs at full price.
>
> A catalogue is sent to the members every month containing around 50 CDs, some at full price and others at half price. Members fill in an enclosed order form, calculate the total including the carriage charge and then send a cheque with their order.
>
> There is a small warehouse attached to the offices of the club and the CDs are placed in boxes on shelves. The CDs are picked from the shelves and orders made up. The parcels are then dispatched by either of two parcel firms.

The above is all you know about the system. Notice it gives no information about whether it is a manual or computer system. The present system was set up when the company started and had only a few members; it is now having problems dealing with the workload and you have been asked to design a new system to process the orders.

Before you can design a new system you need to find out more about the present arrangements and you intend to do this by asking the Managing Director of the club a series of questions. You have arranged an interview and are in the process of formulating a list of questions which will reveal more about the existing systems used.

Here is some advice before you start composing your list of questions:

- Try to arrange your questions in a logical sequence. General questions about the business should come first.
- There may be a temptation to write the questions and leave a space for the answers. Since you do not know the length of the answers it is better to list question reference numbers along with the answers on a separate sheet.
- Make sure that your questions aim at producing answers that reveal important facts about the business. You will use these facts when creating a new system, so

make sure that all your questions are relevant.

- It is a good idea to split the questions up into sections. For instance, you could have a section about how orders come in and are processed; another section could be about stock control and so on.

When you have designed and wordprocessed your question list, let your tutor take a look at it.

Recording

During the fact-finding procedure, the systems analyst will accumulate a large amount of detail about the existing system and all this material will need to be assimilated during the analysis phase. For instance, during the fact-finding stage the analyst could have collected the following:

- questionnaires;
- interview notes;
- observation sheets;
- samples of forms used (invoices, order forms, stock lists, payslips, etc.);
- charts and diagrams to illustrate the existing system (flow charts, organisation charts, etc.).

To make sure that all the details are available for analysis, the data derived from the above must be collected systematically.

Some facts might be recorded using narrative (i.e. a description in words), others using a variety of formal diagrams available to the systems analyst. It is said that a diagram is worth a thousand words, and this is certainly true when describing systems. There are many different types of diagram and chart which can be used during investigation and these will be looked at in the next two chapters.

Analysis

When all the facts concerning the existing system have been collected, the analyst should have a clear idea of what is needed for the new system. A 'requirements specification' for the new system is now agreed between the management and the analyst.

System design

After the requirements have been agreed, it is possible to set about designing the new system. The choice of input devices, computers and output devices should be made in this design. Any communications links should also be mentioned. A detailed specification for each piece of hardware should be given.

Software specifications should also be given to enable a programmer to write the program code. An unambiguous statement outlining what the program should do is provided at this stage. Various diagrams are included in this such as decision tables; structured English is also used as an aid to program design.

Analysis documentation

To produce a new system that replaces an existing one you first need to understand the existing system fully. The process of finding out and documenting the existing system is called analysis and this is done by a systems analyst. There is a variety of diagrams and charts which can be used to document a new or existing system and these include:

- data flow diagrams (DFDs);
- data models (entity relationship diagrams, data dictionary);
- process specification (structured English, structure diagrams, decision tables, flow charts);
- system flow charts.

Some of these important techniques are described below.

Analysis documentation is used repeatedly in systems analysis, at different levels in the system. The first level usually gives just an overview of the whole system, but as the system is developed more detail is added.

In structured systems analysis and design methodology (SSADM), the feasibility study forms the first part of the analysis phase, leading on to more detailed analysis in the second phase.

In order to describe the physical system, several techniques and diagrams are used.

Data flow diagrams (DFDs)

An initial investigation of the system is performed in the feasibility study. This looks at the inputs to the system, what processes are performed on them and the outputs from the system. The scope of the system is also specified in this phase. To help further analysis, **data flow diagrams** are drawn. Data flow diagrams are used to consider the data while ignoring the equipment used to store it. They are used as a first step in describing a system.

There is a series of symbols used in these diagrams; unfortunately different authors use different-shaped symbols, which can be very confusing. The convention used in this book is the one adopted for GNVQ and used in the examination questions. The symbols are used in SSADM to describe existing systems and plan new ones.

A process or action
This is a rectangular box (see Figure 9.7) and it represents a process that does something with the data (it could manipulate it in some way or perform calculations on it, for example). The box is divided into three parts, the top left box having a number in it which identifies the box. The main body of the box is used to record a description of the process and the top right of the box is used to record the person or area responsible for the process.

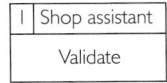

Figure 9.7

An external source of data (where it comes from) or an external sink of data (where it goes to)
This is an oval shape (see Figure 9.8) which is used to describe where, outside the system, the data comes from and goes to. We are not concerned with what happens to the data before it reaches the box (if it is a source) or what happens to it when it goes past a sink.

Figure 9.8

If a data source is duplicated on the diagram, then the oval has a line going through the corner of it, as in Figure 9.9.

Figure 9.9

Data flow

Data flow is shown by an arrow pointing in the direction of the flow (see Figure 9.10). Usually it is advisable to put a description of the data flow on the arrow to aid understanding. By convention, we never use a verb on a data flow.

Figure 9.10

A store of data

The symbol for this is shown in Figure 9.11. A data store can be anywhere data is stored; it could be a drawer where you keep letters, file boxes, folders, books, a filing cabinet (or a certain drawer of a filing cabinet), floppy disk or a hard disk. Again, the symbol bears a number which is used to reference the store when describing it, but there is also a letter placed in front of the number. M is used for a manual store and C for a computer store.

Figure 9.11

Drawing data flow diagrams

To draw data flow diagrams you first need to understand how a system works. If possible, it is best to split the system into smaller subsystems and investigate each of these in detail. These subsystems can then be reassembled to give the whole system.

Let us now take as an example the processes involved in drawing data flow diagrams for a video library. To do this we will divide the system into three subsystems. The subsystems, in turn, deal with new members, record new videos and record loans of videos. There are, in reality, many more subsystems, but to keep things simple we will consider only these three.

Membership recording subsystem

The first task is to investigate the membership system to reveal the following basic information.

Applicants to join the library fill in an application form and show certain documents to provide proof of identity. If the applicant does not have this documentation, the library manager will refuse membership. After the membership details have been checked the new member is given a membership card and the member's details recorded and stored in a filing cabinet. If the member borrows a video and does not return it, this file will be accessed to obtain the member's name and address.

New video recording system

We can now look at the system used when a new video from the suppliers is added to the library. This is a simple manual system, with the details of the video (name, price, etc.) recorded and then stored.

System for recording loans of videos

To borrow a video the member needs two things: the video and a membership card. Each of these items has a unique reference number on it and the borrowing process simply links these two numbers together, recording, for example, that member 34223 has borrowed video 90234.

Notice that the member data and video data are both needed; the 'loans' store of data will contain only the membership number and the video number, so if we need to send a letter demanding return of a certain video the name of the video and the name and address of the member would be recovered from the other recording systems.

We could get an overall view of the system by joining the diagrams together but the system is much easier to understand if the diagrams are drawn separately.

Levels of DFDs

When analysing systems it is usual to draw data flow diagrams at different levels. The level used reflects the depth in which the data flow diagram looks at the system.

We will now look at how to go about drawing a series of DFDs at the various levels for the video library example described above.

Level 0 DFD showing the system boundary

This diagram shows the data flows between sources and sinks (or recipients). A dotted line is used to mark the system boundary, the area inside showing the extent of the system being investigated. In a level 0 DFD no processes or stores are shown so the only shape used will be the ellipse.

All the sources and sinks of data are shown in this diagram, inside elliptical boxes with arrows indicating the directions of data flow between boxes. A brief description of the data is added to these arrows.

When drawing the level 0 data flow diagram it is a good idea to fill in a table like the one below, which lists the name of every external source/sink, whether it is a source or a sink, and the name of the data flow.

Name of external source/sink	Source or sink?	Data flow
Potential member	Source	Application details
Potential member	Sink	Membership card
Video suppliers	Source	List of available videos
Video suppliers	Sink	Order
Video suppliers	Source	Invoice
Video suppliers	Sink	Payments
Manager	Sink	Details of members who have not returned their videos
Manager	Source	Letters to members to return videos
Manager	Sink	Lists of number of times each video is borrowed
Video	Source	Returned video details
Member	Sink	Video information
Member	Source	Fines
Member	Source	Card details
Member	Source	Letters saying to return videos
Member	Source	Video requests

Having completed a table like this, it is easier to draw in the sources and sinks and connect them with the correct data flow lines. Figure 9.12 shows the level 0 DFD drawn from the information contained in the above table.

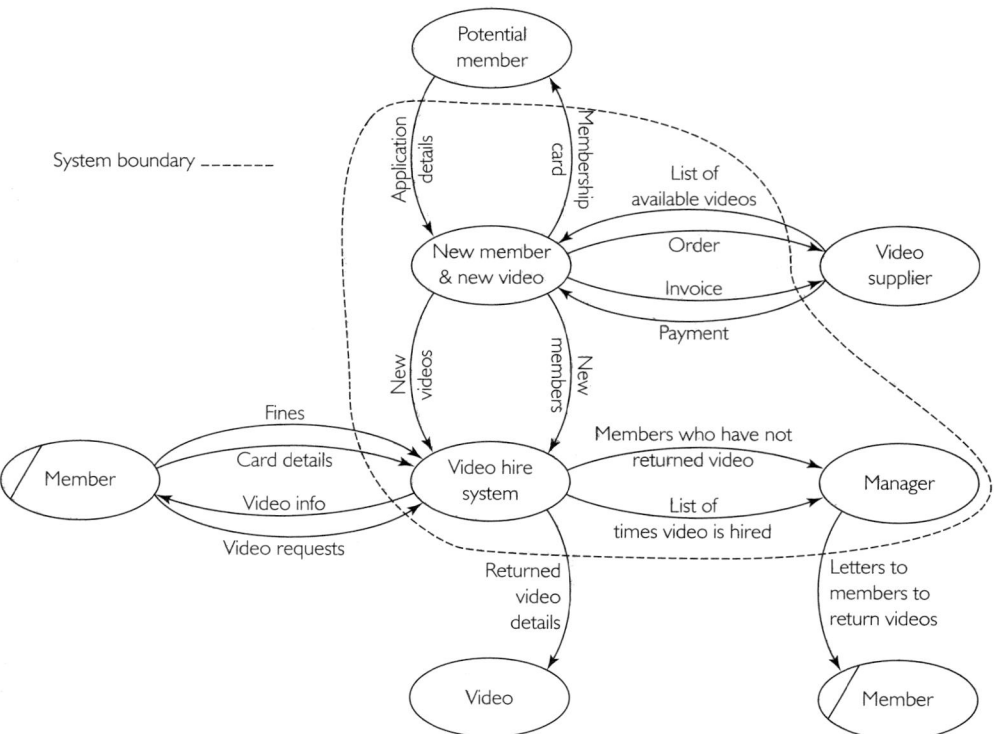

*Figure 9.12 Level
0 DFD*

A broken line marks the system boundary, which in this case separates all the activities that go on inside the video store.

Drawing the context diagram

A context diagram groups everything inside the system boundary and places it in a single process box. A description is added to the box, which takes in the sources and sinks that it replaces. The sources, sinks and data flow lines are now added using the level 0 DFD as a guide.

Figure 9.13 shows the context diagram for the video shop system.

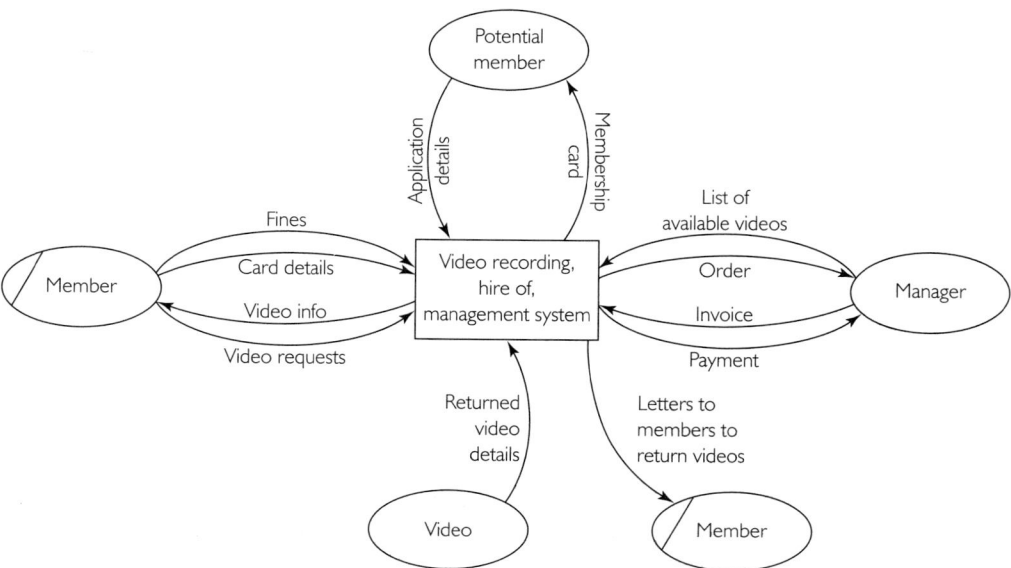

*Figure 9.13
Context diagram
for video shop
system*

The aim of the context diagram is to define the scope of the system and help examine the system boundary.

Level 1 DFD

It is not until the level 1 DFD that the **process** and **store** boxes are encountered. At this stage the rectangle at the centre of the context diagram is broken down into processes and stores, and data flows are added to these. The sources and sinks are also shown along with their associated data flows. Care must be taken to ensure that not too many processes are included. Try to aim for no more than about six. You can use another layer of diagram (the level 2 DFD) to decompose each of these processes further, if needed.

Figure 9.14 shows the level 1 DFD for processing a member's application to join and Figure 9.15 shows the diagram for adding a new video to the library.

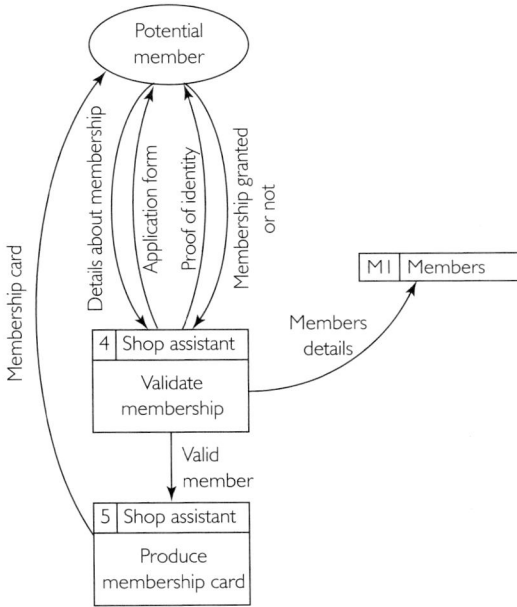

Figure 9.14 Level 1 DFD for processing membership application

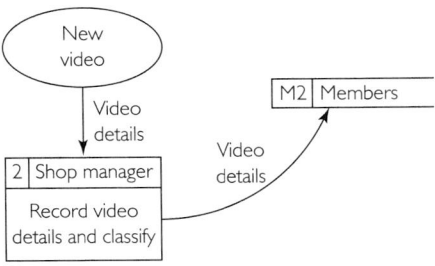

Figure 9.15 Level 1 DFD for adding a new video

Figure 9.16 shows the level 1 DFD for borrowing a video and Figure 9.17 combines the entire system as a level 1 DFD by joining together all the component level 1 DFDs for the subsystems.

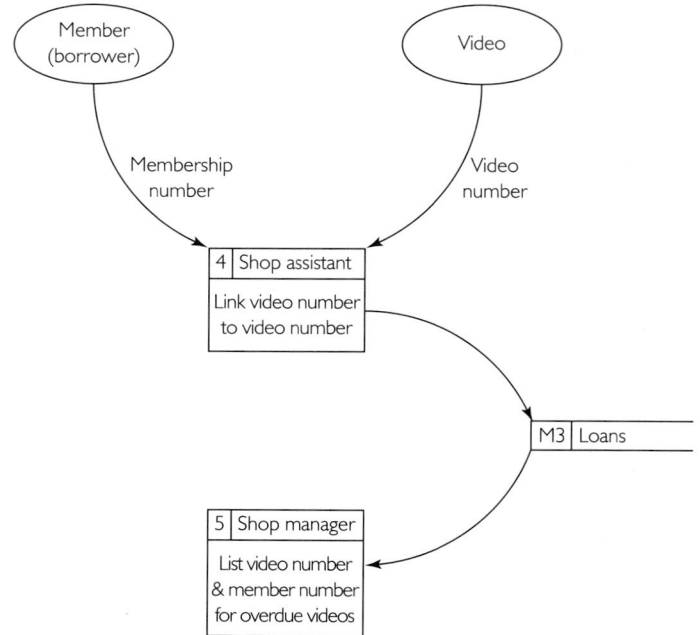

Figure 9.16 Level 1 DFD for borrowing a video

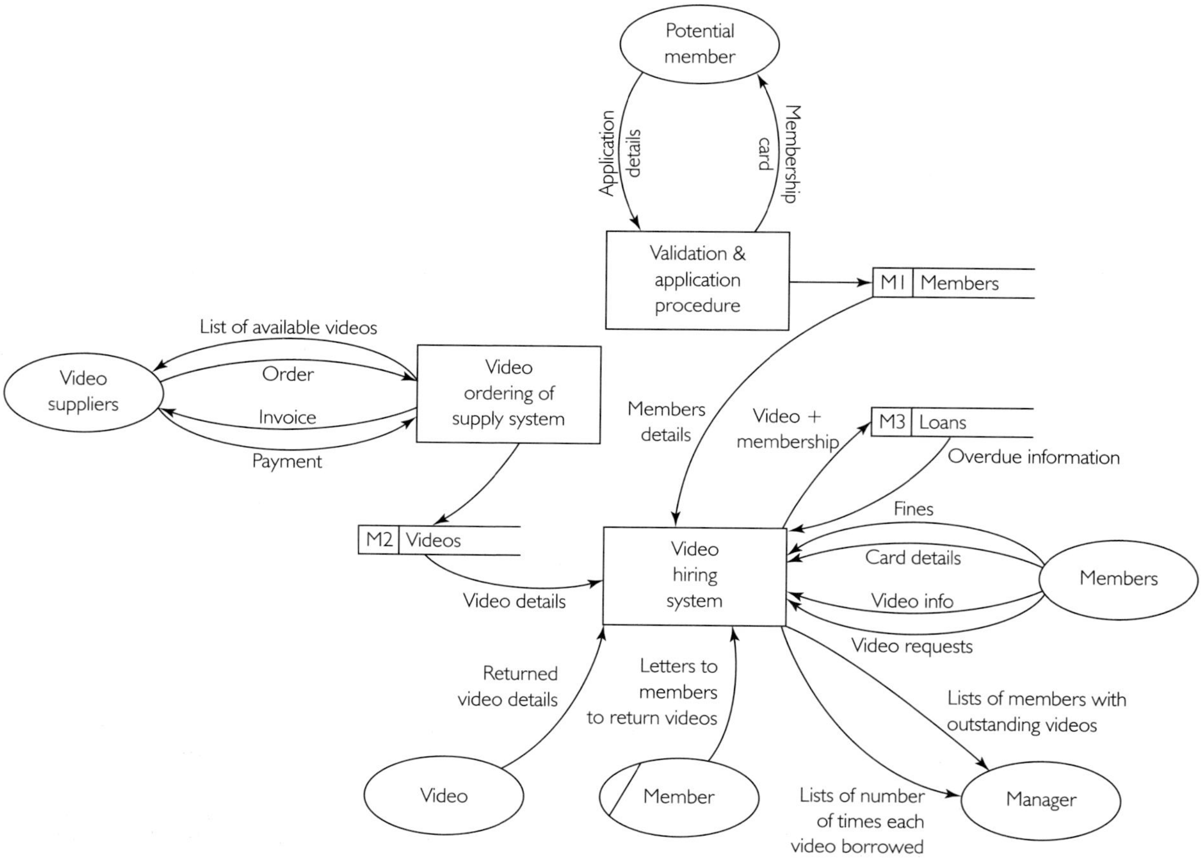

Figure 9.17 Level 1 DFD for entire system

Activity 9.10

Here is a description of a simple order processing system:

> The system receives orders from customers. Orders are validated to make sure all the items on the order are valid stock items and that they are actually in stock; this is done using the stock file. Customers are checked against a customer file to ensure that they are account holders and creditworthy. The order is processed, the stock file updated and the goods sent to the customer with an invoice.

1 Draw a level 0 DFD for this system.
2 Using the level 0 DFD, draw the corresponding context diagram.
3 Using the context diagram to help you, draw a level 1 DFD.

Level 2 DFD

A level 2 DFD breaks down the process boxes in the level 1 DFD. To do this one of the process boxes (i.e. the rectangular ones) from the level 1 DFD is taken, and the process it represents is, if possible, broken down into a series of more detailed sub-processes. The resulting diagram is a level 2 DFD.

If required, the processes can be taken one step further to produce level 3 DFDs by expanding the process boxes to show still more detail.

The advantage of this 'zooming in' approach is that, by looking at each level starting with the outline DFD, we can gradually build up a complete picture of the information flows through the system.

Using data flow diagrams

Data flow diagrams can be used:
- during system investigation to record findings;
- during system design to illustrate how a proposed system will work;
- when outlining the specifications of new systems.

Activity 9.11

Task 1

When drawing data flow diagrams, it helps to write down in a table the sinks/sources, data flows, processes and stores. This has been done for the CD club encountered earlier.

Sink/source	Data flows	Processes	Stores
Member	Stock details Orders Credit status Delivery note	Process orders	Stock Customers

Draw the above (very simplified) data flow diagram. The diagram you draw will show only the information flows from the club to the members and vice versa.

Task 2

Study the details of the CD club outlined on page 291. Now produce a data flow diagram for the system specified.

To recap, the system must:
- process customer orders as they arrive;
- check that the CDs ordered are currently in stock;
- provide a picking list for the warehouse staff;
- update the sales ledger with details of amounts owing;
- send an account to each customer every month;
- send a delivery note with the order and also issue one for the carriers;
- remove the items sold from the stock file;
- send out the bonus CD provided that the customer has not cancelled it on their last order form.

To make the system easier:
- assume that there is no part delivery of orders;
- assume that the initial processes for the free CDs on joining have been sent;
- do not be concerned with the purchasing of CDs from suppliers.

Tip
You will be unlikely to produce a good drawing on your first attempt. Try a rough one to start with and then look at it carefully to see if anything has been left out or if it could be drawn with the symbols arranged differently so that the diagram is less cluttered.

Entity relationship models (ERMs) and entity relationship diagrams

An accountant often produces a financial model to see the effect of changes to the finances of a business, and the models for this are usually created using spreadsheet software. Systems analysts also produce models, called **entity relationship models**, which represent a view of the organisation. A model is a simplification of a real system which can be used to understand how the real system works. Good models reflect the real world and bad models do not. When creating a model, it is unusual (or lucky!) to get it right first time, so the process of producing a model is one of continual trial and improvement.

An **entity model** is an abstract representation of the data in an organisation and the aim of entity relationship modelling is to produce an accurate model of the information needs of an organisation which will aid either the development of a new system or the enhancement of an existing one.

Entity models are particularly useful because they are independent of any storage or ways of accessing the data. They are thus not reliant on any hardware or software at this stage.

An entity relationship model (ERM) describes a system as a set of data entities.

Entity relationship diagrams
Entity relationship diagrams look at any components important to the system and the relationships between them.

So what is an **entity**? An entity can be anything about which data is recorded. It could include customers, sales, payments or employees. Each entity has some associated **attributes**. An attribute is detail about an entity. Let us look at an example. In the following table the attribute for the entity 'customer' contains further details.

Entity	Attributes
Customer	Customer number
	Name
	Address
	Telephone number
	Credit limit
	Amount owing

Each entity is represented in an entity diagram by a soft rectangle (a rectangle with rounded corners) with the name of the entity written inside. The relationship between the entities is shown as lines between these boxes. The entity is always written inside the soft rectangle in capital letters and always in the singular because the use of plural would imply a certain type of relationship. So instead of CUSTOMERS we would need to use CUSTOMER.

Figure 9.18 shows the properties of an entity box.

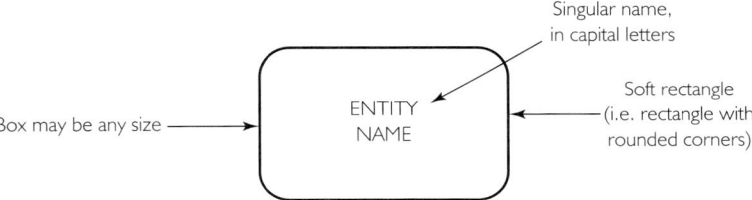

Figure 9.18 An entity box

The relationships between the entities are drawn as lines between the boxes; a solid line indicates that half of the relationship is mandatory (must be) and a broken line indicates that half of the relationship is optional (may be).

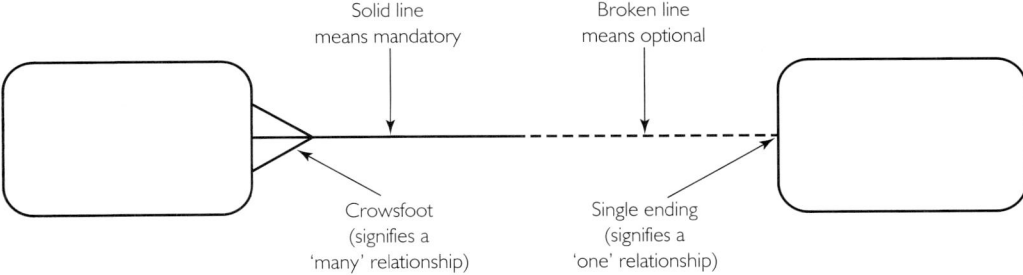

Figure 9.19 Entity diagram for a many-to-one relationship

Take a look at the simple entity relationship diagram shown in Figure 9.19. The boxes show two entities and the line shows the relationship between them. Notice that on the left-hand side the line has a forked ending (called a crowsfoot) while on the right it has a single one. This relationship is called a many-to-one relationship.

It is important to note that each line in an entity relationship diagram has two ends and to describe these you will need to decide on the following:

- name
- degree (how many?)
- optionality (is it optional or mandatory?).

It is important to make sure that both ends of the relationship are defined. Look at the relationship shown in Figure 9.20.

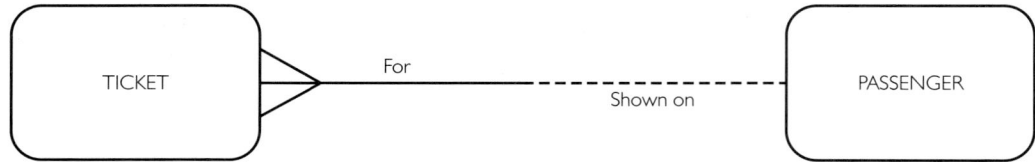

Figure 9.20

Following the diagram from both ends we can see that:
- each TICKET is for one and only one PASSENGER;
- each PASSENGER might be shown on more than one TICKET.

Let us now consider the CD club we met earlier. It can be described as consisting of the following four entities: member, order, CD and delivery. These could be connected by lines in the way shown in Figure 9.21.

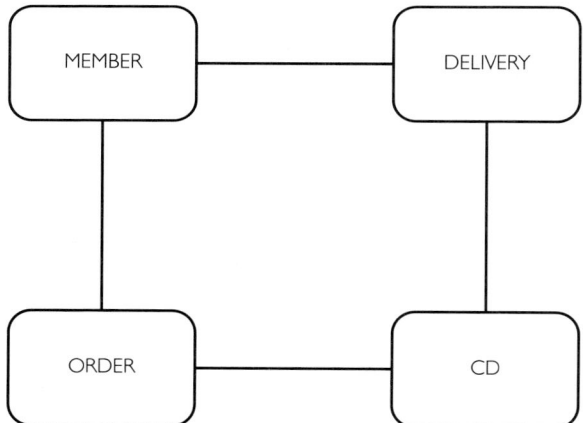

Figure 9.21 Simple entity relationship diagram for CD club

The diagram above is based on the following set of relationships:
- member makes an order
- order consists of CDs
- delivery consists of CDs mentioned in the order
- delivery is straight to the customers.

The diagram is far from perfect. If an order consists of several CDs this is not indicated. In addition, if the club runs out of a popular CD the part of the order that is in stock will be sent, with any out-of-stock CDs to follow.

Let us now look at the relationship between two of the entities: ORDER and CD. We need to examine the relationship from both ends. Looking in the direction from ORDER to CD we can see that one order can be for many CDs. Looking in the reverse direction we can see that a particular CD (that is a particular title) can be in many different orders. In other words, the relationship between ORDER and CD is many-to-many.

Figure 9.22 shows the entity diagram for a many-to-many relationship. We can see from the diagram that many members order many CDs. This would imply that an order is for many CDs but it is impossible to say which CD the order is for. There needs to be a way of linking the CDs to each order so that they can be cross-referenced. We do this by creating a new entity called ORDER LINE. This entity indicates the CD which is on a particular line in a particular order.

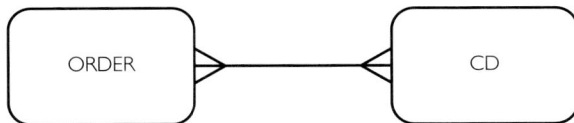

Figure 9.22 Entity diagram for a many-to-many relationship

We try to avoid many-to-many relationships because it is difficult to implement them. Instead we use an intermediate stage which is related to the two entities. This intermediate stage consists of intersection data and is also an entity. For example, in Figure 9.23 you can see that another entity called ORDER LINE has been produced. We must now look at the relationships between ORDER and ORDER LINE. This relationship is one-to-many because one order may consist of many order lines. Looking at the relationship between ORDER LINE and CD we can see that this is also a one-to-many relationship because a particular CD can be in many different order lines.

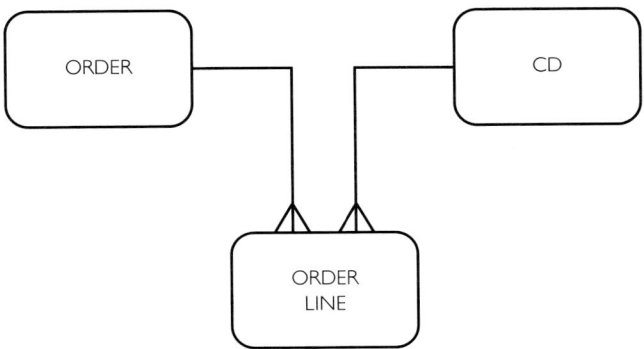

Figure 9.23

The complete entity diagram now becomes the one shown in Figure 9.24.

Entity diagrams are quite complicated and time needs to be spent drawing them; in fact you often need to devote as much time to them as when learning a new programming language. This section presents a superficial and perhaps over-simplified view of entity diagrams, but a more detailed study of them is given in Chapter 13 on database design.

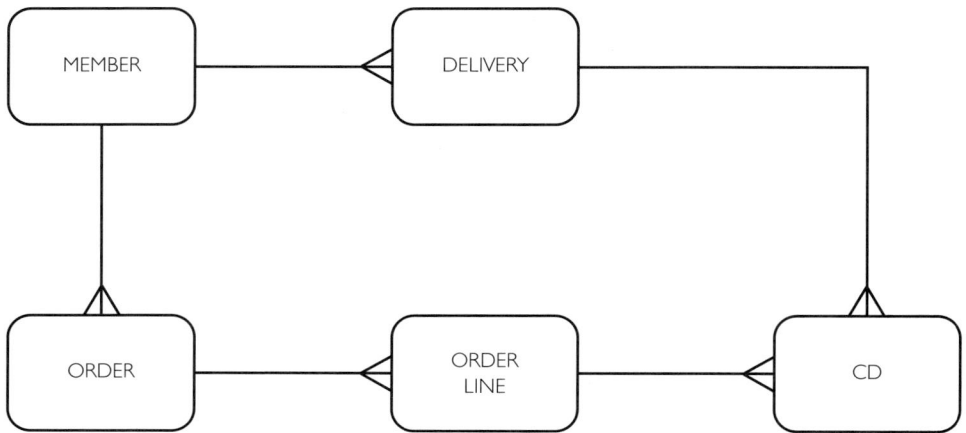

Figure 9.24 Complete entity relationship diagram for CD club

Activity 9.12

Draw entity diagrams to show each of the following relationships:
1 Classes consist of many students.
2 One customer has many orders.
3 One tutor lectures on many courses.
4 Each module is taught by one tutor.
5 Many students enrol on many courses.
6 Many customers order many products.

Data dictionaries

A **data dictionary** system is a tool used during systems analysis and particularly during database design. It is quite frequently provided as development software, called **CASE tools** (see Chapter 11).

The purpose of a data dictionary is to provide information about the database, its uses and participants in the system. A data dictionary could be said to provide 'data about data'.

A data dictionary also provides descriptions of all the entities and their relationships to each other, along with information about which programs use which items of data. Data dictionaries will be looked at in more detail in Chapters 13 and 14.

Process specification

All systems require a certain amount of data processing to be performed and the systems analyst needs to describe this processing. It can be done in a variety of ways which are outlined below.

Structured English

Structured English is used as a way of describing the processes involved in a system as a series of statements from which a programmer can write the program. It can also be used where diagrams are inappropriate to describe the results of systems analysis.

In some ways structured English looks a bit like the pseudocode which programmers often write on paper as a fist step in program development. The main difference is that with structured English there are not as many control structures, although those used are very similar and often interchangeable.

Structured English uses a number of key words. These are: DO, REPEAT, UNTIL, IF, THEN, ELSE, SO. Structured English and structure diagrams are used together to outline the system's programming requirements.

Structure diagrams

Structure diagrams can be used to describe information systems. The overall task is taken and broken down into smaller, more manageable tasks, which can then be broken down further. This is called the **top-down approach**.

The top-down approach

Let us take a look at drawing a structure diagram for a task with which we are all probably familiar: doing the weekly shopping. To begin we place the overall task at the top and describe it briefly in the box 'Do weekly shopping', as in Figure 9.25.

Figure 9.25 A simple structure diagram

The task is then divided into the sub-tasks necessary to complete the whole. For instance, to do the shopping we may have to:

- prepare a shopping list
- do the shopping
- put the shopping away.

So, we now have something like Figure 9.26.

Figure 9.26

These sub-tasks may again be split up into the stages shown in Figure 9.27.

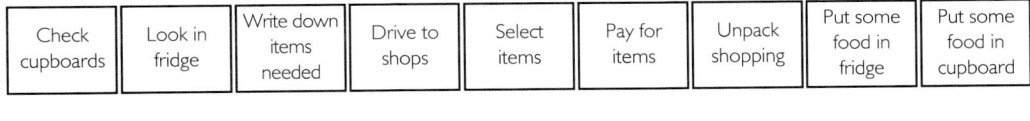

Figure 9.27

We can now put all the stages together to produce a final structure chart as shown in Figure 9.28. Do not worry if your structure diagrams look different from this; two sets are rarely the same.

305

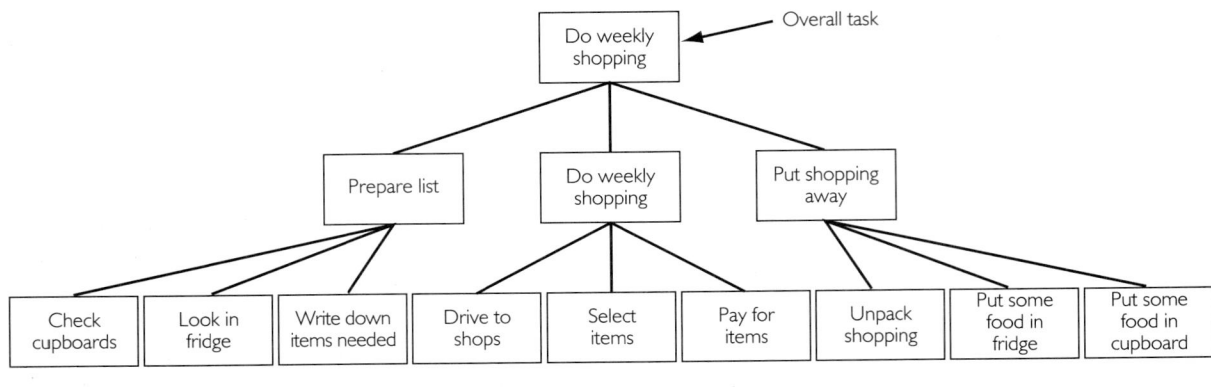

Figure 9.28 Final structure chart

As you can see, the purpose of a structure diagram is to show the tasks in more detail as you move down. The top box is the overall view, hence the term 'top-down approach'. You could carry on breaking each task down, but there comes a point when you have sufficient detail.

Activities 9.13

Task 1
Pick one of the following tasks (preferably the one with which you are most familiar) and draw a structure diagram for it:
- renting a video from a video shop;
- borrowing a book from your local library;
- programming your video recorder to record a television programme;
- getting ready to go for a night out;
- washing the dishes.

Task 2
Draw a structure diagram for making a roast dinner with turkey, roast potatoes, carrots, sprouts and gravy.

Figure 9.29 shows the top part of the diagram to start you off.

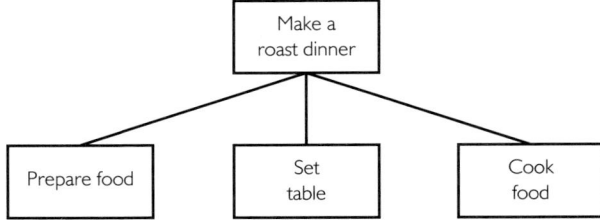

Figure 9.29

In the structure diagrams shown on the previous pages only one sequence is shown; the top parts are done first then, within the same level, the tasks are performed in order from left to right.

There are situations that might be difficult to represent in this way alone, so the concepts of selection and iteration are introduced.

Selection

Selection is indicated by placing a small circle in the top right-hand corner of the box concerned. Taking the example of 'doing the weekly shopping' let us look at the task of putting the shopping away. Two of the tasks are optional: we can put the food in either the fridge or the cupboard. We draw the circle in both of these boxes to show that a choice is made between them. The problem with this representation is that it looks as if the food (as a whole) is put in either the fridge or the cupboard where in fact the selection is made for *each* item of food.

Iteration (repetition)

Iteration is indicated by placing an asterisk in the top right-hand corner of the box concerned. This shows that the task written inside the box needs to be repeated several times. We could have an iteration mark on the box for 'put food in the correct place'.

Figure 9.30 shows a sequence which may be described in the following way: A is made up of B followed by C and then D.

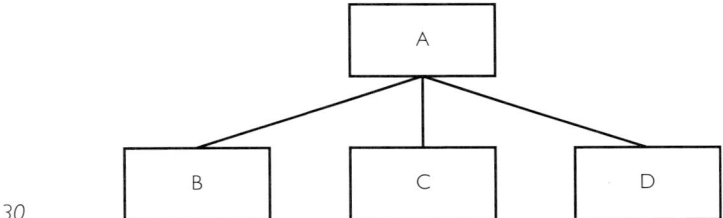

Figure 9.30

Figure 9.31 shows a selection which may be described as: A is made up of B or C but not both.

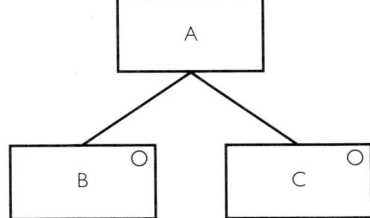

Figure 9.31

Figure 9.32 shows iteration and may be described as: A is made up of B repeated zero or more times.

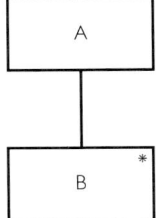

Figure 9.32

Rules when putting the boxes together

Selection and iteration should not be mixed together at the same level of diagram within the same path. Figure 9.33 suffers from this fault and is therefore not allowed. You can however mix them in different paths.

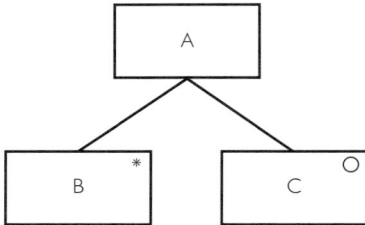

Figure 9.33 Mixing selection and iteration at the same level is not allowed

Activity 9.14

Task 1
Redraw the structure diagram for doing the weekly shopping, adding both selection and iteration in the correct way.

Task 2
Using narrative (explanations in ordinary language), explain what each of the diagrams in Figure 9.34 represents.

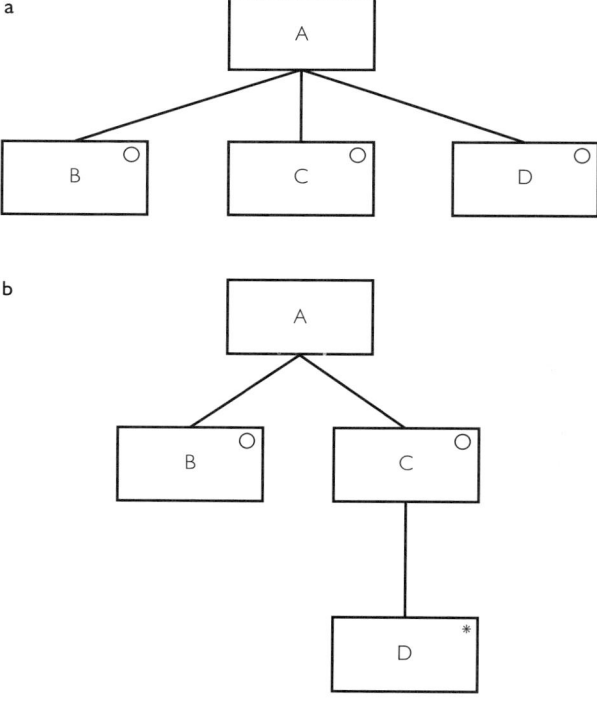

Figure 9.34

Decision tables

A decision table provides a simple way of displaying the actions to be taken when certain conditions occur. The National Computing Centre (NCC) recommends a standard way of laying out decision tables, the framework for which is shown in the diagram below.

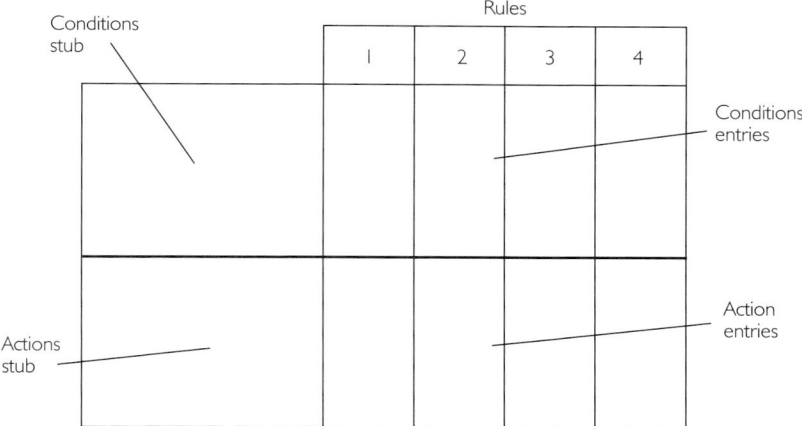

Looking at the diagram you will see the following sections:
- **Conditions stub**: the situations or events that need testing are entered here. They are the cause of the actions which need to be taken in the 'actions stub' section. A typical condition might be 'Is person's age over 18?'.
- **Actions stub**: entered here are the actions that are taken depending on the combination of general conditions that apply in the 'conditions stub'. For instance 'May be served alcoholic drink.' could be an action.
- **Conditions entries**: these give an indication of which of the conditions apply. This is done by placing Y or N next to each condition depending on whether the condition applies or not.
- **Action entries**: these give the action to be taken depending on the conditions that apply. A cross is marked in the decision table to show which action or actions should be taken.

This sounds complicated, but decision tables are more difficult to describe than to construct or use. So let us now look at a simple example with which you should be familiar.

Example of a decision table
Let us draw a decision table to show the operation of a set of traffic lights. The general conditions are the colours of the lights and whether or not to stop.

The first step is to write in simple English the general conditions; these will be the possible colours shown. Similarly we write the general actions to be taken. So in the conditions stub we have:

    RED
    AMBER
    GREEN

and in the action stub we have:

    STOP
    GO
    CALL POLICE (since lights are not working properly)

To set out the table we need to know how many rules there will be. We can work this out theoretically by putting two to the power of the number of conditions in the conditions stub. In this case there are three conditions, so:

$2^3 = 8$

i.e. with three conditions there are eight rules to consider. For the sake of simplicity we will assume that all these rules are possible (there are, in fact, fail-safe systems in use in actual traffic light systems so some of these rules will be impossible).

We can now draw the grid and fill in the conditions stub, action stub and the combinations of Ys and Ns which make up the condition entries. When putting the Ys and Ns in, it is best to adopt a system. You could put all the Ys in first, for example, then the three combinations with two Ys and one N, then one Y and two Ns and finally all three Ns.

To fill in the action entries we look at the combinations to see what particular action or actions should be taken if this combination of conditions applies. We mark a cross to show the action or actions that should be taken.

		Rules						
	1	2	3	4	5	6	7	8
RED	Y	Y	Y	N	N	N	Y	N
AMBER	Y	Y	N	Y	N	Y	N	N
GREEN	Y	N	Y	Y	Y	N	N	N
STOP	X	X	X	X		X	X	X
GO					X			
CALL POLICE	X		X	X				X

Advantages of decision tables
- You can make sure that all the combinations of conditions have been considered.
- They are easy to understand as all the information presented is held in one table.
- They share a standard layout so everyone uses the same format, making them more readily understood.
- Programmers may use them to write programs.
- They show cause and effect and are therefore understood by most people.

Activity 9.15

Task 1
To pass a course in computer studies at college, a student must satisfy the following conditions:
- the student must pass all the computing units;
- the student must pass English and maths;
- the student must have at least 80 per cent attendance (they must still satisfy this attendance rule even if they pass all the units).

The actions that can happen are:
- pass course;
- repeat English or maths or both;
- repeat computing modules failed;
- fail course.

Remember that unless the student passes the course, they will fail. Draw a decision table to show these rules.

Task 2

A mobile phone service provider will allow a person to be a subscriber to their network provided that the following conditions are met:
- they must have a bank or building society account;
- they must have lived at the same address for at least one year;
- they must be a home owner.

Draw a decision table to show these rules.

Task 3

A car insurer who specialises in older drivers will insure only people who are 50 or over, who have been accident-free for at least five years and who hold a clean driving licence.

Draw a decision table to summarise these facts.

Task 4

An examinations board will satisfy an order for syllabuses and past examination papers, provided that:
- they are in stock;
- the correct amount of money accompanies the order;
- the correct amount of postage has been sent.

Draw a decision table which could be used to determine if a particular order should be satisfied.

Impossible rules

In some situations there is no point in writing down and considering all the rules since some may be impossible. Take the following example:

Suppose the carriage to be paid when ordering a CD from a club is as follows:
- 1–3 CDs carriage is £2.50
- 4–6 CDs carriage is £3.00
- 7 or more CDs carriage is £4.00.

Since there are three general conditions there are eight (2^3) rules. If we look carefully, we find that some of these rules are impossible. For instance YYY would be impossible since the number of CDs cannot be 1–3, 4–6 and more than 7. We get impossible rules when the questions in the decision table are related to each other.

To take account of these impossible rules, we leave them out of the decision table. In the above example if the impossible rules are eliminated the following decision table is obtained.

	Rules		
	1	2	3
1–3 CDs ordered	Y	N	N
4–6 CDs ordered	N	Y	N
Over 7 CDs ordered	N	N	Y
Carriage of £2.50	X		
Carriage of £3.00		X	
Carriage of £4.00			X

Activity 9.16

A CD club offers members the following discounts as part of a pre-Christmas special promotion.
- An order for 3–6 CDs qualifies for a discount of 5 per cent;
- An order for over 6 CDs qualifies for a discount of 10 per cent.

The special offers are available only to those who have been members for 12 months or more. Orders for one or two CDs are acceptable but no discount is given.

Draw a decision table which will enable a programmer to understand the rules immediately. Your final decision table should not contain any impossible rules.

Redundant rules

In some cases rules may be combined and this results in a much simpler-looking decision table. See how this works by considering the following example.

With a particular insurer, a person under 25 years old applying for car insurance must have a clean licence to be accepted. Their premiums will in any case be loaded (increased) to take account of their inexperience. Applicants of 25 and over who do not have a clean licence will also have their premiums loaded. Since this insurance is available only to careful motorists, anyone who has had an accident in the last two years which was their fault will be refused insurance. Everyone else is accepted on normal premiums.

A decision table can be drawn up as shown below.

	Rules							
	1	2	3	4	5	6	7	8
Age ≥ 25 years	Y	Y	Y	N	N	N	Y	N
Clean licence?	Y	Y	N	Y	N	Y	N	N
Blame-free accident record for at least 2 years?	Y	N	Y	Y	Y	N	N	N
Normal premium	X							
Loaded premium			X	X				
Insurance refused		X			X	X	X	X

If you look at rules 6 and 8 you can see that they only differ in the second row of condition entries. So applicants will be refused insurance if they have had an accident in the last two years *regardless* of whether they are under 25 or not or have a clean licence or not. We can therefore combine rules 6 and 8 to give a single rule and put a dash to represent Y or N. The dash means that it makes no difference if the answer to the condition is Y or N.

The decision table can now be altered to take account of these redundant rules and the slightly trimmed down version is shown below.

	Rules						
	1	2	3	4	5	6	7
Age ≥ 25 years	Y	Y	Y	N	N	N	Y
Clean licence?	Y	Y	N	Y	N	–	N
Blame-free accident record for at least 2 years?	Y	N	Y	Y	Y	N	N
Normal premium	X						
Loaded premium			X	X			
Insurance refused		X			X	X	X

When eliminating redundancy you look for action entries which are the same where the condition entries differ only in one respect. Examination of this decision table reveals that rules 2 and 7 can be combined, and when this is done the following simplification is obtained.

	Rules					
	1	2	3	4	5	6
Age ≥ 25 years	Y	Y	Y	N	N	N
Clean licence?	Y	–	N	Y	N	–
Blame-free accident record for at least 2 years?	Y	N	Y	Y	Y	N
Normal premium	X					
Loaded premium			X	X		
Insurance refused		X			X	X

Redundancy can be taken a stage further in this example. If you look at the above decision table you can see that the new rules 2 and 6 differ only in their first lines and their action entries are the same, so these too can be combined. The final version of the decision table, eliminating both impossible and redundant rules, is shown below.

			Rules		
	1	**2**	**3**	**4**	**5**
Age ≥ 25 years	Y	–	Y	N	N
Clean licence?	Y	–	N	Y	N
Blame-free accident record for at least 2 years?	Y	N	Y	Y	Y
Normal premium	X				
Loaded premium			X	X	
Insurance refused		X			X

Activity 9.17

Task 1

A finance company will grant a loan to applicants who have a bank account or are married house owners. A partly completed decision table applying these rules is shown below.

				Rules				
	1	**2**	**3**	**4**	**5**	**6**	**7**	**8**
Bank account?	Y	Y	Y	N	Y	N	N	N
Married?	Y	Y	N	Y	N	Y	N	N
Home owner?	Y	N	Y	Y	N	N	Y	N
Loan granted								
Loan refused								

1 Complete the decision table by filling in the action entries.
2 Are any of the rules impossible?
3 Some of the rules are redundant. Identify these rules and draw a revised decision table eliminating these rules.

Task 2

A CD club offers members the following discounts as part of a pre-Christmas special promotion:
- an order for 3–5 CDs qualifies for a discount of 5 per cent;
- for an order of 6 CDs and over, the discount is 10 per cent;
- this special offer applies only to members who have been members for 12 months or more.

1 Write down the conditions and actions.
2 Calculate the number of rules and use this to help you draw the decision table.
3 Redraw your decision table removing any rules that are impossible.
4 Look carefully at your decision table drawn in **3** and locate any redundant rules. Redraw the final decision table with the redundant rules eliminated.

Task 3

To pass an Access course in computing, students must satisfy the following conditions:
- they must pass in a minimum of 21 computing modules;
- they must pass all the modules in English and maths;
- they must have at least 80 per cent attendance throughout the course (unless they do they will fail even though they have satisfied the other conditions).

The actions that can happen are:
- pass the course;
- repeat some or all computing modules;
- repeat English, maths or both;
- fail course.

Produce a decision table to show these rules and actions. Make sure that you have removed impossible rules and eliminated any redundancy.

Systems flow charts

Systems **flow charts** are used to show input and input data files, all the files used such as transaction and master files and, finally, output. In addition, they show the flow of processing, so it is possible to see what is happening at each stage. Unlike data flow diagrams, which show only the flows of data, systems flow charts give some indication of the hardware employed by using shape-coded symbols. You can, for instance, tell if a particular system uses disk or tape storage media. The systems flow chart symbols along with their meanings are shown in Figure 9.35.

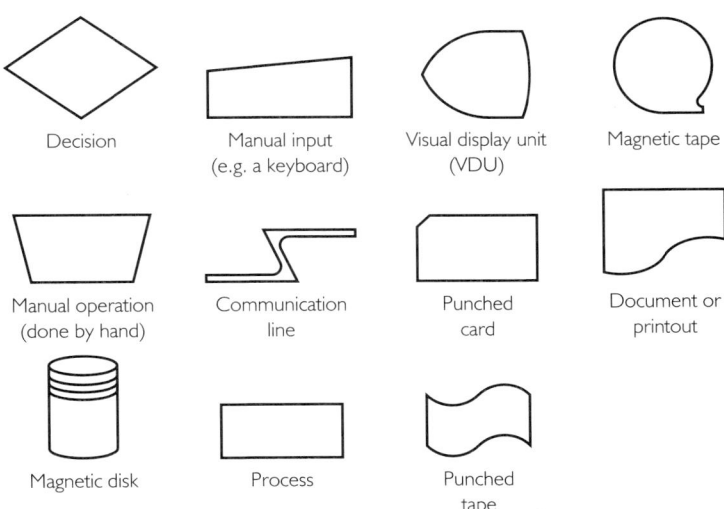

Figure 9.35 Systems flow chart symbols

When there is a single program system (a single PC used to do one task at a time for instance) the systems flow chart is very simple. An example is shown in Figure 9.36.

Look at the systems flow chart showing the order processing for a CD club in Figure 9.37.

315

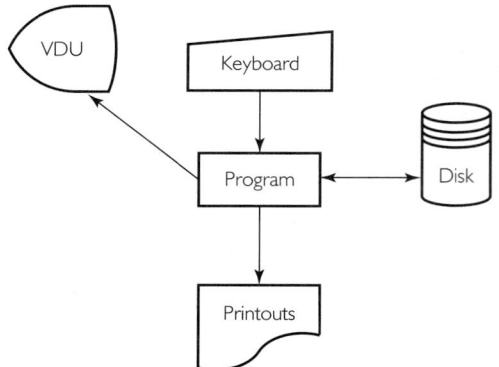

Figure 9.36 A simple systems flow chart

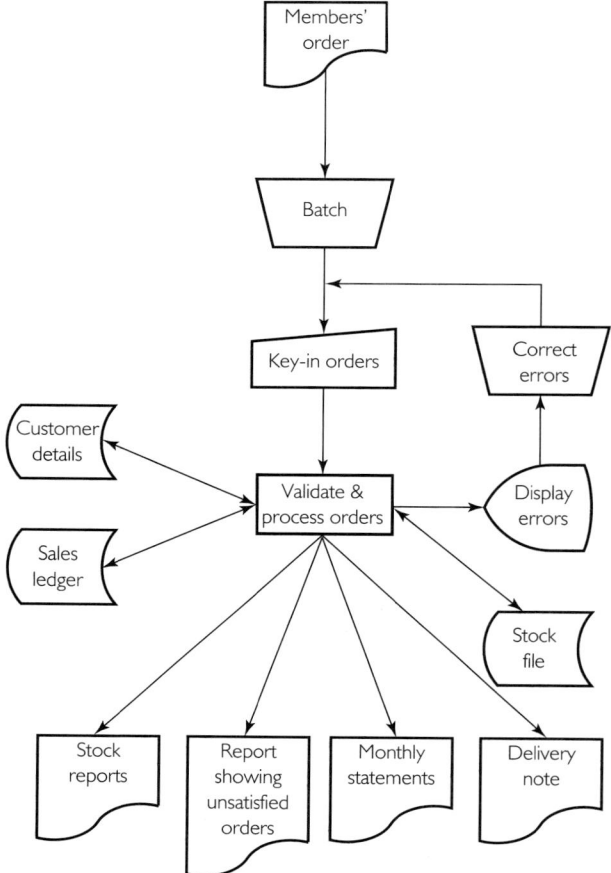

Figure 9.37 Systems flow chart showing order processing for a CD club

From the systems flow chart we can see that:
- the system is disk based;
- the data capture method is key-to-disk;
- orders are checked against the stock file to make sure they can be satisfied;

- once goods have been sold they are removed from the stock so this is a real-time system;
- a delivery note is sent with the goods and this will probably be used as a pick list by the warehouse staff when selecting the CDs to make up the order.

Systems flow chart for producing gas/electricity bills

The production of gas or electricity bills is an example of batch processing. In batch processing, once the inputs have been batched, the processing and the output are produced without any human intervention. The processing is therefore carried out overnight when computer power is not being used for on-line tasks.

Figure 9.38 shows the systems flow chart for producing bills. The diagram itself is fairly easy to understand. Because every customer gets a bill and there are so many customers, batch processing will be used with magnetic tape as the storage media. The transaction file containing all the meter readings has to be sorted into the same order as the customer master file, otherwise tapes would need to be wound backwards and forwards until the records matched and processing would be very slow.

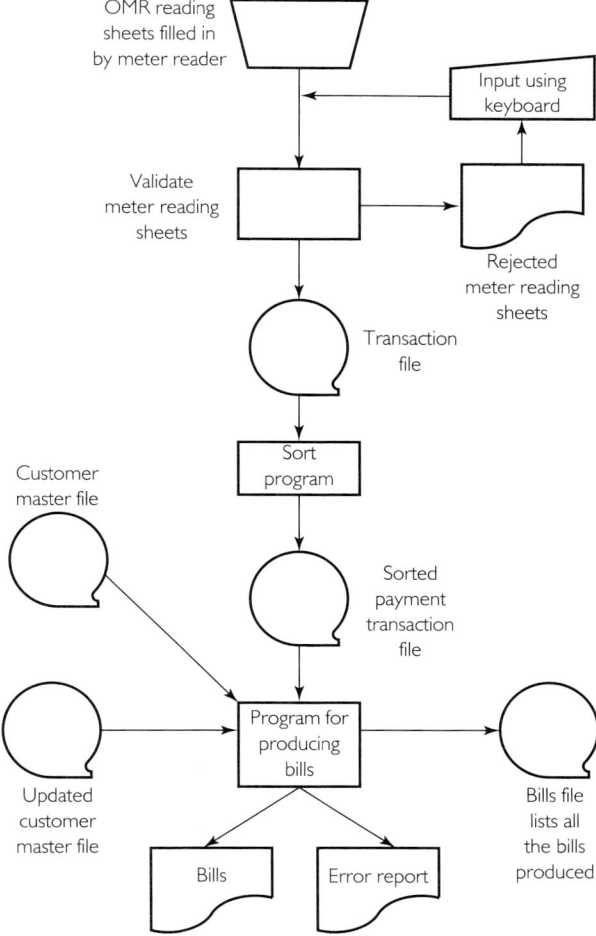

Figure 9.38 Systems flow chart for producing bills

The bills file, also on magnetic tape, contains details of the amounts owed by the customers and this needs updating as the customers pay their bills. Figure 9.39 shows the systems flow chart for processing the bills file. Notice that there are several ways of making payments and the payments must be validated before recording on the **transaction file**. The update program is used to produce reminders and final demands for customers who have not yet paid their bills.

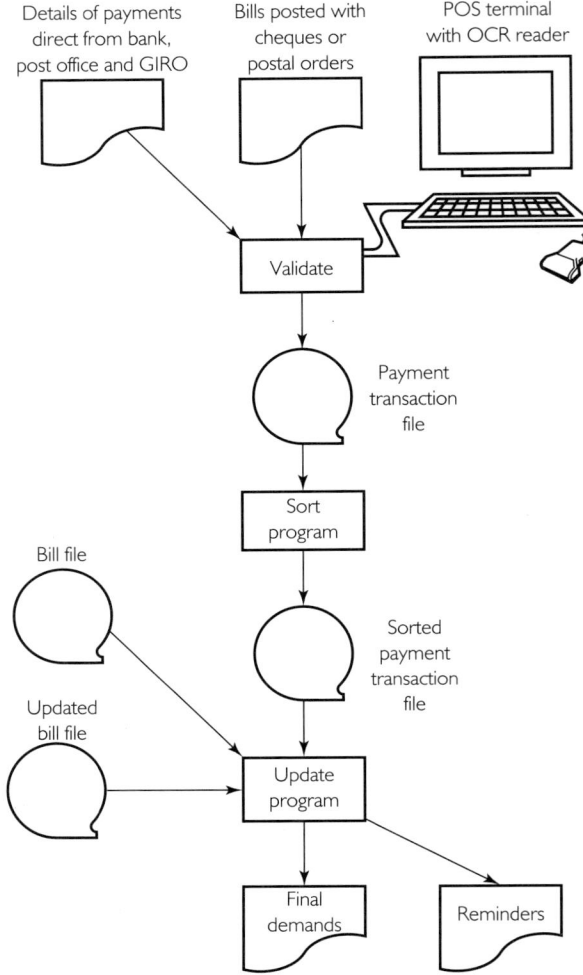

Figure 9.39 Systems flow chart for processing bills file

Systems flow chart for a payroll system which uses batch processing

The following system is used for the weekly wages for a large number of factory staff.

Each employee is given a clock card at the start of each week which contains the employee's name and works number. This card is placed into a special machine which records their arrival and departure time and also the date. For a complete five-day week, there will be ten times recorded on the card. The process of recording the times is called 'clocking in' and 'clocking out'. The clock machine punches holes in the card to record each time; the cards are placed directly into a machine which is able to read this coded data. By this means the data is transferred directly to a transaction file which could be on either magnetic tape or disk.

The transaction file is validated and then sorted by employee works number. Any incomplete clock cards (e.g. someone who has forgotten to clock out) will be output as a list called an 'error report'. Clock cards on the error report will need to be dealt with by a separate system. A disk file is used to hold details of employees' hourly rates, tax codes, taxable pay to date, etc.

The systems flow chart used to represent the above system is shown in Figure 9.40.

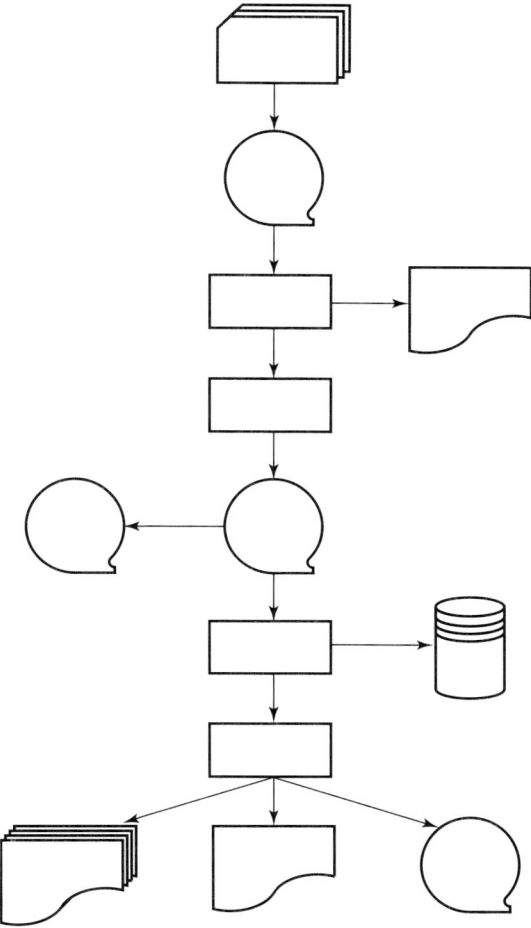

Figure 9.40 Systems flow chart for payroll system using batch processing

Activity 9.18

Task 1

Copy out the systems flow chart shown in Figure 9.40 using a flow chart stencil. Put each of the descriptions shown in the list below into the correct box on the flow chart you have drawn.

Transaction file	Sorted transaction file	Wage slips
Error report	Tax tables on disk	Clock cards
Calculate wages	Validation program	Sort program
Employee master file	Update master file	Error report
Updated master file		

Task 2

The following system is used by a small firm to update the files for payments received from customers. Customers send their payments to the firm's offices where the details are entered into the computer using key-to-disk. These entries form the payments transaction file. After validation, the records are output to a second disk file. Any errors are corrected and re-input. The valid fields are then sorted and used with the customer master file to produce an updated file and a list of people who still owe money.

! Copy out the systems flow chart shown in Figure 9.41 using a flow chart stencil. Insert the letter for the correct expression into each space in the systems flow chart you have drawn.

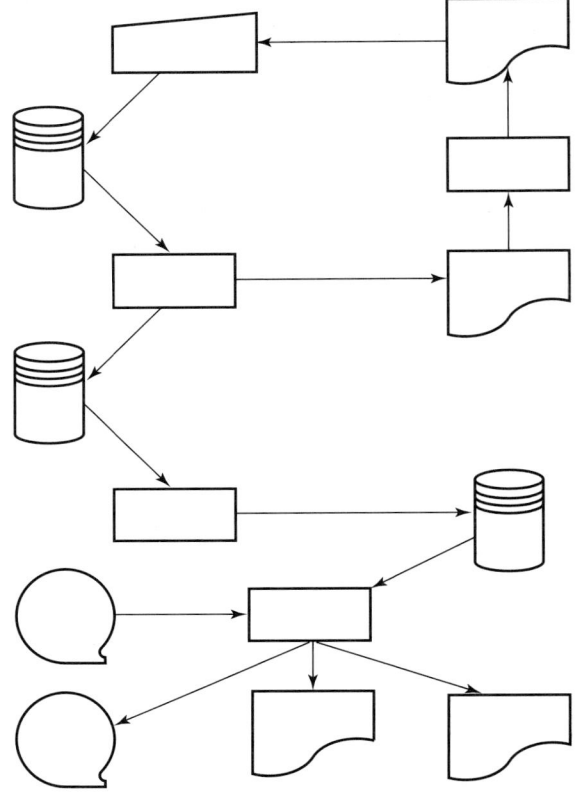

Figure 9.41

A sort payments records into customer account number order
B old customer file
C updated customer file
D error report
E error report
F validated payments transaction file
G payments transaction file
H payment records
I corrected payments records

J   correct errors
K   update
L   sorted valid payments transaction file
M   list of people who owe money
N   validation

2 Why is the payment transaction file sorted into customer account number order?
3 If customers do not send part of the bill back when they are paying, which one piece of information is needed before the payment can be processed?
4 What name is given to the field which contains that piece of information?
5 Three days after paying her bill, a customer receives a request for payment. Why has this happened?
6 The flow chart shows three disk files and two magnetic tape files in use. Which file will become the new 'son' file?
7 Which file will be the new 'father' file?
8 After which two stages are errors found?
9 Name the three files which *must* be kept for security reasons.

Task 3

The systems flow chart shown in Figure 9.42 shows the process of updating the master file at the Driver and Vehicle Licensing Authority (DVLA) using a transaction file.

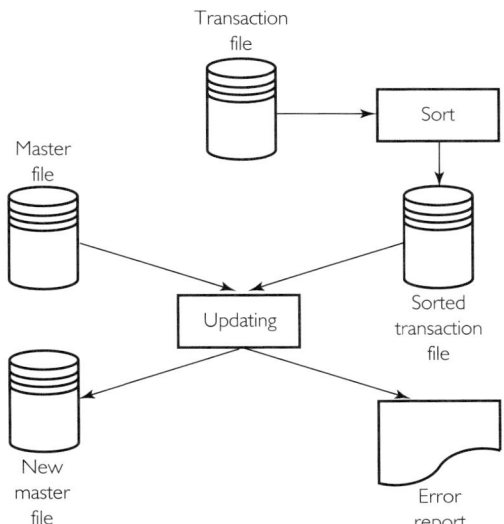

Figure 9.42

1 Explain why it is necessary to sort the transaction file.
2 Three different types of process are undertaken during an update. Name these three processes.
3 Give two examples of errors that could occur during updating and which might be included in the error report.

Elements of a system specification

What is a system specification?

A system specification consists of the data and information used by both systems analysts and programmers to enable them to design and produce a system that meets the user requirements.

The specification will usually include some or all of the following: data definition model, process specification, input specification, output specification and resource requirements.

Output specification

The following items of documentation are included in the output specification.
- If the output is on the screen, then the screen layouts should be included.
- Any bills, invoices, picking lists, management reports, etc. are designed and included.

This is the first stage in the design process since it determines how the rest of the system must operate. To produce a certain type of output it is necessary to start with the inputs and then to perform a variety of processes on them. If the system does not produce the outputs required by the user, then it is no use.

The user requirements will have been investigated before this stage so the output can be designed using the requirements specification.

What type of output?
There are many different types of output media, but by far the most common are output on paper (called hard copy) and output on screen. There are various questions that need answering when deciding about output.
- Are paper documents needed, and if so what quality is required? A document that is being sent out to customers may need to be of a much higher quality than one being used internally. Also, is multi-part stationery being used (e.g. where several copies such as white, green and yellow are produced)?
- What volume of output is required and how often? Each different form of output needs to be investigated to gain some idea of the capacity and speed of the printer needed. For instance, for a CD club, each member will be given an account at the end of each month, so the volume of this output would be the same as the number of members.
- Is the output subsequently used as an input document to be read using OCR (optical character recognition)? This is the case with the tear-off sections of bills which are returned with the payment and are used as input media for the system. Such a document is called a **turnaround document**.
- What is the content of each form of output? Here we need to specify what information is displayed on the screen and what is printed out for each form of output.
- The format of the output. Here we would actually design the layout of any screens and forms used as output.
- What conditions prompt the production of output? Some reports are needed only now and again. For instance, a company may want to produce a list of customers who have overdue accounts at the end of every month.

It is always a good idea to show the user the designs of screens or documents since they will be the best people to spot any omissions and they will be able to comment constructively on your proposed designs.

When designing all the different output formats you should bear in mind that all forms of output cost money and try to economise wherever possible.

Activity 9.19

The operation of a video library can be summarised as follows:
- recording new videos ordered from the suppliers;
- recording new members and any changes to existing members' details;
- recording the borrowing of the videos;
- writing letters to members who have not returned their videos.

1 List the possible contents of a report for a shop manager on overdue videos.
2 List the possible contents of a screen layout for adding new members' details to the members file.

Input specification

An input specification details how the input of data is to be done and the measures taken to ensure that only valid data is accepted for processing. The following pieces of documentation would normally be included in the input specification:
- how the data is captured;
- what the input screens look like;
- what processing, if any, is performed before the data is input.

One of the main purposes of input design is to decide how to get the inputs into a system accurately and in as short a time as possible. Traditionally, most people use keyboard entry as the method of data capture, but for large amounts of data this can be very costly so alternative methods such as OCR, OMR and barcoding should be looked into (see page 280). Sometimes it may be possible to use a combined method. For instance, a student enrolment form could have the course code, fee and number of hours coded in a barcode; other information, supplied by the student, would need to be typed on to the form.

Once the method of data capture has been chosen, you can start actually designing the input media. The data needed depends on the output specified above, so we need to make sure that all the data needed to produce the output has been entered. We can get this information from the data flow diagrams, entity charts or any of the other diagrams we used while designing the system. We could use the context diagram to get information about the functional areas and then use the level 1 DFD to describe the input in more detail.

Methods of data preparation

These are the stages of preparing the data ready for processing by the computer.

Transcription of data
Transcription is the process of transferring information either from a document (such as an order form) or from a conversation directly onto a disk by keying in the details. Such a method is tedious, but more and more transactions are now being done over the phone and the keyboard operator types in the details directly while talking to the client. The rise in direct insurance and mortgage companies shows there are savings to be made in cutting out as much paperwork as possible, and often some of these savings can be passed on to the customer.

For direct methods of data capture such as OCR, OMR, etc. data tends to be input in large batches. There are disadvantages with these methods and the main one is that the rejection rate can be quite high, so there has to be another system in place to cope with these rejections.

Validation techniques

Validation is an important factor when looking at input. Although it is impossible to produce checks that guarantee to pick up every mistake made, it is possible to reduce errors to a minimum. If keyboard entry is used as the data capture method, then transcription errors are bound to occur, so use of this method needs to be kept to a minimum if at all possible.

For more information on validation checks, see Chapter 6.

Process specification

In this element of the systems specification all the clerical and computer procedures necessary to produce the output are outlined. This is necessary so that programs can be written for those tasks performed by the computer, and the clerical procedures for the manual tasks are in place.

The computer and clerical procedures can be described using flow charts or by a series of written steps.

Resources

Resources are the tools, equipment and suitably qualified people needed to do a job. If a job is to be completed quickly and efficiently, then it is necessary to have all the resources available. When a particular resource is unavailable, it is called a constraint on the system.

The types of resource can be divided into three areas:

- hardware
- software
- people.

Hardware resources include computers and their peripherals such as printers, scanners, modems, etc. and any other additional equipment such as communication lines.

Software resources include programming languages, operating systems, applications packages and any tailor-made software.

People resources are important because although there may be enough people to perform a job, they may not have the necessary expertise. For instance, if orders are to be processed quickly using keyboard entry, then it will be essential that the people performing this task can type at high speed and with a high degree of accuracy.

The resources needed to analyse, design and implement a system are hard to estimate at first and it is not until the project is well under way that the resource implications can be assessed accurately. Once the process specification has been produced it is possible to gain some idea of the amount of programming code needed and the number of man hours. The use of applications packages with applications generator features will reduce both these considerably, but the final system will be inferior to bespoke software.

Constraints

Look back to page 282 for details about the constraints imposed on a system.

Assignment A9.1

This assignment develops knowledge and understanding of the following element:
5.1 Investigate principles of systems analysis and specification

It supports the development of the following key skills:
Communication 3.1, 3.2 and 3.4
Information technology 3.1, 3.2 and 3.3

Read the case study about Tesco in Chapter 1 which is fairly typical of most of the larger retailers. The systems used exploit all the latest developments in information technology. In the case study we identified the main areas of the business and how IT is used in each area to make it as efficient as possible.

There are many much smaller retailers who have to make do with manual systems or systems that are only partly computerised. Although these businesses are much smaller, they still experience the same problems as the larger retailers and have the same functional areas such as stock control, recording purchases at the tills, payroll, purchasing, working out staff rotas, etc.

For the following assignment you need to do some research into the way that a small retailer would perform the tasks necessary during the running of their business. In order to do this, you need to contact the owner of a small shop and ask if it would be possible for them to show you how their various systems work.

Task 1
Figure 1.1 on page 11 shows a till receipt from a Tesco point-of-sale terminal. Examine this receipt and produce a report outlining the types of processes that a computer will have performed in order to produce it.

To recap, the processes that can occur are manipulation (sorting, selecting, merging), calculation, interrogation and repetition.

Task 2
A small shop owner, Harry Jones, decides to automate some of the processes that are at present performed manually and has asked you for your advice. Harry has taken an introductory course in the Basic programming language. He suggests that you could give him a hand to write a program in Basic which could sort out a number of problems.

1 You tell Harry that Basic is just one of a range of languages that are available and each one has its advantages and disadvantages. Research the range of programming languages available and produce a brief description of each one.

2 After further discussion with you, Harry comes round to the idea that designing and writing software from scratch is both complicated and time consuming. He has heard about applications packages and how they can be adapted for different types of businesses. Write brief comments on this.

Task 3
Harry has agreed to look at computerising the present manual system, especially for recording purchases as they are made and for stock control, although he is willing to look at other areas of the business as well.

To be able to help him do this you will need some information from him about the following:

Purpose of the system
- a description of the present system (inputs, processes and outputs);
- expectations for the new system;
- constraints (timescale, costs, etc.).

You send the shopkeeper a list of these, expecting him to supply you with a list of answers, but instead he sends the following note:

> Dear Student
>
> You're going to have to help me with this. I don't understand what the above list means. Maybe I'm being stupid but could you please spell out in language that an idiot like me can understand what each of the items in your list means.
>
> If you could give me some ideas of the answers, it would help but as things are I'm completely lost.
> Regards
>
> Harry Jones

Produce a more detailed explanation of the information you supplied which will enable Harry to supply you with the required information.

Task 4

Harry is enthusiastic about the whole project and suggests that you both go to a computer superstore and buy a computer and any software he might need.

You are against this idea since you have no idea of the type of system needed without further careful analysis and design. You tell him that this is the wrong way to go about computerisation of the business and suggest that you tell him how to go about it in the right way. Someone suggested to Harry that he gets a book out of the library on systems analysis but he says that he finds it difficult to understand all the computer jargon and would prefer to be told about it by someone who knows what they are talking about.

Produce a wordprocessed document which explains the stages involved in systems analysis, making it as easy to understand as possible. Any technical words, abbreviations, etc. should be fully explained and remember to make your explanation relevant to Harry's type of business (i.e. the running of a small shop).

10 Systems analysis in practice

What is covered in this chapter

This chapter looks at the steps you will need to take when performing your own systems analysis, along with the production of a system specification.

Element 5.2: Undertake systems analysis

- Getting to grips with systems analysis
- Purpose of a new system
- Investigating and recording information about the present system
- Production of the systems analysis report

Element 5.3: Produce a system specification

- Producing a system specification
- Data definitions.
- Producing a process specification
- Producing an output specification
- Producing an input specification
- Resource implications
- Tutorial Services case study

Resources you will need for your portfolio for Element 5.2
- Your written answers to the activities and assignment in this chapter.

Getting to grips with systems analysis

In this section we will look at the stages involved in performing your own systems analysis on an organisation of your choice. It is best that the business or organisation you look at is small and does not use computers at present. Before the analysis can take place you need to record details about the existing system and its operation and also determine from the owner or directors their expectations of a new system. You should look at the elements covered in this chapter as practical work, building on the theoretical framework of Chapter 9, so you will need to look back to that chapter to refresh your memory.

Purpose of a new system

If you are analysing a system prior to upgrading it you first need to produce an outline of the part of the old system that the new system is designed to replace. The reasons for replacing the old system should be stated and could include some of the following:

Increased speed of processing

With the proposed new system, throughput of customers' orders could be greater so less staff time per order would be needed, or staff could have more time when talking to customers to concentrate on selling or promoting products. In addition, customers' orders might be delivered more quickly.

You need to specify the particular advantages that increased speed could bring.

Reduced costs

The new system could have lower running costs than the present system. If manual administrative tasks are computerised, fewer staff will be needed. A new system would probably have lower maintenance and support costs than an older system. For instance, a company could decide to use dumb terminals and a network to discourage users making alterations and in this way reduce user support costs (such as help desk enquiries). Large, mainframe-based computer systems can incur huge maintenance costs: sometimes their annual maintenance cost approaches the cost of a brand new mini computer with the same processing power!

Whatever the cost savings, they should be specified and quantified (i.e. the actual cost savings should be given) if possible.

Improved efficiency

This could include such things as being able to find customers' orders more quickly, not losing vital information and being able to store files for a longer period.

Improved quality of information

The quality of the information that the system gives might be improved. For example, most video libraries will record new videos, new members and borrowings, but a manager might like to know how many times a certain video has been taken out over a period of time so they can decide whether to buy extra copies or reduce the number if it has not been borrowed for some time. Many new systems are developed to give such management information.

The above are only four of the numerous reasons for replacing an existing system and the system you examine might produce different reasons which need to be identified and recorded in the documentation.

Investigation and recording information about the present system

Analysis of the existing system, whether manual or computerised, is necessary because it is only when the systems analyst fully understands the existing system that an attempt can be made to plan out a new system.

Investigation

A range of methods of investigation can be used to find out about an organisation's existing systems. To recap, the following techniques are available but it may not be appropriate to use them all.

- interviews
- questionnaires
- inspection of documents
- observation sheets.

The results of the investigation might be presented in an initial study, although much of the material will be processed to give the flow diagrams, entity diagrams, etc. with which systems analysts describe systems. Most of the investigation takes place in the initial stages of systems analysis but you may have to go back and find out further information if questions crop up during analysis.

Flow of information

It is important when explaining an existing system to look at the information flows within an organisation and this is often done diagramatically using data flow diagrams. At this stage, high-level data flow diagrams are needed to indicate the general data flow between entities, the processes performed on the data and the data stores used. Data flow diagrams are quite difficult to draw, but are a necessary part of your evidence, so you should persevere with them and let your tutor see them at various stages for comments and help.

The data flow diagrams for the performance criteria in this element have to refer to an existing system only and not to the proposed system.

Types and sources of data

In analysing the existing system you need to look at the types and sources of data used by the system. Chapter 5 explains the various types of information/data. The term 'sources of data' refers to how and where the data originates and whether it comes from an internal or an external function. Both type and source of data are needed when drawing the series of data flow diagrams (level 0, context, level 1, level 2).

Data collection methods

You need to look at how data enters the organisation. For example, orders for goods might come into the organisation by: telephone, fax, paper documents such as order forms, or even electronically using e-mail. Make sure you have covered all the possible ways that data can enter the organisation.

Documents used

Documents used by the organisation are a useful source of information about the detail that needs to be recorded and the processing needed to produce the output. Such documents could include order forms, invoices, stock pick lists, delivery notes and letters.

Looking at letters (particularly letters of complaints from customers) can reveal useful information about the shortcomings of the existing system. For instance, many complaints about the wrong goods being sent may point to bad stock control with unsuitable alternatives being sent to replace goods which are out of stock.

If you are going to base your project on a real organisation, ask if you can see some of the documents which it uses in the course of its business. Look at the design of these, particularly if they are used for output such as quotations, statements or invoices, since these can tell you a lot about the information flows to external organisations. With the organisation's permission, photocopy any documents and include these as evidence in your analysis documentation.

Personnel and skills

In your initial analysis you should outline the staffing arrangements for the existing system. It is a good idea to include an organisation chart. You need to investigate the qualifications of the staff and in particular their computing expertise, since this will tell you about their training needs. It will, for example, be difficult to computerise an organisation where none of the staff have any experience of computers. However, this situation is much less common than it used to be.

If a new computer system is to be introduced, it is essential to find out what computing skills the staff have. You may think that this could be obtained from the personnel department, but their records may not be up to date and people may only put down their skills in the particular area in which they work, or else only if they have a qualification on paper. Computing, for instance, might be a hobby of which personnel have no records. Technical staff are usually computer literate, but seldom have a formal qualification, and often omit it when stating their qualifications. You could put together a simple questionnaire to enable staff who will be using the new technology to assess their computing skills and knowledge. This might be particularly useful later on, when you need to work out how much training to provide.

Operations

The operations to be carried out on the data need to be investigated. In a manual order processing system we would look at what information is copied down. Orders might not always arrive in the normal way on an order form. They might sometimes be phoned through, for instance, so some record needs to be kept of the transaction. Many companies now record the telephone conversations their staff have with customers, particularly when selling financial services such as insurance, mortgages and loans. In this way if a dispute arises over what was said, there will be a copy of the tape that can be played back in the absence of paperwork.

If products are ordered from a catalogue, some check is needed to make sure that the catalogue number quoted on the order exists, and that the catalogue number matches up with the goods' description. If invoices are used you need to find out how the VAT is calculated, how the order is totalled up and how it is checked. Records of transactions might need to be communicated to other departments and the way in which this is done might need to be investigated.

Decisions and their context

It is important to discern from the user information any critical decisions that are made during the running of the operation. Such a decision might be 'IF the total invoice cost is more than a certain amount, delivery charge = ZERO'.

These decisions, and the context in which they are made, need to be noted so that decision tables can be produced summarising the rules and corresponding actions. The construction of decision tables was covered in Chapter 9 and such tables should be included in the systems analysis documentation.

Processing

The processing needed in the system should be outlined. An understanding of the system's processing requirements is built up using the following documents and diagrams:

- structure diagrams
- decision tables
- screen reports and printed report layouts.

Storage

All the paperwork associated with a manual system needs to be stored somewhere for a certain period of time. This can be done using filing cabinets, account books, card files, box files, cardboard folders, etc. During the investigation phase you need to find out what information is stored and where it is stored. It is also important to ask why it is stored and not disposed of. Sometimes, storage is less formal and small businesses might even keep details of orders in the manager's head, or an old shoe box. However informal the method, it is just as important that the developer knows where all the information is stored.

One problem with any storage system is knowing how long to keep material before it is disposed of. Computerised storage is useful in this respect because much less space is taken up than in a manual system and it is possible to delete a whole store of data at the press of a button.

Type of output

Sometimes the output is on paper or screen, but it could be in the form of electronic signals transmitted by telephone. You need to include a description of the various forms of output used by your system. Examples of the paperwork developed as a result of processing should be kept for further reference.

Production of the systems analysis report

The systems analysis report is a synthesis of the documentation created during the investigation and subsequent analysis of a system. The systems analysis report is laid out in a standard way and consists of the following sections, which have already been dealt with in Chapter 9:

- problem statement
- feasibility study and report
- analysis (data flow diagram, resources, costs, constraints and the expectations of the new system).

Producing a system specification

You will be required to produce a system specification, a refined data flow diagram, data definitions, entity relationship diagrams, data dictionary, process specification, input specification, output specification and an identification of the resource implications of the new system. All of these are covered in detail in Chapter 9.

Data definitions

To define the data it is first necessary to construct a data model in first normal form and use a data dictionary to describe all the data attributes which are part of the system. With 'first normal form' there are no many-to-many relationships (see Chapter 9). The following pieces of documentation can be used to describe the data and should be included:

- an entity relationship diagram in first normal form
- a data dictionary (see Chapters 13 and 14).

Producing a process specification

This includes all the clerical and computer procedures necessary to produce the output. It is important not to neglect the manual systems (not computer-based) that need to be put in place at the same time as the computer system.

Once the data has been entered it will be subject to various processes. The data flow diagram can be used to identify the processes that need to be described in more detail. Processes should be described in enough detail that no further analysis is needed and a programmer could, if necessary, write suitable program code to process the data.

The process specification consists of a series of techniques which are used to define each process in the data flow diagram. Where processes are not clearly indicated on the diagram, they must still be defined with a process definition. Any decisions that need to be made during the process should be identified and a decision table drawn up to summarise these. An overall structure diagram is usually produced, together with structured English descriptions of each subsection.

The process specification for your project should be accompanied by the following documentation:

- structured English description
- structure diagrams
- decision tables
- flow charts.

Producing an output specification

The production of an output specification is the first stage in the design process since it determines how the rest of the system must operate. To produce a certain type of output it is necessary to have inputs then to perform a variety of processes on them. If the system does not produce the outputs required by the user, it is of no use.

You need to say what sort of output is required and whether it is hard copy (i.e. a printout) or on a screen. In many systems it will be both. For instance, a customer might ask a travel agent for the availability and price of a holiday. If it comes up on screen as being too expensive they may not be interested, otherwise they may want the details printed out so they can take them away to consider. The output needs to be determined in advance since it is possible to output information only if the required data has been input and the correct series of processes applied to it.

What type of output?

There are various questions that need answering when making a decision about output. These were covered in detail in on page 322, and can be summarised as follows:
- Are paper documents needed and if so what is the required quality?
- What volume of output is required and how often is the output required?
- Is the output subsequently used as an input document to the system, and read using OCR (optical character recognition)?
- What is the content of each form of output?
- What should the output screens or forms look like?
- What conditions prompt production of the output?

Reports

A report is defined as the production of output from software (such as a database) for a specific purpose, such as a telephone list, a list of orders, an invoice or a statement of account. Reports can be divided into two types: screen reports and printed reports.

Screen reports

In many cases the information from a computer can be displayed as a screen report provided that it is brief. Lengthy reports, containing large amounts of factual information, may be too difficult to absorb from the screen and might need printing out for the contents to be analysed and studied at length. Screen reports are ideally suited to on-line enquiries such as:
- Is a particular book in stock?
- When is the next train from A to B?
- How many articles of item X do we have in stock?
- What is the balance in my account?
- I would like to pay off my car loan. How much do I still owe?

All these basic, short requests can be answered quickly and a brief on-screen report is usually sufficient. As more and more business is conducted over the telephone, screen reports have increased in importance. Direct insurance and mortgage companies are now very popular and details given over the phone can be confirmed later in writing, if required.

Printed reports

Many reports are lengthy and need to be taken away and studied; this is easier if the data is on paper. Printed reports include the following:
- lists of goods on order
- lists of customers with overdue accounts
- lists of members of a video club who have not brought their videos back
- bank statements
- a list of students enrolled on a college course.

We still rely on reports printed as paper documents for external communication so they remain an important part of the output from any computer system.

Producing an input specification

The production of an input specification was covered in detail on pages 323-4. We would normally include the following parts in the input specification.

Data source

This gives information about the origin of the data and the transcription method used.

Data capture methods

In this part you need to specify how the information is converted into a computer-readable form, so that the data can be processed by a computer. You are most likely to use keyboard entry as the data capture method for the system you will be developing.

Screen layout

A screen with fields for the user to type into directly is used in many applications. Data is then obtained either from source documents or by direct communication with the customers in person or over the phone.

Verification

A system is needed to ensure that no errors are introduced during data entry. In most cases this means that the keyboard operator will proofread the data entered against the source document. Sometimes, as with business conducted over the telephone, the keyboard operator will read the data back to the customer to confirm its accuracy.

Data can also be verified by two operators keying information from the same source documents. In this case only if both sets of information are the same will it be accepted for processing. This used to be the only method of verification but the cost implications of using double the number of staff for input tasks means that it is now seldom used.

Validation

Although it is impossible to produce checks that will pick up every mistake, it is possible to reduce them to a minimum. If keyboard entry is used as the data capture method transcription errors are certain to occur, so alternative methods should be used wherever possible. If keyboard entry is the only feasible method, validation checks should be made on all input data.

There are various validation checks that can be performed on data once it has been entered depending on the database software used. If you are going to write the program code using a programming language, you will need to ensure that rigorous validation checks are used to prevent the processing of inaccurate data. Such validation checks would, for instance, pick up a character being entered rather than a number.

For more information on validation checks, consult Chapter 6 for general information and Chapter 13 for validation checks for databases.

Activity 10.1

You are required to research the range of validation checks available to a programmer or database designer. Produce a brief report outlining your findings.

You should state on what types of data it is possible to perform a validation check and what types of data cannot be checked.

Resource implications

In your system specification you need to mention what hardware, software and people will be needed by the system. Also any constraints on the system should be mentioned – this usually means some limit on either or both the time and the costs of the project. Look back at page 324 for more information on resources.

Tutorial Services case study

John, who was the Head of Mathematics at a large comprehensive school, decided to take early retirement and start a tutorial agency matching private tutors to students. His business has been great success and he has had to develop an administrative system to cope with the increase in paperwork.

At the moment he advertises in all the local papers around Merseyside and these adverts produce about 50 enquiries per week, although there is a peak in the number of enquiries between Christmas and the exams in June. The enquiries are answered by a team of advisors (usually people who are at home all day). These advisors collect information about the student such as name, address, telephone number, age, subject, etc. and fill in a form which they send to head office. At head office another form is filled in, photocopied and sent to any tutors able to teach the student (usually the ones chosen are in the student's area). The tutors then contact the student with information on their rates and availability. If the student and tutor are able to make suitable arrangements another form is sent back to the agency, informing them that the student has been taken on.

As well as advertising for students, the agency also advertises for suitably qualified and experienced tutors. This is done in the same advert and the advisers also fill in a form and record brief details for applicant tutors. This form is also passed to head office which sends a more detailed application form for the potential tutor to fill in, along with a covering letter. John looks at each tutor's application form and decides whether to place them on the file of available tutors. If an application is successful, the new tutor's form is transferred to a card file in a filing cabinet called the 'main tutor file'. Each tutor is given a unique tutor number and tutor details are stored in number order. In addition to this file, there are sections in another filing cabinet which contain the numbers of tutors who are able to teach a certain level and subject. The main headings for these files are:

- infants
- junior
- lower secondary level
- GCSE
- A-level, BTEC, Advanced GNVQ
- degree and professional qualifications.

These files are further divided by subject into which the tutor numbers are written. When a tutor is needed for a particular level such as GCSE, the file is located, the subject is found and a list of tutor numbers retrieved, which can be looked up in the tutor file to obtain personal details.

This approach is now giving rise to a variety of problems. If someone from a certain area rings up and wants a GCSE maths tutor, head office needs to look though the GCSE file and locate the list under the maths section. Staff must then look through all the addresses and, with the aid of a map, produce a list of suitable tutors, with their addresses and phone numbers, to send to the enquirer. The whole process is time consuming, especially now that the files have become so large.

Once payment has been agreed between tutor and student (or the student's parents), a form is filled in and sent back to the agency informing it of the arrangements made. Each month the tutor fills in a form which gives the personal number and name of the student and the number of hours' tuition provided. The agency charges ten per cent of the fee negotiated with the tutor, and this is returned as a cheque to the agency. This does rely on the honesty of the tutors but the system is fairly simple and it is easy to check by asking the students or their parents about the tuition completed during the month.

This is the system used at present, as described by the owner of the business. The owner is prepared to change the existing system if it will help run the business more efficiently. He has a limited knowledge of computing but has agreed to take on a full-time member of staff with some experience of setting up databases, etc. In addition to this he has set aside £5000 for the purchase of equipment, specialist training and any other goods or services needed.

Activity 10.2

Having read the case study above, attempt the following tasks.

Task 1

The case study might not reveal all the facts about the business. Are there any other questions you would like to ask about the business before continuing?

Write a list and discuss them with your tutor.

Task 2

Draw a diagram to illustrate how the system works. (Make up your own. It need not conform to any standards so you are free to use your artistic talents.)

Task 3

Produce a systems analysis report for this system, making sure that all of the following are included:

- problem statement
- feasibility study
- analysis (data flow diagram, resources, costs, constraints and expectations of the new system).

You need to make sure of the following in your report:

- that you have established clearly, the purpose of the new system
- that you have investigated and recorded information
- that you have reviewed the systems analysis in the light of feedback from users.

Task 4

To encourage established and experienced tutors to stay with the agency rather than advertising for students on their own, the following arrangement has been proposed:

If the tutors have been with the agency for three years or more *or* they have achieved a total of 400 or more tutorial hours since they started, they will pay the agency only a five per cent fee.

If the tutor teaches professional courses only, the fee will drop down to five per cent after 300 hours. The time period proviso is, however, the same.

Draw a decision table to illustrate these rules, making sure that both impossible rules and redundancy are eliminated.

Task 5
Produce a refined data model in first normal form for the proposed new system.

Task 6
Produce a system specification for the system outlined in the case study. Normally, the user will let you know what is required, but in this case he has left it entirely up to you.

Make sure that all parts of the system specification are included. Here is a check list to help you.
- input specification
- output specification
- process specification
- resources
- constraints.

Assignment A10.1

This assignment develops knowledge and understanding of the following elements:
5.2 Undertake systems analysis
5.3 Produce a system specification

It supports the development of the following key skills:
Communication 3.2 and 3.3
Information technology 3.1, 3.2 and 3.3

This project will be developed further in Chapter 13 on database development where the analysis will be used for the design and eventual implementation of a database.

The following tasks are to be performed in groups/pairs. Your tutor will let you choose who you want to team up with and you will need to tell them the names in each group.

Each group needs to contact a business or organisation in your local area to arrange an interview to gain information about the type of organisation, what it does and what data processing requirements it has. The organisation chosen should be fairly small, or a department of a larger organisation, and should either be using computers already or be capable of using them in the future if they had the expertise. In some ways it may be easier to find a business which uses a manual system at the moment but may not have the need for a computerised one. If you have no luck in finding such a business, your tutor may be able to create a fictitious company, in which case you will use the tutor as your contact for the business.

When contacting businesses you might have more success if you make use of friends or relatives to arrange an introduction. You could, as an alternative, look at a business where you have worked in the past or where you now work part time. If the business is part of a large organisation you will need to investigate just a small part of it, perhaps just one department.

The whole group should perhaps attend the interview; one can take notes while the other/others ask the questions.

Task 1

Design a questionnaire to be used to find out about the type of business (or the area of business) you are looking at. Remember that you need to determine not just the way computers are or could be used, but also something of the nature of the organisation: what it does, how many people it employs, etc.

Task 2

From the information gleaned in Task 1 identify either a new system or an alteration to the existing system which can be taken further to form part of an ongoing project that will be assessed in the form of assignments. Your system should have a relational database at its centre, so identify a problem (or problems) that can be solved using a database. Make sure that you keep your tutor informed regarding your choice of project. If it is too ambitious, your tutor may recommend that you investigate and produce a system specification for only part of the system. You should be realistic in your choice of project and what you will be able to achieve in the time available.

For this task you will need to produce a systems analysis report which covers all the range in Element 5.2. To recap, the systems analysis report needs to cover the following:

- establishing the purpose of the system;
- investigating and recording information about the system;
- producing data flow diagrams to illustrate the system;
- producing the system analysis report;
- reviewing systems analysis in the light of feedback from the user.

Task 3

Now that you have identified a particular problem which can be solved using a relational database solution, you need to extend your project to the production of a system specification.

Prepare a system specification for the new system which includes the following:

- a refined data flow diagram;
- data definitions (this would be an entity relationship diagram in first normal form and a data dictionary);
- process specification (including any three of the items covered in the range for Element 5.3);
- an input specification covering all the range for Element 5.3;
- an output specification covering all the range for Element 5.3;
- the resources implications of the new system.

Sample unit test

This set of test questions covers material in Chapters 9 and 10 and therefore should be attempted only after studying both chapters.

1 Which one of the following is *not* a constraint of a proposed new system?
   a it must cost no more than £30 000
   b it must be completed in six months

   c only two development staff can be allocated to the project

   d the new system will enable more management information to be obtained

2 There are various ways that a computer can be used to carry out processing activities. Which one of the following requires the greatest amount of programming expertise?

   a writing software using a high-level programming language such as C or Visual Basic

   b buying an off-the-shelf package

   c using an applications generator to generate the program code

   d using a database with a report generator facility

3 Which one of the following is *not* part of the systems development life cycle?

   a feasibility study

   b systems analysis

   c system investigation

   d system security

4 The purpose of the stage in systems analysis known as the feasibility study is to:

   a see if it is possible to write a program to solve the problem

   b outline the benefits of the new system and to make sure that these outweigh the costs

   c convert all the manual records to computer ones

   d fully document the new system

5 The diagram used during systems analysis to show the inputs to a system, what processes are performed on them and the outputs from the system is called:

   a an entity relationship diagram

   b a data flow diagram

   c an input/output diagram

   d a CPA chart

6 In a data flow diagram, which symbol is used to represent a process or action?

   a circle

   b rectangle

   c ellipse

   d arrow

7 A new system is developed for dealing with orders for books in a book club. Which of the following is unlikely to be an entity in this system?

   a CUSTOMER

   b BOOK

   c ORDER

   d ADDRESS

8 In a student registration system, which one of the following is least likely to be an attribute for the entity STUDENT?

   a date of birth

   b telephone number

   c credit limit

   d student number

9 Which one of the following is a stage of systems analysis used to document decisions made in specifying a system?

a recording
b implementing
c selecting
d identifying   *(RSA, December 1995)*

10 A consultant has just completed a systems analysis. Which two of the following items of documentation should be produced?

1 a staffing specification
2 a process specification
3 a systems flow chart
4 an organisation chart

a 1 and 2
b 2 and 3
c 3 and 4
d 1 and 4   *(RSA, December 1995)*

11 Structured English is used with analysis documentation and is associated with:
a resource specification
b output specification
c input specification
d process specification
(RSA December 95)

Questions 12–15 are based on the following information:
A systems analyst has just completed a system specification for a manufacturing organisation producing machine parts.

12 Part of the system specification will be the input specification. Which two of the following are parts of this?

1 capture methods
2 screen layouts
3 flow charts
4 decision tables

a 1 and 2
b 2 and 3
c 3 and 4
d 1 and 4   *(RSA, December 1995)*

13 A printed report is produced weekly to show different parts available in stock. This would be specified on the:
a stock specification
b output specification
c software specification
d equipment specification   *(RSA, December 1995)*

14 The system specification gives details of how to calculate stock levels. These will be contained in the:
a procedure specification
b hardware specification
c staff specification
d process specification   *(RSA, December 1995)*

15 The hardware and software requirements will be specified in the section of the report dealing with:

    a machine operating procedures
    b machine part suppliers
    c equipment resources
    d human resources   *(RSA, December 1995)*

16 Which two of the following are purposes of a new system?

    1 to improve quality
    2 to increase workload
    3 to improve work environment
    4 to increase speed of processing

    a 1 and 2
    b 2 and 3
    c 3 and 4
    d 1 and 4   *(RSA, December 1995)*

Questions 17–19 are based on the following information:

An organisation in the retail trade is planning to set up an order processing system. It has asked a computer consultant to assist it and to write a report with recommendations of how to proceed.

17 The organisation has requested that order information is entered via a barcode system. This would be classed as:

    a a data collection method
    b a data output method
    c a data encryption method
    d a data flow method   *(RSA, December 1995)*

18 Data entered by a barcode system results in automatic adjustment to stock levels. Which one of the following items of information is requested for automatic re-ordering to take place?

    a decisions on minimum stock levels
    b decisions on number of sales staff
    c decisions on size of display
    d decisions on outlet location   *(RSA, December 1995)*

19 If the consultant recommends weekly reports to management, which two of the following would the consultant specify?

    1 processing methods
    2 type of output
    3 storage medium
    4 sources of data

    a 1 and 2
    b 2 and 3
    c 3 and 4
    d 1 and 4   *(RSA, December 1995)*

20 A systems analysis report is produced. Which two of the following are determined in the analysis stage?

    1 programming costs
    2 personnel training programme

3 implementation procedures
4 memory constraints

a 1 and 2
b 2 and 3
c 3 and 4
d 1 and 4 *(RSA, December 1995)*

21 A data flow diagram is part of a systems analysis report produced:
    a from the identification of resources
    b from the problem statement
    c during the analysis stage
    d during the feasibility study *(RSA, December 1995)*

22 Which two of the following are contained in a data dictionary?

1 data flow diagram
2 data item size
3 data item type
4 data processing system

a 1 and 2
b 2 and 3
c 3 and 4
d 1 and 4 *(RSA, December 1995)*

23 A data dictionary is a file containing descriptions of the data in a database. Which one of the following would be included?
    a entity description
    b system specification
    c hardware requirement
    d software description *(RSA, December 1995)*

Questions 24 and 25 are based on Figure 10.1.

24 Which one of the following actions would be applied if a cheque for £20 was offered by a customer who had bills overdue by more than 60 days?
    a no action required
    b extend credit
    c refuse credit
    d get manager's approval *(RSA, December 1995)*

Conditions	Rules			
Cheque £50 or more	Y	N	Y	N
Bill overdue by more than 60 days	Y	Y	N	N
Actions				
No action required				Y
Extend credit			Y	
Refuse credit	Y			
Get manager's approval		Y		

Figure 10.1 Example of a decision table for giving a customer credit

25 Which one of the following actions would be applied if a customer's bill was overdue by more than 60 days and their cheque was £65.50?

    a no action required

    b extend credit

    c refuse credit

    d get manager's approval   *(RSA, December 1995)*

26 Which one of the following describes the processing required in Figure 10.2 of the numbers indicated by X?

    a optical character recognition (OCR)

    b magnetic-ink character recognition (MICR)

    c optical mark recognition (OMR)

    d magnetic strip recognition   *(RSA, December 1995)*

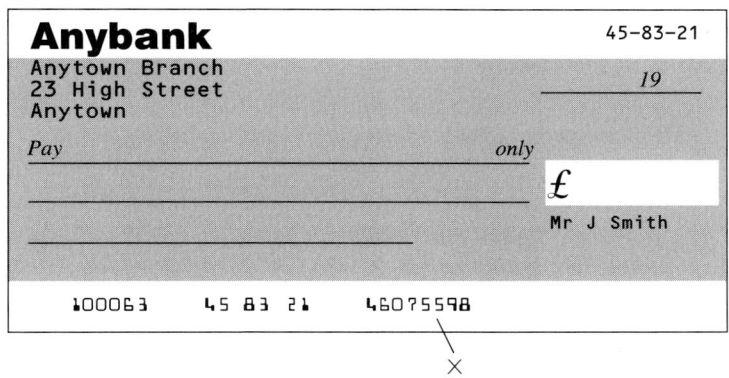

Figure 10.2

27 Which one of the following is required to process the numbers chosen on board A in Figure 10.3?

    a optical character recognition (OCR)

    b magnetic-ink character recognition (MICR)

    c optical mark recognition (OMR)

    d magnetic strip recognition   *(RSA, December 1995)*

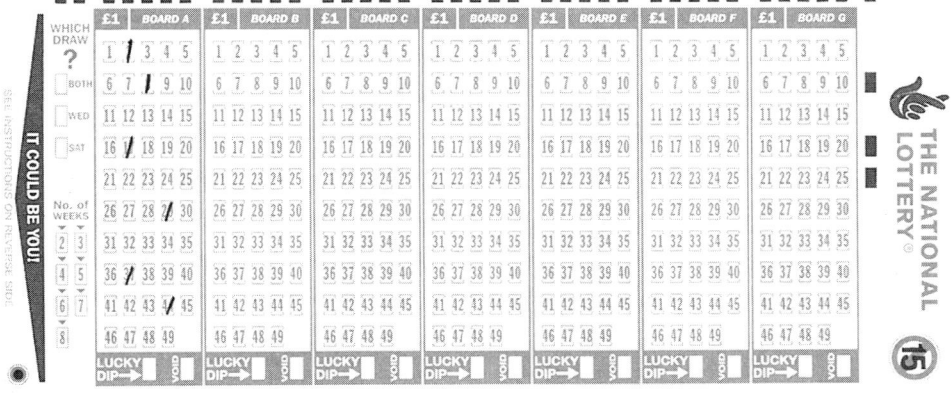

Figure 10.3

343

28 A computer consultancy company based in Coventry has decided to open regional offices in Carlisle, Chatham, Cambridge and Cardiff. Which two of the following are resource implications for this expansion?

1 data
2 hardware
3 people
4 layout

a 1 and 2
b 2 and 3
c 3 and 4
d 1 and 4   *(RSA, December 1995)*

29 A company is upgrading its computer facility and will be installing a new operating system. Which one of the following is a resource implication of this upgrade?
a software
b people
c environment
d layout   *(RSA, December 1995)*

30 A systems analyst is asked to look at an organisation's cash control systems. During the systems analysis a number of members of staff are interviewed. This is done as part of:
a the introduction stage
b the inspection stage
c the installation stage
d the investigation stage   *(RSA, December 1996)*

31 Which two of the following may form part of a process specification?

1 data dictionary
2 data model
3 flow chart
4 structured English

a 1 and 2
b 2 and 3
c 3 and 4
d 1 and 4   *(RSA, December 1996)*

32 Which one of the following is the constraint when installing a new piece of computer hardware that has to be in place by a predefined deadline?
a costs
b time
c staff
d training   *(RSA, December 1996)*

33 An organisation prints payslips for its employees. Data from two different computer files are combined to provide information to go on to the payslip. This process is known as:
a merging
b appending
c calculating
d interrogating   *(RSA, December 1996)*

34 A stock control system is used to produce a number of stock reports each week. One report identifies all items of stock that have not been sold in the previous week. This activity is known as:

a repeating

b collecting

c selecting

d identifying *(RSA, December 1996)*

35 A retail business uses a barcode reader to collect details about products in order to provide customers with a bill. This is known as:

a data control

b data capture

c data selection

d data manipulation *(RSA, December 1996)*

36 A computer programmer is asked to produce a report detailing all items of stock that cost over a certain amount, and to provide a total at the end of the report. Which two of the following processes is the report using?

1 calculating

2 specifying

3 creating

4 selecting

a 1 and 2

b 2 and 3

c 3 and 4

d 1 and 4 *(RSA, December 1996)*

37 A consultant is asked to identify a computerised accounting package for use by a client. The client specifies the price range within which the consultant can look. This is an example of:

a a constraint

b a specification

c a description

d a restraint *(RSA, December 1996)*

38 After a systems analyst has conducted an investigation of an organisation's dispatch systems, a list of recommendations is produced for management. This is an example of:

a classifying

b collecting

c reporting

d recording *(RSA, December 1996)*

39 A reduction in costs is one of the purposes of a supermarket's stock control system. Which two of the following will assist in achieving this purpose when introducing a new stock control system?

1 reducing levels of stock being held

2 reducing the number of repeat orders

3 reducing the number of customers

4 reducing the overtime hours being worked

a 1 and 2

b 2 and 3

    c 3 and 4

    d 1 and 4   *(RSA, December 1996)*

40 Which two of the following will be included in the feasibility study of a systems analysis report?

    1 details of the present system

    2 cost effectiveness of the proposed system

    3 installation procedures for the proposed system

    4 logical design of the proposed system

    a 1 and 2

    b 2 and 3

    c 3 and 4

    d 1 and 4   *(RSA, December 1996)*

11 Understanding software

What is covered in this chapter

In this chapter and the next we will be looking at various aspects of computer software and we will also look at how such software is developed. In these two chapters you will have the chance to develop your skills in producing automated procedures to speed up the performance of certain routine tasks.

Element 6.1: Investigate software

- Categories of software
- Applications software
- Operating systems (systems software)
- Utility software
- User interface software
- Programming languages
- Program generators
- Purposes of the categories of software
- Purposes of applications software packages
- Features of computer programs
- Modes of operation of software

Resources you will need for your portfolio for Element 6.1
- Your written answers to the activities and assignment in this chapter.

In this chapter we will look at the different categories of software, the purposes of software and **applications software** packages. We will also look at the features of a computer program and the different modes of operation of software.

Categories of software

Although some items of software are easy to categorise, others are more difficult. The problem arises mainly with operating systems software which itself often contains utility software as an integral part. This aside, we can consider the main categories and the factors that determine the category to which particular pieces of software belong.

Applications software

Applications software is the name given to the type of software that equips the computer to tackle a particular kind of problem. Such software is therefore used for a specific purpose or application. Examples of applications software include:

- textual document processing (wordprocessing);
- text and graphic printed presentation (desktop publishing);
- numerical analysis processing (spreadsheets);
- record and transaction processing (databases);
- computer-aided design and graphic drawing (vector graphics);
- graphics/artwork processing (bit-map graphics);
- slide/picture presentation (bit-map graphics);
- accounts processing.

Applications software can be further classified into three groups:

- **general purpose software** which might be used in any kind of business or organisation and includes wordprocessing, database, spreadsheet, graphics and integrated software;
- **specific task software** used for a particular task such as stock control, payroll, CAD, modelling, etc.;
- **bespoke (tailor-made) software** written by the user for a specific application.

The main disadvantage of applications packages is that they offer only a standard approach. Some packages, particularly database packages, can be customised by the user, who needs no programming knowledge but should have a detailed understanding of the package. Such packages enable the user to build customised applications and offer a compromise between a package and bespoke software.

General purpose software

General purpose software is designed to be used in a wide range of applications and most organisations will have a range of such software for staff to use. General purpose software is usually bought 'off-the-shelf' either from a computer store or by mail order and provides a cheap way of tackling many general, everyday administrative tasks in the office or at home.

Such software is often referred to as **software packages** and these often provide the best solution to many problems. For example, no one who wants to manipulate, save and print text would dream of writing their own program. They would instead go along to their local computer store and buy a wordprocessing package. This has the advantage of being much cheaper because the development costs are spread among all the purchasers of the package and it is unlikely that anyone could develop a better package without using many experienced programmers. In addition, the software is less likely to contain errors, or bugs as they are often called. If the package is a popular one, it will be easy to find courses to learn about its use, and if the manual which accompanies the software is too complicated there is likely to be other material available to consult.

Wordprocessing software

Wordprocessing software is designed for the entry, storage, manipulation and printing of text and is by far the most popular application used on PCs. A wide range of documents can be produced, including letters, memos, reports, price lists, minutes of meetings, books, articles, mailing lists and tables.

For many people wordprocessing software is the only software they use; it is loaded as soon as they arrive for work in the morning and is not switched off until they go home at night. It is hard to think of a single job where some use cannot be found for wordprocessing.

Many people now type their own documents directly into a computer rather than giving them to a typist, and this can save time if a person can type quickly. Because the text is stored in memory, adjustments can be made before finally saving and printing.

To some extent even printed letters produced by wordprocessors are being superseded as electronic mail is used to send wordprocessed documents directly, in electronic form. There is no need for an envelope or a stamp, delivery is quick and the recipient can store the letter on disk for future reference, thus saving valuable office storage space.

Advantages of wordprocessing

- A more presentable result can be obtained by everyone, and not just experienced typists, since mistakes are easily rectified on the screen before printing out.
- Fewer resources are used, provided the material is carefully proofread on the screen before printing out; this reduces the amount of paper that needs to be used. Most large companies now send all internal letters and memos by electronic mail. The widespread use of electronic mail can help to conserve valuable resources.
- More people are able to produce their own documents rather than passing them to someone else to type. This can save both time and money.
- Wordprocessing software now often has basic desktop publishing features. Extra facilities enable the production of notices, posters, tickets, etc. with very little training.

What can you do with wordprocessing software?

Wordprocessing software allows the user to store, edit, manipulate and print out text. Some wordprocessing packages are **WYSIWYG** which means 'what you see is what you get'. This means you are able to see on the screen exactly what the page will look like when it is printed out.

Most wordprocessors allow you to change fonts (type styles) and sizes of type. Figure 11.1 shows some of the many features you might find in a typical wordprocessing package.

Activity 11.1

Find out how to do each of the following using your wordprocessor. For future reference, write down how each task is performed.

1 Load the wordprocessing software.
2 Edit a document.
3 Alter the margins.
4 Apply special text effects such as:
    bold type
    underlining
    italics.
5 Centre text.
6 Insert a line.
7 Produce a temporary indent.
8 Save text.
9 Load previously saved work.
10 Move blocks of text around (called 'block moves' or 'cut and paste').
11 Print a document.

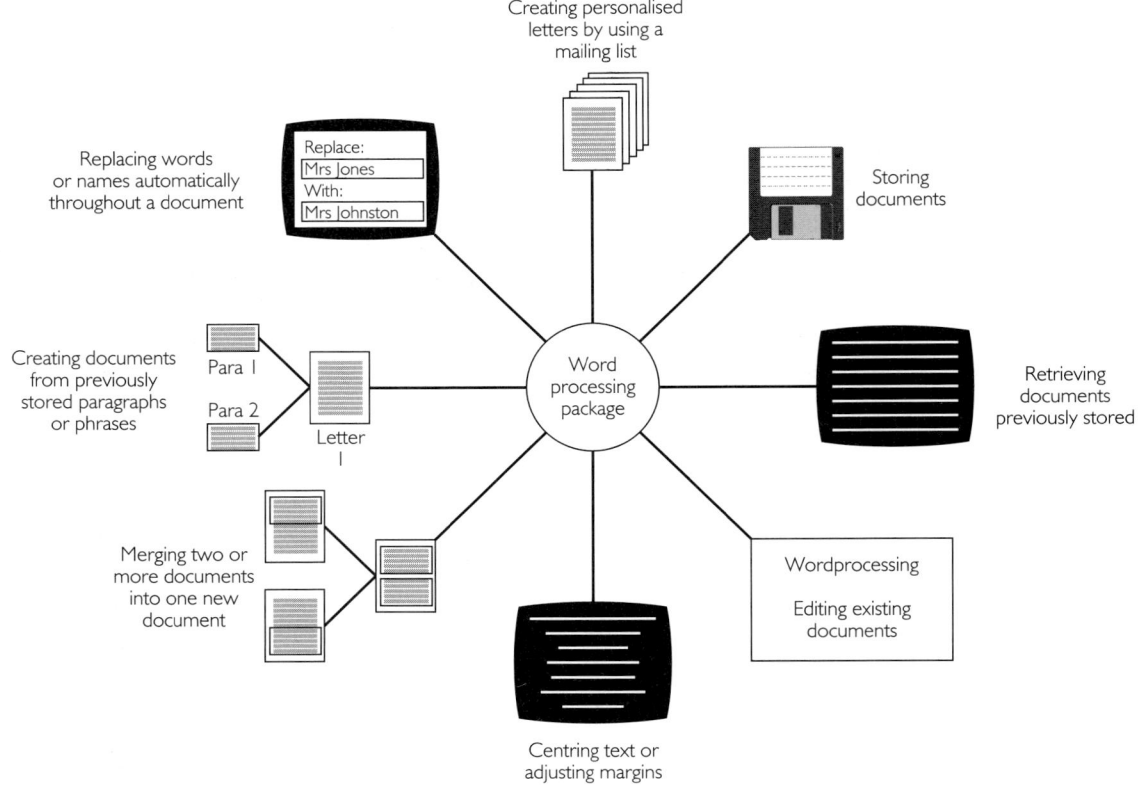

Figure 11.1 Features of a typical wordprocessing package

Some of the more advanced features you will find in a wordprocessing package include:

Spell checkers

Nearly all wordprocessors contain a dictionary against which all the words in a document can be compared to check their spelling (see page 81). Most allow you to add words to the dictionary, which is particularly useful if you use specialist terms.

Thesaurus

A **thesaurus** is only really useful for creative writing. It allows you to highlight a word in a document and the computer lists alternative words with similar meanings (called synonyms).

Mail merge

A general letter can be typed using a wordprocessor, leaving blanks where information from a list is to be inserted. The list is either created using the wordprocessor or imported from a database. For example, a database containing names and addresses can be merged with the letter file to create a set of personalised letters.

Indexing

An indexing feature allows you to highlight words which you would like to use in an index. The wordprocessor keeps a record of the words with their page references and when instructed to, creates an index.

Macros

Macros allow you to automate a sequence of keystrokes so that, for instance, your name and address can be printed at the top of a page by just pressing a key. Macros are very useful for repetitive tasks.

Grammar checkers

Some of the more sophisticated wordprocessors have a feature called a grammar checker. If the wordprocessor you use does not have this facility, you can buy a separate grammar checking package to use with it. Figure 11.2 shows a grammar checker being used. Because of the complexity of the English language, grammar checkers have their limitations. As yet they find only a few faults and often provide an incorrect analysis of the grammar. You therefore need to exercise care when using them.

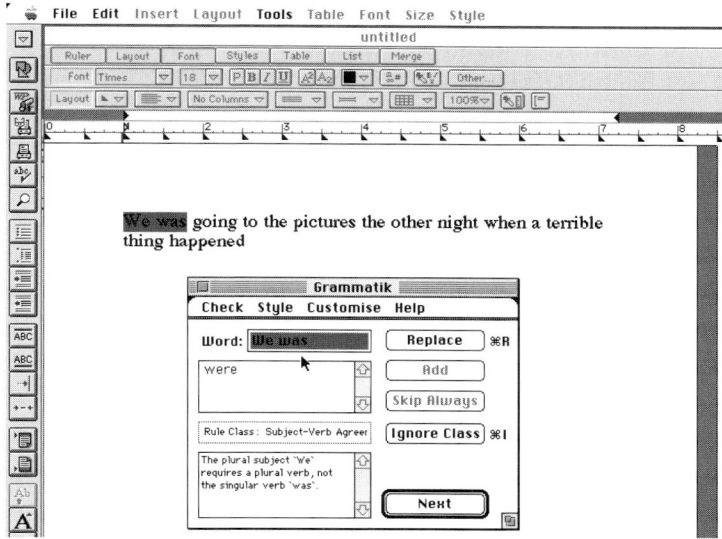

Figure 11.2 A grammar checker

Activity 11.2

This task concerns the more advanced features of the wordprocessor.

Find out how to do each of the following using your wordprocessor and, for future reference, write down how you would perform each task.

1 Spell check a document.
2 Use the thesaurus.
3 Use the search and replace facility.
4 Use macros.
5 Use mail merge.

Database software

Database software allows data to be entered and stored in a structured way which aids its retrieval. Databases may either be **flat file**, which are simple to set up since they resemble a card-box file, or **relational databases**, which are much more flexible but need specialist knowledge to set up.

Many packages incorporate a special programming language so that a whole application can be built around the database (see below). We will look at this again in detail in Chapters 13 and 14, which cover the design of relational databases.

Database management system (DBMS)

Database management systems (DBMSs) are applications packages based around the need to hold a collection of centralised and structured data for further manipulation in various ways. All database management systems allow the user to set up their own databases and most packages are fairly flexible as to how this is done. Database management systems keep the data separately from the programs, which means that when programs are developed, they are independent of how the data is stored.

Since most commercial databases are relational databases, this type of software is often referred to as a relational database management system (RDBMS) and such a package is able to:

- allow the database to be defined;
- allow users to query the database;
- allow data to be appended (added), deleted and edited;
- allow the user to modify the structure of the database;
- provide adequate security for the data held;
- allow the user to import and export data.

A DBMS consists of two parts: the **data description language (DDL)** and the **data manipulation language (DML)**. The data description language specifies the data to be included in the database while the data manipulation language is used to access the required data. Data is usually accessed using a series of statements in **query language**, although a programming language such as Cobol can be used to write statements and extract the data. The query language usually used is **structured query language (SQL)** and this is the agreed language used for the interrogation of information contained in databases. Many DBMSs use a data dictionary held on a mini-database and this is used to hold information about the database. SQL is looked at more closely in Chapter 14.

Spreadsheet software

Spreadsheet software is used to manipulate numerical information. It presents the user with a huge grid containing **cells** in which data can be placed. This data could be a label (consisting of alphanumeric characters), a number or a formula; reference can also be made to other cells. The contents of cells can be related to other cells by using formulae, so that when the value in one cell changes the values in related cells also change.

As well as performing calculations, spreadsheets can also be used to present data in the form of pie charts, bar charts, line graphs, etc. Spreadsheets are particularly useful for 'what if' calculations since the same complex operations can be repeated at little extra expense. Spreadsheet software is ideal for small businesses since it can be used to produce budgets, forecasts, accounts and break-even charts economically. In fact, a spreadsheet can be used in any application which involves the manipulation and calculation of numbers.

There are many different spreadsheet packages on the market, but Microsoft Excel and Lotus 1-2-3 have established themselves as the most popular.

Graphics

'Graphics' is a word used for all types of artwork, including line diagrams, bit-map images (made up of numerous tiny dots), photographs, graphs and charts.

Often pictures are able to communicate ideas and concepts to an audience much better than the written or spoken word alone; this is the purpose of presentation graphics packages. They are useful if you want to incorporate some ready-made, digital artwork (called clipart) into your documents. Presentation graphics packages are designed to produce either eye-catching slides for an overhead projector, or a screen display which can involve many images and give a timed 'show'.

Activity 11.3

For the categories of applications software described above, give the names of two popular software packages which fall into each category. Advertisements for software in computer magazines may be useful for this activity.

Desktop publishing (DTP)

With desktop publishing software, high quality documents can be produced without having to involve a typesetter, so saving time and money. Desktop publishing (DTP) can be used to produce pages that combine text and graphics (photographs and line drawings) for books, magazines, posters and leaflets. Different typefaces, or fonts, can be used to add interest, and diagrams positioned with text flowing around them. Photographs can be scanned in, cropped and their size adjusted so that they fit in a particular position on the page. Figure 11.3 shows the types of document which can be produced using desktop publishing and Figure 11.4 shows the range of sources of text and graphics that can be integrated in a document.

Advantages of desktop publishing

Here are just a few of the many advantages of using a DTP package to design and lay out pages compared with using a wordprocessing package.

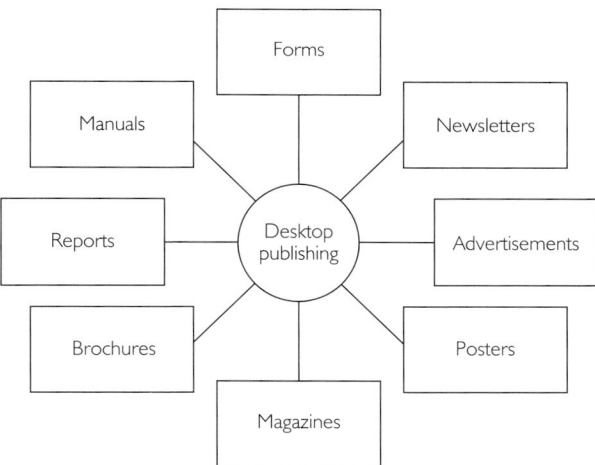

Figure 11.3 Range of documents that can be produced using desktop publishing

- With DTP you have much more control over the way in which text is laid out and especially over the formatting and arrangement of text.
- DTP can be used to bring a number of different files together in the same document.
- DTP can be used to produce output in a certain way so that the material can be professionally printed if required. If your work is going to be output professionally, you will need to make sure that you use one of the main DTP packages such as QuarkXPress, Microsoft Publisher or Adobe PageMaker.

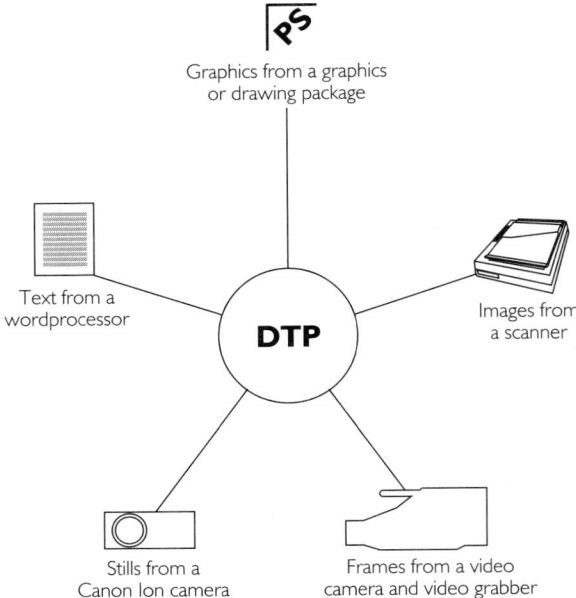

Figure 11.4 *Desktop publishing can integrate text and graphics from various sources*

Bespoke (tailor-made) software

If there are no suitable pre-written packages available to do a particular job it may be necessary to think about developing and writing software that is specifically designed for the task. In this section we will compare bespoke software with off-the-shelf applications packages.

Writing applications programs

This has become a less popular option with the improved availability of off-the-shelf software. Most applications you might need have had software written for them and writing another program is like reinventing the wheel. If, however, the application is unique or available programs do not suit your existing system, there may be no alternative but to write the programs.

Specially written software (called tailor-made or bespoke software) allows organisations to specify exactly what is required rather than having to modify their system to fit in with the existing package that most closely suits their needs.

Before you even consider writing an application program from scratch, you should make sure that you or someone else in the organisation has the following:

- the ability to decide which computer language to use;
- the ability to design a solution to the problem being considered;
- the ability to write technically correct program code;
- the time needed to undertake such a task;
- suitable expertise to train users and provide help if things go wrong when the program is implemented.

Specific task software

Although mass produced like general purpose software, specific task software is developed with a specific application in mind. Stock control, accounts and computer-aided design (CAD) software are all examples of specific task software. Such software can be bought off the shelf, but in many cases is obtained via a trade or professional magazine. So, for instance, if a dentist or a solicitor wants a package designed solely for their line of work, they would probably find suitable software advertised in their professional periodicals rather than the general computer magazines.

Operating systems (systems software)

Operating systems (sometimes called **systems software**) are collections of programs which control the operation of computer hardware. Without operating systems, it would be impossible to run applications packages. In fact, without systems software, computer systems would be useless.

The operating system controls the handling of input, output, **interrupts**, storage and files. In general, the degree to which we are unaware of the actions of the systems software is a measure of its effectiveness. In other words, a machine that runs efficiently without us knowing too much about it must have a good operating system.

An operating system performs two groups of functions:

1 The operating system ensures the efficient management of the computer's resources such as internal memory, input and output devices and files. Operating systems are frequently multitasking, enabling the user to do one task while another task is being performed. For instance, up until a few years ago, you had to wait for one document to be printed from your wordprocessor before another could be typed in; now the two tasks can be carried out simultaneously.

2 The operating system 'protects' the user from the complexities of the hardware. This means that the user need only consider the operation of the applications package being used. For instance, the user does not have to worry whether a file is being stored in a vacant part of a disk; the operating system does this automatically.

At times the operating system needs to perform certain tasks such as formatting disks, deleting files and copying disks. For these there are special programs called **utility programs** (known simply as 'utilities'). The ease with which these tasks are performed is a measure of an operating system's success.

Examples of operating systems include:

- MS-DOS
- UNIX
- OS/2
- Windows 95
- Macintosh System 7.6.

These are some of the detailed tasks performed by an operating system:

- Performing certain diagnostic tests when the computer is first switched on (or 'booted up'). The operating system checks devices attached to the computer, and checks the memory by writing data to the memory locations and then reading it back to see if the data matches. If there are any problems, an error message appears on the screen.
- Scheduling and loading jobs which are to be executed, thereby maximising the computer's power and time.
- Selecting and controlling the operation of any peripheral devices.
- Dealing with any errors that arise and keeping the system running should any fault occur.
- Maintaining system security by checking passwords.

- Loading program files and data files into memory from backing storage devices.
- Handling the interrupts which occur when there are problems with the applications software due to bugs or problems with the computer itself.

Microsoft Disk Operating System (MS-DOS)

MS-DOS was the original personal computer (PC) operating system developed by Microsoft (a large American software company) and it required users to type in commands at a prompt on the screen. Users of MS-DOS need to have a fair amount of knowledge of the system.

Commands in MS-DOS are of two types: internal and external. Internal commands are always immediately available to the user since they are held in internal memory, whereas external commands refer to larger programs which are held on backing store and therefore take longer to execute. The command DELETE is an internal command used to erase a file or a group of files, whereas FORMAT is an external command used to format a magnetic disk.

MS-DOS was developed as a single-stream operating system which means that it can perform only one task at a time. However, software such as Windows 3.1 (not Windows 95) is a graphic user interface and this enables the user to run several tasks simultaneously (this is called multitasking).

MS-DOS uses a hierarchical or tree file structure. To understand how this file structure works, it is necessary to understand what is meant by file, directory and subdirectory.

A **file** is a unit of storage on the computer. Some files are program files, which can be run on a computer to perform a task, whereas other files are documents, storing data in one form or another. All files stored using MS-DOS are given filenames, and the filename ought to bear some resemblance to what is stored in the file. As you store more and more programs and data on a hard drive you can very soon have several thousand files. Keeping these in some sort of organised structure is extremely important and it is here that the operating system can help.

Directories are used to group together files containing similar material. For instance, a directory could be set up for games, another for wordprocessing software and yet another for letters. When a disk is formatted using MS-DOS, a **root directory** is created on the disk and from this root other **subdirectories** can be specified. Look at the directory structure in Figure 11.5.

This tree structure is organised into areas with all the programming languages in a subdirectory called LANG. The LANG directory is divided into two further subdirectories, one for all the Pascal programs and data and the other for Cobol with its programs and data.

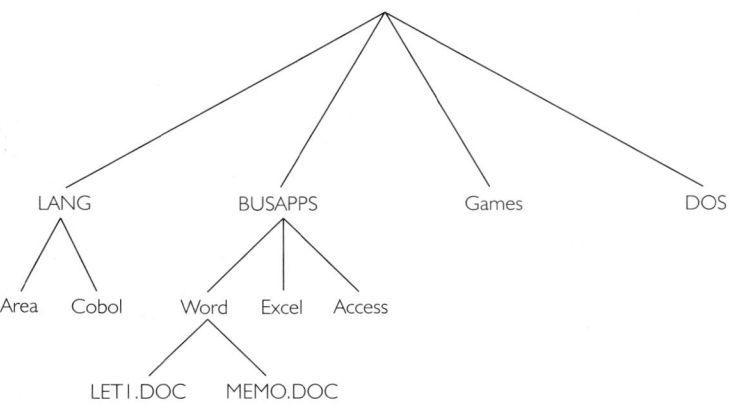

Figure 11.5 The tree directory structure

In order to locate files in certain directories it is necessary to use a path. For example, to select the letter with the filename LET1.DOC you could use the path:

CD\BUSAPPS\Word\EXT.DOC

A sound knowledge of MS-DOS produces a deeper understanding of how computers work, and it is for this reason we will take a brief look at some of the commands available and how they can be put together. You need this knowledge to understand some of the tasks an operating system can perform, and also for the next chapter where we will look at how a sequence of commands is collected together to form a program (called a batch file) which can be used to automate a process.

In order to use MS-DOS commands you must be at the command prompt which appears as C:\>. If the computer uses Windows you must first exit to Windows and go to MS-DOS.

As with all modern software, there is an on-line help facility and this can be accessed by typing HELP at the command prompt. If you know the command name with which you require help, it is quicker to type HELP followed by the name of the command. So, for help on the command to copy disks you type:

HELP DISKCOPY

To write batch files successfully using MS-DOS, it is necessary to understand a little about how certain operations are tackled. For this reason a brief guide to MS-DOS is provided here.

A quick guide to MS-DOS basics
Viewing the contents of a directory
Type **dir** at the command prompt.

Changing to another directory
cd\windows

This changes to the windows directory ('cd' stands for 'change directory').

Changing back to the root directory
cd

No matter which other directory you are in, this moves you back to the root directory.

Creating a directory
Suppose you want to create a directory called 'games', this could be done using the command **md games**. Notice that the command prompt now changes to **C:\games>**. If you now type **dir** at the command prompt, you get a list of all the files in the games directory.

Removing a directory
You can only remove a directory if there are no files contained in it. If there are files in it they must all be deleted first. For example, if you want to remove the games directory, not only must it be empty of files but you must also be in the root directory. The command for removing the games directory is **rd games**.

Copying files
For this you use the copy command which has the format **copy** (source destination). The source needs to specify the drive and directory of the file to be copied; the destination needs to specify the drive and the directory to which the file is to be copied. The following command shows this arrangement:

copy a:task1.doc c:\mydocs

The above copies a file called task1.doc on drive A, to a directory on the hard drive called mydocs. Because no name is specified for the file in the destination, the file will be called the same as the original.

Using wild cards for copying groups of files

Suppose we had ten files with the file extension .doc which we wanted to copy. Doing them one at a time would be tedious, so we look for something the files have in common; in this case it is the .doc file extension. The command for this is:

copy a:*.doc c:\mydocs

The asterisk means the computer will recognise any group of characters before the .doc file extension, so all such files will be copied, in this case into a directory on the hard drive called mydocs. If you wanted to copy all of the files you could use:

copy a:*.* c:\mydocs

There are various ways you can find out about MS-DOS:
- the MS-DOS manual supplied with your computer;
- the on-line help facility;
- books available from the library;
- notes provided by your tutor.

Activity 11.4

Use any of the above methods to answer the following questions.
1 Explain how MS-DOS organises files in directories and subdirectories. What is meant by the 'root directory'?
2 What are the commands to:
   a select the A drive
   b select the C drive
   c create a directory on the C drive
   d remove a directory from the C drive
   e change to a directory
   f list all the files on a disk in the A drive
   g format a disk placed in the A drive
   h list all the files in a certain subdirectory on the C drive?

Windows 3.1

Windows 3.1 is not an operating system as such, since it requires MS-DOS to enable it to run. Windows 3.1 is best referred to as a **GUI (graphic user interface)**. The main advantage of Windows is that it is easy for beginners to use. There is no need to remember the commands for copying files etc. or to be concerned about whether or not to leave a space between commands. With Windows you simply point to the relevant icon on the screen using the mouse and click to make your selection. All applications software in the Windows environment has a similar look, and it is much easier to transfer from one Windows package to another than it would be with the corresponding MS-DOS packages.

Another advantage of Windows is that it is able to run several tasks concurrently (multitasking). For instance, if you want to incorporate a spreadsheet in one package into a wordprocessor in another, using Windows each can be active in its own separate window and combining the documents becomes much easier.

Windows 95

To make computers as easy to use as possible, a very sophisticated and powerful operating system is needed which 'shields' the user from the intricacies of the hardware. The operating system should ideally be compatible with all the existing software, easy to use, fast and powerful. Windows 95, the latest operating system for PCs, has all the above features and is set to become the standard operating system for the latest PCs with large memories (typically 8 to 32 MB), large hard disk capacity (2 GB) and high-speed processors (typically the Pentium with a clock speed of 200 MHz).

Windows 95 is a fully integrated 32-bit multitasking operating system that does not need MS-DOS (unlike the older versions of Windows) but can nevertheless run any of the applications which require MS-DOS.

In the Windows 95 interface, everything hinges on the start button of the taskbar, and pressing this gives access via a series of menus to all the utilities and applications on the system. When a new application is installed, it is automatically added to the menu list. The screens in Windows 95 are less cluttered than in many similar interfaces and the design is the result of thousands of hours of usability testing and careful analysis of the kinds of tasks which users perform regularly.

The main features of the Windows 95 operating system are described below.

Support for 32-bit applications

This means that new software can be used which makes use of 32-bit architecture, providing higher speed than 16-bit applications. With 32-bit applications it is possible to use longer filenames, up to 255 characters long. With MS-DOS, filenames are restricted to eight characters followed by a three-character file extension, making it hard, sometimes, to identify a particular file from its name.

Plug and play

The 'plug and play' feature of the operating system allows you to connect any hardware (printers, scanners, graph plotters, etc.) to the computer while the operating system automatically allocates the hardware resources needed for the device.

32-bit architecture

The 32-bit architecture means that memory use is optimised.

Multimedia

Multimedia was not widely used when early versions of Windows were developed; the new version makes more economic use of the CD-ROM for multimedia applications.

New utilities

New utilities provided within the operating system include disk compression, defragmentation and back-up tools. A new wordprocessor with many more facilities has been included, and a communications utility which enables access to the Microsoft network.

Networking

Support is provided for multiple network servers and there are features which improve compatibility between devices attached to a computer.

Activity 11.5

For this activity you are required to compare and contrast certain routine file management tasks using two different operating systems, one making use of a graphic user interface such as Windows, the other using a command-driven interface such as MS-DOS.

For you to form your own opinion of the two operating system interfaces, you need to perform the following file operations using each interface:
- list the files on a floppy disk
- copy the entire contents of one floppy disk to another
- format a floppy disk.

UNIX

UNIX is an operating system which is more widely associated with mainframe and minicomputers. There is a version available for PCs called **XENIX**. UNIX is written in the high-level programming language C, and its main strength is that it is a multiprogramming, multitasking operating system that can run several hundred terminals if necessary.

Standardisation is one major problem, which has hampered the widespread acceptance of UNIX in the business world. There are three current UNIX standards and this means that any software developed may have to be produced in three different versions to match them. Some software developers stick with a particular manufacturer and develop UNIX-based software that will run only on one type of machine (called a **platform**).

One of the main advantages of UNIX is its portability and this means that it can run on many different types of computer. There is a powerful user interface (called the **shell**), and this is useful to experienced users but can be quite difficult for beginners to grasp. UNIX generally is hard work for beginners to learn and many users describe it as 'an operating system designed by programmers for programmers to use'.

Activity 11.6

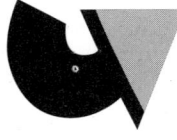

There are many different operating systems on the market, some of which have been covered in this section. There are others, however, which have not been mentioned. In particular:
- Windows NT
- OS/2
- VMS.

You need to find out about each of the above operating systems. Write a short paragraph outlining your findings including what type of system each one is (single user, multitasking, multiprogramming, etc.), what their strengths and weaknesses are and to which situations they are best suited.

Utility software

Utility programs perform common tasks such as file management, editor facilities and diagnostic routines. Such utilities are now often included with operating systems software, whereas previously they would have been bought separately. Other examples of utility software are virus checkers, hard disk doublers (programs that effectively double hard disk capacity by compressing data), and programs such as Cyber Patrol (used for preventing Internet access to pornographic material).

Here are some useful utilities that may be included within an operating system, or perhaps as part of some wordprocessing software.

Antivirus utility

This type of program might be provided as part of an operating system or bought separately; its purpose is to detect and remove computer viruses. Since viruses are being created all the time, many of the virus checkers provided with an operating system are unable to detect the newer viruses, so it is wise to buy the latest checkers separately. Because it is so important to protect data and programs, many of these come with quarterly or even monthly updates.

Scandisk utility

This utility, provided as part of the operating system MS-DOS, detects, diagnoses and repairs disk errors.

Undelete utility

This useful utility can restore the data on an inadvertently formatted floppy disk and is often packaged with the main operating system.

Back-up utility

This backs up programs and data files from the hard disk to a back-up medium such as a floppy disk or tape drive.

Table utility

This utility is often provided as part of a wordprocessing package and creates tables using a matrix of rows and columns. The advantage of this particular utility is that it features 'word wrap' within each cell, so when text is entered it automatically moves down to the next line.

User interface software

This software simplifies the way the user interacts with the system. There are two types in common use: a **graphic user interface (GUI)** such as Windows 3.1 and a **menu selection interface**. These are distinct pieces of software whose purpose is to facilitate use of the systems software; however you still need to load an operating system before they can be used.

A further development is to combine the user interface software with the operating system to produce a single product, such as Windows 95. Unlike Windows 3.1, Windows 95 is an operating system incorporating a graphic user interface. The Macintosh operating system is another example of an operating system that incorporates a graphic user interface.

Programming languages

A program is a set of sequenced instructions that a computer can understand and a programming language is the notation used to specify these instructions. Because, fundamentally, all computers can understand only binary code (i.e. a series of 0s and 1s), computer instructions written in any language must ultimately be reduced to this machine language.

There are various languages the programmer can choose, each suited to a certain type of application. The choice of language must also take account of the programmer's expertise. Many programmers are able to program in several languages, and although the actual statements and syntax differ the principles are often the same.

Program generators

Program generators are programs which help users to write their own programs by expanding simple statements into program code. There are many different types of program generator but most can be classified as either **fourth generation languages** or **prototyping software**. Both perform the same function in that the user specifies what the program has to do in general terms and the program generator works out the program in detail.

Fourth generation languages (4GLs)

Fourth generation languages (4GLs) are programming tools that allow programmers to develop their own applications programs more quickly and hence cheaply. This is possible because the user does not have to be concerned about the structure of the program. All that is needed is a clear idea of the required result. Fourth generation languages are more easily understood by beginners than older languages and usually centre around a database, although some computer-based training development software has a 4GL attached. There are three common language tools which fall into the 4GL category: query languages, report generators and applications generators.

Query languages

Query languages allow the user to ask questions about information stored in a database and retrieve it. In some ways it is not so different from asking questions in English. Although such a language is easy to learn and understand, it still has its own vocabulary (a list of allowable commands), grammar (the way the commands are put together) and syntax (the commands must be spelt correctly). Some query languages allow the user to alter or add data to the database.

Report generators

Report generators are in some ways similar to query languages in that they enable the user to ask questions about the contents of a database, but in this case the results are output in the form of a report. The user can either let the software decide how the report should look or can specify the layout themselves. Unlike query languages, report generators cannot be used to alter or modify the data in a database in any way.

In many reports the user can specify subtotals and totals, and perform calculations on the data before it is output in the report.

Applications generators

Many tasks such as data input, sorting, searching, file management and reporting are common to a wide variety of applications. Applications generators make use of standardised programs to perform these common tasks, while allowing the user to alter the routine slightly to suit their particular system.

Applications generators reduce the amount of time needed to build an application by letting the user specify in general terms what the program should do, and then using these general instructions to automatically create a block of program code to achieve the desired results.

Prototyping software

Prototyping software allows programmers to produce software quickly without having to spend time on coding. Because many programs contain common features, these tools offer the programmer a choice of program parts from a list of possibilities and this helps speed up the writing process.

Purposes of the categories of software

In the previous sections we looked at the various categories of software; here we examine the purposes to which software can be put.

Common data processing tasks

There are certain tasks that are common to nearly all organisations, such as storing and manipulating files, stock control, producing budgets and forecasts, writing letters, reports, memos, etc., producing company brochures and advertising literature and so on. Because most organisations process their data in a similar way, software packages have been developed to help with each of these tasks, and in most cases software packages are an appropriate and economic solution.

Common data processing software includes:

- wordprocessing (for letters, memos, reports, minutes of meetings, etc.);
- databases (to store data in a structured way and then output it in a variety of different formats);
- spreadsheets (used when figures need to be manipulated, for example working out loan repayments, preparing budgets and forecasts, analysing data statistically, etc.);
- presentation graphics (for slides, screen displays, quick posters, etc.);
- desktop publishing (used in preference to wordprocessing when more design features are needed for magazines, company newsletters, brochures, etc.);
- computer-aided design (for maps, plans, drawings, product designs, engineering drawings, etc.).

System control

Systems can be controlled using facilities provided by the operating system. For example, the print manager is part of the operating system and is used to control the operation of the printer using software rather than the printer's own controls.

Simplification of the user interface

Some software, such as Windows 3.1, was designed to simplify use of the operating system. Windows 95 has taken things further, since not only is it a GUI, but it also incorporates its own operating system. Much time and effort goes into the development of a new user interface, the aim of which is to make life easier for the inexperienced user. The move from keyboard to mouse has made it easier for inexperienced typists to use a computer; the next stage must be an interface which allows the operator to talk to the computer, telling it what to do in everyday spoken language.

Software production

Development software is used to write new programs, and as well as containing the instruction set for the computer language it also provides other tools which contribute to making the programmer's job easier.

Activity 11.7

A Cobol programmer is flicking through the job pages of *Computer Weekly* when she notices advertisements for programmers with experience in the following languages:
- Delphi
- Mosaic

- Oracle
- Visual C++.

These languages seem to crop up in many advertisements, so she feels that to keep her skills up to date she must investigate them further. In particular she would like to find out the following:

1 what hardware (networks, mainframes, PCs) the software will run on;

2 what groups of applications the language is ideally suited to.

Research each of the languages given above based on the information outlined in 1 and 2.

Management of shared data

On a network both data and programs are accessed by many users, sometimes at the same time, so special software is needed to deal with this. If, for instance, two users in a travel agent are looking at the same holiday and their customers both decide to book the holiday, the system needs to operate in real time so that any changes are seen there and then on the screen. In this case, which customer will get the holiday? The answer is the first person who books it, since as soon as the transaction is recorded by the system the file is updated, so a second user is unable to make the same booking.

The software also needs to allow the network manager to assign rights to certain files. For instance, some files may be designated read-only, meaning that the user can look at but not alter the contents of the file. Some files may only be viewed and altered by certain users while other users are excluded from the system using a series of user names and passwords.

Purposes of applications software packages

In this section we look at what tasks can be performed using applications software.

Processing documents, numerical data, graphics and structured data

The majority of applications software packages are designed to process documents, numerical data and graphics and structured data. Wordprocessors, databases, spreadsheets, desktop publishing and graphics software all do this.

Modelling

Modelling means using software to represent a real situation or system which can be used for further investigation. Examples of models include looking at the way supermarket queues form, investigating the build up of traffic at junctions, and producing a perspective view of a building to see how it fits into the landscape.

Many models, particularly financial ones, can be built using ordinary spreadsheet software but others need specialist software.

Controlling

Some software is used to control the parts of the computer system. For instance, the print manager in Windows 3.1 controls the operation of the printer, and with this software the printer can be paused or stopped completely.

Controlling software is provided as part of the operating system. Some software can also be written to control various devices connected to the computer, and this includes process control systems in which entire chemical processes are controlled from a computer terminal, or robot arms used to weld body panels together in a car factory.

Expert systems

Expert systems apply artificial intelligence, where a computer is programmed to carry out certain logical processes normally associated with human intelligence, such as learning, adaptation and self-correction.

Expert systems are applications programs that mimic the intelligence of a human expert in a specific field of knowledge. For instance, an expert system could be set up to give medical advice based on the answers given to a series of questions asked by the computer. The computer is supplied with a knowledge-base derived from human experts, and the rules needed to process the information.

Applications of expert systems are given below.

Medical diagnosis systems
The software presents the patient with a series of questions, just as a doctor would, and then comes to certain conclusions. Such a system can be used to save time, although a doctor would still need to perform a medical examination.

Legal systems
Using these systems a person can obtain legal advice on certain situations without the expense of consulting a solicitor.

Tax advice
Here the software is able to assess the tax liability of an individual or a company based on the answers to certain questions.

Features of computer programs

There are certain features which are common to all computer programs.

Code
Once the design of a program has been sketched out, the programmer needs to convert this into the code of the chosen language. In this sense the code is a series of step-by-step instructions written using the correct syntax. 'Syntax' refers to the rules and patterns which are used to form the statements in a particular language. Since syntax varies enormously between languages, programmers have to learn a whole new syntax for each new language, although the principles behind the programs may remain the same. It is common for programmers to learn many languages during their careers.

Program structures
These are the building blocks of any computer program and are common to all computer languages. In Chapter 12 we look at program structures in detail.

Data types
In many programming languages it is necessary for the programmer to define the data type of a piece (or element) of data. Examples of data types include character, number (integer, real or both), graphic, logic (sometimes called Boolean) and date. These are explained fully in Chapter 12.

Data structures

It is logical to group together certain elements of data which have characteristics in common and this can be done using a variety of data structures including arrays, lists, queues, records, stacks, strings, tables and trees. These data structures are examined in detail in Chapter 12.

Method of translation

The job of any computer language is to translate relatively comprehensible statements such as PRINT "HELLO" into a string of binary digits that the computer can understand. The piece of software that converts the 'normal language' instructions into binary instructions is called a **translator**. There are three types of translator: **assembler**, **compiler** and **interpreter** and they are examined in detail in Chapter 12.

Constructs

When a program is written, certain structures will usually be incorporated and these are the building blocks of the program. Because the structures are used to build the program they are sometimes called **constructs**.

Constructs are control structures whose purpose is to alter the sequence in which the instructions within a program are executed. Using the three main building blocks of program construction it is possible to construct any program. The main programming constructs are as follows:

- sequence
- selection
- iteration (sometimes called repetition).

Sequence

This is simply a list of program instructions in which each instruction is always carried out after another, and the program always takes the same path. The various processes are placed in the correct order and are obeyed in sequence. So if we wanted to design a program to do three processes in the order X, then Y, then Z, we would need to put the program statements into this order. A flow chart for this sequence is shown in Figure 11.6.

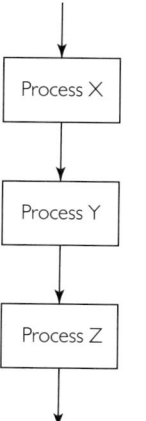

Figure 11.6 Flow chart showing three processes in a sequence construct

Selection

Sometimes it is necessary, within a program, to decide whether to take one particular path or another, depending on a certain condition. If this condition or factor is 'true' then one path will be taken, and if 'not true' then the other will be put into effect. In other words, depending upon conditions, the computer is able to decide which path to take through the program. If several selections are included the number of possible paths through a program increases.

Take the following English description of a selection: 'If condition X is true then do process B'. Figure 11.7 shows a flow chart for the above selection construct.

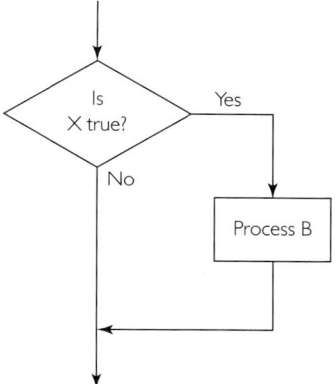

Figure 11.7 Flow chart section showing a selection construct

Another form of selection can be represented by the following English statement: 'If condition X is true then do process B otherwise do process A'. Figure 11.8 shows the corresponding flow chart.

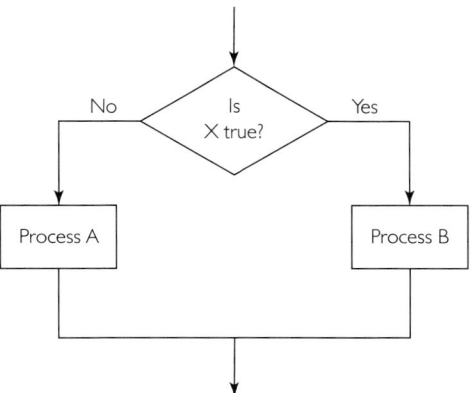

Figure 11.8 Flow chart section showing another selection construct

Iteration (repetition)

An iteration is a section of a program which is repeated a number of times. The following English statement represents a typical iteration statement: 'While condition X is true, repeatedly do process A'. Figure 11.9 shows the flow chart for this construct.

Iteration of a set of program instructions can take place in one of three ways:

1 a condition is tested for after the first run of the sequence;
2 a condition is tested at the start of a sequence;
3 an instruction is given for the sequence to be carried out a certain number of times.

367

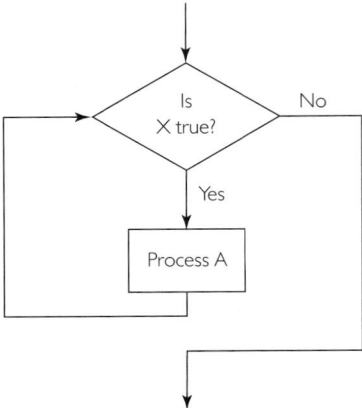

Figure 11.9 Flow chart section showing an iteration construct

Modes of operation of software

There are three main modes of operation by which commands are given to software:
- **Commands**: commands are keyed in and the computer complies with the commands issued.
- **Menus**: here the user is presented with a list of options from which to make a selection. The selection is usually made by typing in either a number or a letter.
- **Graphic interface**: in this mode, the user is presented with a series of graphics which can be pressed or selected using a mouse.

Commands

Instructing a computer using commands involves typing in an abbreviated instruction, which can either be a single letter or a combination/series of keys such as Alt followed by a certain letter. Issuing commands using the keyboard is not the easiest way of controlling a computer, since many commands have to be remembered and this slows down new users who may need to spend time looking up commands in the manual. However, those who have been using the software for some time tend to remember the keystrokes, and can find the keyboard quicker to use since they do not have to move a hand away from the keyboard to use a mouse.

Another disadvantage of commands is that they differ from one piece of software to the next, so the command for saving may well be different in different packages. This can be confusing if the user operates several different packages in the course of their work.

Many command-driven programs make use of the function keys found at the top of the keyboard, with a command assigned to each of the keys, so F1 could be pressed to access the help screens, F2 could produce a printout and so on.

Menus

With a menu a list of commands or options is presented to the user and the user has to make their selection from the list by highlighting the one they want, typing in the number or letter of their selection or sometimes selecting the first letter of the required option.

Graphic interface

The graphic user interface provides a way for the user to communicate with the computer through pictures called icons, and pull-down menus. The icons look like buttons and can be activated by clicking on them with a mouse; they can be either on or off and clicking on them reverses their current status. Windows is an example of a GUI and all Windows software provides a common way of communicating with the computer which makes the software easier to learn and use.

Toolbars also feature in GUIs and are used to contain one or more rows of small buttons within a particular application. Applications can have a huge range of toolbars and buttons; in many cases the user is able to group their most frequently used buttons to produce a tailor-made toolbar.

Activity 11.8

As we have seen in this chapter, the main categories of software are as follows:
- applications software
- operating systems software
- utility software
- user interface software
- programming languages
- program generators
- database management software.

For this activity you are required to place the pieces of software shown below into one or more of the above categories. Some of the following are trade names so you may first need to find out what each is used for.
- Microsoft Office
- Windows 3.1
- Windows 95
- Dr Solomon's Anti-Virus Toolkit
- XTreeGold (A file management suite of programs)
- Novell Netware
- Microsoft Publisher
- OS/2 Warp
- Microsoft Visual Basic
- Lotus 1-2-3
- Sage Instant Accounting
- Adobe PageMaker
- CorelDRAW
- Microsoft Word

Assignment A11.1

This assignment develops knowledge and understanding of the following element:
6.1 Investigate software

It supports the development of the following key skills:
Communication 3.2 and 3.3
Information technology 3.1, 3.2 and 3.3

Task 1

It is important to be aware of the wide variety of different categories of software available for use with computers. For this assignment, you are required to investigate the software on the hard drive, or available over the network, for the computers you use at your college.

Put each piece of software into a category according to the following list:

- applications software
- operating systems
- utilities
- user interface software
- programming languages
- program generators
- database management software.

Load each of the programs you find, try to find out a little about what it does and then write a short paragraph explaining its purpose.

Also state the mode or modes of operation of each piece of software. For instance, if the package requires MS-DOS, then it may be command- or menu-based, whereas Windows-based software will use a graphic interface with toolbars, icons and pull-down menus.

Task 2

You will be given some programs written in a programming language with which you are familiar. Your task is to examine the code and identify the main features of each program. To recap, the main features are as follows:

- code
- program structures
- data types
- data structures
- method of translation
- constructs.

For each program, identify the features by copying sections of code where each feature can be found, and explain why it has been included in the program.

Sample unit test

1 Which category of software consists of collections of programs which control the operation of computer hardware?

   a an operating system
   b applications software
   c file management software
   d database management software

2 A garage uses specialist software to send out reminders of when MOTs and services are due. What category would this software be in?

   a applications software
   b utility software

c systems software

d network management software

3 A piece of software which is able to recover files that have been accidentally erased and which can be used to try to recover corrupted files is best described as:

a applications software

b utility software

c file management software

d a programming language

4 A graphic user interface:

a makes software easier to learn and use

b enables high quality graphics to be produced

c enables commands to be keyed in at the command line

d uses a graphics tablet as an input device

5 A company wishes to produce its own company newsletter. The newsletter is to contain pictures, photographs, cartoons and text in a variety of different fonts. The most appropriate software to use for this task would be:

a desktop publishing software

b wordprocessing software

c presentation graphics software

d expert systems software

6 Which one of the following would *not* be classed as general purpose software?

a wordprocessing software

b bespoke software

c spreadsheet software

d presentation graphics software

7 An applications generator is an example of which type of language?

a high-level language

b low-level language

c fourth generation language

d machine language

8 A program instruction that can be recognised and used without translation is written in which one of the following languages?

a assembly language

b Cobol

c C

d machine code

9 Which of the following best describes a piece of software that converts the whole of a program written in a high-level language into machine code in one go?

a a compiler

b an assembler

c an interpreter

d a utility program

10 One of the following is considered to be not an operating system, but a graphic user interface. Which one is it?

a Windows 95

b UNIX

    c Windows 3.1

    d OS/2

11 Which one of the following general purpose software packages is best suited for modelling activities?

    a spreadsheet

    b database

    c wordprocessing

    d desktop publishing

Questions 12–15 refer to the following options:

    a iteration

    b selection

    c sequence

    d translation

12 What is the name given to the program construct where the program instructions are carried out in the exact order in which they are written?

13 In a program, a decision sometimes needs to be made and the program then proceeds along either of two paths. What is the name of this construct?

14 What process needs to take place before a program written in a high-level language such as Cobol can be executed?

15 In many programs, a particular section needs to be repeated several times. What name is given to this programming construct?

16 The following line is written in a high-level language:

    IF QUANTITY_ORDERED <= 100

Which program construct starts with IF?

    a iteration

    b selection

    c sequence

    d repetition

17 When a computer runs a certain program, it changes each instruction in turn to machine code and then carries it out. Which type of translator is being used?

    a an interpreter

    b a compiler

    c an assembler

    d none

18 An engineer wishes to design a component and then look at it in three dimensions. Which software is the most appropriate for this purpose?

    a presentation graphics

    b a DTP package

    c CAD

    d spreadsheet software

19 When a user logs onto a system, the first screen they see is the one shown in Figure 11.10. Which of the following best describes this screen?

    a a graphic user interface

    b a main menu

    c an input screen

    d a print preview screen

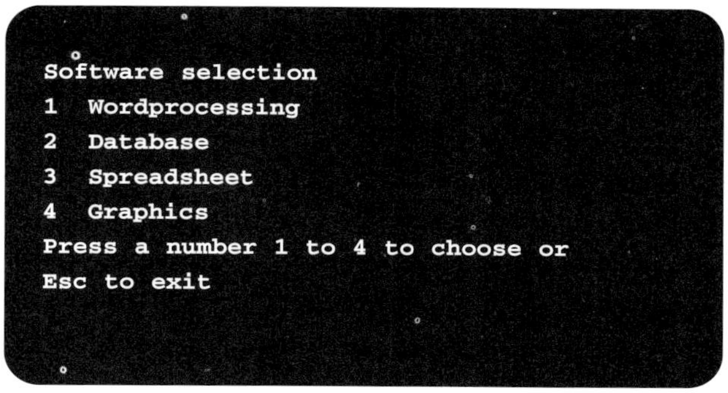

Figure 11.10

20 A database program has its own language to enable users to produce their own applications. This software is known as:
  a a database management system
  b utility software
  c an applications generator
  d an operating system

21 In which category of software would a virus checker be placed?
  a wordprocessor
  b file management software
  c utility software
  d database software

22 A small business buys a stock control package from the local computer superstore. In which of the following categories would it be?
  a general purpose software
  b specific task software
  c tailor-made software
  d bespoke software

23 Which two of the following are tasks performed by systems software rather than applications software?

  1 managing files
  2 dealing with interrupts
  3 production of a computer model
  4 changing the font size

  a 1 and 2
  b 2 and 3
  c 1 and 4
  d 2 and 4

24 An accountant needs to produce a break-even chart for a management meeting. Which one of the following pieces of software would be the most suitable for this task?
  a wordprocessor
  b spreadsheet
  c database
  d utility software

25 Which one of the following categories of software is used for the creation and conversion of code?
  a use interface software
  b applications software
  c database management systems
  d program generator   *(RSA, June 1996)*

26 Which one of the following categories of software is used for system control?
  a operating system
  b database management systems
  c user interface software
  d applications software   *(RSA, June 1996)*

27 Which one of the following categories of software is used for the management of shared data?
  a utilities
  b user interface software
  c database management systems
  d languages   *(RSA, June 1996)*

28 A computer-aided design (CAD) package is used mainly for:
  a manufacturing products
  b modelling products
  c processing documents
  d controlling documents   *(RSA, June 1996)*

29 A desktop publishing (DTP) package is used:
  a to process numerical data
  b to integrate text and graphics
  c to convert code
  d to control databases   *(RSA, June 1996)*

12 Creating and automating software procedures

What is covered in this chapter

In this chapter we will look at the concepts involved when producing software and the creation of automated procedures.

Element 6.2: Examine software production

- Programming environments
- Programming languages
- Features of program execution
- Program constructs
- Types of data
- Data structures
- Expressions and operators

Element 6.3: Investigate the production of automated procedures

- Introduction to automated procedures
- Facilities for creating automated procedures
- Running and stopping batch programs
- Evaluating automated procedures

Resources you will need for your portfolio for Elements 6.2 and 6.3
- Your written answers to the activities and assignments in this chapter.

In the following sections we will look at categories of software, the purpose of software and applications software packages. We will also look at the features of a computer program and the different modes of operation of software.

Programming environments

A programming environment is the set of conditions in which a program is developed and run. These include the programming language used, the method of translation and any special programming languages (e.g. 4GLs) or software routines used. All these factors need to be considered, in addition to the construction of the program itself, when producing software.

Programming languages

Programming languages are the codes in which computer software is written. These must be translated into machine code for execution.

The programmer can choose from many different programming languages, each with its own strengths and weaknesses and each suitable for certain types of task. Programming languages fall into two groups: **low-level** and **high-level** languages. An alternative classification would be into **procedural**, **declarative** and **object-orientated** (object event) languages.

Procedural languages

Procedural languages use a series of steps, to be executed in a certain order by the program, although control of the program can be altered in certain places by the use of control structures such as loops, jumps, etc. The program steps are executed sequentially and the order of the steps is vital to the operation of the program.

Procedural languages include:

- Cobol
- Pascal
- C
- Fortran
- Basic
- C++.

Declarative languages

Declarative languages are high-level languages where the order of the programming steps is not important. The code consists of a set of declarations about *what* needs to be done rather than a set of detailed instructions defining *how* everything should be done. To solve a problem using a program written in a declarative language the problem must first be clearly defined. One of the main advantages of declarative programming is that since instructions are not carried out in a particular order it is possible for the computer to process them in parallel if needed. **Turbo Pascal** (the other versions of Pascal are procedural) and **Prolog** are classed as declarative languages.

Object-orientated programming languages (object event)

Object-orientated languages have become very popular over the last few years and are now the most popular type of programming language for writing commercial software. They combine some of the concepts of structured programming with sophisticated data structures to produce a language which attaches data to the programming routines used to manipulate it, thus producing what is called an **object**. Because the data and the structure used to manipulate it form a single unit it is self-contained, and it can also have 'descendants' with the same characteristics as their 'parents' and so have both the same data members and structures.

C++ is the main object-orientated programming language.

Activity 12.1

You are required to research the three main categories of programming languages: procedural, declarative and object-orientated languages.

Using guides to these categories, produce short sections of code for a language which falls into each of the categories and explain how the programming concepts differ, making reference to your sections of code where appropriate.

As well as defining a particular programming language as procedural, declarative or object-orientated, we can also classify languages according to the method of translation they use. This divides languages into high- and low-level categories.

Low-level languages

Low-level languages are languages that are easy for a computer to understand but more difficult for the programmer to understand. They are used mainly because they give the programmer more control over the way the program runs, directly accessing memory locations and the computer's hardware. Assembly language and machine code are both low-level languages. In a high-level language a simple statement such as PRINT "HELLO" would need several assembly language instructions.

A program in a high-level language is built from pre-packaged blocks and is thus much larger than an assembly program which performs the same job. As a result the assembly language program will run much faster and use less memory, and these are the main reasons for its use.

Machine language (machine code)

Machine language is the language that is directly understood by a computer and consists of a series of 1s and 0s (i.e. binary digits). All other languages must be translated into machine code before the instructions can be carried out. Machine code is often machine specific which means that one computer's machine code is not understood by another computer. A program written in machine code needs no translation and is therefore very fast. Many games and simulation programs are written in machine code for this reason.

Assembly language

An assembly language is a language which uses simple instructions such as ADD, SUB and LDA and is often used in preference to machine code as it is easier for a programmer to write and debug. It still needs translating into machine code and this is done by software called an **assembler** (see page 384).

High-level languages

A high-level language is developed with the programmer rather than the computer in mind. Such languages have the advantage that they are not so machine dependent, so once a program has been written (or a language learned) it can be used on different computers with very little alteration.

High-level language instructions bear a similarity to standard English which makes programming easier. Instructions in Basic, a high-level language, include such commands as PRINT, GOTO and READ which are easy for people to understand.

Some high-level languages have been developed with a particular task in mind. Here are some of the most popular languages, along with their main uses.

Cobol

Cobol is an acronym for Common Business-Oriented Language and is a language mainly used for business data processing because of its excellent file-handling abilities. The main features of Cobol are given below.

The use of statements which are similar to English
This feature means that it is obvious from reading statements what they are designed to do and this avoids the need for further explanation. In this respect Cobol programs may be thought of as 'self-documenting'.

The separation of instructions and data

A Cobol program is separated by function into divisions. Data items contained in the data division are instructions used to manipulate the data contained in the procedure division; machine-dependent information is contained in the environment division. This division by function means that Cobol applications are more portable and will run on a wide range of systems with little or no adjustment. There is one more division, the identification division, in which documentary information about the program is kept.

Access to secondary storage

Cobol was designed to manipulate non-numeric data stored in files contained on backing storage. Manipulating files is the basis of many commercial applications and this is the main reason for Cobol's popularity as a business programming language.

Pascal

Pascal was originally developed as a language for teaching structured programming techniques and therefore does not enjoy much popularity in the commercial world. There are various Pascal language products, but Turbo Pascal is the most popular.

Pascal is a high-level compiled language which means that instead of the program being converted to machine code one line at a time as the program runs, the whole program is converted first then the machine code program is run when required. The word 'turbo' indicates the high speed at which programs are compiled.

The structure of Pascal encourages the programmer to design a program piece by piece, writing sections of programming code which are later joined together.

Pascal programs all start with the keyword PROGRAM (or program; the case does not matter with Pascal) followed by the name of the program, for example:

PROGRAM Calculate_area;

Notice the semicolon at the end, which tells the computer to move on to the next instruction. Semicolons only end executable instructions.

Here is how the program statements are inserted between a BEGIN and an END statement:

PROGRAM Calculate_area;
BEGIN
.
.
.
END.

Types of data allowable in Pascal

There are many different types of data which can be declared in a Pascal program and the following table shows about half of the complete list.

Type of data	Examples	Description
CHAR	'*', 'R', 'y'	A single character (letter, number, punctuation mark or symbol)
STRING	'John'	A group of zero or more characters
INTEGER	−20, 86	Whole numbers; positive, zero or negative
BYTE	30, 0	Positive whole numbers from 0 to 255
REAL	23.85, 0.85, −3.201	Real numbers with decimal points

Variables and constants

Pascal requires all variables to be defined before they are used and the definitions listed at the top of the program. Each variable is listed with its corresponding type.

Examples of variables being declared are:
     VAR   Radius: REAL;
              Circumference: REAL;

or:
     VAR
     Quantity: BYTE;
     Price;   REAL;
     In_Stock: CHAR;
     Item_description STRING;

The names of constants always contain the same value and can be defined as follows:
     CONST pi = 3.142;

In this case, every time the name pi is used in the program it will take the value 3.142.
     Variables held in strings (i.e. groups of characters) must also be declared in the variables section at the start of the program, and, as well as declaring that the variable is a string, you need to specify the maximum length of the string in the following way:
     VAR
     Name: STRING [35]

Here is a selection of programs written in Pascal.

Example 1
The program below is used to find the area of a triangle if the size of the base and perpendicular height are known (see Figure 12.1).

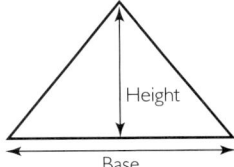

Figure 12.1

     Area = ½ × base × height

```
PROGRAM Triangle;
USES CRT;
VAR
   base,height : real;
    Area         : real;
BEGIN
   CLRSCR;
   WRITE('Enter the base of the triangle ');
   READLN (base);
   WRITE('Enter the height of the triangle ');
   READLN(height);
   Area:= 0.5*base*height;
   WRITELN('The area of the triangle is ', Area);
READLN
END.
```

379

There are some important features in this simple Pascal program:
- WRITE and WRITELN are two different ways of writing text to the screen. WRITE sends a line of text to the screen without performing a carriage return at the end, whereas WRITELN puts a carriage return at the end of the line.
- END must have a full-stop inserted after it (i.e. END.).
- Notice the way the program has been indented to make it more readable.
- Notice the third line down, USES CRT, which tells the computer to use the screen for the output. If the output is to be printed the command USES PRINTER is used.
- The CLRSCR instruction clears the screen for each program run.

Choice and repetition

Pascal utilises various constructs to alter the control of the program. These constructs change the path through a program, and include:

```
IF ... THEN ... ELSE
WHILE ... DO
REPEAT ... UNTIL
FOR ... TO
```

The format of the IF ... THEN ... ELSE statement is as follows:

```
IF condition THEN
    BEGIN
    .
    .
    .
    END:
    ELSE
```

Where the dots represent the main body of statements.

As you can see from the framework, a condition is tested and if it is true the mini-program between the BEGIN and END is carried out. If the condition is false, the mini-program is skipped.

Example 2

A salesman is paid a bonus of £200 only if the total of his sales for the month is over £5000. We can write a program using an IF ... THEN ... ELSE statement which prints out whether or not he receives the bonus.

```
PROGRAM Bonus;

VAR
    Sales : INTEGER;

BEGIN
    WRITELN('Enter the value of the monthly sales ');
    READLN(Sales);

    IF Sales < 5000 THEN
        WRITELN ('Bonus is £200')

    ELSE
        WRITELN ('No bonus. Better luck next month.');
    READLN
END.
```

There are some important features in this simple Pascal program:
- The IF ... THEN ... ELSE statement only needs the semicolon placed at the end.
- READLN waits for the user to type in a number which is then assigned to a variable called 'Sales'. The READLN just before the END means that the program will wait for the user to press any key before it reaches the end of the program. Without this the program goes so fast that none of the messages on screen can be read.

The format of the WHILE ... DO statement is as follows:

```
WHILE condition DO
   BEGIN
      .
      .
      .
   END;
```

Using the WHILE ... DO loop, the program keeps returning to the WHILE as long as the condition is true, but as soon as it is false the loop ends and the rest of the program is carried out.

Example 3
The following program uses a WHILE ... DO loop to produce an asterisk each time the program goes round the loop. A counter is used which is set to 10 initially and each time the asterisk is printed the value stored in the counter variable is reduced by one. When the counter reaches 0, the instructions in the loop are no longer repeated and the rest of the instructions are then carried out. The READLN instruction is used because the program runs so fast that you cannot see results on screen. This command is used to allow a pause while a key is pressed before the program returns to the edit screen.

```
   PROGRAM Example_while_do;

   VAR
      Count:Integer;
   BEGIN
      Count:=10;

   WHILE Count>0 DO
      BEGIN
         WRITE('*');
         Count:=Count-1;
      END;
   READLN
   END.
```

The format of the REPEAT ... UNTIL loop is as follows:

```
   REPEAT
      .
      .
      .
   UNTIL condition is true;
```

Unlike the previous statement, the REPEAT ... UNTIL loop continues so long as the relational condition tested is false. This is useful if you only want to stop the program from looping until a certain number or string is entered.

Example 4

The following program performs the same task as Example 1, except this time the program asks if you want to work out another area using a REPEAT ... UNTIL loop.

```
PROGRAM Triangle;

VAR
   base,height : real;
   Area        : real;
   Ans         : char;
BEGIN
REPEAT
   WRITELN('Enter the base of the triangle ');
   READLN(base);
   WRITELN('Enter the height of the triangle ');
   READLN(height);
   Area:= 0.5*base*height;
   WRITELN('The area of the triangle is ',Area);
   WRITE('Have you finished? ');
   READLN(Ans);
UNTIL UpCase(Ans) ='Y';
END.
```

The format of the FOR ... TO loop is as follows:

```
FOR counter := start TO last DO
   BEGIN
   .
   .

   .
   END;
```

This uses a start value, and the instructions within the mini-program between the BEGIN and END are repeated, adding 1 to the start variable each time. When the start variable eventually equals the last value, then the loop ends.

Example 5

This program produces a list of measurements from 1 to 24 inches, and the corresponding values in centimetres, using the conversion 1 inch = 2.54 cm. A FOR ... TO loop is used for the number of inches and this starts at 1 and goes up to 24.

```
PROGRAM Conversion;

Var
   Count     : Integer;
   Centimetres: Real;
BEGIN
   FOR Count := 1 TO 24 DO
      BEGIN
      Centimetres := Count * 2.54;
      WRITELN (Count, Centimetres);
   END;
READLN
END.
```

Notice the following points in the above program:

- The count holds only integers so it needs to be defined as such in the variables section of the program.
- The centimetre values include decimal points, so they need to be declared as 'real variables'.

Example 6

```
PROGRAM Boolean_variables;

USES CRT;
VAR Age,Height      :real;
    Young,Tall      :boolean;
BEGIN
  CLRSCR;
  WRITE('What is your age in years? Please type it in ');
  READLN(Age);
  WRITE('What is your height in metres? Please type it in ');
  READLN(Height);

  Young:=(Age<=20);
  Tall:=(Height>=1.8);

IF Young AND Tall THEN
  BEGIN
    WRITE('Have you ever thought about ');
    WRITELN('being a basketball player?');
  END;
IF NOT Young AND NOT Tall THEN
  BEGIN
    WRITE('Have you thought about ');
    WRITELN('playing bowls?');
END;
READLN
  END.
```

Basic

Basic (Beginners' All-purpose Symbolic Instruction Code) is mainly a teaching language and is the most widely known (as opposed to *used*) language since it has been taught in many schools, and early home computers used Basic. In its initial form Basic was an interpreted language, which means that the computer worked through a program a line at a time, converting each line to machine code and then carrying it out (see page 384). The early versions of Basic often led to programs that were poorly structured, making it difficult for someone new to a particular program to grasp how it worked. Basic programs were also difficult to **debug** and it was therefore not taken on board by commercial programmers.

Newer versions of Basic have overcome many of the earlier problems; they support structured programming and provide programmers with a number of tools to aid program development. There are now various versions of Basic in use: **Qbasic,** which is an interpreted language, **QuickBasic** which can be interpreted or compiled, and the most recent version **Visual Basic** which makes use of the Windows environment.

Fortran

Fortran is a language used mainly for mathematics and quantitative science, and you are unlikely to come across it unless you work in these fields.

C++ and C

C++ is an increasingly popular language, particularly good for graphics and for developing commercial software. It is an object-orientated language which has the power and control of an assembly language with the readability of a high-level language such as Pascal.

C (there used to be an A and a B!) has become the 'industry standard' language used for building software on personal computers. C is a **block structured** language and a program is made up of a series of program blocks which are linked together.

There are various reasons for the popularity of C and C++, and these include:

- the availability of high quality **library routines** containing sections of programs which can be used within other programs, thus reducing the amount of writing that needs to be done from scratch. Most C programs consist of these library routines;
- it is easy to transfer C programs from one machine to another;
- being in a low-level language, programs are more direct and hence faster.

Translators

Translation programs are part of the systems software and are used to convert program commands into machine code. There are three common types of translator: interpreters, compilers and assemblers.

Compilers and interpreters

These are both types of program which change high-level language instructions into machine code, although the way they do this is different.

An interpreter takes each instruction in turn, converts it to machine code and then carries it out. It is rather like a person who cannot read French taking each word in turn, translating it using a dictionary, then moving on to the next word, with no records being kept. If the document is read again at a later date the same process is repeated.

A compiler is software which converts the whole of a high-level program into machine code in one go. Provided that there are no mistakes in the program, this results in a new version in machine code. The original file contains the program written in the high-level language (called the source code); as a result of compilation another file is produced with the program in machine code (called the object code). Whenever the program needs to be run, the file containing the machine code version is used. Drawing on the foreign language analogy, the compiler is like a person translating the whole of a document from French to English, writing it down, then using the English version when the document needs to be read again.

If the program needs to be altered at a later date, then the original source code can be altered and the program recompiled.

Assemblers

Assemblers translate assembly language instructions into machine code, with each instruction in assembly language usually corresponding to one machine code instruction.

Special programming languages

Many applications packages, especially database management software, provide special facilities called applications generators (see page 362) which are a form of programming language in their own right.

Automated software routines

There are various software routines which a user can develop and run within applications software. They include macros, templates, styles, forms, wizards, etc. These routines will be looked at later in the chapter.

Features of program execution

Run-time system

A run-time system is one which uses software that must be available to run in primary storage to enable a program to be executed. Examples include some graphic presentation packages, interpreted programs and all applications software-run macros.

Executable file

An executable file is one which is ready to be run without the need for an application to be loaded first. In MS-DOS you can tell whether a particular file is executable or not by looking at the file extension: files with the suffix .EXE or .COM are executable files.

Program constructs

Constructs are sections of a program and are covered in Chapter 11. They include:
- sequence
- repetition
- selection.

Types of data

All data is fundamentally of two types: non-numeric and numeric.

Non-numeric data

Non-numeric data usually consists of single characters or groups of characters called strings (see page 387). Each of the characters has a binary code associated with it (the ASCII code is often used) and this is the code in which it is stored by the computer. For instance, the number 12 stored as characters is represented by the ASCII code for 1 followed by the ASCII code for 2. When numbers are stored as characters, the computer is unable to perform any calculations on them and this system is usually used only for 'identification' numbers such as telephone numbers, postcodes and order numbers. These are non-numeric because they can contain non-numeric data, such as dashes and leading zeros, as in the case of many order numbers; such numbers do not need to be dealt with arithmetically.

There are other types of non-numeric data besides strings such as dates and logical values which stand for true/false conditions. Dates, although non-numeric in one respect, can still have calculations performed on them; someone's age can be calculated from their date of birth and today's date.

Numeric data

Numeric data consists of numbers, which can take any value and have any degree of accuracy depending on the context in which they are used. With numeric data the computer stores the binary equivalent of the number. The number 12, for example, is 001100 in binary. Data stored in this way can be used in calculations.

There are several types of numeric data, which are described below.

Integers

Integers are whole numbers, either positive or negative and including zero. Examples are 1, 9, 1099, –2, 0, –200.

Real numbers

Real numbers (sometimes called **floating point numbers**) are numbers which contain decimal points. Examples include 12.0, 112.222, –0.09, 14.008, 0.0. Notice that 12.0 and 0.0 are real numbers *and* integers.

Variables

Variables are locations in the memory where a single item of data can be stored. For example, one variable might hold the integer 5 while another might hold the real number 12.533. These storage locations are normally referred to by the name which is allocated to the variable itself rather than the address of the storage location. So we can have variable names such as net_salary, tax_paid, balance_at_end_of_month and so on. Whenever you enter a new value for a variable it automatically replaces the previous version, so a variable can only ever hold one value at a time. When a program is being executed (carried out), variables can change their values all the time but they are still restricted to one value at any particular time.

Constants

Constants are memory locations which contain values that do not vary. For example, the value of pi (i.e. 3.14) would be classed as a constant since it never changes.

Data types in Cobol

Cobol is a programming language which is ideally suited to dealing with characters. Character data in Cobol can be numeric, alphanumeric or alphabetic. Character strings are manipulated in Cobol as a single unit and they can be declared in the following way:

```
01 TITLE          PIC XXXX
01 EMP_SURNAME    PIC X(40)
01 TAX_CODE       PIC 9999
01 SEX            PIC X
```

- The first line sets up a character variable called TITLE which consists of four characters. We could also have declared this as 01 TITLE PIC X(4), where the number in the brackets is the number of characters.
- 01 EMP_SURNAME creates a character variable which is able to hold up to 40 characters.
- 01 TAX_CODE PIC 9999 creates a numeric integer variable which can store whole numbers from 0 to 9999.
- 01 SEX PIC X creates a single character variable.

Data structures

In the last section we looked at types of data; in this section we look at the way programs are able to structure the variables to make it easier for a computer to organise them in the memory and process them when required. The main structures we will consider are strings, arrays, records, tables, stacks, queues and trees.

Strings

A string is a group of characters that is treated as a single item by a computer; strings are used to hold non-numeric data items. The characters within a string can be any of the characters on a computer keyboard. The start and end of the string are usually identified using special characters, such as quotes. Examples of strings are:

"Stephen Doyle"
"0151 924 0098"
"14th December 1998"

Strings allow applications programs to store and manipulate non-numeric data. Strings can be compared and this is important when searching and manipulating data. When two strings containing letters are being compared, a string whose initial letter comes first in alphabetical order is considered to have a lower value than one which is further on in the alphabet. If two strings with the same initial letter are compared, the program looks at the next letter, and so on until the letters differ. Hence from the computer's point of view, the following is true:

"DOG" <> "DOGS"
"CAT" = "CAT"
"Stephen" < "Steve"
"Stephen"> "John"

Arrays

An array is a structure used to store a collection of data objects of the same type. These data objects are normally stored in consecutive cells within the computer's memory and the position of a data object is identified by its position in the array. Let us look at an example.

Suppose we need to keep track of the weekly sales of a particular book over a 12-month period. From this we have to find the highest and lowest weekly sales and also the average weekly sales over the whole year. You could use 52 variables with different names to hold the weekly sales. However, this is clumsy, and to compute the average all the sales would have to be added up in a statement like this:

total = sales1 + sales2 + sales3 + ... sales52

A better way of doing this is to make use of an array. Using an array, we can produce a list of variables all with the same name but including a 'subscript' (i.e. a number in brackets after the name). This means that each variable can be given the name 'sales' but with a subscript attached (e.g. sales(1), sales(2), etc.). To add up these sales you need only do the following:

FOR subscript = 1 to 52
total = total + sales(subscript)
NEXT subscript

The above is classed as a one-dimensional array because a single number (1, 2 ... 52) in the variable is used to define the position of the data in the array.

In a two-dimensional array, two numbers are needed to identify a particular position in the array which is a matrix; an example of such an array is shown below.

	1st quarter	2nd quarter	3rd quarter	4th quarter
Product 1	280	405	418	301
Product 2	320	420	500	424
Product 3	608	501	630	209

The above array is used to hold the details of three products over four quarters. To set up the array, it is necessary to declare that it is made up of three rows and four columns.

Records

A record is a collection of data objects that are not necessarily of the same type and can be identified by their individual names. This allows related sets of data of different types to be grouped together. For example, in the same employee record you could have a person's name (stored as a string), their department (stored as a string), their salary (stored as a real number) and their sex (stored as a single character). To store this record in Pascal you could use the following:

```
TYPE Employee = RECORD
    Name        : STRING [30];
    Department  : STRING [35];
    Salary      : REAL;
    Sex         : CHAR;
END;
```

Tables

Suppose we want to write a simple program which, when the number of a month is entered, gives us the month's name. This cannot be done by calculation, rather it is simply a matter of correlating two sets of data. For this we use a table instead. The month numbers are stored as integers and the month names are stored as strings; the two lots of data are placed in a table as shown below.

JAN	FEB	MAR	APR	MAY	JUN	JUL	AUG	SEP	OCT	NOV	DEC
1	2	3	4	5	6	7	8	9	10	11	12

This table can then be used by a program to find a particular name of month from its number or vice versa.

Lists

A list is a collection of data arranged in a certain order and is one of the most useful data structures. There are various types of list available to the programmer, including **arrays** and **linked lists**. Linked lists contain two parts: the data itself and a pointer which 'points' to the next chunk of data.

The main advantage of using a linked list is that the data can be manipulated easily and this enables data to be sorted without needing to move it around in the memory. The use of lists is quite complicated, and if you are interested in how they work you should consult a specialist book covering programming concepts.

Stacks

A stack is a bit like a list which can only have data added and taken away at one end. To get to the 'bottom' of the stack it is necessary to remove all the data items one by one from the top. Suppose the letters of the alphabet were stored in a stack. The letter A is inserted first, then B and so on until Z. The letter A would be at the bottom of the stack and Z at the top; when the stack is emptied, it will be emptied in reverse order so the letter Z will be first out. For this reason, stacks are sometimes referred to as 'first in last out' (FILO).

Queues

A queue is similar to a stack in that it contains data in a list. The difference is that in a queue the data is added at one end and removed at the *opposite* end. The effect of this is that the first data item inserted in the queue is the first to be removed, hence the other name for a queue is 'first in first out' (FIFO).

Trees

A tree is a data structure consisting of sets of junctions called nodes, with branches which then end in further nodes with their own branches, and so on. The initial node from which the first branching occurs is called the root node.

Figure 12.2 shows a typical tree structure. Notice that trees are normally drawn upside down with the root at the top and the branches moving downwards. The tree structure is used by MS-DOS for the directory/subdirectory structure in which files are stored.

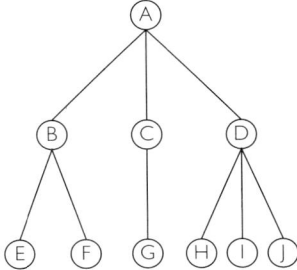

Figure 12.2 Typical tree structure

Expressions and operators

Expressions and operators fall into several categories, which are discussed below.

Arithmetic operators

Most programming languages support the basic arithmetic operations which are $+$, $-$, $*$, $/$. Notice that there is no multiplication symbol because it might be confused with the letter x, so an asterisk ($*$) is used instead. Many programming languages also support the exponent operator which is represented by the symbol $\wedge$ and means 'to the power of', so 2^3 means two to the power of three (2^3, that is $2 \times 2 \times 2$).

Relational operators

Symbol	Meaning	Examples
=	Equals	5 + 5 = 10
>	Greater than	5*3 > 2*3
<	Less than	−6 < −1 or 100 < 200
<>	Not equal to	"Red" <> "White" or 20/4 <> 6*4
<=	Less than or equal to	"Adam" <= "Eve"
>=	Greater than or equal to	400 >= 200

The most common relational operator by far is the equals sign (=). Sometimes a comparison needs to be made between two items of data; for example, we may need to find a list of employees whose salaries are greater than a certain amount.

Operators can also be used with characters or character strings, so one character can be compared with another. Since each character has a binary code associated with it, the computer can work out that A comes before B and so on. This is used when conducting searches where one character string needs to be compared with another, and also when sorting lists of items into alphabetical order.

Logical (Boolean) operators

Logical operators are used to specify a logical relationship between expressions or quantities and include the operators AND, OR and NOT.

AND

The AND operator is used to compare two expressions to determine if they are both true. If they are, then one action is taken, if they are not, an alternative action is taken. For an AND to be true, both conditions must be satisfied and this is shown in the following example:

IF A = 5 AND B = 6 THEN expression_true

Here the variables A and B are tested to see if A is 5 and B is 6. Only if both conditions are true will the expression be true and all other combinations will result in the expression being false.

We can summarise all the possible combinations of true and false for A and B, and the resultant truth of the whole expression in a truth table. The truth table for the AND operator is shown below.

A	B	A AND B
T	T	T
F	F	F
T	F	F
F	T	F

OR

OR is an operator which will return a true provided at least one of the expressions is true.

A	B	A OR B
T	T	T
F	F	F
T	F	T
F	T	T

NOT
The NOT operator reverses the truth value applied to it. Its truth table is the simplest and is as follows:

A	NOT A
T	F
F	T

Concatenation
Concatenation is the process whereby two character strings are joined together to form a single character string. For example, the character strings 'ABC' and 'DEF' can be combined to give the concatenated string 'ABCDEF'.

Activity 12.2

Here is a program written in the high-level language Turbo Pascal:

```
program number one;
Var
    A, B : integer;
    Ratio: real;
begin
    Writeln ('Enter two whole numbers:');
    Readln(A, B);
    Ratio := A/B;
    Writeln ('The ratio is:' Ratio)
end.
```

By referring to the lines as line 1, line 2, etc. answer the following questions on the above program.

1 Which line of the program contains an arithmetic operator and which operator is it?
2 Which line of the program contains a relational operator and which operator is it?
3 In which two lines are variables defined?
4 A and B are defined as integers. Explain what this means.
5 On line 4 the ratio is defined as a real number. Explain what this means. Are all integers real numbers and vice versa?

Assignment A12.1

This assignment develops knowledge and understanding of the following element:
6.2 Examine software production

It supports the development of the following key skills:
Communication 3.2 and 3.3
Information technology 3.1, 3.2 and 3.3

For this assignment you are required to produce a report covering all of the following:
- two types of programming environment;
- the features of program execution;
- an explanation of the term 'program constructs' and one example of each type of construct;
- an outline of the different types of data and data structures available to the programmer;
- a description of the expressions and operators available to the programmer for use in software production, together with one example each of an arithmetic, a relational and a logical operator.

Introduction to automated procedures

In this section we will look at specifying and creating automated procedures to speed up processing, reduce errors and generally make life easier for ourselves when using computer software. These automated procedures include the use of **macros**, **batch files** and programming.

Purposes of using automated procedures

There are various reasons for using automated procedures and these are described below.

To reduce input error

When a user enters a string of characters there is always the possibility that a mistake will be made requiring subsequent editing or re-entering. In order for instructions to be accepted they have to obey certain rules, and it can prove frustrating for the less experienced user who may make a number of mistakes in the construction of a command before eventually getting it right. Each time the user types in an error, the computer will either report that the command cannot be carried out because it is wrong, or carry it out wrongly. Either way, time is wasted so it is much better to let the computer issue long instructions or series of commands, using a pre-stored program, list of keystrokes or mouse movements.

Automated procedures should be used as much as possible to reduce input error. Such procedures include macros, which provide automated procedures with an applications program, and batch files, which are used to automate procedures given to the operating system. Both of these will be looked at in more detail in the next section.

To speed up processing

Suppose we want to write a letter. There are parts of the letter which are common to all the letters we write, such as the address at the top, with its telephone, fax and e-mail numbers, and the name of who the letter is from at the end. Rather than typing these in each time, we can use an automated procedure called a **template** where they are pre-stored together with details of the page setup.

There are many features of applications software which automate procedures and therefore speed up processing. The suite of programs Microsoft Office has **wizards** which are used within each module to automate tasks that would have previously been performed manually. For instance, there is a wizard in Microsoft Word for setting up tables with which you choose the style of the table from a selection and select the number of rows and columns, after which the computer will automatically set out the table.

Batch files also speed up processing by automatically loading the applications software without the user having to issue long and difficult instructions via the mouse or keyboard.

To standardise procedures

We have already come across the use of templates as a way of speeding up processing, but they can also be used to standardise procedures. As well as holding various pieces of text, templates can also hold style data, variable data and even macros. Templates provide a quick way of making sure all company documents and screens look the same, regardless of the operator or machine/terminal through which the document is entered.

Batch files can be created using the operating system MS-DOS to produce simple menus which enable users to load software without issuing commands or making complicated selections with the mouse.

For convenience

Automated procedures are used because, basically, they are more convenient. Using macros you do not have to remember the construction of commands, and you do not need to worry that company documents will not look the same if you use templates.

Facilities for creating automated procedures

There is a wide range of facilities for further automation present in operating systems software and applications software. A little time needs to be spent finding out about these and how they may help you in the future; the time you spend developing such expertise is time well spent.

Automated procedures include macros, batch files and templates but there are also other types.

Macros

A macro is a program written using applications software tools to automate a sequence of keystrokes, mouse movements and clicks or events, thus extending the instruction set of the machine. Macros are very powerful tools, yet not many people use them because they simply do not understand them or see the need to spend time setting them up.

The popular wordprocessor, Microsoft Word, has its own special language called WordBasic for writing macros. Using this macro language it is easy to produce a macro which could, for example, convert dollars to pounds, which might be useful if you were a UK company exporting to the USA. Once you have created the macro, it can then be used repeatedly in your documents.

Some wordprocessors, including Microsoft Word, allow you to develop your own macro toolbar, which makes it very easy to select your macros once created and saved.

There are three common ways you can select a macro:

- using a toolbar
- using a menu
- using multiple key combinations.

Batch files

Batch files are usually provided as part of an operating system. Their purpose is to automate a processing activity by issuing a sequence of commands. Any valid sequence of commands is allowable and the operating system will obey them in exactly the same way as if they had been entered at the keyboard.

There are several advantages in using batch files and these are as follows:

- Their use saves time. Once a batch file has been created it can be used over and over again.
- There is no need for the user to remember a sequence of commands.

The main disadvantages of batch files are:

- It is necessary to understand the commands available in the operating system before the programs can be constructed.
- A mistake in a program can seriously damage files, so careful checking is needed before any program is run.

If you have the operating system MS-DOS on your computer, you will also have a program called AUTOEXEC.BAT which is used to customise the computer when the system is started up. This file is loaded immediately after the operating system and the computer then carries out the instructions contained in this batch file. The batch file facility could be used, for instance, if you use your wordprocessor every day, so that the computer automatically loads the wordprocessing software as soon as the operating system is loaded.

Batch files in MS-DOS are a group of commands, executed one after another, and it is possible to make up small programs using these commands. A batch file can be created either using the editor provided with the operating system or using one of the popular wordprocessing packages, saving the resulting file in ASCII code. All batch files written in MS-DOS have a .BAT file extension and once the file has been created using the editor (or wordprocessor) it is then passed to the command interpreter for execution.

Activity 12.3

Find out what commands are available in the operating system MS-DOS for making up batch files.

Task 1
'Batch files are interpreted.' Explain what this means.

Task 2
Write a batch file which will *either*:

1 enable your computer to load automatically the piece of software you use most frequently, without the need for any input from the user apart from turning the power on; *or*

2 automatically copy any data files you have altered to a back-up disk once you have finished working with one of the programs you use regularly.

MS-DOS batch file commands

ECHO

This command sends a message to the screen and the syntax is:

ECHO (put the message you want printing out here)

The echo command is very useful when combined with the control character ^G in the following way:

ECHO ^G

When this instruction is reached there is a bleep, which is particularly useful if you want the computer to tell the user when it has completed a particular process, such as copying a disk. ECHO ON switches the command on and ECHO OFF switches the command off.

CLS

This is the 'clear screen' command used to clear commands from the screen.

TYPE

If, within a batch program, there is a lot of text to be printed out, it might be easier to create it using wordprocessing software and save it as a text file which can then be summarised from within the batch file. The command TYPE is used to call the text program and after the command comes the name of the text file to be loaded.

A typical batch file to load a piece of text stored in a text file called MESSAGE.TXT might be:

ECHO OFF
CLS
TYPE MESSAGE.TXT

The TYPE command is useful for storing a menu or a series of instructions as a text file.

PAUSE

This command causes the batch file to wait at a certain point until the user instructs the program to continue by pressing any key. This is useful if the user needs time to read something on screen or insert/remove a floppy disk when making back-up copies.

You do not need a message with the pause command as the computer automatically puts up the following message:

Press any key to continue ...

If the user does not want to continue with the batch program, it can be terminated by pressing Ctrl-Break and the following message will then appear:

Terminate batch job (Y/N)?

If the user types in Y, the program will stop.

GOTO

Batch programs need not always be carried out in strict sequence. In many cases the user might want to jump from one part of the program to another and the instruction for this is the GOTO command.

FOR

This command widens instructions to a group of files or directories.

REM

This is short for 'remark' and is used to hold messages within the program; such messages help explain what each part of the program does.

PROMPT

The structure of this command is:

    PROMPT (text)

where 'text' is the message to be displayed before the symbol for the prompt. Prompts are used when the user needs to type something in, usually a number from a menu selection.

Running and stopping batch programs

To run a batch file you type in the name of the file without the extension .BAT; to stop it before all the commands have been executed, you type Ctrl-C or Ctrl-Break.

In this section we will look at some examples of simple batch files to give you an idea of how the commands are put together.

Example 1

This is a useful program whose purpose is to create a menu system so that simple commands can be used to call up your most regularly used programs. These simple menu systems are ideal for novice users since they only have to type in a number to make their selection.

Suppose you want to create the following menu:

MENU

1 Start Microsoft Word
2 Use MS-DOS
3 Back up your document files

Press a number (1 to 3) to make your selection and then press ENTER.

Here is the batch program to produce this menu:

    ECHO OFF
    CLS
    ECHO MENU
    ECHO.
    ECHO.
    ECHO 1.   Start Microsoft Word
    ECHO 2.   Use MS-DOS
    ECHO 3.   Back up your document files
    ECHO.
    ECHO.

    PROMPT Press a number (1 to 3) to make your selection and then press ENTER.

The above program can be saved, with the name MENU.BAT.

You now have to create the three separate batch files, calling them 1.BAT, 2.BAT and 3.BAT. If the user types in 1, for example, at the prompt in the batch file, file 1.BAT is automatically loaded and run, which contains a program taking the user straight to their wordprocessing package.

You can also put a short message in each of these batch files, so that if, for example, the number 1 is typed in, the message 'This loads the wordprocessing software' is displayed on the screen.

Example 2

The following batch file takes a floppy disk and prepares a back-up copy on a second floppy disk. The program works in the following way. First a directory is made on the hard drive (drive C), and all the files on the floppy are copied to this. After copying, this disk is removed. The floppy disk for the back-up copy is now inserted and all the files held in the temporary directory copied onto it. To prevent the hard drive becoming cluttered with temporary files, all the files held in the TEMP directory are then deleted and the directory removed.

See if you can work out what each step in the following program does.

```
CLS
ECHO OFF
ECHO This batch program will take a copy from your workdisk
ECHO and copy it onto another floppy.
C:
CD\
MD TEMP
CD\
ECHO Put the floppy disk you wish to take a backup copy into drive A.
PAUSE
COPY A:*.* C:\TEMP
ECHO Put the floppy on which you want the backup copies placed in drive A.
PAUSE
COPY C:\TEMP\*.* A:
REM This part deletes the files placed in the temporary directory
C:
CD\TEMP
ECHO These files have been stored on the hard drive as a temporary
ECHO measure in a directory called TEMP and if you want these
ECHO files deleted type Y at the prompt.
DEL *.*
CD\
RD TEMP
ECHO File copying is now complete
```

This program needs to be saved in the root directory of the hard drive under the name BACK.BAT and can be run by typing BACK.

If you intend to run this program make sure that you show it to your tutor so that your tutor can check it first.

Activity 12.4

Task 1

For this task you are required to use the operating system MS-DOS and create some batch files using the following procedures.

1 Create a subdirectory called a:\courses on a floppy disk.

2 Create three text files in this subdirectory; maths.txt, computer.txt and accounts.txt. Each of these files needs to contain the following three lines:
   - the course name (e.g. mathematics)
   - the name of the contact tutor (e.g. Mr H Williams)
   - the telephone number of the tutor (e.g. 0151 987 9100).
3 Now create the following course selection menu:
   COURSE SELECTION
   1. Mathematics
   2. Computing
   3. Accounts
   4. Exit

Upon selection of one of the options in the menu, the appropriate batch file should run (e.g. 1.BAT for menu selection 1), typing out the appropriate text on the screen and then pausing for the user to read the screen. When the user presses any key, the screen should then return them to the above menu.

It is important that the batch file is stored in the root directory and the text files are stored in a subdirectory.

Task 2

For this task you are required to investigate the following packages for automated procedures.
- wordprocessor
- spreadsheet
- presentation graphics.

For two of these, find out how to create a macro using the software and then develop your own macro to automate a series of commands. As evidence, you should supply:
- brief notes explaining how to create and run the macros;
- an outline of the macros you have created and the advantages of using them rather than issuing commands in the usual way.

Evaluating automated procedures

Evaluating automated procedures involves assessing the quality of the software and making sure that it meets certain standards. Software that is bought is like any other consumer item, but deficiencies in software may not be so obvious.

When software is bought the purchaser normally assumes that it will do the job for which it is advertised; a wordprocessing package should perform wordprocessing without any problems. You might think this is obvious, but there have been occasions when large software manufacturers have supplied software that still contains bugs and which does not always perform in the way it is supposed to. Sometimes certain conditions cause programs to crash with a resulting loss of data.

Some software might only run with equipment above a certain specification, and even if the minimum specification is met, the software might run so slowly as to be practically useless. Other software might have a user interface that is difficult to learn or use.

It is important, therefore, to evaluate software, and you might have to do this as part of your job in computing. Software can be evaluated in terms of the criteria described below.

Costs

Although the purchase cost can be a factor in selecting a piece of software, it is usually other costs that increase the cost of developing a software solution more significantly. These include:
- the cost of installation;
- the cost of staff training;
- the cost of developing tailor-made software as opposed to using a software package;
- the cost of supporting, through help-desks, software which has a poorly designed user interface;
- the cost of the software compared with the benefits the software is likely to bring;
- the cost of the package compared with software that does a similar job.

Benefits

The use of automated procedures will confer a range of benefits on the user, probably including some or all of the following:
- faster data processing data;
- fewer administrative staff needed to process the same quantity of data;
- more accurate results;
- better presentation of work;
- easier use;
- no duplication of work;
- provision of management information;
- faster access to stored data.

Fitness for purpose

'Fitness for purpose' means making sure that software is suitable for the job it is being used to do. This is particularly relevant when it comes to packaged software, because often the use of such software represents a compromise, with the existing system having to be adjusted to accommodate the software.

Possible improvements

The more types of software you use, the better you become at recognising any deficiencies and knowing what adjustments to make to improve things. With specially written software, it is possible to get the programmer to make improvements, but if packaged software is being used you can only wait for upgrades or new versions of the software to become available.

Activity 12.5

The table on the next page summarises the main features of several popular programming languages. Your task is to copy and complete this table. Some of the details have been included to help you.

Name of language	High-level, low-level or object-orientated	Procedural or declarative	Main uses for the programming language
Basic	High-level	Procedural	Teaching computer languages in schools and colleges
Fortran			
Cobol			
Turbo Pascal			
Pascal			
C			
Prolog			
C++			

Assignment A12.2

This assignment develops knowledge and understanding of the following element:
6.3 Investigate the production of automated procedures

It supports the development of the following key skills:
Communication 3.2 and 3.3
Information technology 3.1, 3.2 and 3.3

Modern software usually contains a wide range of automated procedures to make the user's life easier. Your task is to investigate these procedures within your wordprocessing package and to make use of them in a real situation.

On The Move, a small group of estate agents, has a range of letters that it writes to both buyers and sellers. Many of these letters are similar and differ only with respect to the names, addresses, prices, commission percentage rates, etc. The area manager has asked you to develop software which will facilitate some routine computer tasks.

Task 1
One letter is sent out to all the sellers of properties, outlining the price at which the company intends to put the property on the market and the commission rate. Details such as name and address of the seller and the member of staff sending the letter are also included.

Here is a set of variable data required for one of the letters. The bracketed text describes what the information is.

(Seller's name and address)
Miss G Roberts
23 Moordale Ave
Great Crosby
Liverpool
L23 5RR

(Person to which the greeting is directed, e.g. Dear ...) Miss Roberts
(Price of property) £68,950

(Commission rate) 2.25%
(Name of sender) Mrs Johnston (Sales Negotiator)

Produce a template or style sheet which will set the position, font, style and fixed text and put in variable fields so that the user can insert only those items which change from one document to another. You will have to make up the main body of the letter yourself, bearing in mind the purpose of the letter.

Task 2
Using MS-DOS or another non-Windows operating system, produce a simple batch file which could be used at the end of each day to back up wordprocessing documents from the hard drive to a floppy disk.

Task 3
Produce a series of batch files so that the user can identify which software application they wish to access. They should be able to type in the first letter of the choice, from which the software should go to the required application. The area manager would like the menu system to look like this:

On The Move
Type in the first letter of your selection.
Wordprocessing
Database
Spreadsheet
Exit to the operating system

You should create simple text files with a brief message to appear once the software has been loaded. Note that you do not need to access the actual programs on your hard drive.

Sample unit test

1 A programming language where the order in which the program steps are carried out is important, is best described as:
   a a procedural language
   b a declarative language
   c a high-level language
   d a low-level language

2 The following programming languages are all of the same type. Which type is this?
   Cobol
   Basic
   Pascal
   C++

   a procedural languages
   b object event languages
   c declarative languages
   d object-orientated languages

3 Which two of the following are examples of translators?

1 compilers
2 assemblers
3 applications generators
4 utility programs

a 1 and 2
b 1 and 3
c 2 and 3
d 3 and 4

4 You are writing a program in a high-level language such as Pascal, and when it is run a syntax error is reported. Which of the following reports the syntax error in the program?
a an editor
b a compiler
c an assembler
d an applications generator

5 A program is written to determine the area of circular windows and uses pi in the calculation. The value of pi in the program would be stored as:
a an array
b a real number
c a record
d a constant

6 A program used in a college holds student details for funding calculations. It needs to hold brief details such as student number, name, date of birth and address. Which is the most appropriate data structure for storing this information?
a records in a file
b an array of numeric data
c a string of characters
d a table of constants

7 Numbers such as 3, 34, −100, 0 and 5 are best stored as:
a real numbers
b constants
c integers
d negative numbers

8 The concept of 'first in last out' is encountered when dealing with the data structure called:
a a stack
b a list
c an array
d a string

9 The concept of 'first in first out' is encountered when dealing with the data structure called:
a a stack
b an array
c a queue
d a tree

10 The pay of all employees in an organisation is set to increase by 5 per cent. Which of the following steps will work out the new pay from the old pay?
   a NEW_PAY = OLD_PAY*1.5
   b NEW_PAY = OLD_PAY*0.5
   c NEW_PAY = OLD_PAY*1.05
   d NEW_PAY = OLD_PAY*5/100

11 A program used in a school needs to report all the pupils who are 16 or over but under 18. Which one of the following steps selects the required pupils?
   a IF AGE <> 18
   b IF AGE >= 16 AND AGE < 18
   c IF AGE > 16 AND AGE < 18
   d IF AGE >= 16 AND AGE <= 18

12 The process of joining two strings together, e.g. joining 'John' and 'Smith' together to give a person's full name, is called:
   a adjusting
   b concatenation
   c using a macro
   d deleting

13 Which one of the following is *not* an example of a translator?
   a assembler
   b compiler
   c interpreter
   d macro

14 A program contains the following expression:
   A = B ^ 3

   If B has the value 3, which would be the value of A?
   a 9
   b 6
   c 27
   d 1

15 An insurance company will only insure drivers over 25 years of age. Which programming construct would be used to decide whether a particular applicant could be accepted or not?
   a selection
   b sequence
   c repetition
   d iteration

16 An organisation decides to give all its employees an extra week's holiday. To do this the following expression is written in the program that gives each employee's holiday entitlement:
   new_entitlement = entitlement + 1

   Which is the arithmetic operator in the expression?
   a equals
   b addition
   c subtraction
   d exponentiation

17 An insurance company will only insure drivers who are 25 or over and have been accident free. Which one of the following expressions will select such people?
   a IF AGE >= 25 AND ACCIDENT FREE = "YES"
   b IF AGE = 25 AND ACCIDENT FREE = YES
   c IF AGE >= 25 AND ACCIDENT FREE = YES
   d IF AGE = 25 AND ACCIDENT FREE = "NO"

18 A user-friendly screen is created to enable users to enter data into a database. What is the main advantage in doing this?
   a to enable all the information to be printed out
   b to make the database easy to use
   c to make the database faster
   d to enable a password to be used in order to gain access to the data

19 Here is an arithmetic expression used in a program:
   Amount = Principal*(1+interest_rate/100) ^ number_of_years

   Which one of the following arithmetic operands is *not* present in the above calculation?
   a exponentiation
   b division
   c subtraction
   d multiplication

20 In a payroll program, tax is calculated on a month-by-month basis. Month 1 is April, month 2 is May, etc. Which is the most suitable data structure for doing this?
   a a string
   b a numeric array
   c a record
   d a table

21 Which one of the following is *not* an arithmetic operator?
   a +
   b =
   c ^
   d *

22 Which one of the following is *not* a Boolean (logical) operator?
   a AND
   b NOT
   c OR
   d THEN

23 The following list gives the reasons for using automated procedures. Which one is the main reason for using templates?
   a to reduce input error
   b to speed up the task
   c so that the user does not have to remember a list of commands
   d so that the user does not need to type anything in

24 A program written using applications software to automate a series of keystrokes or mouse movements is called:
   a a utility program
   b a batch program

c a macro

d a pointer

25 A writer uses her PC primarily as a wordprocessor and she is frustrated that she has to move a mouse and click each time she wants to load the wordprocessing software. Which one of the following would she need in order to go straight to the wordprocessing software?

a a batch file

b a macro

c a file manager

d an applications package

26 A travel agency uses a program to change currency from sterling to a variety of foreign currencies. The most appropriate data type used for the exchange rate would be:

a an integer

b a real number

c a logical expression

d a character string

27 A credit card company prints out a message if a customer exceeds their credit limit by £20 or more. Which one of the following could be used to test whether the message needs to be printed?

a IF AMOUNT_OWED – CREDIT_LIMIT > 20'

b IF AMOUNT_OWED – CREDIT_LIMIT > = 20'

c IF AMOUNT_OWED – CREDIT_LIMIT < 20

d IF AMOUNT_OWED – CREDIT_LIMIT < = 20

28 Which two of the following are used to translate high-level languages to machine code?

1 interpreter

2 assembler

3 modem

4 compiler

a 1 and 2

b 2 and 3

c 1 and 4

d 3 and 4

29 Which two of the following are part of the programming environment?

1 assembler

2 programming language

3 logical operator

4 array structure

a 1 and 2

b 2 and 3

c 3 and 4

d 1 and 4

(RSA, June 1996)

30 Which two of the following are examples of translators?

1 interpreter

2 Boolean

3 Pascal

4 compiler

a 1 and 2

b 2 and 3

c 3 and 4

d 1 and 4   *(RSA, June 1996)*

Questions 31 and 32 are based on the following information.

In the programming language Logo

REPEAT 4 [FD 25 LT 90]

has the effect of drawing a square with side lengths 25. FD stands for 'forward' and LT stands for 'left turn'.

The following procedure, called SHAPE, has the effect of drawing a regular shape according to the number of sides in 'SIDES', the length in 'LENGTH' and the angle in 'ANGLE'.

TO SHAPE 'SIDES' 'LENGTH' 'ANGLE'

REPEAT: SIDES [FD:LENGTH LT:ANGLE]

END

This instruction will draw a pentagon with side length 15:

SHAPE 5 15 72

31 FD and LT are examples of:

   a programming constructs

   b program code

   c program structure

   d programming types   *(RSA, June 1996)*

32 The procedure SHAPE is an example of:

   a programming constructs

   b program code

   c program structure

   d programming types   *(RSA, June 1996)*

Questions 33 and 34 are based on the following information.

Two students are using a wordprocessing package on their PC to produce a piece of coursework. The heading they are typing is to appear in bold. Student A presses a single special key before entering the heading, and the same special key afterwards. Student B clicks onto an icon before entering the heading, and clicks onto the same icon afterwards.

33 Which one of the following is the mode of operation that student A uses?

   a function key

   b menu driven

   c graphical interface

   d multiple key combinations   *(RSA, June 1996)*

34 Which one of the following is the mode of operation that student B uses?

   a function key

   b menu driven

   c graphical interface

   d multiple key combinations   *(RSA, June 1996)*

Questions 35 and 36 are based on the following information.

This pseudocode reads a series of numbers. Each sequence of three numbers represents the sides of a triangle, in order of size. Using Pythagoras' theorem, the program decides whether the triangle is right angled or not.

```
REPEAT
    read 1st number
    read 2nd number
    read 3rd number
    IF (1st number) ^2 + (2nd number) ^2 = (3rd number) ^ 2
THEN print 'Right angled triangle: '
    ELSE print 'Not right angled triangle: '
    print 1st number, 2nd number, 3rd number
    UNTIL no more numbers
```

35 Which one of the following is an example of the programming construct 'selection'?

a read 1st number, read 2nd number, read 3rd number

b print 'Right angled triangle'

c IF ... THEN ... ELSE

d REPEAT ... UNTIL   *(RSA, June 1996)*

36 Which one of the following is an example of the programming construct 'repetition'?

a read 1st number, read 2nd number, read 3rd number

b print 'Right angled triangle'

c IF ... THEN ... ELSE

d REPEAT ... UNTIL   *(RSA, June 1996)*

Questions 37 to 39 are based on the information below.

This is part of a Cobol program which prints out examination results:

```
'DATA DIVISION'
FILE SECTION
FD   EXAMRESULT-FILE
        BLOCK 10 RECORDS
        DATA RECORD INDIV-RESULT
        LABEL RECORD STANDARD.
01   INDIV-RESULT
        03  CAND-REF         PIC X(5).
        03  CAND-SURNAME  PIC X(50).
        03  EXAM-CODE       PIC 9999.
        03  GRADE             PIC X.
```

37 Which one of the following has a numeric data type?

a INDIV-RESULT

b EXAM-CODE

c EXAM RESULT-FILE

d CAND-REF   *(RSA, June 1996)*

38 Which two of the following have a character data type?

1 LABEL RECORD

2 CAND-SURNAME

3 GRADE

4 BLOCK 10

    a 1 and 2
    b 2 and 3
    c 3 and 4
    d 1 and 4   *(RSA, June 1996)*

39 Which one of the following is an example of a variable?
    a X(5)
    b PIC 9999
    c GRADE
    d PIC X   *(RSA, June 1996)*

40 A milkman keeps daily records of the number of bottles of milk delivered to each address, categorised by type (i.e. full cream, semi-skimmed and skimmed). Which one of the following is the data structure that would be used to store this data?
    a constant
    b string
    c Boolean
    d array   *(RSA, June 1996)*

41 A milkman keeps information on customers. This information includes name, address, regular milk order details and amount of outstanding bills. Which one of the following is the data structure that would be used to store this data?
    a array
    b variable
    c record
    d statement   *(RSA, June 1996)*

Questions 42–44 are based on the information below.
    Bonuses are paid to employees who work more than 35 hours in a week, provided that they have taken no sick leave during the previous four weeks. The bonus is calculated as 25 per cent of the hours worked over 35, at the employee's normal hourly rate. This pseudocode shows how the bonus is calculated:
    IF sickrecord = "good" AND hoursworked > 35
    THEN bonus = (hoursworked - 35) * payrate * 25/100
    ELSE bonus = 0

42 Which one of the following is an arithmetic operator used in the pseudocode?
    a *
    b AND
    c 25/100
    d "good"   *(RSA, June 1996)*

43 Which one of the following is a relational operator used in the pseudocode?
    a >
    b THEN
    c /
    d bonus

44 Which one of the following is a logical operator used in the pseudocode?
    a IF
    b AND
    c ELSE
    d 0   *(RSA, June 1996)*

45 Refer to Figure 12.3. Which one of the following logical expressions represents the circuitry shown and if true would result in the light being on?
  a C = ON
  b A = ON OR B = ON
  c A = ON AND B = ON
  d (A = ON AND B = ON) OR C = ON   *(RSA, June 1996)*

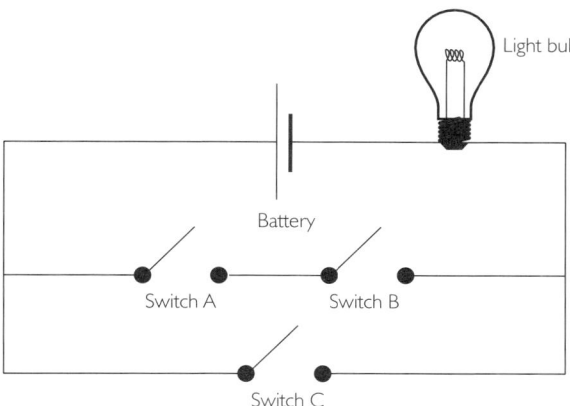

Figure 12.3

Question 46 is based on the information below.
  A card manufacturer offers a choice of greeting. The messages available are stored as variables:
  BW$ = "BEST WISHES"
  MX$ = "MERRY CHRISTMAS"
  NY$ = "HAPPY NEW YEAR"

46 Which one of the following will print the message "MERRY CHRISTMAS AND BEST WISHES FOR A HAPPY NEW YEAR"?
  a PRINT BW$; MX$; NY$
  b PRINT MX$; AND; BW$; FOR A; NY$
  c PRINT MX$; " AND "; BW$; " FOR A "; NY$
  d PRINT MX$; "AND"; BW$; "FOR A"; NY$ *(RSA, June 1996)*

47 In an auction, each item for sale is numbered (ITEMNUM) and has a reserve price (RPRICE). Bids are taken and the item is sold when the highest bid (HBID) at least matches the reserve price. Otherwise the item is returned to the original owner, unsold. Which one of the following expressions will identify an unsold item?
  a HBID < ITEMNUM
  b ITEMNUM < RPRICE
  c RPRICE < HBID
  d HBID < RPRICE   *(RSA, June 1996)*

48 In a software package, the following sequence of commands is necessary to print out a document:
    menu/print/final

The operator can type MPF (the initial letter of each command) or a macro could be written. Which of the following would be the purpose of the new macro?

   a to increase convenience for the operator
   b to reduce the amount of memory used
   c to reduce the processing speed
   d to increase printing speed *(RSA, June 1996)*

49 When entering details of a new customer on a bank's computer, the operator is presented with a template which offers some default values, e.g. today's date. Which one of the following is the purpose of using default values?
   a to ensure validity of the customer's account number
   b to save memory space
   c to reduce the possibility of input error
   d to speed up the production of new cheque books *(RSA, June 1996)*

50 A recruitment agency has set up templates for letters such as those inviting applicants for interview and confirming placements with clients. Which one of the following is the purpose of using templates?
   a to improve security
   b to increase the number of placements made
   c to standardise procedures
   d to reduce the number of vacancies *(RSA, June 1996)*

51 A computer is set up to display a 'welcome page' on power-up. The operator has to enter their ID code and password, and, if both match, can then select an application which is automatically loaded and run. Which one of the following would be written to make this happen?
   a applications software
   b batch file
   c check digit routine
   d data file *(RSA, June 1996)*

52 A florist plans to use a computer to schedule deliveries of bouquets in the local area. Which one of the following would be written to make this happen?
   a a template
   b a program
   c a macro
   d a batch file *(RSA, June 1996)*

53 A macro has been written to print an address label for the current document. Which two of the following would be given in the user specification of this macro?
   1 a method of executing the macro
   2 commonly used variable data
   3 repetitive routines
   4 the purpose of using the macro

   a 1 and 2
   b 2 and 3
   c 3 and 4
   d 1 and 4 *(RSA, June 1996)*

13 Creating databases

What is covered in this chapter

In this chapter we will look at the creation of database structures. There is always a temptation to try to create databases without giving enough thought to their development and expansion. Although a simple database (such as one for names and addresses) could be developed in this way, a larger application created without careful planning and design may not be able to do what is eventually required, and much time and money can later be wasted trying to get it to work.

This chapter begins looking at database design by building a data model. Later in the chapter we look at how this data model can be converted into a valid data model on which a database structure can be based.

Element 7.1: Create relational database structures for a given specification

- Creating a data model to meet the specification
- Refining the database using normalisation procedures
- Building a relational database

Resources you will need for your portfolio for Element 7.1
- Your written answers to the activities and assignment in this chapter.

In the following sections you will be required to produce a data model to meet a given specification, refine the data model using normalisation procedures and produce relational database structures to suit the data model.

Creating a data model to meet the specification

Before a database can be designed and built, a clear idea is required of what it needs to do. This understanding is obtained by careful systems analysis and culminates in the system specification. A system specification consists of the data and information needed to allow that system to be analysed and for the subsequent design and development of a database system to meet user requirements. The specification can include some or all of the following: a data-definition model, a process specification, an input specification, an output specification and resource requirements.

This chapter builds on the system specification developed in Chapters 9 and 10 and looks at how a data model is created and refined, and how database structures are then created using the model.

Data model

A **data model** is used to give an insight into the way data is used within an organisation and, like all models, it can be progressively refined in the light of further investigation until it represents as nearly as possible the real system. The GNVQ syllabus defines a data model as follows:

> The purpose of a data model is to identify and present user requirements in a way easily understood by users and computer professionals. It is also important that the model can be easily converted to a technical implementation and provide rules and criteria for implementing the system. A data model may consist of some or all of the following: high-level information flow diagrams, data flow diagrams, data dictionary and entity relationship diagrams.

Entity relationship diagrams

We have already looked at entity relationship diagrams in Chapter 9 and it would be advisable for you to re-read this section to refresh your memory.

Entity relationship modelling is a technique for defining the information needs of an organisation to provide a firm foundation on which an appropriate system can be built. Putting it simply, entity relationship modelling identifies the most important factors in the organisation being looked at. These factors are called **entities**. Also looked at are the properties which these factors possess (called **attributes**) and how they are related to one another (called **relationships**). Entity models are logical, which means that they do not depend on the method of implementation. If two departments in an organisation perform identical tasks but in different ways their entity models would nevertheless be identical since they would be using the same entities and relationships. But their data flow diagrams could be different since their information flows may well differ.

There are two main objectives when producing an entity relationship model (ERM). The first is to provide an accurate representation of the information needs of the organisation. The second objective is to provide a model which looks at the data independently of the method of storage or subsequent access to the data.

Entity relationship modelling, although important, is only an intermediate step towards the successful implementation of a system. However, a carefully thought out system can be developed faster and will work better, so the extra time is well spent.

At the core of entity relationship modelling is the **entity relationship diagram**. Although the drawing of these diagrams has been covered in Chapter 9 we will look here at some simple examples. Before we do this, though, we will define a few key terms.

Entity

An entity is an object of the real world that is relevant to an information system, e.g. a customer, invoice, product, etc. Entities are written in a softbox (a box with rounded corners), with the name of the entity in the singular and in capital letters.

Attribute

An attribute is a single item of data which represents an individual property of the entity. For instance, the entity STUDENT could have the following attributes: student number, student address, telephone number, date of birth, tutor, course number.

An attribute can be thought of as something which adds further detail to the entity.

Activity 13.1

A college library borrowing system has been looked at and was found to have the following entities:

- MEMBER (a person who is a member of the library and eligible to borrow books);
- BOOK (a book which may be borrowed);
- LOAN (a link between a particular book and the person borrowing it);
- RESERVATION (books may be reserved by members, so that when brought back they are kept aside for another person).

The above system is only part of the whole library system.

For this activity you have to identify and list the attributes for each of the above entities. You will need some attributes which uniquely define the entities MEMBER and BOOK. Although the ISBN (International Standard Book Number) is used by bookshops to identify book titles, a library might have many copies of the same title, in which case the ISBN could not be used to distinguish each copy.

Produce your list and show it to your tutor.

Relationships

A relationship is the way in which entities in a database system are related to one another to form a complete relational database. The relationship may be one-to-one (1:1), one-to-many (1:m), or many-to-many (m:m).

Each relationship has two ends and for each end there is a name, i.e. what the relationship is, the degree (how many) and optionality (whether it is optional or mandatory).

Drawing entity relationship diagrams

Let us now look at how to construct an entity relationship diagram. In this section we will be adding more detail to the material in Chapter 9 on entity relationship models and diagrams.

Relationships are represented by lines which join the softboxes (rectangular boxes with rounded corners), as in Figure 13.1.

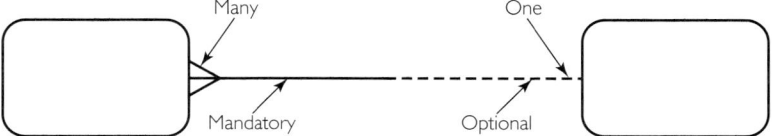

Figure 13.1

A mandatory relationship means that the relationship always holds and is represented by a solid line, whereas an optional relationship is represented by a broken line. Figure 13.1 represents a many-to-one relationship with the many side being mandatory and the one side optional. Many-to-one relationships are by far the most common type of relationship.

Common relationships

There are three kinds of relationship possible between two entities, A and B, as shown in Figures 13.2 to 13.4:

- one-to-one
- one-to-many
- many-to-many.

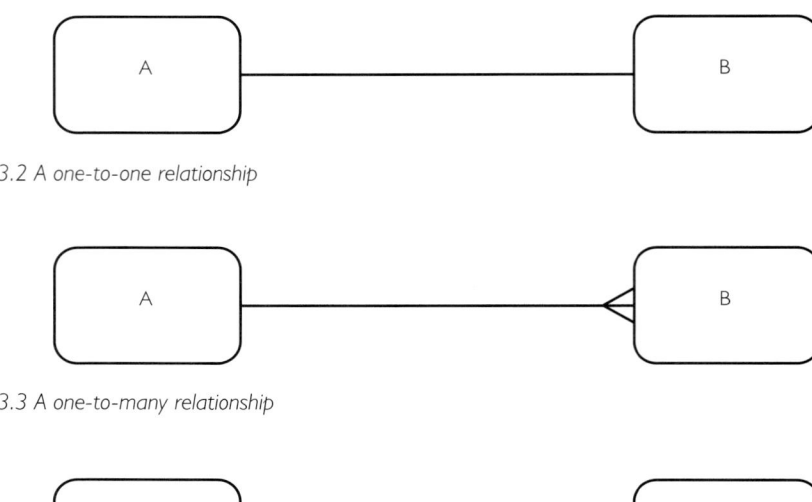

Figure 13.2 A one-to-one relationship

Figure 13.3 A one-to-many relationship

Figure 13.4 A many-to-many relationship

In practice, two of these relationships cause problems. The one-to-one relationship, when looked at more closely, will reveal that the entities A and B are really different views of the same thing. In this case, since they are not really separate entities, A and B need to be combined. Consider the relationship within a personnel system shown in Figure 13.5. The diagram shows that each employee has one address. In fact the address is better thought of as an attribute of the entity EMPLOYEE rather than a separate entity, so two entities can be combined into a single entity EMPLOYEE.

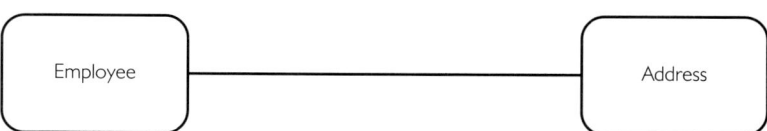

Figure 13.5 One-to-one relationship between EMPLOYEE and ADDRESS

The many-to-many relationship implies that no instance of A can occur without B and that no instance of B can occur without A. In practice it is found that this can never be so, so instead the many-to-many relationship is broken down into two one-to-many relationships.

Suppose we have two entities in an order processing system, ORDER and PRODUCT. Each product could be given a number which uniquely defines which particular product it is. For instance, 1231 could be a floppy disk and 1234 could be a copyholder. On an order for goods there will probably be several lines, with one line for each type of product. If we look at the two entities from either end you will see that one order can be for many different products and that one particular product can be in many different orders. We therefore have a many-to-many relationship between ORDER and PRODUCT, as shown in Figure 13.6.

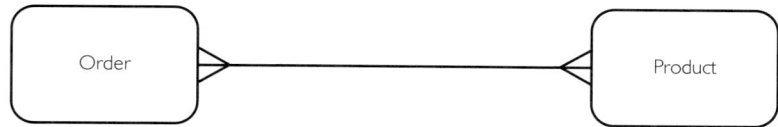

Figure 13.6 Many-to-many relationship between ORDER and PRODUCT

Many-to-many relationships are impossible to implement so we solve this problem by using a new entity called ORDER LINE. We can now see that a particular product can be in many order lines and that one order consists of many order lines (see Figure 13.7).

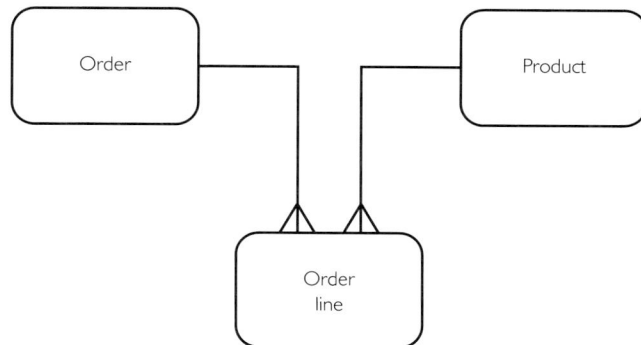

Figure 13.7 The inclusion of the new entity ORDER LINE. Notice that we now have two one-to-many relationships.

Optionality

As well as deciding on the relationship degree (one-to-many, many-to-many, etc.) we also have to decide about optionality by looking at both ends of the relationship to establish whether the relationship is mandatory (compulsory) or optional.

Suppose that we are looking at a system for booking airline tickets and the relationship between the two entities TICKET and PASSENGER. Each ticket is for one (and only one) passenger and each passenger may be shown on more than one ticket (a passenger may have two tickets, one for the forward and another for the return journey). The above situation is shown in the entity relationship diagram in Figure 13.8.

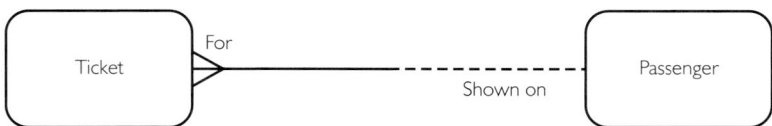

Figure 13.8

In this simple introduction to entity diagrams we will not concern ourselves with any other than the one-to-many relationships. There are several combinations of optionality to consider within one-to-many relationships.

Optional-to-mandatory
This is the most common form of relationship and implies that several Bs are related to one A and that A can exist without B (see Figure 13.9).

In Figure 13.10, we can see that a customer can exist without making an order.

415

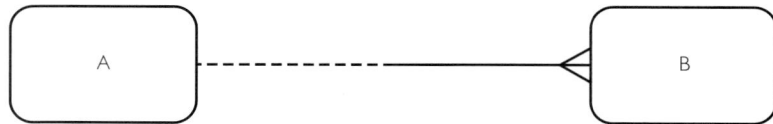

Figure 13.9 Optional-to-mandatory relationship

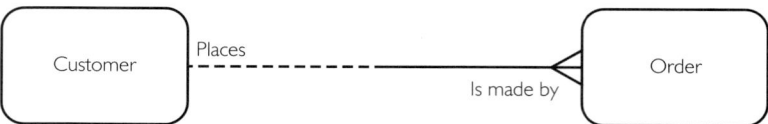

Figure 13.10

Optional-to-optional

In Figure 13.11, A and B can exist on their own without any relationship between them.

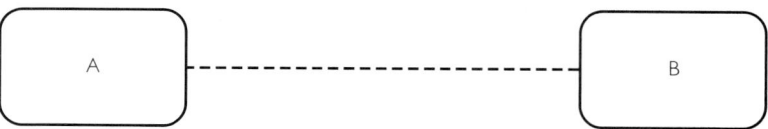

Figure 13.11 Optional-to-optional relationship

Mandatory-to-mandatory

In the mandatory-to-mandatory relationship shown in Figure 13.12 an instance of A cannot be created without one or more associated entries of B.

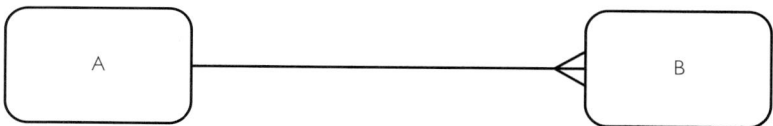

Figure 13.12 Mandatory-to-mandatory relationship

The entity relationship in Figure 13.13 shows that stock consists of many CDs and that without one or more CDs there can be no stock.

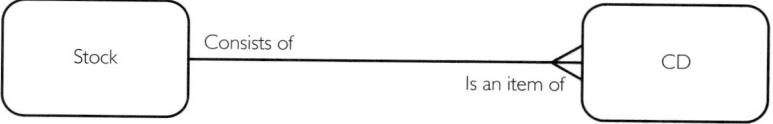

Figure 13.13

Deciding on the type of relationship

In entity modelling it is necessary to decide on the type of relationship between entities. This is best done by looking at the entity from both ends. Take the relationship between students and courses in a college. Looking at the relationship from the student end first we can see that a student could take more than one course. Looking at the relationship from the college end, we see that a single course can be taken by many students. So the relationship between COURSE and STUDENT is many-to-many.

We can describe the relationship between the entities COURSE and STUDENT using the diagram shown in Figure 13.14.

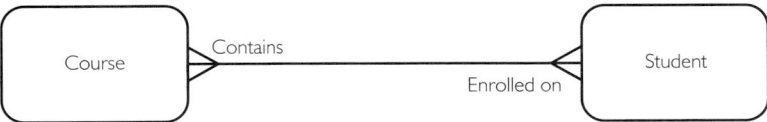

Figure 13.14

Notice that the names of the entities are always written inside their boxes in the singular form, hence STUDENT rather than STUDENTS.

As we have already seen, many-to-many relationships cannot be implemented, so in this case we need to create a new entity called ENROLMENT. If a student takes several courses, there will be an enrolment for each course and the attributes of the enrolment record will include the student number (to identify the student) and the course number (to identify the course) as the primary keys.

The entity diagram now becomes as shown in Figure 13.15.

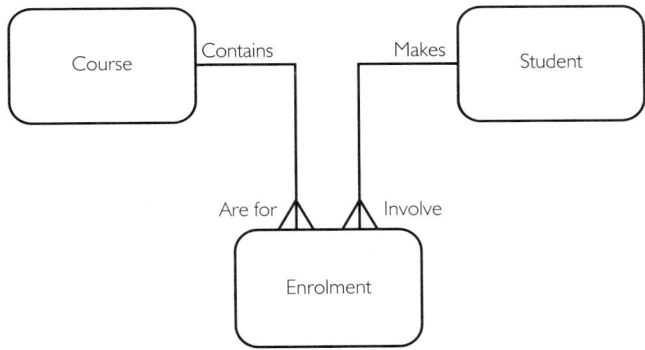

Figure 13.15

Example

An agency employs temporary staff to conduct market research for its clients. The staff are employed only on a 'per job' basis, although as one job finishes another one starts. It has asked a consultant to build a database system to store details about staff, jobs, rates and the hours that staff have worked. Initial analysis reveals the following entities:

- EMPLOYEE
- DATE
- HOUR
- JOB
- RATE.

Further investigation reveals the following:

At a given moment one employee can work on only one job with that job having only one rate. The one job can have many hours and can be done over many dates. The one rate can also be paid over many hours and worked over many dates. Finally, one employee can work many hours over many dates.

417

Figure 13.16 shows the entity relationship diagram for this situation. The situation has been simplified, so optionality is not shown in the diagram nor are the names of the relationships included.

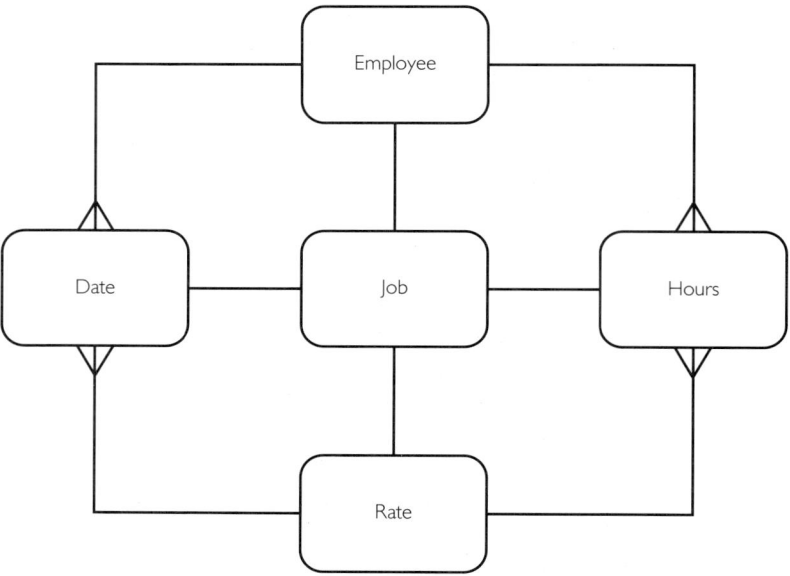

Figure 13.16

Activity 13.2

1 Look at Figure 13.16 and redraw it, but this time include suitable names on both sides of the relationships.
2 The above situation applies only to a momentary point in time. Taken over a period of time the situation is slightly different, so the entity relationship diagram will need to reflect this. Modify the diagram to take account of the following:

Over a period of time, one employee can have many jobs which have many pay rates. The many jobs will also be worked over many hours with many rates involved for those hours. The many rates will also be paid over many dates. As before, the one employee works many hours over many dates.

Relational databases

The basic component of any relational database is the table, which is a collection of information arranged in rows and columns. Relational databases can consist of many tables containing related data.

In a video library, for instance, we might assign each video a unique number and list its details (title, category and hire price) in one table. Another table could list the members, who are also each given a unique reference number along with information such as name, address and telephone number. A further table, called rentals, can be used to record which member has which video, using the appropriate customer and video numbers. The rental table would also record the date when a video is borrowed so that the library knows when it is overdue.

It might be thought that all the information can be most conveniently kept in a single table, but there are problems with this. First, only a few members may have a video at any one time, with the result that much of the part of the table devoted to video details would be blank. A second problem arises because the video library has no limits to the number of videos a particular member can borrow at once, so for each member many sections would have to be provided, although most of the time this space would not be needed. There is, in addition, one very serious problem. When a new video arrives from the supplier it must be given a unique code number and its details recorded on the database, but since members, videos and rentals are recorded in the same file, we cannot add a video without a member borrowing it. For these and similar reasons relational databases use several separate tables for information storage.

Although tables are the basic building blocks of relational databases they do include other features such as queries, reports and forms which are also stored as part of the database. These tools allow the user to view and manipulate the data in a variety of different ways.

Once the data model has been created and refined using the normalisation process (explained later in this chapter) we then have a series of entities, each with its associated attributes. We can now turn our attention to the design and structure of the relational database. When talking about database structures we now use the term 'table' in place of 'entity' and 'field name' instead of 'attribute'.

With a **relational database management system (RDBMS)** (see page 352) data from different subject areas is first placed in tables and relationships which link the tables are then constructed. Creating separate tables rather than combining all the information in a single table avoids duplication of data so saving storage space and increasing the speed of the machine when accessing data.

Database relationships

Most databases allow the user to create either a one-to-many relationship or a one-to-one relationship. These were defined earlier (see page 413).

To link tables a relationship must be created between them and this is done by having a matching field: a field which appears in both tables. To create the link the primary key field in the primary table is related to the same field in the related table. If such a field does not appear in the related table, it will need to be added.

In most databases, key fields (ones through which the tables are related) cannot be altered or deleted without first deleting the relationship between the tables. It is also necessary to make sure that the data in linked key fields is of the same type in both tables, that is, character fields should link only with character fields, etc.

Keys

A key is any attribute of an entity with which an index has been created or a relation has been set. There are three main types of key: primary, secondary and foreign.

Primary keys

The primary key is the set of mandatory columns that make the rows in the table unique. Rows in the table are normally accessed using the primary key. If, for example, a surname were chosen as the primary key, the database would not allow details to be entered for two people with the same surname. To avoid this problem it would be necessary to a create a unique reference, such as an employee number, member number or customer number. Database software allows users to create their own primary keys or instead will supply a sequential number, called the record counter, which is automatically used as the primary key.

Secondary keys

A secondary key is a key that can identify more than one record. If, for example, an employee number is the primary key then a surname could act as the secondary key. In this case the surname might not be unique since several employees may share the same surname.

Foreign keys

A foreign key is a column in one table which contains data that corresponds to a key in another table (the key can be either primary or secondary).

Consider the two tables shown below, which we will come across later when we study the development of a database for a video library. Here we have two tables with their various fields.

In the MEMBER table, Membership_number uniquely defines a row (which can also be called a record) and this is chosen as the primary key for this table. In the VIDEO RENTAL table, Video_number is the primary key because it uniquely defines a particular video being borrowed. A member can borrow more than one video, as shown with Membership_number 0001 who has borrowed two videos, 0004 and 0005. With respect to the VIDEO RENTAL table, Membership_number is a foreign key.

MEMBER table

Membership _number	Surname	Forename	Title	Street	Town	Postcode	Date_of_birth	Tel_no
0001	Bell	John	Mr	12 Queens Rd	Crosby	L23 6BB	12/12/56	924-8882
0002	Smith	Jenny	Ms	1 Firs Close	Crosby	L23 5TT	01/08/79	924-9090

VIDEO RENTAL table

Video_number	Membership_number	Date_borrowed
0004	0001	12/01/98
0001	0002	12/01/98
0003	0005	12/01/98
0005	0001	12/01/98
0002	0006	12/01/98

Refining the database using normalisation procedures

Normalisation of data

Normalisation is a mathematical technique for analysing data.

Reasons for the normalisation process

- Normalisation minimises the duplication of data. You may think that each table will need to have all its data input, so there will still be duplication of data. However, although there is some duplication, we need only type the data in once. Where the same data is needed in several tables, the computer will be able to read the data into the different tables automatically.
- The normalised data enables the data model to be mapped onto a wide variety of different database designs.
- The final tables in third normal form (see page 422) provide the flexibility to enable data to be extracted efficiently.

A simple database containing the records of students in a college would contain the data in an un-normalised form. Since each different course a student takes has a different number, this part of the student record would need to be repeated for any student enrolled on more than one course. If, for instance, a student is taking five GCSEs each one will have a different course number and course title. The un-normalised data would be as follows.

Un-normalised data
STUDENT
Student_reference
Surname
Forenames
Address
Tel_no
Course_number
Course_title
Lecturer_name
Lecturer_number

Instead of the above, a shorthand method is often used which would be written as follows:
STUDENT (<u>Student_reference</u>#, Surname, Forenames, Address, Tel_no, Course_number, Course_title, Lecturer_name, Lecturer_number)

Notice the following in the shorthand method:
- The entity is written in capital letters and in singular.
- The attributes of the entity are placed in brackets with the attribute which uniquely defines the entity (the primary key) underlined.
- The hash (#) symbol is short for a numeric attribute.
- The items in the above list are in their un-normalised form.

Going from un-normalised form (UNF) to first normal form (1NF)
The first stage of normalisation is the removal of repeating items, instead showing them grouped together by the creation of a new entity. The attribute used as the key from the original entity will still need to be included as this is used to provide the link between the two entities. So in this case we have the original key field as Student reference# and this must be included under the courses record entity ENROLMENT.

Data in first normal form
STUDENT (<u>Student_reference</u>#, Surname, Forenames, Address, Tel_no)
ENROLMENT (<u>Student_reference</u>#, <u>Course_number</u>, Course_title, Lecturer_name, Lecturer_number)

Going from first normal form (1NF) to second normal form (2NF)
To go from first normal form to second normal form the entities containing more than one key must be examined (in this case the two underlined in the ENROLMENT entity) to check if each attribute relates to only part of the key. In our example, Course title refers to part of the key attribute Course_number. When this happens the attribute is removed with its key attribute and transferred to form a new entity, which in this case is called COURSE.

Data in second normal form
STUDENT (<u>Student_reference</u>#, Surname, Forenames, Address, Tel_no)
ENROLMENT (<u>Student_reference</u>#, <u>Course_number</u>, Lecturer_name, Lecturer_number)
COURSE (<u>Course_number</u>, Course_title)

Going from second normal form (2NF) to third normal form (3NF)

To reduce the data to third normal form, entities must be examined to see if any of the data is mutually dependent. Mutually dependent items are moved to a separate entity, leaving behind one of the items in the original entity to use as the key for the newly created entity. Lecturer_number and Lecturer_name are mutually dependent because each lecturer has a number and for each lecturer number there is a corresponding name.

Data in third normal form

STUDENT (<u>Student_reference</u>#, Surname, Forenames, Address, Tel_no)
ENROLMENT (<u>Student_reference</u>#, <u>Course_number</u>, <u>Lecturer_number</u>)
COURSE (<u>Course_number</u>, Course_title)
LECTURER (<u>Lecturer_number</u>, Lecturer_name)

Notice that there are now four entities where previously there was one.

The beauty of the normalisation process is that all the entities and attributes can now be used when designing the relational database. Looking at the entities it is clear that these could be used as the names of the tables and that attributes can become the field names. This defines four tables in which to store all the data with a minimum of duplication.

Summary of the normalisation steps

1 Conversion into first normal form removes all repeating data elements.
2 Conversion into second normal form ensures that the data items are all dependent on the primary key.
3 Conversion to third normal form removes any mutual dependence between non-key attributes.

To understand the above steps it would be advisable to look back at the previous example to see how they are actually accomplished.

Example of normalisation

A book publisher decides to keep records on each of its authors using a relational database such as Microsoft Access. After conversations with users about the attributes for the entity AUTHOR the following list was obtained:

AUTHOR (this is the name of the entity, which is the name of the proposed table)
Author_number
Surname
Forename
Address
Phone_number
ISBN
Book_title
Book_category
Royalty_rate
Agent_number
Agent_name
Agent_address

A shorthand way of writing the above is as follows:

AUTHOR (<u>Author</u>#, Surname, Forename, Address, Phone_number, ISBN, Book_title, Book_category, Royalty_rate#, Agent_number#, Agent_name, Agent_address)

Notice that AUTHOR is the name of the entity and in the brackets is a list of the attributes (i.e. further information about the entity) with those attributes that are numeric having a # symbol after the name. The unique identifying attribute, the primary key, is underlined.

We now need to go through the process of normalisation. Before attempting to normalise, however, it is important to note the following:

- An author may have written more than one book (this is important when converting into first normal form).
- The ISBN is different for all book titles and is used by bookshops to identify a certain book. To convert data elements into second normal form the non-key attributes are examined to make sure that they have full functional dependency.
- When the data is in second normal form each of the entities is checked to see if there are any functional dependencies between pairs of non-key attributes. In this case the Book_category determines the Royalty_rate, for instance a paperback might have a royalty rate of 15 per cent, while hardbacks have a rate of 20 per cent and textbooks 10 per cent.

We will now work through the normalisation process.

Un-normalised form (UNF)

   AUTHOR (<u>Author</u>#, Surname, Forename, Address, Phone_number, ISBN, Book_title, Book_category, Royalty_rate#, Agent_number#, Agent_name, Agent_address)

The above is not in first normalised form because the book details (ISBN, Book_title, Book_category, Royalty_rate#, Agent_number#, Agent_name, Agent_address) are a repeating group since one author could have written more than one book.

First normal form (1NF)

Each of the books an author has written will have a different ISBN, Book_title, etc., so this is the repeating group. We need to create a new entity called PUBLICATION but still include the key of the original entity. We now obtain the following:

   AUTHOR (<u>Author</u>#, Surname, Forename, Address, Phone_number, Agent_number#, Agent_name, Agent_address)
   PUBLICATION (<u>Author</u>#, <u>ISBN</u>, Book_title, Book_category, Royalty_rate#)

Second normal form (2NF)

To move the data elements from 1NF to 2NF any entities containing more than one key need to be examined. PUBLICATION contains two keys, <u>Author</u># and <u>ISBN</u>, so all its attributes must be checked to make sure they all depend on both keys and if not that they are taken out with their key to form a new entity.

In this case we do not need to be concerned with the entity AUTHOR, since it has only one key.

The attributes Book_title, Book_category and Royalty_rate# are dependent only on the ISBN, so these need to be removed with their key and a new entity BOOK created. We now have the following:

   AUTHOR (<u>Author</u>#, Surname, Forename, Address, Phone_number, Agent_number#, Agent_name, Agent_address)
   PUBLICATION (<u>Author</u>#, <u>ISBN</u>)
   BOOK (<u>ISBN</u>, Book_title, Book_category, Royalty_rate#)

The above is now in 2NF.

Third normal form (3NF)

To go from second normal form to third normal form all the attributes are checked in case any of them are mutually dependent. Any that are mutually dependent need to be moved with their keys to a newly created entity. For instance, in the entity BOOK, the Royalty_rate# is determined by the Book_category, so we move these to a new entity called COMMISSION, leaving Book_category in the original entity and then use it as the key for the newly created attribute.

The attributes Book_category and Royalty_rate# are mutually dependent, because for a particular book type there will be a certain royalty rate. Also, in the AUTHOR entity we find that Agent_number# determines both the Agent_name and Agent_address, so these can be moved to a new entity called AGENT. All these features should have come to light during analysis.

So, in third normal form (3NF) we have:

AUTHOR (<u>Author#</u>, Surname, Forename, Address, Phone_number, Agent_number#)
PUBLICATION (<u>Author#</u>, <u>ISBN</u>)
BOOK (ISBN, Book_title, Book_category)
ROYALTY (<u>Book_type</u>, Royalty_rate#)
AGENT (<u>Agent_number#</u>, Agent_name, Agent_address)

Activity 13.3

The following data items are in un-normalised form. They need to be fully normalised (converted to 3NF) so that tables can be created which minimise data duplication across them, thereby solving many of the problems associated with data redundancy.

CUSTOMER ORDER (<u>Customer order#</u>, Customer#, Customer_name, Customer_address, Customer_tel_no, Depot#, Depot_name, Product#, Product_name, Product_quantity#, Product_price#)

Go through the process of normalisation showing the various stages (1NF, 2NF and 3NF). To help you through the processes, here are a few reminders:

- primary keys are underlined;
- # means that the attribute is numeric;
- **1NF**: a table is in 1NF if it contains no repeating groups;
- **2NF**: the table must first be in 1NF and then have non-key attributes removed which are dependent on only part of the primary key;
- **3NF**: the table must be in 2NF and in addition have no non-key attributes which depend on other non-key attributes.

Defining normalisation

Now that we know what the normalisation process entails, it is possible to define what normalisation is. Here is the definition suggested by the GNVQ syllabus:

Normalisation is the process of converting an invalid data model into a valid data model, ensuring consistency and integrity of the data model. Normalisation reduces the entity to an atomic structure (i.e. the entity cannot be broken down any further) and it removes any repeating groups of attributes.

It could be argued that the results of carrying out the process of normalisation on a set of attributes could have been arrived at equally well by a good systems analyst. However, by normalising data you ensure that the solution is one that can be implemented successfully.

Activity 13.4

A data model is to be constructed for a new in-patient system in a hospital. Each ward in the hospital has its own name and a unique reference number. The number of beds in each ward is also recorded, along with its name and reference number. Each ward has a complement of nurses who are given unique staff numbers which are recorded along with their names. Each nurse works only in one of the wards.

In-patients are given a patient number when they arrive and this is recorded with each patient's name, address, telephone number and date of birth. When admitted to one of the wards, each patient is assigned to one consultant who is responsible for the medical care of his or her patients. Consultants have their own unique staff numbers recorded with their names and specialisms.

1 Draw an entity relationship diagram for this system.
2 Write down the names of all the attributes and put them in one entity, called PATIENT.
3 Go through all the stages of normalisation from the un-normalised form to third normal form. You should show the names of the entities and their corresponding attributes in each form and also explain what you are doing at each stage.

Building a relational database

A considerable amount of analysis is needed to build a relational database successfully, and only when this has been done will the developer know what fields are required within the tables. When devising the fields, the developer needs to ask 'what output is needed from the database?' Remember that nothing can be output which has not been input, or cannot be obtained from the input. The following steps should then be taken:

- List all the fields likely to be used. Do not include any fields that are unlikely to be used.
- Try to put the fields into some sort of order, grouping those that go together logically.
- Normalise the data, converting it from the un-normalised form to 3NF. The normalisation process ensures that data is in a form that can be successfully and efficiently implemented, and places data in groups that can be used as tables in a relational database.
- Determine the relationships between the tables and create them using the database software.
- Refine your design. It is quite hard to get everything right first time, so you may have to make changes to the structure as you go along. Do not worry about this too much as most databases are flexible and it is easy to make changes to the structure even once data has been entered in tables.

Relational database structures

All relational database management systems (DBMSs) have a framework (or structure) which has to be created before it is possible to enter data. The basic structures are as follows:

- tables (records, fields)
- indexes
- relationships (see page 419)
- keys – primary, secondary and foreign (see page 419).

Tables

Entity types in a relationship model are represented by a table of values, where the columns represent attributes of the entity and each row of the table corresponds to an entity occurrence. The table below is used to hold details about members of a video library.

MEMBER table

Membership _number	Surname	Forename	Title	Street	Town	Postcode	Date_of_birth	Tel_no
0001	Bell	John	Mr	12 Queens Rd	Crosby	L23 6BB	12/12/56	924-8882
0002	Smith	Jenny	Ms	1 Firs Close	Crosby	L23 5TT	01/08/79	924-9090
0003	Cannon	Paul	Mr	12 Bells Rake	Crosby	L23 5FD	09/03/65	924-0098
0004	Charles	Steve	Mr	8 Moor Grove	Crosby	L23 7YY	02/07/69	924-1121
0005	James	Karen	Miss	3 Meols Rd	Crosby	L23 4RR	01/09/45	924-8111
0006	Brady	June	Mrs	9 Fox Close	Crosby	L23 5EE	20/01/59	924-0232

The columns represent attributes of the entity MEMBER. When we come to implement the database the entity name MEMBER can be used as the table name and the attributes (the column headings) used as field names. Each table needs to have a primary key which uniquely defines each row or record in the table and in this case it will be Membership_number.

We have already seen how easy it is to convert the fully normalised data model into a table structure, using entities and attributes for table names and field names. Within a relational database, the data is held in tables consisting of columns which represent the fields of information, and rows which represent the individual records. Each record consists of a number of fields which are determined by the columns in the table.

Relationships between tables can be established and this enables data from more than one table to be combined for queries, forms and reports. In many cases a relationship involves tables where the primary key in one table matches a field called a foreign key in another.

Indexes

Suppose you want to find a particular topic in a book. One way to do so would be to look through the whole book until you find what you want. It would be faster, however, to use the index at the back of the book, and it is for exactly the same reason that we construct and use an index within a database.

Data is usually put into the various tables in chronological order, i.e. it is arranged according to time or date. This makes it harder for the database to locate the record since the date need not be unique, like the primary key field. There is, however, a way round this. If the rows in the table are not in the primary key order, the database will automatically create an index which can be used to locate them quickly in primary key order. An index is always created on the primary key but other fields can also be indexed. The database software can process queries and searches much faster if a field has been indexed.

Any field can be indexed provided that it is of one of the following types: text, numeric, currency or date. However, the temptation to index all fields should be resisted because any subsequent editing or adding of records will be slowed down. This is because an index table is created at the same time as the original table, so in any subsequent operations two tables are being manipulated. For this reason indexes should be created only on fields which are used repeatedly for searching, sorting, etc.

Let us now have a look at how an index works. Suppose we have a personnel file with the first two columns containing the record number and surname, as shown below.

Record number	Data
1	Pearson
2	Jones
3	Edwards
4	Jackson
5	Adams

Suppose we want to create an index according to surname so that we can print out the employee details in surname alphabetical order. A new table is created with a new record number and the index referring back to the original record number. Adams comes first, so the record number in the index table is 1 and the index refers to 5, which is the record number in the original table. This process is repeated until all the fields on which the index has been created have been dealt with. The final index table is shown below.

Record number	Index
1	5
2	3
3	4
4	2
5	1

Example of building a database

A video library operates in a similar way to any other library, with members, videos and rental details to record. There are many more things we might want from such a system but for now let us narrow the scope and just look at a system for recording members, videos and borrowings.

The first thing is to write down a list of attributes for the whole system. It is tempting to immediately put the attributes into separate tables, but although in this case it is fairly obvious which tables are required it is not always so simple, so first we write down all the attributes. In choosing attributes, again it is tempting to include every attribute that could possibly be needed, but this should be resisted: we only specify those that are definitely needed. If the database develops, it is better to add other attributes as they are needed.

For the video library system we could have the following attributes:
MEMBER (<u>Membership number#</u>, Surname, Forename, Title, Street, Town, Postcode, Date_of_birth, Tel_no, Video_number#, Video_title, Category, Cost_price#, Rental_price#, Date_borrowed)

Looking at the above, we have placed all the attributes in an entity called MEMBER. We must now go through the normalisation process to determine how many tables to use and what attributes should go into each table.

The video details are repeating attributes and therefore need to be removed into their own entity to give the data in the 1NF, thus:

1NF

MEMBER (<u>Membership_number#</u>, Surname, Forename, Title, Street, Town, Postcode, Date_of_birth, Tel_no)

VIDEO RENTAL (<u>Membership number#</u>, Video_number#, Video_title, Category, Cost_price#, Rental_price#, Date_borrowed)

We now look at the VIDEO RENTAL entity with the two keys and check to see if the attributes depend on both of the keys. Video_number, Video_title, Category, Cost_price and Rental_price only depend on the Video_number and therefore need to be placed in a new entity which we will call VIDEO. This converts the data to 2NF.

2NF and 3NF

MEMBER (<u>Membership_number#</u>, Surname, Forename, Title, Street, Town, Postcode, Date_of_birth, Tel_no)

VIDEO RENTAL (<u>Membership_number#</u>, <u>Video number#</u>, Date_borrowed)

VIDEO (<u>Video number#</u>, Video_title, Category, Cost_price#, Rental_price#)

To convert the data to 3NF we look to see if any of the non-key attributes are dependent on other non-key attributes. In this case no change is needed and so the 2NF becomes the 3NF and the data is now fully normalised in the form shown above.

We now have three tables: MEMBER, VIDEO RENTAL and VIDEO, and we can use the attribute names as the field names in the tables.

MEMBER (<u>Membership_number#</u>, Surname, Forename, Title, Street, Town, Postcode, Date_of_birth, Tel_no)

VIDEO RENTAL (<u>Membership_number#</u>, <u>Video number#</u>, Date_borrowed)

VIDEO (<u>Video number#</u>, Video_title, Category, Cost_price#, Rental_price#)

The following tables are set up; the MEMBER table is the same as that on page 426. Notice the columns contain the attributes or field names, and the rows represent a particular record in each table.

MEMBER table

Membership_number	Surname	Forename	Title	Street	Town	Postcode	Date_of_birth	Tel_no
0001	Bell	John	Mr	12 Queens Rd	Crosby	L23 6BB	12/12/56	924-8882
0002	Smith	Jenny	Ms	1 Firs Close	Crosby	L23 5TT	01/08/79	924-9090
0003	Cannon	Paul	Mr	12 Bells Rake	Crosby	L23 5FD	09/03/65	924-0098
0004	Charles	Steve	Mr	8 Moor Grove	Crosby	L23 7YY	02/07/69	924-1121
0005	James	Karen	Miss	3 Meols Rd	Crosby	L23 4RR	01/09/45	924-8111
0006	Brady	June	Mrs	9 Fox Close	Crosby	L23 5EE	20/01/59	924-0232

VIDEO RENTAL table

Video_number	Membership_number	Date_borrowed
0004	0001	12/01/98
0001	0002	12/01/98
0003	0005	12/01/98
0005	0001	12/01/98
0002	0006	12/01/98

VIDEO table

Video_number	Video_title	Category	Cost_price	Rental_price
0001	Independence Day	12	13.99	1.00
0002	Eraser	PG	13.99	1.00
0003	Bambi	U	13.99	1.00
0004	Evita	U	35.00	1.50
0005	Brave Heart	U	13.99	1.00

The relationships between the tables must now be devised. Let us look first at the relationship between the MEMBER and VIDEO RENTAL tables. They both contain the <u>Membership number</u> field and this is used to provide a link between the tables. Although <u>Membership number</u> is the primary key in the MEMBER table it is a foreign key in the VIDEO RENTAL table. The field <u>Video number</u> is the primary key in the VIDEO RENTAL table.

We now need to assess the relationship between the MEMBER and VIDEO RENTAL tables. Since one member can borrow more than one video at a time, one row in the MEMBER table could correspond to several rows in the VIDEO RENTAL table. This situation arises with member number 0001 who has two records in the VIDEO RENTAL table. The relationship between members and videos is clearly a one-to-many relationship.

Let us now consider the relationship between the VIDEO table and the VIDEO RENTAL table. Since each video has a unique Video_number, it can appear only once in the VIDEO table and once in the VIDEO RENTAL table so it follows that the relationship between these tables is one-to-one.

Tables can be created once the tables have been named, fields devised and primary keys identified. After the tables have been created using the database software it is next necessary to establish the relationships between tables. In Microsoft Access (which is part of the Microsoft Office Professional suite) we place on screen those tables being used, then form relationships by drawing lines between fields we wish to connect in the tables. In our video rental system, a one-to-many relationship line would be drawn between the MEMBER table and the VIDEO RENTAL table because one member can borrow more than one video. The relationship between the VIDEO and VIDEO RENTAL tables would appear as a one-to-one line.

Figure 13.17 shows the screen used in Microsoft Access to establish the relationships between tables.

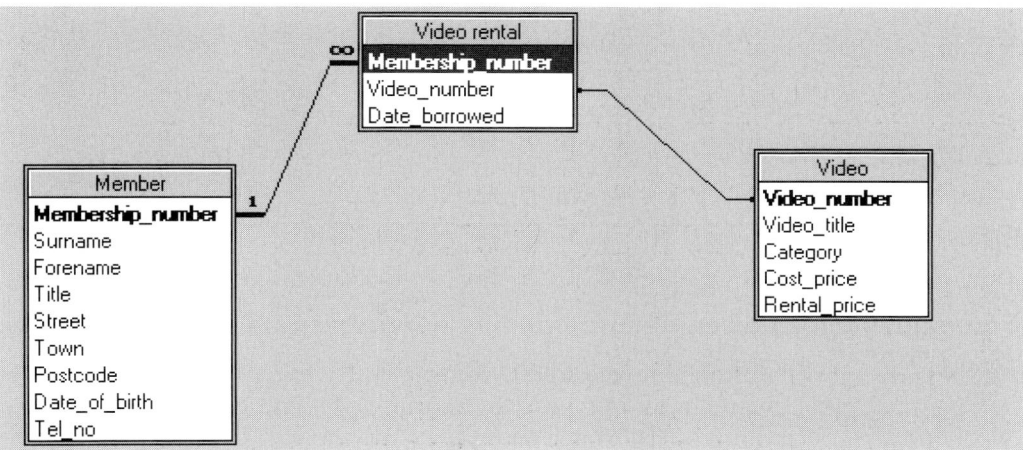

Figure 13.17

Data dictionary

To describe the properties of the fields used in a database, a data dictionary can be used. The data dictionary holds data *about* data and can be made to appear as a table either on paper or on the computer screen.

A data dictionary is a file containing descriptions of all the data items in a database. The descriptions might include:

- data type
- element size
- validation range of values
- entity descriptions
- attribute–entity relationships
- purpose.

When setting up the database structure, various features of the fields have to be defined, such as type (numeric, character, logical, etc.) and this is used to help create the data dictionary.

Here is a part of the data dictionary for a temporary survey staff database. We will look at data dictionaries again in Chapter 14.

Attribute	Description	Format	Length	Key	Validation
PAYROLL NO.	A unique number given to an employee e.g. 356991	Number	Double	Primary	N
FIRST NAME	The first name of the person to be employed	Text	30		N
LAST NAME	Family name of the person to be employed	Text	50		N
STREET	Street or house name of the person to be employed	Text	50		N
POSTCODE	Postcode of the person to be employed e.g. L15 5TR	Text	7		Input mask

Some advice for designing and building a database

- Before listing the fields, think about what you want to get out of the database: remember that you cannot output something that has not been input to the system or derived from such an input.

- When choosing fields, consider how the data in each field will eventually be used. You may, for example, think of having a field for addresses. It is, however, much better to break this into smaller elements, such as street, town and postcode, as the data is more flexible arranged in this way. Having the address stored as one line means it will be printed out this way, which is not the usual format for the top of a letter or an envelope. Include forename, surname and title in preference to just 'name'. You should try, if possible, to break down larger chunks of data into several fields.

- Any calculations that need to be performed on the data (such as adding VAT or totalling an invoice) should not be put in a table; they should be added at the report stage.

- Make sure that any field you choose as the primary key is unique. It is usually best that a number rather than text field is used and that this number is not too large. You should consider using the record counter as a primary key for some tables. In tables where records are not uniquely defined by one field, you need to incorporate more than one field as a primary key.

Assignment A13.1

This assignment develops knowledge and understanding of the following element:
7.1 Create relational database structures for a given specification

It supports the development of the following key skills:
Communication 3.2 and 3.3
Information technology 3.1, 3.2 and 3.3

This assignment builds on the system specification developed in Chapter 10. You will implement the system already suggested in your assignment submitted at the end of that chapter.

The purpose of this assignment is to prepare the relational database structures ready for implementation, which is covered by the assignments in Chapter 14.

You have to produce:

- a data model diagram which meets the specification developed as the assignment in Chapter 10;

- a list of the un-normalised attributes followed by their conversion into first, second and third normal form, along with an explanation of how each of the normalisation stages has been achieved;

- an outline of relational database structures which suit the data model.

Sample unit test

Questions 1 and 2 refer to Figure 13.18.

1 Which one of the following is represented by the boxes in the diagram?
   a entities
   b data elements
   c relationships
   d primary keys   *(RSA, December 1995)*

2 Which one of the following is represented by the lines joining the boxes in the diagram?
   a entities
   b data elements
   c relationships
   d primary keys   *(RSA, December 1995)*

Figure 13.18 An entity relationship diagram

Questions 3–5 refer to Figure 13.19.

3 A surgery has three resident doctors. Appointments are booked at ten-minute intervals for patients to see their own doctors. Which one of the following describes the relationship between appointment and doctors?
   a many-to-many
   b many-to-one
   c one-to-many
   d one-to-one   *(RSA, December 1995)*

4 Patients are always seen by their own doctor. Which one of the following describes the relationship between doctors and patients?
   a many-to-many
   b many-to-one
   c one-to-many
   d one-to-one   *(RSA, December 1995)*

5 Records are kept of each patient's medical history. This includes notes made during an appointment, results of tests, treatment given and so on. Which one of

the following describes the relationship between medical history notes and patients?

a many-to-many

b many-to-one

c one-to-many

d one-to-one

(RSA, December 1995)

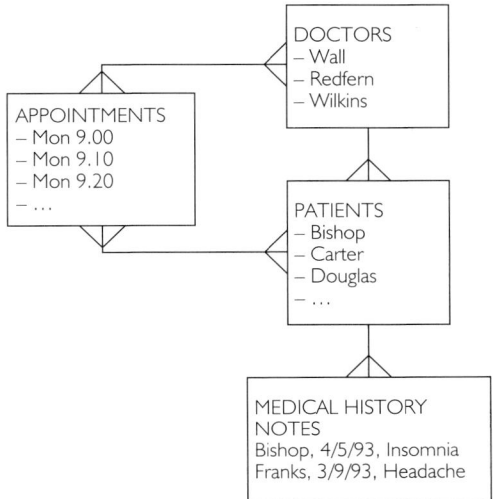

Figure 13.19 A medical records and appointments system

Questions 6 and 7 refer to Figure 13.20.

6 The information in Column 2 specifies for each data item:

   a element size

   b entity description

   c validation requirements

   d data type

(RSA, December 1995)

7 The information in Column 4 specifies for each data item:

   a element size

   b entity description

   c validation requirements

   d data type

(RSA, December 1995)

Extract from data dictionary

Column 1	Column 2	Column 3	Column 4
Patient date of birth	date	DD/MM/YY	UK date format
Patient surname	text	40	alpha only
Doctor's surname	text	40	alpha only
Appointment date	date	DD/MM/YY	UK date format
Appointment time	numeric	HH/MM	HH = 09–11 or 14–17
			MM = 00, 10, 20, 30, 40, 50
....	....	....	
....	....	....	....

Figure 13.20

Questions 8 and 9 refer to Figure 13.21.

8 In the new database, primary key dependence has been achieved. Which one of the following data items would be used as the primary key?

a employee name

b employee number

c date of birth

d NI number *(RSA, December 1995)*

9 In the planned database the employee name appears only once (in Table 1), but in the original system the employee name appeared in each of the three files. This is because:

a during normalisation repeating data elements are removed

b the data entry clerk might make an error typing in the name

c each employee is known by their employee number only

d the employee name takes up more space on the disk *(RSA, December 1995)*

Extract from data dictionary
Three separate files of records of employees are kept by three departments

File 1 – Personnel	File 2 – Training	File 3 – Salaries
employee name	employee name	employee name
employee number	employee number	employee number
date of birth	qualification/skills	NI number
		rate of pay

A relational database is being planned to meet the needs of all the three departments and the following tables are suggested

Table 1	Table 2	Table 3
employee number	employee number	employee number
employee name	qualification/skills	NI number
date of birth		rate of pay

Figure 13.21

Questions 10 and 11 refer to Figure 13.22.

10 The invoice data '118909, 27/08/95, £37.50' shown shaded is called:

a a record

b a field

c an index

d an attribute *(RSA, December 1995)*

11 The customer data 'Aye Company Ltd ... Gee Graphics' shown shaded is called:

a a record

b a field

c an index

d an attribute *(RSA, December 1995)*

The following is an extract from a relational database

INVOICES

Invoice Number	Invoice Date	Customer Number	Invoice Amount
1118907	26/08/95	500025	£400.50
1118908	26/08/95	109028	£92.75
1118909	27/08/95	501441	£37.50
1118910	27/08/95	231230	£1098.00
....	....	....	....
....	....	....	....

CUSTOMERS

Customer Number	Customer Name	Address
109028	Aye Company Ltd	....
....		
....		
231230	Bee plc	....
....		
....		
500025	Dee Enterprises	....
....		
501441	Gee Graphics	....

Figure 13.22

Questions 12 and 13 refer to Figure 13.23.

12 'Invoice Amount' shown shaded is called:

    a a record
    b a field
    c an index
    d an attribute   *(RSA, December 1995)*

13 The data '231230' shown shaded in both tables is called:

    a a record
    b a field
    c an index
    d an attribute   *(RSA, December 1995)*

Questions 14 and 15 are based on Figure 13.24.

14 In Figure 13.24 'Engineer' is an example of:

    a a key
    b an entity
    c a record
    d an attribute   *(RSA, June 1996)*

The following is an extract from a relational database

INVOICES

Invoice Number	Invoice Date	Customer Number	Invoice Amount
1118907	26/08/95	500025	£400.50
1118908	26/08/95	109028	£92.75
1118909	26/08/95	501441	£37.50
1118910	26/08/95	231230	£1098.00
....	....	....	....
....	....	....	....

CUSTOMERS

Customer Number	Customer Name	Address
109028	Aye Company Ltd	....
....		
....		
231230	Bee plc	....
....		
....		
500025	Dee Enterprises	....
....		
501441	Gee Graphics	....

Figure 13.23

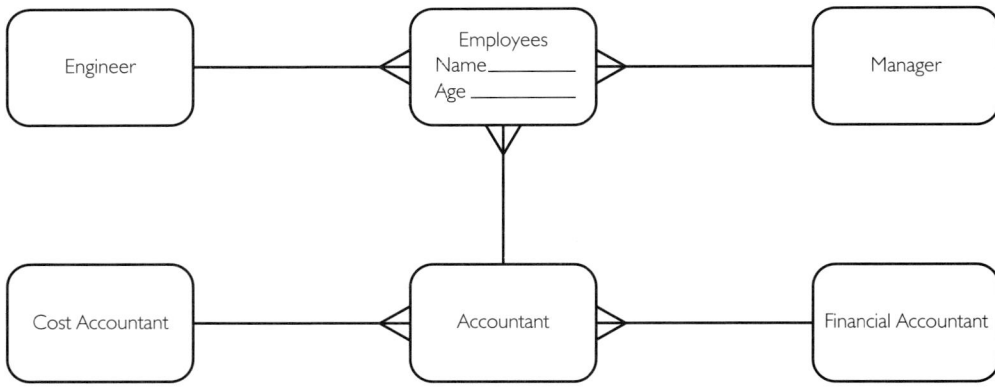

Figure 13.24

15 In Figure 13.24 'Age' is an example of:
  a a key
  b an entity
  c a record
  d an attribute

(RSA, June 1996)

Questions 16 to 18 are based on Figure 13.25.

16 The bank has a number of employees and a number of branches. Which one of the following describes the relationship between employees and branches?

   a many-to-many

   b many-to-one

   c one-to-many

   d one-to-one   *(RSA, June 1996)*

17 Each employee has a new clock card each week. Which one of the following describes the relationship between employees and clock cards?

   a many-to-many

   b many-to-one

   c one-to-many

   d one-to-one   *(RSA, June 1996)*

18 Which one of the following describes the relationship between clock cards and bank branch?

   a many-to-many

   b many-to-one

   c one-to-many

   d one-to-one   *(RSA, June 1996)*

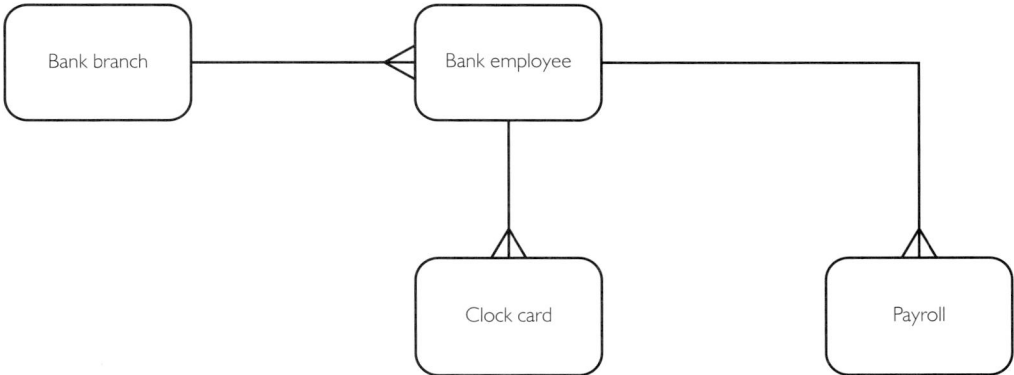

Figure 13.25

Questions 19 and 20 are based on Figure 13.26.

19 The information in Column 2 specifies for each data item:

   a a data type

   b a data diagram

   c a data element

   d a data attribute   *(RSA, June 1996)*

20 The information shaded on the line beginning 'Patient code' can be described as:

   a a data type

   b a data entity

   c a data element

   d a data attribute   *(RSA, June 1996)*

Column 1	Column 2	Column 3	Column 4
Patient code	Numeric	999999	≥ 100000
Last name	Text	X(25)	
Initials	Text	X(5)	
Date entered	Date	DD/MM/YY	UK date format
Ward number	Alphanumeric	A99	A–D 1–14

*Figure 13.26
Extract from a
data dictionary
from a hospital
patients system*

21 In the extract from an entity type ORDER (Figure 13.27), which one of the
following best describes 'Product Name'?
a entity relationship
b repeating data element
c record
d primary key

(RSA, June 1996)

ORDER

Product Code	Product Name	Quantity Ordered
1396	Cup	56
1478	Badge	23
1396	Cup	78
1578	Flag	15

*Figure 13.27
Extract from a
stock system*

22 In the extracts from the entity types PRICE and STOCK LEVEL (Figure 13.28),
which one of the following best describes 'Product Code' for the entity PRICE?
a entity relationship
b repeating data element
c record
d primary key

(RSA, June 1996)

PRICE

Product Code	Product Name	Price
1396	Cup	1.25
1478	Badge	1.65
1396	Flag	3.95

STOCK LEVEL

Product Code	Bin Location	Qty in Stock
1396	L	826
1396	M	14
1478	U	19
1578	M	416

*Figure 13.28
Extracts from a
stock system*

14 Input and retrieval of data from a database

What is covered in this chapter

In this chapter we move away from the theory towards the practical side of databases. Since it is difficult to discuss databases without referring to a particular package, Microsoft Access has been chosen to illustrate this chapter and all the examples, screenshots, etc. are from this package. Microsoft Access was chosen for its widespread use (it is the most popular database package for PCs) and availability.

Element 7.2: Create data input forms for a database

- Creating input forms for data entry
- Modifying form fields to enable accurate input of data
- Ensuring data entry fields comply with the data dictionary
- Creating and using special fields

Element 7.3: Create database reports

- Database reports
- Designing database report layouts
- Specification of a report

Resources you will need for your portfolio for Elements 7.2 and 7.3
- Your written answers to the activities and assignments in this chapter.

Creating input forms for data entry

Figure 14.1 shows the screen when an existing database is opened. From this window all the main functions of the RDBMS (relational database management system) can be accessed. In this case the 'table' option is selected; there are three tables already stored and we are given the option of creating another, opening the existing tables or altering the design of one of the existing tables.

Creating tables

Relational databases store all data in tables, so once the contents of each table (i.e. the filenames) are decided, we can design the tables using the database software. We have first to plan out the structure of each table and save each table structure separately.

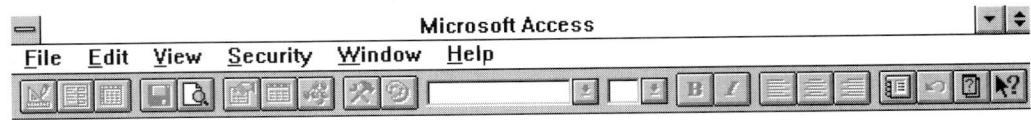

Figure 14.1 Opening an existing database

Starting with entities and their fully normalised attributes we can refer to entities as table names, and instead of attributes, talk of filenames.

Activity 14.1

Find out how to load your database software and produce a brief user guide, making use of screendumps. Screendumps can be produced using the following procedure:
- If you are using Access (or any other Windows-based database), you can press Alt + PrintScrn and the screen design will be pasted into the clipboard.
- Exit the database package and load your wordprocessing software.
- Open a new document and select 'paste' from the EDIT menu (if you are using Microsoft Word) and the screen will be placed into your document.

Next, the structure of the tables used to hold the data is created; this is done in Microsoft Access using the table definition window shown in Figure 14.2.

Using this window, table structures are created for all the tables in the database. As you can see from Figure 14.2, the window is divided into two parts. The upper part is used to define the field name and the type of data allowed in that field, and to give a brief description (with examples) of the data that the field can hold. The bottom part of the screen is used to define the field properties for each field in turn and ensure that only allowable data is entered. Only the default values are shown and these need to be changed depending on the type of data to be entered.

Choosing field names

Field names should always be descriptive to identify the field. Try to avoid using spaces in fields; instead use dashes or a combination of upper- and lower-case letters. In Access, the maximum size of a field name is 64 characters.

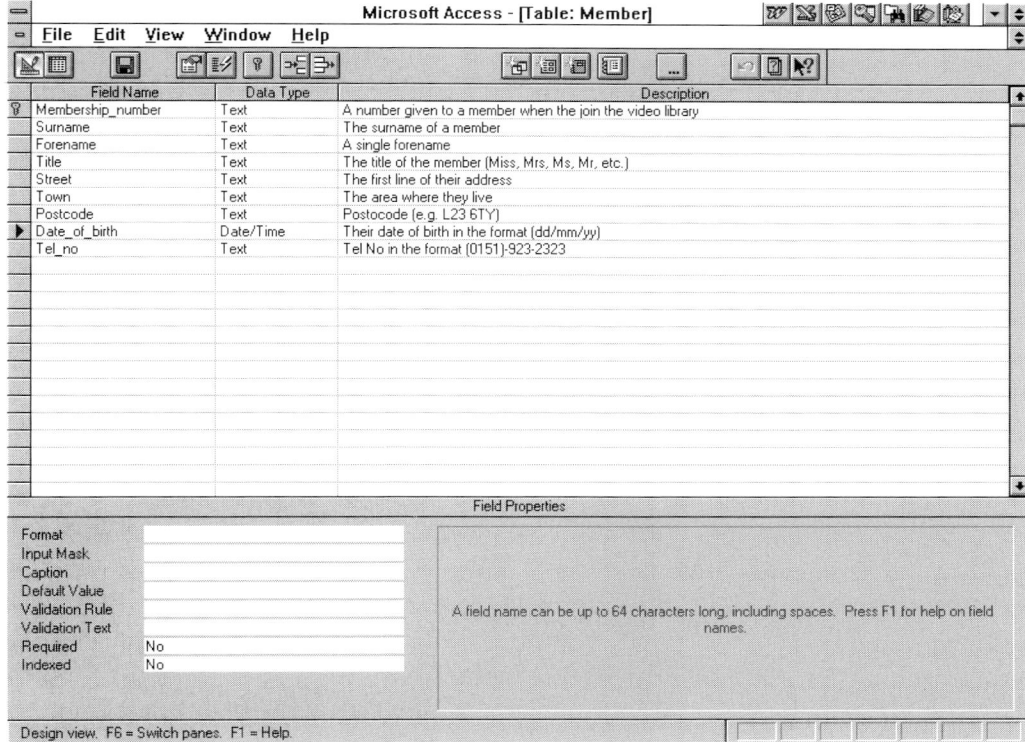

Figure 14.2 The table definition window in Microsoft Access

Choosing data types

Once a field has been named, the type of data that can be entered has to be specified. In most databases, the data can be of the following types:

- text (alphanumeric characters);
- memo (used for data in note form; a window will usually open where messages which do not conform to any particular format can be typed in);
- number (for numeric values such as integers, real numbers, etc.);
- date/time;
- currency (monetary values to two decimal places);
- counter (a numeric integer value which the computer automatically increments for each record added);
- yes/no (Boolean values);
- OLE (OLE objects, graphics and other binary data).

Figure 14.3 shows the data type being selected from the pull-down menu for the field Membership_number. Data type 'counter' has been chosen because the database designer wants each member to be given a sequential membership number when they join the video library. Notice also that a brief description of the field name is given.

Important note

There are many situations in which we use a number that is not numeric. A proper number, i.e. one that is numeric, contains no spaces, no leading zeros, no letters or non-numeric characters, and can have calculations performed on it. The simple test is to ask yourself 'am I likely to perform a calculation using the field?' If the answer is 'yes', you need to store it as a proper number, if 'no', it is best stored as text.

441

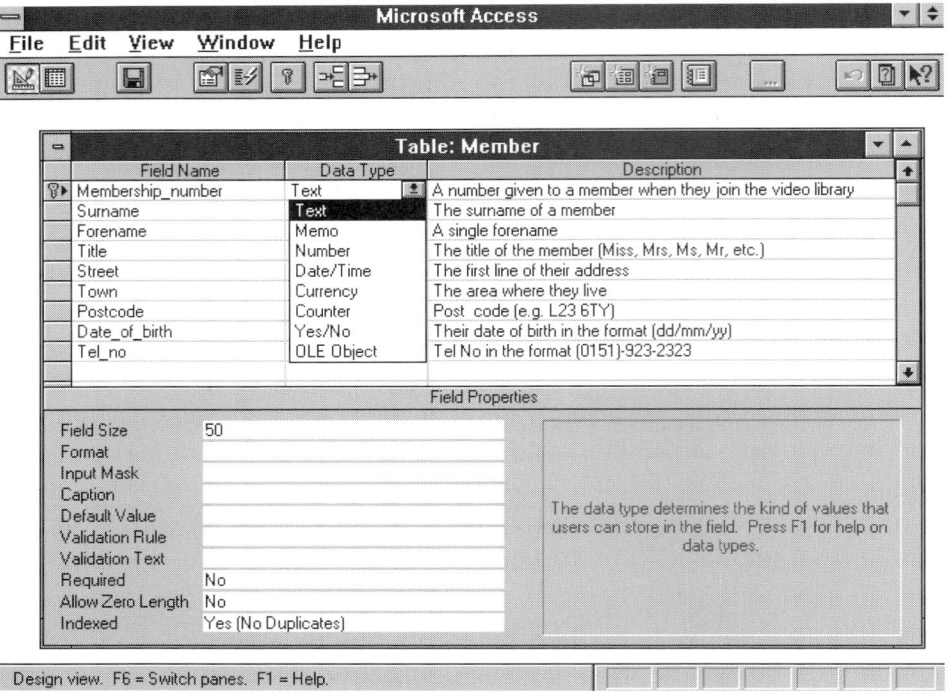

Figure 14.3 *Selecting the data type*

Activity 14.2

Here are some items of data which are to be stored in tables in a database. Your task is to identify whether they should be stored as text or numbers. Examples of the data to be entered are shown in brackets.

- the number of units in stock (234)
- an invoice number (0001 to 9999)
- a telephone number (0161 876 2302)
- a tax code (488H)
- an employee number (00234442)
- the rate of VAT (17.5%)
- the rate of pay (£10 per hour)
- a National Insurance number (TT232965A)

Description of fields

When you are designing the structure of the fields in Access, there is a section where a description of the field can be added to give more information about the field name. For instance, you might have a field called 'street' with the description 'this is the first line of the address'. Adding field descriptions in this way makes the tables you create easier to understand.

Choosing the field size

Some fields such as date and currency have their field sizes preset, but others (such as numeric and text fields) need to have their field sizes specified unless the default value is to be used.

When you are choosing the field size for text, the number of characters likely to be required should be considered. If the field size is not set, a default value is entered, which for Microsoft Access is 50. If a field size is chosen which is too small, you can modify the structure of the table once data has been entered. Any data entered will remain intact when the structure is changed provided that a field is not reduced in size so as to 'chop off' any data already entered.

Some fields must always contain a fixed number of characters and in this case the field size should be set to this value. This ensures that only a certain maximum number of characters can be entered, thus providing a form of validation.

Numeric field sizes determine the range of values which can be stored in a numeric field; whether or not the value should contain decimal points can also be specified. In Microsoft Access, the following field size settings are possible:

Field size setting	Range of numbers	Number of decimal places	Size of storage needed
Byte	0 to 255	None	1 byte
Integer	−32 768 to 32 767	None	2 bytes
Long integer	−2 147 483 648 to 2 147 483 647	None	4 bytes
Single	-3.4×10^{38} to 3.4×10^{38}	7	4 bytes
Double	-1.797×10^{308} to 1.797×10^{308}	15	8 bytes

Data types and validation checks

When data is being entered into a field, either in a table or a form, before you can move on to the next field the computer checks to make sure that the data entered is allowable. If it is not, the computer will alert you to this with a message which you can specify in the validation text.

There are various reasons why data might not be allowed:

- Data may be of the wrong type for the particular field. For instance, a field that is to hold telephone numbers may have been set up as a numeric field. If a user then tries to enter the telephone number 0151-929-6758, which is not numeric (it contains a leading zero and dashes), it will be refused. If this happens the type of field will have to be altered; telephone numbers should be stored as text.
- The data may break a rule for the field set up in the field properties section.
- The field properties section may or may not demand that a particular field be filled. For instance, a telephone number field can be left blank if the person does not have a phone, but an employee number field in a personnel system should require the employee number to be entered. An error will be reported if a field that always requires data to be entered is inadvertently left blank.
- The user may have tried to enter the same data more than once into a field set as a primary key. Since the primary key must be unique, the same data is not allowed twice in such a field.

Figure 14.4 shows the structure for a table called MEMBER in the video library database. In the main body (the top half of the screen) the field names, data types and descriptions of the data are input.

Notice the small key at the side of the Membership_number field, which indicates that this field is set as a primary key. The data type for the field is set as a counter which is automatically numbered sequentially by the computer. Note also that the description provides some brief explanation of the field.

443

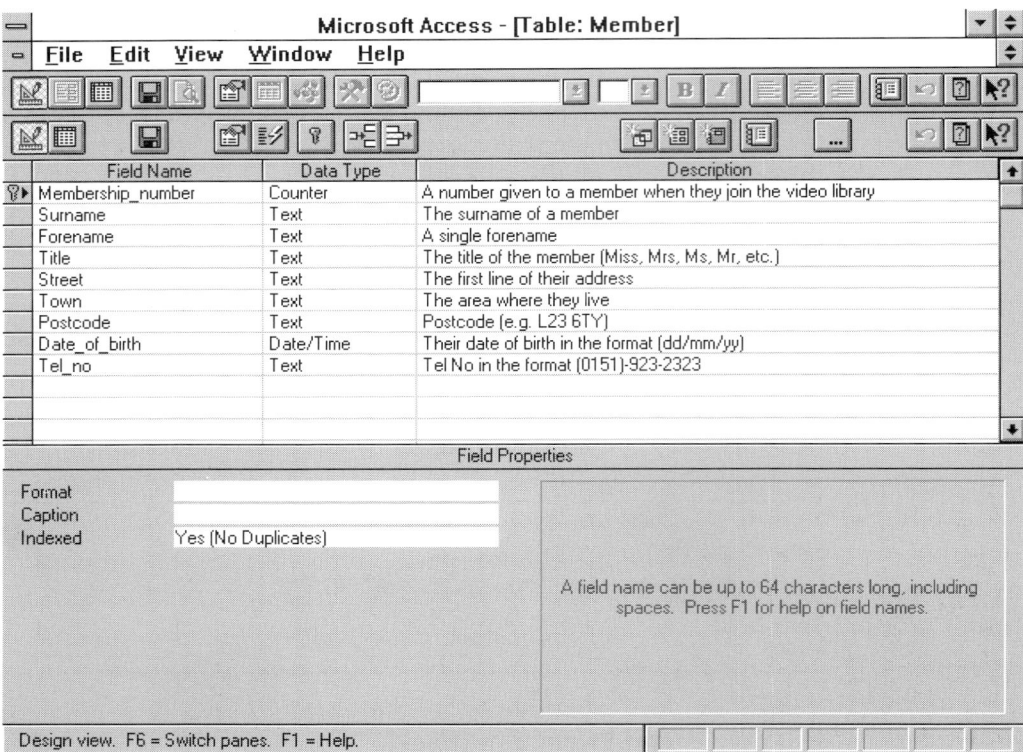

*Figure 14.4 The
completed
structure for the
MEMBER table*

You will already have created a data dictionary, but in setting up the database you may find you need to go back to the structure to make changes. If you do, make sure that the structure screen is the same as your data dictionary; if it is not the dictionary will need altering.

As well as limiting the type of data that can be entered into a particular field, other validation checks can be performed on the data by making use of **validation rules**. Validation rules are specified as validation expressions. For instance, the following validation expressions could be employed, which will produce the text if the rule is not obeyed (these expressions can be used only with Microsoft Access).

Validation expression	Validation text (appears if the data being entered is not allowable)
>100 And < 200	The value entered must be between 100 and 200 but not including 100 or 200
>=100 And <=200	The value entered must be between 100 and 200 including 100 and 200
>0	The value entered must be positive
<>0	A non-zero value must be entered
<#12/1/98#	The date entered must be before 12/1/98
Like "A????"	The data entered must be 5 characters long beginning with the letter A
='2.5' Or '5.0'	Value must be 2.5 or 5.0
>=#1/1/97# And <=#31/12/97#	The date entered must be in the year 1997

Screen input forms

Screen input forms are effectively electronic forms which enable data to be entered directly into a computer via the keyboard. They are similar to paper forms, with boxes

444

to be filled in by the user. The screen design will usually incorporate a title for the form and have prompts (usually the field names) for the data which the user has to add. Many database packages allow the user to enter data directly into tables, but it is usually better to create special forms to allow records to be entered one at a time.

Figure 14.5 shows data being entered into a table via a screen input form.

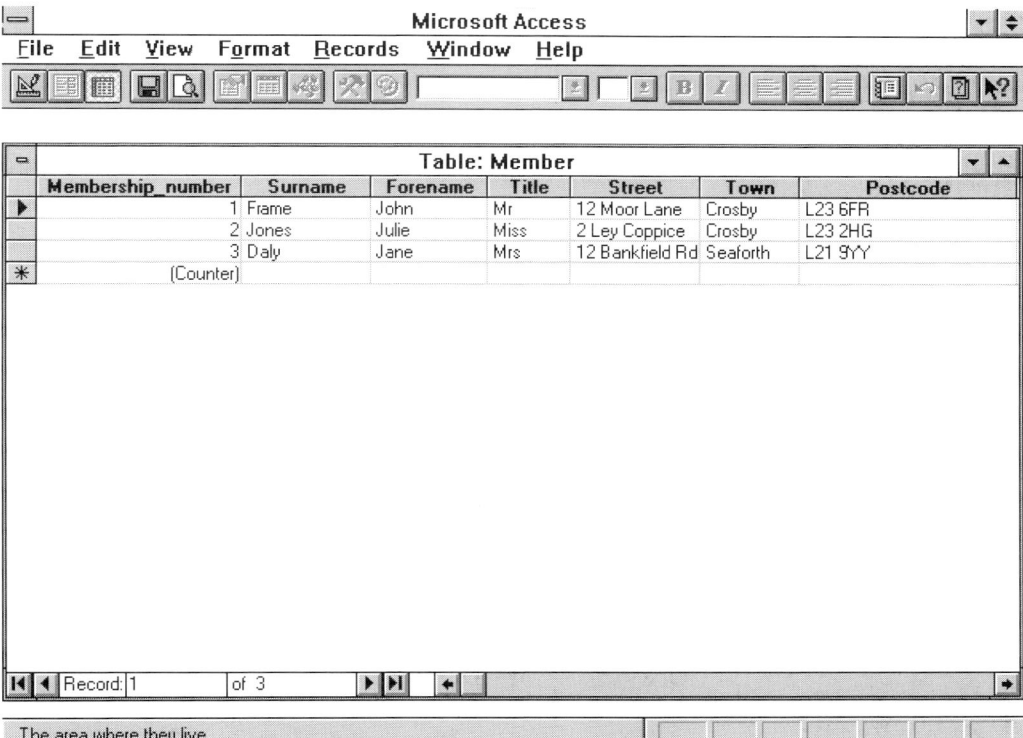

Figure 14.5
Screen input form
being used to
enter data into a
table

Most database software allows the use of text, data, pictures, lines and colour to improve the appearance of input forms, and this is particularly important if the screen faces the customer. As well as being used for data entry, input forms can also be used to view data on screen. Data for a form can come from a table or a query, while information such as company logos, titles, etc. are stored in the form design itself.

Forms can be used to view a single record or all the records for that form. Figure 14.6 shows a form being used to input data into a MEMBER table, one record at a time.

Single data entry forms

Single data entry is where the data entered into a screen input form goes to a single table, where it is stored and can be accessed as required.

Multiple data entry forms

These are input forms which enable data to be entered into more than one table at the same time. Suppose two tables need to contain the customer number. Rather than using separate forms to enter this data into each table, a single form is employed which automatically passes the data to both tables. This saves time and reduces the chance of an error occurring. Multiple entry forms can be used only with relational databases; for flat file databases single data entry forms have to be used.

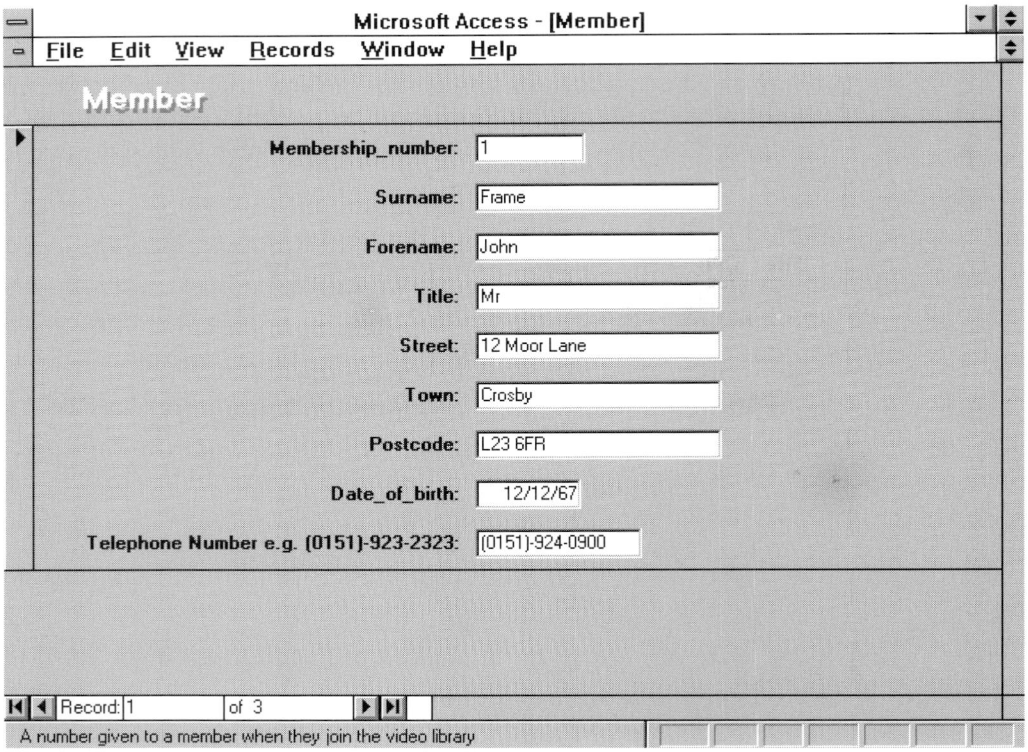

Figure 14.6 Form being used to input data into a MEMBER table

Modifying form fields to enable accurate input of data

Form fields are the blank spaces included in the form design on the computer screen, into which variable data can be added. The added data is then passed to the records contained in one or more tables, where it is stored for further use. Like a paper-based form, form fields also have headings and prompts so that you know what sort of data should be keyed into the boxes.

Figure 14.7 shows a form designed to input the hours worked by a temporary worker over a certain week. Notice the last two fields: Total (the total number of hours worked that week) and Total Pay. These are not entered but calculated from other fields. The total hours are worked out by adding the numbers in the Number of hours worked fields on each of the five days, while the total pay is the total number of hours worked multiplied by the rate of pay.

Field length

Field length (also known as field size) is usually taken to be the maximum number of characters an entry is likely to occupy within a field. This is usually specified when the database is set up, but most databases allow the field length specified in the structure to be adjusted without damaging the data already entered.

Data entry fields

Some fields, such as today's date or a sequential order number, can be filled in automatically by the computer. Many fields, however, need to have their data keyed in by the user.

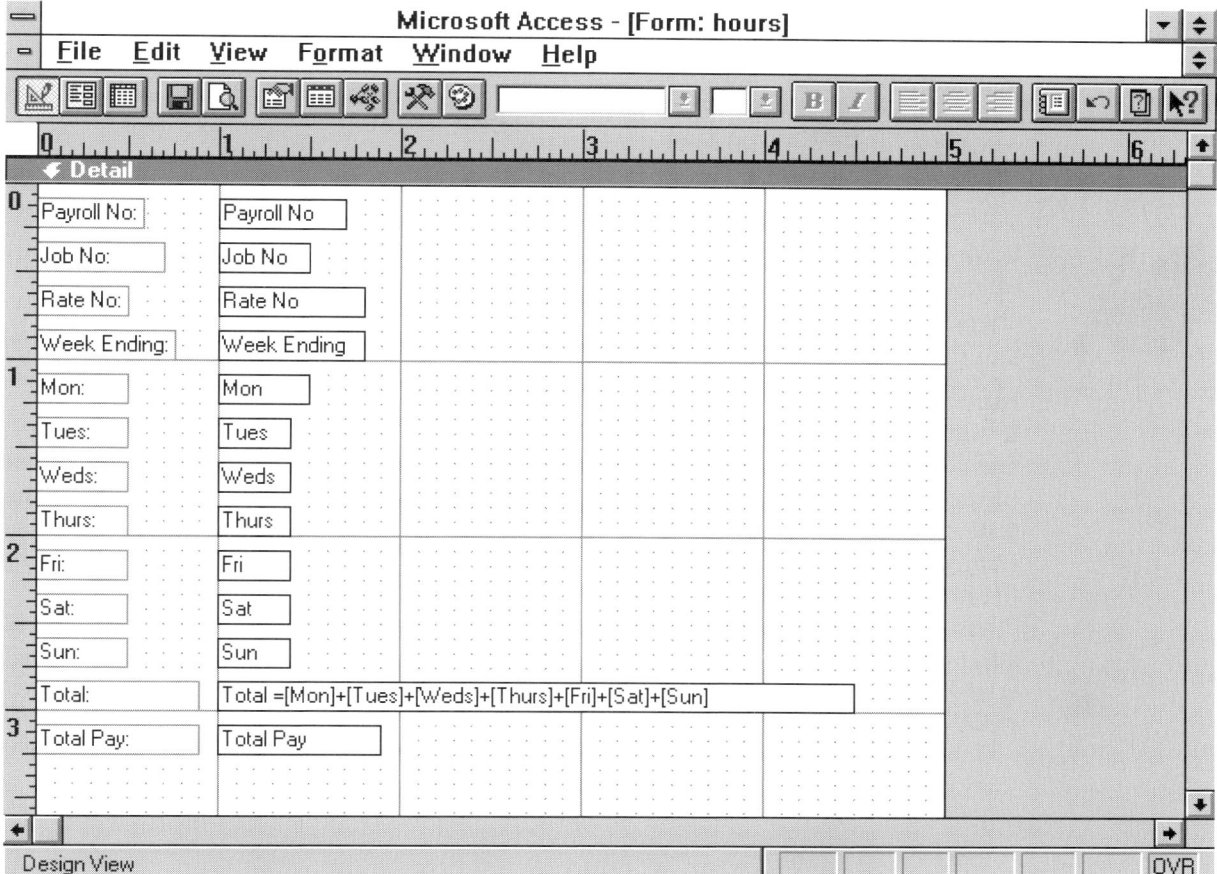

Figure 14.7 Form designed to input hours worked in a week

Instruction fields

All screen forms should include instructions to let the user know what each field requires. Sometimes the field name alone is sufficient. 'Surname' is self-explanatory but 'date' can be problematical to an inexperienced user not familiar with the 'dd/mm/yy' format. Any fields with field names which are not obvious need an example to give the user an idea of the type of format required for input.

Field titles

Field titles are usually the same as the field names, or they can be more detailed. It is more convenient if field names are kept short, as they have to be typed in when performing searches, but the actual field titles can be longer and offer further explanation.

Validation checks

Validation checks are used to prevent inaccurate data from being entered into tables. Although staff who enter data should ensure that it is accurate by checking the completed form against the source document, each field can also have certain validation rules attached to it, allowing only data which conforms to the rules to be entered (see page 444). If the data entered does not conform to the validation rule for a particular field, a message appears informing the operator why the data is incorrect.

447

There are various validation checks which can be performed on data, for example a credit limit field may have a range check to make sure that no credit limits are entered that exceed a predetermined value.

Chapter 6 contains further information on validation checks.

Activity 14.3

Look back at the section on validation checks in Chapter 6. There are four types of validation check. Using manuals, books or on-line help, find out how each of these checks is performed. Outline your findings in a brief report.

Input masks

In some fields data might all have the same format, so to simplify data entry an input mask can be used. The input mask supplies the invariable characters in a field so that the user need only enter the data that differs from one field to another. This is best illustrated by taking an example of entering telephone numbers. If all the telephone numbers to be entered have the same format, (0151) 876 2341 for example, we can use the input mask to supply the brackets and spaces between blocks of numbers.

As well as saving some input time, input masks help to ensure that the data entered adheres to a format. If an order number field contains customer numbers which each start with a single letter of the alphabet followed by four numbers, this can be specified in the input mask.

Microsoft Access uses the following mask characters. Note the difference between 'may be entered' and 'must be entered'.

Mask character	Can be used in the input mask to mean
0	A digit must be entered here
9	A digit may be entered here
#	A positive (+) or negative (−) sign may be entered here
L	A letter must be entered here
?	A letter may be entered here
A	A letter or a digit must be entered here
a	A letter or a number may be entered here
&	Any character or space must be entered here
C	Any character or space may be entered here
<	All characters to the right are converted to lower case
>	All characters to the right are converted to upper case
. , : ; - /	Decimal point, thousands, date and time separators
!	Mask fills from right to left (useful if the optional characters are on the right-hand side of the mask)
\	Character to the right is interpreted as an ordinary character and not part of the mask

Let us now look at constructing some input masks using these characters. For a telephone number such as (0151) 876 2341 we could use the following input mask:
    (0000) 000 0000

But if we want dashes between the groups of numbers we should instead use this mask:
    (0000)-000-0000

Activity 14.4

Task 1
Suppose we need to store a postcode. Our first task is to find the formats for all postcodes. Our input mask would need to take account of the following possibilities:
- L23 8VY
- GL50 1YW
- L9 0BQ.
- EC1X 4BD

Your task is to design a single input mask suitable for the entry of the above postcodes.

Task 2
Using your database software, find out which validation checks can be performed on the data entered into the following fields:
- date of order (dd/mm/yy)
- order reference (a letter followed by four numbers e.g. A1729)
- postcode (e.g. L23 5GT).

Ensuring data entry fields comply with the data dictionary

We have already come across the description of a data dictionary, but what is its purpose? Data dictionaries provide a valuable reference because, even within an organisation, IT users might define an element of data quite differently. (An element of data is a unit of data which cannot be decomposed any further.)

Take, for instance, a college principal who needs to know how many students the college has. They could do a simple count of students on the register, but since some of the students may well appear on more than one class register, there is a danger of counting them more than once. Another approach would be to obtain a total of the student hours attended by all students in the college over a one-week period, and divide this by the number of hours per week a full-time student would normally attend. This method would not be accurate, however, if some courses, classed as full-time, require 16 hours attendance while others are based on 24 hours or more per week. As you can see, data that at first sight appears relatively simple can easily be misunderstood and misused. Two people often think they are talking about the same thing when in fact each has a different definition of the item under discussion. Taking again the example of full-time students, all members of staff need to agree a definition if they are not to risk talking at cross-purposes. A data dictionary would help by defining a student, a full-time course and all the other data elements in the system.

The contents of the data dictionary

Data dictionaries usually contain some or all of the following features:

Field names
Field names become the headings of the various columns in the table. They should be chosen so that they describe the data as fully as possible without being too long, since as column headings they may determine the width of the columns, which in turn governs how much data can be fitted onto the screen at any one time. It is best to avoid leaving spaces in field names, using - or _ to separate the words instead.

Synonyms

Synonyms are alternative names for the same thing. In many large organisations, the database is at the centre of the computer system and is used by different departments for various activities. It is therefore common to find users in different departments employing a different name for the same concept; this can be very confusing for systems analysts trying to design and build a new system. To prevent confusion, users should list any alternative names in the synonyms section of the data dictionary.

Data type

A data type needs to be specified for each field; sometimes it is set automatically by the software, otherwise the user needs to select the type from a list. It is very important that once a field's data type is set, it has the same data type wherever it occurs in other tables. In most cases, relationships can be made only between fields with exactly the same field names and data types.

Format

Details of formats should be included in the data dictionary for those fields which have formats set by the user. For instance, a numeric field can be a short integer, long integer, currency, etc. and dates can be given as 12th June 1997, 12/06/97, etc.

Description of the field

Each field in each of the tables usually has a description, and these descriptions can be transferred to this section of the data dictionary.

Field length

Here we specify the length of the field for those fields which can have their lengths set.

Table name

Here we list the names of all the tables in which the field can be found.

A summary of what should be included in the data dictionary about a particular data element is shown below.

Field name	This is usually the same as the name given to the data element
Synonyms or aliases	Alternative names for the same thing
Data type	Data may be numeric, character, date or logical (Y/N), memo, etc.
Format	Currency, number of decimal places, standard form (a way of storing very large or small numbers)
Description of the field	Information about what the data element is and how it is used
Field length	The number of characters needed for the text or the number of digits used for numbers
Table name	The names of any tables where the data element may be found

Here is a data dictionary entry for a data element called REORDER_QUANTITY:

Field name	REORDER_QUANTITY
Synonyms	None
Data type	Numeric
Format	0 decimal places (i.e. an integer)
Description of the field	The number of units of a stock item which can be ordered at any one time
Field length	4 digits
Table names	STOCK_LIST
	STOCK_LIST_EXCEPTION
	REORDER

Data dictionaries are always created when large commercial databases are being built, especially if the databases are to be used in many different applications. The purpose of the data dictionary is to make sure that data across the whole system is consistent. Large systems are built by large project teams, with each team working on a part of the whole system; in this situation consistent terminology is vital, and the data dictionary is invaluable. The data contained in data dictionaries is often referred to as **metadata**.

Data dictionaries can be built as a manual system but there are clear advantages in maintaining a computerised data dictionary. Most relational database management systems have software which creates and maintains a data dictionary. It is kept as a separate database and automatically updated as changes are made to the structure of the main database.

As part of the evidence indicator for Element 7.2, you will have to make sure that data entry fields comply with the data dictionary which was created for the system in Assignment A13.1.

Optional features of the data dictionary

In addition to the essential features listed above, some data dictionaries provide the following additional information:
- validation checks;
- details of the validation checks performed on data entered into each field;
- a key;
- the type of key specified.

Creating and using special fields

Special fields are form fields which are designed to contain special data such as date, time, page number, or calculations like column total.

Calculated fields

Calculated fields are calculations which the database software performs, based on fields in the table. It is important to note that calculated fields are *not* stored in the table. Figure 14.7 shows a form containing two calculated fields of this type.

Date

Sometimes it is necessary to enter a specific date such as a date of birth, but in many situations a current date ('today's date') is all that is required and this can be done by default, using the system date. It should be noted that much of the software used is from the USA where the MM/DD/YY format is used rather than the DD/MM/YY format used in Europe. If you have problems with this, you will need to check that the system clock in the operating system of your computer is set to the DD/MM/YY format.

Time

When many transactions are taking place on one date it is useful also to record the time of each transaction so that different transactions by the same person can be differentiated. In most database systems the time field is tagged onto the date field; the time on its own is not very useful without the date to which it refers. When creating the database structure you normally include a date/time field.

In Microsoft Access, the following times are possible:

- long time, e.g. 2:30:00 PM
- short time, e.g. 14:30
- medium time, e.g. 02:30 PM.

You can use the date and time together to group records producing, for instance, a list of transactions in complete chronological order.

Assignment A14.1

This assignment develops knowledge and understanding of the following element:
7.2 Create data input forms for a database

It supports the development of the following key skills:
Communication 3.2 and 3.3
Information technology 3.1, 3.2 and 3.3

This assignment is part of the project developed in stages in Chapters 10 and 13. You were working in groups for these assignments and should continue in the same group for this assignment (if this is not practical consult your tutor), which takes the system a stage further.

In Chapter 13 you developed a data model and produced relational database structures. You will now produce the tables in accordance with your structure using relational database software.

Task 1
For this task you will create tables in accordance with the database structures described in the assignment in Chapter 13, nominate the primary keys for each table and then set up relationships between the tables.

Task 2
For this task you have to produce input screens to allow data entry into your tables. The input screens should cover single table entry, multiple table entry or a combination of the two.

Task 3
You are now required to produce a data dictionary for your database system. Make sure that all the fields in your database conform with the definitions contained in the dictionary.

Task 4
The fourth task requires you to show that you have created and used special fields (time, date, calculations) in your database.

Database reports

This section examines how a database can be interrogated using queries to produce appropriate reports which meet the requirements of a system specification.

Queries

Queries are requests, written in a special language, for specific information, posed to databases. For instance, from a database containing names and addresses, you may want to obtain a list of all those entries with the surname 'Jones' or details of accounts where outstanding credit exceeds the credit limit. Database software allows users to design specific queries; the following should be considered when designing such queries:

Choosing fields

You can choose any combination of fields stored in one or more tables. Provided that the data has been stored, it can be retrieved and put into a query. Figure 14.8 shows how a query is set up in the query design screen while Figure 14.9 shows the results when this query is used to interrogate the database.

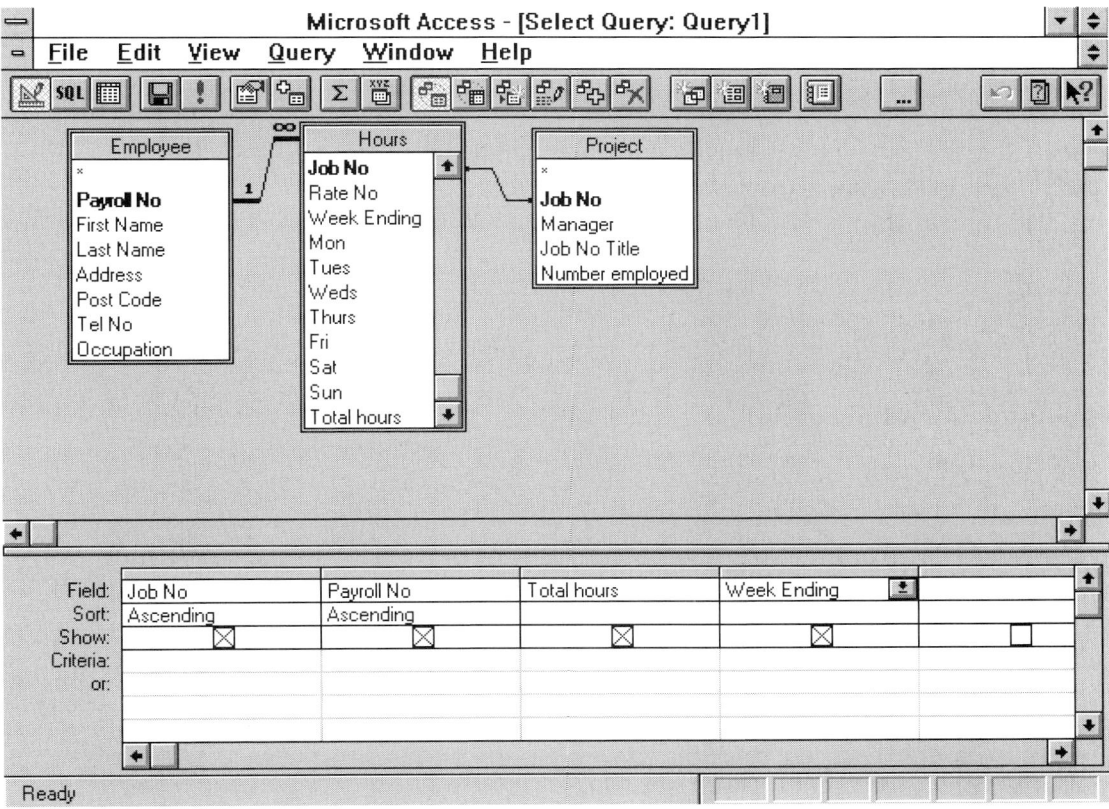

Figure 14.8 Setting up a query in the query design screen

Notice the tables in the upper part of the screen along with the relationships between the tables. In the lower part of the screen we can choose which fields we wish to display and also order the data in one or more fields. In Access the fields you want are marked by clicking on 'Show' after which a cross appears to indicate which field will be shown.

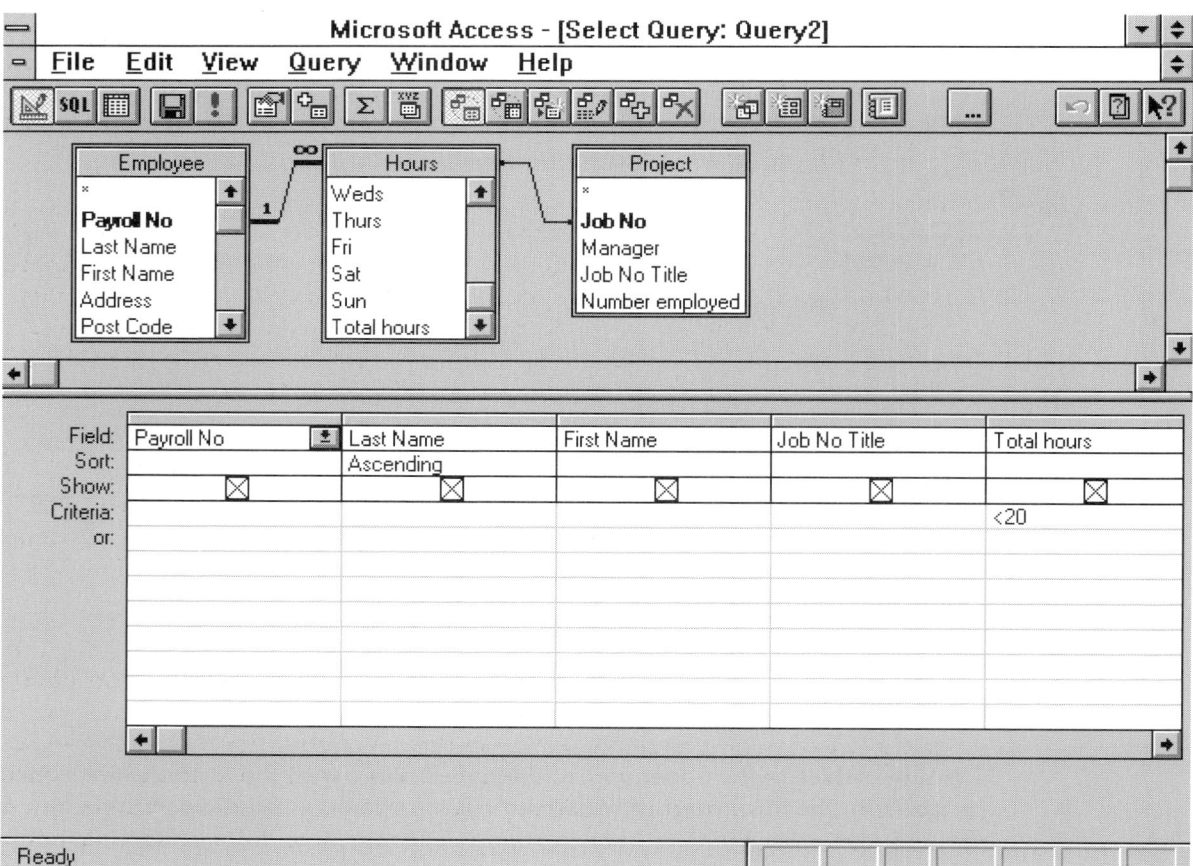

Figure 14.9 Results obtained when a query is used to interrogate a database

Choosing records

You can choose data within a field to form a group of records. For example, those items sold over a certain week can be selected and listed.

Using Access you can enter criteria for the search into the query design shown in Figure 14.10 where, for those employees who work fewer than 20 hours, the payroll number, first name, last name, job number, title and the total hours worked are picked out in order of last name.

Figure 14.10 Entering criteria for the search

Figure 14.11 shows the results obtained using the query described above.

	Payroll No	Last Name	First Name	Job No Title	Total hours
▶	131234	Harris	Peter	Skills Survey	19
	132121	Hughes	Dawn	Skills Survey	15
	132241	Jackson	Jane	Crosby Herald Survey	14
	223242	Johnston	Pamela	Crosby Traffic Survey	14
	122243	Owens	Jane	Skills Survey	15

Microsoft Access - [Select Query: Query2]
File Edit View Format Records Window Help

Figure 14.11 The results from a query

Sorting the data

Records are usually most useful if they are sorted into an order related to the main field or fields used for the query. For example, if we have obtained details of customer accounts to determine who owes the most, it would be helpful to place these in order of the balance, with those customers owing the largest amounts placed first. If the list were to be used to answer customer enquiries regarding their balances, alphabetical order according to surname would be more useful. Sorted data can be displayed in a form by creating a query to sort the records, then using the query as a source of data for the form.

Look back at Figures 14.8 and 14.9. Figure 14.9 shows the results from a query. Notice that there are two orders being used. The first is in order of job number, and within this (because several jobs have the same number) the order is ascending payroll number.

Asking questions about the data and deciding which tables to use

Questions can be asked about the data contained in more than one table and the results viewed either on a form or in a report.

Using calculated fields

New fields can be created containing the results of calculations and these are called 'calculated fields'. For example, you might want to multiply the price of an individual article by a quantity to give the total price. To do this a new 'total' field would be created to contain the results of a calculation involving the other two fields. In order to show the calculated field, you need first to construct a query which contains the calculated field and then base a form or report on the results of the query.

Deciding whether to present the search in a form or report

As we have already seen, queries are used to extract certain data from tables. When the query is run, the results are presented in a table with columns for each field and with records for the tables in the rows underneath. You can also print out the results from the queries, but it is usually better to load the query into a report and this enables more flexibility as to the arrangement of the data on the page.

Other uses for queries

One very useful feature of queries is that they can be used to update, delete or add to (append) the group or record specified by the query.

Queries are of two types: select queries and action queries. Select queries are used to find and extract certain information, whereas action queries perform actions such as deleting or updating a record. Action queries enable you to make changes to many records in just one operation. For example, if all the employees of a certain organisation were given a 5 per cent pay rise, all the salaries contained in the personnel records can be increased in one operation rather than through altering each record separately.

Activity 14.5

Classify the following queries according to whether they are select or action queries.
1 Increase the salary of all employees working in the sales department by 5 per cent.
2 Identify all the records of employees who have attended a first-aid training course.
3 Identify all those sales staff whose sales are below target.
4 Delete all those members' details in a video library who have not borrowed a video in the last two years.
5 Alter all the telephone numbers for a certain area from 051 to 0151.

Structured query language (SQL)

Structured query language consists of a small number of commands which the user can combine in order to extract particular details from a database. It is now the industry standard language for the extraction of information from databases.

In SQL, the SELECT command is used to query the database and this command is constructed in the following way:

SELECT attribute list
FROM table list
WHERE condition

The attribute list is used to list the attributes (i.e. the fields) we want to retrieve, while the table list indicates in which table the listed attributes can be found. The condition is a Boolean expression used to identify those records to be retrieved.

Structured query language also allows the logical operators AND, OR and NOT to be used to combine relational expressions.

AND

Two expressions are combined with AND when both must be true for a record to qualify. For example, we might want a surname Jones AND the town Crosby.

OR

Two expressions are combined with OR when either one needs to be true for the record to qualify. For example, we might want the surname Doyle OR Prescott.

NOT

NOT can be used to display all the records that do not meet a criterion. For example, we may want details of all people who live in a town which is NOT Crosby.

Suppose we want to extract the name and address of a video library member whose membership number, stored as text, is 0001. If the table containing the member's details is MEMBER we can use the following SQL statement:

SELECT Surname, Street, Town, Postcode
FROM MEMBER
WHERE Membership_number = '0001'

The following example shows how Boolean expressions can be used to narrow down a search.

Example 1

It is necessary to extract the names of all employees earning over £30 000 per year in the production department of a company. The employees' details are stored in a table called PERSONNEL. The SQL instruction to do this is as follows:

SELECT EMPLOYEE_NAME
FROM PERSONNEL
WHERE DEPARTMENT = 'PRODUCTION' AND SALARY >30000

Example 2

Suppose we want to extract a list of the names and addresses of employees who work in the production or marketing departments from the PERSONNEL table. We could use the following SQL statement:

SELECT Surname, Street, Town, Postcode
FROM PERSONNEL
WHERE Department = 'Production' OR 'Marketing'

Activity 14.6

The table shown below was looked at in the last chapter. It is called MEMBER and is used to store the details of the members of a video library.

Write down the SQL statements which could be used to query the data contained in the table in the ways described below.

1 A query to extract all the members' membership numbers and surnames, sorted into alphabetical order according to surname.
2 A query to produce a list of the membership numbers, surnames and dates of birth of all the members born before 12/12/70.
3 A query to extract the names and addresses of all the female members of the video club.

MEMBER table

Membership _number	Surname	Forename	Title	Street	Town	Postcode	Date_of_birth	Tel_no
0001	Bell	John	Mr	12 Queens Rd	Crosby	L23 6BB	12/12/56	924-8882
0002	Smith	Jenny	Ms	1 Firs Close	Crosby	L23 5TT	01/08/79	924-9090
0003	Cannon	Paul	Mr	12 Bells Rake	Crosby	L23 5FD	09/03/65	924-0098
0004	Charles	Steve	Mr	8 Moor Grove	Crosby	L23 7YY	02/07/69	924-1121
0005	James	Karen	Miss	3 Meols Rd	Crosby	L23 4RR	01/09/45	924-8111
0006	Brady	June	Mrs	9 Fox Close	Crosby	L23 5EE	20/01/59	924-0232

Query by example (QBE)

The queries we have constructed so far are all of a type called **query by example**. Query by example (QBE) is a simplified method of entering SQL queries and enables users to enter a query using a menu or keystroke sequence which is automatically converted into an SQL command. With the RDBMS Microsoft Access it is possible to use either SQL or QBE, although, because it is so easy to use, the majority of users prefer QBE. Nevertheless some experienced users accustomed to programming and building large applications still prefer SQL.

When you create a QBE query in Microsoft Access, the database constructs an SQL statement and carries this out. The SQL statements are not shown on screen as this might confuse the user. However, users familiar with SQL statements may want to use them rather than QBE, and the system allows you to do this by opening an existing query then selecting the SQL option from the view menu.

Activity 14.7

For the database system you are developing as part of your on-going assignment, you are to extract the required data from the tables using queries.

For this activity, write down the SQL equivalent of each of the queries used.

Statements can also be constructed in SQL to perform action queries. In the following example the holidays for those workers who work in the production or marketing departments is increased by five days.

UPDATE Personnel
SET No_of_days_holiday = No_of_days_holiday + 5
WHERE Department = 'Production' OR 'Marketing'

Designing database report layouts

Reports are used to extract information from a database and produce a printout on paper or on the screen. Reports can be used to extract and print information in a single table or a number of tables and can also be used to present the results of a query. Apart from the data itself, other information can be included on a report, such as headings on the top of the report and graphs showing numerical data.

Most people consider a report to imply a printed copy, but it may be sufficient to display a report temporarily on screen rather than producing a hard copy.

Screen reports

Screen reports are only really suited to small quantities of information, where the report is easily assimilated and does not need to be taken away. Screen reports are ideal for summarised data and answers to simple queries such as 'how many of item X do we have in stock?'

Printed reports

Many reports are lengthy and may need to be taken away and studied or used for future reference; such reports are always printed out. Some reports are the result of complex file interrogations and manipulations, and the grouped or sorted data is finally printed out as neatly formatted hard copy.

It should always be remembered that a table is a way of storing data with a minimum of duplication. It is easy to be confused by relational databases, and it is common to think that you can only print out data from a single table at a time. This is not the case. The table structure allows any data, in any of the tables, to be printed out, provided that relationships exist between them.

How is a report laid out?

There are certain design features of reports and these include the following.

Pagination

Pagination involves deciding which parts of the report should be on each page. You should try to keep related data on one page if at all possible.

Footers

There are three types of footer: group footer, page footer and report footer. The group footer appears at the end of each group of records and usually gives the total of a particular group. The page footer appears at the bottom of each page in a report, and is normally the page number in a multi-page report. Report footers appear only once, at the end of the whole report. They are usually placed above the page footer on the last page of a report and are normally reserved for items such as report totals.

Headers

There are three types of header: the report header, the page header and the group header. The report header appears at the beginning of a report and usually contains a logo, the report's title and its date. The page header appears at the top of every page in the report and includes the column headings in the case of a tabular report. A group header appears at the start of a group of records and here you would normally put the name of the group.

Totals

Most reports contain some numerical data and group totals are often useful. Such group totals can be specified in the report design. Figure 14.12 shows a report of the pay earned for the week ending 11/02/96. Notice that records are ordered according to last name and that totals are calculated, along with a grand total at the end.

Single Pay for Week Ending 11/02/96
23-Apr-96

First Name	Last Name	Payroll No	Job No	Total Pay
Gareth	Bean	233478	S727	£127.50
Peter	Belling	711234	S729	£133.28
Jan	Chilcott	823456	S727	£142.50
Anna	Coleman	286752	S729	£145.04
Rolph	Harris	987654	S727	£146.52
Miriam	Higgins	356991	S728	£122.85
Amanda	Jones	982345	S729	£152.88
Stephen	Morris	243167	S727	£105.00
Harry	Secombe	762345	S728	£119.34
Mike	White	234567	S727	£123.75
Dave	Williams	923452	S728	£98.28
Dave	Wood	678213	S729	£156.80
			Grand Total =	£1,573.74

Figure 14.12

Calculations

Rather than perform calculations on the data in the database itself, it is easier to do any necessary arithmetic at the report stage. To produce an invoice or bill the quantity is multiplied by the cost per item, each line in the order totalled and the VAT calculated and added to give the final amount. As well as performing simple sums, the reporting process can be used to carry out more complex statistical calculations.

Data groupings

The ability to be able to group records in some way in a report can be very useful. For example, you might want a list of customers who are over their allowed credit limit in order of the amount they owe. The person using the report can immediately see the important ones at the top of the list. Customers could also be grouped logically according to their department or job title.

Sometimes reports which show overdue accounts are useful if the accounts are ordered according to how overdue they are, and this is done using the date field.

Figure 14.13 shows a report with data groupings according to job title. The report shows how much the staff working on each job earned in the week ending 11/02/96. Totals are also included for the cost in wages for each job, for that particular week. A grand total comprises the wages for all the jobs carried out that week.

The report in Figure 14.13 demonstrates the wide variety of ways that data held in tables can be extracted and presented and illustrates the power of a relational database.

Project Group and Individual Pay by Week Ending 11/02/96
23-Apr-96

Job No Title	Week Ending	Payroll No	First Name	Last Name	Total Pay
Bootle Town	11/02/96	233478	Gareth	Bean	£127.50
Centre Traffic		823456	Jan	Chilcott	£142.50
Counts		987654	Rolph	Harris	£146.52
		243167	Stephen	Morris	£105.00
		234567	Mike	White	£123.75
					£645.27
Netherton	11/02/96	711234	Peter	Belling	£133.28
Residents Skills		286752	Anna	Coleman	£145.04
Survey		982345	Amanda	Jones	£152.88
		678213	Dave	Wood	£156.80
					£588.00
Southport	11/02/96	356991	Miriam	Higgins	£122.85
Visitors		762345	Harry	Secombe	£119.34
Survey		923452	Dave	Williams	£98.28
					£340.47
				Grand Total:	£1,573.74

Figure 14.13

Print preview

Print preview is a feature included in most RDBMSs and allows the user to view a database report screen before printing. Adjustments can then be made if needed, so using print preview can save both time and paper.

Specification of a report

Whether a report is being produced for your own use or someone else's, you need to consider the purpose of the report and who it is aimed at, and adjust the arrangement of the fields and other information to suit these requirements. The specification of the report needs to cover the following areas.

Order

Reports can be arranged in any order so it is best to consider the purpose of the report and order the information accordingly. For instance, customers who have not paid their end-of-month account could be placed in order of how overdue the account has become or in order of the amount owed. Either way, it will help the person who has asked for the report. If the purpose of the report is known, the process can be taken a step further and an exception report produced which prints only items of interest.

The order in which the fields should be printed is also important. If, for instance, there are columns of fields, the more important and unique fields should be positioned to the right-hand side of the report.

Fields

Before creating a report you need to decide which fields should be included in the report. There is a tendency to try to cram in as many fields as will fit into the report, 'just in case they are needed'; this should be resisted. Reports should contain only information that is essential to fulfil their purpose; adding non-essential information only serves to obscure the main points.

Field positions

Rather than have field names at the tops of columns with their respective data in rows below (much as data is arranged in tables), it is often better to specify where the data is to appear in a report. Many reports contain data in various places. Consider an invoice, for example: details such as customer number, name and address appear only once but the order line for the various items on the order appears many times, usually across the page in the following order:

product_number, product_description, unit_price, qty, cost.

Assignment A14.2

This assignment develops knowledge and understanding of the following elements:
7.3 Create database reports
3.3 Use information technology for a data handling activity

It supports the development of the following key skills:
Communication 3.2 and 3.3
Information technology 3.1, 3.2 and 3.3

This assignment follows on from Assignment A14.1 and also provides evidence for Element 3.3, the theory for which was covered in Chapter 6. Before attempting this assignment you will probably need to look back at Chapter 6 as well as at the material contained in this chapter.

In the previous assignment you set up tables and created forms to allow the input of the data to the database.

Task 1

To produce reports you need to enter some data using the forms created as part of the previous assignment. Enter data for about 30 typical records into each of the tables. You can invent the data yourself, but the data should be sensible and realistic.

Task 2

This task provides evidence for Element 3.3. You are required to undertake some field maintenance activities. These are listed below. You have already entered data in Task 1, so the first item in this list has been covered.

- data entry
- amending
- deleting
- appending.

For any three of the above (two and data entry) you should simulate the file maintenance activities and provide evidence, in the form of printouts, showing the contents of the tables (or individual records) before and after the changes have taken place. You should also show what data needed changing and why. Examples of this might be 'to delete the record of member no. 1234 because they have moved to another area' or 'a new member 4563 has joined so the data needs appending', etc.

Task 3

This task provides evidence for Element 3.3. You are required to use a minimum of six data handling procedures, which to recap are as follows:

- calculating (numerical fields, totals)
- converting (number to character and vice versa)
- sorting (one field or multiple fields)
- searching ($=$, $<$, $>$, AND, OR)
- selecting
- merging
- grouping.

You need to provide evidence in the form of a brief description of what you are trying to do and a printout showing the results for each process.

Task 4

Using the output specification from Assignment A10.1 as a guide, produce report layouts and save each report for later use.

Task 5

To produce reports showing only certain fields you have to interrogate the database to extract the information. This task involves creating at least two queries which can be used to produce reports that are appropriate to your particular system. You need to make sure that the reports you produce meet the requirements of the specification outlined in Assignment A10.1.

Task 6

This task provides evidence for Element 3.3. You are required to apply appropriate security checks to your database system, covering the following range:

- confidentiality (passwords, non-disclosure)
- regular file saving
- back up
- theft (equipment, software)
- copyright (software, data)
- access rights.

Task 7

This task provides evidence for Element 3.3. You are required to evaluate the effectiveness, compared against the specification, of the data processing activity (i.e. using the database you have created).

Sample unit test

Questions 1–4 relate to the following information:

A student database is set up by a tutor of the GNVQ Advanced Information Technology course. The database is to hold information on each student, such as student number, name, address, telephone number, date of birth and qualifications.

1   When choosing a field size for the student surname it should always be:
   a the size of the largest surname currently on the course
   b the size of a randomly picked student's surname
   c the size of the largest surname you are ever likely to come across
   d the size of the smallest surname currently on the course

2   A telephone number should be stored as which data type?
   a number
   b text
   c a counter
   d memo

3   Each student is given a number when they join the course and this is called the student number. The best data type for this would be:
   a a counter
   b currency
   c text
   d memo

4   Since all the students live in the Liverpool area, the area telephone code is always (0151). To avoid unnecessary typing, this can be added automatically by making use of:
   a a macro
   b an input mask
   c a validation check
   d a primary key

Questions 5–7 refer to Figure 14.14.

5   On joining a college, students are given an enrolment number and their name and address details are entered. Details of available courses are entered separately using a course code as a key. Students are then allocated to courses using the sample data entry form shown in Figure 14.14. Which two of the following are data items which would be entered via this input screen and validated in input?

   1   student enrolment number (e.g. 4379)
   2   course code (e.g. CSA)
   3   student name (e.g. John Peterson)
   4   course name (e.g. Comp St A Level)

   a 1 and 2
   b 2 and 3
   c 3 and 4
   d 1 and 4   *(RSA, December 1995)*

 6 Which one of the following is an example of a title field?
   a COURSE ENROLMENT 1995/96
   b CSA
   c Press F2 to save
   d Course code: *(RSA, December 1995)*

 7 Which one of the following is an example of a data entry field?
   a COURSE ENROLMENT 1995/96
   b CSA
   c Press F2 to save
   d Course code: *(RSA, December 1995)*

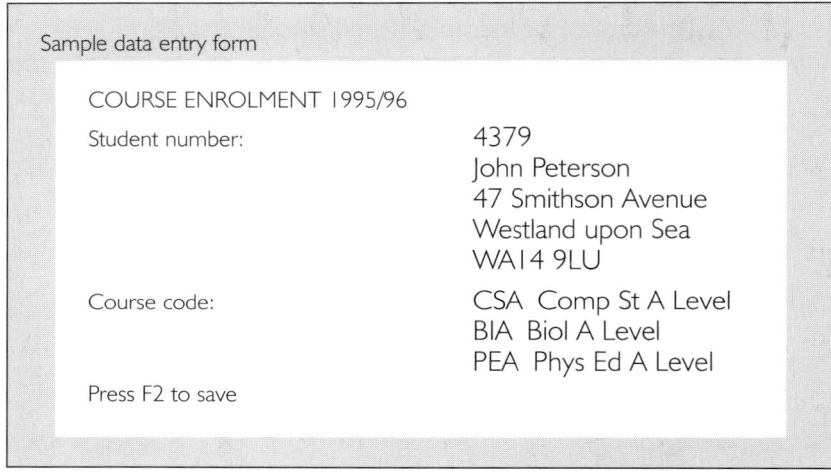

Figure 14.14

Questions 8–10 are based on Figure 14.15.

 8 Which one of the following best describes 'ENTER ALL DATA IN CAPITAL LETTERS PLEASE'?
   a instruction field
   b data entry field
   c header section
   d title field   *(RSA, June 1996)*

 9 Which one of the following best describes 'SA12'?
   a instruction field
   b data entry field
   c header section
   d title field   *(RSA, June 1996)*

 10 Which one of the following fields could be validated using a check digit?
   a 139786 (Employee number)
   b PATEL (Employee name)
   c 12/03/65 (Date of birth)
   d F (Male/female)   *(RSA, June 1996)*

Employee Data Entry Form

ENTER ALL DATA IN CAPITAL LETTERS PLEASE

Employee number:	139786
Employee name:	PATEL
Department code:	SA12
Date of Birth:	12/03/65 Male/female: F
Annual Salary:	15000

Figure 14.15
Example of a
screen input form

Questions 11–13 are based on Figure 14.16 below.

11 Which one of the following would be the missing entry shown as * in Column 1?
   a Smith
   b alpha
   c XXXX...
   d surname   *(RSA, June 1996)*

12 Which one of the following would be the missing entry shown as ** in Column 4?
   a 0
   b 11
   c 110
   d 1100   *(RSA, June 1996)*

13 Which one of the following would be the missing entry shown as *** in Column 2?
   a date
   b age
   c 25/06/80
   d 16   *(RSA, June 1996)*

Figure 14.16
Extract from a
data dictionary
for membership of
a club

Column 1	Column 2	Column 3	Column 4
membership number	numeric	000001-999999	6
*	alpha	AAAAA...	45
address	alphanumeric	XXXX...	90
telephone no	numeric	NNNN...	**
date of birth	***	dd/mm/yyyy	10

14 A number of employee time cards are input to a computer during a batch run. As part of the run, a number of administrative fields are entered by an operator. Which one of these fields is a calculation field?
   a batch number
   b control total
   c operator number
   d system name   *(RSA, June 1996)*

Questions 15 and 16 are based on Figure 14.17 below.

15 Which one of the following describes the field marked by X?

   a group

   b calculation

   c header

   d footer   *(RSA, June 1996)*

16 The information marked Y is contained in each page of the report. Which one of the following describes this information?

   a total

   b calculation

   c header

   d footer   *(RSA, June 1996)*

Figure 14.17 Extract from a report taken from an organisation's employee file

March 1996

Page no. 1   }Y

EMPLOYEE DETAILS FOR THE SALES DEPARTMENT

Name	Salary this month	Commission this month	Commission to date
Eric P	1,750	420	2,310
Fearns J	1,500	290	1,940
Fenlon D	1,500	450	2,500
Gallagher J L	1,750	600	3,200
Orritt D	1,500	240	1,720
Percival J	1,500	130	1,460
Pritchard G	1,750	330	2,170

X

Questions 17 and 18 are based on Figure 14.18 opposite.

17 Which one of the reports taken from the Employee and Payroll files is produced by the following procedure?

    SELECT emp_name, dept, bon, sal_ban FROM emp, payroll
    WHERE bon > 150

   a report 1

   b report 2

   c report 3

   d report 4   *(RSA, June 1996)*

18 Which one of the reports taken from the Employee and Payroll files is produced by the following procedure?

    SELECT emp_name, dept, bon, sal_ban FROM emp, payroll
    WHERE bon < 250
    AND dept <> 'Marketing'
    ORDER BY sal_ban

   a report 1

   b report 2

   c report 3

   d report 4   *(RSA, June 1996)*

Report 1

Employee Name	Department	Bonus Earned	Salary Band
Smallthwaite J	Computing	200	B01
Ezard G	Marketing	180	A05
Collins G	Personnel	155	A04
Williams J	Sales	140	A03

Report 2

Employee Name	Department	Bonus Earned	Salary Band
Smallthwaite J	Computing	200	B01
Ezard G	Marketing	180	A05
Collins G	Personnel	155	A04
Williams J	Sales	140	A03
Ireland G	Purchasing	260	A02

Report 3

Employee Name	Department	Bonus Earned	Salary Band
Williams J	Sales	140	A03
Collins G	Personnel	155	A04
Smallthwaite J	Computing	200	B01

Report 4

Employee Name	Department	Bonus Earned	Salary Band
Ireland G	Purchasing	260	A02
Smallthwaite J	Computing	200	B01
Collins G	Personnel	155	A04
Ezard G	Marketing	180	A05

Figure 14.18

19 Which one of the following reports taken from the Employee and Payroll files is produced by the following procedure?

SELECT emp_name, dept, bon, sal_ban FROM emp, payroll
WHERE bon < 250
AND dept <> 'Purchasing'
ORDER BY dept

a report 1
b report 2
c report 3
d report 4

(RSA, June 1996)

Questions 20–22 are based on the information below.

The following procedures are used to access the contents of two files. One is a staff file called EMPLOYEE and the other is a project file called ASSIGNMENT. A number of reports are produced from the procedures below using SQL.

Procedure 1
SELECT EMPLOYEE.emp_no, EMPLOYEE.emp_name, ASSIGNMENT.proj_no, ASSIGNMENT.proj_name
    FROM EMPLOYEE, ASSIGNMENT
    WHERE ASSIGNMENT.proj_no < 1315

Procedure 2
SELECT EMPLOYEE.emp_no, EMPLOYEE.emp_name, ASSIGNMENT.proj_no, ASSIGNMENT.proj_name
    FROM EMPLOYEE, ASSIGNMENT
    WHERE ASSIGNMENT.proj_no > 1385

Procedure 3
SELECT EMPLOYEE.emp_no, EMPLOYEE.emp_name, ASSIGNMENT.proj_no, ASSIGNMENT.proj_name
    FROM EMPLOYEE, ASSIGNMENT
    WHERE EMPLOYEE.emp_no > 1386

Procedure 4
SELECT EMPLOYEE.emp_no, EMPLOYEE.emp_name, ASSIGNMENT.proj_no, ASSIGNMENT.proj_name
    FROM EMPLOYEE, ASSIGNMENT
    WHERE EMPLOYEE.emp_no <> 1387

20 Which one of the procedures would produce the report shown below?

emp_no	emp_name	proj_no	proj_name
1387	Jones J	1279	dynamo
1489	Poole P	1386	alternator
1579	Benz P	1298	carburettor
1794	Kenny N	1316	dynamo

a procedure 1
b procedure 2
c procedure 3
d procedure 4

(RSA, June 1996)

21 Which one of the procedures would produce the report shown below?

emp_no	emp_name	proj_no	proj_name
1212	Sankey C	1102	dynamo
1316	Bailey A	1145	carburettor
1387	Jones J	1279	dynamo
1579	Benz P	1298	carburettor

a procedure 1
b procedure 2
c procedure 3
d procedure 4

(RSA, June 1996)

22 Which one of the procedures would produce this report?

emp_no	emp_name	proj_no	proj_name
1212	Sankey C	1102	dynamo
1316	Bailey A	1145	carburettor
1489	Poole P	1386	alternator
1579	Benz P	1298	carburettor
1794	Kenny N	1316	dynamo

a procedure 1
b procedure 2
c procedure 3
d procedure 4

(RSA, June 1996)

Questions 23–25 refer to Figure 14.19.

The following is an extract from a data dictionary

Column 1	Column 2	Column 3	Column 4
Invoice Number	INVNO	numeric	1110000-1119999
Invoice Date	INVD	date	DD/MM/YY
Customer Number	CUSTNO	*	000000-999999
Invoice Amount	INVAMT	numeric	**
Paid?	PD?	***	YES/NO

Figure 14.19

23 Which one of the following would be the missing entry in Column 3, shown as *?
  a date
  b currency
  c numeric
  d logical

(RSA, December 1995)

24 Which one of the following would be the missing entry in Column 3, shown as ***?
  a date
  b currency
  c numeric
  d logical

(RSA, December 1995)

25 Which one of the following fields might appear automatically on an input form during data entry of sales invoice data?

a order quantity

b customer account number

c today's date

d product order number *(RSA, December 1995)*

Questions 26 and 27 refer to Figure 14.20.

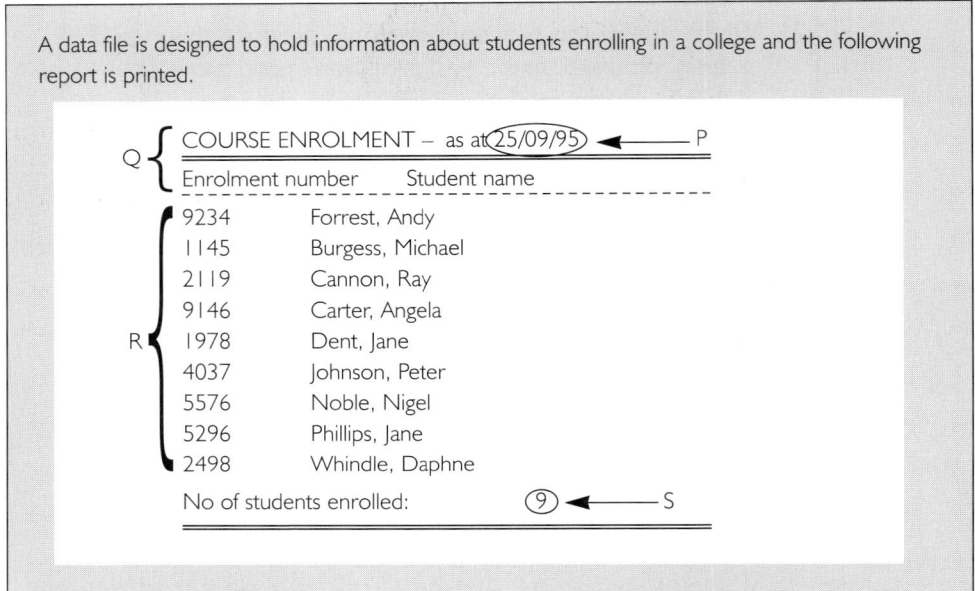

Figure 14.20

26 Which one of the following points to the header of the report?

a P

b Q

c R

d S *(RSA, December 1995)*

27 Which one of the following involves a calculation during the production of the report?

a P

b Q

c R

d S *(RSA, December 1995)*

28 The purpose of a multiple data entry form is to:

a enable many forms to be printed out to send to customers

b enable the data to be entered into a single table

c enable the data to be entered into several tables at the same time

d enable more than one person to enter data at the same time

29 It is important, when creating a database, that everyone in an organisation uses the same definition of a data element.In which of the following are data elements and terms defined?

a thesaurus

b data dictionary

c table

d report

30 A query which deletes all the records of people over sixty-five years of age would be classed as:

a a select query

b an action query

c a report

d an index

31 A company is setting up a table to hold the prices and descriptions of all the goods it sells. A typical price would be £34.78 and this would need to be held in one of the fields. Which one of the following data types would be most suitable for storing the price?

a integer

b character

c string

d real

15 Project work in information technology

What is covered in this chapter

Element 8.1: Explore information technology team projects

- Purpose of planning
- Project organisation activities
- Project scheduling
- Methods of controlling projects

Element 8.2: Contribute to an information technology team project

- Project objectives
- Roles and responsibilities
- Performance

Element 8.3: Evaluate an information technology team project

- Evaluative comments
- Comments on performance
- Areas of improvement
- NHS case study

Resources you will need for your portfolio for Elements 8.1, 8.2 and 8.3
- Your written answers to the activities and assignments in this chapter.

In the following sections we will look at the purpose of planning activities, project organisation activities, project scheduling and methods of controlling projects in the context of information technology team projects. A team is a group of people who are united by a common purpose; in this case, using IT to solve a problem. This may include hardware design, software design, system implementation or user training.

Most information technology projects cannot usually be undertaken by a single person, mainly because they are so large and would never get completed in a reasonable timescale, and the technology might change in the intervening period. It is common in IT to talk about the size of a project in terms of the number of 'man years' it takes to complete. The largest IT projects can take around 200 man years and this means it would take one person 200 years to complete, two people 100 years, four people 50 years and so on. It is usual for the people involved in an IT project to work in teams, with each team member being allocated a proportion of the overall task. In some ways, working as a team member can be harder than working as an individual since you may have to work closely with someone you do not necessarily get on with. In life, you can choose who your friends are but you can seldom choose who you work with.

Another problem is that there might not always be equal division of the overall task and some team members can find they have to work harder than others.

Purpose of planning

For an information technology project to go smoothly, it must be well planned. Without such planning the project might not be completed in the time available or it might go over budget. To be able to plan a project successfully, it is necessary to break it down into a series of smaller tasks and determine the order in which these smaller tasks need to be done. The time and resources needed for each of these smaller tasks also need to be estimated. The tasks then need to be divided among the project team members on the basis of their suitability and expertise.

The planning process needs to take into account all of the following factors.

Controlling resources

Resources include some or all of the following:

- accommodation
- equipment
- finance
- material
- people
- software.

Projects have to produce results within a reasonable timescale to a preset budget and using limited resources.

Accommodation

The project team may need to use existing offices rather than purpose-built accommodation, and this could result in team members working in different offices in different parts of the building. This could cause communication problems, though the use of e-mail can go some way to solving this. Regular meetings will be needed, where all the team members are able to get together, so meeting rooms need to be booked in advance. Video conferencing helps keep costs down by allowing team members in another part of the country, or even the world, to take part.

Many offices are now open plan, with 'closed' offices available only to senior members of staff or on a bookings basis. Open-plan offices help ease communication problems as staff are able to discuss their work frequently with other team members.

Equipment

Sometimes a test computer is used by a development team to produce a working system, but many systems have to be tested on a computer which is also being used operationally. This means that any development work needs to be fitted around the essential tasks that have to be performed on a day-to-day basis. It is therefore important to ensure that the appropriate equipment will be available when a project is undertaken.

473

With the decreased cost of hardware it is now feasible for companies to have a spare machine called a 'test machine' which is used only for development work and system testing and not operationally.

Other equipment such as printers, photocopiers, fax machines, video conferencing equipment, PCs, coffee machines, etc. also need to be made available.

Finance

Once a decision has been made to go ahead with a project, the senior managers or directors who have given the project approval will allocate a certain amount of money to it: this is called a budget. All projects are given a budget to finance them, and it is usually essential that projects do not go over budget. All the costs attributed to a project have to be taken out of the budget, and this usually includes the wages of the staff involved in the project, even though many of them may be employed by the organisation already.

Going over budget can pose serious problems. The costs and benefits of the system being developed have to be worked out in advance of the project being started, and any subsequent increase in the costs might mean that the project is no longer feasible and should be abandoned.

People

Suitably qualified and experienced staff must be available to take on the project. Many development staff now work freelance on a contract basis and most large companies now have a proportion of freelance (or contract) staff working in their computer departments at any one time. Many large-scale computing projects are passed on to outside organisations: this is called **outsourcing**. Outsourcing is now very popular since the development staff need be paid only while working on the project, and the wages they would have been paid in-between projects can be saved. However, because contract staff have less job security and yet are often highly experienced, they can demand high rates of pay, and rates of £300 per day are not uncommon.

One problem which many organisations experience is that while staff are developing new systems that are often at the leading edge of technology, they are acquiring skills that are in great demand by other organisations, and this means staff are often tempted to move to other companies that offer them more money and perks. The effect of this is that experienced staff can be lost before a project is completed, leaving gaps in expertise that are often very difficult to fill. Experienced development staff are therefore very much in demand, and their pay is usually well above what you could expect for the same level of responsibility in a non-computing role.

Material

A project might need special materials, such as specially printed input documents that can be read directly by a computer. MICR, OMR and OCR forms need to be designed and printed by specialist companies, and a certain amount of time and money will need to be allocated to this. Other materials that might be needed include photocopier paper, computer disks, whiteboard markers, flip charts, overhead projector slides and all the usual stationery.

Software

There are many software packages designed to help development teams in some way, ranging from special project and time management software to CASE tools, which provide a variety of development tools for database designers or programmers. Project management software is also available for personal computers and this is used to plan and organise projects. Other packages include special flow charting packages and packages for designing the layout of offices.

Software must be made available to the development team if needed. Sometimes it will be bespoke software that has been specifically written for the organisation, but in most cases 'off-the shelf' packages are used.

Value for money

One of the main purposes of careful planning is to make sure that an organisation developing a new project receives value for money. Any project that is not carefully planned and controlled, without deadlines and budgets, will eat up money and take an unlimited amount of time. Careful planning ensures that the project solves the problem at reasonable cost and in a reasonable time period.

Meeting deadlines

A deadline is a date set by the senior management of a company, by which the project should either be completed or reach a certain predetermined milestone. The **milestones** or **mileposts** mark the ends of logical stages in the project, and their main purpose is to establish whether the project is on time or not. If there is any slippage, then the time might be made up in the next stage and the project could still meet its deadline.

In business, deadlines are very important and everyone involved in a project needs to be constantly aware of them. Contract staff may only be available for a certain period to work on a project, and there may not be enough money to pay staff their wages after a certain date. Planning activities should therefore be centred on achieving the preset deadlines.

Securing consensus

It is an important part of any project manager's job to try to obtain consensus from other departmental managers who will all be competing for budgets. There is never an unlimited amount of money, and sometimes organisations may have to choose between, say, a new computer system, a new fleet of lorries, or a new piece of equipment in the production department. In some ways the project manager needs to be a salesperson, because they have to sell the benefits of a new system to managers both on the same level as themselves and also at a higher level.

For a project team to work together harmoniously, it needs to reach a consensus on the overall aims and goals of the project. The team members should agree on a certain solution to the problem and stick to it. If the project involves a customer, then consensus should also be obtained from them, and the customer should be involved throughout the whole project. A customer who is kept informed in this way is much less likely to be disappointed, and have less cause for complaint if the new system does not match their expectations.

Project organisation activities

Various activities need to take place throughout a project, and these are outlined below.

Role definition

Team members are picked because of their skills and experience in a particular area and it is necessary to specify the role each person is going to play in a project. Each team member has an important role in the development of a new system, and it is important that they fully understand what their role is. Each person is given a **role definition** by the project manager, which outlines the part played by that particular team member within the project team together with a list of their responsibilities. In this way, each team member understands what is expected of them.

For larger projects involving more than one team, each team reports to its respective team leader who in turn is part of a steering committee with all the other team leaders and other senior managers involved in the project. Overseeing the whole project there is a project manager who takes full responsibility for its overall success.

Examples of job roles include:

- writing programs which meet a specification for an applications system;
- designing a specification for a program to solve a particular business need;
- managing day by day a company's relational database management system;
- having overall responsibility for the day-to-day operations of the whole IT function within an organisation.

Role assignment

Role assignment involves allocating certain tasks to the member of the project team who is most able to carry them out, and this is done by the project manager. To assign roles, the project manager needs to have a detailed knowledge of the strengths and capabilities of each team member. Personal preferences can be taken into account, and there needs to be a certain amount of flexibility to allow for team members falling ill or leaving before the project is completed.

Team building

Team building aims to increase the effectiveness of a team. All the members of a team are dependent on the other members, and each member has other people dependent on them. Working in a team involves using a high degree of interpersonal skills and can lead to greater creativity, improved job satisfaction and increased energy and excitement than when working individually.

Good teamwork involves coordinating the activities of all the team members and ensuring that there is no duplication of any of the tasks. Most teams are made up of around five to seven members, and larger IT projects will involve two or more teams. The leaders of these teams need to meet together regularly to coordinate their activities and assess progress.

Planning

The planning of a project is the project manager's job, whose aim is to complete the project successfully within the predetermined timescale and budget. Without careful planning projects can eat up large amounts of money. Projects that go seriously over budget may have to be abandoned without anything being achieved, and this has serious repercussions for all the team members. Contractors, for example, could find it difficult to get another contract if word spreads that the last project they worked on failed.

A detailed plan of the activities that need to take place and when needs to be drawn up, and various milestones need to be established at which a review of the tasks completed to date can be compared against the original plan. Any slippage in the timing of the project can be identified, and steps taken (e.g. taking on extra staff, working overtime, etc.) to try to bring the project back on schedule.

There are various techniques and tools available which can be used to help manage projects, and these will be investigated later in this chapter.

Design

Design of a new system encompasses the planning and preparation required before a new system is developed and eventually implemented, and usually comes after a rigorous analysis of the existing system has taken place. There are various ways a new system can be designed (called a **methodology**) and it is important that all the team members share a common approach. Every organisation should have a set of standards which describes the methodology used when designing a new system.

Ensuring consistency of approach is made easier by the use of special software packages which aim to document the system at the same time as it is being designed. These are called CASE tools.

Task assignment

For a team to work on a project it is first necessary to break the overall task down into a series of smaller tasks. With larger projects, each person or group is assigned one or more of these smaller tasks. The timing for completion of each task has to be adhered to since a delay in any one of them could cause a delay in the completion of the whole project.

Project evaluation

Once a system has been developed and implemented, it is useful for the project team to reflect on how the project went in order to learn lessons for the next project undertaken. One way of doing this is to perform an evaluation. Basically the team needs to ask itself the following questions:

- Has the system realised the system objectives (i.e. does it do what it was originally intended to do)?
- Was the project completed within the allocated timescale and budget?

Evaluation is covered in more detail on pages 493–5.

Project scheduling

A full schedule must be drawn up for all projects to ensure that all the resources (human and equipment) are available at the right time and that the project follows a pre-agreed timetable.

Large projects seldom run smoothly. It is very difficult to anticipate the time needed to complete a project and the likely costs encountered. There are many reasons why projects do not go according to plan and many of them are beyond management control. For instance, important staff leaving half way through a project can give rise to gaps in expertise that are impossible to fill. Staff absences due to sickness can also delay the completion of a project. Some problems, however, can be put down to bad management, such as critical equipment not arriving on time because it was ordered too late.

Task analysis

It is generally much easier to estimate the time needed to complete a small task than a large one, so by breaking a project down into a series of smaller tasks and estimating the time and activities needed to complete them, we can get a far better estimate of the time needed to complete the whole project. This process is known as **task analysis**.

Work study

Work study, as the name suggests, looks at the way a job is done to ascertain whether the methods used to do it could be improved upon. Work study usually involves looking at the way the job is being done at the moment and comparing it with the proposed system. For instance, with a manual system you may find that a person spends too much time searching for documents to sort out customer queries.

Letters of complaint from customers provide a useful way of identifying the worst aspects of any system from the customer's (i.e. an independent) point of view.

Time and cost estimating

To assess the feasibility of a project it is necessary to have some idea of how long it will take to complete and how much it will cost. Many people think that the cost of the hardware is the most expensive part of developing a new system. Although this may have been the case ten years ago, hardware costs have fallen and the wages of computer development staff have risen, so the wages of the staff involved in a project are now usually by far the greatest part of the cost.

Estimating costs can be quite difficult, and can only be done accurately on the basis of the costs of similar activities. Yet costs do have to be estimated accurately so that the go-ahead can be given and a budget can be allocated to a project. The time taken to complete a project also needs to be estimated accurately since if it runs over the allotted time, then the costs will also rise because of increased staff wages, etc.

A good project manager will have experience of a number of projects, so they should be able to estimate fairly accurately the time a project is likely to take and how much it will cost. However, unexpected problems can still arise, that no amount of experience or planning can allow for.

Mileposts (milestones)

On long projects, it is always hard to assess whether the whole job will be completed on time, so mileposts are used to break it up into smaller tasks. The mileposts mark the points in the project where progress is assessed. Mileposts usually mark the end of a logical section, and from the timing of the mileposts the project team can assess the progress of the overall project.

Critical paths

Determining the **critical path** involves analysing a large project to identify those tasks that can be undertaken in parallel, and which of these parallel tasks are critical to the project timescale.

Calendar of events
The start and finish times of the various tasks that make up a project are noted on a calendar, so, for instance, you might know that the feasibility study is due to start on Monday 9 November and is due to be completed by Friday 27 November. This is known as a calendar of events.

Order of events

When constructing a critical path diagram, you need to decide on the tasks which make up the whole project, produce an estimate of the duration of each of these tasks and put them into order. Putting events into order is not that easy. Some tasks automatically follow on from others, while some can be carried out simultaneously. Others will appear to be independent and therefore stand on their own.

More information on critical path analysis is provided on pages 481–7.

Activity 15.1

Select one of the tasks from the list below (preferably the one you know most about) and write a list of the main activities that make up the overall job. Once you have done this, make up a new list putting the activities in the order in which they would normally be carried out and put them in a table like the one shown. In this table you will need to allocate a letter of the alphabet to each activity and also give the letters of any activity or activities that directly precede it.

Pick your overall task from this list:

- preparing a Sunday lunch for four people
- decorating a room (wallpapering and painting)
- repairing a puncture in a car or bicycle tyre
- making a dress or other item of clothing.

Activity	Preceding activities	Estimated time needed
A Measure job and estimate materials	None	0.25 hours

Managing slippage

If the estimated timings for the mileposts are not being achieved it is likely that the project will not be completed on time. This is known as slippage. In order to complete the project by a certain date it might be necessary to do something drastic, such as paying the development staff overtime or bringing in contractors. Implementing a smaller version of the overall project might also be considered.

Slippage nearly always results in project costs going over budget, and there may even come a point when abandoning the project needs to be considered as a serious option. Many projects are started and never completed for a variety of reasons, but abandoning a project is very expensive because there are no benefits to outweigh the costs, and it should only ever be a last resort.

Methods of controlling projects

To control a project it is necessary to produce a plan and time schedule for the various activities that make it up. There are various aids that the project manager can use to do this, and some of the main ones are outlined below.

Coordination

Since many tasks in a project are dependent on other tasks being completed first, coordination of the various activities is important if the project is to be completed on time. If all the tasks are to be performed in-house then it is much easier to coordinate a project than if part of the work is to be done outside the organisation. Contract staff may have different methods and styles of working.

To coordinate the various activities, regular team meetings need to be held. At these team meetings various strategies are looked at, such as re-deploying staff or bringing in contractors to help bring back on target any activities that are starting to slip.

A steering committee is often set up whose purpose is to approve or reject any project whose budget costs look like outweighing the benefits of the proposed system. It also monitors the progress of the project. Steering committees are mainly set up in large organisations where there is a separate and clearly defined IT function.

Cost control

Most companies include every cost (staff wages, rental of accommodation, use of consumables, bills, etc.) in the costs of a project, so it is important to keep a careful check on the project costs and monitor them throughout the project's duration.

The project manager needs to keep accurate records of the costs as they mount up and this is usually done using a special software package or sometimes using an ordinary spreadsheet.

Recording

Various records must be kept, for example to provide evidence of the costs involved in case there is a dispute at a later date over what was agreed. Records are also needed to provide information for the evaluation of the project when it is completed.

The following records are usually kept:

- time sheets for each member of staff showing the time that they spent on each activity
- minutes of team meetings;
- action plans;
- agreements made with the users, customer or project sponsor
- memos, letters, faxes, etc.;
- progress reports;
- cost breakdowns (usually for each team in the form of a spreadsheet).

Gantt charts

Gantt charts are horizontal bar charts which are used to plan and schedule jobs. They show diagramatically when the tasks that make up the whole job start and finish. They have a timescale going across the page and a list of the activities to be done going vertically down the page. The blocks that show the duration of the activities are shaded to show the time taken on each task.

Gantt charts are usually constructed on squared paper so that times can be read off accurately. By placing a transparent ruler vertically at the point on the chart representing the present time, it is possible to determine which jobs are behind schedule and which are ahead.

The main problem with Gantt charts is that they fail to show the dependence of one activity on another, but combined with critical path analysis they can be a useful aid in project management. In fact, most project management software makes use of Gantt charts in some way. An example of a Gantt chart is shown below.

Tasks	WEEKS												
	1	2	3	4	5	6	7	8	9	10	11	12	13
1 Investigate existing system													
2 Feasibility study													
3 Fact finding													
4 Analysis													
5 Output design													
6 Input design													
7 File design													
8 System design													
9 System testing													

Project evaluation and review technique (PERT)

Project evaluation and review (PERT) is a project management technique that involves charting out the time and other resources needed to complete a project. Although you can perform PERT just using a pen and paper, there are now many project management software packages which contain PERT features.

Critical path analysis (CPA)

Critical path analysis (CPA) is a system developed to find the minimum time necessary to complete a project. The techniques for CPA are simple and can be performed without a computer, although for larger projects it is best to use the software packages that are available.

To find the minimum time for the completion of a project, it is necessary to find the 'critical path'. The critical path is the sequence of activities that takes the longest time from beginning to end. The critical path is determined by time only; it does not assume that any one activity is more important than another. If any activity or activities along the critical path are delayed for whatever reason, then the whole project will be delayed.

To calculate the critical path, you need to take the following steps:

1 Break the project down into its component activities.
2 Arrange the activities in a logical sequence, each being represented by an arrow. This is known as a network diagram.
3 Estimate the duration of each activity.
4 Identify each path through the network and calculate the time for each path. The path with the greatest duration is the critical path. The difference between the duration of the critical path and that of the other paths is the spare time or 'float' for the other paths.

The advantage of the critical path method is that it highlights those activities that have a direct effect on the timing of the whole project.

Let us now take a look at the symbols used in network diagrams.

481

Arrows

Figure 15.1

Arrows (Figure 15.1) are used to represent activities. If the arrow is long enough the activity can be written along it, or you may prefer to letter each arrow and have a key at the side to show what the activity is. Note that the length of an arrow is not related to the duration of the activity it represents.

Circles

Figure 15.2

Circles (Figure 15.2), called nodes in the critical path analysis diagram, are used to denote events which mark the end of one activity and the start of another. They are divided into quadrants and a number is placed in each quadrant. This will be dealt with in more detail later in the chapter.

Deciding on the sequence of arrows

To be able to draw the arrows in the correct sequence, it is necessary to determine what activities need to be done directly before each arrow, so in other words you need to determine the preceding events. In Figure 15.3 you can see that activity B cannot be done until A has been carried out.

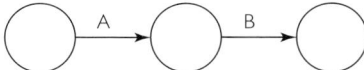

Figure 15.3

In Figure 15.4, activity C can only be started when both A and B have been completed.

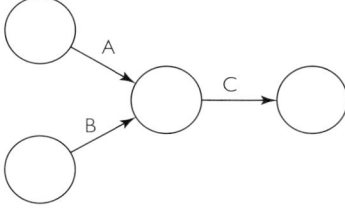

Figure 15.4

Activities B and C in Figure 15.5 can only be started after activity A has been completed.

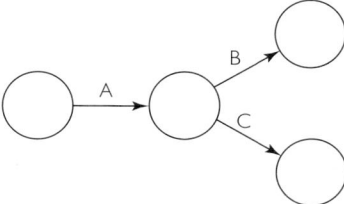

Figure 15.5

Dummy activities

Dummy activities are broken or dashed arrows and are used to show an activity that takes no time to complete and uses no resources. Take the following example: activity A precedes activities B and C; in their turn activities B and C both precede activity D. You could draw a diagram like that shown in Figure 15.6. However, this is not allowed because activities B and C both have the same start and finish node, so instead you have to use a dummy activity and draw the diagram as shown in Figure 15.7. Activity E is the dummy activity, which takes no time and consumes no resources and is shown as a dashed line.

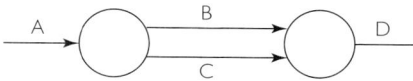

Figure 15.6

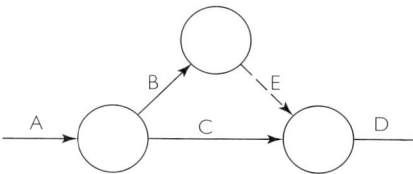

Figure 15.7

Activity tables

An activity table breaks down the whole job into a series of smaller activities and shows the estimated duration of each activity, and the activity or activities that have to be completed directly before each activity can be started.

Example 1

An old tarmac drive is starting to break up and needs replacing. Sarah, who is a systems analyst and keen on DIY, decides to do the job herself. The activity table for doing this job is given below.

Activity		Preceding activities	Estimated number of man days
A	Measure job and estimate materials	None	0.25
B	Find cheapest suppliers	A	0.5
C	Order skips and await delivery	B	1.0
D	Dig up old drive	B	2.0
E	Order materials and await delivery	C	1.0
F	Dig trench for edging stones	D	0.5
G	Lay and cement in edging	F and E	1.0
H	Spread sand, compact and level	G	1.0
I	Lay blocks	H	3.0
J	Compact paving	I	0.5
K	Brush sand into cracks	J	0.5

Figure 15.8 shows the network diagram. It is quite a simple network diagram because Sarah is working on her own and the only time she can do things in parallel is when she is awaiting delivery of the skips or materials. Most of the activities are therefore performed end to end. The times can be inserted on the diagram underneath the activity letters.

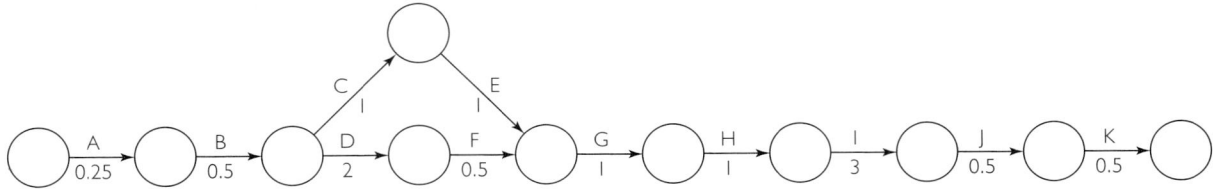

Figure 15.8

Example 2

You are investigating a computer project and have drawn up the following activities table.

Activity	Preceding activities	Estimated duration in weeks
A Feasibility study	None	3
B Decide on computer equipment	A	2
C Prepare site	B	1
D Order and await delivery of equipment	B	2
E Decide on staffing	A	1
F Order consumable materials and await delivery	E	1
G Train users	C	2
H Install equipment	F, D and G	1
I Test system	H	1
J Implement system	I	3

The next stage is to work through the activities table and prepare a sketch as you go along. The nodes (i.e. circles) are not put in at this stage since the diagram will probably need changing.

Activity A has no preceding activity so it must be the first activity. It is therefore represented by a single horizontal line (Figure 15.9).

A

Figure 15.9

Activities B and E are both preceded by A, so you now have a branch (Figure 15.10).

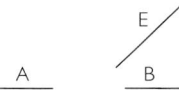

Figure 15.10

Activities C and D are preceded by B, so you need another branch (Figure 15.11).

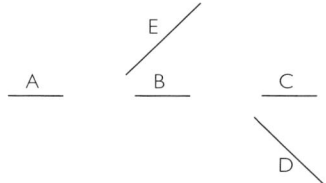

Figure 15.11

Activity F is preceded by E, so you draw a horizontal line (Figure 15.12).

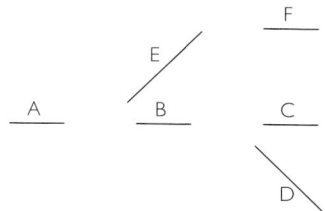

Figure 15.12

G follows C, so you draw another straight horizontal line (Figure 15.13).

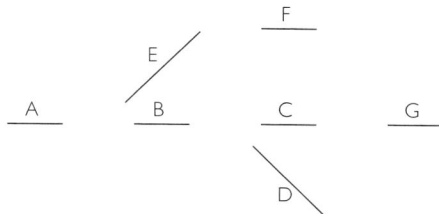

Figure 15.13

Activity H is preceded by the three activities D, F and G. You now have to bend the line for F around to join to H, and activity D will need a dummy activity (Figure 15.14). Don't worry about the curved line at the moment since you can straighten it later.

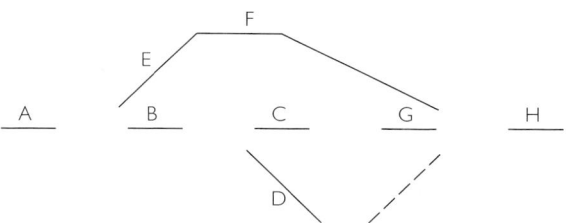

Figure 15.14

I is preceded by H, so a horizontal straight line is drawn (Figure 15.15).

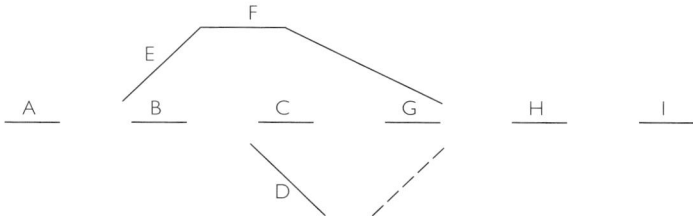

Figure 15.15

J is preceded by I, so you draw another a horizontal line (Figure 15.16).

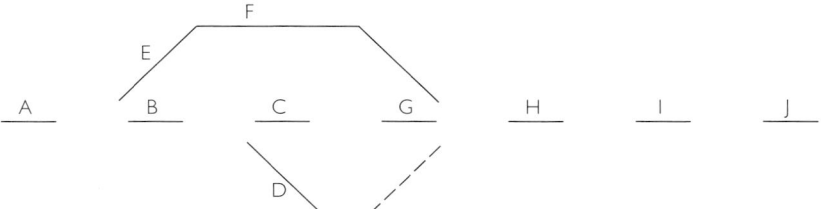

Figure 15.16

You can now draw the neat diagram using straight lines, and putting in the nodes, arrowheads and duration of each activity. Figure 15.17 shows this.

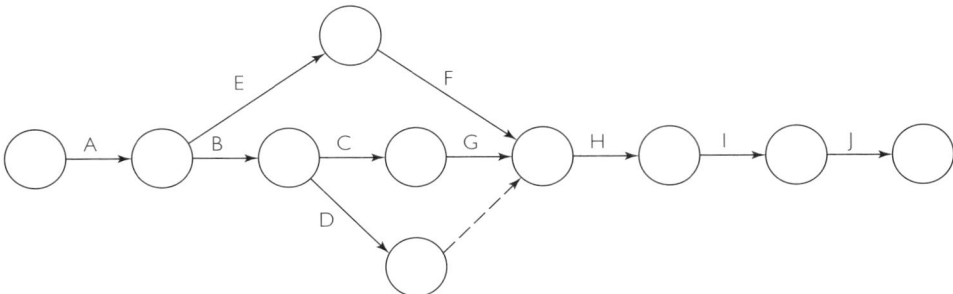

Figure 15.17

You now need to add some other parts to be able to use the diagram. Each node is divided into quarters, like that shown in Figure 15.18, and these quarters are used to contain the numbers described below.

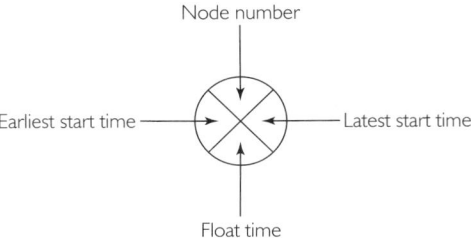

Figure 15.18

Node number
The nodes should be numbered, preferably sequentially in the order of the events, but do not worry if this is not possible since the main purpose of the node number is as a reference point. This makes it easier when referring to specific nodes.

Earliest start time
This gives the earliest time an activity can start, measured from the beginning of the project.

Latest start time
The latest start time is the latest time the previous activity can finish or the latest time the next activity can start, if the total duration of the project is to be unaffected. Any delay in this time will result in the whole project being delayed.

Float time
The float time is found by subtracting the earliest start time from the latest start time. It gives you the amount of time by which the start of an activity, or the finish of the previous activity, can be delayed without it affecting the duration of the whole project. If the float time is zero, this means there is no float, and any delay in the activities connect ing nodes that contain zero float times will cause a delay in the completion of the whole project. The path which joins up the nodes with zero float times is called the critical path.

Completing the diagram

The earliest start times are put into the left-hand side of the nodes as follows: first you place a zero in the first node since this node marks the start of the whole project. Activity A takes 3 weeks, so in node 2 you place the number 3. Activity B takes 5 weeks so you add this to the value of the previous node and enter the earliest start time of 5 into node 4. Activity C takes 1 week so you insert 6 into node 5. This process is continued until you come to a point where several different paths join. When this occurs you always put the latest of the earliest start times in the node. The reason for this is that the next activity cannot be started until all of the preceding activities have been completed, so it is necessary to wait for the latest of them.

When the last node is reached, the number you insert here is the earliest time for the completion of the whole project, which in this case is 13 weeks.

You now start to enter the latest start times, working from the end of the diagram back towards the start. In the end node you place the same value as the earliest start time into the latest start time. You now start to work from right to left, subtracting the times for each activity. When you reach a join you insert the earliest of the latest start times. In other words, the whole process is exactly opposite to the way that the earliest start times were calculated. When you get to the first node in the network you should get a value of zero. If not, then you need to recheck your work.

The float times are now inserted and these are easily calculated. You simply subtract the earliest start time from the latest start time and insert this number into the appropriate space in the node. Nodes with zero float times mark the critical path and any activity along this path which is delayed will delay completion of the whole project. In this example the critical path is A to B to C to G to H to I to J, and the earliest time in which the whole project can be completed is 13 weeks. Figure 15.19 shows the completed diagram with all the numbers inserted into the nodes.

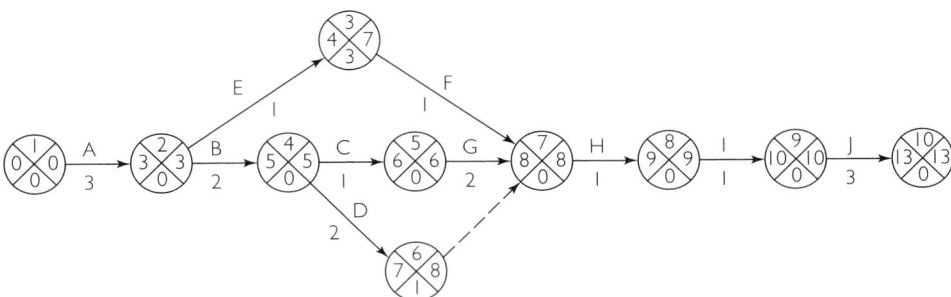

Figure 15.19

Assignment A15.1

This assignment develops knowledge and understanding of the following element:

8.1 Explore information technology team projects

It supports the development of the following key skills:

Communication 3.1, 3.2 and 3.3

Information technology 3.1, 3.2 and 3.3

Most of the IT projects you will come across when you start work will be team projects, so it is important that you know what it is like to work as part of a team. Here is a list of some IT projects which could be developed using a team approach.

- Analysis and design of a relational database system to replace an existing manual system.
- Creation of a training program for a popular software package.
- Creation of standard documents to be used throughout a new company.
- Creation of a help desk monitoring system to cope with the change to a new operating system, such as the change from one operating system to another (e.g. Windows 3.1 to Windows 95) or from one applications package to another.
- Creation of a new computer magazine.
- Making a new computer system by buying and assembling the separate components.

You are required to choose one of the above projects, or provide one of your own which should be discussed with your tutor first, and then develop it as the evidence for Elements 8.1, 8.2 and 8.3.

Before starting the project you will need to form a team. Your tutor will tell you how many team members you are allowed to have and whether you are free to choose them yourselves or whether they will be chosen for you.

You will need to:

- produce a report which describes the purposes of the planning activities;
- produce a description of the project organisation activities needed;
- perform the project scheduling activities for your chosen project, making sure that you include an example of each activity;
- produce a report explaining the methods that you could use to control your project.

In the following sections we will look at the various things you need to be aware of when working as part of an IT project development team. This involves defining the project objectives and the roles and responsibilities of the project team, and also recording your own and your colleagues' performances on a project.

Project objectives

Before starting a project everyone in a team has to be clear about what they are hoping to accomplish, and this is usually summarised as a set of brief project objectives. To define the main objective you can look at the overall aim of the organisation: what is it trying to do? It could, for instance, be trying to produce an end product such as a tin of beans, or the organisation could be providing a service such as insurance, health care, education, etc.

Once the overall objective has been identified you can look at the objectives of the system needed to produce the end result. These can be given in terms of the following criteria, although other objectives can be defined that may be more specific than these.

Timescale
A project might have to be completed by a certain date. For example, when the National Lottery was set up, it had a fixed date for the first weekly draw, so all the systems for selling and recording tickets had to be working by this date.

Costs
Money is always limited, so there is a cost objective in all IT projects.

Specifications

The aim of a project might be to produce a set of specifications. For example, you could be involved in networking an office with 20 PCs. You would have to decide what equipment you would need and the specifications of each of the machines.

Methods

A 'method' is a way of doing something and this might have to be decided in advance.

Roles and responsibilities

Various staff are involved in an IT project, some of them working as part of the team and others providing the team with support. The types of roles that are generally required by an IT team project are described below.

Accountancy

Although overall responsibility for the costs of a project usually lies with the project manager, someone in an accounts department keeps detailed information on the amount spent, and supplies this information to the project manager as and when required. Some details, such as the hours worked by each member of the team, are kept by the project manager, who checks them and passes them on to the accounts section for payment.

Administration

The development of a new IT system generates huge amounts of paperwork, and often each team member will need a copy of every document or report. The task of producing photocopies can be extremely time consuming, so administrative support is often essential. The role of administration is generally to provide wordprocessing facilities, arrange meetings, produce and copy reports, produce standard documents such as contracts, and make sure that office resources such as stationery are always available.

Development

Many of the team members will be involved in development work, which usually includes systems analysis. System development requires a high level of expertise, and this is reflected in the status and salaries offered to such staff.

Design

Design involves both systems design and program design, and the design stage of any project has an important bearing on its implementation. Design also includes looking at the way a problem is to be solved, and choosing the most appropriate method of systems analysis.

Production

Production is the name given to the series of steps that needs to be performed after completion of the devlopment stage to produce the final working system. Production is usually the most time-consuming part of an IT project, and involves integrating the work of all the team members to produce a working system.

Management

The project manager ultimately takes responsibility for the outcome of the project, whether successful or not, and depends on all the project team members. A good project manager will have excellent leadership skills, be good at communicating (both in writing and in speech), delegating work, listening and decision making, and be able to work under immense pressure.

Many of the team members will be given a 'free reign' to use their time effectively, so these staff will manage their own time to some extent. Contractors are often 'results orientated' and tend to work well with little management. The main responsibilities of the project manager should therefore be coordinating activities and dealing with problems.

Working as part of a team

A team is built up of various people, each with some knowledge of part of the system being produced. It may include technical staff, systems analysts, programmers, shop managers, users, etc., and there will be senior staff who chair meetings etc.

Many of the team members might not know each other or might not have worked together before, so in order for them to work effectively as a team they may first need to get to know each other and perhaps spend some time socialising away from the office before the start of the project.

Why work as part of a team?
- Many IT tasks or projects are far too big to be performed by a single person.
- A team brings together people with expertise in different areas.
- Members of the team are able to 'bounce' ideas off each other and this can produce better solutions to IT problems.
- Effective teams can produce work which is far superior to that which could be produced by individual members of the team.

Team building
Team building is covered on page 476.

Activity 15.2

You are involved in the selection of a football team (or another team sport). What qualities in the team members will you be looking for? Are you just concerned with technical skill, or are there other qualities which the team members must have?

Performance

The performance of a team member can be judged in a variety of ways, one of which is by other members of the team. Another way is for the project manager to assess a person's contribution to the project. If the project is being developed for a customer, then the customer could comment on the overall way the project was run.

Performance can be broken down into the factors discussed below.

Interpersonal skills

Interpersonal skills are those used in dealing with and getting along with people. An effective team will consist of people with a good range of interpersonal skills. Some team members, for example, will exhibit skills of leadership by offering to take over meetings or to coordinate activities. Some members may be particularly enthusiastic about the project and this may mean that they are popular members of the group.

Within a group of people, you will find some who have a positive attitude to their work and get on with the job while others sit around moaning about other members of the team, the management or the way the project is being developed. Such people always see the disadvantages rather than the advantages of doing a particular task and can be quite disheartening to work with. Good team members participate in the project and are active members of the group.

Cooperation

Teams are put together by team leaders or senior managers with the aim of accomplishing a certain task, so they are not necessarily made up of people who know each other or who are friends, yet to work together successfully it is necessary for team members to get along with each other. One of the main problems faced by people working in teams is that they may have to work with people they dislike and this can cause tension within the group. Good cooperation is therefore required to ensure that all the team members are able to mix and work well with each other.

Leadership

Someone with good leadership skills is able to assume the role of group or team leader, and be readily accepted in that role by the other members of the group or team. To provide leadership, a person needs to serve the members of the group and induce or motivate them to work effectively. The team will have its own expectations of a good leader and these might include someone who will inspire them, coordinate their efforts, help them when a problem occurs, set a good example, be fair and have a high degree of integrity.

Enthusiasm

Enthusiasm can be infectious. People like working with enthusiastic people, and it tends to motivate them.

Adaptability

People working in computing need to be adaptable to change, and they constantly need to develop new skills in programming languages, and the use of new hardware, software packages, etc. Adaptability is also important if a team member leaves or falls ill, and someone else needs to take over their role.

Technical skills

Teamwork brings together people with a wide range of experience and skills in different areas of the organisation. Sometimes, however, to get people with the necessary skills and level of technical expertise, it is necessary to look outside the organisation for contract staff who may have worked on similar projects in other organisations. In fact, many contractors specialise in a particular area of work, so for example a contractor could have an in-depth knowledge of system testing for large insurance companies. Such expertise does not come cheap, with many contractors earning over £1000 per week, so using contractors could mean that the cost of the project is a lot higher, but the benefits could far outweigh the costs.

Technical skills need to be constantly developed and updated, and staff should be positively encouraged to attend training courses regularly.

Effort

A considerable amount of effort needs to be put into a project by all the team members, and this effort needs to be sustained throughout the project's duration. Sometimes, a project may start to run late and a considerable amount of overtime may be needed, often at weekends, to bring the project back on course again.

Some people work better under pressure, but the work produced may not be of as high a quality as that performed at a more leisurely pace. Some people are also better at meeting deadlines than others, and will put in any amount of effort needed to meet them.

Economic factors

Left to themselves, many members of a project team might prefer to take a more leisurely approach to their work, in which case the project could drag on and subsequently cost more. The project team needs to always be aware of the financial implications of what it does and the necessity of completing the project on time and within budget.

Use of resources

Many people take less care when spending company money than when they are spending their own. For example, when buying hardware or software, they might decide to use one supplier rather than to approach various suppliers and negotiate the best deal. All the team members must be careful in the way that the money is spent because they may have to economise later if the project looks like going over budget.

Use of time

Most people tend to take their time during the early stages of a long project and then speed up as the deadline approaches. The result of this is that people tend to have to work under a huge amount of pressure towards the end of a project, and may not even complete it on time.

All team members should work at a pace which leaves some margin for unforeseen problems and delays. There should be regular mileposts at which the progress of the project is reviewed and any remedial action taken if the project looks like going off course.

Assignment A15.2

This assignment develops knowledge and understanding of the following element:
8.2 Contribute to an information technology team project

It supports the development of the following key skills:
Communication 3.1, 3.2 and 3.3
Information technology 3.1, 3.2 and 3.3

This assignment follows on from Assignment A15.1.

For Element 8.2 you will need to demonstrate the following:
- that you have contributed to defining the project objectives and roles and responsibilities of the project team covering each of the following range statements: objectives, roles and responsibilities, performance;
- that you have improved your personal performance following critical comment.

In order to provide evidence of the above, you will need to keep records in your portfolio regarding:

- personal and colleagues' performance in the project;
- comments obtained from tutors and colleagues on your personal performance.

In the next sections we will look at the ways in which a team project can be evaluated and how the contribution made by each team member to the whole project can be judged.

Evaluative comments

Evaluation is the act of reviewing what has been achieved, how it was achieved and how well the system or product operates. Good evaluation requires comment from everyone concerned in the project, e.g. users, developers and producers. Evaluation looks at two things: the project itself and the way the project was conducted.

Quality

There are various questions which need to be posed in order to evaluate the quality of the results of a project, and these include:

- Is the solution a quality solution or have compromises had to be made?
- Has the whole of the project been completed or are there any loose ends to tie up?
- Does the project satisfy the original objectives?
- Has the final system been thoroughly tested and any problems been rectified?
- Is the customer/user happy with the final system?

Cost

The main question to ask is 'has the project gone over the budget allocated to it, and if so, by how much?' If the project manager has been prudent and kept a careful eye on costs, then there may even be money left over. On the other hand there may have been unexpected costs due, for instance, to a technical problem, and these could have pushed up the project's total cost. If a project does go over budget then the project manager will be asked why, so detailed breakdowns of the figures will be needed.

One useful exercise when evaluating cost is to compare the actual figures for such things as hardware, software, wages, photocopying, administrative support, etc. with the budgeted figures to see how accurate the estimates were. This is useful for estimating costs in any future projects more accurately.

Time taken

The main question here is 'was the project completed on time and to a satisfactory standard?' Predictions as to how long each of the activities would take can be compared with the actual times taken, and any reasons for slippage can be identified. There may be costs associated with the slippage resulting from overtime payments or fees paid to contractors brought in to bring the project back on course.

Project organisation

The answer to the question 'was the project properly organised?' can vary according to who you ask, so you need to get answers from all the project team members and the customer or project sponsors. (The project sponsor is the person in an organisation, usually a director or senior member of staff, who requested that the project be carried out.)   Ultimately, the project organisation is the project manager's responsibility so in effect it is a reflection of the project manager's organisational skills. Some questions that might be asked include:

- Were the team members given the right roles and responsibilities?
- Did all the team members understand the part they had to play in the whole project?
- Did the project manager liaise well with the customer/project sponsor?
- Could the team members rely on the support of the project manager when problems occurred?
- Did the project manager motivate the team successfully and provide effective leadership?

Methods used

There are many different ways to solve a problem, and in the case of computer systems each of these is called a methodology. The main question is whether the project manager used the most suitable methodology for solving the problem. You could also ask whether the team members were consistent in their methodology, and if not, what was done to redress the problem.

Interpersonal relationships

Questions that might be asked in this context are:
- Did the project manager keep up good relations with the customer/project sponsor?
- Were there any serious disagreements between members of the project team?
- Did the members work as a complementary team rather than just a group of individuals working on the same project?
- Was the team composition correct?

Constructive comments

Comments about a person's work require a certain amount of diplomacy, and you can never be quite sure how they will react to them. Comments should always be constructive, i.e. positive and helpful, so that the person takes on board any criticism and can hopefully learn from their mistakes. Comments can be made either orally or in written form.

More and more people in work are used to having a review or an appraisal at the end of each year, at which their superiors look at their strengths and weaknesses and offer help to improve their weak points by perhaps sending them on a training course. During an appraisal it is important not to get upset about any adverse comments you receive, rather you should learn from them and strive to correct your weaknesses.

These are the important things to consider when making constructive comments:
- **They should be clear**: comments should be clear so that they cannot be misinterpreted.
- **They should be objective**: your comments should not be clouded by your own prejudices or beliefs. So if you have had an argument with someone in the team and are then asked to comment on that person, you should do so on the basis of their work and not on how you feel about them personally.
- **They should be accurate**: no one likes to have a comment made about them which is unjustified or untrue, so any comments made about a person should be accurate and backed up by documentary evidence if possible.

- **They should be concise**: you should be able to make your point in as few words as possible; reiteration will simply reduce the impact of what you have to say and will irritate the reader.

Comments on performance

For a detailed analysis of performance criteria, see the section beginning on page 490.

Areas of improvement

It is important that any evaluation of an IT team project includes suggestions for improvements in one or more of the following areas.

Accountancy

All projects are given a budget and it is important that all the money spent on such things as hardware, software, wages, administrative support, materials, training, etc. is properly accounted for. The amount of money spent on a project is the responsibility of the project manager who, with the help of the accounts department, keeps track of what has been spent and how much is left. After a project has been completed, the project manager will compare the budgeted with the actual costs, and this will enable more accurate estimates to be made at the feasibility study stage of any future projects, thus avoiding projects going wildly over budget.

Usually costs start to excalate when projects start missing their milestones, since to bring them back on target again often involves paying overtime rates (which are higher than normal rates) or using contract staff. Careful project planning goes hand in hand with making sure that budgets are not exceeded.

Administration

It is useful after the completion of a project to reflect on the project team's administrative back-up and to assess its performance. If highly paid development staff have spent too much time typing memos, letters and contracts, arranging meetings, etc., then this is not a good use of their time. In future, development staff may need to delegate more of their work to administrative staff so they can concentrate on the job they are being paid to do.

The use of modern software development tools allows a lot of the documentation for the system to be produced automatically, and this cuts down on administration and ensures that the documentation is accurate and standardised across the whole project team.

Development

It is during the development stages of a project that the initial design is transformed into the final working system. After completion of a project, the team can look back on these stages to see how the planning and preparation for the project that took place during the design stage were actually implemented. How accurate were the time and cost estimates? How closely did the final system match the original design? How much modification was required to arrive at the end product?

Design

If the initial design is wrong, then this may not come to light until after the system has been implemented, when the team finds that the system cannot do what it was intended to do without making major changes to it. Some design problems do not become apparent until the system has been passed to the customer.

The number of people involved in the design of a system is critical: just enough to generate a good range of ideas that people can 'bounce off' one another, but not so many that it becomes difficult to coordinate people's activities and to reach a general consensus on important issues.

Production

Producing the final working solution within the time and budget allocated to it is the aim of any IT project.

Production can always be improved by making use of the technology available, for example to automate procedures which would otherwise have to be performed manually. CASE (computer-aided software engineering) tools, for example, consist of a series of software tools whose aim is to automate much of the software development and production process. These tools provide facilities for modelling and design, creating and maintaining a data dictionary, producing documents automatically, enforcing the standards of a certain methodology, and performing critical path analysis and using this to schedule the various activities involved in the project.

Management

The responsibility for the success or failure of an IT project rests with the project manager, so it is extremely important for any organisation to ensure that their managers are of the highest calibre. A good project manager will have worked on many similar projects before and therefore built up skills and experience directly applicable to the project in hand. The project manager needs to reflect on their own performance at the end of a project and analyse what they did well and what they handled badly. They need also to look at the relationships they built up with the customer and project sponsor. Did they involve the customer enough in the project, or did the customer get too involved and interfere with the way the project was run?

Activity 15.3

For this activity you need to carry out some research using back issues of the professional computing magazine *Computer Weekly* and research articles on any two IT projects which have gone seriously wrong. Produce a short report outlining what the projects were, why they went wrong and what the final consequences were. You may also use back copies of newspapers available on CD-ROM for your research.

NHS case study

The following article is a summary of one that appeared in *Computer Weekly* on 12 September 1996.

Some of the projects which have been identified as causing problems include:

- A project to give everyone in the UK a unique NHS number led to thousands of duplicate numbers being issued.
- A rushed hospital information management system cost £106 million but only saved £3.3 million.
- A series of executive information systems have had to be aborted before completion.

NHS project prompts audit probe

The Audit Commission, which is a government watchdog that makes sure public money is spent wisely, has been investigating a series of computer project disasters at the National Health Service. They centre around the main NHS executive systems.

Hospital managers, doctors and nurses and MPs have all condemned the Information Management Group (IMG) which they claim wastes public money on over-ambitious projects. When the projects fail, they claim they try to cover things up. The NHS has tried to prevent leaks to the media by reminding the staff that they are covered by the Official Secrets Act.

Assignment A15.3

This assignment develops knowledge and understanding of the following element:
8.3 Evaluate an information technology team project

It supports the development of the following key skills:
Communication 3.1, 3.2 and 3.3
Information technology 3.1, 3.2 and 3.3

This assignment follows on from Assignments A15.1 and A15.2.

For Element 8.3 you will need to evaluate your information technology team project. To provide evidence for this element you will need to produce records relating to the following:
- evaluative comments obtained on a team project covering everything included under the heading in the chapter;
- constructive comments on the performance of the project team covering interpersonal skills, technical skills and economic factors;
- appropriate suggestions for areas of improvement to the team project.

Glossary

Absolute referencing A formula is told to use a certain cell and when this formula is copied to a new position, it will not alter the address of the cell to which the formula refers.

Actuator Hardware device, such as a motor, which reacts according to signals given to it by a computer.

Address The location of an item in a computer's memory.

Algorithm A set of rules which gives a sequence of operations for solving a problem.

American Standard Code for Information Interchange (ASCII) A code for representing characters in binary.

Analogue computer Computer that works on data represented by a continuous physical quantity such as electric current.

Analogue-to-digital converter (ADC) A device that changes continuously variable quantities (such as temperature) into digital quantities.

Antivirus software Software used to discover and then delete computer viruses.

Application What a computer can be used to do.

Applications software A program or a set of programs to carry out a particular application such as accounts or payroll. Also known as an **applications package** or **package**.

Applications software routines Routines that provide user automation facilities such as macros, styles and templates.

Arithmetic and logic unit (ALU) Part of the central processing unit. It performs all the arithmetic and logic operations.

Array A structure used to store a collection of data objects of the same type. An array can be one dimensional or two dimensional.

Artificial intelligence (AI) The science of developing computers that 'think' like humans.

Assembler A program that converts assembly language into machine code.

Assembly language Low-level language where one programming instruction corresponds to one machine code instruction.

Asymmetric duplex Transmission of data in two directions at the same time.

Asynchronous transfer mode (ATM) A high-speed method of data transmission making use of packet switching which uses fixed-length packets.

Attribute A single data item representing an individual property of an object or entity.

Audit trail The documentary evidence which enables the path of a particular transaction in a system to be followed.

Automatic access control Controlling access to a computer room automatically, usually by the use of a code being entered via a keypad.

Auxiliary storage Storage that is in addition to the normal storage facilities on a file server.

Backing store Memory storage outside the CPU. It is non-volatile which means the data does not disappear when the computer is switched off.

Back-up file A copy of a file which is used in the event of the original file being corrupted (damaged).

Bankers' Automated Clearing Service (BACS) Service set up by the major banks to deal with the payment of wages directly into employees' accounts, the payment of standing orders and direct debits, etc.

Barcode Lines of varying width used to encode data such as the price of goods.

Barcode reader An input device used to scan a barcode. Also known as a **laser scanner**.

Basic A high-level programming language.

Batch file A file, created using operating systems software in order to automate a processing activity.

Batch processing Collecting jobs over a period of time and then processing them in one go.

Baud rate A data transmission rate; the number of bits per second.

Bespoke software Software specially written for a particular user.

Binary code Code made up from a series of binary digits – 0 and 1.

Bit A binary digit; 0 or 1.

Bit-map image/graphics An image represented by patterns of tiny dots called pixels.

Block structured A type of language where the program is made up from sections called blocks that are linked together.

Boolean operators The operators AND, OR and NOT. Also known as **logical operators**.

Break-even analysis Technique to determine the number of goods to be sold in order to just offset the costs.

Bridge A hardware device used to link LAN segments together to form a single logical LAN.

Broadcast service A service where all users receive the same information but only the person to whom the address refers, acts on it.

Buffer A storage area where data is stored temporarily. Printers have buffers so that the user can get on with something else while data is waiting to be printed.

Bug A mistake or error in a program.

Bulletin board service (BBS) A noticeboard and message system run by volunteers.

Bus A high-speed transportation system for sending data and control signals in a computer.

Bus topology A type of network arrangement where the terminals are connected off a main wire.

Byte The amount of memory needed to store one character such as a letter or a number. A **kilobyte (KB)** is 1024 bytes and a **megabyte (MB)** is 1 million bytes.

C A block-structured programming language used mainly for producing applications software for PCs.

C++ A general purpose programming language which is easier to understand than assembly language but runs almost as fast.

Cache A special part of the memory where a computer can store data temporarily to avoid accessing much slower storage such as hard or floppy disks over and over again.

Carrier sense multiple access/collision detection (CSMA/CD) A method for sensing when two or more terminals are transmitting simultaneously.

Carrier wave A wave with a constant frequency which can be modulated and used to carry a data signal.

CD-ROM Abbreviation which stands for compact disk read-only memory.

Cell An area on a spreadsheet produced by the intersection of a column and a row in which data can be placed.

Central controller Hardware device that enables LANs to be linked together to form WANs. Also known as a **hub**.

Central processing unit (CPU) A computer's 'brain' where data is stored and processed. It has three parts: the ALU, the control unit and the memory.

Character Any symbol that can be entered into a computer via a keyboard.

Characters per second (cps) A measure of the speed of data transfer between hardware devices.

Check digit Number placed after a string of numbers to check that they have all been input correctly into the computer.

Client/server A network where several PCs are connected to one or more servers.

Clipart Predrawn computer artwork that is available for people to use.

Clones Computers that are copies of the original IBM personal computer.

CMOS RAM Abbreviation for complementary metal oxide semiconductor random access memory. It is used to store the date and time, for example, because of its very low power consumption.

Cobol A high-level programming language used mainly in business because of its good file handling facilities.

Comma separated variables (CSV) A way of holding data so that it can be transferred into databases or spreadsheets.

Command line The place on a computer screen where an instruction is typed in.

Communications software Software which, with the use of modems, allows computers to communicate with each other.

Compiler Software that converts a high-level language program into machine code.

CompuServe An Internet service provider.

Computer-aided design (CAD) Using a computer to design a system and produce technical drawings.

Computer-aided system engineering (CASE) A software tool used by programmers to help in the analysis, planning, design and documentation of computer programs.

Concatenation The process whereby two character strings are joined together to form a single character string.

Concentrator A hardware device that enables LANs to be linked together to form WANs.

Configuration The pieces of hardware that are needed to set up a computer system. Also, the setting variables that need to be altered to enable software to be used with particular hardware.

Consistency check Check to ensure that an item of data is compatible with all other occurrences of the data item.

Constructs The structures which are the building blocks of a program.

Contention Competition between terminals on a network.

Control device A device connected either within the main processor housing (e.g. disk controller, video card, input/output card, serial and parallel output cards) or to the input/output port of the main processing unit via a buffer.

Control procedure Program created to operate a process control system.

Control system A computer system which automatically controls a process or mechanical device by sensing the need to vary the output.

Control unit Part of the central processing unit used to control the pulses which travel around the CPU.

Controller board The circuit board which contains the circuits responsible for controlling data transfer to and from the disk drives.

Copyright, Designs and Patents Act 1988 An act which, amongst other things, makes it an offence to copy or steal software.

Critical path analysis (CPA) A method used to control and schedule large projects. The project is broken down into a series of smaller activities and a diagram constructed to determine the order in which they need to be carried out. The path along which delay in any one activity will cause a delay in the whole project is known as the **critical path**.

CR/LF Abbreviation for carriage return/line feed. Command issued to tell a computer to return to the start of the line and then to move down a line.

Current instruction register (CIR) A memory location within the CPU which holds the instruction currently being executed and which is also responsible for decoding it.

Data Information in a form a computer can understand.

Database Series of files in which data is stored and which can be accessed in a variety of different ways.

Database report Output from a database that is to be used for a specific purpose.

Data bit lengths The number of bits used to store an item of data.

Data capture The way a computer obtains its data for processing.

Data compression Using software to reduce the size of files so that they take up less space on a disk.

Data description language (DDL) A language used to describe data and its relationships within a database.

Data dictionary A document or file which contains descriptions of all the data items in a database. The descriptions can include data type, element size, format of data, validation range of values, entity descriptions, attribute–entity relations, purpose and synonyms.

Data flow diagram (DFD) A diagram showing the information flow in an organisation.

Data logging A system which collects data automatically over a period of time. Remote weather stations use data logging.

Data manipulation language (DML) A programming language, supported by a database management system, for accessing, deleting data, etc.

Data model A series of diagrams and text (information flow diagrams, data flow diagrams, data dictionary, entity relationship diagrams, etc.) which are used to describe a system.

Data processing Doing something with data to produce some form of useful output.

Data Protection Act 1984 An act which restricts the way personal information is stored and processed using a computer.

Data representation Using a code such as ASCII to represent characters.

Data terminal equipment (DTE) The equipment which acts as a terminal at the end of a communication line.

Data transmission media The media through which data is transmitted from one place to another.

Data type The type of data, including character, number, graphic, logical and date.

Data type check A check performed to make sure that data is of the correct type for processing, e.g. that numbers have been entered in numeric fields etc.

Debug Remove all the errors in a program.

Decision table A table which shows the relationships between variables and the actions which must be taken under certain conditions.

Declarative language High-level language, such as Turbo Pascal and Prolog, where the programming steps can be in any order.

Dedicated leased line A line reserved for a single use or user.

Default settings The settings a computer automatically reverts to, unless instructed otherwise.

Desktop publishing (DTP) The use of software to combine text and graphics on a computer screen to produce posters, newsletters, brochures, etc.

Digital computer Computer that works on data represented by numbers. Most ordinary computers are digital.

Digital-to-analogue converter (DAC) A device that changes digital quantities into analogue ones.

Digital simultaneous voice and data (DSVD) The ability to transfer both voice and data simultaneously using a single telephone wire.

Directory A list of the programs and files stored on a disk. The directory enables the operating system to retrieve files from backing store.

Disk Storage medium used to hold data.

Distributed system Data processing system where the processing, storage, input/output devices, etc. are dispersed geographically.

Document A text file produced by a wordprocessor.

Document imaging system System whereby all paperwork (letters, bills, etc.) are scanned into a computer system and then disposed of.

Documentation The documents that accompany a system explaining how the system works. It can also be the manuals that accompany a program.

Disk operating system (DOS) A program which tells a computer how to work. Controlling data storage on the disk drives is one of the many tasks it performs.

Dot matrix printer A printer which uses numerous tiny dots to make up each printed character.

Dots per inch (dpi) Used to describe the resolution of printers. A 600 dpi printer will produce a clearer image than a 300 dpi printer.

Drum plotter Type of plotter in which paper is rolled backwards and forwards over a drum while pens draw lines on the paper.

Dry run Checking the results of each step of a program manually to make sure the program is correct.

Dumb terminal A terminal which has no processing power of its own.

Duplex Allows signals to be sent along a communication line in different directions at the same time.

Echo Enables transmitted characters to appear on the sender's screen for checking.

Edit Change something stored on the computer.

Electronic data interchange (EDI) Network link that allows shops to pay suppliers electronically without the need for invoices and cheques.

Electronic funds transfer (EFT) The process of transferring money electronically without the need for paperwork

Electronic funds transfer at point of sale (EFTPOS) Electronic funds transfer that takes place at a point-of-sale terminal.

Electronic mail (e-mail) Messages and documents that are created and sent electronically and read on screen, eliminating the need for them to be printed out.

Electronic point of sale (EPOS) A computerised till that can be used for stock control.

Emulation Software or hardware which acts in the same way as another system.

Encrypt Encode. Sensitive files can be encrypted, which means they have to be decoded in order to be read.

Entity An object of the real world which is of relevance to an information system, e.g. customer, invoice, goods.

Entity relationship diagram (ERD) A diagram showing the relationships between entities and their attributes in a system.

Entity relationship model (ERM) A model which represents a view of an organisation based on its entity relationships.

Execution error An error detected during the running of a program.

Executive information system (EIS) A system used to extract strategic information for use by senior executives or directors of a company to aid decision making.

Existence check Check to ensure that a certain field in a database contains data.

Expert system A program designed to behave like a human expert in a specialist field.

Fact finding Investigation of a system prior to performing a feasibility study.

Feasibility study Study carried out before a new system is developed to see what type of system is needed.

Fetch/execute cycle The cycle of events a computer carries out when executing a program.

Field A space in a database in which data is entered. For instance, you may have a field for surname, date of birth, etc.

Field check A check performed by a computer to see if data is of the right type to be put into a field, e.g. that numbers only are entered into a numeric field.

File A collection of related data.

File protection A facility offered by some networks to enable only certain users to see particular directories, subdirectories and files.

File server A network computer used for storing all the users' programs and data.

File transfer Using communications links to transfer a file from one computer to another.

Flat file database A database that is only able to use one file at a time, unlike a relational database which is able to use two or more files at a time.

Floating point number Another name for a real number such as 12.0, 112.22, –0.09, 14.008, 0, etc.

Floppy disk A magnetically coated disk used to store data. The 3.5 inch disk is inside a hard case.

Flow chart Chart or diagram used to break down a task into smaller parts. Also known as a **flow diagram**.

Flow control Controlling the flow of data so as to prevent data from being sent too fast or from being lost due to the receiving device not being ready to accept it.

Folder A name for a subdirectory on a Macintosh computer.

Form field A space on a data collection or data entry form into which data can be entered.

Format The process of allowing the operating system to electronically mark out the surface of a disk ready to store data.

Fortran A high-level programming language mainly suited to mathematical or scientific programs.

Fourth generation language (4GL) Software tool that allows applications programs to be developed more quickly.

Gantt chart A type of chart, with horizontal bars, used to plan and schedule jobs.

Gateway The computer link which connects and translates between two different kinds of computer network.

General purpose software Software such as spreadsheets, databases and wordprocessing software which can be used for many different applications.

Generation Every time a file is updated, a new generation of the file is produced.

GIGO Abbreviation for garbage in garbage out, which means that if you put rubbish into the computer then you get rubbish out.

Grammar checker A program (usually part of a wordprocessing package) which checks a document for grammatical errors and suggests corrections.

Grandfather-father-son principle A method of backup where the last three versions of a master file are kept along with their transaction files, so if one file becomes corrupt it is possible to recreate it from the others.

Graph plotter A device which draws by moving a pen. It is useful for scale drawings and is used mainly with CAD packages.

Graphic user interface (GUI) Interface that allows users to communicate with the computer using icons and pull-down menus. Windows is a GUI, and Macintosh computers use a GUI.

Graphics Diagrams, charts and graphs that are either examined on screen or printed out.

Graphics adapter A circuit board that contains the electronic circuitry needed to supply data in a form that the monitor can display.

Graphics tablet An input device which makes use of a large tablet containing a number of shapes and commands that can be selected by the user by moving a cursor and clicking. It works by moving the toolbars onto the tablet rather than cluttering up the screen when doing large technical drawings using CAD software.

Hacker A computer enthusiast who tries to break into a secure computer system.

Half-duplex Two-way communication, but only one way at a time.

Handshaking Process whereby signals are sent between devices to indicate that successful data transmission can take place.

Hard copy Printed output from a computer.

Hard disk A rigid magnetic disk which provides more storage and faster access than a floppy disk.

Hard drive Unit containing a hard disk.

Hardware The physical components of a computer system.These include the VDU, processor, printer and modem.

Hash total A meaningless total of numbers used to check that all the numbers have been entered into a computer.

Hexadecimal Base 16. A number base system used by computers.

High-level language Programming language where each instruction corresponds to several machine code instructions.

Icons Symbols displayed on a computer screen in the form of a menu.

Immediate access store Storage in the memory of the CPU.

Impact printer Any printer that relies on a character pressing against an inked ribbon for its operation.

Import Load a file into one package from another.

Index A table which aids the manipulation of data in a database.

Information Processed data.

Information retrieval The process of recovering information after it has been stored.

Information technology (IT) The application of computing, electronics and communications.

Ink-jet printer A printer that works by spraying ink through nozzles onto the paper.

Input Data fed into a computer for processing.

Input mask A preset format for data being entered into a database. Brackets, dashes, etc. are added automatically, with the user having only to type in the variable data.

Integrated services digital network (ISDN) A completely digital system which allows data to be sent along telephone lines at high speeds without the need for a modem.

Interactive A program or system that allows the user to respond immediately to questions from the computer, and vice versa.

Interface The hardware and software used to enable devices to be connected together.

Internet Worldwide network of networks. The Internet forms the largest connected set of computers in the world.

Interpreter Program that converts a high-level language into machine code. The interpreter is different from a compiler because it translates each instruction and carries it out before moving on to the next instruction. Compilers translate the whole program first and then carries out each instruction.

Interrogation The process of getting information from a file.

Interrupt An instruction given to a computer telling it to stop whatever it is doing.

Intranet A network used within an organisation which makes use of Internet technology.

I/O controller The link between a microprocessor and its surrounding components.

Jackson structured programming (JSP) A method of using structure diagrams for analysing data and programs.

Java A programming language.

Joint Academic Network (JANET) A network serving the Higher Education Funding Council and the research councils and institutions, with links to international networks.

Joystick An input device used instead of the cursor keys or mouse as a way of producing movement on the screen.

Key One of the attributes of an entity on which an index has been created or a relation set.

Keyboard The set of keys used to input data into a computer.

Keypad A miniature keyboard or set of keys grouped in a certain way.

Key-to-disk A way of putting data directly onto disk using the keyboard.

Local area network (LAN) A network of computers on one site.

Laptop A computer small enough to fit on your lap. Laptop computers use rechargeable batteries.

Laser printer A printer which uses a laser beam to form characters on the paper.

Library routine Part of a program that is kept so that it can be copied and used in other programs, thus speeding up the writing of new programs.

Linear bus Type of bus network where terminals are connected off a single cable called the bus.

Linked lists A collection of data stored in a certain order, with a pointer which points to the next set of data.

Logo A simple language which enables a 'turtle' to move according to the instructions given to it.

Loop A sequence of steps in a program which is repeated once or more.

Low-level language A programming language very similar to the machine language of the computer. Each low-level instruction can be easily converted into a machine code instruction.

Machine code The language a computer can understand without it being translated. Each type of computer has its own machine code.

Machine readable Data that can be input directly into a computer without any data preparation, e.g. the magnetic ink characters on cheques.

Macro A program written using applications software tools to automate a collection of keystrokes or events.

Magnetic media Media such as tape and disk where the data is stored as a magnetic pattern.

Magnetic strip A strip containing magnetically encoded information which can be read by a special reader. Cards such as credit cards have a magnetic strip.

Magnetic strip reader Device that reads the data contained in magnetic strips.

Magnetic-ink character recognition (MICR) Method of input that involves reading magnetic ink characters from a document.

Magneto-optical disk Combines the technologies of magnetic media and CD-ROM to produce a disk that looks like a CD-ROM but which you can read and write to.

Mail merge Combining a master file with a secondary file containing variable data such as names and addresses to produce multiple documents such as mail shots.

Mainframe A large computer system with a number of dumb terminals attached to it.

Mainstore Memory inside the CPU.

Management information system (MIS) System, usually centred around a database, that is able to extract information in a way which enables management decisions to be made.

Master file The main source of information; the most important file.

Maths coprocessor Incorporated as part of most chips to perform calculations at very high speed.

Medium The material on which data can be stored such as magnetic disk, tape, etc.

Megahertz (MHz) One million cycles per second. The speed of the internal clock that controls the speed of the pulses in a computer. Chip design and clock speed determine the overall performance of the CPU.

Memory Area of storage inside chips, consisting of ROM and RAM.

Memory address register (MAR) The part of the memory responsible for giving the address of the memory location where data is either put into the memory or taken from it.

Memory buffer register (MBR) A place in the memory through which data must pass when it is being moved between memory locations, the data bus and the memory address register.

Menu selection interface Interface which provides the user with a list of options to choose from.

Merge To combine data from two different sources.

Mesh topology Network arrangement where each computer has many wires connecting it to other computers.

Methodology The method used when investigating, developing and documenting a system.

Microcomputer A cheap, relatively slow computer with limited memory that is only able to work on one program at a time. Includes home computers as well as personal computers.

Microsoft Disk Operating System (MS-DOS) An operating system used by personal computers.

Milestones Points in a project which mark the ends of logical stages in the project. Also known as **mileposts**.

Mode A particular way of running a program.

Model A software representation of a real situation or system which can be used for analysing its operation and for investigating its behaviour under certain conditions.

Modem MODulator/DEModulator. A device which converts data from a computer into a form that can be passed along a telephone wire.

Modem response string A string of bits given out by a modem which is used to tell a computer if the modem is on-line.

Modulated signal The signal produced when a carrier signal is used to carry a data signal.

Motherboard The main circuit board of a computer into which most of the devices are connected.

Mouse An input device which is moved over the desk top to create equivalent movement of the cursor on a computer screen. Buttons on the mouse are pressed to make menu slections.

Multi-access system System which allows many different users to gain access to the computer. Because of the high speed of the CPU, each user has the equivalent of sole access, even though the time is being shared between a number of users.

Multimedia Software that combines more than one medium for presentation purposes, such as sound, graphics and video.

Multiplexer Hardware device used to allow simultaneous transmission of multiple messages using a single communications channel.

Multi-user processing Processing which makes use of programs and operating systems that are able to support more than one user at a time.

Netscape Navigator A program which can be used for searching for information on the Internet.

Network A group of computers that are able to communicate with each other.

Network administrator The person responsible for the running and administration of a network. Also known as a **network manager**.

Network computer Computer which is to be connected to a network.

Network interface card (NIC) Card which slots into a motherboard and is used primarily to reduce the amount of cabling in a network.

Network management software Software used to help the network manager/administrator in their job of looking after a network.

Network operating system A special operating system with all the features of an ordinary operating system but with additional facilities to deal with the problems encountered when communicating with other computers connected on a network. Also known as **networking software**.

Normalisation The process of converting an invalid data model into a valid data model, ensuring data consistency and integrity of the data model.

Novell A company that provide networking solutions.

Null modem A cable used to allow two computers to communicate with each other by emulating a modem.

Object The data, and the structure used to manipulate it, as a single, self-contained unit.

Object orientated language A language which attaches data to the programming routines used to manipulate it.

Object linking and embedding (OLE) Where one application can be linked directly to another. For example, a spreadsheet can be linked to a wordprocessing document, and if the figures are changed in the spreadsheet, then the figures will be changed automatically in the document.

Off-line/on-line Terms used to describe whether a device is under the control of a computer or not.

Operating system The software that controls the hardware of a computer and runs the programs. The operating system controls the handling of input, output, interrupts, storage and file management. Also known as **systems software**.

Operator A symbol which represents an arithmetic operator (+, -, /, * etc.) or a relational operator (=, <, >, >=, <=, <>).

Optical character recognition (OCR) A combination of software and a scanner which is able to read characters into a computer.

Optical mark reader Device used for detecting marks on a sheet of paper and putting the data contained in them into a computer.

Optical mark recognition (OMR) Method of data input that involves detecting marks, usually shaded areas, on a piece of paper.

Optional relationship A relationship that may or may not exist.

Oracle Sophisticated database used for large networks that has its own programming language.

OS/2 An operating system used with PCs.

Output The results from processing data.

Outsourcing Using an outside organisation for the development of new computing facilities.

Parallel processing Processing which allows a computer to carry out more than one task at a time.

Parallel transmission Transmission of bits side by side.

Parity bit An extra bit added at the end of a group of bits to keep the number of binary digits in the transmission either even or odd.

Peer-to-peer Network arrangement in which each computer is of equal status.

Pentium Computer based around the Intel Pentium or Pentium Pro chip.

Peripheral A device connected to and under the control of the CPU.

Permanent storage Place where permanent data such as boot programs is stored.

Pixel The smallest dot of light on a computer screen that can be individually controlled.

Platform The hardware used by an operating system, or the operating system used by an applications programs.

Plug and play A system whereby an operating system is able to recognise the peripherals attached to it automatically. Windows 95 makes use of plug and play.

Point-to-point topology Network arrangement where each terminal can send data to any other terminal on the network using a single link.

Police National Computer (PNC) The central computer system used by the police which holds details of criminals, etc.

Polling A system where each station on a network is invited to transmit data.

Port An external connection point on a computer to which peripheral devices are attached.

Primary storage Storage area in ROM or RAM for holding data and instructions.

Printer server The computer which contains the printer server software and controls for a local area network (LAN) and which controls the printer queue.

Piracy The illegal copying and use of software.

Private wide area network A network which makes use of communications that are not shared by anyone else and are either owned or leased from a telephone company.

Problem statement An outline of the problem to which an IT solution needs to be found.

Procedural language Language made up from a series of steps placed in a certain order that can be changed by using jumps, loops, etc.

Process Something that is done to raw data, e.g. calculating, sorting, etc.

Process control software The program which controls a certain process.

Program A complete set of structured instructions given to a computer to tell it how to carry out a particular task.

Program generator A program which expands simple statements into program code, enabling inexperienced programmers to write their own programs.

Programmer A person who writes computer programs.

Project brief An outline of a project supplied by the senior managers or directors of an organisation.

Project evaluation and review technique (PERT) A project management technique that involves charting out the time and other resources needed to complete a project.

Prolog A declarative programming language used primarily for expert system programming.

Protocol A set of standards that allow the transfer of data between computers on a network.

Prototyping software See fourth generation language.

Proximity sensor A sensor consisting of two parts which detect the nearness of one part to the other.

Pseudocode A combination of English and programming language used to express the flow of a program.

Public switched telephone network (PSTN) The ordinary telephone system.

Qbasic A version of the Basic programming language which can be interpreted or compiled.

Query A request for specific information from a database. Action queries peform certain actions such as deleting or updating, and select queries find and extract certain data.

Query by example (QBE) A quick way of entering SQL commands in order to extract certain information from a database.

Query language Language used to construct queries to a database.

Queue A list of data in which the data is added at one end and taken away at the other.

QuickBasic A version of the Basic programming language which can be interpreted or compiled.

Random access memory (RAM) A fast temporary memory area where programs and data are stored while a computer is switched on.

Range check Data validation technique which checks that the data input into the computer is within a certain range.

Read-only memory (ROM) Computer memory that cannot be changed by a program.

Real time A real-time system accepts data and processes it immediately. The results have a direct effect on the next set of available data.

Record A set of related information. Records are sub-divided into fields.

Relational database Database where data is stored in separate tables and the tables are related to each other. The use of tables cuts down on data duplication and enables access to the data to be more flexible.

Relational database management system (RDMS) Database system where the data is held in tables with relationships established between them. The software is used to set up and hold the data as well as to extract and manipulate the stored data.

Relationship The way in which entities are related to each other. Relationships can be one-to-one, one-to-many or many-to-many.

Relative referencing When a cell is used in a formula and the formula is copied to a new address, the cell address changes to take account of the formula's new position.

Remote sensing The process whereby sensors are connected via communication lines to a main computer.

Repeater Device used to increase the strength of a data signal sent through a wire over a large distance.

Repetition Repeating program statements until a certain condition is satisfied. Also known as **iteration.**

Report Printed information extracted from a database.

Reservation Process whereby a terminal keeps exclusive use of a communication line while it is sending data to another computer or terminal in a network.

Ring bus Type of network bus topology where terminals are connected in a circle or a loop.

Ring topology A type of network arrangement where the terminals are connected together with wires in a ring.

Root directory The first directory on a magnetic disk.

Router Hardware device that is able to decide which path an individual packet of data should take so that it arrives in the shortest possible time.

Run-time error An error detected during the running of a program (e.g. division by zero).

Screendump A printout of what appears on the screen.

Search To look for an item of data.

Search engine Program which searches for specific information on the Internet.

Secondary storage Storage outside the CPU such as magnetic disk, CD-ROM, tape, etc.

Sensor Device that measures physical quantities such as temperature, pressure, etc.

Serial access Accessing data in sequence; the time it takes to locate an item depends on its position.

Serial transmission Transmission of bits simultaneously.

Service provider A company which provides a service enabling connection to the Internet.

Share level security Security system provided by many network operating systems which gives each resource on a network its own password.

Shell The name given to the program used to control the operation of a computer.

Simple network management protocol (SNMP) Manufacturers' standards for operation of all network management software.

Simplex Transmission in a single direction or one direction at a time.

Simulation An imitation of a system or phenomenon produced using computer software, e.g. a flight simulator used to train airline pilots.

Single-user processing A system with single user processing can only carry out processing for one user at a time. It is used by stand-alone machines.

Software The programs used by a computer.

Software package Software that can be bought off-the-shelf to solve a business problem.

Sorting Putting data into ascending or descending order.

Sound card An add-on card used in multimedia applications to output high quality sound through speakers.

Sound sensor A sensor used to detect a certain level of sound.

Source document The original document from which data is taken.

Special fields Form fields designed to contain special data such as date, time, page number or calculations.

Spell checker A program, usually included with wordprocessing software, which checks the spelling in a document and suggests corrections.

Spreadsheet A software package, often used to produce financial predictions, which consists of a grid used to contain text, numbers or formulae.

Stack A list of data items that allows data to be added to and taken away from the list at one end only.

Stand-alone computer A computer system which is self-contained, e.g. a PC which is not connected to a network.

Star topology Network arrangement where the cabling looks like a star with the terminals at the points of the star.

Start bit Bit used to signal the start of data transmission.

Stop bit Bit used to signal the end of data transmission.

String A group of characters.

Structure diagram A diagram showing how a job can be broken down into smaller tasks.

Structured English A shorthand form of English used to define the elements of a computer program.

Structured query language (SQL) A special language used for extracting specific information from a database.

Structured systems analysis and design methodology (SSADM) The most popular way of going about systems analysis.

Subdirectory A directory within or under the main directory.

Syntax error An error reported by a computer due to the incorrect use of the rules governing the structure of the language. Similar to the rules governing grammar in English.

System Hardware and software working together to do a job.

System specification The data and information used by analysts and programmers to produce a systemwhich meets the users' requirements.

Systems analysis Investigating and analysing the requirements for an information system.

Systems analyst A person who studies the overall organisation and implementation of a system.

Table Used in a relational model to represent an entity type.The columns represent attributes of the entity and each row corresponds to an entity occurrence.

Tailor-made software Software specifically written to solve a particular problem.

Tape Magnetic media used to store data.

Task analysis Breaking a project down into a series of smaller tasks to estimate the amount of time and resources to be allocated to the project.

Team building The process of enhancing the ability of team members to work together in a coherent and positive way, rather than as a collection of individuals.

Telecommunications The field of technology concerned with communicating at a distance (e.g. telephones, radio, cable, etc.)

Teleconferencing System enabling two or more people to hold a conference using the telephone system.

Teletext Information sent by means of a television signal and displayed on a specially equipped television set.

Template An electronic file which holds a standardised document layout or screen format.

Temporary storage Storage on a medium which allows data or files to be deleted.

Terminal A computer on a network, or a keyboard and VDU connected to a mini- or mainframe computer.

Terminal adapter (TA) A piece of equipment needed for ISDN.

Terminal emulation The type of terminal selected will set the character and control codes used in transmission and reception.

Terminal equipment (TE) A piece of equipment needed for ISDN.

Test data Data used to test a program or flow chart for logical errors.

Thesaurus Software which suggests words with similar meanings to the word highlighted in a document. Usually included with wordprocessing documents.

Timesharing A system whereby the processing time of the CPU is divided among many terminals.

Time-slice The time given to a particular terminal. Also known as a **time slot**.

Token-ring A network where a token (a signal which gives workstations permission to transmit data) passes around a ring network.

Top-down approach Problem-solving strategy whereby an overall problem is broken down into progressively smaller and more manageable problems.

Topology The way a particular network is arranged.

Trace A check performed by a computer program whereby the path through the program is followed and the line numbers recorded in the order in which they are carried out. Useful for checking the logic of a program.

Tracker ball An input device somewhat like an upside down mouse.

Transaction file A file on which all the transactions (bits of business) over a certain period of time are kept. It is used to update a master file.

Transaction processing A real-time system where transactions are processed as soon as they are received.

Translator A program used to convert a program written in a high- or low-level language into machine code.

Transmission modes Configuration settings used with networks.

Transmission rate The speed of data flow in bits per second (bps) through a medium.

Tree A data structure consisting of a set of junctions called nodes, with branches which end in further nodes and so on.

Tuple A row of data in a table of a relational database.

Turbo Pascal A declarative high-level programming language.

Turnaround document A document produced by a computer which is subsequently filled in manually and used as the input to the computer.

UNIX An operating system used in multi-user computing.

Update Changing details which have become out of date.

User interface system A system used to improve the ease with which users can interact with the system.

User level security Level of security provided by a network operating system where each user is given a user name and a password in order to gain access to the network.

Utility program Software which helps the user perform tasks such as virus checking, file management, etc.

Validate A check performed by a computer program to make sure that data is allowable.

Video compression card Used to compress the large amount of data needed to store a video sequence so that it can be stored on disk or sent over a network.

Vector graphics Graphics which are defined using co-ordinate geometry. They are easy to scale without any loss of resolution. Each part of a vector graphic can be manipulated individually.

Verification Checking the accuracy of data entry.

Video conferencing System enabling meetings to be conducted without leaving the office, using video cameras and special computer software.

Video sensor A sensor used to detect the outline of an object. Used by 'intelligent' robots to position components accurately when assembling products.

Viewdata A computer-based information retrieval system such as teletext which uses screen messages to display information.

Virtual reality Computer technology which creates a simulated multi-dimensional environment for the user.

Virus A program that has been created to do damage to a computer system.

Virus checking The process of using software to scan for computer viruses.

Visual Basic A version of Basic which makes use of the Windows environment.

Visual display unit (VDU) The screen on which data is displayed. Also known as a **monitor**.

Voice recognition The ability of a computer to 'understand' spoken words by comparing them with stored data.

Wide area network (WAN) A network where the terminals are remote from each other and telecommunications are used to communicate between them.

Windows A graphic user interface which provides a common way of using programs.

Windows icons menus pointing devices (WIMP) Using a graphic user interface (GUI) rather than typing in commands at the command line.

Wizards Programs within Microsoft Office which can be run to speed up certain tasks.

Wordprocessor A program that allows text to be entered, styled, displayed on a VDU and edited before being printed out.

Workstation A computer or terminal at which a user works.

Wrap The process by which a computer starts a new line automatically.

WYSIWYG Abbreviation for 'what you see is what you get'; what appears on the computer screen is exactly what is printed out.

XENIX A version of the UNIX operating system.

XON/XOFF A system which makes use of handshaking for flow control.

Index